D1603602

PRIMO LEVI

An Identikit

MARCO BELPOLITI

Translated by Clarissa Botsford

LONDON NEW YORK CALCUTTA

The Italian List
SERIES EDITOR: **Alberto Toscano**

Seagull Books, 2022

Originally published in Italian as Marco Belpoliti,
Primo Levi: Di fronte e di profilo, 2015

© 2015 Ugo Guanda Editore S.r.l., Via Gherardini 10, Milano
Gruppo editoriale Mauri Spagnol
www.guanda.it

First published in English translation by Seagull Books, 2022

English translation © Clarissa Botsford, 2022

Photographs © Individual proprietors; reproduced here with kind permission

ISBN 978 0 8574 2 899 8

British Library Cataloguing-in-Publication Data
A catalogue record for this book is available from the British Library

Typeset by Seagull Books, Calcutta, India
Printed and bound in the USA by Integrated Books International

CONTENTS

NOTE ON THE ENGLISH EDITION

Primo Levi: An Identikit is very different from the first Italian edition published by Guanda in 2015 and from subsequent editions over the following years. The chapters regarding the books Primo Levi published in his lifetime have been completely rewritten, starting from my notes to Einaudi's three-volume *Complete Works* (2016–2017), for which I was the general editor. There are 11 chapters that present the results of further research carried out on previously unavailable material from the Einaudi Archive, in addition to new critical studies relating to Levi's multiple drafts. Some chapters of the Italian edition have been excluded from this edition, in agreement with Seagull Books, while two new short chapters have been added: 'Levi, the Ecologist' and 'Artist'. The publication of the volume in this edition would not have been possible without the contribution of the Bridge Award and, above all, the support of Ruben Levi, to whom all my gratitude goes. I thank Clarissa Botsford for her excellent translation and for the forebearance she has shown over the years. Roberto Gilodi, my literary agent, and Luigi Brioschi, editor of Guanda, were also key figures in this massive undertaking. However, without the enthusiastic support of Alberto Toscano, this edition would never have seen the light in English, a language that allows as many readers as possible to approach the writer and witness, Primo Levi.

Marco Belpoliti, 2022

PREFACE

The first edition of *If This Is a Man* came out two years after the end of the Second World War, before I was born. I belong to a generation that came across Levi's books much later, when I was at high school in the 1970s. A second edition was published in 1958, and from then on, even after the author's death, it became one of the best-known books ever, read by every Italian school child across the country.

Immediately after the war, the predominant theme of the book was seen as the imprisonment and forced labour of anti-Fascists, members of the Resistance, workers, union leaders, ordinary people, and Italian soldiers who had defected from Mussolini's Salò Republic, propped up by Hitler after the Armistice. The Shoah was not a dominant paradigm between the 1950s and the 1970s. Even though Primo Levi was a Jew, and the testimony he gave in his book was about the Nazi extermination of European Jews, *If This Is a Man* was held up as a symbol of anti-Fascist resistance against the Germans and against Italian Fascists who joined the Salò Republic. In the meantime, Levi had published *The Truce*, which was taken to be a sequel to *If This Is a Man*, a book of short stories that was largely ignored (*Natural Histories*), and a second collection of fantasy stories (*Flaw of Form*) in 1971.

I came across Levi at high school thanks to a teacher who had been deported by the Germans as a young soldier after the 8 September 1943 Armistice because he had refused to sign up with Mussolini's puppet state. The teacher did not read the book in class; he recommended it to those of us who wanted to find out more about the Nazi concentration camps. 'It's essential reading,' he told us. From that moment on, my parents bought and I read Levi's work as it came out: *The Periodic Table* in 1975, *The Wrench* in 1978. This book in particular was a favourite at home because its subject was work. My parents' generation had participated in the reconstruction of Italy after the war, and played a part in what was known as the 'economic boom'. Like millions of other Italians, they worked tirelessly to rebuild the country and guarantee a future for the generations to come, for their children.

The 1970s was a decade of social conflict, during which Italy underwent a prolonged period of political turmoil. There were neo-Fascist bombings, and Red Brigade terrorist attacks and kidnappings. Levi's books were read in this political and historical context. He was considered to have something to say about fascism, racism and labour relations. The Jewish question was certainly present, but neither I nor my schoolmates saw it as the most important element of his work. At the time, Levi was not deemed a great writer. In the pantheon of Italian literature, Alberto Moravia, Italo Calvino, Pier Paolo Pasolini, Leonardo Sciascia, Elsa Morante, Goffredo Parise, Natalia Ginzburg were all much higher up in the firmament.

My reading of Levi changed in the early 1980s, when Levi published two books which are still little-known today but which were well suited to a cultural climate that contemplated theories of complexity: *Other People's Trades* and *The Search for Roots*. In these works, Levi revealed that he was a more complex author than he had previously been given credit for, far more than just a memoirist of Auschwitz atrocities. Furthermore, he had been a professional chemist all his life since returning from the Lager, but in his work, he amalgamated science, technology, linguistics and foreign literature—to name just a few of the layers.

During the 1990s, after Levi's death, I tried to reconstruct the path he had followed as a writer. His vast range of interests—from anthropology and ethology, to language games—made him a highly unusual writer in Italy where scientific and literary cultures have traditionally been in eternal conflict. Calvino, who had welcomed and accepted Levi as an Einaudi author in 1958, and whose ties to the Turin publisher made him a close reader of Levi's work, was perhaps the only other Italian writer with similar interests.

In 1996, after publishing a book on Calvino's visual images with Einaudi, I started work on editing the edition Einaudi was planning of Levi's *Complete Works*. That same year, I edited a collection of essays by writers, critics and researchers—mostly my peers—which presented a new, less traditional interpretation of Levi's work. In our view, Levi was not just a witness and survivor of the Lager experience; he was also a fully-fledged writer in his own right. Published by Riga Books, the volume influenced a new generation of readers who began to rediscover Levi's work.

I edited the two-volume edition of the *Complete Works* in 1997, which comprised, in addition to the better-known novels and short-story collections, a vast array of unpublished or re-published material and a detailed apparatus of Notes on the Texts. W. W. Norton's 2015 English edition of the *The Complete Works of Primo Levi*, edited by Ann Goldstein, was based on this. After Levi's death, Einaudi published several other books of mine, including a travel diary of a road trip through Europe following Levi's journey in *The Truce*, which was the basis of a film *La strada di Levi*, directed by my travel companion, David Ferrario. Thirty years after Levi's death, Einaudi asked me to work on a third volume to add to the collection, which included new material, revised and extended Notes on the Texts for each piece of work and a wide selection of interviews and conversations, which integrated the partial selection Einaudi had published in 1987. The third volume was entitled: *Complete Works* III. *Conversations, Interviews, and Declarations*.

Primo Levi: An Identikit was published by Guanda in 2015. It won the Bridge Prize for Italian non-fiction, promoted by the American Initiative for Italian Culture in 2017.

PORTRAIT WITH HIS MOTHER

Primo was born in Turin on the last day of July 1919, a year after the end of the First World War, while the so-called 'Spanish Flu' was sweeping through Europe and Italy, after killing millions all over the world. His mother, Ester Luzzati, had married the engineer, Cesare Levi, two years before, in 1917. Primo doesn't say much about her in his books. She is hardly ever mentioned, while Primo talks about his father much more. Both parents are Sephardic Jews. The family tree—part heraldry, part fantasy—can be found in 'Argon', the first story in *The Periodic Table*. The family is not particularly religious; they celebrated the Jewish festivities out of tradition and habit.

The photograph was taken in 1920, when Primo was a year old, or a little younger. Ester holds her son on her right arm, supporting and sustaining him, and yet the picture suggests something different. Primo's mother is looking at the camera, straight into the lens; her gaze is shyly seductive. What strikes the viewer are her big, deep, dark eyes and the fact that her head is leaning slightly towards Primo. A light shawl of some kind is wrapped around her shoulders, showing off her figure beneath. Primo, by contrast, is looking off to the right, his eyes wide open. He is wearing a white dress and a necklace, and is holding something like a rattle in both hands. As was common in those days, clothes are not markers of gender, leaving the young child suspended in some kind of limbo. He looks uncertain. It's hard to see his character in this shot. There is, however, already a hint of that perplexed amazement, that kind of curiosity and detachment, often bordering on remoteness, visible in other photographs from his youth.

In Susan Sontag's view, photographs are images of images. When we see photographs of Levi in books that is what we are seeing. We can't touch the portrait of Levi with his mother published here. There is no contact with the cardboard on which the printed photograph is mounted. 'Collecting photographs is collecting the world', Sontag wrote at the beginning of her essay in *Plato's Cave*.

Looking at the portrait more closely, one can almost sense a divergence between the mother's gaze, which is self-aware, and that of the baby boy. Norberto Bobbio, who knew Levi, told Levi's biographer, Carole Angier, that Ester was both highly intelligent and imperious. This photograph reveals her strong character, kind but firm. Mother and son occupy the same space in the same photograph, but it is as if they are separate. Yet, we know that they had, and would continue to have, a deep, almost symbolic relationship—embodied in this photograph.

Ester outlived her son. She died after Primo, challenging the norm whereby children push their parents out of their life as they grow up, and generations pass on the baton of life and death. Pier Paolo Pasolini, a very different writer to Levi, and not much liked by him, wrote: 'It is absolutely necessary to die [. . .] only thanks to our death does our life serve to express ourselves' (*Empirismo Eretico*). It is hard to leaf through a private album made public by biographers and researchers without thinking about the different destinies of the two people portrayed in this photograph, the final outcome of the existence of mother and son.

If This Is a Man

When Primo Levi came back to Italy in October 1945, he has no idea that several other testimonies of former deportees like him had already been published. In the year that marked the official end of the Second World War, 11 books were published or printed by local publishers or presses. We do not know if Levi knew of any of these testimonies, as they were little more than pamphlets circulated locally. Only a few were distributed to bookstores.

The first work to be published was by a chemist like Levi. Alberto Cavaliere was a member of the Communist Party who had told the story of his sister in law, Sofia Schafranov, a Jewish doctor of Russian origin. The title of the 92-page book published by Sonzogno in 1945 was *I campi della morte in Germania: nel racconto di una sopravvissuta* (Death Camps in Germany: The Story of a Survivor). The second title (*16 ottobre 1943*), an 82-page story by the writer and critic Giacomo De Benedetti, had already been published in Rome by OET, in the journal *Mercurio* in December 1944. Neither Cavaliere nor De Benedetti had experienced the Lager first-hand, however. Gaetano De Martino, a Theosophist lawyer and militant communist, was the first genuine eyewitness to publish his account alongside testimonies from other deportees. Published by Edizioni Alaya, the book was called *Dal carcere di San Vittore ai 'Lager Tedeschi': sotto la sferza nazifascista* (from San Vittore Prison to the 'German Lager': Under the Nazi-Fascist Whip). The literary critic Silvio Guarnieri wrote a 23-page account after hearing Luigi Rozzi's experiences as a deportee and prisoner at Monowitz, where Levi, whom he later met in Romania, had also been held. The pamphlet was printed in Salò, at the Ebranati Printing Press and was entitled *Campi di eliminazione nella Germania nazista* (Elimination Camps in Nazi Germany).

Levi, the young Jewish chemist who had made it back to Italy after being deported to Monowitz, also wanted to tell the story of his imprisonment: his journey to Auschwitz and the time he spent in the death camp working in the German synthetic rubber factory. His earliest works, written almost as soon as he set foot in Turin on 19 October 1945, revealed this need. One of the first was a report written for the Turin Jewish Community, where, after a brief introduction, he provided precise information garnered from fellow prisoners about other deportees. It was a formal 'deposition', as Levi himself called this report: a list of names and a series of events that then found their way into a narrative in *If This Is a Man*, both in the first edition in 1947 and in the later, expanded edition in 1958.

Alongside, Levi wrote a first draft of what would later become Chapter 17 of *If This Is a Man* ('The Story of Ten Days'). At the end of the typescript he put the date, February 1946. This piece of writing was not strictly private, even though he was writing about his personal experience. It was already a story, written in the form of a diary. In the same period, Levi wrote several poems which he kept private and which remained unpublished for three decades: 'Buna' (28 December 1945); 'Singing' (3 January 1946); 'February 25, 1944' (9 January 1946); 'Song of the Crow I' (9 January 1946); 'Shemà' (10 January 1946); and 'Get Up' (11 January 1946). They were finally published under these dates in the collection *L'osteria di Brema* (The Brema Tavern) by the Milan-based publisher Scheiwiller after they had been rejected by Einaudi, his publisher since 1958.

A third text in a vestigial form that would later become *If This Is a Man* was co-authored with his friend and fellow concentration-camp survivor, Leonardo De Benedetti. Also known as the *Auschwitz Report*, it was a medical report on the sanitary and medical organization at

Monowitz (*A Report on the Hygenic-Sanitary Organization of the Concentration Camp for Jews in Monowitz* [*Auschwitz–Upper Silesia*]). It was published in a medical journal in November 1946, but was also distributed in manuscript form to various Turin organizations with ties to the Resistance and the Jewish community. This was a clear sign that, as early as 1945/1946, both authors wanted their experiences to be more widely-known.

Levi was so disturbed on returning home that he felt the urgent need to eliminate the toxins forced into his system at Auschwitz by writing about his experience. The aim of writing was thus to free himself of the poison. And yet his urge to write—not just testimonies—was already there at the camp. As Levi himself reminded us many years later in his Appendix to *If This Is a Man*, the young deportee had a notebook and the stub of a pencil inside the death camp. The expression he used to communicate with his readers when they would one day read the result of his note-taking was that he was writing 'what I could never tell anyone' (p. 135). The idea was implicit in the very act of writing. Writing, with its distancing and objectifying stance, stood in for the direct, oral account of events—which would have been obsessive and impelling in his first few months back in Turin. Levi's eye-witness stories were reflective, and for Levi reflecting on his past was his way of going back in time to the episode that he wanted to relate.

The body of work Levi produced in the early months of his return to Turin took the form of written reports and testimonies and were an act of denunciation; writing these was an essential part of his return. The image of the pencil stub would return in later stories set in the Lager. The letters he managed to write to his family in Turin when he was imprisoned at Monowitz, and was even able to send with the aid of a volunteer at the factory, were physical evidence. Sending letters was by no means a common occurrence in the Nazi extermination camps.

Several chapters of *If This Is a Man*, if not all, were written in a small town in the Piedmont region called Avigliana where Levi found a job in 1946. Two months after his gruelling but ultimately fortunate journey home, Levi was employed by Montecatini, the company that owned the chemical plant there. Years later, Levi wrote about the period when he was writing his first book in a short-story called 'Chromium' (in *The Periodic Table*). Levi's duties in the noisy paint factory were not particularly pressing ('No one paid much attention to me', p. 877), and he found time now and then to dedicate to his writing. It is likely that some chapters were written by hand while others were typed, especially in the evening in the factory dormitory where he stayed during the week. The 'maniacal scribbler who disturbed nights in the dormitory' (p. 881). Since he had just come back from Russia, some suspected him of being a Soviet agent. He was in no hurry to finish, but told his story 'giddily' (p. 876), almost compulsively. He had no precise plan. The chapters of *If This Is a Man* he produced 'little by little' (p. 876) in Avigliano were still very much fresh reports of facts, impressions, reflections and eyewitness accounts which would only take on a cohesive form when the final project was completed.

Levi also 'scribbled' on his commutes from Turin to Avigliano and back. As he himself would later relate, one important chapter, 'The Canto of Ulysses', was written in a lunch break. He finished his meal in 15 minutes and then retired to his dormitory to write the story of Pikolo and how he attempted to use Dante's Canto XXVI to teach Italian to his French fellow prisoner. These impressions linked to facts, as he liked to say, were exactly what Levi was extracting by writing a testimony in the guise of a story.

Before examining the work-in-progress that was the 1947 edition of *If This Is a Man*—the one published by De Silva after Einaudi rejected the manuscript—let us take a few steps back in time and look at the text known as the *Auschwitz Report*. This is because there is an important link between this more 'technical' witness statement and the first edition of *If This Is a Man*.

WRITING THE *AUSCHWITZ REPORT*

In the Katowice concentration camp where Levi was held after Auschwitz was liberated by the Red Army in January 1945, Leonardo De Benedetti and Primo Levi were commissioned by the Soviet officials who managed the camp to write a report on the sanitary and medical conditions at Monowitz where they had been imprisoned. The Soviet government requested a similar report from all the doctors who had been held at Monowitz. De Benedetti, who was a doctor, had worked in the infirmary there, and Levi had been his assistant.

We do not know what language the report handed over to the Soviet officials was written in. It may have been in French, a language both sides were familiar with. What we do know is that the initial report served as a palimpsest for a later report better-known as the *Auschwitz Report*, written by the same two former prisoners who had worked at the Buna synthetic rubber factory at Monowitz.

De Benedetti and Levi sent the *Report* to the medical journal *Minerva Medica* in 1946, after they had been introduced by Silvia Pons, a doctor and former partisan. The article was reviewed by the board and published in the 26 November edition under the section 'Original Work'. The article was signed by the two authors, although De Benedetti's name was spelt wrong. De Benedetti was credited as being a 'surgeon' while Levi was referred to as a 'chemist'.

In the opening sentence of the *Auschwitz Report*, the co-authors stated that, owing to photographic evidence and depositions provided by former prisoners, readers already knew about the existence of extermination camps instituted by the Germans in order to wipe out all Jews in Europe. It is true that, after 1945, there were a number of photographs that circulated in newspapers and magazines as well as short films that were included in news-reels. Clément Chéroux (2001) examined the impact of these pictures in Europe while Elisabetta Ruffini (Ruffini et al. 2016) conducted research on Italy in particular. Numerous photographs were published in the Italian daily press from May 1945 onwards. In the following years, books and pamphlets with printed photographs began to circulate. In 1945, a book by Giancarlo Ottani, *Un popolo piange: la tragedia degli ebrei italiani* (A People Weep: The Tragedy of the Italian Jews) was published in Milan by Spartaco Giovine. This was a collection of witness accounts of the persecution received by men and women 'of the Jewish race' in the San Vittore Prison in Milan, in the transit camp at Fòssoli and in the concentration camps. The book also reported Princess Mafalda of Savoy's imprisonment and death at Buchenwald, and the Nazi massacre at Meina. In 1948, a book entitled *Nei campi della morte* (In the Death Camps) was printed by Tipografia Lucchi. The author, Angelo Colleoni was a writer and journalist, correspondent for the Rome daily *Il Messaggero* at the Russian Front, who received the first witness statements from former concentration-camp survivors who were still in the Russian-occupied territories liberated from the Germans.

When De Benedetti and Levi wrote the *Auschwitz Report*, there were already several testimonies circulating. Elisabetta Ruffini (Ruffini et al. 2016) and her Bergamo team confirmed that there were 16 books or pamphlets on the deportation and concentration camps, eleven of which were specifically about the Lager experience, and five written by people who did not have first-hand knowledge of the facts. Most of these texts concentrated on deportation for political rather than racial reasons. In 1946, Luciana Nissim and Palagia Lewinska co-authored *Donne contro il mostro* (Women against the Monster), published by Vincenzo Ramella in Turin. Nissim, who was a doctor, was deported to Auschwitz on the same transport as Levi, a friend of hers. Her section of the book was called *Ricordi della casa dei morti* (Memories of the

Death House), and her testimony as a doctor and a Jewish prisoner made specific references to the medical and health conditions in the camp where she had been held. De Benedetti and Levi may well have read her account in manuscript form before they wrote and published their *Report*.

One of the most interesting elements about the *Auschwitz Report* is the authors' point of view. They announced themselves from the start as both witnesses and victims, thus placing themselves inside and outside the text at the same time. This dichotomous point of view would later be replicated in a more complex literary form in *If This Is a Man*. The *Report* is co-authored by De Benedetti and Levi, but it is possible, with a certain degree of approximation, to deduce which parts were written by which author. There are several textual indications that, once the two had finished writing, Levi edited the entire *Report*, making corrections, adding factual details or changing the lexis in a way that revealed his aspirations as a budding writer.

The more specifically technical or medical sections were presumably written by De Benedetti; the more narrative or meditative parts, with greater attention to details relating to people or things, were most likely Levi's. The longest central segment of the *Report*, listing the prevalent diseases and their development in the context of the concentration camp, was almost certainly written by De Benedetti. In addition, the clinical descriptions of the effects of deprivation, starvation, insanitary conditions, violence and fatigue on prisoners at Monowitz were certainly the doctor's. The account of the journey to Auschwitz, however, was clearly Levi's, to the extent that one can draw a parallel between the story as it was reported here and the story at the beginning of *If This Is a Man* as it was told a year later.

The band playing 'infernal' marches and 'popular songs dear to every German' described in the chapter 'Ka-Be' (p. 48) appeared in the *Auschwitz Report* in more general terms. Likewise, Levi's focus on shoes, which returned in many of his works, as well as the German soldier who offered friendly advice on what to do with their money and jewellery to deportees as they were leaving. The figure in this early sketch resembled the soldier 'bristling with arms' (p. 17) in the 1958 edition of *If This Is a Man*, who asked the thirty prisoners 'if we have any money or watches to give him, seeing that they will no longer be of use' (p. 17) in the truck that would take them to Monowitz. This detail was added 11 years later, showing how Levi's mind processed successive waves of memories.

Some of the expressions used in the *Auschwitz Report*, such as 'impartial and affectionate advice', 'the group was tough', 'imprisoned here', 'dark' or 'tragic presentiments', sound like phrases from *If This Is a Man*. Many years later, further details emerged in other works, such as a reference to improvised shoe laces made with twisted paper strings or, when possible, electric wire. All these clues put together allow us to attribute the first and the last section of the *Report* to Levi. Clearly, his narrative style had not yet been as honed as it would be when he came to write *If This Is a Man*, but these are early experiments. Writing improves with practise, and as we shall see, the young chemist from Turin would go on to work hard on the various versions of his books in the future.

Robert Gordon (2006) analysed the *Auschwitz Report*, comparing the text with later work. He highlighted the progressive sharpening of Levi's prose style in terms of concision, rhythm and balance. There were already several specific traits of the author's style in the *Report*, which owed as much to his training as a chemist as to his natural precision and seriousness: his technical lexis, and his wide reading. These features tend to confirm the hypothesis that Levi edited the entire *Report*, including the technical parts written by De Benedetti. Another quality of the *Report* is ascribable to Levi: the underlying irony of the text, highlighting his natural sense of humour. An example of this was when he stressed the Germans' obsession with form and appearance. The double layer that irony and humour provided meant that Levi's prose was not tainted by moralism, here or in later works. It also allowed him to grasp the comic or ridiculous aspects of human behaviour—as he did so patently in his later writing. Levi had a flair for subtle irony which saved him from deep pessimism, and helped him relativize—or at least judge from a distance—the things that happened to him.

As Gordon noted, the *Auschwitz Report* was a call to be heeded. Both authors felt an urgent need to testify; at the same time, they took nothing for granted. Both mentioned the gas chambers that then figured in *If This Is a Man*. In the *Report*, Levi made every effort only to include details he had witnessed; he mentioned them but did not describe them. In the medical section, the *Report* talks about the special Kommando responsible for the gas chambers and the crematoria. One detail in particular is inexact, as it was probably second-hand information. That is, that the Sonderkommando was made up of criminals with blood on their hands. In 1945–46, not much was known about the running of the camps, nor about the number or provenance of those prisoners that Levi would go on to describe in detail 40 years later in 'The Gray Zone' (*The Drowned and the Saved*). When the two authors talked about the crematoria, they adopted the formula 'we understand that', or 'we have heard that', so that it is clear they are writing about other people's experiences and not their own. In the case of the diseases prevalent in the Ka-Be hospital wing, by contrast, the diagnoses and details were extremely precise because Levi and De Benedetti had seen them with their own eyes.

How should one classify the *Auschwitz Report*? Some critics have referred to it as a 'proto-document' or 'ante-text', but if we see it as a work-in-progress over the first few months after his return to Turin (together with the poems, stories and the various chapters that would them comprise *If This Is a Man*), then it could be seen as a 'parallel text'. Levi worked, if one can put it this way, at different tables, in different genres. When he decided to write down his memories of the concentration camp, he had not yet established what genre or style he would adopt for this purpose.

The *Auschwitz Report*, at least the parts he most likely wrote, was a 'technical' or 'scientific' text, in line with the two authors' professions. Another text written in the same period, 'The Story of Ten Days', was a diary. Added to these were the poems and stories, such as 'The Mnemagogs', where Levi experimented with other literary forms that he hoped might be complementary, or even parallel, to the other tables he was working on in those early months, both with his notebook and pencil and his typewriter.

A vital difference, on the other hand, between the *Auschwitz Report* and the other pieces he was working on at the same time, and which would evolve into his first book, was with regard to the grammatical subject. The *Report* was written in the third person, given that is precisely that: a report. In *If This Is a Man*, by contrast, the dominant person is the first-person singular and plural: the I/We that constituted the grammatical fulcrum of the narrating subject (La Fauci 2015).

A DIARY AND EARLY TYPESCRIPTS

The first text narrating the deportation was 'The Story of Ten Days'. The first typescript, in the archives of the Turin Jewish Community, bears the date February 1946. Levi chose the form of a diary which is very different and yet parallel to the form of the *Auschwitz Report*. The two texts, in fact, are closely linked, even though the *Report* was co-authored. Both typescripts were deposited at the same time in two different places: the offices of the CLN (National Liberation Committee), where the memory of the partisan struggle was kept alive; and the offices of the Turin Jewish Community, where two other depositions by Levi and De Benedetti were held (2015). Both these places were highly symbolic and reveal Levi's dual group identity: as a Partisan (a brief interlude of his life he did not write anything about until the 1958 edition of *If This Is a Man*), and as a Jew (the reason he was deported to Monowitz).

It is not by chance that Levi chose the diary form as his first narrative tool, starting in his final days in the Lager before the chaotic evacuation that followed the German Army's hasty flight. It was a story of salvation, as he himself called it, a rare moment of optimism that provided a counterpoint to the terrible stories of deportation and imprisonment in the concentration camp. The first things Levi wrote about were in fact the last things to happen to him, as he himself pointed out later. He was well-aware of the importance of the prisoners' return to humanity in the overall picture of the 1947 book.

Various typescripts of 'The Story of Ten Days' circulated, as we shall see. Levi typed his manuscript and may well have written the *Story* in one sitting, with very few corrections—perhaps owing to the positive nature of the events he was describing. An indicator of this was his use of the simple past tense (*passato remoto*) in most of the story, as if to indicate completed events distant in time. The other chapters of *If This Is a Man* were mostly written in the present indicative, with some verbs in the imperfect and present perfect form, and a few in the simple past.

Levi's writing of the various chapters that made up *If This Is a Man* took place at different times and in different places. Owing to the fact that Levi sent several typed chapters to his cousin, Anna Yona (né Foà), who lived in the United States with her husband after fleeing the racial laws in Italy, it is possible to reconstruct the dates and examine the way Levi worked on the texts which would later comprise his first book. Anna Yona and her two daughters held on to the typescripts of 10 out of the 17 chapters that were finally published by De Silva. These typescripts are dated, presumably indicating the date the manuscript was typed up into a final version. Thus, we learn that Levi finished 'The Canto of Ulysses' on 14 February 1946; 'Kraus' was completed on 15 February; 'Chemistry Examination' was dated March 1946; 'October 1944' was typed up between 5 and 8 April of the same year; 'Ka-Be' between 15 and 20 June. Among these chapters sent to his cousin in order to spread the word about his testimonies, but also in the not-so-veiled hope that a US publisher might be interested, there were also the two chapters that would open *If This Is a Man*: 'The Journey' and 'On the Bottom', neither of which are dated. It is possible that these were the two chapters Levi wrote immediately after 'The Story of Ten Days', though it is hard to know for sure. It is likely, however, because some of the events described there also appeared in the *Auschwitz Report*, although in a more concise, less narrative form.

Did Levi start from the end and then go back to the beginning of his story? The only way to answer this question is to examine the original manuscripts and typescripts. In the last few years of his life, Levi stated in several interviews that he had no particular plan in mind when he started writing *If This Is a Man*. If anything, he chased his memories while attempting to cover the main issues of his deportation. This leads us to suppose that the more obvious time linkers were added while the chapters were being assembled, or at least in the context of the intense editing that the book underwent over the course of just a little more than a year. In the 1958 edition, the author added a reference to when and where *If This Is a Man* in its entirety was composed (Avigliana–Turin, December 1945–January 1947), which did not appear in the 1947 edition.

Anna Yona was not the only person to receive typescripts from Levi. Domenico Scarpa (2015) discovered that he also sent 'The Story of Ten Days' to Laura Capon Fermi, the Nobel Prize–winning physicist's wife, who also lived in exile in the US with her husband after escaping the Fascist racial laws against Jews, and after Capon Fermi had received the Nobel Prize in Stockholm. Laura Capon Fermi's papers, together with her English translation of the chapter, were donated to the University of Chicago library, but the original typescript is not among them. A comparison between the 1947 edition published by De Silva and her English translation, however, reveals some discrepancies which could prove that the text she translated was identical to the one in Anna Yona's possession. Capon Fermi's papers also include a summary of

If This Is a Man, chapter by chapter. This must mean that she had received the 1947 edition. There is also a heavily corrected first draft of a translation into English of the chapter 'Chemistry Examination' in the Chicago papers, which looks as if a native speaker—which Laura Capon Fermi was not—did the editing. These various versions show the extent to which Levi wanted his testimony to be known, and how much he wanted to be considered a writer—to the point that he sent the typescripts to people outside Italy, who were a part of his network of friends and family, and members of the Jewish diaspora.

Another person to receive Levi's typescripts was Silvio Ortona, a Jewish friend from his youth who then became a partisan commander, a high-ranking member of the Vercelli Federation of the Italian Communist Party (PCI), and later a Representative of the PCI at the Lower Chamber of the Italian legislature. Ortona became, to all intents and purposes, Levi's first publisher when he published a few 'chapters' of Levi's typescript versions in a local weekly magazine he directed called *L'amico del popolo* (Friend of the People) between March and May 1947, five months before *If This Is a Man* was to come out. The first episode was presented with a brief note stating that the text was granted 'courtesy of the author' and belonged to a forthcoming book entitled *On the Bottom* (which became instead the title of the second chapter of *If This Is a Man*) about the 'Auschwitz elimination camp'. The excerpts published by the magazine were given titles by the editors, or perhaps by Ortona himself. 'The Journey' was published on 29 March 1946; 'On the Bottom' on 5 April 1947; 'Häftlinge' on 17 May 1947; 'Our Nights' on 24 May 1947; 'An Accident' on 31 May 1947. All these correspond to the titles of the chapters that were to make up *If This Is a Man*, except 'An Accident' which was incorporated into one of the longer chapters, 'Ka-Be'. 'Häftling', likewise, became a subsection of 'On the Bottom'. This leads one to suppose that 'On the Bottom' was originally written as a chapter on its own, and that the magazine layout required two sections, with the sub-title 'Häftling' added as the first word of a new paragraph in italics.

The chapters that comprised the De Silva edition of *If This Is a Man* that came out a few months later, in October 1947, were mostly the same length—about nine pages each. The exceptions were 'The Story of Ten Days', which was the longest at 31 pages, and four others which were between 15 and 19 pages long. Publication of the instalments in the magazine came to an abrupt halt, even though the latest episode to come out, 'An Accident', bore the postscript 'to be continued'. This must mean that other episodes had been planned. The reasons for the interruption are unknown; it is possible that the De Silva publication was brought forward.

There are several notable differences between the episodes published by Ortona and the De Silva edition. These were most likely cuts required by the magazine layout, with the collaboration of the author or at least his consent. The Vercelli magazine did not publish the more meditative sections—an important aspect of Levi's prose style—that would then find their way into the De Silva edition. The publication of these edited excerpts, preceded by the one-off publication of a poem called 'Buna'—Levi's very first published work—probably aimed to tell the story as it was, raw and unfiltered. An interesting example of the changes include the omission of the section on 'perfect happiness' and unhappiness, alongside other significant cuts which contributed to giving the text a feeling of precision, of hard truth.

Some of the missing details in the Vercelli magazine versions invite us to believe that the typescripts sent to Ortona were similar to the ones sent to Anna Yona, and may even be the same versions that were sent to Einaudi in 1946. This work-in-progress approach to writing, which was typical of Levi in all his books, was particularly evident in the development of the chapters for his first book. The manuscript of *If This Is a Man* was the most heavily edited, with the exception of some sections of *The Truce*, which were also heavily revised.

Another interesting feature to emerge from a comparison of the De Silva and the earlier magazine versions is the different punctuation. In the De Silva edition, Levi punctuated more liberally, with the effect that his sentences are generally longer, with sub-clauses separated by commas and semicolons, and with explanations following colons. This punctuation shows greater attention was paid to the De Silva edition than to the previous magazine versions.

The following two sections will deal with the first edition of *If This Is a Man* and the events surrounding its publication. Further sections will be dedicated to the various chapters of the book, and will look into the differences between the various versions of 'The Story of Ten Days' and the final version that went to print, which is a perfect example of Levi's work-in-progress approach to writing. The chapter will then look into the 1958 edition and other versions of *If This Is a Man*.

THE 1947 EDITION OF *IF THIS IS A MAN*

By the end of 1946, the manuscript of *If This Is a Man* was almost complete, as the dates on various chapters, subsequent interviews and letters to Jean Samuel (the character Pikolo in 'The Canto of Ulysses') reveal. Levi had typed up all the material previously written by hand in notebooks, and the manuscript was therefore ready to send to a publisher.

As we have pointed out, in the two years after the war, 1946–47, the publication of testimonies and books by concentration-camp survivors reached a peak—29, including *If This Is a Man*, in that period alone. Only nine of these, however, were included in a publisher series (Ruffini et al. 2016). At the end of 1947, there was a blackout in publications on the subject of the deportation and nothing else was printed until 1952. By the time Levi had completed his manuscript of *If This Is a Man* in 1946, three books had already come out specifically regarding the deportation of the Jews: *Tra gli artigli del mostro nazista* (In the Claws of the Nazi Monster) by Frida Misul; *Donne contro il mostro nazista* (Women against the Nazi Monster) by Luciana Nissim and Pelagia Lewinska, already mentioned at the beginning of this chapter; and

24029 by Alba Vecchi Capozzi. All three of these books were written by women who had transited through Fòssoli and then gone on to Auschwitz. Did Levi read all three? Or only Nissim and Lewinska's? We will never know the answer.

Unlike the four Jewish women authors who published their testimonies with small, local publishers, Levi had every intention of getting his book published by a major publisher with distribution across the country. As Levi said years later, he sent his book to 'big publishers'. The only one we know for sure was Einaudi, but it is possible he also sent his manuscript to Arnoldo Mondadori and Edizioni di Comunità, both founded in 1946. Einaudi was not, in fact, a 'big publisher' at the time, but it had a good reputation, and its offices were in Turin. Moreover, friends of Levi's that he admired, such as Cesare Pavese, worked there. Levi took his manuscript to the offices in via Biancamano, a parallel road to Corso Re Umberto where he lived. Years later, he said he couldn't remember who received the package. He did recall, however, that a subsequent meeting took place with Natalia Ginzburg who was a family acquaintance: Ginzburg's brother was the Levi family doctor. Natalia handed the manuscript back to Levi, saying that Einaudi was not interested in publishing it.

In an interview with Nico Orengo many years after this rejection, Levi said:

> I had written some stories after I came back from Monowitz. I wrote them without realizing they could be turned into a book. My friends in the Resistance after they had read them suggested filling them out and making a book out of them. It was '47, and I took the book to Einaudi. Various people read it, but it was my friend Natalia Ginzburg who was tasked with telling me they weren't interested. So, I went and asked Franco Antonicelli at De Silva. Malvano, Anita Rho, Zini and Zorzi read the manuscript and they decided to publish it. Antonicelli

chose the title of one of my poems, 'If This Is a Man', as the title of the book. They printed 2,500 copies (Orengo 1985).

Levi's description of events contained at least two interesting points. First, that Levi felt he had written 'stories' rather than a book; or rather, by writing separate 'stories' he didn't realize they formed a book. At least that is what he says. Are we to believe him? I think we should, at least in principle, because the form of the single manuscripts was probably not yet that of a book. The second point is the suggestion his friends made to 'fill out' the stories, meaning to give the manuscript a more literary form.

We know from various testimonies, and from the author himself, that he started by talking about the deportation and his life in the camp, and only later prepared himself to write about the experience. Levi often talked about the act of writing, including in *If This Is a Man*. The first mention of it in the book was when he wrote that he tried to take notes when he was imprisoned in the Lager; the second was when he referred to himself sitting at a table writing. Nearly every one of Levi's books contains the story of how it came to be written. He tended to authorize the very act of writing by means of a meta-textual tool: writing about writing the book as he was writing it.

Natalia Ginzburg was often asked why she and Cesare Pavese rejected *If This Is a Man*. Answering Orengo in an interview (1987), she said:

> I remember that as well as myself, Pavese also read the book, and others did too, though I can't remember who. Pavese said it was perhaps not a good moment to publish *If This Is a Man*, not because he was censoring a book about Jews but because he thought it would get lost among the many testimonies that were being published at the time on the Lager experience. He said it was better to wait. Whether we made a mistake is another question, but I repeat, it was not out of censure.

After Einaudi's rejection, Levi sent the manuscript to the De Silva publishers via his sister, Anna Maria, who was a friend of Alessandro Galante Garrone, a member of the National Liberation Committee (CLN) who had read the book and strongly recommended it to the publisher.

Established in 1942, the De Silva publishers were named after the first printer in Piedmont to produce a book in Italian. Their founder, Franco Antonicelli, was an influential cultural figure in Turin who had published the most important literary discoveries in the 1930s with Frassinelli, including Kafka, Melville, Joyce, Anderson and Babel. With ties to the anti-Fascist movement, Antonicelli was arrested and later played an important role in the Resistance. When publications resumed after the 8 September 1943 Armistice, De Silva became a promising publisher with literary and cultural influence. They published five books in 1946, and eleven in 1947, including Levi's *If This Is a Man*, which was printed in the series dedicated to Leone Ginzburg, Antonicelli's friend who had died in the anti-Fascist struggle, who was one of the founders of Einaudi and Natalia Ginzburg's husband. Two other books on military history were published in the same series: General Antonio Trabuchi's 'I vinti hanno sempre torto' (The Vanquished are Always in the Wrong), and Giusto Tolloy's 'Con l'armata italiana in Russia' (With the Italian Army in Russia).

Antonicelli grasped the importance of Levi's book from the start. He appreciated its literary value, and was enthusiastic at the idea of publishing it. His marketing blurb called it 'an exceptional book, perhaps the most important since the war, together with the far more famous *Cristo si è fermato a Eboli* [. . .] together a memoir, documentary and work of art. The concept of non-professional men of letters has become more common in Italy, and Primo Levi is first in line.' Antonicelli was well-aware that Levi did not belong to literary circles, but in his eyes this made Levi even more of a novelty in the publishing world of the day.

Once the book was printed, it comprised 107 pages. The hard cover was white with red lettering for the title, the simplest possible. The dust-jacket illustration was a Goya drawing taken from the preparatory sketches for the etching series known as *Disasters of War* and depicted a man lying dead, face down in a pool of blood, his arms outstretched. The publisher added a publicity belly band with four sides, in red, yellow and black, and on one side the words:

> Primo Levi wrote this cold and terrifying account of the most tragic experience a man could ever experience. Is a man that is hour by hour, trial by trial, stripped of his physical appearance and destroyed in his moral existence still a man? This is the question that a stunned and bitter Primo Levi asks himself and all his brothers in the world: If This Is a Man?

'Cold and terrifying.' The choice of these two adjectives is interesting. The first, in particular, grasps an important aspect in the way Levi's testimony was perceived. On the other face of the belly band the publisher stressed that Levi was a 'new writer' and continued: 'Primo Levi wrote this narrative with the simplicity of one who has adjusted his memory to the extent of the reality he has suffered, but his testimony succeeds in being both that of a person and that of a writer.' The publicity material was most probably written by Antonicelli himself.

If This Is a Man was printed in 2,500 copies, an average run for De Silva, but there are no available sales data. Many years later, Levi spoke of 1,500 copies sold and a total of 3,000 readers. In 1949, De Silva was sold to the Florence-based publisher, Nuova Italia, where the excess books were transferred. Levi claimed that 600 books still in stock were lost in the disastrous 1966 flood. One in-house document claimed that there were only 80 copies of *If This Is a Man* in stock, while another stated that, in 1951, there were still 562 (Mazzoleni 1998). In any case, the book appears to have circulated very little outside Turin, and its lack of success was a heavy burden for Levi, to the point that years later he would claim that the low sales of the book meant he had to abandon the idea of living by his writing, and devote himself instead to his profession as a chemist (Caccamo De Luca and Orangiero 1984). In 1959, he confided his secret dream of retiring early in order to write in a letter to his German translator, Heinz Riedt (Letter, 25 November 1959).

IF THIS IS A MAN (1947–58)

Most readers come across Primo Levi in the 1958 edition. Only 3,000 or so readers ever set eyes on the 1947 edition; since then, only researchers working on comparisons between the two editions have read it. Until the beginning of the 1970s, very few people knew there were any differences between the two. The 11 years that went by between the first and second editions meant that people generally thought they were the same book. But as we now know, this was not the case. The additions Levi made to the 1958 edition transformed the book: the order of the chapters was changed, a whole new chapter was included, numerous details were added, more characters were described and the sections on Alberto were reinforced, all strongly modifying the perception of the book.

The 1947 De Silva edition of *If This Is a Man* was drier and harsher than the 1958 edition. The editors of the Italian edition of Levi's *Complete Works* decided to open with the 1947 edition, so that readers—not just critics—could experience first-hand the difference. It was, after all, the first book Levi had written: the young chemist's springboard as a writer that revealed for the first time a new narrative voice. The book lived up to that expectation. The additions, changes and corrections he made over the 11 years between the two editions did little to modify this voice; they simply altered some of his inflections. The voices in the 1947 edition and in the 1958 edition everyone knows are hard to distinguish, but if it were possible to listen to his voice as if it were the first time we had ever heard it, the 1947 edition would be the best possible starting point.

Levi was a tireless editor of his own texts, adding, cutting, correcting—a constant fine-tuning that made him more than just a witness. He was already a writer. Once he found a form for his story, he would revise it constantly. This was partly because his memories surfaced at different times, and partly because it was his interpretation of the act of writing. This was evidenced in the early typescripts of some of the chapters that he sent to Anna Yona, by the various versions of 'The Story of Ten Days' and by the single chapters he shared with family and friends. Levi also kept a notebook with 'For Einaudi' written on the cover, which dates back to the early 1950s when he started editing the 1947 edition, where he noted possible edits in pen. Further evidence was the version that Levi finally gave to Einaudi—the manuscript used for the 1958 edition we all know and still read today.

Before examining the preparation process for Einaudi's publication of *If This Is a Man*, however, it is important to clarify that the 1947 and the 1958 editions were two different books, and not two versions of one. The only way to highlight their differences is therefore to compare them, as we will do. The unique features of the 1947 edition, in fact, only emerge by comparison to the later edition: its literary impact, grasped by some of the earliest reviewers (Calvino and Cajumi), and its structure, which is more direct and has less internal articulation than the 1958 edition. Likewise, in order to appreciate the extent of Levi's fine-tuning over the intermittent years, it is equally necessary to go back and forth between the two editions.

Let us start, then, with a formal detail. Levi did not re-type the whole of *If This Is a Man* for Einaudi. He gave the Turin publisher a copy of the De Silva edition, with the Goya sketch on the cover (now in the Italian State Archive, where the Einaudi archive is held, File n.1502, Folder n.3003). The copy was probably his wife, Lucia's, as the frontispiece is dedicated to her: 'To Lucia, October 26, 1947, (signed) Primo.' Levi's changes were indicated with strips of typed paper stuck onto the printed edition. Every strip, or new sheet, was marked with progressive numbers corresponding to the page numbers in the De Silva edition, with the exact point in the page where the text was to be added. This annotation was probably carried out by an in-house editor tasked with preparing the new edition, though the method may have been suggested by Levi himself who was very pragmatic in these matters. Some paper strips were typed using black carbon paper. Corrections, or the editor's proofreader's marks, were in red. An example of this method is an insert with a passage about Emilia Levi, one of the most touching passages in the whole 1958 book, which is a paper strip with seven lines typed on it, indicated as number 8.

We will now proceed to examine the changes between the two editions chapter by chapter.

'The Journey'

The poem that opened *If This Is a Man,* later entitled 'Shemà', was written in 1946. In the 1947 edition, it was placed after the Preface while in the 1958 edition it preceded it. The shift in position alters the significance of the text. In the 1947 edition, in fact, the poem followed the author's declaration in the Preface that the book was 'A detached study of certain aspects of the human mind' (p. 5). Before embarking on his story, but after his 'detached' preface, Levi addressed his readers harshly in the poem—especially in the last lines. The only change between the two editions was that the 1958 Preface is untitled.

There is a marked difference between the typescript sent to Yona and the 1947 De Silva edition, however, at the very beginning, in the chapter called 'The Journey'. The opening phrase of the version sent to his cousin—'at Fòssoli talking about leaving was considered a serious breach of etiquette'—was later cut. The incipit of the De Silva edition was more effective in its precision regarding the facts: 'In the middle of February 1944, there were roughly 600 Italian Jews, in addition to about 100 Yugoslav internees and a few other foreigners who were considered politically suspect.'

Further changes, additions and clarifications were made but they were not significant. The 1947 edition opened in the Fòssoli transit camp, with an estimation of the number of Italian Jews being held there. Levi thus included his own eye-witness account in the general testimony of the deportation, a duality that ran throughout the book, even though the title contained the word 'Man' and not 'Jew'. The 1947 edition used the noun 'Jew' (or adjective 'Jewish') more than 40 times; the 1958 edition used the words a little more often, but the difference was not enormous.

Levi attached a page and a half of typed text to the 1947 edition that Levi gave Einaudi 11 years later. The text was marked up in blue biro, indicating where the old text needed to be integrated with the new. This extra page and a half changed the framework of the entire work. Levi had already written a new incipit in the early 1950s, but by the time the book was being prepared for print in the 1958 edition, the perception of the deportation had changed: an anti-Fascist paradigm of the Resistance had replaced the idea of an anti-Nazi struggle. In the 1947 edition, there was no trace of Levi's partisan experience, except at the very end, in 'The Story of Ten Days' which we will analyse later. Apart from the useful historical reference, Levi added to the impact of the narrative when he included a significant episode: his capture by the Fascist Militia, his interrogations, his declaration that he was 'an Italian citizen of Jewish race' and his transfer to Fòssoli. In addition to these freshly added facts were also some meditative passages in the 1958 incipit, which was typical of his style. In these he reflected on his experience, asking himself what he had learnt from the failure of 'the nonexistent organization' (p. 9) that was 'supposed to become a partisan band' (p. 9): 'At that time I had not been taught the doctrine that I learned very quickly later in the Lager' (p. 9).

There are further short but highly significant additions confirming the rounder tone of the 1958 edition. In these sections, Levi talked about the feelings shared by his friends in the camp, adopting the first-person plural ('we' and 'us') which included himself and other deportees. He talked about their 'fear and desperation'. The journey by train was 'unnerving' (p. 13) and the 'hours of darkness were a nightmare without end' (p. 14).

Another paper strip added to the De Silva edition contained an important passage that strengthened a previous section by introducing a moralizing, psychological tone:

> There are few men who know how to go to their death with dignity, and often they are not those you would expect. Few know how to stay silent and respect the silence of others. Our restless sleep was often interrupted by noisy and futile disputes, by curses, by kicks and punches delivered blindly to ward off some troublesome and inevitable contact. Then someone would light the mournful little flame of a candle, to reveal the obscure swarming of a confused and indistinguishable human mass, sluggish and aching, rising here and there in sudden convulsions and immediately collapsing again in exhaustion (p. 14).

This passage was one of those literary threads—both meditative and narrative—that Levi wove into the structure of his first book. His close attention to moral, ethical and psychological detail added to the impact of his writing without altering its nature.

A further passage that was woven into the earlier text struck critics to the point that it became one of the most common quotes from *If This Is a Man*: 'that barbaric barking of Germans in command which seems to give vent to a centuries-old rage' (p. 15). Just as memorable was the inserted phrase describing the SS officers at Auschwitz as having 'faces of stone' (p. 15). We have already spoken about the passage that threaded Emilia into the story. It was a fine example of the more emotional tone Levi introduced into the new edition, the result of his constantly honing his literary skills. The last 15 or so lines of the chapter were also added: the description of the German 'Charon' mentioned previously, who asked the prisoners, on his own 'small private initiative' (p. 17), for their money and watches. The passage opened with an expression of speed—'the truck took off into the night at full speed' (p. 16)—which allowed the narrator to expand his metaphor of the prisoners in the truck 'all going 'down' and showed greater literary skill than similar passages in the 1947 edition. Another remarkable stylistic feature was the way he effortlessly shifted from direct speech to reported speech without losing any of the immediacy of the narration.

'ON THE BOTTOM'

Several changes were made to this chapter. Some were small details (hair 'clippers' [p. 19] rather than 'machines'); others were whole new passages. One of these, for example, was the passage on Flesch, the interpreter, whom Levi described as being 'reluctant to translate into Italian the icy German phrases' (p. 20), thus revealing his state of mind. These textual integrations enriched the writing while revealing the narrator's feelings. They also underlined how important Levi considered words themselves: 'He is a closed, taciturn man, for whom I feel an instinctive respect because I am aware that he began to suffer before we did' (p. 21).

The most important addition, however, regarded the process of tattooing. The addition to the new edition was four printed pages which radically altered the chapter. In the 1947 edition, after stating the number of the tattoo on his left arm, Levi went straight to the phrase: 'There are many things still to learn, but many things we have already learnt.' He then said the operation was 'painful' and 'rapid' and provided information regarding the numbers that were tattooed onto the arms of prisoners from various nationalities (which he then came back to in other parts of the book). This information turned out to be invaluable for ascertaining the numbers of prisoners who went through the camps.

Without going into the details of the many, substantial additions to this chapter, we will limit our analysis to a few significant points. Levi added information regarding the Birkenau crematorium; used expressions in French, one of the many languages used in the camp; and adopted the expression 'destruction of European Judaism' (p. 24), which he probably derived from his post-1947 reading (The word Shoah was already in use in the 1930s and 40s, but Levi preferred to use a historical reference). Moreover, in a conversation with a young Polish Jew, Levi referred to his mother as 'a Jew in Italy'. Another addition was the much-cited phrase '*Hier ist kein warum*' (here is no why here [p. 25]), followed by the quote from Canto XXI:48 of Dante's *Inferno* ('The Sacred Face has no place here!' [p. 25]).

A further addition was the image of the band at the camp entrance playing 'Rosamunde' (the 'well-known sentimental song' [p. 26]). The theme of music and sounds penetrating the camp was picked up later, almost as if re-reading the early edition induced Levi to re-think the details which he then added to this chapter and to the following entirely new one. In the dialogue with the young Polish boy, Schlome, who was sitting 'against the wooden wall of the barrack' (p. 26) and had already spent three years in the Lager, Levi stated that he was a chemist ('*Ich Chemiker*'). After their 'timid embrace', Levi wrote that he was 'filled with a serene sadness that is almost joy' (p. 27), again extending the range of emotions contained in the book. There was already irony in the 1947 edition, presented in the phrase about the 'many things we have learnt' which recalls the ending of Manzoni's *The Betrothed* where Renzo makes a list of the things he has learnt.

A final interesting addition was the section about shoes, one of those subjects that recurs in *If This Is a Man* and in *The Truce*. Considering that it was a footsore that led him to the Ka-Be infirmary, it was clear why shoes were so essential in the camp. 'And do not think that shoes constitute a factor of secondary importance in the life of the Lager. Death begins with the shoes' (p. 30), Levi wrote in the 1958 edition. In this chapter, there was already a marked tendency to versify his prose, creating what was almost a parody of the poems he knew by heart. One example was 'I get tired in the rain' (*mi fiacco nella pioggia*) taken from Canto VI:54 of Dante's *Inferno* (p. 32).

'INITIATION'

There were four typed carbon-copied sheets stuck into the 1947 book in this chapter, which was all completely new material. This chapter not only provided a great deal of information—such as the Babel of languages present in the camp, the dream, the passage about bread being used as currency in the camp and its various names—but it also allowed us to appreciate how attentive Levi was to words and to things. His attention to the latter became a distinctive feature of his journalistic writing in the 1970s and 80s. The climax of the chapter took place in the washhouse with the description of the 'curious didactic frescoes' (p. 35), with 'an enormous white, red, and black louse', together with the 'inspired distich' in German reminding prisoners to wash their hands (p. 35). The most significant additional figure was the ex-Sergeant Steinlauf, whom Levi introduced at the focal point when 'the instinct for cleanliness disappeared in me' (p. 36); a point towards which the whole chapter converged from a narrative point of view. After Flesch, he was the second German 'of goodwill' (p. 37) in the camp, who had fought in the First World War in the Austro-Hungarian Army.

This new passage was one of the most remarkable in the book. It was clearly the fruit of reconsideration and afterthought which had impelled him to add the new pages. For the first time, the concept of bearing witness was explicitly brought into the story: 'One must want to survive, to tell the story, to bear witness' (p. 37). A survivor can bear witness, and therefore it was necessary to survive. This passage feels like *a posteriori* justification for placing himself as a witness in the story. There is, however, another important aspect: as time passed, Levi's way of viewing the Lager experience shifted. The 1958 edition that people still read today made it clear that Levi did not agree with Stanlauf's doctrine that is was essential to 'wash our faces', and 'walk erect, without dragging our feet, not in homage to Prussian discipline but to remain alive, to not begin to die' (p. 37). He justified this by saying that this moral system could be 'understood and accepted only in part' because it was 'softened by an easier, more flexible, blander doctrine, which for centuries has drawn breath on the other side of the Alps' (p. 37) According to this, 'there is no greater vanity than to force oneself to swallow whole moral systems elaborated by others, under another sky' (p. 37)—the 'other sky' being Italy, of course.

The conclusion of the chapter is interesting because, after 11 years of re-writing and re-elaborating, Levi confessed that he was still bewildered by the hellish experience of the Lager: 'In the face of this complicated netherworld my ideas are confused: is it really necessary to elaborate a system and put it into practice? Or would it not be better to acknowledge that one has no system?' (p. 37). These questions were highly significant for Levi who was a creature of the Enlightenment.

There was a different ending to the chapter, however, that was never adopted. Levi had stuck a strip of paper on top of the previous correction, with the following text typed on it:

> He kept to these principles, and translated them into practice, day by day, because they suited him; and thanks to these he was able to last, as the good soldier he was, to the end of the Lager at Buna-Monowitz. Until the day when he too was overthrown by the final convulsions of vanquished Germany, nobody knows how or where, and his wisdom and valor was extinguished by blind violence.

Why did Levi then change the text again into the passage we now read? Did he rethink the whole section on Steinlauf? Did he decide to leave him alive, in the narrative space of this chapter, rather than report his death? Was it that he didn't want to anticipate an important narrative element of the final chapter, that is, the destruction of Germany? It is more likely that Levi, 11 years after writing the first version, wanted to close the section devoted to his reactions to Steinlauf's doctrine with a significant addition to his concept that the Lager was senseless.

The chapter 'Initiation' underwent many revisions, as Giovanni Tesio (1977) demonstrated after studying Levi's notebook entitled 'For Einaudi.' His handwritten notes can thus be dated between 1955, when, as we shall see, Levi signed a contract with Einaudi for a new edition of *If This Is a Man,* and 1958 when the new edition was published. The beginning of the chapter that Levi wrote in the notebook was different:

> All I remember about the first months in the Lager are a series of leaden days, a constant feeling of being crushed, of being shipwrecked. It seemed absurd to hope to survive, and the attempts made by my stronger companions to improve their condition felt ridiculous and pathetic, like the retching of a mouse as it spins uselessly around the trap.

This was followed by still another version: 'Buried by the interminable hours of labour under the thick mantle of acute physical discomfort, the awareness of my desperate condition burned like a red-hot iron in the few minutes a day we could relax, especially on waking up after the clement truce of sleep.'

The notebook contained other pages that Levi considered adding to the 1958 Einaudi edition, as Tesio argued (1977). There is one passage that was a likely candidate but never saw its way into print: 'The spectacle is horrific, unforgettable, vile. What evil genius was able to conceive of this barbaric parade, this dance of spectres in the red twilight?' This phrase confirms the development of an essential element of Levi's style: the way he built up his sentences with short phrases, almost aphorisms, as if they were 'mosaic tiles', as Tesio calls them. It was not just a matter of writing 'economically' but also of thinking 'economically'; creating memorable images in crisp, concise turns of phrase that were both form and content, word and thought—if it were possible to separate the two, which it is not. Levi thinks and writes 'economically'. To find a form of thought that is similar, we need to look at the ethical nature of his writing, in a moral and not a meditative sense. Many of the phrases that were added, or written to be added and then perhaps never used, had a strong meditative significance.

Analysing Levi's constant revision process—from the early typescripts in 1947, to the additions in 1958, including the passages not used in the Einaudi edition—allows us to appreciate the extent that Levi worked by means of accumulation. He would add details, or insert whole passages, as if his book were a score where the addition of a note, or a whole musical phrase, did not alter the overall impact of the piece, and yet the sonata or symphony would not be what it was without them. This process of accumulation means we must consider each and every phrase in its own right, which is what lends his writing such strength. At the same time, every phrase—even the ones that were eventually thrown out—reflected the general design of the work. The book was like a hologram. Its component parts—broken down from the page to the passage, and then further down to phrase level—form the overall picture.

This is why Levi went on editing his texts for years, adding or taking away (more the former than the latter) without modifying the palimpsest. This approach is confirmed even by the way the book was conceived. It was written in individual, separate parts, which Levi originally called 'stories'. They were then assembled and 'filled out' with subsequent revisions until the complete version was ready. In this sense, the text was never closed but always open to changes and additions. The structure of *If This Is a Man* is therefore unique. No other writers in the 'literature of memory' genre, who published fiction or witness accounts of the deportation and the 'extermination camps' in Italy and elsewhere after the end of the Second World War experimented to the same extent as Primo Levi.

'KA-BE'

'Ka-Be' was the longest chapter in *If This Is a Man*, as well as being the most articulated and filled with facts. It is in this chapter that Levi introduced the figure of Null Achtzehn ('Zero Eighteen, the last three figures of his entry number'), the Muselmänn. In the 1958 edition, Levi added details, such as the fact that Null Achtzehn was very young, as well as a further consideration on the 'grave danger' (p. 40) of being young in the camp. He also included a description of his bed companion, Chaim, who was defined as being 'Polish, a religious Jew, a student of rabbinical law' (p. 44) as well as being a watchmaker' whom Levi admired greatly for many reasons, including his profession. As we have mentioned, there were also an increased number of references to the Judaism of various characters in the 1958 edition compared to the earlier one. Levi also added a detail regarding the fact that it was 'strictly forbidden to enter Ka-Be with shoes on' (p. 43) and changed the wording for 'sent from Ka-Be to the gas' (in the 1947 edition) to 'sent from Ka-Be to the gas chambers' (p. 43) in 1958. Another interesting intertextuality can be seen in the words 'mala novella' (bad news) which linked *If This Is a Man* to the poem 'Song of the Crow I'.

'OUR NIGHTS'

This chapter in the 1947 edition opened with the words, 'In the Winter, the nights are long and we are allowed a considerable period of time to sleep' (p. 55). Levi inserted almost three pages before this opening line in order to create a link with 'Ka-Be', the chapter that preceded 'Our Nights'. The figure of Alberto was fleshed out considerably in the 1958 edition, to the extent that critics later remarked that Alberto could represent an alter ego of the author. Levi filled almost a whole page with his description, thus giving him a more complete identity than many other characters. What purpose did Alberto, almost a co-protagonist, serve? Memory doubtless played a part, but there was also a narrative strategy that Levi developed in the years between the 1947 edition—where there were no fully fleshed-out characters besides the narrator—and the 1958 one. The character introduced a novelistic element to the text, which in its turn persuaded Levi to add narrative passages to link the various chapters. This probably took place after re-reading the separate stories years later, when he had matured as a writer, and after they had been gathered together as a whole. Alberto's presence somehow 'sweetens' the narrative at certain points in the story, such as in the penultimate chapter, 'The Last One', as we shall see. It was also a sign that Levi had developed greater detachment from his own eye-witness accounts. Telling his story had become less urgent than it had been when he had just got back home after the traumatic experience.

This chapter too, in its 1958 edition, provided us with more detailed information regarding names. Engineer Kardos was written with a K, and the storyteller's name was given for the first time (Wachsmann). The passage about Levi's dream, already present in the 1947 text and not revised at all in the later edition, is highly significant as a further element of intertextuality, and as a *fil rouge* in Levi's body of work (Belpoliti 2015). In the paper strips stuck into the 1947 book for the 1958 edition were several corrections made by hand to the typed passage. When Levi had written about adaptation, he added in blue pen the word 'unconscious' ('It is an invaluable exercise of adaptation, partly passive and unconscious, partly active' [p. 53]). The adjective is fitting in the new edition. Similarly, Levi substituted the word 'reason' with 'intelligence' to describe the narrator's friend Alberto, perhaps in order to avoid repetition ('He is sustained by intelligence and intuition. He reasons correctly; often he does not even reason but is right just the same' [p. 54]).

'THE WORK'

The 1958 edition of this chapter is almost identical to the earlier one. He substituted a more technical word for the tools they were handed at work with a more commonplace word: 'jacks'. He also cut the word 'everyday' from the phrase ('and then the usual everyday things began') so that it became 'and then the usual things began' (p. 62). Finally, he added that Meister Nogalla was 'the Polish foreman' (p. 62).

'A GOOD DAY'

This chapter was also hardly revised, confirming that it was already well-established in the 1947 edition. Like the three chapters preceding it, 'A Good Day' provided a great deal of detail about life in the camp. One addition regarded the presence of 'German managers and technicians' (p. 68) in Buna, a subject that would return in future research on the people Levi had come across in the Lager, such as in 'Vanadium' (*The Periodic Table*). Another inclusion was the description of Buna as a city surrounded by different Lagers for the various foreign prisoners working there. The Buna factory 'which never produced a kilo of synthetic rubber' (p. 69) was the other topographic centre of the book, and Levi's memories continued to revolve around it.

'THIS SIDE OF GOOD AND EVIL'

This chapter, devoted to describing the barter economy and market laws in the camp, was substantially unchanged, aside from small corrections. It is worth noting that, for the school edition Levi, cut the ten lines on prostitution in the Frauenblock. In the margin of the 1947 book with paper additions that Levi used as a master copy for the 1958 edition, there was a line written in pencil and then crossed out: 'Story of broom and file'. This may have been a note to himself for a story to develop further, which later found its way in an addition to *The Last One* with Alberto as its protagonist.

The Drowned and the Saved

This is without doubt the most important chapter in terms of Levi's 'theory', and few corrections were made in the 1958 edition. The only significant change regarded political prisoners, i.e. those prisoners who were held in the camp for political reasons rather than owing to their race or religion. Levi had already written in the 1947 edition that some Jews became 'Prominents' in the camp, stressing the fact that the camp was run along the corrupting lines of 'divide and rule', according to which some prisoners were offered privileges in exchange for undertaking certain tasks. Levi's analysis of the forms of power operating in the camp was made almost 40 years before he wrote the chapter 'The Gray Zone' in the 1986 edition of *The Drowned and the Saved*.

In the 1947 edition, the passage on the 'politicals' read: 'The "real" politicals lived and died in special camps, in conditions notoriously no better than the Jews.' This was information that Levi had gleaned after he returned to Turin, and was therefore not part of his direct experience. In 1958, the passage was changed to: 'The "real" politicals lived and died in other camps, with names now sadly famous, in notoriously harsh conditions, which, however, differed in many aspects from those described here' (p. 87). Levi felt, years later, that clarifying this issue was necessary. He cut the word 'Jews' and made the distinction between the treatment reserved for political prisoners and that received by the Jewish prisoners clearer. The paradigm of the Shoah had not yet been developed, but the theme was already there, despite the framework whereby Levi had been captured as a partisan introduced in the 1958 version.

'Chemistry Examination'

In this chapter, as in others, there are reverberations with Levi's poetry: the phrase 'we are capable of waiting for hours with the complete, dull-witted inertia of spiders in old webs' (p. 99) finds an echo in Levi's 1981 poem 'Arachne', showing how Levi recycled ideas and themes. One addition rounded out the sensation of feeling like 'Oedipus in front of the Sphinx' (p. 100) before the chemistry exam. It was an interesting re-definition of his state of mind 11 years later: 'My ideas are clear, and I am well-aware even at this moment that the stakes are high; yet I feel a mad desire to disappear, to avoid the test' (p. 100). If he knew how to 'explain fully' the nature of the look that passed between the chemistry examination candidate and Doktor Ingenieur Pannwitz, Levi wrote in 1947, he would be able to understand 'why wars are started'. In 1958, the result, if he were able to 'explain fully' the look, changed: 'I would also be able to explain the essence of the great insanity of the Third Reich' (p. 101). This was a significant change, including the word 'Germany', which appeared here as well as in the chapter 'Initiation'. Another interesting addition to the theme of how Jews were differentiated in the camp. When Alex 'flies down' the stairs after the exam, Levi stated that he could do so since 'he has leather shoes because he is not a Jew' (p. 102). In the 1947 edition, the phrase was 'because he is an Aryan'. We will be looking at this aspect in the following chapter.

'THE CANTO OF ULYSSES'

Levi claimed to have written this chapter directly on his typewriter, in one sitting, during his lunch break in Avigliana. Perhaps for this reason it was the most heavily revised. It was not entirely rewritten, but there were many edits which can be traced through two different versions of the typescript (there was also a handwritten version in a notebook that is not in the archive). One typescript is the four-page text that Levi sent to his cousin, Anna Yona; the other is a typescript Levi sent to his friend, Jean Samuel which Samuel later reproduced in a book (Samuel with Dreyfus 2008). The version Levi sent to his cousin was almost identical to the one in Samuel's possession, although it may have been written earlier because one or two lines were in pen. The version sent to Samuel was completely re-typed, and the first page was a few lines shorter.

Comparing these early versions with the printed 1947 edition, several differences can be seen. Most of these are descriptive add-ons, such as 'The powdery rust burned us under our eyelids and coated our throats and mouths with a taste almost like blood' (p. 103). There is also some significant fleshing-out of the figure of Alex, the Kapo of the Chemical Kommando where Jean Samuel and Primo Levi worked, and of Pikolo—details which were not present in the typescripts but were included in the 1947 De Silva edition. The extra description of Pikolo opened with 'It should be noted that the post of Pikolo represented quite a high rank' (p. 104) and continued for more than half a page, describing the young Alsatian student and Alex, the Kapo. Various changes were made, and the whole passage was preserved in the 1958 edition.

There are two interesting differences in the Yona typescript: Samuel was described as being 'a Jew from Strasbourg', with a degree in physics, 'he was in quite good shape, and wore his camp clothes with a certain flair.' Moreover, his name was still Piccolo, in its Italian form, when later he adopted the German form Pikolo. In the typescript, Levi had written that the post of Pikolo 'was usually taken by boys under 15' but this annotation did not find its way into the De Silva edition.

One of the most interesting things to emerge from the Yona typescript that was not in the 1947 printed edition is a comparison between Piccolo and the Old Testament Joseph: 'Piccolo, like Joseph in Egypt, succeeded in making himself indispensable.' One must assume that the reference to Joseph was cut, because, in the context of a chapter with Dante's Christianized Greek Ulysses as its fulcrum, a further element—Jewishness—must have felt out of place. Nevertheless, at the end of the chapter, Levi did hypothetically introduce the theme of Jewish destiny when he wrote that the chosen people had been condemned for their 'anachronism' (p. 109). It may appear that the reference to 'our fate' alludes to Piccolo and Primo's deportation, but it is more likely that 'our' means 'us Jews', the 'Jewish people' evoked in the first chapter of

If This Is a Man in the Gattegno family ceremony. The expression 'something gigantic' (p. 109.) certainly feels like a confirmation that Levi was indeed writing about the fate of the Jews. By identifying with Ulysses, Levi suggested that the entire Jewish people may have been struck down by divine punishment. The reference to Joseph and his brothers in Egypt, on the other hand, was most likely derived from Levi's early reading of Thomas Mann's four-part novel, *Joseph and his Brothers*, the influence of which can be traced at various junctions in Levi's work (the book was included in his personal anthology, *The Search for Roots*, published in Italy in 1973).

There were numerous other differences between the Yona typescript and the 1947 printed edition. 'I then try to translate' became 'Here I stop and try to translate', for example. Or again, 'And after "when"? Who knows! A hole in my memory. 'Before Aeneas gave that place a name.' Another hole. A fragment surfaces. 'Nor pity for my old father nor the love I owed Penelope. Can that be right?' became 'And after 'When I departed'? Nothing. A hole in my memory. 'Before Aeneas gave that place a name.' Another hole. An unstable fragment floats in my mind: 'Nor pity for my old father nor the love I owed Penelope which would have gladdened her. Can that be right?' There are about ten of these differences, including: as the euphemism 'perdinci' (for goodness' sake) cut, making the phrase: 'Pikolo stops' starker; 'it makes you want to curse' edited out; and the addition of the description of the mountains 'which would appear in the evening dusk as I returned by train from Milan to Turin'. They were all interventions that shifted the chapter onto a higher plane and gave greater precision to the account.

A few changes were also made for the 1958 edition of this chapter. In the first paragraph, for example, the phrase 'It wasn't one of the worst jobs' was changed to 'It was a luxury job' (p. 103). The 1947 edition mentioned the fate of Pikolo's mother ('His mother ended up in Birkenau') while in the 1958 edition this was cut. There was also a significant passage that was added:

Or perhaps it is something more: perhaps, despite the feeble translation and the pedestrian, rushed commentary, he has received the message, he has understood that it has to do with him, that it has to do with all men who toil, and with us in particular; and that it has to do with us two, who dare to talk about these things with the soup poles on our shoulders (p. 108).

In the 11 years that separated the two editions, Levi perfected the details of his account, but he also honed his language, enhancing the more 'sublime' elements of the chapter, and driving his point home with the expression 'perhaps the reason for our fate, for our being here today' (p. 109) that we discussed earlier. There are two different registers in this chapter: one is a high, literary register, where Levi's memory of Dante's verses and the thoughts his 'terzarima' induced in him created a sense that Levi was speaking to a double of himself rather than to Pikolo; the other is a low, everyday register, used by Levi to describe Pikolo and Primo's daily life in the Lager.

As far as the Dante citations from Canto XXVI are concerned, there were a few differences between the Yona typescript and both the 1947 and the 1958 print editions. The first quote, 'just like a fire whose flame struggles' was corrected to 'just like a fire that struggles in the wind' (p. 106). Another addition included in the 1947 edition was the expression 'like the voice of God,' which substituted the previous 'like a sip of warm wine' ('As if I, too, were hearing it for the first time: like the blast of a trumpet, like the voice of God. For a moment I forget who I am and where I am' (p. 108). This change altered the meaning of the whole chapter. Was Levi invoking the Christian God or the Jewish God? One must suppose he was referring to Dante's God. In the final part of Levi's comment on Dante's verses, after the triplet that starts with the line 'Three times it turned her round with all the waters' where Levi mentioned the anachronism Dante appeared to have fallen into, in the Yona typescript Levi wrote 'the anachronism thrown in as a betrayal,' which then became 'about the so human and so necessary and yet unexpected anachronism' (p. 109). Finally, the critic Alberto Cavaglion thought that the edition of Dante's *Inferno* Levi used was the *Divina Commedia* commented by Giuseppe Vandelli in its ninth edition for Hoepli in 1929 (2012).

'THE EVENTS OF THE SUMMER'

Only one addition was made to this chapter between the 1947 and the 1958 editions, and this regarded the relationship between prisoners and civilians in the Lager: the way the 'means to survive' could be obtained by prisoners from civilians, and the fights that took place to obtain these favours. The passage that was added starts on p. 114 with 'There are also some who specialize in complex and patient campaigns of spying' and ends with 'capable of overcoming the caste barrier' (p. 115). In the 1958 edition, Levi made some further revisions in order to link the new paragraph with the text that followed it, as well as small alterations such as the story of Primo's relationship to Lorenzo being 'banal and enigmatic' to being 'plain and enigmatic' (p. 113), as well as adding the word 'modesty' to the phrase 'he shows a serious lack of modesty and tact,' (p. 114) which evoked the opening of the first chapter of the Yona typescript that was then cut.

'OCTOBER 1944'

Five lines were added to the 1958 edition of this chapter, and these were important because Alberto figured in the scene where Primo discussed with him the 'hypothesis' that there 'could have been a mistake with our cards' (p. 122) because René had been selected for the gas chamber. Another line that was added was: 'It must likewise have been a mistake with Sattler' (p. 123). Furthermore, the second paragraph in the 1947 edition began with the words 'we were here last year', whereas then 1958 edition was corrected to the starker, harsher 'we were here last winter' (p. 117).

'KRAUS'

The manuscript of this chapter was dated 25 February 1946. This might signify that he wrote it in a day in a moment of inspiration that Levi once referred to as 'trances' in an interview. He wrote many pages in this state (the theme of inspiration returns in a comical and sarcastic form in the short story collection).

There are no differences in this chapter between the 1947 and the 1958 editions, but there are some changes, mostly additions as we have noted, that took place between the Yona typescript and the 1947 edition. These revisions added significant details that were probably the result of memories surfacing, which were then translated into words. In the early version, there was no 'roof', the water was up to his 'shoulders' and not his 'head', 'parts of the body' became 'portions of the body'. Levi always paid attention to details regarding the parts of the body. Another revision regarded the prisoners' shovelling while they were 'stuck in the mud', with its obvious reference to Dante.

The chapter revealed an important element of Levi's approach to writing. Never one for exaggeration, he always knew when to stop, when not to overwork his point, demonstrating a strong sense of measure. In his revision of the Yona typescript, in preparation for the 1947 edition, he re-assessed the sequence of actions he had used to describe the prisoners toiling in the mud and decided to add 'so that our shoes don't get sucked in' after the phrase 'we extract our feet cautiously'. He would fiddle with the single parts of his construction, as if he were working on a Meccano model made of words. Other revisions include 'Now we are leaving. "Links, links, links", the first steps our feet hurt, then slowly we warm up and our nerves relax' in the 1947 edition became 'The Kapo marks our time in a harsh voice: "Links, links, links"; at first our feet hurt, then slowly we warm up and our nerves relax.' Cutting 'Now we are leaving' and opening with the realistic words spoken by the Kapo, presented as if they were the prisoners' interior monologue, gives the phrase an entirely different rhythm. The adverbial phrases 'to start with' ('dapprima') and 'slowly' ('piano piano') add to the rhythm. Both are composite adverbs in the Italian, and the former was often used by the eighteenth-century dramatist and poet, Vittorio Alfieri, adding a literary echo to the passage—whether Levi was aware of it or not.

In this chapter, as in many other points in the book, Levi's memories of phrases or verses of poetry re-emerged almost unconsciously, giving the text a literary gilding. Levi built his phrases up with a scaffolding of adverbs—which are invariable parts of speech—using them to modulate the temporal rhythm of the action he was describing. At times he used them to slow the action down, so that readers could follow the sequence. Levi's analytical approach to his prose, his capacity to break down the actions he was writing about into their component parts, examine them and then put them back together again, derived from his innate observation skills. Not only did Levi study the Lager experience as an animal behaviourist would study wildlife, he also reflected this discipline in the language he used to describe it.

Another change in the text concerned Kraus, the protagonist of the story and the only character whose name was used as a chapter title. In the Yona typescript, the passage went like this: 'What a good boy Kraus must have been as a civilian: I'm sorry I don't know Hungarian, he expresses himself in a flood of words in his outlandish language, I only understand my name, from his gestures one would say that he is making promises and prophesies.' The 1947 edition was corrected to:

> What a good boy Kraus must have been as a civilian: he won't last long here, it's obvious at first glance, as demonstrable as a theorem. I'm sorry I don't know Hungarian, for his emotion has overflowed the banks, erupting in a flood of outlandish Magyar words. I cannot understand anything except my name, but from his solemn gestures one would say that he is making promises and prophecies (p. 129).

The revised passage included a harsh evaluation of Kraus's chance of survival in the camp. The overall tone of the chapter was harsh. We see a different Levi, one that already announced himself in the last sentence of the chapter before 'Kraus': If I were God I would spit Kuhn's prayer out upon the ground' (p. 124).

'Die Drei Leute vom Labor'

The most significant inclusion in this chapter again regarded Alberto, who was presented in an extremely positive light, almost as a co-protagonist—his companion in symbiosis, a 'simbionte' as Levi would later call him. The change from 'the new silence of Buna' to 'the empty silence of Buna' (p. 134) is also interesting. In this chapter we find a reference to the fact that *If This Is a Man* was first conceived in the Lager: 'Then I take my pencil and notebook and write what I could never tell anyone' (p. 135). Writing substituted speaking, as if Levi were already objectifying the experience—the phrase certainly seems to suggest it—although we will never know whether this was the case.

'The Last One'

Almost three pages were added to the 1958 edition of this chapter, beginning on page 139 with 'We talk about three new undertakings of ours' and ending with 'isn't it well thought out?' (p. 141). The inclusion revolved entirely around Alberto, the absolute protagonist of the passage. Alberto already figured in the 1947 edition, opening the chapter. This expanded chapter with its account of the 'three undertakings' Primo and Alberto had carried out, had a more flippant tone, in marked contrast with the gloomy De Silva version. All the inclusions that regard Alberto throughout the book have the function of rounding the rough edges of the 1947 text and creating a better narrative. The link with the previous section featuring Alberto and Lorenzo, and the subsequent section which talks about their empty bowls is also interesting owing to its note of colour, which is more literary in style: 'We talk about these things, stumbling from one puddle to the next, between the black of the sky and the mud of the road' (p. 141).

'THE STORY OF TEN DAYS'

We have already written about this chapter, the first account he wrote when he got back to Turin. Several versions survive: the typescript held in the Turin Jewish Community archive, the typescript deposited at the CLN, the Yona typescript, and the 1947 De Silva edition. Comparing the two typescripts, it is evident that they were typed on different typewriters. Moreover, the CLN edition has a handwritten addition: the date of his illness, 11 January 11 1945. Apart from this, there are not that many differences between them: the handwritten corrections can be read under the lines of x's used as cancellations. The main difference is the finale. In the CLN version, it was a separate section under the heading 'Epilogue'. An extra 15 lines had also been added to the account of events that took place on 21 January, which were maintained in the De Silva edition. The new passage begins: 'I was thinking that life outside was beautiful and would be beautiful again, and that it would be truly a pity to let ourselves be submerged now' (p. 157). This has every appearance of being a positive commentary that was added to the original text. Whatever the case, it reveals the fact that Levi tried to convince the 'sick men' in the infirmary Ka-Be that they should all now think about returning home. It is hard to evaluate the text deposited in the CLN archive. Was it simply an eye-witness account, or was it already a part of a book in Levi's mind? It is hard to gauge that a witness account and the story for a book came into being at the same time. It was only when he started to write about his experience that Levi began to introduce those literary elements that were already a part of his cultural heritage.

The typescript preserved in the Turin Jewish Community archive was written with a different typewriter from the other two, and could well have been given to a typing agency. The most interesting comparison, however, is between the Yona typescript and the text that became the basis for the 1947 De Silva edition. Twenty months went by between the first editorial drafts and publication, and the text underwent heavy revision over that period. There were many new details: the 'belt of braided electric wire' (p. 144) (in the typescript, leather), or the 'eighteen flints that I had stolen from the Laboratory' (p. 144), which became the basis for a later story, 'Cerium'. New characters were also introduced: the 'two Frenchmen with scarlet fever' (p. 145), Arthur and Charles, 'who had entered the camp only a few days before, with a large convoy of civilians swept up by the Germans in their retreat from Lorraine' (p. 145) Again, the revisions tended to increase the literary impact of Levi's writing. 'It was not worth it' became 'it was clear he did not think it worth doing'; 'the metal hurt to touch' became 'the icy metal stuck to the skin of our fingers' (p. 152); 'hardly able to walk' became 'infirm on our feet'; there were more dramatic descriptions such as 'after a long search, we finally found a small area of floor that wasn't excessively soiled' (p. 157).

Another addition regarded Levi's experience as a partisan. In the CLN and Yona typescripts, Levi wrote: 'Charles almost cried when I reached the part about my arrest', while in the De Silva edition Levi went into more detail: 'Charles almost cried when I told him the story of the armistice in Italy, of the grim and desperate beginning of the partisan Resistance, of the man who betrayed us and our capture in the mountains' (p. 164).

Levi referred to the revisions he made to the 1947 edition of in a 1966 letter to Gianni Polidori, who had staged *If This Is a Man* using several of Levi's drawings to help him create the play. In this chapter, the style of an eye-witness account dominated the narrative, making it similar in many ways to the *Auschwitz Report* he had written with De

Benedetti. Levi's ethical and moral meditations were limited to short phrases which did not interrupt the flow of the account, unlike in other chapters. There were few further additions in the 1958 edition, proving that the editorial revisions made by Levi and by the De Silva in-house team had already achieved the right balance. Details were honed in the 1958 edition: the doctor was the only 'Greek, the translation was 'unwilling', the wall that separated them from the dysentery patients was 'wooden', 'the man Charles, our active, trusting friend' (p. 156). As we have already stated, the date and the place where the chapter was written ('Avigliana-Turin, December 1945–January 1947') was absent in the 1947 De Silva edition.

A SEQUEL?

Levi's copy of the De Silva edition of *If This Is a Man* contains a hand-written annotation, probably in fountain pen, but the ink has been almost entirely absorbed by the paper. It looks like a note to himself: themes and situations to come back to in a future edition, which he called *Addenda*.

The note reads as follows:

(1) The 1st (?) night. Shoe polish: Templer. Wash your face. Liko, the Glückman. Ernst's speech. 'Mararin'. Luria's death. Dierna's death. Chaim.

(2) Distribution of bread in the morning. Other people's bread bigger.
Sunday day of 'rest'. Schreiber: 'Pech'. Labour without privileges.

(3) Rudimentary organs. Cabbages on the ground. The two Tischlers. The acid soup of the bombs.

Capaneo

These notes were presumably details and little stories that, in a few cases, such as in the story dedicated to Capaneo and the character of Tischler in 'Lilith', were later to be developed—though they were originally planned as possible expansions for *If This Is a Man*. As Cavaglion points out, Levi's first book is a container for stories, many of which later found their way into other forms. Some of the episodes and characters, however, were never developed further.

THE 1948 EDITION

After having rejected the book in 1946, Einaudi accepted publishing a new edition of *If This Is a Man* 11 years later. What had taken place in the meantime to make the Turin publishers change their mind? In an editorial board meeting in 1952, Paolo Boringhieri, the chief science editor, proposed the book for re-publication. In the minutes of the meetings held between 16 and 23 July, we can read that

> Boringhieri told the board that Primo Levi, who is also a fine translator of scientific texts, would like to know whether we are willing to publish a new edition of *If This Is a Man*, published by De Silva and almost out of print. The board is willing but Einaudi points out that, from a commercial point of view, De Silva has been bought up by la Nuova Italia and that therefore if we publish a new edition of the good book by Primo Levi after it has gone through two other publishers it would not stand a good chance of success. No decision is made on the subject' (*I verbali del mercoledì* 2011).

Boringhieri's proposal shows that Levi never stopped thinking about his book and continued to hope it would one day get back into the bookshops under the Einaudi imprint—despite the fact that the publishers had rejected it six years before. Six more years were to pass before this happened. In 1955, on the 10th anniversary of the liberation of the concentration camps, an exhibition on the Resistance and the

Deportation was held at Palazzo Madama in Turin. Another decade later, Levi said in an interview:

> They invited me to comment on the photographs in the exhibition, and to talk about this book that some of them had read; they were nine years older, but they had read it. I found myself submerged by questions from young people, people who were younger than me [...] I still remember how scared I was. It was my first public appearance, I found myself under siege, literally bombarded by questions. And they asked: 'Why is this book lying there buried?' So, I took it to Einaudi, and at that point there was another editorial team. There was Luciano Foà. They accepted it (Paladini 1987).

As Ruffini has shown (2016), the April 1955 exhibition at Palazzo Madama was not about the deportation at all—it was about the Resistance in Piedmont. The exhibition on the deportation was actually inaugurated in November 1959 at Palazzo Carigliano, when *If This Is a Man* had already been published in its new edition by Einaudi. The show was a huge success and many young people went to see it.

The contract Levi signed for the new edition of *If This Is a Man* was dated 11 July 1955, three years after Boringhieri pleaded his case at the editorial board meeting. The date of the publication launch was given as 31 March 1957. However, Einaudi was going through financial straits at the time, and a new contract was signed on 9 May 1956 with no publication date indicated. The book was initially assigned to the series 'Piccola Biblioteca Scientifica' (A Little Scientific Library) but then re-assigned to the 'Saggi' (Essays) collection. Before publishing the book, Einaudi asked Levi to buy some of its shares as an advance on his royalties. Levi accepted the request in a letter dated 16 March 1955. Part of his advance was paid in shares to the value of 40,000 lire, but the book did not come out that year, nor in 1956. In February 1947, Levi solicited Einaudi who answered that *If This Is a Man* would see publication by the end of that year. Levi had a meeting with Luciano Foà, an editor at Einaudi, who played an important role in recuperating the book. It was Foà who, together with Boringhieri, insisted that the book be published. After this meeting, the publisher sent a letter to Levi, addressing it 'Dear Engineer,' stating that the book would indeed be published in the first half of 1958. Levi continued to solicit Einaudi insistently and finally, in June 1958, *If This Is a Man* was published.

The book was 251 pages long. The dust jacket had an abstract picture by Bruno Munari on the cover: grey, red, blue vertical blocks rising and overlapping, with black vertical and horizontal bars superimposed, giving the idea of a fence or a prison. The name of the author, the title and the publisher were negative images—white lettering on a black background. The copy on the inside flap, almost certainly written by Calvino, read:

> There was a recurrent dream, Primo Levi tells us, that often came back to haunt the nights of the prisoners in the annihilation camps. The dream was that they had returned home and were relating their past sufferings to loved ones, but they soon realized, with a sense of punishing desolation that they were not believed, their loved ones couldn't grasp the truth.
>
> With things like the annihilation camps it would seem that any book has to represent somewhat less than reality in order to be able to be read. Still today, in attempting to evaluate the literature on the concentration-camp experience, there are at least two books that rise above the others in our time. One is the French, *The Human Species*, by Robert Antelme, already translated by Einaudi; the other is the Italian *If This Is a Man*, by Primo Levi, published for the first time in 1947 by De Silva and out of print for years. We are very pleased to be presenting the book to a wider readership, as a text of exemplary value in Italian literature.

Primo Levi, a chemist from Turin, was deported to Auschwitz at the beginning of 1944, together with a transport of Italian Jews from the transit camp in Fòssoli. The book opens with the biblical scene of the departure from Fòssoli, and goes on to describe the journey and arrival at Auschwitz, where a devastatingly powerful scene takes place: the separation of the men from the women and children, whom they would never see again. Null Achtzehn, Zero Eighteen, Levi's companion in the labour camp who was reduced to an automaton and no longer reacted, marching to his death, was the type of human being most prisoners modelled themselves on during that slow process of physical and moral annihilation that led inevitably to the gas chambers. The opposite paragon was the Prominent, the man of privilege who 'organized' himself and managed to increase his daily ration of food just enough to not be eliminated; who succeeds in acquiring a position of supremacy over others; whose every faculty is honed towards one aim only: survival. Primo Levi describes the figures who become the real protagonists of the book. The Engineer Alfred L. who maintained the position of authority in the camp that he had held in his life before; the absurd Elias, who appears to have been born in the mud of the camp and who is impossible to imagine as a free man; Doktor Pannwitz, with his chilling scientific fanaticism. Some scenes recreate the atmosphere of the prisoners' world: the sound of the band playing while the prisoners march to their forced labour, a surreal symbol of the geometric insanity of the camp; the anguished nights in the narrow bunk, with a bedfellow's feet in your face; the terrible scene of the selection of men to go to the gas chambers, and that of the hanging of the man who had found the courage, in that hellhole of resignation and annihilation, to conspire and to resist, shouting on the gallows—'Kamaraden, ich bin der Letze!'—(Comrades, I am the Last One!)'

This is the first book written by Primo Levi, born in Turin in 1919, a graduate in Chemistry who now practices that profession in Turin.

On the back of the dust jacket were various quotes from reviews of the De Silva edition: the reviewers cited were Aldo Garosci (*Italia Socialista*, 27 December 1947); Lorenzo Gigli (*Gazzetta del Popolo*, 18 April 1948); Italo Calvino (*l'Unità*, 6 May 1948); Arrigo Cajumi (*La Stampa*, 26 November 1947); Cesare Spellanzon (*Corriere d'informazione*, 6 August 1948). In later reprints, Calvino and Garosci's blurbs were cut, as well as all the publication dates for the various reviews. The book was numbered as the 232nd book in the 'Saggi' series, the same collection *The Diary of a Young Girl* by Anne Frank had been published four years earlier, again at the insistence of Foà. The book that followed *If This Is a Man* in the series was *Ricorda cosa ti ha fatto Amalek* by Alberto Nirenstein, on the Polish ghettos (published in English by Orion in 1959 as *A Tower from the Enemy: Contributions to a History of Jewish Resistance*). The first edition of *If This Is a Man* was 2,000 copies, which sold out by the end of the year. Einaudi informed Levi that they wanted to print a second edition, and Levi consented in a January 1959 letter, expressing his gratitude to the publisher and asking if he could correct a couple of words in the dust-jacket blurb: the German word *Prominenten* was changed to *Prominent*, and *Letze* (a mistake in the German) was corrected to *Letzte*. By the end of 1959, the second edition was also sold out. More than 6,000 additional copies were printed between 1958 and 1961.

In 1963, after the success of Levi's second book, *The Truce*, published that year, Einaudi moved *If This Is a Man* to a more literary series, created in 1947 for contemporary fiction, called 'Coralli'. From 1963 to 1970, there were 12 reprints of the book, with a total of 95,000 copies sold, until it found its way into the series 'Nuovi Coralli', where Einaudi's top sellers were published. There were 30 further editions over the subsequent 23 years—until 1994—with 330,000 copies sold. In order to appreciate the full extent of the book's success in Italy, however, it is necessary to add to these sales' figures the 427,000 copies of the school edition, published in the series 'Letture per la scuola media' (Readings for Middle Schools) in which Einaudi had published since 1965 some of their most successful books for junior-high and high-school students with additional notes and appendices. The 1973 school edition of *If This Is a Man*, edited by the author, was printed in 32 editions.

In 1972, a joint edition of *If This Is a Man* and *The Truce* was published in the 'Supercoralli' series founded in 1948. The joint edition was reprinted in three editions between 1972 and 1977, with a total of 14,000 copies, while as the second book to be published in the pocket-book series 'Einaudi Tascabili' (founded in 1972), it sold out 13 editions by 1996 with a total of 48,000 copies. Further copies were sold from 1985 onwards under the imprints De Agostini (in the series 'Tesori della narrative') and Mondadori (in their 'Evergreen' series), as well as by Einaudi Scuola, a branch of the publishers dealing with school editions, which had split from its mother company. Einaudi Scuola printed 12,000 copies of the joint edition, with commentaries and notes by Carlo Minoia and Fabio Cereda for junior-high school students, while Giovanni Tesio annotated a new edition in 1997 for the series *Libri da leggere* (Books to Read) which was printed in an edition of 10,000 copies. In 1997, on the 10th anniversary of Levi's death, when the film of *The Truce* directed by Francesco Rosi came out, a further 100,000 copies of the joint book were printed. In total, counting only the Einaudi editions, 1,379,000 copies were sold between the first edition in 1958 and 1997. Sales over the 20 years that followed were constant, reflecting the rising fame of the author. From 1997 to 2015, 920,651 copies of the joint edition of *If This Is a Man* and *The Truce* in the 'Einaudi Tascabile' series were sold. In between 2005 and 2015, 678,953 copies of the pocket edition of *If This Is a Man* on its own were sold. The *Opere*

(Complete Works) of Primo Levi was published in 1997 and 4,000 copies were printed, with the edition of *If This Is a Man* commented by Alberto Cavaglion.

OTHER VERSIONS

'*If This Is a Man* is a book of modest dimensions but, like a nomadic creature, it has left behind a long and tangled trail for forty years now,' Levi wrote in 1986 (p. 2535). This trail was scattered with crumbs, which reappeared throughout his work (*The Periodic Table, Lilith*, his short stories and essays) but also in a radio version and a theatrical production of the book. The radio version started out as an adaptation proposal made to the author in 1962 by Radio Canada. Levi liked the Canadian script, especially the multilingual structure that attempted to reproduce the Babel of languages described in the book. Levi then went on to write an Italian radio adaptation based on the earlier Canadian version for the regional production office of Italian State Television (RAI). This was broadcast on 24 April 1964 as part of a series of programmes on the Resistance and memories of the Second World War (Scarlini 1997). The radio play was recorded outdoors, in a small town outside Turin called Brozolo, between 9 p.m. and midnight, which was extremely unusual at a time when recording studios were still dominant. Levi participated enthusiastically and local newspapers wrote about the live recording session (Appiotti 1964). The director was Giorgio Bandini, who was committed to renewing the theatrical repertoire of the RAI, and who also directed the first Italian performances of Samuel Beckett (Scarlini 1997). The two pages that introduced the script contain a Preface:

> The following script is a radio adaptation of Primo Levi's book *If This Is a Man* in the Einaudi edition. The story is about the concentration camp in Auschwitz, where the author was held prisoner for a year. Adapting the text for radio has meant

bringing events and thoughts from that distant time back to life as faithfully as possible, reconstructing the atmosphere and the meaning of his inhuman experience. This is why the scenes we broadcast the confusion of languages is a dominant element: it was a fundamental element of the way of life in the German concentration camps, and strongly contributed to the incomprehension, discord, and hatred sown there in order to weaken the ties of natural solidarity, obstruct any attempt to organize resistance, and increase the sense of isolation and suffering. For this reason, many of the dialogues will be heard in the language in which they originally took place: German, French, Polish, Yiddish, Russian. Who do not believe, however, that this effort to adhere to reality will be a hindrance to listeners' understanding, even if their only language is Italian. The meaning of what is being said will be clear at every point in the story, aided by the context and the narrating voice. The counterpoint of the foreign, incomprehensible voices will transport listeners right into the middle of the hostile, barbaric environment of the camp, making them direct participants for a while in the condition of an infinite number of people today. They will be a part of the conscious project to ban the prisoners from the human community, to destroy their identity, to attack and demolish their human essence.

As the author has made clear, the feature of multilingualism is paramount. In this radio adaptation, the narrating voice has two identities: Primo Levi who is the protagonist of the action, and the external narrator who comments on the events using the words in the book, taking on the meditative role of the author. The narrative complexity of the book has been reduced. The episodes from the book that have been preserved are: leaving Fòssoli, Journey to Auschwitz, arriving in Auschwitz, working in Buna, the Resnyk episode, the Ka-Be infirmary, the episode in 'The Canto of Ulysses', selections, the hanging of the 'Last One', 'The Story of Ten Days'. Levi is most interested in the phonic aspects of the recording, the overlapping of voices, the linguistic Babel of the Lager, the diametric opposite of the vocal qualities that he sought in so many of his works.

The theatrical adaptation was written in 1966 by Levi with Pieralberto Marché (the actor Pieralberto Marchesini's stage name). Unlike the radio adaptation, however, the stage version of *If This Is a Man* was published by Einaudi the same year as the play was produced. The play was directed by Gianfranco De Bosio, with the collaboration of Giovanna Bruno and Marta Egri, under the aegis of the Teatro Stabile di Torino. Gianni Polidori was the costume designer, and Paolo Ketoff together with Gino Marinuzzi Jr was the sound engineer. The opening was supposed to be in Prato, but, because of the disastrous Florence flood, it was moved to the Carignano Theatre in Turin, with the first night on 18 November 1966. The reviews were not very enthusiastic, but the play was very successful with the general public, with 50 repeat performances. Owing to the complex staging, however, the company did not go on tour. The stage production required many actors, as did the radio adaptation. In order to maintain the multilingual approach of the radio piece, the actors were selected from theatres throughout Europe. Marché had been one of the actors in the radio production and he was the one who convinced Levi that *If This Is a Man* could also be produced in the theatre, as the programme notes explain (*I quaderni del Teatro Stabile della città di Torino*, 1966). Marché produced an outline that Levi used as a basis for his first script. The two authors went back and forth making innumerable changes until a final version was printed. Levi wrote a letter to Einaudi on 23 November 1965 recommending the theatrical version for publication: 'I myself worked intensely on the theatre version,' he wrote, 'seeking solutions to staging problems which were not always obvious: it was almost a year's work.'

The chorus was the central feature of the play, taking on the role played by the narrator in the radio adaptation: commenting on what was happening on stage, providing a point of view revealed in the patterns of stress and intonation. Passages from the original book were recast in a rhythmic, cadenced style by alternating voices, with the effect of accentuating the choral quality already present in the book. Another effect created by the chorus was that, in addition to references to the Bible and to Dante's *Divina Commedia*, there was a resonance of Ancient Greece—not only in the representations of mythological figures such as Tantalus, Oedipus and Ulysses, but also in the very language and rhythmic force. The two authors made the decision not to have the SS officers on stage, but to represent them off-stage with loudspeakers, their harsh voices rendered incomprehensible. With this device, they were faithful to the spirit of the original work which accentuated the physical nature of the cacophony of the concentration camp.

Unlike the radio version, the play did not feature Primo Levi as one of the characters. The equivalent role was played by Aldo, who was also a chemist. The language of the play was complex, and there were a great number of characters and episodes, each of which was developed into a story that was only outlined in the 1958 novel. Some of these characters later found their way into a few short stories Levi published in the Turin daily *La Stampa* which were then published in *Lilith and Other Stories*, such as 'Capaneus'. Meister Nogalla, for example, was an insignificant character in *If This Is a Man*, but became more important in the play. Others do not appear at all, or play a different role, such as Null Achtzehn or Lorenzo, the builder, who speaks in the first person in the play and tells a different story to the one in the book which later re-surfaced in 'The Return of Lorenzo' (*Lilith and Other Stories*).

The episodes the authors chose to represent in the play followed the same outline as the radio adaptation. While sound prevailed over everything else in the radio version, which glossed over details, leaving them to the listeners' imagination, the staged play inevitably gave a greater role to the dialogues which provided both a narrative framework and a visual impact. The episodes that made up the various scenes of the play were Leaving for Fòssoli, Arriving in Auschwitz, 'The Initiation', 'The Chemistry Exam', 'The Canto of Ulysses', the infirmary 'Ka-Be', The Prisoners' Marketplace, The Selection, The Buna Chemistry Laboratory, The Hanging of the Last One and 'The Story of Ten Days'. The play is divided into two acts: Act I closed with the scene in Ka-Be and the selection of the sick; Act II with Elias and the chemistry exam. Levi cut some sections of the book and filled out others that were barely mentioned. Marché's role was to write detailed stage directions for each scene, with precise indications for the actors' gestures and blocking. Levi's presentation, which was published as a Preface to the Einaudi edition of the play (no. 99 in the series 'Collezione di Teatro' with a picture of the theatre production on the cover) was interesting because it presented a detailed re-visitation of *If This Is a Man* by the author eight years after the 1958 edition, and because it revealed the relationship that Levi continued to have with his first book throughout his life. His letters from the year of the production, in particular to the costume designer Gianni Polidori, are also significant. Preserved in the Genoa Museo dell'Attore (Actors' Museum), these 1966 letters described the prisoners' clothes and their precious objects, and included Levi's drawings. Levi also reconstructed the publication odyssey of *If This Is a Man*, including the radio adaptation, and reminded Polidori of the book's roots in the oral tradition, commenting that he was an 'indefatigable, imperious, and maniacal narrator'. Levi and Marché's play won the Saint Vincent Prize for the best theatrical piece of the season. The Einaudi publication in the 'Theatre Collection' series was reprinted and sold over 8,000 copies.

In 1973, Levi drafted a school edition of *If This Is a Man*, with an apparatus of notes and an entirely new preface. Levi, like other authors before him, such as Calvino who was also published by Einaudi, adapted the text for young readers. The brothel scene was cut, as were other passages considered too harsh. The cuts were relatively limited and did not change the substance of the book. The new preface placed the book firmly in the historical context in which it was written, and underlined the historical significance of the deportation and the concentration camps. Levi also introduced two maps representing the layout of the concentration and extermination camps, and the region around Auschwitz. These maps were kept in subsequent editions. The 1973 school edition also featured a short bibliography on the subject. The notes were particularly significant because they provided a commentary on the text at a distance of nearly 30 years. The idea for these notes probably came to Levi at the end of the 1950s when he answered some of the questions posed by his German translator Heinz Riedt, explaining several terms and expressions coined in the Lager. Many of the details noted in the school edition were already present in these letters, such as the Decauville locomotive, the reference to the painting of Sodom and Gomorrah, the explicit and implicit references to Dante and the technical chemical terms. The notes, of course, had a different purpose. Some provided a translation of German or Yiddish expressions which formed the basis of the multilingual layers of the book; others explained the meaning of the acronyms (Stefano Bartezzaghi [2010], has pointed out the importance of acrostics in Levi's works) and of the technical terms; others again revealed direct or indirect allusions to passages from Dante's *Inferno*. We might call some of Levi's notes meta-textual, with explicit references to other works of his, such as *The Truce*, as well as critical comments on his own writing which help us understand the way Levi continually reappraised his first book.

At the end of 1975, Levi added an Appendix which became an integral part of the book in 1976. This was a self-interview, which comprised Levi's answers to the most common questions readers and school pupils had put to him over the years in Italy and abroad: a kind of 'conference circuit' he once called his 'third job'. A shorter version of the Appendix was published on 28 February 1976, before the school edition came out, in *Tuttolibri*, the literary pages of *La Stampa*. The text shows once more Levi's refined self-critical approach—both as a witness and as an author. In 1986, Levi updated the Appendix for the US double edition of *If This Is a Man* and *The Truce*.

Levi spoke about *If This Is a Man* on many occasions, adding a great deal to our knowledge and understanding of his work. His interviews, in particular, are a useful tool for critics and ordinary readers. The following are interviews in which Levi speaks specifically about the content of the book: in an interview with students from Indiana University (Rosenfeld 1986) he talked about Lorenzo; with Vera Székacs (1987) he talked about the Hungarians; a long interview on his detention in the Lager was conducted by Anna Bravo and Federico Cereja, first published in a journal and then in book form (1987); a conversation with Risa Sodi (1988) covered the subject of his imprisonment in the Fòssoli transit camp; finally, a more general and highly revealing interview on these themes took place with Ferdinando Camon (1989).

LEMMAS

The Deported

Ever since Primo Levi returned from the Lager, he felt it was his task to remind people what had happened. This was especially true in the years when the subject of the deportation of Jews to Nazi concentration camps was avoided. Not by chance, one of his first articles, published in a newspaper in 1955, bore the title: 'The Deported. Anniversary' (*Uncollected Stories and Essays*). Further articles appeared in ANED, the journal of the Association of former deportees, and in *Triangolo Rosso*, a journal that Levi supported and contributed to (*Uncollected Stories and Essays*), as well as in a 1997 ANED publication called *Primo Levi per l'ANED, l'ANED per Primo Levi*. Another important piece on the subject was the text written for *Il Memoriale*, inaugurated at Auschwitz in 1980 in honour of Italians who died in the Nazi concentration camps. This text appears anonymously on a memorial stone in the Italian block in Auschwitz (*Al Visitatore*). *Triangolo Rosso* published Levi's last article on the Lager, 'The Last Christmas of the War' in 1986 (*Uncollected Stories and Essays*).

Friends of Levi's who were former deportees included: Lidia Beccaria Rolfi, whose book of testimonies, *Le donne di Ravensbrück* (The Women of Ravensbrück, co-authored by Anna Maria Bruzzone) he reviewed in 1978 in 'Women for Slaughter' (*Uncollected Stories and Essays*) and for whose posthumous book *Broken Future*, he wrote a foreword (*Uncollected Stories and Essays*); Liana Millu, who wrote *Smoke Over Birkenau*, which first came out in 1947 and which Levi reviewed in the daily *La Stampa* when it was reprinted in 1979; and the writer, Edith Bruck, for whom Levi wrote a brief foreword to her book of short stories, *Two Empty Rooms*, and who, in her turn, published an interview of Levi on the subject of Judaism. Another important figure in ANED was Bruno Vasari to whom the poem, 'The Survivor' (1984) was dedicated.

Many of Levi's poems dealt with themes linked to deportation. The shame deportees felt was the subject of the chapter 'Shame' in *The Drowned and the Saved*. Two further posthumous texts are also worth mentioning in this context: the foreword to a volume collecting the testimonies of deportees from the Piedmont region, *Offended Life*, to which Levi contributed with a conversation (published after his death in 1987 by Bravo and Cereja), and a speech given at a conference on the topic of 'Lived History' entitled ' "Our Generation . . ." ' (*Uncollected Stories and Essays*).

Lager

On the platform at Auschwitz, a small town in Poland not far from Cracow, Primo Levi was selected alongside other men, and separated from the women and the rest of the trainload, to be taken to hut 30. Auschwitz was the biggest camp in the entire German concentration-camp universe, comprising 39 minor camps. The extermination camp was not far away, in Birkenau, where the gas chambers and cremation furnaces had been built. In Monowitz, a camp that Levi once called 'Auschwitz III' in a conversation with two historians, Bravo and Cereja, was established at the behest of the chemical factory, I. G. Farben, which bankrolled the construction of the Lager and exploited slave labour for its synthetic rubber production. (Levi went into this subject further in his Appendix to the 1976 School Edition of *If This Is a Man*). Surrounding this camp were 30 to 35 smaller Lagers, each of them with links to mines, factories, farms and weapons' factories. The population of Monowitz alone was of approximately 10,000 prisoners.

In 1944, when Levi arrived at Auschwitz, the progress of the war and subsequent industrial expansion made it impellent for German industrialists to exploit the slave labour provided by Jews, thus postponing the plan to eliminate them on the spot. Experts in the SS calculated that the average life span of an underfed prisoner in harsh working conditions was approximately three to four months. The group to which Levi had been assigned was selected for forced labour and was subjected to a terrifying initiation: their identity was stripped, and a new identification number was tattooed onto their forearm. They were then thrown into the infernal circle of the Block without any warning or guidelines. Levi was immediately struck by the Babel of languages: most Italians spoke neither German nor Yiddish, which was the mother tongue of the majority of the inmates, nearly all Jews from Eastern Europe.

This new phase of industrial expansion, however, did not mean that the mass elimination of Jews deported from Nazi-occupied countries came to a halt. Trains continued to arrive at Auschwitz station, and the selections went on. The old, the sick, the disabled, women and children were sent straight to the gas chambers. Only a small minority was selected for forced labour. The structure of the Lagers, their internal hierarchies, their methods for eliminating victims and their gratuitous violence, were all covered in *The Drowned and the Saved* as well as in Levi's interviews.

When he was asked about the function of the Lagers, Levi said these institutions had three aims: to terrorize (quash political resistance, especially of the Communists), to exterminate (destroy the Jews), and, from 1943 onwards, to obtain low-cost, or rather zero-cost, labour. Talking to schoolchildren, he was always asked the same questions: 'Did the Germans know? Did the Allies know? How could the genocide, the extermination of millions of human beings have taken place in the heart of Europe without anyone knowing anything?' (pp. 169–70). His answers in the 1976 Appendix to the School Edition of *If This Is a Man* and in *The Drowned and the Saved* are complex. This is partly because Levi insisted that trying to understand the past with the categories of the present often leads to stereotyping, or simplification. Levi answered the first question by saying the Germans knew. 'The whole country knew it, and knew that in the Lager people suffered and died' (p. 171); 'In Hitler's Germany a particular code of behaviour was widespread; those who knew didn't speak, those who didn't know didn't ask questions, those who asked questions didn't get any answers' (pp. 173–4).

News of the horrors taking place in the Lagers, aired by Allied radio, was so overwhelming that it was generally not believed. To the question, 'Were there prisoners who escaped from the camps? Why were there no mass revolts?' Levi responded with the emblematic episode in 'Stereotypes' (*The Drowned and the Saved*). To the student who told Levi exactly how he could have escaped, Levi rebutted by describing the state of physical and moral prostration of the Jews who were held in the labour camps, and reminded readers of the ritual of selection on the Auschwitz station platform already described in *If This Is a Man*. 'To reproach the prisoners for failing to rebel represents an error of historical perspective; it means expecting from them a political consciousness that today is a nearly common heritage, but at the time belonged only to an élite' (p. 177).

Muselmänn

Levi explained in his Appendix to the 1976 school edition that the term Muselmänn was used by camp elders to denote the weak or inept, those who were destined for selection. The Polish writer, Tadeusz Borowski, in a glossary he added to his short-story collection on his experiences in the Lager (Borowski 1988), defined the term as referring to a man who was physically and spiritually weakened and demoralized, who had neither the strength nor the will to continue his struggle for existence. The Muselmänn usually had dysentery, scabies or abscesses, and was ready for the ovens. Borowski stressed that no exemplification could render the extent to which a Muselmänn was despised by the community: anyone who had ever been in a Lager and survived had been, at least for a brief period, a Muselmänn, even though they may not have wanted to admit it in their memoirs. Without somebody's help, without tangible gestures of support, none of them would have managed to survive their state of prostration.

Levi talked about this figure in *The Drowned and the Saved*. Elsewhere he explained that the origin of the term is not known, although some people say that the first 'Muslims' had a head covering that looked like a turban—hence the name. In camps other than Auschwitz, there was another word that indicated the same extreme condition. Bruno Bettelheim in his *The Informed Heart: Autonomy in a Mass Age* (1960) claimed that the term derived from the state of resignation attributed to Muslim populations. 'Null Achtzehn' (Zero-Eighteen) was the Muselmänn protagonist in the opening paragraph of the chapter 'Ka-Be' (*If This Is a Man*).

First Names

The primary aim of the Lager was to deprive prisoners of their identity. A number tattooed on the arm was a new name-giving ceremony: 'I have learned that I am a Häftling. My name is 174 517; we have been baptized [. . .] my new name, ironically, appeared instead, a number tattooed in bluish characters under the skin' (p. 24). This was why, in *If This Is a Man* and in later books and short stories on the Lager experience, Levi insisted on using people's names. He constantly referred to his characters with their first name, and often with their surname (family name) or at least a nickname. *If This Is a Man,* entirely devoted to the vicissitudes of the Lager, was interwoven with names. Readers pay little attention to this feature to start with. It soon becomes clear, however, that it is, first and foremost, an act of salvation: remembering people's names brings back to life, at least on the page, those who are no longer with us.

In the chapter 'Shame' (*The Drowned and the Saved*), Levi called the 'drowned' by their first name and surname, citing at times their profession as a further element of identification. The significance was to give each person a well-defined identity, precisely in that place where identity had been obliterated. First names are the personal identity of each and every person, more than their bodies. Even a Muselmänn who was 'drowned' by definition, was given a kind of name in *If This Is a Man* ('Ka-Be'): 'Null Achtzehn' (Zero-Eighteen). Levi thus preserved the semblance of a first name and a surname, or nickname (which is what the two German numbers sound like to us), even though he was no longer a man because he had forgotten his own name.

Levi often changed people's names, or substituted them with a nickname, out of discretion or respect. Examples include the Galician ('The Last One'), and the Hungarian Doctor. He never forsook the idea of giving his characters an identity, however, since the uncertainty of people's identity which has always puzzled biographers, was a defence against the natural forgetfulness of that termites' nest that was the Lager.

In *Lilith and Other Stories* and in *Uncollected Stories and Essays*, most of which dealt with the concentration camps, this aspect was even more marked. While in *If This Is a Man*, the element of personal testimony was at one with the need to describe the actual exterminations in the Lager, the stories in *Lilith* were portraits of the inhabitants of the Lager. This same attention to names returned in the article 'The Squirrel' (*Other People's Trades*) where the origin of a Piedmont surname, Perrone, is discussed. In 'Argon', which opens *The Periodic Table*, the names and nicknames of Levi's Piedmont ancestors (often reinvented in the fantasy of a heraldic tale) are significant in that they outlined an aspect of their personality, or reiterated something curious that had happened to them. Saving names was a distinguishing feature of Levi's style, which no doubt pre-existed his experience of the Lager—at least in terms of his focus and sensitivity—but it was given further motivation by that experience.

Holocaust

Levi rejected the word commonly used to indicate the extermination of the Jews in Europe. In an interview with Marco Vigevani, he stated that this term—which literally means 'everything burnt'—irritated him precisely because of its reference to animal sacrifices made to the gods. He reminded his interviewer that Elie Wiesel, who was the first to coin the word, later regretted it, and would have liked to have withdrawn it from circulation. In fact, as Anna-Vera Sullam shows in *I nomi dello sterminio* (The Names of the Extermination, 2001) the word had been in circulation since 1947 in journalistic circles, and was always linked to the idea of fire. It then reappeared in a 1951 text in French by Léon Poliakov, and subsequently appeared in 1958 when François Mauriac used the word 'holocauste' in an article that later became the preface to the French translation of Wiesel's book, *Night*.

Levi's 'secular' nature rebelled against the sanctification of the Nazi extermination programme, which was carefully planned and scientifically implemented by means of the concentration camps. In 1979, when the TV film *Holocaust* was shown on Italian television, Levi returned to the question in three articles, two of which were published in *La Stampa* (*Uncollected Stories and Essays*). He cited the word in these articles in order to widen its meaning. He talked about a 'European holocaust' in which, together with 6 million Jews, 50 million Europeans died in the Second World War, more than 10 million of whom were Germans (on another occasion, in *The Drowned and the Saved*, he talked about a 'massacre of the first-born' in the German population). Levi hardly ever used the Hebrew word 'Shoah' (Destruction); when he does, it is only in interviews where it was generally introduced by Jewish interviewers.

Time

In the Lager, prisoners had no watches. Time was kept by daily activities in the camp. Levi could not fail to mention this aspect in *If This Is a Man*. In the Lager, time never seemed to pass; it felt as if it stood still forever. Boredom was the most common psychological condition for prisoners. An obsession with time is present in almost all Levi's stories. In *Natural Histories*, 'The Mnemagogs' explored the possibility of recovering the past through a collection of smells. In 'Angelic Butterfly', the Nazi scientist experimented with manipulating evolutionary time, and in 'Sleeping Beauty in the Refrigerator: A Winter's Tale' Levi played with the concept of time through the myth of eternal youth, exploring the erotic aspect of temporal manipulation—a theme which is common in the fantastic tales of the nineteenth and twentieth centuries.

The problem of time presented itself dramatically in *If This Is a Man*. The prevalence of the present tense denounced the stasis of a context that never evolved, even in Levi's own narration. The Lager was always there, right next to the narrator in terms of time and space so that he could not separate himself from the experience even in the therapeutic act of telling his story. Pier Vincenzo Mengaldo has written that Levi's present tense 'slides invisibly from historic to a-chronic, to eternal' (*Lingua e scrittura in Levi*, 1990). In 'Creative Work', literary activity in itself is seen as a vehicle for achieving eternity, that condition 'without time' of an eternal present. The Vilmy, the imaginary animals in the story with the same name (*Flaw of Form*) which make their owners lose their sense of reality, are fascinated by clocks. Similarly, Mendel, the protagonist of *If Not Now, When?*, is a clockmaker. There are countless mentions of time in Levi's works

(Bartezzaghi compiled a brief catalogue in his entry in *Tempo di Cosmichomiche*, 1997). In one of his last short stories, 'Time Checkmated' (*Stories and Essays*) he described—part seriously, part facetiously—an invention called the Parachrono which had the power to accelerate, slow down or stop subjective time at pleasure. Levi went on to relate a series of experiments undertaken with this machine.

I/We

One of the stylistic features Levi adopted in *If This Is a Man*, in order to shift both the narrative point of view and the thought process itself, was to move between the autobiographical first-person singular to the inclusive first-person plural. The critic, Cesare Segre (Segre 1996), and other scholars, such as Alberto Cavaglion, have written about this feature. Two linguists, Nunzio La Fauci and Liana Tronci (2014) analysed the use of the pronoun 'we' on the first page of the 1958 edition. They commented that the first-person singular and the first-person plural, or the 'fourth person' indicating generic referents, are dichotomous. The I/narrator describing his deportation and the situation in the Lager is the most evident voice throughout the book: the 'I' that readers identify with Primo Levi, the protagonist and author. 'I' is thus the subject and the object of his experience. It is split into a double, not only grammatically speaking but also in terms of Frege's 'sense and reference'. There is an 'I' that implies 'us' at the beginning of the book, which embraces all the victims of the Lager, 'The need to tell our story [. . .] took on for us [. . .] the character of an immediate and violent impulse' (p. 6), which is different from the 'us' that regards everyone in general: 'as long as the conception exists, the consequences remain to threaten us' (p. 6). La Fauci and Tronci referred to the latter as an 'inclusive us', which they claim has both conative and affective value, in Roman Jakobson's classification of the functions of language.

The two linguists explored the 'fourth person' and made an interesting point. In their view, there is an 'us' that indicates Levi's fellow deportees in the Lager, which is in contrast with the 'I' that implies 'us'. There are two distinct subsets within this implied 'us': the 'saved' and the 'un-saved' whom Levi calls the 'drowned'. Just as 'I' plays a double role, so does 'we', 'us' or 'our'. On the one hand, it reduces the 'level of personalization of the text', as La Fauci and Tronci put it, to the point where it refers to 'non-persons' ('we have been baptized, we will carry the mark tattooed on our left arm until we die.' [p. 23]), thus creating a kind of objectivity. On the other hand, it melds with the narrator's 'I', and somehow personalizes the text.

The figure of the narrator, in its turn, is equally dichotomous: an 'I' narrator and an 'I' that is being narrated. In *If This Is a Man*, in fact, we have Levi the prisoner and Levi the writer, who was describing the events in another time frame and in another place ('Today, this very day, as I sit at the table and write, I myself am not convinced that these things really happened.' [p. 98]). It was as if Levi were never alone. He was always accompanied by his alter ego, the Levi that experienced Auschwitz about whom he was writing. This split in grammatical subjects was one of the qualities of Levi's prose. It allowed him to modulate his written testimony, making the book unique among all the books written about the concentration-camp experience.

There was another aspect that La Fauci and Tronci underlined in their essay: the fact that the 'saved' and the 'drowned' appeared together, unlike in his final book, *The Drowned and the Saved* (1986), where Levi claimed the 'drowned' should be the ones to speak. In the text carved on the Auschwitz memorial stone, Levi used 'we' even more decisively as a way to indicate all the dead ('We bear witness, we Italians who died'). He explicitly adopted the voice of the 'drowned' by using the 'fourth person': 'In this place, where we the innocent were killed [. . .] See to it that your journey is not in vain, that our death has not been in vain'. According to La Fauci and Tronci's analysis, the voice of the drowned had already been used in the chapter 'Ka-Be', where 'we' was used very often: 'we look at each other', 'we know', 'we are aware'. The 'fourth person' here indicated both the deportees imprisoned in Ka-Be, and the victims in general of the Lager, a 'we' which is used in an identical fashion to the 'we' on the memorial stone.

This dichotomous system was entirely built on the experiential 'I' of the narrator, the clearest voice in the book. The 'I' of the prisoner who has direct experience of being deported to the camp is the main voice in the text. 'We'—in its turn split into two different referents—is thus generated from the eye-witness 'I'. Cavaglion, in his critique of *If This Is a Man* (Cavaglion 2012) considered the 'fourth person' 'we' as 'dual', a possible reminiscence of classical Greek as taught in high school. Classical Greek, in fact, has dual agreements, an intermediate level between singular and plural. La Fauci and Tronci observed that this was a 'grammatical number', not a 'person'. Cavaglion used the 'dual' figure to account for characters who were highly significant for Levi, such as Pikolo, Alberto, Charles and Leonardo in *The Truce*. In this sense, the grammatical 'we' is perfectly compatible with the context. Cavaglion found a similar 'dual' form in Luciana Nissim's *Ricordi della casa dei morti* (Memories from the House of the Dead) where Vanda Maestro was the 'dual' of the narrator—who also appears in *If This Is a Man*.

Another well-known feature of Levi's style was how close his prose was to poetry. His continuous shifts between 'I' and 'we' were one element of this, creating what has been called 'an exact vagueness'. In La Fauci and Tronci's view, the vagueness was linked to the reiterated use of oxymorons, considered by Mengaldo (1990) to be the main stylistic figure, both in terms of frequency and quality in Levi's works. Oxymorons created a correspondence between the way the text was presented on the surface (and in its details), and the hypothetical process that went into producing it. In other words, the shifts between the dual first person and the dual 'fourth person' created an energy field that captured readers, showing them the different faces of the subject implied in the narration, from close-up (the identifying 'we') to far away (the experiential 'I' of the narrative voice). The strong emotional impact of Levi's writing was reinforced in a highly complex way by his shifting of tenses, from present to past, and of grammatical person ('I' and 'we'). A further effect was created by shifting tone. One tone was calm, such as in the Preface, and another was harsh, such as in the invective of the poem 'Shemà' that opened the book. Again, the conative and the affective functions of language are both present, and this melding is achieved without ever creating an ideological contrast between 'us' and 'them'—except when the grammatical person 'they' or 'them' refers to the Germans.

La Fauci and Tronci also remarked on the significance of the third-person plural in the first chapter 'The Journey' ('their number rose to more than six hundred' [p. 10]). 'Their' refers to the number of Italian Jews imprisoned in Fòssoli, a category to which Levi belonged inasmuch as was an Italian Jew held in that transit camp. The third person has a distancing effect, but in the next paragraph is transformed by Levi's use of the impersonal form of the verb into a wider, more inclusive 'we'. This constant zooming in and out, from close-up to far away, is part of the duality that connoted all of Levi's work. It is what makes his writing so classical and yet so problematic, so closely sealed and yet so readable. In short, it is what makes it 'like a centaur', half-human, half-horse, as Levi himself, doubtless with a different aim in mind, once defined it.

Depositions

'Human memory is a wonderful but fallible instrument' (p. 2420). Primo Levi opened the first chapter of The Drowned and the Saved ('The Memory of the Offense') with this axiom, and he always abided by it. He took enormous care to review every detail, including his own memories, even when he had the opportunity to testify about his experiences as a partisan and as a deportee. Levi gave at least six depositions in the years between returning to Turin in October 1945 and 1971, the year Colonel Friedrich Bosshammer, Eichmann's close collaborator was put on trial. In addition, Levi contributed a report, co-authored by Leonardo De Benedetti, on the Hygienic-Sanitary Organization of the Concentration Camp for Jews in Monowitz (Auschwitz–Upper Silesia)' which was published by Levi and in Minerva Medica in 1946.

The first deposition was a report providing the names, and describing the personal experiences, of 30 Italian Jews deported to Germany on the same transport as his, whom he then got to know in the Monowitz camp. For each person, Levi gave the age, geographical origin and occupation. He also offered a preliminary hypothesis on the fate of the column of prisoners who had been held there since January 1945, and who had been forced to evacuate the camp with the Germans as they escaped from the

Allied Forces. The deposition, which also comprised De Benedetti's eye-witness accounts, is housed in the Terracini Jewish Archive in Turin. It was later published in *Così fù Auschwitz* (Fabio Levi and Domenico Scarpa eds 2015), and translated into English, edited by Robert Gordon, as *Auschwitz Report*, 2006. At some point between mid-November and mid-December 1945, at the request of the Rome-based Jewish Deportee Research Committee (CRDE), Levi wrote *Deposition*. This was a more detailed account, containing for the first time a precise description of Zyklon B, the pesticide used by the Nazis to gas the deported. As a chemist, Levi was able to outline its composition in a few succinct sentences, reporting on its more common uses before it was used in the gas chambers, which Levi called 'asphyxiation chambers', reporting the agonizing final moments of the prisoners who were condemned to death there. In 1947, commissioned by Massimo Adolfo Vitale (as a footnote in *Auschwitz Report* revealed), Levi sent a typed report to be used in a potential deposition for the trial against Rudolf Höss, the Auschwitz Commandant. In 1985, when Einaudi decided to reprint Höss's autobiography (*Commandant of Auschwitz: The Autobiography of Rudolf Höss*, published in English in 1959), Levi wrote a foreword where he commented on the 'bright idea of trying Zyklon B, the poison used to kill rats and roaches, and that works well' (p. 2709).

In 1953, he wrote an anonymous witness statement—not a formal deposition—about the partisan fighter, Vanda Maestro, who had been captured in Valle d'Aosta and deported to Auschwitz with him. Levi's deposition for the war criminal Adolf Eichmann's trial, now preserved in the Jerusalem Yad Vashem Archive, was deposited in June 1960. It is likely that Levi dictated the text to Vitale, who then consigned the papers to the prosecutor's office in Jerusalem. In his note on the text, Domenico Scarpa notes that it was almost certainly not typed by Levi, pointing to the abundance of exclamation points as evidence, but that the tone and style are those of the author of *If This Is a Man*. Levi started the deposition with his experience as a partisan in Aosta, going over the details and filling in some of the names he had left out in his first book, some of whom he would later refer to in *The Periodic Table*. He provided the surname, occupation and destiny of each of his fellow prisoners. He also referred to the spy, Meoli, ironically—irony is so important for Levi—calling him 'our man' in inverted commas. He also cited the Fascist centurion by name and, despite everything, betrayed neither hatred nor contempt. He went on to report that the centurion was killed by partisans in 1945, adding that Fascist soldiers were as inexperienced as the partisans. Levi stated that the centurion treated them well because they were all college graduates.

Levi was not only balanced in his judgement, he was also attentive to detail. Minutiae of historical significance emerge from the deposition. He described how a Jewish prisoner from Turin held in Fòssoli, Arturo Foà, was kept at a distance because of his Fascist sympathies—it is interesting to note that many Jews adhered to Fascism. He made references to Yugoslav and British prisoners, calling them 'subjects' to indicate that they were civilians. In his notes, Scarpa rectified various names cited in the deposition. There were also pointers to the climate of fear the prisoners lived in at Fòssoli, such as the observation that 'nobody tried to escape'.

In its third section, after his capture by the Fascist militia and his imprisonment at the transit camp at Fòssoli, the deposition turned to the journey to, and internment at, Auschwitz. Levi gave precise numbers: there were 650 Jews, 96 of which were set to work 7 kilometres from the main Lager, in addition to 26 women who had already passed through other camps. He listed the names of the Jewish doctors working in the Buna-Monowitz camp, their provenance—Athens, Strasbourg, Poland—and their academic qualifications. He also noted that one doctor from Thessalonica did not behave well. The Kapo was a Dutch Jew, Josef Lessing, who had played trumpet in an orchestra and was a *musiker* in the camp whom Levi described as punitive and evil. He would return to this in a later story: 'A "Mystery" in the Lager' (*Stories and Essays*).

The 'Grey Zone', the forced collaboration of Jews in the inner workings of the concentration camps, denied in Israel until the Eichmann trial, was already present in this deposition, even though the expression had not yet been coined. There were more names of deportees, further memories saved from oblivion. When Levi was unsure of a name, he added 'a certain' before the name. He used the expression 'a half-Greek from Trieste' to add detail to the identity of a 'so-and-so' called Venezia. He stated clearly that 95 per cent of the deportees in the camp were Jewish, when in the 1960s when he was writing the only talk was of political deportees.

The rest was related in a few succinct lines: the liberation of the camp by the Russians, the prisoners' transfer and odyssey to get back home which became the subject of *The Truce*. To describe the strange behaviour of the Russians—which was in positive contrast to the conduct of the Germans described in *The Truce*—Levi reported that prisoners were given the option of being sent back home by sea, but they would be directed to embark in Odessa. This was pure geographic nonsense. We know this is not what took place. The deposition provided a detail that was missing in *The Truce*: the prisoners were actually taken to Minsk. The deposition closed with words that were worthy of a narrator 'when, God willing, we finally returned to Italy'. There was irony, and an audible sigh of relief.

In addition to the 1960 deposition, an important article published in the journal *Il Ponte* in 1961 is worth mentioning. *Testimonianze per Eichmann* (Testimonies for Eichmann) responded to a series of objections to eye-witness accounts given by former concentration-camp prisoners. In this article, Levi referred to the camps as places of perdition as well as of torment and death. This was an early hint of the debate that would develop around the issue of the 'Grey Zone'. In order to explain his concept, he quoted Karl Jaspers and Thomas Mann, both of whom gave up trying to describe Hitlerism in rational terms. He described the Jewish function-aries in the camp and the reverse selection effected by the Nazis, who chose the worst of them as their collaborators. This reference to the Sonderkommando was the same as the one he would make 25 years later in *The Drowned and the Saved*, with the difference that in this deposition Levi stated that the SS contaminated the deportees who collaborated with them.

The Bosshammer trial called for three successive depositions. The first was his November 1965 *Dichiarazioni per il processo Bosshammar* (Declarations for the Bosshammer Trial) probably at the request of Eloisa Ravenna who was then general secretary of the Milan-based Contemporary Jewish Archive (CDEC). This was followed by his 1970 answers to questions in German in *Questionario per il processo Bosshammer* (Questionnaire on the Bosshammer Trial) and then by *Deposizioni per il processo Bosshammer* (Depositions on the Bosshammer Trial). The third was the text of an oral deposition given in May 1971 in Investigating Magistrate Barbaro's office in front of the West Berlin State Prosecutor, Dietrich Hölzner. Hölzner had been conducting an inquiry for the previous year on the SS Colonel, Friedrich Bosshammer, who had been identified and arrested in Germany where he had been living undisturbed since the end of the war. He was accused of being directly responsible for the death of 3,500 Italian Jews. The former SS Colonel was sentenced to life imprisonment at the end of the trial in 1971, but died soon after of a heart attack. The transcription of Levi's deposition was in Eloisa Ravenna's hand, written in a notebook.

The striking thing about the deposition is the absence of emotion or superfluous comments. Levi never plays the role of the victim, nor does he take on the guise of inflexible judge. Even though Levi was testifying in a trial, the style of the oral account was clearly Levi's, focusing as always on the details and on the truthfulness of his testimony. He cogently balanced the things he knew against those he did not. He was probably one of the only eye witnesses who, on his arrival in Auschwitz in the midst of all the confusion, actually counted the prisoners as they were being selected. He was only 25 years old, but he possessed the mentality of a chemist, and maintained it even at the threshold of the gas chamber. This is probably why, on his return, he was so meticulous in reconstructing the names of those who were deported; it was important to him whether there were 95 or 96 other prisoners interned alongside. As Fabio Levi and Domenico Scarpa remind us in their note, the numbers are different from one deposition to another—a sign of his continuous attention to memory, which is a wonderful instrument but also, as Levi knew well, fallible. He attached the list of names to his deposition and used letters of the alphabet to document the fates of each individual. He exploited the opportunity to testify to state that it would have been perfectly possible back in the forties in Italy to have received news of the deportation of Jews in Italy. At the end of his deposition, with a highly effective, dry phrase, Levi measured the distance between the prisoners' expectations and what actually took place in the camps. When the meeting came to an end—a newspaper of that time refers—Levi handed a copy of *If This Is a Man* to Prosecutor Hölzner as an appendix to his testimony. 'In Germany,' he said, 'the book is no longer in print. It is sold out.' This legal deposition was to be his last.

All the themes that were covered in his many depositions, alongside others touched on in newspaper and journal articles published between 1959 and 1974, were to return in his last book *The Drowned and the Saved*, although in a more mature, complex and problematic form. This reveals how Levi continued to mull these issues over for decades on end. His was, if one can put it that way, a work-in-progress, a construction to which he would ceaselessly add details and thoughts, well-aware of the swings in perspective and context in the debate regarding the deportations and the extermination of the Jews. There is one theme that inhabited and tormented him more than any other. That is, understanding why people like him accepted collaborating in the elimination of millions of human beings. This would become the subject of his exchange of letters with Hety Schmitt-Maass, his German correspondent from the 1960s to the 1980s.

Heinz Riedt

When Levi found out in 1959 that a German publisher had bought the translation rights to *If This Is a Man,* he was 'overcome by a violent new emotion, that of having won a battle' (p. 2535). However, his main concern at the time was: who could be trusted with the translation? Levi knew German sufficiently well to be able to evaluate the work, and was determined to do so every step of the way. The German edition was too important an opportunity to take lightly. As he said in a series of interviews during the 1980s, *If This Is a Man* was written as an act of accusation against the Germans, as if it had been a legal deposition. Germans were the audience 'at whom the book was aimed, like a gun' (p. 2536).

In 'Letters from Germans', Levi confessed that he had written a letter 'bordering on insolence' to the publisher Fischer, 'warning him not to remove or change one single word of the text [. . .] I wanted to check its fidelity not only to the words but also to their innermost meaning' (p. 2537).

The publisher duly sent the first translated chapter to the author, with a letter from the translator, 'in perfect Italian' (p. 2357.) Levi responded appreciatively, making a few suggestions for corrections. Heinz Riedt, the translator, introduced himself and told Levi that he had been a partisan in Padua, and that his father-in-law had been sent to Auschwitz: 'a singular coincidence that I estimate will bring us together so many years after the events' (13 August 1959). Levi's answer was enthusiastic. Riedt was not, as Levi had expected, simply a 'public defender'; he was a man who was alive to the things he cared about most. His joy at meeting a German of this calibre is such that he wrote, 'Perhaps you are the person I have been hoping to meet for years.'

Their correspondence continued throughout the translation process, until it was completed in June of the following year. Most of the translator's queries regarded how to render certain expressions and which verb tenses to adopt. Levi suggested direct and indirect quotes from the Italian classics cited in the book, especially Dante. Riedt was an expert on Ruzante and Goldoni, and was familiar with Venetian dialects, as Levi explained many years later. He had also translated modern Italian authors such as Collodi, Gadda, D'Arrigo and Pirandello. He was, as Levi put it, 'an anomalous German who had feigned illness to avoid being called up and had been given permission to convalesce in Italy, studying Italian literature at Padua University'. This is where he came into contact with an anti-Fascist group led by Concetto Marchesi, Egidio Meneghetti and Otello Pighin. After the 1943 armistice, he 'naturally joined the Paduan partisans of Justice and Liberty which fought in the Euganean hills against the Fascists of the Republic of Salò and against his fellow Germans' (p. 2538).

Once the translation was completed, Levi and Riedt agreed to use an extract of one of Levi's letters to his translator as a Preface to the German edition. In this short piece, Levi stated: 'I can't say I understand the Germans. [. . .] I hope that this book will have some kind of echo in Germany' (p. 2541). In Riedt's response to this letter, he thanked Levi for his collaboration in the translation but claimed he would have to disappoint the author for not finding an inner motive in the 'German character'.

Riedt worked for many years in theatrical circles until the 1960s when, after the Berlin Wall had been erected, he was persecuted by the East German authorities for his past as an army 'deserter' and a partisan. He was finally forced to leave his home and country and defect to the West, where he carried on his work as a literary translator, translating several other books by Levi throughout the 1960s and staying in contact with the author. He died in 1997 on the Italian island of Ponza, where he had lived for many years.

Germans

'In your book, there are no expressions of hatred or bitterness towards the Germans, or a desire for revenge. Have you forgiven them?' (p. 168) This question, included in the Appendix to the School Edition of *If This Is a Man* epitomized the many questions readers sent him or asked him in person (the many letters sent to *La Stampa*, and published in the letters section 'Specchio dei tempi' are a case in point). Levi's answer was short and to the point: 'I believe in reason and discussion as supreme tools of progress, and so I place justice before hatred' (p. 169).

This is why, Levi claimed:

> in writing this book I deliberately assumed the calm and sober language of the witness, not the lament of the victim or the anger of the avenger: I thought that my word would be more credible and useful the more objective it appeared and the less impassioned it sounded; only in that way does the witness fulfil his function, which is to prepare the ground for the judge. It is you who are the judges (p. 169).

If This Is a Man, however, leaves one crucial question unanswered. This was addressed explicitly in the Preface to the 1961 German edition, taken from one of his letters to his German translator:

> I can't say I understand the Germans. Now, something that one does not understand becomes a sore point, a sharp pain, a permanent itch that asks to be satisfied. I hope that this book will have some kind of echo in Germany; not only because of my ambitions

but also because the nature of this echo will perhaps allow me to understand the Germans better and to soothe the itch (p. 1151).

Levi received 40 or so letters from German readers between 1961 and 1964, and considered collecting this correspondence into a volume that Einaudi then decided not to publish. The chapter 'Letters from Germans' in *The Drowned and the Saved*, which was published in 1986, was thus the only place where the letters were cited. Levi took nine correspondents expressing different points of view into consideration, starting with Dr T. H. from Hamburg, and concluding with Hety Schmitt-Maass from Wiesbaden, who was his most interesting interlocutor and with whom he exchanged numerous letters.

In Levi's view, the German population was culpable mainly because people had lacked the courage to speak out. To those correspondents who objected that it was not fair to generalize in his censure, in this chapter and elsewhere in interviews and various other articles, Levi agreed that it is 'dangerous' and 'illegitimate' to talk about 'the Germans', or any other people, as if they were a single, undifferentiated entity' (p. 2550) 'Yet,' he maintained, 'I do not feel I can deny that a spirit of the people exists (otherwise it would not be a people' [p. 2550]: a 'cautious, probable expectation' (p. 2550) with individual exceptions was possible. During his exchange of letters with H. L., a young Bavarian student, Levi had the opportunity to experience what he called Masslosigkeit, or excessiveness. The girl sent him a 23-page letter, 'a doctoral thesis, almost' (p. 2553) on the behaviour of the Germans. H. L.'s letters triggered 'ambivalent reactions' (p. 2555) and he decided to break off the correspondence. With Hety Schmitt-Maass, Hermann Langbein's friend, on the other hand, he enjoyed an intense correspondence, which was interwoven with the letters of Jean Améry, who was also a personal friend of hers and whose address she had given Levi. (Hety demanded a carbon copy of every letter the two Auschwitz survivors exchanged, and both Levi and Améry agreed to her stipulation.) In her first letter, Hety opens in a similar manner to Riedt: 'You will certainly never succeed in understanding "the Germans", not even we Germans are able to. So much happened in those years that never should have happened, at any price.' (p. 2556). What made their epistolary friendship 'long, rich, and often joyous' was the fact that 'she, of all my German readers, was the only one who was pure of heart and therefore unencumbered by guilt' and that 'her curiosity is mine' (p. 2562).

When the Nazi war criminal, Herbert Kappler, escaped from prison, Levi wrote two articles. The first was an open letter to the Italian Minister of Justice, Vittorio Lattanzio, published in *La Stampa*. The second was more complex and interesting, written for the Turin Jewish Community newsletter *Ha Keillah*, and entitled 'The Germans and Kappler'. In this article, Levi expressed sharp criticism of the German reaction to Kappler's escape. The Germany that applauded Kappler's escape, organized and implemented by his wife, was 'not neo-Nazi Germany'; it was 'the self-righteous and legalistic Germany, the same one that wasn't National Socialist but offered Nazism a warm womb, fertile and welcoming' (p. 1235). Writing an Afterword to the New German Edition of *If This Is a Man* in 1979, Levi said he felt a 'painful curiosity' about the reactions of his new German readers. 'The second German edition will be read by a new generation, freed to a great extent from the guilt feelings of their fathers, open to all European influences, more receptive but at the same time more ignorant of their past, perhaps even more indifferent' (p. 1331).

In a 1986 recorded conversation with the writer, Ferdinando Camon, edited by Levi himself (Camon 1987 and 1989), Camon provoked Levi by asserting that German culture and civilization had always had certain satanic traits. Levi dissented: 'If I may,' he answered, 'I do not agree with this interpretation. Germans in Goethe's day were not affected. Germany started deviating in this direction much later on.' Camon insisted that anti-Semitism was a component of German culture. Levi found it 'curious' that he should be defending the Germans, but believed it was his responsibility to do so.

> I believe that to start with, even under Hitler, anti-Semitism was not widespread. German Jews were highly integrated, there was a widely assimilated Jewish bourgeoisie in the German nation [. . .] In my view, Hitler's personality carried great weight and was a decisive factor in this regard. I don't believe in Tolstoy's theory that history is bottom-up, that a tidal wave sweeps all our various

Napoleons along as if they were floating corks. Experience has taught me otherwise. I was clearly convinced when I witnessed the rise of Nazism in Germany, when I experienced it personally, and when I read about it afterwards: I had the impression that there was an evil spell, something demoniacal—you yourself were talking about demons as being a constant in German culture—but this was incarnated in Hitler.

In 1979, the East German publisher, Aufbau, founded in 1945, published *The Periodic Table*. Immediately following this, Aufbau decided to publish *If This Is a Man* and translate *The Truce*, neither of which had been published in the German Democratic Republic. In order to go to print, especially for *If This Is a Man*, which had already been published in West Germany by Fischer in 1961, permission had to be granted by the relevant authorities. An in-house editor, Joachim Meinert, who had worked on the Aufbau edition of *The Periodic Table*, was entrusted with the task of preparing the application. Following a procedure which was typical in the DDR, Aufbau was required to obtain a written opinion from an expert outside the publishing house. Fred Wander, a writer of Austrian origin, who was both communist and Jewish, and had been, like Levi, imprisoned in a Nazi concentration-camp, was chosen. As Gabriella Berolatti (2008) related, Wander immediately provided positive feedback, suggesting a few changes to be submitted to Levi. In his view, the condition of the 'privileged prisoners' described by Levi in *If This Is a Man* did not correspond to his experience. He also proposed eliminating the descriptions of the Russian soldiers in *The Truce*. Levi was so anxious to see his books published in the DDR in addition to West Germany—it was, after all, still Germany, and he felt keenly the urgency that all Germans be able to read his first book— that he answered Wander, who had written to him in 1982, and accepted all his edits.

In the DDR, there was absolute control over publishing, which was overseen by both the state apparatus and the Communist Party, and therefore Aufbau proceeded with extreme caution: the two books were highly sensitive, owing to their take on German history. The editorial director contacted the president of the Arts Academy, Konrad Wolf, asking him to write a favourable report on *The Truce*. Wolf had not been a random choice; he was a Party apparatchik, son of a communist writer, Friedrich Wolf, who had emigrated under Nazism to the Soviet Union, and above all brother of the famous secret service agent, Markus Wolf. Konrad Wolf stated that some parts of the two books were too 'subjective', but concluded that, with some significant edits, publication could go ahead. With these two opinions in hand, the publishers forwarded their application to the Hauptverwaltung, whose imprimatur was required. Typically, the Hauptverwaltung then sent the application on to the 'territorial' anti-Fascist committee, a representative of which, Otto Funke, declared that the figure of the political prisoner described in *If This Is a Man* did not correspond to the reality of the concentration camps. For publication of *The Truce*, Funke gave a green light, provided that some sections were cut and others rewritten by the author. However, the anti-Fascist committee went on to discover that Levi was a member of the international committee of Auschwitz survivors but that he was not a member of the anti-Fascist association with ties to the Communist Party. This finding brought the whole procedure to a grinding halt. The two books in the end never obtained permission to be published in the German Democratic Republic.

In a November 1984 letter to Meinert, Levi expressed his dismay at the failure of *If This Is a Man* to be published in East Germany, even though, on rereading Wander's letters from two years before, he had understood that there was only a remote possibility that the DDR would ever give permission to publish the book. In the same letter, he explained to the Aufbau editor that his views on the 'political' prisoners in Auschwitz were dictated by 'local conditions and were strongly influenced by the behaviour of Polish political prisoners who, as we now know, were mostly nationalists, almost fascists, and not only anti-Soviet but even anti-Semitic.' He repeated to Meinert that he was willing to rewrite or cut all together the part about the 'political' prisoners if this would serve to save the publication. 'I beg you to forward my proposal to the one who "judges and sends according as he girds him",' Levi wrote, quoting from Dante's Inferno.

The following year, in March 1985, Levi wrote back to Meinert, saying that he understood perfectly why the book had been rejected. He also added a detail explaining what he had written about the political prisoners in his camp. At the end of the letter, Levi thanks Meinert for the 'serious and honest' missive he had received a few days earlier. It was not until after the fall of the Berlin Wall that his first two books began to circulate.

PORTRAIT OF A STUDENT (c. 1937)

Primo was a sickly child, and missed many days of elementary school. In Grade One, his parents kept him home for several months, and later he had tutors to help prepare him for the middle-school entrance exams. There are several middle and high-school class photos of him. The high school he attended in the late 1920s and early 1930s was the prestigious Massimo D'Azeglio Classical Lyceum, which bred and educated many famous anti-Fascists. Levi had just enrolled in the Chemistry Faculty of Turin University in 1937, after graduating from high school. In this picture, he's staring into space, a little dismayed it seems—an adult version of the expression he already revealed aged one with his mother. He looks shy and reclusive, but not aloof. He is staring obliquely at the camera which is not directly in front of him. But his gaze is not absent. As Roland Barthes would say, the eyes are the focal point of the picture, taken by an anonymous photographer in Turin. Primo's eyes are similar to Ester's, but they do not have the bravado of his mother whose gaze is nonetheless shy and feminine. His wavy hair is striking; it continued to be wavy even after he had gone completely grey.

It is hard to gauge the image that the young student held of himself at the time this photograph was taken. Many years later, Levi wrote *The Periodic Table*, an autobiography of his life as a chemist which would reveal something about his younger self. And yet, it was a different self that was telling the story, a self that had been forged out of Auschwitz and the long journey home. In this identity-card sized photo, there is an identity that would not vanish, but which would become one of the many layers of a stratified personality where nothing of the past was lost but where every experience accumulated into a plural identity. Rather, a double identity comprising the Ego and the Id. In 1938, the Fascist Racial Laws forbade Jews from enrolling in college. A loophole in the law, however, exempted those of the 'Jewish Race' who were already signed up. Levi managed to graduate in June 1941, *summa cum laude*.

Is *If This Is a Man* Really 'A Detached Study of Certain Aspects of the Human Mind' as the Author Claims?

What is *If This Is a Man*? 'A detached study of certain aspects of the human mind', the author stated in his Preface to the 1947 De Silva edition. Levi, a 28-year-old graduate in Chemistry, explained that the book was not written 'to formulate new accusations', but rather to 'furnish documentation' (p. 5). The adjective 'detached' is vital, as is the word 'fortune' that Levi used in the first line ('It was my good fortune').

One of the most important, if not the most important, witness accounts of the Nazi concentration camps was not only a true story describing the personal experience of the author. It was also, above all, an anthropological and ethological document-report. In the chapter at the heart of *The Drowned and the Saved*, Levi explicitly talked about the 'human animal' and described the Lager as being a 'gigantic biological and social experiment' (p. 82). Readers may thus think, as they start reading the book, that it is the work of a 'detached' person, who has achieved a distance from his devastating experience of extermination—of Jews, Russian soldiers, Ukrainian women, homosexuals, partisans and political prisoners. And yet, when they turn the page, they will come across the poem that, stripped away, gives the title to the book: 'You who live safe in your heated houses . . .'

The last three lines are an invective, or rather a curse. Adopting a biblical tone, 'Scemà' condemns those who refuse to carve the author's words into their hearts or tell their children. The curse is ultimately aimed at them: 'Or may your house fall down, May illness make you helpless, And your children turn their eyes from you.' The words Levi uses at the opening of the book are incredibly harsh and contradict the detachment he claims to have. As Mario Barenghi (2000) claimed, there is a marked contradiction, a two-fold tension, in *If This Is a Man* and throughout all his testimonies and literary work. It is almost an ambivalence between composure and severity, which are the twin poles of his personality as a writer. The tension is stretched to the limit, both here in his first book and later, in his greatest and last, which was not published until 1986, *The Drowned and the Saved*. The ambivalence allows us to view the book on two different levels: as one of the masterpieces of the Italian language, as well as a witness statement presented by a man with both acute observation skills and the tough temperament of the biblical prophet, even though he had no desire to play that role. The book has the effect of a slow, unstoppable percolator, penetrating our emotions and our intelligence, judging while helping us to feel.

Barenghi explains how this autobiographical text is substantially based on an 'experience of extreme impoverishment, taken to the point of demolition'. Traditional autobiography, as it emerged in the eighteenth century (such as in Rousseau) relied on the idea of exemplarity or exceptionalness. In the nineteenth century, on the other hand, the genre comprised mostly memoirs of conspirators and patriots, while in the twentieth it was increasingly defined as an autobiography of victimhood, men and women who had helplessly suffered the fury of historical events.

Levi's ambivalence is profound. On the one hand, there is a search—however difficult—for a rational thread when describing and attempting to understand what he had experienced, which takes the form of a 'detached study of certain aspects of the human mind'. On the other, there is the total absurdity of his experience of the concentration camps. Moreover, Levi's reminiscence of his experience in the Lager is, as Barenghi puts it, 'constricted and obsessive'. Right at the threshold of his first book, Levi is unable to free himself of the unreality that had captured and imprisoned him for months in the camp. In order to free himself, at least temporarily, of this unreality, he assumes the tone of a biblical prophet and launches himself in an invective against his readers, pronouncing an incredibly harsh curse.

The ambivalence between the various levels of Levi's work, the ambivalence he talks about in a series of interviews in the 1960s immediately after publishing *The Truce*, could well be the stigma Levi himself attached to his first book of witness accounts and his later short stories. The split between Levi the chemist and Levi the writer, between witness and narrator, between scientist and man of letters, could well be a replica—on different, not necessarily overlapping, planes—of the separation that Levi himself offered in a literary form at the opening of *If This Is a Man*. Barenghi adopts one of Bettelheim's phrases in *Surviving and Other Essays* (Bettelheim 1980) referring to his deportation ('unforgettable but unreal') when he lists the various ways in which Levi's memory works, highlighting the lacerating, almost schizogenous, nature of his memory of the Lager.

When the young chemist got back to his native city, back to his friends and loved ones, back to his work, he discovered that telling his story—for which he felt a vital need—was also saturated in pain. 'Rather than bringing about a liberating sense of satisfaction, it can also be prelude to a kind of loss of contact with reality' (Barenghi 2013). This is apparent at the end of his second book, *The Truce*, as his real life, in his own house, is contaminated by the memory of his experience. Psychologists who have researched the reactions of former deportees have found that it is not possible to 'attribute the same level of reality to the real world and to the hellish world of the Lager. It is not possible to inhabit two worlds so alien to each other at the same time, even in one's memory' (Barenghi 2013).

This division between telling and understanding, between remembering and testifying, was destined to return in different ways in Levi's work. In his short stories, it took on the guise of unusual fantasies (objects, characters, animals, situations). In his poems, it was the false bottom of the terrible, teeming memory of the Lager, as evidenced by the poem that opens *If This Is a Man*. In his autobiographical texts in *The Periodic Table* that try so hard to contain his initial unease, and in particular in *The Drowned and the Saved*, his greatest work, which is honest even against his own interests, it is saturated to the very last word with the memory which had never healed of Auschwitz.

Levi started explicitly referring to himself as 'The Ancient Mariner' in interviews and statements during the 1960s. Coleridge's hero was a kind of alter ego, representing the split in himself between being a writer and being a witness, always on the ready to tell the story that needed telling, but punished with an albatross round his neck holding him back on the threshold of yet another study of 'certain aspects of the human mind'.

WHY *IF THIS IS A MAN* WAS REJECTED BY EINAUDI
AND OTHER PUBLISHERS, OR WHY SO MUCH TIME WENT BY
BEFORE IT WAS UNDERSTOOD AND APPRECIATED

Looking back over cuttings of reviews, leafing through old newspaper and magazine articles, rereading the cultural climate and literary criticism of the time, it becomes clear that Levi was not fully accorded the status of writer until the beginning of the 1980s. This corresponded almost perfectly with international recognition of his work, which came about even though the early translations of his books in the United Kingdom and the United States had soon gone out of print. It was a random event—a book blurb written by the Nobel Prize–winning novelist Saul Bellow for *The Periodic Table* (not a book on his experience in the concentration camps)—that shot Levi's star up into the international literary firmament.

It is important, therefore, to analyse more closely why Einaudi rejected Levi's first book. Examining the publisher's reasons is rather like finding Edgar Allen Poe's 'Stolen Letter', because all the facts (nearly all of them) have always been there right under our noses. The real scandal, if we can call it a scandal (rejecting a book, even when it turns out to be an important book, is not in itself scandalous because significant books sooner or later have a way of resurfacing) lies in the fact that nobody ever looked for them in the right place.

A good place to start is in the general cultural climate in Italian post-war society. Levi described it in an interview in the 1980s, when he had already been hailed as a great writer. In this conversation, Levi was conciliatory, not just because he had achieved recognition and had been gratified by it but also because he naturally sought explanations for things rather than recriminations. After touching on the difficulties that Natalia Ginzburg, a Turin Jew like him, had met with after her husband Leone's death, Levi said that he understood why his book had been rejected. In his words, 'it expressed a wider, collective rejection. At that time people had other things to do [. . .]. A book like mine, and like many others that came along after mine, was almost an act of rudeness, it was like spoiling a party.' Levi was expressing a form of pietas (duty) not only towards what took place in the concentration camps but also towards those who wanted to forget (the theme of voluntary oblivion, and the conflictual relationship between memory and oblivion, was to return in *The Drowned and the Saved*).

A play written by Eduardo De Filippo, *Napoli milionaria!*, Provides ample evidence of this cultural attitude towards concentration-camp survivors, Italian soldiers (an estimated 700,000 of whom were deported to Germany after the 8 September 1943 armistice), and war veterans in general. Written hastily and staged in Naples in March 1945 (later published by Einaudi in 1950), the play's protagonist comes back from the war to find his wife and daughter so busy making money in various ways that they have no patience with his stories, and refuse to listen to them (Levi has referred to De Filippo's piece as 'fraternal work').

More in general, events of the Second World War were 'shared memories', as historians put it. Italy had lost the war, negotiated the Armistice with the allied forces in 1943, and transitioned from a Fascist to a post-Fascist regime which left all the state structures intact under Marshall Badoglio's command. It had then suffered terrible bloodshed under German occupation in the centre and north of the country, followed by a civil war in a country divided between the Kingdom of the South, under the Italian King and the Allied Forces, the Republic of Salò, and the Partisan Resistance. The situation was complex, to say the least, and the memories of ordinary Italians were not necessarily 'shared'.

The post-war period was equally drawn out, marked by a highly charged political conflict between the parties that had participated in different ways in the Resistance. The Christian Democrat Party, and other parties on the right, largely discredited the experience of the Resistance, while the other side of the political spectrum—the Action Party, the Socialist Party and most of all the Communist Party—enshrined and exalted it.

Memories of war are often suppressed in a divided country, and this has repercussions on the collective memories of the most atrocious elements of the Second World War. The first book about the deportation of Italian Jews and soldiers came out in 1944. *October 16, 1943*, was written on the spur of the moment by the writer and literary critic Giacomo De Benedetti. Ten books on the subject were published in 1945, fourteen in 1946, only three in 1947, including Levi's, and then nothing until the early 1950s. Only four books were published up to 1954, including *Oblìo e colpa* (Oblivion and Blame) edited by the association of former deportees (ANED). A decade after the end of the war, in 1955, Levi wrote an article in a pamphlet distributed in Turin entitled 'The Deported. Anniversary'. The text is heartfelt, dignified and filled with moral fortitude. At the same time, it reveals an important consideration on the relationship between victim and executioner that was developed 20 years later in *The Drowned and the Saved*. Levi quite simply reminded his readers that the concentration camps had been completely forgotten.

The suppression of memory was thus still firmly in place; part of the generalized oblivion concerning the Second World War. While the First World War altered Europe's memory, as historians have shown, the Second World War was relegated to oblivion in at least the 20 years that followed. This is a very important aspect that historians will have to shed light on in the future, as the linguist Harald Weinrich pointed out in *Lete* concerning the construction of a European identity,

Returning, however, to the circumstances of *If This Is a Man*'s early rejection, the book was read by Franco Antonicelli, who had founded the De Silva publishing company in 1942 but also collaborated with Einaudi and later joined their author list. Unlike Cesare Pavese, Antonicelli had taken part in the Resistance efforts to free the country of Nazi control and was thus more likely to have been willing to accept Levi's work bearing witness to Nazi atrocities. Pavese was Einaudi's editorial director at the time, and Levi's book was most probably placed in his hands. The question of why Pavese, who was a declared anti-Fascist and exiled by the regime, never took part in the Resistance is too loaded to go into here. This question, alongside his repeated declarations that he was extraneous to politics, certainly contributed to Pavese's attitude towards manuscripts written by partisans and deportees that arrived on his desk at Einaudi in the immediate post-war years.

The first series to be published by the Turin-based publishing house Einaudi in 1933 was called 'Problemi Contemporanei' (Contemporary Problems). It comprised mostly books on economics and politics, and the series continued until 1944 when it ceased for two years and then reopened in 1946. In 1934, a second series of scientific, economic and financial monographs was launched, followed by the third in 1935 called *Memorie di guerra e documenti* (War Memories and Documents) which was closed almost immediately after the Fascist regime confiscated Leonida Bissolati's *Diario di guerra* (War Diary). Immediately after the Second World War, Einaudi editors felt it was essential to launch a new series, to be called *Testimonianze* (Testimonies), and to include works on fascism, war and the partisan struggle.

In 1945 alone, five books were published in the series, including works by the secretary of the Italian Communist Party, Palmiro Togliatti, and by Luciano Bolis, *Il mio granello di sabbia* (My Little Grain of Sand) on his experiences with the partisans and the torture that was meted out to him by the Nazi-Fascists. This book was re-printed several times in the years to follow. However, the series did not meet with commercial success. Nothing came out in the series until 1955, when 'I coetani' (The Peer-Group) by Elsa De' Giorbi was published in the series because nobody knew where else to place it. A similar series, which aimed to use testimonies as a way to narrate recent historical events, was launched in 1946 with the name 'Mondo Contemporaneo' (The Contemporary World). The only work to be published before a similar market failure shut it down was a book by the Socialist Party leader Pietro Nenni entitled *Storia di quattro anni* (A History of Four Years).

The Einaudi archive, painstakingly researched by Luisa Mangoni (Mangoni 1999), reveals that, in October 1945, Lisa Dresner asked Elio Vittorini where the two books about Polish concentration camps she had talked to him about when she was in Milan had got to. These two books were the abridged and translated version of the book published in Germany by a committee of former internees, and another book about Auschwitz written by Dresner herself. Vittorini answered in a letter that he had spoken to his editors 'rather hastily' and that he didn't think it was possible to publish them in the series he was responsible for. He went on to reassure Dresner that he had written to Antonio Giolitti and Felice Balbo to see whether the two books might come out in the 'Testimonianze' series. The distinguished series editors answered that, by the time the editions were ready for print, 'the subject would already be out of date'.

Anybody with any experience in publishing in Italy knows that finding the right series for certain books is a recurrent problem. Einaudi, moreover, had always promoted a holistic cultural project. In-house debate about which series to publish new arrivals in was of vital importance, as all the various histories of the publishing house prove. Giolitti and Balbo's answer, highlighting what they saw as being the speed of change in the publishing world, just goes to show how confused and uncertain the cultural climate was at the time. There was certainly anxious internal debate about the 'Testimonianze' series. Giolitti called for the urgent publication of a book on the partisan war, while Balbo was better disposed to a collective volume on the same subject. And yet the impression gleaned from the correspondence among Einaudi editors and consultants is that the need to keep up with events, not to be left behind by the times, and to break with the past, meant that editors were highly susceptible to market response and reader opinion—following the natural inclination in the population to suppress the memory of the war.

It is not by chance that the first book on the history of the Resistance movement by Roberto Battaglia did not come out until 1953. This was precisely when Einaudi decided to recover the memory of the Partisan war, with its militant anti-Fascist tradition, by publishing and continuously reprinting books which were destined for new generations of readers. Einaudi had its wake-up call in 1960 when the Christian Democrat leader Tambroni was propped up by the neo-Fascist party, Movimento Sociale Italiano, whose votes saved the government. This was when the decision was taken to publish the series 'Letture per la scuola media' (Readings for Middle Schools), which was the vehicle used to bring Levi's works into schools.

After the 'Testimonianze' series, which had been the most suitable for publishing memoirs of the deportations, was closed, testimonies regarding concentration camps were invariably rejected. Rousset's book on the subject was considered, and Vittorini even reputed it to be an important piece of work with historical significance, but he doubted it would enjoy commercial success (the final decision not to go ahead with publication, in Pavese's papers at Einaudi, was made in December 1946). In-house papers in the archive up to 1948 tell the same story. The importance of testimonies of concentration camps was recognized, but it was felt they would not be a commercial success. Antonio Bandini Buti, chief editor at the Italian Touring Club magazine, sent Einaudi a manuscript in 1948 written by a Jew from Zagabria, Egon Berger, who had spent four years in a concentration camp run by the Ustasha regime and told the story of the atrocities committed there. Pavese wrote back: 'We generally reject every book on this subject. Primo Levi's book, *If This Is a Man*, published by De Silva, had been previously submitted to us and rejected. We advise you to try De Silva.'

The rejection of *If This Is a Man* was not the fruit of incomprehension but, rather, a deliberate editorial decision. The trend is confirmed by

Natalia Ginzburg's letter to Sergio Antonielli, author of *Il Campo 29* (Camp 29). Ginzburg provided detailed feedback on the book but advised the author to send it to De Silva, whose general editor, Franco Antonicelli, 'publishes a series with contemporary documents where your book would fit perfectly'. The book was finally published in 1949 by the Milan house, Edizioni Europee, and won the Bagutta Prize in 1950.

In 1947—as a letter later published by Einaudi in 1977 under the title *Gli anni del 'Politecnico'* (The Years of 'The Polytechnic') proves—Vittorini proposed Roberto Antelme's book, *La specie umana* (The Human Species), which was not published until 1954 in the series *Gettoni* (Tokens). In the letter, Vittorini explained that Antelme's book was rejected at the time, as *If This Is a Man* had been, because there was no suitable series to publish it in. The other reason he cited was that, in 1947, 'the subject seemed to us to be unbearable for the general public; it had become over-exploited and rhetorical, while nowadays, with distance, it can be read with its interest intact.' A few years later, Levi's books were reprinted by Einaudi.

There's another more subtle, but equally important, issue that influenced the attitude of Einaudi editors, especially Pavese, towards literature in general in the early post-war period. Today we consider that period one of great literary ferment, when many of the most influential writers of the second half of the twentieth century published their first novels. The fact of the matter is that 1945 to 1950 was a period of inertia—the kind of sudden stasis that is typical of transitions. In order to understand what took place, in particular at Einaudi, it is necessary to go back a few years to the outbreak of the war and examine the fiction series and authors Einaudi started to publish then.

In 1941, in the early stages of the war, Cesare Pavese debuted with *Paese tuoi* (Your Country), Natalia Ginzburg, under a pseudonym because she was Jewish, published her first novel *La strada che va in città* (The Road that Leads to the City), and Arrigo Benedetti, future editor of the weekly news magazines *Europeo* and *L'Espresso*, also became an Einaudi author. By 1946, however, the series *'Narratori Contemporanei'* (Contemporary

Narrators) had become inactive. Both Pavese and Vittorini, who had pub-lished his *Uomini o no* (Men and Not Men) in 1945, were well-aware, as Mangoni reveals after studying Einaudi's publishing correspondence, that Italian literature was undergoing a period of crisis, and that their own novels were part of that same crisis. The crisis was more in general that of European culture since the 1930s, which had been the starting point for all Italian writers and intellectuals born in the first decade of the century. The Second World War could have been a turning point, but in the early post-war years Einaudi editors were increasingly convinced that real-life accounts were beginning to prevail over novels. Manuscripts poured in reporting war experiences and recounting the Resistance, but there was nothing 'new' on the literary front. Literature seemed to have been confined by its content, as Mangoni put it.

This was one reason why Pavese pushed for Calvino's *Il sentiero del nido di ragno* (The Path to the Nest of Spiders), which Vittorini did not like at all, to the point where it was nearly rejected. It was finally published in 1947, owing in part to Giulio Einaudi's enthusiasm. At the same time, however, Pavese rejected yet another war account which, as he wrote to the author, Costanzo Aurelio in 1947, had the same 'defect' as 'nearly all the novels inspired by the civil war period. 'For the last two years,' the editor continued,

> we have seen innumerable manuscripts on partisan, clandestine, prison, or zebra-striped life—and the author has always been convinced that the enormity of the things they experienced, or believed they experienced would be enough to produce a piece of literature. It is not the case. These books oscillate between news reporting and venting steam. They are essentially 'senti-mental' and, apart from their political point of view, they are all the same.

Mangoni, who reports this extract of Pavese's letter, stresses that Vittorini felt very much the same way. It was not until the early 1950s, in fact, with the launch of the series 'Gettoni' (Tokens) that the new post-war generation of writers began to emerge. Vittorini, 10 years after his 1947 letter, writing in *Diario in pubblico* (Public Diary) defined this new crop of writers as 'youth without a past', with 'no roots in anything but their own generation'.

Returning to *If This Is a Man* , one could say that the book fell into Einaudi's hands at an unfortunate time, owing to both the editorial difficulties in keeping the 'Testimonianza' series going and to the fear that the manuscript did not have the requisite literary value (which, however, two critics as influential as Calvino and Cajumi, recognized immediately). Unfortunately, we do not have Natalia Ginzburg's report on her reading of the manuscript, if it was ever compiled. We can conjecture at least one thing, however: the manuscript of *If This Is a Man* did not resemble any other book of that period, neither in its language nor in its narrative style.

Nowadays, the label 'neorealist' is used more often for the films of the post-war period, while it seems to be used less and less in literature. In Calvino's Preface to the 1964 reprint of *The Path to the Nest of Spiders*, he denied the very existence of neorealist literature. What is certain is that writers sought a new voice, and tried to adopt a 'new language' in their stories and testimonies of that time. This language was more immediate and fresher than before, and bore a close relationship to spoken Italian, with a great deal of dialogue and rapid descriptive sketches.

Not everyone succeeded, but the search for a 'new' voice in literature was on. The manuscript that Levi submitted to Pavese and Natalia Ginzburg was very different from the neorealist works of the time. It was full of explicit and hidden literary references (to Dante, Manzoni, Foscolo, Gozzano, and Latin Classics, among others), which were more common than they are now. *If This Is a Man*, as has already been observed, was carved in marble. It was tainted here and there with technical terms, but Levi's style aimed to achieve extreme precision, at the same time relying on the concise, effective style of the Italian tradition. It is the language of the Classical *liceo*, the most traditional branch of high school, the same language adopted by Fascism in its intent to train a new elite. In this sense, in its classicism, Levi's style is related to the language that lost the war. It is the rhetorical language of the nineteenth century, that of Carducci (an important influence on Levi's poetry), which was appropriated and later owned by Fascism. There's nothing fascist in Levi's style—far from it. And yet the lexical and syntactical similarities are so evident that it would be impossible for Pavese or Ginzburg, with their sensitive ears, not to detect them. After all, these two authors were themselves trying to find a very different style in their own writing. Levi's language would have sounded 'old-fashioned' to them, and this may well be the primary reason for their rejection of his work.

Just as Franz Kafka wrote in a foreign language, as Giles Deleuze and Félix Guattari pointed out in *Kafka, per una letteratura minore*, Levi's language in *If This Is a Man* was equally 'foreign' to the period when it was written. It is not by chance that the book did not meet with critical success for many years: very few critics understood the linguistic significance of Levi's style. Readers, by contrast, took immediately to his style, partly because many of them were his contemporaries. It was in fact his readers who decreed the slow but inexorable success of the book.

The origins of Einaudi's notorious rejection of *If This Is a Man*, as we have seen, are complex. Responsibility did not lie so much with a publisher and two illustrious authors as with an entire epoch and its intricate issues. Aside from this historical context, and the problems related to a brief period of this era, *If This Is a Man* later imposed itself as one of the greatest books in Italian post-war literature. The real scandal was not that it was published by De Silva and not by Einaudi, but that so many critics for so long, with so few exceptions, parroted the same old clichés about Levi, without ever stating simply and clearly why his books were important. Easy inclusions in a publisher's author list are as suspect as exclusions. Often sanctifying authors is the quickest and most effective way to avoid settling accounts with them.

Is *If This Is a Man* a Comedy or a Tragedy?

If This Is a Man is an unequivocally Italian work, within the rich seam of the Italian literary and intellectual tradition. It is no chance, then, that Levi's guide, moral and linguistic yardstick and putative mentor of the terrible journey into the abyss of Auschwitz—the *anus mundi*—is Dante. Even though it deals with one of the most tragic episodes of twentieth-century history, from a literary point of view Levi's first book is a comedy. While there are plenty of grim descriptions that often evoke the themes of classical tragedy, there is always an element of comedy in them.

A good example can be found in the bleakest chapter of all, 'The Last One', where Levi in the 1958 edition added the 'three undertakings' with the anecdote of the stolen broom and the trade in shower discs 'organized' by Alberto. Another is at the end of the chapter 'On the Bottom', with the apparition of the German Cerberus (again, added in the second edition) whose demands for money and watches are met with hilarity among the deportees on the truck. There are further examples in 'Our Nights' and 'The Story of Ten Days', as well as in the tragicomic chapter 'Kraus', where the false dream Levi describes to the poor Hungarian prisoner is a piece of comedy within the overall tragedy of the Lager.

As with Kafka, the term 'tragedy' in the classical tradition does not apply to Levi. This is because neither Levi nor Kafka adopt the notion of *guilt*, which is a prerequisite for tragedy. This absence is abundantly evident in Levi's work, while Kafka admits the existence of guilt but makes it clear that there is no way, even if anyone wanted, to atone for it: it is guilt without redemption. In *If This Is a Man*, Levi denies the very idea of guilt, and never uses the term 'innocent' to describe the victims of the

Lager. The idea of sacrifice, with its veneer of sacredness, was alien to Levi's moral framework.

Nor is *If This Is a Man* a drama, since the medieval concept of drama was that victims' suffering—their martyrdom—is an expiation that will be compensated by eternal bliss (there are no 'tragedies' in the literary sense in medieval literature). Levi rejects the idea that deportees are saints, martyrs, or heroes; their death is never glorious.

As Giorgio Agamben demonstrates in his book on *The Divine Comedy* (1996), with Dante's choice of title—which was to have a huge impact on Italian literary tradition—the poet advances an idea of moral redemption that is categorically anti-tragic. In Dante's view, there is a comic split between human nature (which, according to Christian theology, is innocent) and the person (who, by contrast, is guilty): tragedy appears to be the culpability of what is just; comedy, a justification for guilt.

In *The Death of Tragedy* (1961), George Steiner states that a tragedy is simply the story of an eminent or historical person's life that ends miserably after a reversal of fortune. This is the medieval definition of tragedy. Dante calls his poem *The Divine Comedy* because, as Steiner puts it, the action follows the 'rising path' of the soul from the shade to the light, from doubt to certainty, from joy to grace. Tragedy, on the other hand, moves in the opposite direction: a downward path, from prosperity to suffering and chaos.

In *If This Is a Man*, Levi rejects these models: his 'comedy' has different features. Most importantly, there is no God. In 'October 1944', for example, Levi exclaims to the pious Jew who thanks God for saving him from the selections, 'If I were God, I would spit Kuhn's prayer out upon the ground' (p. 124). Nor is there the idea—developed by other authors who have written about the concentration-camp experience, such as Elie Wiesel—of absolute evil, or of a theology of evil. This does not mean that Levi does not explore the meaning of evil; it is just that he does not presume there is evil. In this sense, he adheres closely to twentieth-century philosophy, although he does not reference it explicitly.

In his personal anthology, *The Search for Roots*, he writes, 'Why start with Job? [. . .] Job is the just man oppressed by injustice [. . .] Job the just, degraded to an animal for an experiment.' This is the clincher that excludes the possibility of defining *If This Is a Man* a tragedy. Levi has an animal-behaviourist view of human beings; human beings are animals, or man-animals. He describes the Lager as a 'gigantic biological and social experiment', an extreme experiment (p. 81). Levi's Darwinian view of humankind also excludes the classical—and Christian—approach to the relationship between human beings and nature. For him, the relationship is not something to strive for; it is the result of behavioural strategies based on biology. Similarly, morality is an ethos that evolved throughout the history of civilization.

As a 'comedy', Agamben writes, Dante's poem represents a path from guilt to innocence, rather than from innocence to guilt. Dante's itinerary as a human being is a comedy, not a tragedy. Ultimately, Agamben concludes, the fact that the title includes the word 'Comedy' calls into question an issue that is at the heart of the work: the guilt or innocence of a human being when facing diving justice. Dante's *Divine Comedy* is rooted in the idea of original sin, while the basis of classical tragedy is the innocence of the individual. Dante contemplates the possibility of a comic reconciliation between personal innocence and personal guilt. Using the theory of *shame*, based on a tragic idea of natural guilt, he shifts towards a comic notion of personal guilt. Similarly, in Levi's approach, 'human nature' is a condition of imperfection. 'Sooner or later in life we all discover that perfect happiness is unrealizable, but few of us pause to consider the opposite: that so, too, is perfect unhappiness. The obstacles preventing the realization of both these extreme states are of the same nature: they derive from our human condition, which is hostile to everything infinite' ('The Journey', p. 13). He continues with a list of the elements that constitute the human condition,

> Our ever-inadequate knowledge of the future opposes it, and this is called, in the one instance, hope and, in the other, uncertainty

about tomorrow. The certainty of death opposes it, for death places a limit on every joy, but also on every sorrow. Our inevitable material cares oppose it, for, as they poison every lasting happiness, they just as assiduously distract us from our misfortunes, making our awareness of them intermittent and hence bearable (p. 13)

Levi's theory is both anthropological and political. As with classical moralists, the two fields meld into a single approach. That is, political theory—the *polis*—cannot exist without a theory of human beings (anthropology). Levi and his mentor Dante, the medieval philosopher, differ on the concept of shame, however. In his *Divine Comedy*, the character Dante goes through an experience of comic humiliation (Agamben 1996). He is ashamed in front of Beatrice as she guides him towards achieving a child-like condition of purity; the journey purifies him. Levi denies the notion of shame. In this respect, he is closer to Oedipus than to the character Dante; he is more the tragic hero than the Christian pilgrim. Since the character Levi in *If This Is a Man* is innocent, he does not accept being diminished by shame (the idea is taken up again in the chapter 'Shame' in *The Drowned and the Saved*).

The issue at stake in the Lager, if anything, is generalized guilt: the grey area. In *The Drowned and the Saved*, Levi cites Manzoni, the author he refers to in order to define the complex relationship between victims and torturers in the Lager. 'The troublemakers, the oppressors, all those who do harm of any sort to others, are guilty not only of the evil they do but also of the perversion of their victims' minds' (p. 2436). But then he immediately adds, 'The condition of victimhood does not exclude guilt, which is often objectively serious, but I do not know a human court that could be delegated to take its measure (p. 2436).

The problem, if anything, is one of *incommensurability*. *If This Is a Man* is Levi's *Human Comedy*, the adjective 'human' being the key shift from Dante's work. Agamben points out that tragedy never became part of

Italian culture, owing to Dante's anti-tragic stance. In contrast to the tragic claim of personal innocence, Dante introduced the Christian idea of the natural innocence of God's creatures. Was Levi faithful to this tradition? Yes and No. On one hand, his view of nature is Edenic, where nature is seen as innocent. On the other, Darwinism is an essential element, and the struggle for survival is unavoidable. In *If This Is a Man* there are numerous passages inspired by Levi's reading of Darwin. Steiner ends his essay, *The Death of Tragedy*, with a personal episode that took place on a train journey through southern Poland, when a fellow traveller told him a terrible story involving a German prison camp for Russian officers, and others in the compartment recounted comparable or worse incidents. Steiner's conclusion was that, 'Tragedy is that form of art which requires the intolerable burden of God's presence. It is now dead because his shadow no longer falls upon us as it fell upon Agamemnon or Macbeth or Athelie' (p. 352).

Perhaps we should start thinking of Levi, a secular Jew, as the writer who decreed the end of tragedy within the tragic and senseless game of history.

PHOTO OF THE FALSE IDENTITY CARD (c.1942)

Primo is wearing what looks like a mountain jacket, with the zipper open, revealing a striped shirt with a pointed collar and a tie with a thin knot, which resembles the one he was wearing in his student portrait. Philippe Mesnard (Mesnard 2008) informs us that this was the picture stuck into the false identity card Primo was carrying in 1943. After the collapse of Fascism in Italy on 25 July 1943, and the Armistice signed with the Allied Forces on 8 September of that same year, German troops occupied Italy and discrimination of Jews began in earnest. Levi escaped into the mountains of Valle d'Aosta in order to join a partisan group there, as he described in 'Gold' (*The Period Table*). It was to be a short-lived adventure. Levi was not particularly proud of this experience, calling it an 'escapade', but he never rejected it or tried to hide it. He doesn't mention it in the 1947 edition of *If This Is a Man*, but in the 1958 edition it finds its way into the story. Primo joined a small band of young resistance fighters inspired by the Justice and Liberty movement, who were all socialist and secular. They were 'probably the most poorly armed partisans in Piedmont, and probably also the most inexperienced' (p. 859), it being the very beginning of the Resistance in Italy. Primo was captured during a sweep by military police from the Salò Republic, the newly formed political and administrative entity where Fascist die-hards had joined Mussolini after German troops freed him from his prison in Gran Sasso. He was taken prisoner on 13 December 1943. Three hundred soldiers against 11 resistance fighters: eight managed to escape and three were captured, including Primo. In his account many years later in 'Gold', Levi referred to an episode when two young members of their band were killed by their own companions which distressed him enormously but for which he accepted responsibility (an ugly secret, as he called it). Levi described their capture and described how he 'ate, bit by bit, the patently false identity card I had in my wallet (the photograph was particularly revolting)' (p. 859), referring to the quality of the paper, it seems. If it really was this photograph, it may have been 'revolting' in his eyes, but it is one of the best photos of him. He looks hale and hearty, in the fullness of his youth. He looks almost proud, despite his usual shy demeanour and lowered eyes. It is the youthfulness of a man who cycles for miles and climbs mountains with friends, as the sports jacket shows. You can just see the string which he must have used to pull the collar, and perhaps the hood, tight to protect him from the cold. It is a strange match with the shirt and tie, which marks him as a student, as a member of the Turin bourgeoisie and as a mountain guide. His barely exhibited elegance was typical of his style as he got older, as a chemist and as a deportee. It was a symbol of the multiple layers that were to build up his personality. His gaze is lost and unaggressive and yet he looks decisive and completely sure of himself.

The Truce

In a 1947 letter to Jean Samuel, Pikolo in 'The Canto of Ulysses', Primo Levi told his friend that *If This Is a Man* was at the printers and would be coming out in September or October that year (Samuel with Dreyfus 2008). The publication date was respected: the print date in the colophon was 11 October 1947. Levi also informed his friend that he would probably not write the novella, or story, about the carbon atom he had talked to Samuel about when they were at Monowitz, but that he was thinking of a new piece. 'If my book is successful, I'll try and write a sequel; that is, the story of my long and curious journey back home through Eastern Europe.' Not long after *If This Is a Man* was published, Levi wrote a letter to thank the critic, Arrigo Cajuni, for his review in *La Stampa* of the book. 'As soon as my day job gives me time, I'm intending to write a second book which will complete the first: the story of my long journey home through western Russia and the Balkans. In preparation for this task, I would be extraordinarily grateful to meet you in person' (26 November 1947).

These were the first mentions of the book that we know as *The Truce*, which would not come out for another 16 years. Nevertheless, it is highly likely that at least two chapters were almost completely written between 1946 and 1947, while he was writing the various chapters of *If This Is a Man* and thinking about how to follow it up. The scene that opened Levi's second book was a seamless continuation of 'The Story of Ten Days'. It told the story of the liberation of Monowitz, Levi's illness and his transfer to the Big Camp at Auschwitz after the Soviet troops had arrived. Many years later, in a conversation with Carlo Paladini,

Levi confirmed that he had already written a chapter or two of *The Truce* between 1947 and 1948, spurred on by Franco Antonicelli and Alessandro Galante Garrone, 'to whom I had told the story of my complicated journey home' (Paladini 1987). In the bibliographical review of the first monograph dedicated to Primo Levi, Fiora Vincenti (1973), who was able to consult Levi during her research, wrote that *The Truce* first saw the light between 1960 and 1961, even though the idea was in the author's mind much earlier, as his letter to Samuel shows. The story was born from a scrap of paper on which Levi had scribbled the legs of his journey in 1946. 'I had a railway guide, so to speak, of my journey home. A sort of itinerary: such-and-such a day in such-and-such a place, in such-and-such other place. I found it, and I used it as an outline, almost 15 years ago, for writing *The Truce.*' Fifteen years later, he used the outline as a basis for his written account (Caccamo De Luca and Olagnero 1984). According to Giovanni Tesio, who had it in his possession for many years, in Levi's notebook 'For Einaudi'—where from the mid-50s onwards, he had written notes to himself for a possible new edition of *If This Is a Man*—there was already a sketched-out version of the opening of *The Truce*.

Unlike his first book, *The Truce* came about as the result of a well-outlined plan right from the start. The 1958 Einaudi edition of *If This Is a Man* gave him a boost, and he was keen to get back to work. As Levi himself stated: 'This time I wrote the book methodically, fully aware of the fact that I was writing a book from the beginning. My aim was to write a chapter a month' (Caccamo De Luca and Olagnero 1984).

The first two chapters, already written, or at least outlined, were the link between the first book and its sequel. The second book could only start in Auschwitz, since it was, in many ways, a continuation of the first, though very different. Here too, the origin of the book was oral—perhaps even more so than in *If This Is a Man*—because the picaresque nature of his adventurous journey home lent itself to this type of oral narration. As Levi explained in an interview at the time of publication

(Fabiani 1963), he had often told these stories to old school mates and members of his family, while strolling through the streets, in cafes or at home. Nearly everyone who heard his accounts encouraged him to write them down and publish them.

> Finally, the time came when the equation between free time, desire, and external pressure was perfect. The book cost me 200 hours' work, a chapter a month. Considering, however, that I can only work in the evenings, after a day at my company, and that I take at least an hour to change my skin and transform myself from a chemist to a writer, I would say the book took me three to four hundred days to write.

EDITOR OF HIMSELF

All this time writing, calculated to the day, produced the desired result. The first draft was written in a school, squared-paper exercise book with a thick paper cover in olive green. Written in capitals on the cover were the words: *Giglio—Bella Copia* (Lily—Good copy). On the first line of the frontispiece there was the author's full name, Primo Levi, written by hand, with *Italiano* on the next line (Tesio 1997). The notebook contained the chapters in succession, the date of composition for each, and, next to the titles, even the length of each chapter (number of lines and number of words). With his precision and passion for numbers, or rather for quantity—which, in the eyes of a chemist meant quality—Levi had calculated that each page comprised roughly 170 words. He tallied the total as being 63,000 words. He then converted the numbers to percentages to compare *The Truce* to *If This Is a Man*.

Looking at the sequence of dates, we can ascertain that 'The Greek' was written—or finished, as it is never clear whether the author was referring to the first version or the final one—on 30 March 1961. 'A Little Hen' was dated November 1961, 'The Thaw' (originally called 'Yankel's Cart'), 3 December 1961, 'The Big Camp', 12 December 1961,

'Katowice', (previously Katowice I), 16 December 1961, 'Cesare', 6 February 1962, 'Victory' (then called 'Victory Day'), 11 March 1962, 'The Dreamers', 31 March 1962, 'Heading South', 6 May 1962, 'Old Roads', 25 June 1962. One chapter was later cut. It was called 'Mushrooms and Horses', and was probably an alternative version of the final section of 'The Forest and the Path', which Levi had imagined in another narrative form. 'The Forest and the Path' was dated 18 July 1962, 'Vacation', 14 August 1962, and 'Theater', 19 August 1962.

In the notebook manuscript, the first two chapters were placed consecutively: the first was labelled '1°', and the second 'The Big Camp'. They both followed a chapter called 'The Disciple', a story that was subsequently published as a free-standing piece in the collected stories of *Lilith*. We can presume from the other dates that this story was written somewhere between March 1961 and August 1962, as the writer had told Vincenti. Later we will see how the dates correspond to those typed into the version Levi sent to Einaudi, which were then taken out of the printed edition.

Despite Levi's claims to the contrary, the genesis of *The Truce* has as complex a history as that of *If This Is a Man*. Gathering together the various chapters, which had been written separately without a pre-ordained plan for *If This Is a Man,* was clearly a different process to the clear outline Levi had envisaged for *The Truce*. And yet, some of the chapters of *The Truce* had in fact undergone previous versions before becoming the novel we know today. For example, a part of what was to become the fourth chapter, 'Katowice', was published in *Stampa Sera in* December 1959, with the title 'The Last in the Class' (19–20 December 1959). Levi told the story of the pickpocket known as 'the Ferrari', a mini version of the story that would then find its way into the chapter. There were several differences too, confirming Levi's tendency to work in blocks and then build them together into a narrative construction. According to Levi's biographer, Carole Angier, another chapter, 'The

Greek', had already been composed in 1954 (Angier 2004). This was confirmed by the notes at the end of the Einaudi manuscript.

The dating of the first two chapters of *The Truce*—'The Thaw' and 'The Big Camp', placed by Levi in his notebook in third and fourth position—remains uncertain. In Levi's word count, 'Yankel's Cart', as 'The Thaw' was then called, was expanded from 1,960 words to 2,314 words, which leads one to suppose that the chapter underwent revisions, perhaps precisely in order to place it at the beginning of the book. It is probably not by chance that the two chapters that were placed at the beginning of the notebook were complete in themselves as stories in their own right, rather than being part of a complete work. These two 'stories' were 'The Greek' and 'A Little Hen', which then became Chapter Three and Chapter Ten, respectively. This once again confirms that *The Truce* was built up out of a loose collection of short narrations revolving around individual characters or given events.

The unifying principle of the book was, of course, the journey, which followed the places and dates that Levi had sketched out back in 1946. The temporal and geographical axes thus provided Levi with a scaffolding for his stories, making it into more of a novel than a sequence of episodes. *The Truce* was a construction, put together with the building blocks of his stories, and the map published at the beginning of the book was the cement that held it together. Levi, as always, made adjustments as he went along, but the final effect was one of solidity, owing to both the style and the tight structure created by the building blocks.

In Tesio's description of Levi's notebook, it is clear that he made repeated changes to the titles of the chapters and to the text. For example, Cesare, one of the most memorable characters in the book, was introduced in a chapter that was originally called 'Katowice II'. In his textual revisions, he added a sentence so that he could call the chapter 'Cesare': 'I had met Cesare in my last days of the Lager' (p. 269). Examining the notebook gives a good idea of Levi's writing method.

This method was spontaneous to a certain degree; at the same time, there was some level of standardization—if one can call it that—since every book Levi wrote, even taking into consideration differences in style and form, followed a similar pattern. That is, they were all constructed chapter by chapter, and then the author had the task of juxtaposing them, or rewriting the opening or closing sentences, so that the chapters followed on from one another, always placing great importance in the titles.

The first draft of *The Truce*, as we have seen, was written by hand in the notebook, as the first draft of *If This Is a Man* almost certainly was. The revisions are clearly visible: in the notebook preserved by Tesio, they are marked in blue or red biro. The corrections are clear and untroubled, unlike the tormented, chaotic corrections made by his fellow writer, Calvino. An example of a revision in 'Cesare' was a change from the original text, 'In the neighbouring ward, for patients with dysentery, agony and death prevailed,' where the final words of the sentence were changed to 'death prevailed uncontested' (p. 269). It looks as if the sentences flowed freely from his pen and were almost perfect from the start; as if they had been mulled over at length before reaching the paper. It is almost as if his memory deliberately or unconsciously cited from the Classics. Added to this was his incredible capacity for creating images and writing succinctly. From his first version with hand-written revisions, Levi then produced a typed version of each chapter which he gave to his closest friends to read.

Alberto Salamoni, who would appear later in *The Periodic Table*, held on to three typed chapters of *The Truce*: 'A Little Hen' (dated November 1961 as in the notebook), 'Old Roads' and 'The Forest and the Path'. There are several differences in the typed version compared to the version that finally made it into print, showing again how Levi continued to make changes right to the end. For example, the number of Italians staying at the Red Cross changed, and some names were altered (Luciano became Daniele, Cuzzeri was called Mr Unverdorben, and his friend was defined as 'a friend from Trieste'). In addition, in Salamoni's typescript, the man from Marino (*il Marinese*) was corrected to a man born in Velletri (*il Velletrano*). The original name had appeared in one of Levi's earliest stories published in the journal *Il Ponte* in 1946 entitled 'Fine del Marinese' ('The Death of Marinese', in *Uncollected Stories and Essays, Complete Works* II), in a neorealist style. The additions Levi made to the original text, as we shall see when we examine the typescript sent to Einaudi, may have been made as a result of his rereadings, or on the basis of suggestions made by editors. However, Levi was so deeply engaged in editing his own work that he hardly needed an editor to help him.

WRITING BY HAND

In the notebook containing the first version of *The Truce*, Levi's handwriting was tiny but clearly legible. The handwritten text was filled with corrections, crossings out, and alterations. While this is not the place to go into too much detail regarding Levi's revisions, it is still interesting to examine the changes made to certain passages in order to appreciate Levi's approach to writing his second book.

The notebook contained a complete version of 'The Disciple', and a partial rendering of three other stories: 'Sleeping Beauty in the Refrigerator: A Winter's Tale' (dated 4 December 4, 1960), 'Man's Best Friend' (5 February 1960) and 'Censure in Bithynia' (which is missing its introductory section). On the cover was the title of the whole work, and references to it during his work-in-progress were indicated with the abbreviation LT (for the Italian title *La Tregua*). The actual dates when the various pieces were written are not certain where Levi did not explicitly date them. His practical and parsimonious approach to the tools of his trade could have meant that he actually re-used an old notebook, filling in the blank pages and empty spaces. In any case, many of the dates are the same as the ones indicated in the typescript handed in to Einaudi.

The chapter 'Cesare', as we have already said, was entitled 'Katowice II' and in this version an anthropological comment was included that was later taken out: 'Two emotions: "He is like us", "He is unlike us". The first is more common, because when relating other journeys, the only source of information, the accent is always on what is "different". Thus, the dominating surprise is that of being the same.' In Tesio's view, these and other edits where passages are cut, show that Levi was seeking 'expressive exactitude' in his stories and in his titles, in the rhythm of his speech patterns and in his more refined meditations, in order to achieve an 'epigraphic energy'.

One example of this was the description of the Soviet guard at the entrance of the camp at Katowice. 'The behaviour of the guard was unpredictable,' Levi had written; he had then added a cross inside a circle as a legend indicating a correction at the bottom of the page, which was in the form of short notes, 'a mongol (describe him), never replaced, hence his boredom'. The final printed version reads: 'The sentinel was a gigantic Mongol of around fifty, armed with machine gun and bayonet; he had enormous gnarled hands, a drooping grey moustache like Stalin's, and eyes of fire, but his fierce, barbaric appearance was utterly incongruous with his innocuous duties. He had no replacement, and so he was dying of boredom' (p. 256). This passage was the result of ongoing revisions in the various notebook and typescript versions.

A further example was in the chapter 'A Little Hen', in the description of the latrines at Sluzk. The notebook version was 'Inside there was only a floor of rough boards, and a hundred holes, ten by ten. There were [corrected above] There was no subdivision [corrected above] subdivision between the compartments intended for the three sexes. [added at the bottom of the page] If there were they had disappeared.' The final version ended up as: 'Inside, there was only a floor of rough boards and a hundred square holes, ten by ten, like a gigantic Rabelaisian multiplication table. There were no subdivisions between the compartments intended for the three sexes; or if there had been they had disappeared' (p. 322). The three sexes Levi was referring to, with his well-known sense of humour, were 'For Men, For Women, For Officials' (p. 322). A significant change between the handwritten and the printed version was the reference to Rabelais, whom he had perhaps read (or reread) at the time of writing, giving a refined touch while creating a surreal juxtaposition with the subject of the latrines.

In the same chapter, where Cesare put his horse-trading skills to work by mimicking a chicken in the village square because neither he nor Primo knew the Russian word for the bird, was another revealing revision. In the notebook, Levi wrote: 'And so we got no results. The chatter of the old Russian ladies took on an alarming and worrying colour and it was easy to understand the content. Who were these two beggars from who knows where clowning in their square, and what did they want?' This version was corrected to:

> So we got no results. They looked at us in astonishment, and certainly took us for madmen. Why, for what purpose, had we come from the ends of the Earth to do this mysterious clowning in their square? Now furious, Orazio even tried to produce an egg, and meanwhile insulted them in fantastic ways, making still more obscure the meaning of his pantomime. At this indecorous show, the chatter of the old ladies rose an octave and became the sound of an agitated wasps' nest (p. 328).

The name Orazio was changed to Cesare in the printed version and 'pantomime' was changed to 'performance'. The other revisions created a sense of crescendo in the description of the impromptu theatrical performance, enriching the whole story.

As we have seen, Levi was particularly careful with the beginnings and ends of his pieces. After writing the beginning of *The Truce*, Tesio claims, Levi wrote a note to himself in the margin: 'This is not very clear.' In the notebook version, the grim last page of the printed version was not there. This was so much gloomier than the rest of the picaresque story of Levi's adventures, that it cast a different light on the whole book, retrospectively conditioning its interpretation. The page adopted the tone of *If This Is a Man*, even though in nearly the whole of the rest of the book Levi appeared to have rid himself of the need to bear witness, allowing himself greater narrative freedom and vivacity.

At the very beginning of *The Truce*, when Levi described the shame the prisoners felt at the sight of the Russian soldiers on horseback, the well-known passage ('It was a shame well-known to us, the shame that inundated us after the selections and every time we had to witness or submit to an outrage: the shame that the Germans didn't know, and which the just man feels before a sin committed by another' p. 216) had an additional clause in the notebook version: 'the shame for which Christ asked his father to forgive his tormentors.' The reference to Christ was interesting, and showed Levi's familiarity with Christian themes. Additionally, the fact that the phrase was cut meant that the word 'forgive' no longer figured, which, had it stayed, would have changed the interpretation of the whole passage—one of the most cited in the book. Again in the opening pages, another passage was cut by the author before it reached the printing press:

> There is no defence against injustice: if you give in, you will fall without glory, like a beast at slaughter; if you resist, you may live or die but you will not find no other weapons for the struggle, even for you, than violence or fraud; if you run away to the ends of the earth your human conscience will follow you, and the remorse of the deserter as well as that of the accomplice will weigh in your breast.

From a stylistic point of view, this passage resembles the poem 'Shemà' at the beginning of *If This Is a Man*, with its reiterated first conditional constructions. From a conceptual point of view, it is an embryonic statement of Levi's idea of the 'grey zone', with its reference to the weapons of 'violence and fraud', and the corrupting power of shame in anyone who has been a prisoner and survived the experience ('deserter and accomplice').

Before going on to examine the typescript that Einaudi received from Levi, it is worth looking at one more significant revision in the second chapter, 'The Big Camp'. This was the passage where Olga reported the death of Vanda Maestro, the woman who also appeared in *If This Is a Man* and who was deported to Auschwitz from the Fòssoli transit camp on the same convoy as Levi and two other friends. The passage in the published book reads: 'Vanda had been gassed, fully conscious, in the month of October; she herself, Olga, had obtained two sleeping pills for her, but they were not enough' (p. 233). In the notebook version, there were also the following lines, which were later cut: 'I did not suffer from this news because I felt distant, detached, memories of my previous world were tenuous and sporadic; but I knew with absolute certainty that I would suffer later on.' In this direct autobiographical intervention, Levi explicitly revealed his feelings for Vanda, leaving aside his usual reticence and modesty. Similar, though less direct, autobiographical elements are expressed in the 1946 poems, written immediately after Levi's return from the Lager.

THE TITLE

The genesis of the title of the book is quite interesting. We know that when Levi signed the contract with Einaudi in December 1962, the title was *Vento alto* (High Wind). This was a reference to a passage from Genesis, quoted indirectly in 'The Greek'. In the first paragraph of the second section of that chapter, in fact, Levi had written, 'a high wind blew over the face of the Earth: the world around us seemed to have returned to a primal Chaos, and was swarming with deformed, defective, abnormal human examples' (p. 235). At the end of the book there was a form of explanation for this early title, where the idea of primordial chaos made its comeback: 'Everything has now turned into chaos; I am alone at the centre of a grey and murky void, and, yes, I know what this means, and I also know that I have always known it. I am again in the Lager, and nothing outside the Lager was true' (p. 397). Levi was invoking both the Bible and the Greek creation myths, the four elements of Empedocles and the pre-Socratics—all his great passions. It is a powerful passage, revealing his knowledge of the Classics and of the Bible. The theme of wind recurs in one of Levi's key works: '*Quaestio de Centauris*' (in *Natural Histories, The Complete Works* I) where Levi recounted the myth of the second creation featuring high wind as a regenerating spirit. This theme would return in other works too. And yet, the title *High Wind* would have given a different spin to the whole book.

So where did the title *The Truce* come from? The word 'tregua' appeared in the chapter 'Katowice', in the passage which described the war as it was coming to an end, although this was added as a revision. It is important to remember that when Levi and the other deportees were liberated from Monowitz it was January 1945, while Italy was occupied by the Germans until April of that same year, three months later. Moreover, Levi wrote his second book a good number of years after his return home. In the context of the détente—a kind of truce in the 1960s—Levi wrote about his adventures in Eastern Europe: 'It was the great truce, for the hard time that was to follow hadn't yet begun, nor had the cursed name of the cold war been uttered' (p. 258). The expression 'Cold War' started circulating in 1947, but it is likely Levi introduced it at the end of the 1950s or later. The word 'truce' was already present in *If This Is a Man* in the chapter 'The Events of the Summer' ('in the moments of truce') and is thus part of his lexicon. It is also used in 'Nickel' (*The Periodic Table*) for the period Levi spent between his father's illness and the German victories on various fronts at the start of the war, although this was much a much later work.

In the 1965 comment to the school edition of *The Truce*, Levi explained in a note the 'dream within another dream' (p. 397) of the final pages:

This page that closes the book in an unexpectedly serious tone, clarifies the meaning of the poem at the beginning and at the same time justifies the title. In the dream the Lager takes on a universal significance; it has become the symbol of the human condition ('nothing was true outside the Lager') and can be identified with death which no one can avoid. There are remissions, 'truces' as our troubled sleep at night was in our life at the camp, and human life itself is a truce, a postponement; but they are brief intervals, soon interrupted by the 'dawn command', feared but expected, from the foreign voice ('Watawc' means 'get up' in Polish) that everyone understands and obeys. This voice commands, or rather invites, death. It is quiet because death is inscribed in life, it is implicit in human destiny, inevitable and irresistible. At the same time no one would ever have thought about disobeying the wakeup call in the freezing Auschwitz dawns.

It must be supposed that the final pages of *The Truce* were written deliberately as a foil to the picaresque comedy of the much of the rest of the book—with the exception, of course, of the first two chapters still set inside Auschwitz.

The word 'truce' reappeared at the end of the book: 'Although the months just passed, of wandering at the edge of civilization, were harsh, they now seemed to us a truce, an interlude of unlimited openness, a providential gift of destiny, never to be repeated' (p. 396). Levi also commented on this passage in his notes to the school edition where he associated this truce to the life of young war veterans on returning home, comparing them explicitly to Renzo Tramaglino in Manzoni's *The Betrothed*, who got home to an untended garden run over with weeds. We will see further on when we analyse the Einaudi typescript how Levi wove the word into the material of the book.

In sum, there are three different interpretations of the word 'truce'. One is historical and political and came into circulation in the 1960s with the détente after the cold war, the same period when the final version of the book and its publication took place; another regards the situation in the camp: sleep at night as a remission or suspension of the suffering during the day; still another is a more general meaning referring to a definition of human life as a postponement, which is the implicit message in the final pages of the book confirmed by Levi's commentary. According to a biographer of Levi, Ian Thomson, it was one of his dearest friends, Giorgio Lattes, who suggested the title to him (Thomson 2003). The chapter 'Quaestio de Centauris', where, not by chance, the theme of chaos was explored, was dedicated to this friend.

THE TYPESCRIPT

Levi typed up the manuscript of The Truce and handed the bundle of paper to Einaudi for typesetting. There were 164 pages of different weights, which were numbered by hand, in-house, and stamped with the date 10 January 1963. On the left-hand side, the two punched holes show that they had been gathered into a loose-leaf file (the papers are now in the Turin State Archive, Folder 1052, File 3006). At various points in the typescript, Levi had scotch-taped strips of paper with his additional text directly onto the pages, as he had done for the 1958 edition of If This Is a Man. The typescript had also been revised by hand, with changes marked in different coloured pens. While there is little point in examining these minor revisions, which often involved single words, it is well worth analysing the expansions Levi made.

In the chapter 'The Big Camp', a typed sheet was stuck in alongside the whole passage describing Klein Kiepura from 'A few days after my arrival' (p. 228) to 'We tried in vain to wrench him out of his delirium: the infection of the Lager was too far advanced in him' (p. 230). In the section that follows, where Levi told the story of the two Polish girls, Hanka and Jadzia, there was another 14-line expansion on a stuck-in strip of paper from 'The two Polish girls who carried out (in reality quite badly) the nursing duties' (p. 230) to 'if the man waited for her, Jadzia enveloped him' (p. 230). The additional text was typed onto what looks like an older sheet of paper; it may even be a passage that already existed in a previous version, but this is only a hypothesis. Levi clearly went on tweaking, even after he had typed up his earlier manuscript. Most of his revisions were additions rather than subtractions of text. In this chapter, there are many hand-written corrections in blue ink, in what is often an illegible scrawl. At the end of the typed chapter is the date: December 1961. The editor working on the script cancelled the date in this chapter and in all the others.

Levi wrote a different introductory section to 'The Greek'. In the notebook, the chapter opened with the following paragraph:

> The camp at Auschwitz had already been a month in Russian hands: it was the end of February 1945. After my scarlet fever, I had gone through a series of other strange maladies (it was as if, in the long run, not only our physical appearance and our way of thinking, but our very physiology had undergone an aging process that was unknown in civilian quarters) which, in the absence of doctors or medicine, resolved themselves spontaneously, leaving me in a state of acute physical misery. Like me, many other convalescent or healed former prisoners were progressively sorted into groups by the Russians to be sent to practically unknown destinations. People talked about transit camps for different nationalities situated about 10 kilometres away but since no one came back [illegible] precise news.

This paragraph was cut entirely, so that the chapter opened with 'Toward the end of February, after a month in bed, I felt not recovered but stable' (p. 234) which was identical to the original. Another correction changed the word 'straordinario' in 'extraordinary, defective, abnormal human examples' to 'scaleno' (irregular, with a positive connotation, like a scalene triangle), translated in the *Complete Works* as 'deformed, defective, abnormal human examples' (p. 235). After the last sentence of the chapter ('But he was to reappear one more time, many months later, against the most unlikely background and in the most unexpected incarnation' [p. 255]). Levi had added 'which will be told in time', but then cancelled it. The typescript gave the date the chapter was written as being over the longest period of time of all of them: July 1954 to March 1961.

There were various corrections made to the typescript of 'Katowice', right from the first line. The typescript describing the Soviet guard was a few lines longer than the final version, confirming Levi's tendency to rewrite the links between chapters until they were just right. He also cut some linking devices, such as 'in a way that will be described'. The most significant change was the addition of the passage cited before, where the word 'truce' was introduced: 'It was the great truce, for the hard time that was to follow hadn't yet begun, nor had the cursed name of the cold war been uttered' (p. 258). This correction was written by hand in fountain pen, leading us to suppose that either it was added after the title had been decided, or that the new text itself led to the title being chosen. There were about 20 handwritten revisions in the typescript of this chapter, many of them in green ink and others in blue biro, again showing Levi's tendency to edit right up to the last minute. The date given by Levi for this chapter was written as 14/1/62, then corrected to 14 January 1962.

The typescript of the chapter finally called 'Cesare' was different to the others. It was a carbon copy, as if the whole thing had been retyped and then added to the final version. There are various corrections made with rows of capital X's cancelling the text underneath, additions written by hand in black biro as well as a few lines typed anew at the bottom of some of the pages. However, there are fewer revisions than in other chapters. Most of them regard the protagonist of the chapter, 'Cesare', adding weight to the hypothesis that the chapter had been rewritten entirely. Levi dated the chapter 6/2/62.

In 'Victory Day', Levi censured the name Bocchinara (cock-sucker) from Cesare's list of clients, and made a few other changes of this kind, perhaps out of modesty, but also, in particular, for the school edition. There are only about 10 revisions to the typescript of this chapter. One cancellation is curious: Levi cut a few words 'perhaps theoretically mechanical' from his description of the NKVD captain's 'mysterious interest' in refereeing the soccer match, which was 'perhaps aesthetic, perhaps metaphysical ['perhaps theoretically mechanical']. The date Levi marked as completion of this chapter was 11 March 1962. 'The Dreamers' was very little revised, with fewer than 20 markings on the typescript in blue and black biro. One concerned Ferrari, where Levi cancelled 'already described at the time' and added by hand 'last in the class at the Loreto school'.

In 'Heading South' there were several corrections; some phrases were added in fountain pen or black biro, others were illegible. The most interesting is in the section on Leonardo, from 'On the eve of departure, Leonardo and I handed over the keys to the clinic' (p. 305) to 'and has thereby deserved the gratitude of all the workers of the world' (p. 306). This passage of almost a page gave some very important details. The lines that followed were added to the typescript: 'The next day, the dream we had had forever became a reality. In the station at Katowice the train awaited us: a long train of freight cars, which we Italians (we were around eight hundred) took possession of with noisy cheer. Odessa, and then a fantastic journey by sea through the gateways of the east, and then Italy' (p. 306). Another substitution is revealing. In the published chapter, Gottlieb was described as being 'sharp as a sword', while in the typescript he is said to be 'as quick as an electronic relay switch' which was anachronistic for an account set in 1945. Another change came at the end of the chapter, when the protagonists met the convoy of Italians at Zmerinka. Levi added a phrase in Greek, written by hand, that was later cut. The phrase was an approximate rendering of Odysseus (X, 48) 'and swiftly the storm-wind seized them and bore them weeping out to sea'. Levi later said he had added the episode with the 'wrinkled old crone' of a shopkeeper to this chapter, but that is was actually from a later trip to Germany, and did not take place on his journey home from the camp. The chapter was dated 6/5/62.

'Heading North' also featured a paper strip insertion from 'That groups of former Allied prisoners had embarked at Odessa months earlier, as some Russians had told us, must have been true (p. 316)' to 'They were also Russian transports' which replaced the previous, 'From the station platform, our temporary and not very intimate residence, we watched the arrival and departure of numerous convoys. They were also transports'. The date on the typescript was 15/5/62.

The lines of the typescript for 'A Little Hen' were single-spaced so that each page contained almost double the number of characters than the other chapters. There were more than 10 handwritten corrections in pen. There was one passage that was then cut where the buildings where the former deportees were housed were described. Moreover, several names were changed between the typescript and the published version. The chapter was dated November 1961.

'Old Roads' was double-spaced, unlike the chapter preceding it. The varying interlinear spacing suggests that Levi typed the chapters at different times. There were more corrections marked on this typescript in different coloured inks, including green. These were mostly minor adjustments and clarifications. He added the word 'shame' in pen referring to Cesare's dubious commerce, revealing his sentiment. This was typical of his constant honing of the text, making changes as his memory called details up to the surface. The date was 24/6/62.

'The Forest and the Path' contained a significant correction where, as we have said, 'Marinese' was corrected to 'Velletrano' (born in Velletri rather than Marino) six times. Some adjectives were changed (such as 'bizarre' which became 'senseless', 'fantastic' which became 'interesting') and the phrase 'and other obscene gallantries suitable for restoring his manly honour' to the passage about Cesare and the milkmaid was added in pencil. These corrections reveal different layers of revisions, using the various tools of his trade as a writer. The final date on the typescript was 18/7/62.

'Vacation' was probably the most rewritten chapter compared to the notebook manuscript. The paper on which the chapter was typed was lighter, and some of them were recycled sheets. Page 123, for example, had printed text regarding liquid alkaloids on the back. The longest expansion (just less than a page) was the story of the young Russian sailor that begins with 'Another day, but at the same time and in the same place, I come upon an unusual sight' (p. 352) and ends with 'they are sleeping, the fools, and they don't know what's in store for them' (p. 353). Levi also added by hand the words 'Alberto and me' in blue biro when he was describing Flora, the young prostitute in the camp, as if he wanted to include the name of his symbiotic partner in this book as well as in *If This Is a Man*. The last page bore the date 2/9/62.

'Theater' was typed onto higher quality Fabriano paper and also contained corrections and additions, typed directly onto the page. There were also three paper strips in the passage regarding the performance of *The Shipwreck of the Inert,* when the departure of the ship was announced. At the end of the chapter was the date, as usual: 16/9/62.

The typescript of 'From Starye Doroghi to Iasi' contained the most cancellations. In the passage where Levi described the young Russian guards' fascination for the children's' games during the train journey, a long section was cut after the words 'in any case'. This is the passage that was cut, crossed out diagonally in blue pencil on the typescript:

One of them saw an Italian boy playing the well-known, puerile tie trick on a friend: he went up to him looking slightly worried and stuck his index finger under his chin where the knot of a tie would normally be, as if he had seen a stain there. The friend looked down instinctively in order to see what was wrong, at which the boy hit him on the nose and ran away laughing. The young guard watched him closely and soon after tried out the technique on a fellow soldier. In short, the tie trick became a habit for our guards. First, they practiced among themselves, bringing strange variations and perfections; then they started performing it on us, first shyly, then with increasing energy, choosing the most dignified members of the transport as their victims and bursting out every time into gigantic, innocent laughter. After the first stage [the Russian guards—cancelled] elected their domicile.

In the pages that followed, still dedicated to children's games—a theme Levi would return to several times in the following years—numerous corrections were made to the typescript. The marble shooting course was described in great detail, but an explicit reference to a Jewish prayer was cut ('words of prayer of our fathers, "Shemàm Israel, Adonai Eloem"'. A detail was added in the passage regarding his meeting with Galina, which gave atmosphere to the description: where before the text read, 'also sad' the revised version was 'happy to have seen her again, sad at the memory of the hours passed with her, the things not said, the opportunities not taken.' The apparition of the camel was also corrected: the word 'scemenza' (idiocy) was replaced with 'sciocca' (silly). The date: 4/10/62.

'From Iasi to the Line' had pencil and blue biro revisions, as well as typed corrections, most of which give a sense that Levi was refining his text from a literary point of view. The word 'tregua' (truce) in the title of the book was worked into the text in the description of going over the Transylvanian Alps on the Pradael Pass, as well as on the following page in the episode with the Alpinists and the two 'robust' Russian women soldiers cooking the goose, though it is not reflected in the English translation which translates 'tregua' first as 'halt' (when the engine is detached from the train) and then as 'respite': 'the goose was carved and divided peaceably, then, [after a short respite], the Russians took up their weapons and their duties' (p. 385). The original version in this case was 'after this epicurean parenthesis' and the correction was made in blue biro probably after the date marked on the typescript, which is 3/11/62.

'The Reawakening' had two additions to the typescript, which are significant in the economy of the book as a whole. The first addition was: 'Of six hundred and fifty, the number who had left, three of us were returning. And what had we lost, in those twenty months?' The second was in the passage already cited, where the word 'tregua' was again worked into the text: 'Although the months just passed, of wandering at the edge of civilization, were harsh, [they now seemed to us a truce], an interlude of unlimited openness, a providential gift of destiny, never to be repeated' (p. 396). Moreover, the original phrase 'dream of a dream' was corrected to 'dream within another dream' in fountain pen with blue ink. The date of the typescript was marked as 10/11/62, only a week after the previous chapter.

The typescript was ready to go to print, with its numerous revisions, stuck-in paper strips, new pages glued onto old ones and the editor's proof marks in red. The revisions took place over the course of two years, during which Levi wrote, reread and rewrote his chapters, creating layer after layer of edits. It is not clear from the mark-ups on the typescript whether these were made before or after the typescript was handed in to Einaudi. Hence the idea of Levi as an editor of himself.

PUBLICATION

Levi handed the typescript to Einaudi in the autumn of 1962. In the minutes taken during the editorial board meeting held on 28 November 1962—17 days after the date Levi had given as the completion date of his final chapter—Daniele Ponchiroli wrote: 'Primo Levi has given us a new book which continues *If This Is a Man*, describing the peregrinations and events that took place during his long journey home. It is a fine book, as compassionate as the last, although it lacks the pathos and tension of *If This Is a Man*. It has been decided to place it in the series

"Saggi" ' (*I verbali del mercoledì*, 2011). *The Truce* was published a year later, not in the Essays series but in the contemporary fiction series 'I Coralli', no. 176 of the list. No. 175 was Calvino's 1963 novella *The Watcher,* and it is likely that it was Calvino who opted for the fiction series rather than the essay collection since he appreciated the narrative power of Levi's work. It would prove to be an important decision, though it did not mean that Levi was immediately considered a fully-fledged writer, neither by critics nor by the editorial board at Einaudi. The dust-jacket illustration was chosen by Giulio Bollati, who often worked on cover illustrations with Giulio Einaudi. It was a line drawing by Marc Chagal of a man flying over the roof of a house surrounded by a wooden fence, against the backdrop of a waxing moon. On the back flap there was a full-face photograph of Levi in a shirt and sweater. The marketing slogan: 'The sequel to *If This Is a Man*.'

The front-flap book description has been attributed to Italo Calvino, but it was not signed.

> *The Truce*, a book describing a homecoming, an odyssey of Europe between war and peace, is a sequel to *If This Is a Man*, which remains one of the most powerful books in European literature born out of the extermination camps. Primo Levi continues to call himself 'an occasional writer', and works as a chemist in Turin where he was born in 1919. While his first book was written immediately after his homecoming—as if it were to liberate him, as if it were necessary to bear witness, as one of the few Jews to have survived the Lager, in obeisance to an urgent and immediate need 'to tell other people, to share the story with others'—this second book was written at a distance of years from the events, in a calmer and more detached climate. As the miracle of *If This Is a Man* was a classical equanimity in the face of the atrocious material of the story, here, in *The Truce*, in this lively, colourful account of an unexpected springtime of freedom, there is a poignant note of anguish, of

an incurable sadness. In *The Truce* we see how Levi's Mittel-European adventure did not end with the liberation of Auschwitz by the Russians. For reasons that are never entirely clarified—perhaps simply out of pure negligence or bureaucratic ineptitude—Levi's repatriation, together with many other Italians like him, took place much later, at the end of 1945 after a tortuous and absurd journey home by way of Poland, White Russia, the Ukraine, Romania and Hungary. This book is Levi's travel diary, opening in the fog of Auschwitz which had just been liberated but was still filled with death, and continuing through unheard of scenarios of Europe in a fragile truce, having emerged from the nightmare of a World War and Nazi occupation but not yet paralysed by the new anguish of the Cold War. These include the clandestine markets of Krakow and Katowice; the continuous assignments of quarters by the Red Army, and their biblical and gypsy-like transports, as the Soviets demobilized; the boundless Russian territories, pervaded with glory, misery, oblivion, and vital vigour; swamps and virgin forests; the revelry and singing of Russians drunk with victory; the dormitories filled with dreams of the Italians on their uncertain way home. We find again in these pages Levi's taste for concise and sapid character sketches, in the manner of the moralists of the past. There is The Greek, obedient to his extraordinary code of anarchy and commerce; sunny Cesare, 'friend of the whole world', who pursues his mad ventures with great practical application; the Moor from Verona, the old blaspheme who appears to have stepped out of the Apocalypse; Hurbinek, the child born in Auschwitz who had 'never seen a tree'. The book unfolds along these two tracks: the continuation in hundreds of explicit or hidden ways of the 'pestilence that had prostrated Europe', and the discovery of a new Russia. This discovery was witnessed first-hand and from inside; it was at times comic at others tragic, at still others picaresque, epic or Oblomovian. Far from presenting ideological rigidity, it was far closer to the famous representations of Pushkin, Gogol, or Tolstoy.

The blurb was a splendid description, as well as an effective marketing tool. It was almost a critical review, indicating what, in Calvino's view, were the high points of the book, and, at the same time, orienting the interpretation of the book—at least as far as critics were concerned.

As soon as it was published, the book was selected as a finalist in the prestigious Strega Prize, which was then awarded to Natalia Ginzburg's *Family Lexicon*. *The Truce* came third. A smaller jury went on to select it in September for the Campiello Prize, owing its victory to a wider circle of readers who participated in the judging. Sales were immediately high. Between 1963 and 1967, there were 10 reprints, all of them in the fiction series 'I Coralli'. In 1965, the book was published in the 'Readings for Middle Schools' series as Number 3 in the collection, and from 1965 to 1989, 27 reprints for a total of 200,000 copies were sold. In 1971, the book was moved to the 'Nuovi Coralli' series used for Einaudi's bestsellers, which sold 13 editions with 120,000 copies between 1971 and 1993.

For many years, almost as if the slogan 'a sequel to *If This Is a Man*' had taken hold, the two books were published in a single volume. It was not until 1997 that *The Truce* was re-published on its own, in the paperback series 'Einaudi Tascabili' (n.425). This was the same year that the film of the book came out, directed by Francesco Rosi; Levi had waited in vain. Between 1997 and 2015, 287,534 copies of the paperback version of *The Truce* were sold. After this book, Levi eventually became an affirmed writer. Although his first book sold well, this was the publishing success he had hoped for when he wrote to Pikolo in 1947.

In 1965, Levi prepared a revised edition of *The Truce* for schools. Just as he had done for the school edition of *If This Is a Man*, Levi made some relevant cuts. In particular, he eliminated the passage about Jadzia and her hunger for men, and the reference to the two German auxiliaries prostituting themselves in the chapter 'The Forest and the Path'. He also censored the whole section on Flora, the prostitute held at Monowitz, in 'Vacation', and the sexual escapade between the two Alpinists and the two 'robust' Russian women soldiers before sharing the goose. Levi wrote a Preface for this school edition, which came out two years after the first edition of *The Truce*. In his intentions, the preface served to link *The Truce* to *If This Is a Man*, with the result that Levi returned to the theme of the deportation and extermination of Jews, recapitulating the main events in his life and the vicissitudes that led to his being transported to Auschwitz.

In the Preface, Levi presented himself as a writer who did not 'feel like a 'writer' in full' (p. 1158), or rather as a writer who was not obliged to write for a living, and who only wrote when he felt the 'necessity to tell' (p. 1). He theorized, perhaps for the first time on paper, the important link that existed between his 'daily profession' as a chemist and 'the many things that every writer needs to know' (p. 1159). Twelve years later, he would go on to explore this link in *The Periodic Table*. What Levi was striving for was 'objectivity' in his narrative, 'that is to say, the acknowledgement of the intrinsic dignity not just of people but of things, and to their truth, which needs to be recognized and not distorted if one does not want to fall into vagueness, emptiness, and falsehood' (p. 1159). It was this very definition that led him, 10 years later, to deny that his first book was actually a novel. He preferred to consider *If This Is a Man* a kind of documentary. In a television programme called 'The Art of Storytelling' (Amendola and Belardinelli 1974) that turned Levi into a household name and face even though he already had a great number of readers, Levi once said: 'I wrote [*If This Is a Man*] as a convalescent not as a witness'. He added that his style was 'middle-brow' and that he had 'experimented' with writing 'as he had done with telling his stories'.

In 1978, Edmo Fenoglio directed a radio adaptation written by Levi, who abridged and revised the book himself. The radio version was broadcast in seven weekly episodes by the popular public-radio channel, Radio 1, starting on 25 April (Liberation Day) that year. When an interviewer asked Levi in what way his radio adaptation differed from the book, Levi answered:

> Any adaptation is different from the book, especially for the radio, because the medium limits to a great extent the notions that can be expressed. For this reason, I already knew that the book was condemned to undergoing drastic cuts. I was determined, however, with the agreement of the RAI (Italian State radio and television) to salvage the cosmopolitan and multi-lingual aspect of the book. That is, of all the elements the book may have offered, I decided to concentrate on a series of gatherings among nomads in Eastern Europe and the Soviet Union devastated by the war. Thus, from the start, I asked RAI to source authentic voices for me—not good Italian actors who could speak Polish or German, but real Poles, Russians and Germans even if they were not actors.

The interviewer asked him whether he was satisfied with the radio adaptation. Levi answered:

> I am quite satisfied. Contrary to common opinion, the radio is extremely subtle, far more than television. It triggers emotions and sentiments through subliminal channels. It is in this aspect that I think the essential character of the book is preserved; that is, the character of a journey that is both real and fantastic through a world that is so totally different from today's that it feels almost imaginary. It is certainly true that many of the

conversations that take place in Russian, Polish or even Yiddish will not be understood by Italian listeners, but their value is in re-creating the idea of disorientation, of 'the other', that we perceived when we lived through the events presented in the radio adaptation (Adrian Levi 1978).

The emphasis on recreating the multilingual atmosphere of Levi's direct experience was similar to the importance given to languages in the 1964 radio adaptation of *If This Is a Man*. It is not surprising either, that the radio version of *If This is a Truce* was made just after he had written *The Wrench*, where languages played an essential role. This confirmed Levi's tendency, book after book, to develop the potential of his work.

Among the many interviews Levi gave when *The Truce* was published, and in the years that followed, one in particular, with Ernesto Olivero, is worth mentioning here. In this interview, Levi talked about the incident with the Berlin shopkeeper who had written a letter to Hitler (in the chapter 'Heading South'). This is the only episode in *The Truce* that is not in its rightful place. 'Not because it didn't happen,' Levi commented,

> it did happen, but not there. It took place many years later on a trip to Germany. The shopkeeper in *The Truce* was not a shopkeeper; she was a woman living in an old people's home in Frankfurt. She was incredibly popular there. Everyone knew her story, and she would ask to be paid to tell it. She used to work in a pub there and she would tell her clients, new ones every evening, and they would pay her with a steak or a beer. But the story is true and it came to me that it would fit well in *The Truce* (Olivero 1980).

This inclusion was an example of Levi's 'filling out' of stories, which progressively expanded the narrative and tended to grow with every book. That *The Truce* had intrinsic literary worth, and was more of a narrative than a testimony, was evident to the author who talked about this aspect in the Preface to the school edition. In 1963, however, in another interview with Luigi Silori, he insisted on the book's value as bearing witness to his experience as a deportee. It was almost as if he were retracting his previous claims, or at least attempting to assert the book's value as an eye-witness account—especially in the first two chapters. Levi said to Silori: 'It may be as you say, but, believe me, the experience of Auschwitz, when you were there inside the camp, was not very literary. You should know perfectly well as you too were in a Nazi concentration camp.' Silori answered: 'Yes, but I never thought for a minute about writing the story of my experience. How do you explain that?' Levi rebutted: 'In fact, I can't explain it either. In my view, it is your position that is strange, not mine. Anyway, I wanted everyone to know about all those things I was writing about. It was a kind of message—or, if you prefer, a document—that was necessary' (Silori 1963).

LEMMAS

Mud/Clay

Mud and clay feature in many passages in Levi's work, especially in *If This Is a Man* where mud is a constant physical presence (during every march, the prisoners in their wooden clogs risked getting mired in the stuff). It is also a recurrent presence in *The Truce*, where it became a symbol of the primordial chaos from which God moulded some sort of order—although chaos was always ready to make a comeback.

The short story '*Quaestio de Centauris*' (*Natural Histories*) told the story of the second creation after the flood, when all the seas had withdrawn and 'a deep layer of warm mud covered the earth' (p. 511) ('There was wild, ecstatic fecundity in which the entire universe felt love, so much so that it nearly returned to chaos.') In Levi's last article to be published in *La Stampa* ('Adam's Clay'), Levi reviewed a recently published book, *Seven Clues to the Origin of Life* by A. Graham Cairns-Smith. This book explored the subject of clay silicates: 'yes, that same clay used by God the Father to make the first man.'

Trains

In *If This Is a Man*, trains were a negative symbol that featured right from the first chapter, 'The Journey'. They were also an obsessive leit-motif in *The Truce*, where the symbolism was reversed and became positive but never completely lost its negative connotations. In numerous interviews in later years, Levi confessed to a feeling of anguish whenever he caught sight of a freight train. An eighteenth-century symbol of progress was transformed by Levi into the antechamber of hell, the means by which he was transformed into an animal.

A recurrent theme in Levi's work was the practical and symbolic use of cattle cars by the Germans to transport Jews and other categories of deportees to the concentration and extermination camps. In 'Useless Violence' (*The Drowned and the Saved*), Levi stated that 'The memory's sequence almost always begins with the train that marked the departure toward the unknown: not only for chronological reasons but also because of the gratuitous cruelty by which those otherwise innocuous convoys of ordinary boxcars were employed for an uncustomary purpose' (p. 2488). In an article written in the form of a letter to Rosanna Benzi, Levi returned to his train journey 30 years after the event: 'Our train, made up of freight cars, carried 650 people, 50 in each car; the journey lasted five days, during which food was distributed, but no water' (p. 1297). 'Brief Dream' (*Lilith and Other Stories*) was set in a train compartment, although the context was obviously completely different.

Journeys

Levi often remarked on his sedentary nature. He was never one for travelling or adventure. And yet, writing about his travel adventures he appeared perfectly at ease in this dimension. *The Truce* was, first and foremost, a travelogue, while *The Wrench* also contained travel stories, although they were not always his own (when they were they were mostly trips taken to Germany and Russia for work). The theme of moving through geographical space triggered his attention and curiosity—as if he did not already possess these qualities—and exploring the effects of disorientation was certainly a cornerstone of his vocation as a writer. His science-fiction writing was born of the same curiosity, as well as of a natural talent for microscopic observation which he once defined as being a 'point-type intuition'. It may well be that Levi's natural unwillingness to travel, and his consequent detachment, was precisely what made him more attentive to detail. What is certain is that the *topos* of journeys (described as 'involuntary interruptions' in 'My House', *Other People's Trades*, p. 2015) revealed the duality that was always present in Levi. His sedentary disposition meant he felt the need to challenge his nature by travelling; at the same time, it created a fierce desire to return home. This aspect was particularly relevant in his deportation to Auschwitz. The long, slow journey home described in *The Truce* was mitigated by the pleasure of discovering new countries and unknown peoples; adapting to the journey, without giving in to it, was a healthy form of nomadism after the terrible punishment of imprisonment.

In the three collections of stories (*Natural Histories*, *Flaw of Form* and *Lilith*), the *topos* of journeys symbolized discovery. This was taken to an extreme in the sarcastic narration of the ethnographic adventure in 'The Sorcerers' (*Lilith and Other Stories*) and in 'Heading West' (*Flaw of Form*). Journeys represented a desire not to be oneself, to discover the other; at the same time, they presented the risk of losing one's own identity. Identity was a key concept for Levi, both as a writer and as a memorialist. *If Not Now, When?* was also, in its way, about travel. Moving through geographical space was the narrative thread, as it often was in traditional fiction. One rare report of a journey Levi made simply as a tourist can be found in 'Among Manhattan's Skyscrapers' (*Stories and Essays*).

Space Travel

Over a period of almost 20 years Levi explored the subject of mankind's conquest of space in his different capacities: as a writer of science-fiction but also as a technical expert; as a writer with a scientific background as well as someone always curious about discoveries. His first article came out in 1968, after the Apollo 8 flight. It was entitled 'The Moon and Man' (*Stories and Essays*) and its tone was decidedly optimistic.

From an evolutionary point of view, man was the 'naked ape' (p. 2337), as Levi claimed in the article, citing Desmond Morris, but of all the weapons that nature made available to animals, humans claimed the brain: 'man is strong in and of himself, he is stronger than he thought possible, he is made of a substance that is fragile only in appearance, he was mysteriously designed with enormous, unsuspected margins of safety' (p. 2337). The whole piece was permeated by the spirit of Joseph Conrad, a style which Levi often adopted when he was writing about human feats, technical prowess, individual or collective challenges. This was the other side of the coin from his pessimism when he was dealing with concentration camps and extermination.

In the 1970s, Levi appeared confident in the positive effect of the spirit of competition in the race to achieve scientific and technical superiority:

We are unique, sturdy, versatile animals, motivated by atavistic impulses, and by reason, and, at the same time, by a 'creative force' as a result of which if an undertaking, whether good or bad, can be achieved, it cannot be put aside but must be achieved. This undertaking, the lunar flight, is a test. Others await us, works of daring and brilliance, demanding in a different way, in that they are essential to our very survival: endeavours to eliminate hunger, poverty, and suffering (p. 2337).

There WAS the same ironic, optimistic spirit in the short-story 'The Sixth Day' (*Natural Histories*) on the creation of man.

The next article Levi wrote on the subject was 'The Moon and Us' (*Other People's Trades*), on the eve of the first human moon walk. Levi again adopted an optimistic tone when he examined the dual mechanism that regulated mankind's existence on this earth. On the one hand, self-preservation, which would be favourable to the idea of conquering the moon—'the drive to disseminate and diffuse one's kind over as vast a territory as possible' (p. 2031)—and at the same time the need to rise to ongoing challenges.

In Levi's view, technological leaps forward led to sociological rather than anthropological adaptations. That is, they did not change man's essential nature. By contrast, the four great discoveries of the century ('nuclear power, solid-state physics, anti-parasitics, and detergents', p. 2031) radically changed society. Space travel was not to be counted among these revolutions because it obeyed an irrepressible need of mankind to face challenges and rise to them. If anything, Levi was concerned with the fact that literature was unable to keep up with space exploration in the same way that it did with the great sea voyages or air travel (Levi quoted in this respect the author of *The Little Prince*, Saint-Exupéry, whom he also included in his personal bibliography, *The Search for Roots*). Space travel was by definition 'lunatic', but it was also too planned to offer poets material for their work. The reference is interesting because it confirmed the idea that literature was born from disorientation, from 'recklessness' as Levi put it in this article, including a reference to 'Astolfo's feat' (p. 2032, the reference being to Ariosto). Space travel was destined to be incomprehensible, like the astronauts' voices coming from outer space which 'do not seem like human voices: they are as incomprehensible as space, motion, and eternity' (p. 2033).

In 1972 and 1973, two space probes (Pioneer 10 and 11) were launched in order to study the far reaches of the solar system in a quest to see whether there were other forms of intelligence in the universe. In 1981, Levi was invited by *La Stampa* to write an article on the subject. In 'There is No Other Adam in the Neighborhood' (*Uncollected Stories and Essays*), Levi considered the position of both those who believed that 'other forms of intelligence besides ours exist in the cosmos' (p. 2582), and those who did not. In the latter case, Levi calls this subjective view 'wishes in the form of beliefs.' His conclusion after the results of the probes was that 'There is no other Adam, at least in our neighborhood, and not even his most rudimentary ancestor; there are only moderately complex carbon compounds—that is, the clay with which to make him' (p. 2582).

The 1985 essay 'Man in Flight' (*Stories and Essays*) was triggered by a competition launched by *La Stampa* on experiments in the absence of gravity. The article, which mentioned in passing children's dreams of flying, went on to interpret an episode in Dante's *Inferno* (*Inferno* XVII) where Geryon, the 'brute animal,' actually 'eludes weight' (p. 2385). In Levi's view, Dante described the sensation of flying perfectly. Levi was struck by the human capacity to adapt to weightlessness. Even travelling by sea or by car could create problems, Levi observed, and yet man had adapted to the supremely unnatural condition of being weightless in space.

The theme of human adaptability in the face of extreme, unnatural conditions—like so many of his themes—had a dual value for Levi. Adapting to space travel or adapting to life in the Lager? Humans were capable of both, although not without immense effort. Levi cited the 'Red Triangles' in Auschwitz as a prime example of this. The article ended with a reference to Freeman Dyson in *Disturbing the Universe*, who had the visionary idea of 'a humanity migrating among the stars on vessels with gigantic sails driven free of charge by stellar light' (p. 2386). Calvino was equally fascinated by this book, and also published a review of it. Levi used the expression 'disturbing the universe' in a December 1984 poem 'Still to Do' (*Collected Poems*): 'I wouldn't disturb the universe. I'd like, if possible, to get free silently' (p. 1989).

In the story 'Frogs on the Moon' (*Stories and Essays*), Levi described an early episode in his scientific education when as a child he collected tadpoles and watched their 'metamorphosis' into frogs. He remarked at one point that the urge to get out of their environment in order to survive was 'a completely understandable instinct, the same one that drove us to the moon' (p. 2298).

The last article on space travel was written in 1986 after the Shuttle exploded, killing its entire crew. Levi hadn't lost his optimism about scientific progress, but stressed the risks of using technology to the wrong ends. Nevertheless, he had come to believe that space travel was not as straightforward as he had supposed. In his view, unmanned space travel, such as when the Voyager circumnavigated Uranus, was preferable and less risky.

A comic science-fiction short story also came out in the journal *L'Astronomia* in 1986. This was 'The TV Fans from Delta Cep.' where Levi 'translated' a letter from space addressed to the science journalist Piero Bianucci.

Maps

The first map to figure in Levi's *oeuvre* was published in *The Truce*. Levi had sketched the various legs of his long journey back to Turin from Auschwitz, and together with an itinerary of names and dates, the map became the basis of the book. Levi's passion for maps and other visual representations, such as formulae and models, was evident in many of his works. Maps of the various concentration camps were included in the school version of *If This Is a Man*. There was one showing the locations of the concentration camp, the work camp and the extermination camp in the Polish territory occupied by the Germans during the Second World War. Another indicated where the camps were in relation to the area of Auschwitz. A letter Levi wrote described the publisher's resistance to including these maps in the school edition. Still another map was published in *If Not Now, When?* outlining the journey the protagonist made, partly overlapping with the map in *The Truce*, since the book was set in the same area of former Russia. There were also maps in *The Periodic Table* (the island where Mercury is set is a kind of 'Treasure Island', but also an alchemical Saint Helena). The very title of the book was inspired by a kind of map, or graphic representation at least: Mendeleev's Periodic Table. Again, in *The Periodic Table*, the formula for Alloxan is represented graphically. In *The Wrench*, there is another 'map' of a chemistry formula, a model that the chemist-narrator scribbled onto a sheet of paper for Faussone. Finally, a graph, or table, could be found at the beginning of Levi's personal anthology, *The Search for Roots*. According to the critic, Giorgio Bertone, this was probably inspired by the tables in the 1970s and 80s Einaudi encyclopaedia, where possible links between different entries were indicated. Levi represented a sphere, as Calvino called it in his review, with four potential paths between Job and black holes, four paths to salvation that included most of the authors listed by Levi in his anthology.

All these maps (the definition is inappropriate but effective) show Levi's desire to represent implicit visual aspects of the narrative, or elements of his narrative or conceptual structure, in various graphic forms. Levi enjoyed representing his ideas in drawings. He was a technician who was not only able to express himself through words, using his specific vocabulary and style (precision and concision) but also by means of designs or sketches. In *The Wrench*, this skill is turned into a method to make people understand what the protagonist is trying to say.

Self-Commentary

Many twentieth-century writers, in particular poets, provided a commentary to their own work, either in written form or in interviews or conversations. The special significance of Levi's work as an act of bearing witness meant that Levi gave many interviews and visited numerous schools, especially in the 1970s. Levi's most significant written self-commentary was in the school editions of *The Truce*, published by Einaudi in the series 'Readings for Middle Schools' in 1965; *If This Is a Man*, published in 1973 in the same series; and *The Periodic Table* in 1979. Levi's apparatus of notes gave additional information about history, geography, language or science and made explicit references to literary sources, as well as clarifying points in the text that he thought may have been difficult for students in middle school to understand. Levi presented himself, as he often did in conversations about his work, as an 'archaeologist of himself,' but very rarely offered explanations as to the meaning of his work. One exception was in the final note to *The Truce*. Many of the notes originated in Levi's letters to his German translator, Heinz Riedt, to whom Levi offered elucidations about the Dante quotes and specific jargon from the Lager.

Music

In *If This Is a Man*, when Levi was lying in his bunk at the Ka-Be infirmary, he could hear the band playing as the prisoners were marched to and from their forced labour: 'The beating of the bass drum and the cymbals reaches us continuously and monotonously, but on this weft the musical phrases weave a pattern only intermittently, according to the wind's caprices' (p. 47). The tunes were monotonous and repetitive, mostly marches and popular songs loved by the Germans.

Music, Levi wrote, was one of the most indelible memories of the camp: 'They lie engraved in our minds and will be the last thing in the Lager that we forget: they are the voice of the Lager, the perceptible expression of its geometric madness' (p. 48). It is clear that Levi knew something about music; he had piano lessons when he was young, but never cultivated music beyond going to concerts and listening to records in his youth.

Levi spoke about his relationship to music in several radio interviews: from the first ditty his mother sang to him, which he has never forgotten, and which in his turn he sang to his own children, to the Offenbach arias his father used to sing at home (his father was an amateur pianist). He also described the songs he would listen to on one of the very first crystal radio receivers, as well as the songs that were popular under Fascism. Music was a part of his life in many different ways. It was an important element of a bourgeois education, an essential part of a well-educated man's cultural baggage. It was also a political tool, used for propaganda and mass organization; music was a manifestation of military spirit and the cult of the body. The marches played by the band in Auschwitz brought together these two opposites in an incongruous but paradoxically effective way.

The tune that stuck in Levi's mind the most because he knew it before arriving in the camp was 'Rosamunde'. During a radio programme on Levi's personal musical preferences, he discovered the song was originally a Czech melody known as 'The Beer Barrel Polka'. Sound was an essential element in Levi's work, as was noise. This became clear when Levi created the sound effects for the radio adaptation of *If This Is a Man*. While 'Rosamunde' reminded Levi of his captivity, Tchaikovsky's 1812 Overture was the soundtrack of his Liberation. The Overture was blasted over loudspeakers to celebrate the Soviet victory over the Germans as he pulled into Cracow station. Another tune that stayed in his mind was the folk song 'Kalinka', sung by Russian soldiers on their return from war, which he described in *The Truce*. Finally, Levi talked about music in American films such as *Gilda*.

In the youth groups Levi participated in before the war, and in the chemistry labs where he worked, there was always happy singing. Music was a way to communicate and create a sense of community. In Levi's work, there was always some kind of sound in the background: at times, even in the Lager, it was marked as *allegro*: in his books on his profession as a chemist, it was rather *allegro andante*. This sonorous quality was usually rendered with adjectives and verbs. His very memory was triggered by sounds, such as the Polish or Hungarian words he recognized, having memorized them in the Lager but whose meaning he doesn't know. For this reason, the infernal band music (infernal in the paradoxical, back-to-front way it was used) became the most deeply imprinted and longest lasting mechanical memory of former deportees.

Theatre

As some critics have pointed out (in particular Mengaldo and Scarlini), Levi's work had a precise 'thread of dramaturgic research that runs parallel to that of his fiction'. There were numerous citations of theatrical works in his books, showing how theatre was an important point of reference throughout his life. More in general, Levi often used dialogue in his work to tell a story, and this revealed an underlying sense of theatre that he often developed directly. After all, the world was a 'show' he watched with great curiosity. The rascal Cesare's comic performances in *The Truce* are emblematic of this, and there is a theatrical quality even in *If This Is a Man*, where Levi felt the duty to bear witness most strongly.

In *The Truce*, aside from the description of a performance by Russian soldiers (in 'Victory Day'), there is a chapter called 'Theatre', where Levi described the acts in a revue put on by Italian prisoners in the Russian transit camp. As Scarlini observed, these sketches included choral pieces ('I pompieri di Viggiù' from the Italian popular music tradition), comedy improvisations and the performance of an Italian musical (*The Shipwreck of the Inert*). Of all these acts, the one that stands out the most in terms of its significance for the underlying themes of the book is *The Three-Cornered Hat*, which opened with a nonsensical rhyme and closed with 'absolute silence' that 'was a harrowing death agony, a mortal spasm' (p. 366).

Levi was a 'traditionalist', but when it came to the theatrical versions or radio adaptations of his books, he turned to theatre directors who had staged Beckett's plays and belonged to the experimentalist generation of the 1970s. Scarlini noted that in *The Three-Cornered Hat* there was more than a hint of Beckett (*Waiting for Godot* was translated into Italian by Carlo Fruttero and performed in 1954, directed by Luciano Mondolfo). There are further references to theatre in *The Truce*'s 'twin' *If Not Now, When?* which came out in 1982. In this book, one of the protagonists, Pavel, is a Russian Jewish actor in a 1930s Warsaw cabaret, a member of the Moscow Jewish Theatre who went on tour with his company to Italy under Fascism.

Levi's first direct experience with writing for the theatre was under the aegis of the cultural channel of state radio (Radio Tre) which commissioned a few one-act plays from him. Levi transformed the short stories published in *Natural Histories*, 'The Sixth Day' and 'Sleeping Beauty in the Refrigerator: A Winter's Tale' into short plays. The first was written between 1946 and 1947 and the radio adaptation is dated 22 December 1957, while the second was written in 1952 and recorded as a radio play in June 1961. Other stories were transformed into radio dialogues or theatrical productions after being published in journals or newspapers, such as 'The Versifier', which was then published in *Uncollected Stories and Essays*. Levi spoke about the genesis of these stories in an interview with Edoardo Fadini (*Primo Levi si sente scrittore dimezzato*) when the stories from *Natural Histories* were staged in Turin directed by Massimo Scaglione at the Teatro delle Dieci ('The Sixth Day', 'Sleeping Beauty in the Refrigerator: A Winter's Tale' and 'The Versifier'). Critics did not pick up on Levi's writing for the theatre for many years.

The most significant theatrical writing Levi undertook was the radio adaptation of *If This Is a Man*. Levi worked with the actor Pieralberto Marché and the adaptation was recorded in 1966. It was also published in its own right in Einaudi's theatre collection series, under the title 'Dramatized Version of *If This Is a Man*'. The Preface explained the way the book came to be written and how the dramatized version was adapted from it. Marché's notes, as well as those of the director, Gianfranco De Bosio, were published in the journal *I Quaderni del Teatro Stabile della Città di Torino* (8, 1966). Marché had also taken part as an actor in the radio adaptation of the book in 1964, and asked Levi to work on a dramatized version for the theatre. Initially Levi refused, but a year later he came around to the idea. Work on the dramatized version took about a year, as Levi wrote in a letter to the publisher. Marché worked on the stage directions (printed in italics in the published version) while Levi was responsible for the dialogues. These were then edited together with his co-author, Gianfranco De Bosio, who was the artistic director at the Turin theatre, and who directed the play with the collaboration of Giovanna Bruno and Marta Egri. The scenery and costumes were designed by Gianni Polidori, while the sound effects were created by Paolo Ketoff and Gino Marinuzzi Jr. The Florence Festival Theatre collaborated with the Turin theatre, assisting them with coordinating a cast made up of over 50 actors from theatres from as far afield as Hungary,

Austria and Israel. Owing to the disastrous flood in Florence that year, the first performance was moved to Turin, where more than 50 further performances took place. The company also took the play on tour, but the tour was cut short with the result that Levi and Marché took the Turin theatre to court for failing to fulfil their side of the contract, and won.

Theatre critics were harsh in their judgement. They complained that the two authors had very little experience in the theatre, and commented that the text was an extension of the author's testimony rather than a piece of theatre. In their view, it focused excessively on the multilingual element of the play rather than on its actual staging. The authors' choice had been to keep the SS soldiers off stage and to use megaphones to represent their voices. The stage set featured harshly lit steel pipes; the sound effects— basically adapted from the radio production, but also as a result of the cast of foreign actors creating the Babel that Levi strived for—dominated the scenic design. Despite the criticism, the play was highly acclaimed by the general public and won the I.D.I Prize–Saint Vincent in 1967 for the best play of the season. It was also nominated by the Theatre Biennale although a piece written by Alberto Moravia won First Prize there.

The character of Primo Levi did not feature in the play. His role was taken on by Aldo, a chemist like him. Several other characters that did not figure in the 1958 edition of the book, but were described in *Lilith and Other Stories* made a reappearance in the play. Some of the minor characters in the book were given more important roles in the play, such as Meister Nogalla, while others were totally ignored. In 1980, the theatre director, Massimo Scaglione, adapted several 'theatrical' stories which had already been produced for television into a piece called *Nascere sulla terra*. In 1986, Levi allowed an amateur theatrical group, Gruppo Teatro Studio, made up of factory workers and white-collar workers to put on their own adaptation of *The Wrench*.

In his personal anthology, *The Search for Roots*, Levi included a passage from T. S. Eliot's *Murder in the Cathedral*. He also gave Girolamo Arrigo permission to use his works in a project of 'musical theatre', the opera *Orden*, which he based on parts of *If This Is a Man*. The Cantata *E Venne la Notte*, which was published in its own right in 1973 was derived from this opera. Arrigo also wrote a semi-staged version of *The Truce* called *La cantata d Hubinek* in 1972, and a cantata called *E ciascuno riconobbe nell'altro la vita* in 1974.

DREAMS, NIGHTMARES AND VISIONS FROM
IF THIS IS A MAN, THE TRUCE AND THE SHORT STORIES

If This Is a Man could well be considered a journey to and from the Kingdom of Death: it starts with a departure ceremony—an initiation rite at the Fòssoli transit camp—and ends with a return to life. The journey is like a catharsis that reaches its nadir of inertia in the chapter 'The Story of Ten Days' ('We were lying in a World of dead men and phantoms' [p. 164]) and then swings up again in the last lines of the Epilogue. The impression that the book questions ghosts as if it were a *nekyia* is even stronger in the 1947 edition where the first chapter, 'The Journey', opens with the events at Fòssoli. In this descent to the Underworld, the chapter 'Our Nights' occupies a special place. In the 1947 De Silva edition, this chapter is shorter and plunges straight into the subject of the title with the words, 'In the winter the nights are long and we are allowed a considerable period of time to sleep.' Sleep is the real protagonist of the chapter, and with it, dreams—or rather, dreams, nightmares and re-awakenings.

Dreams played an important role in Levi's work. He returned to the subject repeatedly, not only in his books bearing witness to life in the camps and their liberation but also in other works. Examples include a short-story written in 1976, 'Brief Dream' (*Lilith and Other Stories*), and a 1977 essay, 'Our Dreams' (*Stories and Essays*). There is also an invented dream, that of Mendel the clockmaker in *If Not Now, When?* (1972) and two poems, 'Get Up', written on 11 January 1946, and 'Wait. Get Up' prefacing *The Truce*, while a prose passage paraphrasing it was used as an epilogue. Dreams are also a recurring theme in *The Truce*, for example in the chapter called 'The Dreamers', but also in the revue *The Three-Cornered*

Hat, where Levi commented that the silence that followed the act every time it was repeated was like 'the heavy breath of a collective dream, the dream that emanates from exile and idleness, when work and suffering cease, and nothing places a barrier between man and himself' ('Theatre', *The Truce*, p. 366). This act brought forth 'the crooked, hunchbacked profile of the monsters generated by the sleep of reason' (p. 366), a reference to Goya's famous print series *Los Caprichos*, one of which was used as the cover illustration for the 1947 edition of *If This Is a Man*.

Sleep, dreams, but also rationality were themes shared by Goya, an artist Levi admired (as did Calvino, and an entire generation of writers at the time). Goya denounced the failure of reason in his *Disasters of War*, and reason is almost totally absent in *If This Is a Man*. Rationality is put to sleep, while the whole story takes place in the ambient of a dream, or suspended reality. Pulling into the station platform in Auschwitz, 'Everything was as silent as an aquarium, or as certain scenes in dreams' (*If This Is a Man*, p. 15). The scene that follows, at the beginning of the chapter 'On the Bottom', is depicted as being equally unreal. Before being transformed into a *Häftling*, Levi had to traverse 'Hell [. . .] today, in our time' where there were no horned devils, flames or boiling cauldrons but simply a vast stretch of emptiness: 'a huge empty room' (p. 17). The first few paragraphs of the chapter are a depiction of a dream.

Levi always said the Lager was an upside-down world, with its own logic and rules which were the opposite of those of the civilized world. The shock that the deportees felt as they crossed the threshold into the camp, having survived the initial selections by chance or blind luck, was more like disconcertion. How, they asked themselves, could this actually be happening? Two psychologists, Victor Frankl and Bruno Bettelheim, both of whom were imprisoned in the concentration and extermination camps there, commented, like Levi, on the sense of incomprehension, of unreality, that the Lager produced. In a piece written three years after the liberation of the camps and his arrival in the US ('The Price of Life', later called 'Vigilant Heart'), Bettelheim went back to the theme: the experience if the camp was unforgettable but unreal. If the Lager was a place of unreality, what then were dreams which are life's double?

Frankl and Bettelheim, who both dealt with dreams throughout their professional life, claimed that, while in the Lager, prisoners' dreams did not intermediate reality; the most traumatic events simply did not make an appearance. Bettelheim, who had already suffered the consequences of a terrible accident before he was imprisoned, expected to relive the experience in a long, drawn out re-elaboration of the trauma in his dreams. But this was not the case. Other former deportees when interviewed on the subject reported the same thing: they never dreamt about their journey or about the most traumatic experiences while they were in the camp. Frankl wrote about wish-dreams where everyday activities such as eating, having a hot bath, getting home and being in their own bed were the main subjects. Prisoners never dreamt about sex.

CAN PRIMO LEVI BE CONSIDERED A POLITICAL WRITER?

In 1955, Palazzo Madama in Turin hosts an exhibition on the Resistance Movement in Piedmont organized by the History of the Resistance Institute with the city council. There are posters, flyers, manuscripts, news cuttings, photographs and documents on the birth and evolution of Resistance to Nazi-Fascism in the region. A special issue of the monthly journal *Torino* is published for the occasion and distributed at the entrance. The articles are mostly about partisans and resistance fighters, but one, entitled 'The Deported. Anniversary', is penned by Primo Levi.

Levi—who is credited in the journal as Prof. Levi—is the author of a relatively unknown book published by a small independent press, De Silva, which rapidly went out of circulation. This meant it was only read by friends, political activists and those former deportees who were determined never to forget. This piece, then, is one of Levi's first public statements on the subject.

Ten years have passed since the liberation of the Lagers, and eight since the publication of *If This Is a Man*, but people are still largely unaware of what took place there. In the article, Levi states that the subject of the extermination camps, 'far from becoming history, is starting to be completely forgotten' (p. 1127). The predominant view at the time is an idealized version of the partisan-hero myth: combatants who were deported and tortured for opposing the Nazis. He recalls the near annihilation of 'the Jewish populations of entire nations of Eastern Europe' (p. 1127) and its role in the overall Nazi plan: that is, to test the techniques on these populations before extending them to entire continents.

153

Deportees, he points out, are defenceless men, women and children— not freedom fighters. Hence, nobody is writing or talking about them.

Levi advances the idea that the issue is shame. On returning from the camps, victims are silent because they are ashamed. The decision not to talk is not only the result of what happened to them in the extermination camps. Compared to the achievements of the partisans, the men, women and children who survived the camps feel a double weight of shame: both for what they were subjected to, and for what they were unable to do, i.e. resist or fight the abjection of camp life, or combat its dehumanizing effects. However, there is another factor that the seemingly clear, straightforward article analyses. Faced with the enormity of their executioners' crimes, camp survivors feel like 'citizens of Sodom and Gomorrah' (p. 1128). The Lager experience tainted them to the extent that they feel implicated in the crime committed against them. 'We cannot be exempted from the charge that an otherworldly judge, on the basis of our own testimony, would bring against all humanity' (p. 1127).

A statement of this kind, during the Cold War, and the Korean conflict that pitted the US and its allies against the Soviet Union and China, is not easy to digest for many people. The common view is that anti-Fascist fighters are heroes, but in a world divided into two blocks, civil victims—the Jews themselves—are hard to place. They are neither in the communist nor in the western camp.

When the young chemist writes, 'We are children of that Europe where Auschwitz is: we lived in the century in which science was bent, and gave birth to the racial laws and the gas chambers. Who can say for sure that he is immune to the infection?' (p. 1127), his meaning was not clear even to readers at the time. The condemnation of science is expressed by a graduate in chemistry, but it is really the result of a sense of responsibility, or rather co-responsibility, induced by the experience of being at Auschwitz. The reason why many survivors choose not to speak out—an issue which later becomes vital to Levi—is already clearly set out in this article, as is his animal-behaviourist approach when he states that 'we belong to the same human family that our executioners belong to' (p. 1127). This makes some of the details and ideas contained in the 1947 edition of *If This Is a Man* more explicit.

Levi constantly reflects on the assumptions, premises, and consequences of bearing witness. His testimony takes place within a framework where science, anthropology, ethology, and moral philosophy are more than just academic disciplines. They are never detached from the tangible existence of individuals; rather, they are essential tools for interpreting life. Without forcing these ideas into a straitjacket, echoing those of the Frankfurt School (which Levi would not yet have come across), and without subjecting them to the scrutiny that would take place in the second half of the 1960s after Hannah Arendt's work was published, it is important nonetheless to grasp the fact that this article contains the seeds of a question that was central to his last book. That is, 'It is vanity to call the death of the innumerable victims of the extermination camps glorious. It wasn't glorious: it was a defenceless, naked death, ignominious and obscene' (p. 1127). Deftly, but firmly underscoring this contradiction, Levi's comparing and contrasting the degradation of deportees to the glory showered on partisans, is a significant step forward. It is the 'virtue' of 'ordinary men' (Robert Gordon) that makes Levi a thinker without necessarily being a philosopher. His observations are the fruit of an ordinary man's genius.

That same year, 1955, Levi signs a contract with Einaudi for a new edition of *If This Is a Man*, three months after the article on deportees came out. In preparation for the new publication, Levi gets down to work on the book. In particular, he changes the beginning, adding the passage where he is arrested as a partisan (whereas in the 1947 edition, the book opens with him in the Fòssoli transit camp as a Jewish prisoner). This need for precision is typical of Levi, but it is also a way to encapsulate his story within a double frame: Levi is captured as a partisan, but deported as a Jew in order to avoid a Fascist firing squad. This new focus is the product of a changed political and cultural climate and it hones in on an issue that will become decisive in the future. That is, Primo Levi does not only bear witness to the Shoah, or the Holocaust; he bears witness to the deportations in general, where the Jews are part of a project put in place on a vast scale by Nazi Germany to exterminate enemies and purify the world—a project which fortunately failed.

Levi is witness to human behaviour. 'Man is, and must be, sacred to man, everywhere and always,' he writes in a 18 July 1959 article in *La Stampa*, headlined 'Monument at Auschwitz'. The monument under construction on the 'very site of the biggest massacre in human history' poses a problem that Hannah Arendt later expresses explicitly in the subtitle to her book, *Eichmann in Jerusalem: A Report on the Banality of Evil* (1963). Levi asks the rhetorical question, 'How did [the camps] take place?' and states that the question cannot be answered comprehensively. 'In some way, we can put ourselves in the shoes of the thief, of the murderer, but it's not possible for us to put ourselves in the shoes of the deranged' (p. 1131). Humans can act madly, but their behaviour cannot be explained by using reason. Levi says that the diary of Rudolf Höss, the former commander of Auschwitz, is instructive in this respect. 'The author is not a bloodthirsty sadist, or a fanatic full of hatred, but an empty man, a tranquil and diligent idiot who endeavoured to carry out as carefully as possible the bestial initiatives entrusted to him, and in this obedience he seems to find every doubt or worry put to rest' (p. 1131). He concludes that, 'The Nazi massacre bears the mark of folly, but also another mark. It is the mark of the inhuman' (p. 1132), meaning by 'inhuman' something that is *beyond* human, even though there is a human origin. 'An empty man, a tranquil and diligent idiot.' The definition anticipates the appraisal of essayists and philosophers to come.

Again in 1959, in the month of November, the city of Turin hosts another exhibition on the Deportation at Palazzo Carignano. Levi is directly involved in the preparations, and holds two meetings with young people there. This opportunity to speak in public is probably one of the first times Levi puts into practice what he would later call his 'second job':

bearing witness. We do not know precisely what Levi says in these two meetings with students, but so many of them flock to the talks that the organizers have to provide more spots for him and other speakers, such as Norberto Bobbio. However, we can gain an idea through the articles he publishes later. The first was in *Triangolo Rosso* (Red Triangle), a journal published by the National Association of Former Deportees (ANED) in the same month as the exhibition, on the subject of labour, with reference to the sarcastic slogan posted above the gate at Auschwitz, '*Arbeit Macht Frei*' (Work Makes You Free). In this article, we see the extent to which Levi believes well-performed work is an approximation of happiness on earth, a theme he develops later in *The Truce* (1963) and *The Wrench* (1978).

An article in 1960, published in the *Giornale dei Genitori* (Parents' Newspaper) is based directly on his meetings during the exhibition on the deportation. Levi takes stock of the situation and makes some important points. The first is 'a germ of reproach' (p. 1136) for 'committing the sin of laziness and lack of faith', having been silent for so long on the subject and 'failing to fulfil an expectation' (p. 1136). The second is that former deportees tend to adopt a language that does not belong to them.

Levi tackles a thorny issue when he comments on the kind of language adopted for the Resistance, a language that in his view was 'embalmed' before its time, 'relegating it obsequiously to the noble castle of the History of the Homeland' (p. 1137). His logic is simple and effective: the language used to convey past experience is 'rhetorical, hagiographic, and therefore vague' (p. 1137). A further error, in his view, is calling the Resistance a 'Second Risorgimento.'

Levi reflects here on a topic that must have been debated in clubs and among friends in Turin. Is there 'an ideal continuity between the events of 1848, 1860, 1918 and 1945?'

If there is, is should not be constructed to the detriment of the twenty years of Fascist rule. In order to talk effectively to young people about the Resistance and the Deportation, Levi says, 'we should speak to them a little less of glory and victory, of heroism and sacred ground, and a little more of that hard, dangerous, and thankless life, the daily strain, the days of hope and of despair, of our comrades who died doing their duty in silence, of the participation of the populace (but not all of it), of the errors made and those avoided, of the conspiratorial and military experience painfully acquired, through mistakes that were paid in human lives, of the hard-won (and not spontaneous, not always perfect) agreement among the supporters of different parties (p. 1138).

During the 1960s, Levi starts his pilgrimage from school to school, giving talks. He goes wherever he is invited. After 1963, when *The Truce* is published and wins the Campiello Literary Prize, he becomes increasingly popular. Continuous reprints of *If This Is a Man* are also a clear signal that the perception of the deportation and the extermination camps is changing. The overall situation in Italy has also changed. There are centre-left parties and a Cold War détente. In the meantime, survivor associations have contributed to educating the general public, allowing people to look at recent history in a new light. This change releases some survivors from the burden of silence that they took on when they first returned from the camps. At an international level, the Eichmann trial in Israel contributes to creating a climate that is more favourable to denouncing the 'shameful' history of the Deportation of Jews and the massacre of defenceless civilians in countries occupied by the Germans.

In 1965, the school edition of *The Truce* is published in the highly successful Einaudi series, 'Readings for Middle Schools'. For the occasion, Levi writes a new Preface, which is a potted autobiography. With this publication, Levi is recognized within the school curriculum as being a literary writer as well as a witness, and soon gains a certain popularity among young readers. By this point, his writing career separates into two different areas that sometimes overlap: on one hand, engaging in activities linked to his literary output; on the other, bearing witness and becoming the critical conscience of the deportation.

Levi starts publishing short stories in the Milan daily, *Il Giorno*, and a few years later contributes regular articles on literature, linguistics, anthropology and natural history to *La Stampa*. His approach to this kind of secondary literary activity is mainly artisanal; at the same time, he is increasingly in demand as a public speaker and as an interviewee, especially after the new edition of *The Truce*. One of the first written interviews, perhaps the very first, came out in June 1961 in the magazine *Storia Illustrata* (Illustrated History); Levi answers questions on subjects such as the possible causes of the Jewish genocide, racism and anti-Semitism. His written answers are very direct and anticipate some of the themes he will go on to explore when 'negationist' ideologies become a hot topic in the European press. In the interview, Levi says that the history of humankind is filled with bloodshed and that the genocide represented a return to the barbaric infancy of civilization. Human beings are not naturally good, he goes on to state, while outlining a biological explanation for the mass murders in the camps. Answering a question on the collective responsibility of Germans, Levi says that every human being is individually responsible for his or her actions. In this sense, the Germans (and non-Germans) who played a role in the massacres are fully culpable as are their accomplices.

Levi's interviews through the 1970s and 1980s, whenever a new book is published, or when there are particularly traumatic social upheavals to debate, mark a high point in his role as a communicator and teacher. His answers are always mild-mannered but firm, even though he expresses opinions that are far from mainstream. Italy, in the meantime, is in turmoil, shaken by social conflict and terrorism and Levi's voice speaks to the country. He is openly critical of the Vietnam war, the Soviet Gulags and of the use of torture in Latin America. In a 1974 article published in *Corriere della Sera*, ' "A Past We Thought Would Never Return" ', he writes, 'Every era has its fascism; the warning signs can be seen wherever the concentration of power denies a citizen the opportunity and the capacity to express and carry out his will.' (p. 1199). There are many ways of getting there, he concludes, 'Not necessarily through the terror of police intimidation but also by censoring and distorting information, polluting justice, paralyzing schools, disseminating in many subtle ways nostalgia for a world where order reigned supreme, and where the security of the privileged few rested on the forced labour and forced silence of the many' (p. 1199).

Levi visits Israel in 1967 and publishes two articles (1967–68) on his return for the journal *Resistenza. Giustizia e Libertà* (Resistance. Justice and Liberty) on his relationship to the State of Israel, where he sets out his ideas about Zionism and the construction of a Jewish state. Levi has never been a Zionist, as his first two books, *If This Is a Man* and *The Truce*, make clear. He feels an attachment to Judaism, the religion he grew up with, but also feels a similarly strong connection to Italy. In Levi's view, Israel has a right to exist, even though he is critical of the link between American politics, which he considers 'imperialist', and the state of Israel's very existence. Levi sees the question of Jews in Israel as a symbol of a more universal human history, and considers the country's constitution as having a socialist calling, in line with his political outlook in Italy. The biggest surprise for him is that the country is not European, even though it is born of the traditions of the old continent. Nevertheless, in Levi's view, it doesn't have the layers of history that unites Europe 'from Gibraltar to the Urals'.

As his writing career becomes more prominent—in the early 1980s— Levi turns his thoughts to his identity as a Jewish writer. In this period, there is a boom in interest—both in Europe and in the US—in Jewish culture, especially central European Jewish culture, as well as in Jewish American writers. Publication in 1982 of *If Not Now, When?*—the protagonists of which are Jewish partisans—gives Levi the opportunity to position himself within that Jewish tradition. In a 1984 speech entitled 'The Itinerary of a Jewish Writer', delivered as part of a symposium on the subject in Bellagio (very similar to an article that came out eight years before on his identity as a writer, 'The Writer Non-Writer', 1976), he starts out by saying he accepts being defined as a 'Jewish author', although he feels some resistance to the label. He goes over his life story, and outlines the elements that give his work a Jewish identity, but insists on considering his Jewish identity intrinsic to the Italian cultural and literary tradition. As evidence of this, he cites his most autobiographical work, *The Periodic Table*, and his atypical position with regard to the Jews of the Diaspora.

In 1982, Levi signs a petition against the Israeli invasion of Lebanon, demanding the withdrawal of troops and a political solution to the conflict in the Middle East that recognized a right to sovereignty for all the different populations in the region. Menachen Begin is Prime Minister at the time, and numerous protests break out against the government in Israel, leading to the birth of an Israeli peace movement, Peace Now, after the massacre at the Sabra and Shatila refugee camps. Levi's position meets with criticism in the Italian Jewish community and in Israel. In an interview with the journalist Giampaolo Pansa, published in the Rome daily *la Repubblica* (24 September 1982), Levi attempts to explain his position on the Israeli government and the Palestinians, in particular their leader, Arafat. The interview was triggered by an article Levi published in June 1982 in *La Stampa*, entitled 'Who Has Courage in Jerusalem?' In this article, written on returning from a trip to Auschwitz, Levi outlines the situation in Israel and argues that the Palestinian problem exists and 'cannot be resolved in the Begin manner' (p. 2597).

Two years later, in a conversation with Gad Lerner, a journalist with the weekly magazine *L'Espresso*, Levi painfully returns to the subject. As Lerner recounts, Levi's relationship with Israel is passionate but tormented. It is a complex relationship, despite his reputation as a rational and reasonable writer, with an acute sense of justice. It could be said that, throughout the 1970s and 1980s, Levi engages in a kind of militant anti-Fascism that reveals itself in his measured but precise words. In both his writing and his public speaking, Levi shows a capacity for discernment and analysis based on clear distinctions. In this respect, he is a truly unique figure in the Italian intellectual and literary landscape.

The article Levi publishes in *La Stampa* in May 1978, after the kidnapping and assassination of the politician Aldo Moro, is a vivid example. After describing the 'darkness' the country has been 'groping in' since 1969, Levi indicates a starting point in 'a cynical and merciless game that started in Dallas' with the assassination of John F. Kennedy, stresses 'the inefficiency of the response and the incompetence displayed' and reflects on the lessons to be learned for the Left: letting 'our many wounds fester without responding with timely and organic measures; to forgo justice by relying on oblivion; to set the arrogance of power against the urge to clean house' (p. 1252). The mistakes, he points out, 'are not just of institutions but of all of us citizens', including Levi himself. While indirectly referencing the Piazza Fontana bomb in Milan, the death in police custody of the anarchist Pinelli and other political assassinations that took place in that decade of unrest, Levi denounces the general indifference ('we often shrugged our shoulders') to the transgressions of the terrorists, perpetrated on a daily basis. The Red Brigades 'are not the heirs of the workers' movement; they have nothing to do with it, not in the way they operate and even less so in their language' (p. 1253). As a former partisan and member of the anti-Fascist Action party, Levi condemns the terrorist group's barbarism outright.

In the same period, Levi critiques Liliana Cavani's film, *Il portiere di notte* (Night Porter) and the 'Nazi-porn' genre in an article for *La Stampa* (12 February 1977). Levi firmly contests the idea presented by the film director that there is always a morbid relationship between victim and executioner. Most of the SS, he writes, 'weren't monsters, idiotic lechers, or perverted dandies: they were functionaries of the State, more pedantic than brutal, effectively indifferent to the daily horror in which they lived, and which they appeared to get used to quickly' (p. 1230).

After Jean Améry's suicide, Levi writes a profile of the philosopher who becomes an interlocutor in his last book. In a short article for *La Stampa* (7 December 1978), he discusses why the reasons for suicide are so hard to comprehend. 'Understanding the reasons for a suicide is particularly difficult, since, in general, the victim himself isn't conscious of them, or provides himself and others with explanations that are intentionally or unintentionally distorted' (p. 1262).

Levi reaches a high point in his role as teacher and thinker in a short article for *La Stampa* in January 1979 discussing Professor Robert Faurisson's negationist ideology, which claimed the Nazi Lagers, gas chambers and crematoria were a 'big lie'. Although he has always rejected the idea that he was a teacher with his usual shy humility, the article 'But We Were There' is a lesson. It is more than just a witness statement from a camp survivor—it closely examines the mental mechanisms adopted to deny guilt. Levi dons the cap of a highly effective psychologist.

> We are well-acquainted with certain mental mechanisms: guilt is troublesome, or at least inconvenient; in times long past, in Italy and France, it was also dangerous. One begins by denying it in court; it is denied for decades in public, then in private, then to oneself. Finally, it's done: the spell has worked, black has become white, wrong right, the dead aren't dead, there is no murderer, there's no more guilt, or, rather, there never was any. It's not just that I haven't committed a crime; the crime itself doesn't exist (p. 1266).

The article concludes with an invitation to Faurisson to 'talk to each one of us' survivors. Levi returns to this subject in the following days and months in at least two articles, which is a prolific output for him, given how slowly he usually writes.

In 1978, the novel *Holocaust* is published at the same time as a TV mini-series based on the book. The subject of the extermination of the Jews in concentration camps is beamed to the whole of the western world and Germany in particular, where millions of people watch it and reel in shock. Levi writes a review of both the film and book in *La Stampa* ('So That Yesterday's Holocausts Will Never Return'). Lucid as ever, he distinguishes the value of the book and the film from the impact they had in the various countries where they appeared. He carefully examines the book and highlights the reasons for its success, but also its limits and historical inaccuracies. He discusses the TV production in detail, and underscores the effect it had in Germany, a sign of a change underway among the new generations. He appreciates how a 'story' can be so powerful in a historical context precisely 'because it is a story' (p. 1284), and because television penetrates consciences more powerfully than books can. At the end of the article, Levi wonders 'what might happen if a different or opposite topic were to be chosen, in a country where television is a state monopoly that has no democratic controls and is impervious to public criticism' (p. 1284)

In a longer article commissioned by *Radiocorriere TV* ('Images from *Holocaust*', May, 1979), Levi examines some common explanations for the Holocaust, adopting here the term he has always rejected, and investigates why the Nazis were so determined to annihilate the Jews. 'It can't be explained why, in the tragedy and chaos of a war that was by then lost, the convoys of deportees had precedence over troop and ammunition transports' (p. 1289). Even more radically, he tries to answer a more pressing question posed by many viewers of the series, 'the 'why' of evil in the world' (p. 1289) He concludes that there is no explanation. Levi is not religious, and the theological explanation of 'God's silence' is not, in his view, an adequate response. Historical or sociological explanations are equally insufficient, as is the plumb line of German anti-Semitism.

His answer is on a different plane, and is already present in *If This Is a Man*, where he explores the idea of the man-animal. For someone like Levi with a training in science, who has spent most of his working life in a technical field—Levi always claimed he was a technician, not a scientist, and that he worked with his hands as well as his brain—to claim that at the heart of the tragic events of the Holocaust there is an unassailable hard core that is impossible to explain or comprehend is highly significant.

On returning from the camps, he increasingly suspects that behind the folly of Auschwitz, underpinning the abnormal and absurd extermination project, is a surprising dose of rationality. In his view, the madness of what took place does not exclude rationality; if anything, it assumes it. Writing about Höss, the petit-bourgeois commander at Auschwitz, Levi compares him to an inventor because he was able to solve the practical problem of extermination by inventing the gas chambers. His comment is ironic, of course, but it shows the emphasis Levi places on the rationality of the Lager system. Rationality and irrationality are opposites and yet they are symmetrical: they are equal, though opposing, forces. Auschwitz is symmetrical to the 'normal' rational world; it is simply turned upside-down. At the same time, Auschwitz is dominated by a sort of 'rationality' in the way it managed the camp, eliminated prisoners, exploited labour, paid maniacal attention to violence and recreated circles of Hell for the drowned and the saved. In the eyes of an animal behaviourist like Levi, the camps presented a coherent system, even though the logic of normal life is reversed. Unlike other deportees and survivors, Levi sees the upturned logic of the Lager perfectly. He can understand the uncertain boundary that separates reason from non-reason, good from evil. This is because his approach is both anthropological and scientific. His lucid gaze has always allowed him, from the very first draft of *If This Is a Man*, to analyse human behaviour in an almost detached manner, as if he were indeed an ethologist. As the years go by, Levi becomes increasingly detached and lucid, and this causes him increasingly deep and unbearable pain.

Levi examines human nature as a moralist and not as a psychologist, as an ideal pupil of Montaigne (he does not agree with psychologists such as Bettelheim, for example). This is because his analysis of his fellow prisoners in the camp takes into account a possible reversal of logic in the Lager system. In human rationality, Levi tells us, in civilization itself—and even in science—there is a seed that can spawn its opposite and unleash irrational and destructive forces. These forces need not necessarily be triggered by anger or rage, as studying Homer taught him at school; they can also exist as cold, detached actions. Cruelty is intrinsic in human nature and its mechanisms are unpredictable. Every time he has to answer questions regarding the irrationality of the Lager system in public, Levi is forced to grapple with an enigma. This does not stop him from trying to define and highlight new aspects, however. He never gives up on his search for answers, however provisional and partial they may be.

In the post-war period—from the end of the 1940s to the 80s—dominated by opposing ideologies, Levi presents himself as a thinker outside mainstream systems such as Marxism, Liberalism, Socialist Christianity or Libertarian Socialism. A lecture he gave in Turin in 1979 on the topic of racism, with an audience of non-specialists, shows Levi thinking outside the box while upholding his biological and anthropological beliefs (Darwin is his model in this respect). After humbly confessing his incompetence, Levi separates animal-behaviourist or biological explanations for racism from historical and cultural justifications. As a faithful reader of Konrad Lorenz, mistrusted at the time as being on the political 'right', Levi explores the question of intraspecies aggressiveness, 'evil'—the existence of which he witnessed in the camps. In his view, the biological origins of the phenomenon cannot be dodged. Clearly, Levi's determinism has a positivist origin, but he harbours no doubt that the phenomenon of racial intolerance is pre-human, and prehistoric. The fact that it has always existed, however, only partially justifies the historical intolerance experienced repeatedly by his people—the Jews—over the centuries.

In 1975, Levi translated Jacques Presser's book, *The Night of the Girondists*, published by Adelphi. In his foreword, he takes up an issue he has already raised in his review of Cavani's film. That is, the fine line separating victims and executioners, which he will later call the 'grey zone':

> Only a Manichean rhetoric can assert that that space is empty; it is not, it is scattered with vile, miserable, or pathetic characters (who occasionally possess all three qualities at once) and it is indispensable that we know them if we want to know the human

species, if we want to know how to defend our souls when a similar trial returns (p. 1222).

In 1977, he publishes in *La Stampa* an essay/story dedicated to the figure of Chaim Rumkowski, president of the Lodz Ghetto ('The King of the Jews'). In this piece, the expression 'broad band of gray consciences' (p. 1415) appears for the first time; the phrase, with corrections and variants, is later included in *The Drowned and the Saved*.

In these years of deep crisis in Italian society, Levi is planning to return to the theme of the Lager, having seemingly moved away from it in his writing. In the interviews he gives after publication of *The Wrench* (1979), he mentions a new project, but it does not come to fruition until seven years later.

Levi's state of mind during the decade in which he elaborates the themes of *The Drowned and the Saved* is revealed in a conversation with Giorgio Calcagno published in 1976 in *La Stampa*, the newspaper he now contributes to assiduously after retiring from the chemical factory in 1975. Calcagno asks him why he returns to these issues after stating, on several occasions after *The Truce*, that he had nothing more to say about the Lager experience. There is a need for truth, Levi replies, adding that emerging negationist ideologies have affected him deeply, both personally and as a former deportee bearing witness. But also, to go against the usual rhetoric, he adds, referring to the point he made back in the 1950s:

> We former deportees are equated with former partisans, and that's correct. But there is a substantial difference between the experience of a victorious struggle and the passive and diminishing experience of imprisonment. I wanted to re-establish these points. I am willing to tolerate a certain amount of rhetoric; it is a necessary component of life. We need monuments and celebrations. In the etymology of the word 'monument' there is the word 'admonishment'. On the other hand, we need something to counter it: a prose commentary on the flights of rhetoric.

I have tried to provide this knowing that it will harm certain sensibilities. They are quite taboo subjects (Calcagno 1982).

In parallel, there is another reason that leads him to start writing about the Lager experience again, following a framework that he clearly considers anti-rhetorical: that is, the fact that young people are becoming more detached. He feels that they listen to the story of the Jewish extermination and concentration camps as if it belongs to the remote past, with no links to the present, or to events still taking place in many parts of the world. Schoolchildren are moved, he claims in some interviews, in the same way they are for the Christian martyrs or the prisons of Silvio Pellico. It is clear from the very first chapter of *The Drowned and the Saved* that Levi has realized that memory is fragile, and easily lost; not just collective memory but also individual memory, including that of former deportees. Levi raises the issue of what and how to remember, noting that victims' memories are often seen as antithetical to those of historians. This is what leads Levi to return to writing about the camps, so that he can explore these issues further.

The core of *The Drowned and the Saved*, a unique example in the Jewish literary canon, is Levi's exploration of the theme of the 'grey zone', a concept that will go on to influence literary output on the concentration-camp experience, among other tragedies. Returning to themes that were already present in *If This Is a Man*—in particular to the idea that in the Lager the 'enemy' was not only all around but also inside, so that there were no longer any clear boundaries between 'us' and 'them'—Levi examines the rites and ceremonies that welcomed deportees into the camp, and describes how the reality on the ground was 'an endless struggle' to obtain privileges that were necessary for survival. This is how Levi defines the grey zone: 'The hybrid category of inmate-functionaries is both its framework and its most disturbing feature. This category is a gray zone, with undefined contours, which both separates and connects the two opposing camps of masters and servants. It has an incredibly complicated internal structure, and harbours just enough to confound our need to judge' (p. 2435).

The chapter entitled 'The Gray Zone' is more like a treatise on the anthropology and psychology of prison behaviour, although the same principles apply to any number of situations where people are forced to live together and where there is a power-dynamic between a commanding structure and a base that is required to obey.

Levi is careful to distinguish between making moral judgements on the causes of oppression and his analysis of the mechanisms governing the grey zone. 'It should be clear that the greatest fault lies with the system, the very structure of the totalitarian state. The criminal complicity of individual collaborators, great and small (never friendly, never transparent!), is always difficult to evaluate' (p. 2436). He makes it quite clear that 'The rise of the privileged—not only in the camps but in all human society—is a disturbing but inevitable phenomenon. The only places where you don't find them are utopias' (p. 2434). Levi presents the Lager as a sort of laboratory with a highly complex structure—the experiment he described in *If This Is a Man*—and stresses two aspects: first, that 'the smaller the area of power the greater the need for outside assistance' (p. 2435); second, that 'the harsher the oppression, the more widespread among the oppressed is the willingness to collaborate with power' (p. 2435).

Levi quotes a significant passage from Manzoni's *The Betrothed* in this regard. 'The troublemakers, the oppressors, all those who do harm of any sort to others, are guilty not only of the evil they do but also of the perversion of their victims' minds.' In writing *The Drowned and the Saved*, Levi is propelled by the fear—worse, by the almost certainty—of the failure of his own testimony. Another factor was a prolonged feeling of shame, a subject to which he dedicates a whole chapter in the book. Shame is far more devastating than guilt, and Levi feels a double layer of shame about himself: not only has he been forever tarnished by the violence of the Lager, but he has also survived, while others, perhaps the best of them, have swollen the ranks of the drowned. Like his first book, Levi's last was autobiographical. *The Drowned and the Saved* is undeniably Levi's last word as a writer. It places an onerous seal on one of the most original, and at the same time the humblest, thinkers in the history of the twentieth century.

Natural Histories

While Levi was working with De Benedetti on the *Auschwitz Report* in 1946, he wrote a short story called 'The Mnemagogs'. It was set in a country medical practice, where a young Morandi was about to replace an older doctor named Montesanto. The two doctors recall Levi and De Benedetti, who was a doctor and several years older than Primo, though this may just be a coincidence. It was the first short story Levi wrote after getting back from the Lager, but he later said he had formed the idea for the story before he was deported. He had spoken to friends about it, as he had done with other literary projects of his. 'The Mnemagogs' was published in the left-wing daily *L'Italia Socialista* on 19 December 1948. The paper had previously published another story, 'Maria and the Circle', on 19 September that same year, which was included nearly 30 years later in *The Periodic Table* with the title 'Titanium'.

In those first years back home, Levi wrote several short stories. Some of these were handwritten in the same notebook that contained nearly all the chapters that were to form *The Truce*, as Tesio has pointed out. He did not plan on collecting the stories into a book at the time. 'Sleeping Beauty in the Refrigerator: A Winter's Tale' was originally written in 1952, although the version that came out in *Natural Histories* was probably a rewrite of a text commissioned by the State radio, RAI, and recorded in June 1961. 'Man's Friend' and 'Censorship in Bitinia' were also written in the notebook, accompanied by a comment in Latin on a request from RAI for a new ending to *Sleeping Beauty*: 'Est fabula bifida. Cum exitum novum rogatus essem invenire, novum exogitavi.

171

Volo tamen, quod fines ambo maneant, et valeant, et legantur, et sicut vita haec fabula sit, quae non fluit plane, sed varie ruit et alterna vice inter sese complitur' (Tesio 1997a). Another short story, conceived between 1946 and 1947 while Levi was writing *If This Is a Man*, but finally written in 1957 (the typescript handed to Einaudi is dated 22 December 1957), was 'The Sixth Day'. This may well have been part of the RAI commission, together with 'The Versifier', but it was never recorded or broadcast. 'The Versifier' was published by the liberal-socialist leaning weekly *Il Mondo,* edited by Mario Pannunzio and financed by Adriano Olivetti, on 17 May 1960, while 'The Sixth Day' came out in the Turin-based bimonthly journal *Questioni* in the September–November 1958 issue.

Levi became a regular contributor to *Il Mondo* between 1960 and 1962. In addition to 'The Versifier' and 'Censorship in Bitinia', which was a political satire on the censorship operated by the ruling Christian Democrat Party at the time, the weekly magazine published 'Quaestio de Centauris' (4 April 1961), 'Bear Meat', which was not included in *Natural Histories* (29 August 1961), 'Man's Friend' (16 January 1962) and 'Angelic Butterfly' (14 August 1962). These were the years Levi was working on *The Truce.* When his second book was published in 1962, Levi's reputation as a writer was beginning to grow, although it was still limited to a small circle of professional readers. After winning the Campiello Literary Prize in 1964, Levi was invited to contribute to *Il Giorno*, edited by Italo Pietra and financed by the petrochemical group Eni, whose president at the time was Enrico Mattei. The newspaper hosted articles by many other up-and-coming writers and critics, including Pietro Citati, Luciano Bianciardi, Alberto Arbasino and Umberto Eco. Several of the other short stories included in *Natural Histories* were published there: 'Order at a Good Price' (22 March 1964), 'Some Applications of the Mimete' (15 August 1964), 'The Measure of Beauty' (6 January 1965), 'Versamine' (8 August 1965), and 'Full Employment' (27 February 1966). A further story that was later included in the collection, 'Cladonia Rapida', was published by the Milan-based weekly magazine *Panorama* in August 1964.

Given that Levi sent his short stories one by one to the newspapers and magazines to which he contributed regularly, it is evident that at the time he had no plans to publish them as a collection. Short stories were the third genre that the 40-year-old chemist experimented with, alongside what was still then his very private activity of poetry writing, and his better-known work as a writer of witness narrative, and occasionally—not often, and mostly in Turin—of articles and reports on his experience as a deportee. However, Levi was anxious to be considered a writer of fiction that was not necessarily linked to his Lager experience. This led him to send his early short stories to Calvino for comments. Calvino already had a literary reputation, both as an author and as an editor at Einaudi, and on 22 November 1961 he wrote an affectionate letter to Levi that read as a critical review, with some constructive advice as to how to get the stories published. At the time, Levi was still a one-book author. Even though a new edition of *If This Is a Man* had come out three years before, few readers were aware of the differences between the 1958 and the original 1948 editions. His second book was still in its early stages, as he did not write the final draft of *The Truce* until the end of 1961. The letter was an important boost for Levi's literary ambitions.

There is no record of which stories Levi sent to Calvino. From Calvino's letter we can assume that 'A Disciple' (later published in 1961 from the version in Levi's notebook), was included, as well as 'Capaneus' (already published in the journal *Il Ponte* in 1959) since Calvino suggested leaving them out. Levi obligingly set these two stories aside and did not pick them up again until 1981, when he included them in *Lilith and Other Stories*. We do know that Calvino commented on 'Man's Friend', '*Quaestio de Centauris*' and 'The Mnemagogs', describing them as successful examples of stories in a genre of 'biological fiction': 'a direction in which I would encourage you to work'. By contrast, he felt that the stories based on Levi's Lager experience were little more than 'fragments of *If This Is a Man*' which appeared 'limited to being short sketches without a wider narrative framework'. Calvino's criticism was addressed at an implicit aspect of Levi's literary output, which was his ability to create a story from the most minimal material. In his first book, these micro-episodes were embedded in a wider narrative framework that provided a moral—or even philosophical—commentary. Calvino did not use the word 'sketch' in a derogatory fashion; if anything, he was complimenting the author on his capacity for creating a vivid picture with very few lines. Calvino appreciated Levi's rapid, detailed images, which were not frescoes or paintings but 'sketches'. From 1946 onwards, Levi's output of short stories had been incredibly varied in tone, style and subject matter. He had not established a trademark style, and was unsure as to how to proceed, but he took Calvino's criticism on board and continued to write in different genres. In Calvino's view, however, Levi was not yet ready to publish a short-story collection. In the three years that followed, Levi continued to publish stories, reusing material or ideas from his past.

Calvino's advice was to publish stories as often as possible in order to maintain a dialogue with his readers, and also to very carefully choose the journals he published in. As a well-established author, in fact, Calvino was more media savvy than Levi, and knew how to cultivate a loyal readership. This was decidedly a new direction for Levi, whose literary identity had been forged as a writer of testimonies. The author of *The Path to the Nest of Spiders* was by no means diminishing Levi's literary worth or questioning the value of his output. He was trying, rather, to help his friend find his own literary path, using the parameters of his own taste and experience. There is no evidence to show that Calvino had had the opportunity to read the stories that had come out in *Il Mondo*, but his identification of the genre 'biological fiction' in Levi's writing was an evaluation of Levi's work in itself. What it indicated was that the source of Levi's fantasy world was to be found in life (*bios*); it also implied that the fictional fantasies of Levi's short stories shared some features with the biological and social aspects of *If This Is a Man*. In his letter, Calvino cited the biologist Jean Rostand, commenting on the way Levi's stories built up a fictional world: 'Your fantasy mechanism, which takes off from a scientific-genetic starting point, has a power of suggestion that's intellectual but also poetic, just like the genetic and morphological digressions of Jean Rostand. Your humor and your elegance easily save you from the danger of falling to a level of subliterature' (22 November 1961, cited in *Notes on the Texts*, pp. 2837–38). In later years, Calvino confessed to Levi that reading his stories had been one of the sources of inspiration for his own short-story collection, *Cosmicomics*.

The same year that Calvino wrote to Levi, Einaudi published its second anthology of science-fiction stories, edited by Carlo Fruttero and Franco Lucentini, *Le meraviglie del possibile II* (The Wonders of the Possible). This second edition followed on from the first commercially successful anthology published in 1959, edited by Sergio Solmi and Carlo Fruttero. Calvino's comments on Levi's short stories should also be seen in the light of the publication of these two popular anthologies, because they placed Levi's output in an area between traditional fantasy—which had always been present in the Italian literary canon—and science fiction, a genre which was in the process of being defined by the two Einaudi collections, without locking it into a rigid frame of reference.

SCIENCE FICTION?

When *Natural Histories* came out in 1966, Einaudi had a yellow band placed over the dust jacket with the words 'Science Fiction?' printed on it. The question mark was appropriate, as the short-story collection did not properly belong to the genre—not exclusively, at least. Five years before the collection came out, Calvino had already appreciated Levi's sense of humour, as well as the elegance of his prose, which, in his view, saved his writing from being considered 'sub-literature'. In his 22 November letter-review, Calvino praised Levi for having avoided falling into an 'Anatole France-Walt Disney-type pastiche' but also warned: 'you still lack the confident hand of the writer who has a complete stylistic personality, like Borges'. The most striking passage in Calvino's letter was when he attempted to define the cultural and literary area to which he felt Levi's short stories belonged: 'You move in a dimension of intelligent digression on the edges of a cultural-ethical-scientific panorama that reflects the Europe we live in. Maybe the principal reason I like your stories so much is that they assume a common culture notably different from the one assumed by so much of Italian literature' (p. 2838).

It was difficult to appreciate at the time what was so different about Levi's stories. The 15 stories that made up the collection belong to different genres. They range from the realistic to the fantastic, from exemplary tales to science fiction, from anecdotal to dramatic. In a single story there may be a variety of themes and styles. In addition to their scientific and technical inspiration, the nineteenth-century Italian and foreign short-story tradition, the Scapigliatura movement, Joseph Conrad and Jack London, all played their part. There were even hints of the Picaresque in the stories, which found an original application in *The Truce*. Levi's own definition of the inspiration for his stories, originally in a letter to his publisher and then adopted in the dust-jacket blurb of the book, was interesting: his stories came into his imagination as a 'point of intuition. Levi described this intuition as being a 'perception of a gap in the world we live in' (p. 2841).

Just before the publication of *Natural Histories*, Levi was interviewed by Edoardo Fadini after three one-act plays based on three stories in the collection ('Sleeping Beauty in the Refrigerator: A Winter's Tale', 'The Versifier', 'The Sixth Day') were performed. In this interview, Levi called himself a centaur. Fadini asked him what the 'link between human beings and these stories of machine poetesses, women in a state of permanent hibernation, and bureaucratic creators' might be. Levi's answer was significant:

> I am an amphibian, a centaur (I have even written short stories about centaurs). I feel that the ambiguity of science fiction mirrors our current destiny. I am split into two parts. One belongs in a factory, as a technician, a chemist. The other, however, is totally detached from that part, and it is the part in which I write, accept interviews, and work on my past and present experience. It is really like having two half-brains. It is a paranoid split (like that, I believe, of Gadda, Sinigalli, and Solmi)' (Fadini 1966).

In the same interview, Levi told Fadini he had tried to write stories about life in the factory but had never succeeded. Perhaps the time had not yet come, he concluded.

THE BOOK

The title *Natural Histories* was derived from a citation of a citation: a passage from Pliny's *Naturalis Historia* was cited in Rabelais' *Gargantua and Pantagruel*. Levi played this Russian-doll like game quite often, creating what is now called 'intertextuality'. Levi placed the passage quoted in French at the beginning of the book. He explained the origin of the title in a 1973 letter to the Romanian translator of *If This Is a Man*. It was chosen 'for the following reasons. First, because these stories are about as un-'natural' as could possibly be imagined (although the language they are written in almost always simulates the cold, detached tone of a scientific report); second, because the epigraph I have chosen for them is a citation from Rabelais [. . .] The title is thus loaded with irony' (Letter to Condrea Derer, 29 May 1973). Irony and humour are essential keys to understanding the stories.

The book was published at the end of 1966 in the Einaudi 'Coralli' series, with a collage of by Arno Waldschmidt on the cover. The image was of a white moon face against a black background, with a black crow's head facing the other way as the eye. The figure of a crow, of course, had already appeared in the poems Levi wrote on returning from Auschwitz. The author of the book was given as Damiano Malabaila, a pseudonym adopted by Levi at the request of the publisher. Again, Calvino wrote the copy, as he had for *If This Is a Man* and *The Truce:*

> The fifteen 'entertainments' that compose this book invite us to enter a future that is increasingly propelled by the frenetic impulse of technological progress and is hence a theatre of disquieting or utopian experiments, in which extraordinary and unpredictable machines act. And yet it's not sufficient to classify these pages under the label of science fiction. Satire and poetry can be found here, nostalgia for the past and anticipation of the future, epic and daily reality, scientific formulation and the pull of the absurd, love of the natural order and a taste for subverting it, humanism and polite malice. The author is a chemist, and his profession filters through in the interest in how things are constructed, how they are recognized and analysed. But he is a chemist who knows human emotions no less than he knows the law of mass action, and he disassembles and reassembles the secret mechanisms that rule human vanities, winking at us from the ironic allegories, the smiling morals that he offers (p. 2841).

Calvino then introduced a letter from the author to his publisher:

> I find it quite embarrassing to write about my short stories. Perhaps a description and analysis of my embarrassment will serve to answer your questions. I've written some twenty stories and I don't know if I will write others. I wrote them for the most

part straight off, trying to give narrative form to a point of intuition, trying to recount in other terms (if they are symbolic, they are so unconsciously) an intuition that today is not rare: the perception of a gap in the world we live in, of a small or large fault, of a 'flaw of form' that nullifies some aspect of our civilization or our moral universe. [. . .] In the act of writing them I feel a vague sense of guilt, as of one who consciously commits a small transgression. What transgression? Let's see [. . .] I entered the world of writing (unexpectedly) with two books about the concentration camps; it's not for me to judge their value, but they were undoubtedly serious books, addressed to a serious audience. To offer this audience a volume of joke-stories, of moral traps, entertaining, perhaps, but detached, and cold: isn't this commercial fraud, like someone selling wine in oil bottles? These are questions that I asked myself, in the act of writing and publishing these 'natural histories.' Well, I wouldn't publish them if I hadn't noticed (not right away, to tell the truth) that between the Lager and these inventions a continuity, a bridge, exists: the Lager, for me, was the largest of the 'flaws,' of the distortions I spoke of earlier, the most threatening of the monsters generated by the sleep of reason (p. 2482).

Calvino thus not only mentioned the profession of the author but also the fact that he had already written two books about his concentration-camp experience. This was as close as he could get to revealing Levi's identity, which was accompanied by a 'vague sense of guilt' for being the author of a volume of 'joke stories'. The idea that an author's sense of inadequacy could be revealed in a publisher's presentation was highly unusual. The letter concluded by saying that there was indeed a 'bridge' between the stories in/and the Lager experience. The final reference was to Goya, whose drawing had been chosen as the dust-jacket illustration for the 1947 De Silva edition of *If This Is a Man*. The artist's

Disaster of War etchings were often cited by Italian writers, including Calvino and Sciascia, who were both contemporaries of Levi.

Why did Levi use the pseudonym Damiano Malabaila for his third book? Many years later, Levi confessed the idea was not his but Roberto Cerati's, the director of the Einaudi sales department. In a letter written in August 1966, he wrote to Levi on behalf of the editorial board suggesting the hybrid formula: a pseudonym on the cover and a clear indication in the publisher's blurb as to the real identity of the author by citing his two important books about the Lager experience. Cerati supported this idea with two arguments. First, that by conveying the author's 'reluctance', or 'polite modesty', readers would feel sympathy for the author; second, that Levi's name on the cover was far from being a guarantee of good sales, given that his previous two books were witness narratives—even though *The Truce* was relatively successful.

What the letter did reveal, however, was no great secret at the time. That is, Levi's fantasy tales were not considered to be of the same standard as his first two books. In fact, Calvino—speaking for Einaudi— referred to them as 'entertainments'. Cerati came up with a comparison to illustrate his point, which made the publisher's position very clear: 'If Gianfranco Contini published a wonderful book of recipes, he would get the critical attention worthy of the great philologist, and the attention of a wider audience on both sides.' This point was not far off the mark, as the literary world received Malabaila-Levi's new book with almost unanimous reserve: the stories were interesting, but not outstanding. This was in line with Calvino's by-no-means negative first response to the stories which is worth citing again here: 'Maybe the principal reason I like your stories so much is that they assume a common culture notably different from the one assumed by so much of Italian literature' (p. 2838). It is evident from the letter cited in the publisher's blurb that Levi was equally ambivalent about his latest literary venture. On one hand, he defended the stories as being linked to his witness narratives; on the other, he admitted feeling as though he has committed a 'small transgression' by shifting his perspective from concentration camps to 'joke-stories'. This must be why, in the many interviews that followed publication of *Natural Histories*, Levi always stressed the continuity between his two Lager memoirs and his fantasy stories. When a journalist from *Il Giorno* asked him why he had hidden behind a pseudonym, Levi answered by citing Manzoni's *The Betrothed*:

> Renzo said to Don Abbondio 'I could have failed.' It may have been a mistake; we will soon find out. Basically, I felt faintly guilty, perhaps as a form of respect towards some of the readers of my first two books. What if some of them had been affected in person, or a member of their family had suffered the tragedy of the Lager? They would read my stories in *Il Giorno* and say to me, 'How can you write about these things when you've been to Auschwitz?' I don't share this point of view myself (or I wouldn't have written *Natural Histories*, or I wouldn't have published them at least) but I respect it. In order to distance myself, and to differentiate between the author of *If This Is a Man*, I accepted the publisher's idea of signing the book with a pseudonym. As far as I am concerned, I feel no contradiction between the two topics, and I honestly don't believe I have betrayed any principle or person. In fact, I am convinced that it is possible to find traces of the Lager in many of the stories, such as the acceptance of evil, the 'preposterousness' of the cosmos, geometric madness. For example, 'Versamine' and 'Angelic Butterfly' came to me with a German setting' (12 October 1966).

The journalist went on to ask Levi whether the pseudonym had any significance. Since Levi had already been revealed as the author of the collection, he answered:

> As for the pseudonym, I thought about it a lot. Then it came by itself. Every morning going to work and every evening returning home I pass a car electrician called Malabaila. It

struck me, I appropriated it. Only later did I realize that there was a link between the name and the stories, an allusion that has been appreciated and appraised by some of those deep layers of awareness around which today the debate is raging. Malabaila means 'bad wet nurse'; I now realize that there is the smell of rancid milk in many of my stories, of rotten food, of adulteration, contamination and evil spells. Poison instead of nourishment. I would like to remind people that for we survivors the Lager was precisely this: at its most offensive and unpredictable it was a world turned upside down, where 'fair is foul and foul is fair', where professors wielded a spade, assassins were foremen, and hospitals were the place for killings' [. . .] I feel there is an intimate relationship between my first book and this new one. In both, men are reduced to slavery by 'the Nazi thing' and the 'thing thing'. The conclusion is the same: the sleep of reason generates monsters (D'Angeli 1966).

VARIANTS

The typescript of *Natural Histories* is not available in the Einaudi archive, which means the only comparisons we can make are between the first publication of each story in various newspapers, magazines and journals and the versions then published by Einaudi. As we have already said, 'Sleeping Beauty in the Refrigerator: A Winter's Tale' together with some of the other stories in the collection were originally commissioned for radio. There were few differences between their first appearance and publication in *Quaestio de Centauris*, except for an interesting Latin dedication in the Einaudi version to two 'sodales perpetuos', Levi's dearest friends: 'G.L.' (Giorgio Lattes), and 'L.N.' (Livio Norzi). In 'The Versifier', by contrast, radical changes were made between the version printed in *Il Mondo*, which was in the form of a story narrated in the first-person by the protagonist, a professional poet, and the version included in the collection, which was the radio commission written in the form of a dialogue. This shows the remarkable flexibility with which Levi approached his writing. The opening of 'Censorship in Bitinia' was changed for the Einaudi collection, and the version published by *Il Mondo* did not have the chicken claw printed at the end as a stamp of the censor's approval. In an interview, Levi declared the story was written in protest at the then Minister Mario Scelba's cultural censorship in Italy. 'Man's Friend' came out in *Il Mondo* labelled as a 'novella', which was not the case for the published story. 'Angelic Butterfly' came out in *Il Mondo* but was also part of the radio commission where it was arranged in a chronological sequence. In the Einaudi collection, the last two lines of the story were cut: 'Because there is no seed that does not sprout, be it good or bad, and there is no idea that does not mature'. 'Order at a Good Price', first published by *Il Giorno*, contained the word 'Trovatore' which was then taken out. The finale was also altered. 'Some Applications of the Mimete' is identical in the two versions except for one short sentence. 'The Measure of Beauty' in the Einaudi book contains one small addition compared to the first version: a detail regarding where Mr Simpson's firm was located. 'Versamine' is unchanged, except for one tiny detail. Both of these stories were recorded by State radio RAI in 1965 and 1966.

Natural Histories won the Bagutta prize in 1967, under the jury presidency of Ricardo Bacchelli. The book was reprinted twice in the first two years and sold 12,000 copies. In 1979, after *The Wrench* was published and won the Strega Prize, a version was printed with Primo Levi's name on the cover. Over the following four years there were four more editions, with a total of 16,000 copies sold. It was later reprinted in paperback. The paperback edition in the series 'Einaudi Tascabili' called *Racconti* sold 21,889 copies, while the *Collected Stories* (*Tutti i racconti* in the series 'ET Biblioteca') sold 14,594 copies.

LEMMAS

Science Fiction

Many of the stories collected in *Natural Histories, Flaw of Form,* and *Lilith and Other Stories*—especially those where 'machines' played an important role, from 'Some Applications of the Mimete', written in the 1960s to 'Psychophant', written a decade later—could be called science fiction. There was a vein of fantasy running throughout his work, right up to the late stories, such as 'The Man Who Squeezed Through Walls' or 'The Mirror Maker' collected in *Stories and Essays*, where fantasy prevailed over science fiction, hinting at the way Levi's story telling might have developed.

The element of fantasy was also present in Levi's witness literature; indeed, it was one of its strongest narrative features. The rogue's gallery of characters in *The Truce*, for example, relied on fantastic details in order to expand the boundaries of the realistic. It could be said that Levi was an author of testimonials and a writer of fantasy or science fiction at one and the same time.

Levi's science fiction, however, was not simply technological—although technology was often present, of course. Its roots lay in the Italian short-story tradition, where twentieth-century 'magic realism', and more in general the Scapigliatura literary movement, had elevated fantastic visions over technology or social utopias. Levi's short stories were never really about social issues; rather, they focused on individuals. Utopias were rarely even considered. In addition, his science fiction concentrated on the ethical and anthropological aspects of human interaction, as Rabelais' and Swift's fantasies did. His approach was closer to these writers, or even to Voltaire's philosophical stories, than to the science-fiction genre as it developed in the United States. In this sense, the story that Levi anthologized in *The Search for Roots*—Frederic Brown's 'Sentry', published by Einaudi in 1959—was paradigmatic. When Levi described the genesis of his science-fiction stories, he said they came about through a 'point of intuition'. By this he meant that they were generally born from a minimal idea and then developed around the initial nucleus. This was evident, for example, in the 'The Mnemagogs'. Humour was another element that accompanied the organic process of writing science fiction. It was particularly evident in Levi's short stories, although it was not recognized as a quality when *Natural Histories* was first published. The critic, Cesare Cases, defending the collection in an interview, claimed Levi had created a uniquely Italian strain of science fiction, and that the central nucleus and narrative tone of the stories revealed what he called 'humanist melancholy'. This melancholy was the centre of many of his stories, making them teeter between scientific optimism and apocalyptic pessimism. Levi's melancholy played well with his humour; one could even say melancholy was the effect of his humour. Examples of this include: 'Quaestio de Centauris', 'Best is Water', the stories where Levi effectively predicted a future of virtual reality such as 'Retirement Package', 'Order at a Good Price', which talks about cloning, or again 'The Synthetics', where the same topic took on a different form.

Levi experimented with different narrative techniques in nearly every story. In some, science accompanied myth ('The Sixth Day'); in others, mythological themes transformed the story into an archaic utopia ('Quaestio de Centauris'); in others again, fantastic creatures generated fantastic narratives ('Censorship in Bitinia'). Topics related to Levi's experience in Nazi concentrations camps were thus extended beyond the traditional framework of witness narratives or memoirs and transformed into scientific fantasies ('Angelic Butterfly' and 'Versamine'). There are still other stories that the linguist Stefano Bartezzaghi called 'Cosmicomical' in order to link them to Calvino's short-story collection *Cosmicomics*. In an interview with his Croatian translator, Machiedo, Levi confirmed that Calvino was inspired by his 'biological fantasies' and vice versa.

The biological or organic origins of many of Levi's stories ('Cladonia Rapida', 'Man's Friend', 'Disphylaxis', 'Children of the Wind' and others) was unique in scientific circles, even though the way Levi developed his biological nucleus into a story was predominantly humanistic, or at least, anthropocentric. Race, as a topic, appeared in several of his stories, where the theme of 'disorientation' was one of the narrative tools he adopted, again like Swift. A few other stories, whose prevalent feature was that of a 'joke', in the musical sense of a *scherzo*, did not strictly fit into the category of science fiction. And yet, imagination, or fantasy, did play a role, leading readers to believe there Levi had actually invented the stories, such as in 'Sisters of the Swamp' or 'Our Fine Specifications'.

Levi made two interesting statements regarding science fiction. The first was in an interview with Alfredo Barberis in the daily, *Corriere della Sera*, on 27 April 1972, where he claimed he chose science fiction after he realized he had exhausted his function as a writer of witness narratives:

> When my function as a witness was exhausted, I realized I could no longer insist on writing autobiography. At the same time, however, I realized I was too 'marked' to be able to write orthodox science fiction. I therefore thought that a certain type of science fiction might satisfy my desire to express myself, a desire I still felt, and that it lent itself to a modern form of allegory. Most of the stories in *Natural Histories*, after all, were written before I published *The Truce*.

In the same interview, he claimed that Italians were not keen on science fiction, not because of the 'fiction' part but because of the 'science' part.

The second statement was made in *Conversations* when he claimed that there was no longer a dividing line between science and science fiction, or rather that the line shifted every year. This statement coincided with Levi's abandoning science fiction for fantasy where 'marvellous' or 'magical' elements were prevalent—perhaps temporarily, but we will never know whether this would have been the case. Levi was fascinated in particular by the optical illusions created by mirrors, owing to both their fantastical results and the science behind them.

In the 1960s and 70s, Roberto Vacca—an engineer, technology expert and science-fiction writer—was in close contact with Levi, to the extent that he became a character in one of his stories and was cited in the 1987

Preface to the second edition of *Flaw of Form*. While his book *The Coming Dark Age* influenced Levi considerably, Vacca was also instrumental in the publication of several of Levi's stories in newspapers and magazines and had advised Levi early on to publish them in a collection before *The Truce* came out, promising to present them himself to the Milan-based publisher Rizzoli.

Hybrid

Levi spoke of himself as a hybrid, a centaur, a cross between different parts. 'I believe,' he said, 'that my deep destiny (my planet, as don Abbondio would say, is to be a hybrid, to be split: Italian but Jewish, a chemist but a writer, a deportee, but not so much (or not always) disposed towards lamenting and complaint' (*Conversations*). His intellectual formation was also hybrid in his view: 'I have had hybrid inputs' (*The Search for Roots*).

The theme of blending or mixing is present throughout Levi's work, but is most evident in his moral and intellectual autobiography, *The Periodic Table*, where the word 'hybrid' is linked to the word 'impurity'. The system of hybridism also guided Levi-as-narrator's friendships and relationships, to the extent that one could speak of hybrid couples: Alberto and Primo in *If This Is a Man*; Cesare and Primo in *The Truce*; Emilio and Primo in *The Periodic Table*. Each of these characters was the opposite—in terms of character as well as behaviour—of the narrator.

Explaining his attraction for opposites in his work and in his reading, Levi wrote in the Preface to his personal anthology *The Search for Roots*: 'As a chemist, expert in the affinities among elements, I find myself lost when dealing with affinities among individuals. In this sphere everything is possible. Think, for example, of those improbable but long-lasting marriages, or of some unequal friendships that are so fertile' (Preface, *The Search for Roots*).

Linguistic hybridism was another vital aspect of Levi's writing, as Vincenzo Mangaldo has pointed out. There was hybridism when he explored the Jewish Piedmontese dialect of his ancestors in 'Argon' (*The Periodic Table*) as well as the Piedmontese-Italian adopted in *The Wrench*, but also in his use of technical terms throughout his work. The roots of this hybridism can be found in Levi's anthropological approach to his experience of the Lager, where he saw the dual nature of human beings: rational but bestial. Strange hybrid creatures inhabit the animal world: a woman-swan, an insect-man or a fish-man, a mammal-human, an anti-dog, a ladybird-person, a man-beast, a man-bird (all these appear in Levi's work). In Levi's approach, applying animal behaviourism to human beings, there was no such thing as a monster. The Lager Commanders were not monsters, as becomes clear in *The Drowned and the Saved* and in his Introduction to Rudolf Höss's *Commander at Auschwitz*. Levi was well aware that humans were animals, just a little more evolved than them. He oscillated between serene pessimism and extreme pessimism about mankind, a result, perhaps, of his hybrid nature.

Scientific American

In November 1961, Calvino happened to read the stories that would later make up the collection *Natural Histories* because he was an editor at Einaudi. He wrote to Levi, stating that his approach was similar to the French biologist Jean Rostand's. The book Calvino was referring to was *Artificial Man*, published in 1959 by Einaudi. Claudio Milanini, writing about the sources of inspiration for Calvino's *Cosmicomics* in his book *Cosmicomic Chronology*, claimed that Rostand's book was an important influence in Calvino's stories. Calvino wrote to Levi that his biological fantasies and Rostand's book both have a strong intellectual and poetic suggestion.

The new narrative style Calvino launched in the 1960s had many different sources, including a conference Calvino attended in 1962 held by the philosopher and scientist Giorgio de Santillana (*Ancient Fate, Modern Fate*). Twenty-three years after the conference, Calvino wrote that de Santillana had inspired in him 'the idea of knowledge where the world of modern science and that of ancient wisdom reunite'. This idea of reuniting modern and ancient knowledge was also present in the typescript of Levi's stories that Calvino was given to read. There were contemporary scientific notions mixed with classical mythology, as well as a blend of recent readings and reminiscences from as far back as his high-school studies. Claudio Milanini, after reading a comment by Silvia Mezzanzani, identified entries in the *Encyclopaedia Britannica*, (such as 'Cosmogony') and in the *Encyclopédie de la Pléiade*, edited by Raymond Queneau, as well as a series of books translated, or being translated by Einaudi, as the main sources of inspiration that Calvino acknowledged briefly at the beginning of each story in *Cosmicomics*. All of these sources were texts that Levi may well have read in the same years. Both writers at the time were faithful readers of *Le Scienze*, the Italian edition of *Scientific American*.

Reading the stories in *Cosmicomics* and those in *Natural Histories* in parallel, there are evident points in common, such as their shared passion for science and exploration. There are, however, significant differences too. Calvino was more bound by the images evoked by the scientific texts, while Levi focused on the scientific facts which he then elaborated in a semi-serious or parodying key. Levi behaved more like a scientist and technician and less like a visionary than Calvino. This is not to say that Levi lacked imagination. His *Natural Histories*, as well as the stories collected in *Flaw of Form*, however, re-elaborated the scientific data in a manner that was coherent with their source. This may be why Levi kept his source of inspiration more hidden than Calvino, who acknowledged them as citations at the beginning of each story.

Enrico Mattioda has inspected the issues of *Scientific American* from 1966 to 1983, that is after Calvino would have read Levi's typescript, in order to identify which articles correspond to which of Levi's stories, especially those collected in *Flaw of Form*, written between 1969 and 1971 (Mattioda 2011). Mattioda's research reveals a great deal. One article, for example, '*The Origins of Feedback Control*', by Otto Mayr, published in 1970, inspired several pieces by Levi, such as 'The Molecule's Defiance' and 'Passing Walls'. Another, by Marvin Minsky, the father of artificial intelligence, together with a further, more technical, article by John Pierce (both published in 1966) may have inspired one of Levi's most futuristic works, 'Al Fine di Bene', where the idea of a Network—the future Internet—was put forward. The closest parallel was between the stories 'Recuenco: The

Nourisher' and 'Recuenco: The Rafter', two mysterious science-fiction tales that correspond to a piece by N. W. Pirie published in February 1967. In the stories, Levi talked about an invention of a highly nutrient low-cost synthetic food in order to solve the problem of hunger in the developing world. The food was dispensed from the Rafter, a spaceship invented by Levi.

There was one field in particular where the articles in *Scientific American* influenced Levi's work, and that was the field of visual perception and 'optical illusions'. Mattioda compared several of these articles with a strange drawing by Levi that appeared in 'The Beast in the Temple' (*Lilith and Other Stories*). The drawing was an example of an optical illusions: two columns, with a landscape behind them where birds are flying in a cloudy sky, and a parapet at the bottom of the picture. If you look at the columns, or at the landscape, you are unsure where the parapet or the birds are. The trick lies in the ambiguous drawing of the columns, which trick the eye in the style of Escher.

A famous article by Richard Gregory called 'Visual Illusions' was published in *Scientific American* in 1968, while the publisher Il Saggiatore had already published *The Eye and the Brain: The Psychology of Vision* in 1966 in the series 'The Universe of Knowledge', with one of the famous optical illusions discussed in the book on the jacket cover. It is very likely that Levi had come across this book, where Gregory discussed 'impossible figures', which had previously been presented in 1960 by the art historian Ernst Gombrich in his *Art and Illusion*, later published by Einaudi in 1965, with Fraser's Spiral on the cover. There are other articles that Mattioda identified as having influenced Levi: Fred Attneave (1971) and Irvin Rock (1974) on visual disorientation, as well as Marianne L. Teuber's 1974 article, 'Sources of Ambiguity in the Prints of Maurits C. Escher'.

References to Escher form another link with Calvino's writing. Levi had proposed Escher etchings for the covers of both *Flaw of Form* (1971) and *The Periodic Table* (1975). Calvino's *Cosmicomics*, published by Einaudi in 1965, had Escher's 1947 woodcut, *Another World* (in the Hague's Gemeentemuseum), on its cover. In the image, the visual paradox of the open archways on each side of the cubic architectural structure is taken to an extreme, with stupefying artistic elegance. The metallic sculpture of a bird with a face that is suspended between being humanoid and extra-terrestrial, could be interpreted as a representation of the proteo-protag-onist and narrative voice of the stories. The woodcut was included in Gombrich's book in the section on the 'Ambiguity of the Third Dimension'. It is highly likely that either Calvino, or Giulio Bollati, head of Einaudi design, saw the image there while it was being prepared for publication as the two books came out in the same year.

Mattioda identified the source of the drawing included in *Lilith* as being the French mathematician, René Thom rather than *Scientific American*. The author of *Theory of Catastrophes* became well-known in Italy in the 1980s after Einaudi published his most important work, *Structural Stability and Morphogenesis*. However, Calvino had lived in France and come across Thom's work owing to the intense cultural debate on the mathematician's theories that had raged there in the 1970s, influencing his stories with Palomar as their protagonist which were first published in newspapers and magazines over that same period. An article by E. C. Zeeman on 'Catastrophe Theory was published in *Scientific American* in 1976, which Mattioda surmises was a source for some of the psychological and perspective themes in Levi's work.

In a letter published in the 1987 reprint of *Flaw of Form*, Levi acknowl-edged his debt to *Scientific American*. In his personal anthology, *Flaw of Form*, Levi even included an article by Kip S. Thorne, 'The Search for Black Holes', originally published in the magazine in 1974 and included in the Italian issue a year later. Similarly, he cited an article from the same pub-lication about polyaqua, ('viscous and toxic, similar to what I anticipated'), which he claimed he read a year after writing the short story, 'Best is Water'. Mattioda pointed out that the article in fact preceded the story, as they were published in the US edition of the magazine in 1970, a year before *Flaw of Form* came out. There were three articles on the same sub-ject that year, which may have sown the seed for Levi's story.

What was the real extent of the influence on Levi of these scientific articles? Was Levi's imagination fired up by them? There is no doubt that the articles were primary sources for his stories. From the crude primary material, Levi refined his plots along para-scientific lines in order to give plausibility to his creations. As a backdrop to this process, of course, there was Levi's personality, propulsions and personal curiosity, his scientific training and humanistic culture and his experience both in the Lager and at the Silva plant. All these elements were grafted together, creating a hybrid. Levi's fantasy, however, unlike Calvino's, was not necessarily triggered by images. It may have sprung from, or produced images, but Calvino's short introductory phrases introducing his stories in *Cosmicomics* clearly indicate that images were the direct source of his fiction. Calvino similarly stated that the heraldic trilogy *Our Ancestors* was inspired by cinema, art, and, above all, comics (see 'Visibility in American Lessons'). Images do not play the same role in Levi's work. His fiction has been called 'punctiform'; that is, it was triggered and constructed on the basis of a point of intuition that could be called linguistic rather than visual because sounds, words or phrases were what left an impression on his mind and set him off on a story. Levi said that sounds would catch in his brain, forming the substratum of his memory, and that was why the phrases he learnt by heart in the Lager came back to him verbatim years later.

This does not mean that Levi's visual memory was not important, or meaningful. His memory for details was impressive, as one can verify in his Lager memoirs, from *If This Is a Man* to his last stories, and even in the least visual of his books, *The Periodic Table*. Levi built up his fiction from an intuition, developing the story as if he were in a magnetic field that slowly reveals itself. The construction was methodical, building up the story step by step, without Calvino's flights of fancy, as evidenced in *Cosmicomics*. His method was more like a game of chess, where what really counted were the moves that created the pattern of the story and the relationship between the various parts, the details that lead to further details and that ultimately weave together to thicken the plot of the story. In this sense, Levi's fiction is closer to Nabokov's. Nabokov was trained as a scientist, had a passion for insects, especially butterflies, and word games; he also loved poetry and the close reading required by a translation. The comparison should not be taken much further, given the marked difference between the two writers, but they share *forma mentis* in the way a story is generated.

Having established that *Scientific American* was an important source of ideas for Levi's stories throughout the 1960s and 70s, another possible generator of images and inventions should not be overlooked. That is, the circle of friends that Levi closely cultivated after returning to Turin. There were at least two groups. One, as Alberto Piazza recounted, was a triangle between Levi, Livio Norzi, a mathematician and well-read scientist, and Giorgio Lattes, a designer, who worked at Olivetti. In this group, discussions about science, mathematics, philosophy and politics were frequent. Levi played chess with Norzi—another passion Levi shared with Nabokov—and they enjoyed solving crosswords and other puzzles together. The three men, again in Piazza's account, were truly eccentric, and spent a great deal of time on brain teasers, mental challenges and unusual fantasy or word games: a ludic and intellectual activity in its own right, more common in adolescence than in later age. In Carole Angier's 2004 biography of Levi, *The Double Bond*, she wrote that the trio had invented a secret language, which became the basis for what she described as a 'hermetic friendship'. Piazza, who was to become a well-known geneticist, remembers that the trio often discussed mathematical abstractions and the beauty of formulas.

The other group Levi frequented revolved around Ada and Silvia Ortona, as witnessed in the mysterious short story, 'Psychophant'. Alberto Levi and Giorgio Lattes were part of this group, in addition to Tina Rieser, described by Pavese as being a 'woman with a raspy voice', and her husband Henek. In addition to the ideas that inspired him in *Scientific American*, then, Levi was stimulated by conversation with these friends and undoubtedly assimilated facts and idea from them which he then moulded into his fiction.

Radio

Levi's first piece written for radio was 'Sleeping Beauty in the Refrigerator: A Winter's Tale', recorded in June 1961 and broadcast in November the same year. The radio drama was directed by Marco Visconti, with actors from the Florence state-broadcasting company, RAI, and presented as a 'science-fiction story'. Four years later, in 1965, Massimo Scaglione directed 'The Versifier' with the Turin branch of the same company (broadcast in February 1966). The radio version of 'Angelic Butterfly', directed again by Scaglione and recorded that same year by the same actors, altered the story slightly, evidencing the dialogues. The piece went on air in February 1965. 'Some Applications of the Mimete' was similarly recorded and broadcast in 1965 in a series called 'Humoristic Stories of the Twentieth Century', directed by Scaglione, with two actors playing the narrator and the protagonist, Gilberto. In 1966, 'Versamine' was recorded and broadcast in September, with four actors directed once again by Scaglione.

Levi's short stories were collected that same year under the pseudonym Damiano Malabaila, but critics and reviewers did not catch on to the fact that several of the stories written in the form of dialogues had been written for the radio. One critic, Paolo Milano, writing for the weekly *Espresso*, expressed surprise at how close three stories, 'The Versifier', 'Sleeping Beauty in the Refrigerator: A Winter's Tale' and 'The Sixth Day' were to 'an actual screenplay'. Nor does the dust-jacket blurb of the collected stories mention this feature of the stories. The truth was that Levi had conceived many of his stories as one-act radio or stage plays, perhaps as a response to a commission by RAI in the early 1960s when many writers, including Gadda, Savinio, Patroni Griffi, Manganelli and Pratolini, were called on to produce pieces for radio (Scarlini 1997).

In some cases, Levi adapted existing stories (such as 'The Versifier') for the radio, teasing out the dialogue and theatricality of the original text. In others, he did the opposite. What is almost certain is that many of his radio pieces were originally short fiction, or at least conceived as such ('The Sixth Day'). After publication of his short-story collection, 'The Versifier' was recorded as a radio drama in 1967, directed by Andrea Camilleri and broadcast in November 1967; 'Retirement Package' directed by Gian Domenico Giani, with two actors, recorded and broadcast in 1968; and a later version of 'The Versifier', using a voice synthesizer for the voice of the 'machine' directed by Paolo Cingolani in July 1982, called 'Computer Words: The Versifier'.

In 1968, an interesting experiment in radio was conducted by Carlo Quartucci based on an idea by Levi: 'Intervista Aziendale' (Company

Interview) was recorded in August and broadcast in November. Quartucci was an avant-garde theatre director, active in Turin in the late 1960s where he worked with the Teatro Gruppo and collaborated with several writers from the Gruppo 63. He was co-author of 'Intervista Aziendale', which, as Levi explained in a preface to the text of the play published in a limited edition by Eri, Quadrucci developed on the basis of a 'slender' idea of Levi's. The final product, however, was attributable to the director and the actors alone, who improvised from a minimal script, and the published text was a transcription of a recording of the play, which was submitted to the Premio Italia radio prize. The soundtrack of the radio production was as important as the script, however, as it involved the music of contemporary composers of the calibre of Stockhausen, Kadlec and Berio, which provided the atmosphere and soundscape of modern factory life. Some of the themes covered in the production recall those developed by Levi in *The Wrench*, such as the worker in the towers. The atmosphere, however, was more akin to science fiction, with gimmicks such as a speaking solder-iron. In the play, an interviewer crosses the factory floor asking questions to anyone he meets, from the workers to the chief engineer and CEO. The political debate of the day regarding the alienated condition of factory workers was reflected in the subject matter and dialogue. In the preface to the printed edition, Levi declared he had little to do with the social polemic of the piece, which was 'too strong for the plot'. What Quartucci extracted from Levi's 'slender' idea, which is instantly recognizable in the piece, was a subtle analogy between life in the Lager and life in the factory. Levi later denied this analogy, in particular when he was interviewed after publication of 'The Truce' on the subject of work. Nevertheless, a hint of the analogy resurfaced in *The Drowned and the Saved*.

In 1978, a radio adaptation of *The Truce*, directed by Edmo Fenoglio and written by Levi himself, was broadcast in six episodes from 25 April to 9 May 1978. The radio version highlights the multilingual nature of the book, although it is less agitated and chaotic than the radio version of *If This Is a Man*. In both adaptations, non-professional, mother-tongue actors were selected for the various parts and coordinated by the German actress Eva Herber. In an interview with Giorgina Arian Levi (*The Truce* on Radio, 1978), Levi said: 'Counter-intuitively, radio is extremely subtle. Subtler than television, in fact. It triggers emotions and feelings in the actors through imperceptible channels.'

This and many other statements confirm Levi's sensibility to sound. He was a writer of words rather than of images, and was highly aware of the sound texture of his work, often experimenting with words and language to this end. His attention to sound doubtless derived from his experience in the Lager, with its linguistic babel (such as the carburet tower, the Babel Tower or the many different ways to say 'bread' in *If This Is a Man*). The sounds in the Lager had multiple sources: the work being done, the band playing, the various languages and dialects spoken, the shouts of the Kapos and the SS, the baying of dogs, screams and yells, exclamations and curses, cries of desperation, etc. Radio was thus an appropriate tool for recreating the infernal atmosphere of the place. It is not by chance that, in the stage production, Levi accentuated the auditory aspects over the scenic elements.

In 1988, finally, RAI Radio 3 broadcast an unabridged reading of *The Wrench* with four actors directed by Scaglione. Levi was interviewed on radio repeatedly throughout his life (*Conversations*). Some of these have been transcribed, but they lose the 'viva voce' sonority that was so essential in Levi's work.

Television

The first time Levi appeared on television was in 1958, after Einaudi had issued a reprint of *If This Is a Man* in the 'Saggi' series. The evening news broadcast the ceremony for the Riccione Literary Prize, awarded that year to Levi, without an interview or a direct statement made by the author. After publication of *The Truce*, which won the prestigious Campiello Prize, Levi was interviewed briefly for the main state television channel RAI 1 news. That same year, on 27 September, Levi was interviewed at length in his home in Turin for the most important cultural programme of the week, the Saturday evening 'Approdo'. Levi was filmed sitting at a table repairing a children's toy. The factory where he worked in Settimo also featured. Levi's interviews invariably focused on the ethical aspects of bearing witness. When asked why he had written about the deportation, he answered using an unusual expression: 'I didn't know yet that I was capable of committing the act of writing.'

Three years went by before his face was seen on television again, when Scaglione made a television version of 'The Versifier'. In this interview, Levi spoke about his short stories, but only in relation to his two earlier books. In June 1966, Levi gave another interview. Literary prizes, or radio or television versions of his books were often the occasion for brief interviews, such as the ones he gave in 1967.

It was not until May 1974, after Levi had become better-known as an author, that he began to appear more regularly on television. RAI, broadcast a three-episode adaptation of *If This Is a Man* entitled *The Art of Recounting*. The screenplay was by Anna Amendola and Giorgio Bellardelli, and it was directed by Patrizio Barbaro, who also decided to film Levi on a winter train journey from Milan to Strasbourg to meet Jean Samuel, the character Pikolo in *If This Is a Man*. Trains were used for the Nazi deportations and they therefore lent themselves to portraying the events that took place at the time. The film alternates Levi's memories, quotes from the book read by the author, images of Birkenau and segments devoted to the theme of the 'Drowned', while the landscape rolling by outside the window and the rail tracks themselves are turned into protagonists of the story. The film follows Levi's conversations with Jean Samuel, but also flashes back to his study back home in Turin.

The critic, Frediano Sessi, who has researched Levi's appearances on television, claimed that the directors Barbaro and Claude Lanzmann, who made a later film with Levi called *Shoah*, managed to 'transform the witness into an actor portraying himself' by allowing him to relive his experiences and the things that happened to him in front of the camera. The editors' cuts of the film based on Levi's first book create a sense of speed, with an interplay, as Sessi has pointed out, between past and present.

After this mini-series was broadcast, Levi became a public figure. The television interview gave him far greater fame than his books had ever done at the time. He was in fact known more for his participation in school debates, newspaper articles and the circulation of his works among associations of deportees, trades unions and left-leaning political parties. After the series, Levi became the principal witness of the Nazi deportations in Italy and his fame was constantly on the rise. He was the voice of all deportees, not only of the Jews but also of political prisoners and Italian civilians who had been taken prisoner. This role was helped by his initial choice, expressed in the first lines of *If This Is a Man*, to bear witness not only to the genocide of the Jews but to the Nazi exterminations in general and in particular to the experience of concentration camps.

In 1977, as part of a theatre season broadcast on the second state television channel, RAI 2, Levi adapted three short stories for television: 'Sleeping Beauty in the Refrigerator: A Winter's Tale', 'The Sixth Day' (both from *Natural Histories*) and 'Born on Earth' (adapted from 'The Brokers', in *Flaw of Form*, which had already been adapted for television in 1971 as part of a project that was later abandoned, as Levi stated in several interviews). One of the actors in the adaptations was Franco Nebbia, a cabaret artist who had already appeared in the one-act play 'The Versifier' in Milan. The dialogues in 'The Brokers' give the impression that the story had been commissioned as a radio or television play that was never performed and then written as a short story—the opposite of 'The Versifier' that was written as a short story and then adapted as a play. The television adaptations of Levi's short stories were in fact closely linked to the radio adaptations.

Given Levi's growing notoriety, whenever the subject of the deportation came up on television, he was increasingly called in to comment. On the 30th anniversary of the liberation of Auschwitz, Levi gave an interview for the evening television news. In the same period, Levi appeared countless times in conferences and public speeches, a fact that Levi commented on in the interview. Sessi has observed that Levi was not completely up to date on current historical research. His greatest preoccupation appeared to be the rise of fascism: 'I never tire of going to schools that invite me, or other places, so that I can tell them: watch out! At the end of Fascism there is the Lager.' This statement can be explained by the political climate at the time after the bomb in Piazza Fontana and the rise of neo-Fascism in Italy.

When *The Periodic Table* came out in 1978, it was awarded the Prato Literary Prize. Levi's appearances on television, and the questions asked of him, focus on the topic of Judaism, the Holocaust and the State of Israel. These issues in the late 1970s progressively became the object of heated public debate and private discussions in Italy. Despite his clear success as a literary author in his own right, Levi was first and foremost considered a witness and presented himself as such when he was on air. As he frequently repeated, our task is to remember: there is no rest 'for our generation' he would say in newspaper interviews.

The Wrench came out three years later, and again RAI 2 interviewed Levi, acknowledging that his role as a writer was becoming more important. A television film crew went to Levi's house in May 1979 to interview him on the themes of forgiveness and collective responsibility. After Levi won the most prestigious literary prize, the Strega, Levi's fame was consecrated. In a television interview on the day of the award ceremony, Levi was as humble as ever, surprising spectators. In a documentary on the subject of workers called *With Sweat on My Brow*, directed by Nicola Tranfaglia, and broadcast on the third channel on 22 May 1981, Levi was filmed in the factories, having just retired from the chemical plant where he had worked all his life.

An interesting interview on the life and work of Levi was directed by Bruno Gambarotta as part of the series *Very Important Piedmontese* for the third channel again. The programme was hosted by Claudio Gorlier and Marinella Venegoni and went on air on 21 May 1981. After retirement, Levi was also interviewed on local television, as he had become a full-time writer, contributing assiduously to *La Stampa* with reviews, articles, poems and translations. There were several other brief interviews, but the next important one was after *If Not Now, When?* won the Campiello Prize in September 1982, and the award ceremony was televised.

The most significant television programme Levi participated in was Daniel Toaff and Emanuele Ascarelli's *Return to Auschwitz*, filmed on location during a visit to Auschwitz that Levi made in 1982. The documentary featured on 25 April 1982, as part of the weekly spot dedicated to Jewish questions on Italian state television called *Source of Life*. This was Levi's second return to the concentration camp where he had been held, after the trip he took in 1965 for a commemoration ceremony. The second trip took place in a motor coach with a group of students and teachers from schools in Florence and the Tuscan province. Levi asked the directors not to be interviewed in the camp, but only outside or during the journey. Sessi has commented on the didactic and informative nature of the programme, where Levi as witness prevailed over Levi as writer. Sharp as ever, Levi clarified the relationship between sufferance in the past and remembering today. He used the term 'dislocation' to compare the Holiday Inn where the group was staying to the sheds in the concentration camp. Sessi claimed this interview once again relegated Levi to the limbo of bearing witness, as if he felt having an audience was necessary, when his books had amply demonstrated that he had the stature of a writer.

Levi constantly returned to the problematic nature of the theme of memory in those years, in a spirit of self-criticism, which later found its expression in the book *The Drowned and the Saved*. A 1985 interview with Giorgio Bocca is worthy of note from this period, broadcast on the commercial channel 5. The topic was anti-Fascism, broached by the well-known Italian journalist and former partisan with great fervour. Levi also gave a lecture on chemistry as part of Episode 7 of *University Planet*, directed by Alberto Papuzzi, in September 1984 at the Turin regional headquarters of RAI. He was also invited to participate in Piero Bianucci's science programme, *Journey Inside the Atom*, together with Tullio Regge and Carlo Augusto Viano, revealing a different side of his character. Another particularly interesting interview was recorded for *Focus*, in a segment on the future of humanity hosted by Ennio Mastrostefano entitled *If This Is a Man*, broadcast by RAI 2 on 12 December 1986.

The Drowned and the Saved was published in April 1986 and the book immediately sparked debate on the subject of the 'Grey Zone', an expression many journalists, including Bocca, used inappropriately in Levi's view. Levi often spoke about the fact that ideologies were being watered down, about the younger generations, and the new problems humanity was having to deal with. These were years of insecurity and preoccupation, and Levi launched a proposal when he was live on air to invite scientists to abstain from any future activity that would jeopardize the human race, such as research into nervine gas. Despite this climate of distrust, Levi appeared optimistic about democracy, which he no longer saw as an abstract value but as a technique for governing the people that could be improved in order to be closer to an ideal of true social justice: 'my opinion is that some ideologies have lost their force, while—if you can call democracy an ideology—I still believe in it [. . .] because I cannot represent myself, and I can't imagine a better system than this' (*Conversations*).

Cinema

Films cited by Levi include Marcel Carné's *Il Porto delle Nebbie* in his story 'Phosphorous' (*The Periodic Table*), 'Papillon' and 'I am a Fugitive from a Chain Gang' in *The Drowned and the Saved*. In the chapter 'Vacation' (*The Truce*) the projection of three films are mentioned: an old Austrian film on the First World War, a Soviet war film and a 1930s American film, *Hurricane*. Levi provided a summary, an evaluation of the aesthetics of the film and the audience's reaction in each case, for *Hurricane* occupying four pages of the book.

Levi's passion for the film genre transpired clearly in his summaries, as did his familiarity with movies, at least in the role of spectator, where he was anything but passive. Levi wrote three articles inspired by films he had seen: 'Movies and Swastikas' (*La Stampa*, 1977), on Liliana Cavani's *Night Porter*; 'Close Encounters with Astuteness' (*La Stampa*, 1978, an open letter to Mario Soldati on Steven Spielberg's *Close Encounters of a Third Kind*); and 'Our First Ancestors Weren't Animals' (*La Stampa*, 1982, on Jean-Jacques Annaud's *The War of Fire*) (*Uncollected Stories and Essays*). All three were critical reviews, in Levi's polite and precise style. In the first, Levi decidedly rejected the interpretation of the relationship between victim and perpetrator portrayed in Cavani's film. Levi returned to this subject in various interviews, including one with Risa Sodi, *Interview with Primo Levi*, in which he called Calvani's film 'beautiful and false', as well as in *The Drowned and the Saved*. The other two articles developed themes he was interested in. In *The War of Fire*, for example, he criticized the way early man was represented in the film, in particular their gesticulations.

There was also a review of the television series *Holocaust* based on Gerald Green's bestseller ('A Holocaust That Still Weighs on the World's

Conscience', April 1979, *Tuttolibri, La Stampa*). Levi accepted writing the introduction to the picture-book of the film, published by the magazine *Radiocorriere TV* in May 1979, and commented on the film on the first page of *La Stampa* ('So That Yesterday's Holocausts Will Never Return', 1979). Levi's opinion of the film was divided. On one hand, he criticized the historical errors and the imprecisions contained in the series; on the other, he praised the fact that the topic was being discussed in Europe, especially in Germany. In his leading article in *La Stampa*, however, his critique was more nuanced. The article was not so much about the film, which catered to an American commercial audience, as of the general problem of reactions to the re-evocation of the Jewish genocide.

In the text introducing the series in Italy, Levi commented on the 'sado-pornographic' elements in the series. As Scarlini observed, 'once again, there is a continuous and precise attention towards the dynamics of theatrical representation' (1997). In a long interview with Milva Spadi, Levi critiqued another film for the same reason: Pasolini's *Salò* or the *120 Days of Sodom*.

Flaw of Form

The short-story collection printed in the Einaudi 'Coralli' series (n.270) had Levi's own name on the cover, with an Allen Jones *Double Take* as a dust-jacket illustration: a black-and-white checkerboard against a pink backdrop with two abstract figures in the foreground. The jacket copy—probably written by the author, or at least inspired or revised by him—mused on general topics of the time rather than the collection itself.

> Will there be historians in the future—even, let's say, in the next century? It's not at all certain: mankind may have lost any interest in the past, preoccupied as it will surely be in sorting out the tangle of the future; or it may have lost the taste for works of the spirit in general, being focused uniquely on survival; or it may have ceased to exist. But, if there are historians, they will not devote much time to the Punic Wars, or the Crusades, or Waterloo, but will instead concentrate on this twentieth century, and, more specifically, the decade that has just begun. It will be a unique decade. In the space of a few years, almost overnight, we've realized that something conclusive has happened, or is about to happen: like someone who, navigating on a calm river, suddenly observes that the banks are retreating backward, the water teeming with whirlpools, and hears the thunder of waterfalls close by. There is no indicator that is not soaring upward: the world population, DDT in the fat of penguins, carbon dioxide in the atmosphere, lead in our veins.

While half the world is still waiting for the benefits of technology, the other half has touched lunar soil and is poisoned by the garbage that has accumulated in a decade: but there is no choice, we cannot return to Arcadia; by technology, and by that alone, can the planetary order be restored, the 'flaw of form' repaired. Before the urgency of these problems, the political questions pale. This is the climate in which, literally or in spirit, the twenty stories by Primo Levi presented here take place. Beyond the veil of irony, it is close to that of his preceding books: we breathe an air of sadness but not hopelessness, of distrust in the present and, at the same time, considerable confidence in the future: man, the maker of himself, inventor and unique possessor of reason, will be able to stop in time on his path 'heading west' (p. 2844).

Two editions came out in 1971, with a total of 15,000 copies printed, but the book was not reprinted for several years after that. After winning several literary prizes and becoming better known in Italy and abroad, Levi's popularity grew in Italy. In 1987, Einaudi thus decided to publish the collection in its 'Nuovi Coralli' series (n.386), with a new run in 1988 for a total of 12,000 copies. In 1996, after Levi's death, all the stories from *Natural Histories, Flaw of Form* and *Lilith and Other Stories* were republished in one book in the 'Einaudi Tascabile' series (n.374) with an introduction by Ernesto Ferrero. The run was for 10,000 copies.

There is no typescript for the stories contained in *Flaw of Form* in the Einaudi archive. Unlike the stories in *Natural Histories*, only one of the stories in this collection had previously been published. This was 'Observed from a Distance', which had been included in an anthology called *Italian Short Stories* published in 1968 by the highly popular *Reader's Digest*. This inclusion of one of Levi's short stories in a popular publication of this calibre shows that Levi was already considered an important Italian author at the time, despite the fact that Italian critics and professional newspaper reviewers continued to either ignore or snub him.

LEMMAS

Games

Levi had an almost infantile predilection for games, which he wrote about in an article called 'Children's Internationale', later included in *Other People's Trades* and *Inventing an Animal*. He loved puzzles, anagrams, acrostics and palindromes, about which he wrote essays and stories. He peppered his works with language games (false etymologies, popular etymologies, polyglot chains) as well as literary games, his examples being Rabelais, Borges, Queneau and Wilcock. He also played board games, including chess, later in life against the computer. Levi's poetry was often a catalogue of games and how to play games (such as the use of rhyme in *The Periodic Table*, where chemistry is interpreted as a game that combines given elements).

Levi's love of games would appear to be in contrast with the serious or heavy subjects of his prose, especially of his witness literature. And yet Levi's sense of humour always revealed itself in these works, in his irrepressible pleasure in puns and plays on words, and in his citations. The marked intertextuality in his work is another sign: his citations may be explicit or arcane, they may be of other authors—the game of titles in London, for example (*The Wrench*)—or they may be from his own works.

In his 'catalogue raisonné of the different games in Levi's opus, Stefano Bartezzaghi suggested that language games were top of the list (*Cosmicomiche*, 1997). Reading Levi's opus with this in mind, one could say that he was an inventive writer with an apparently clear and simple style that was actually built on a coplanar system of cross-references, which a linguistically and culturally agile reader would be able to pick up and appreciate. The system also relied on foreign languages, dialects and sectorial jargons, which created a hybrid, blended language that never betrayed the simplicity of style but, rather, wove its linguistic thread invisibly through the weft of the story.

Language games were the basis of the story 'Dizzying Heat' (*Lilith and Other Stories*) which used numerous palindromes showing an unusual talent for the form. As Bartezzaghi has commented, reversibility is connected to time—being able to measure the present and predict the future.

Invention

Bartezzaghi commented that Levi's work was an 'articulated treatise on invention'. There were technological, literary and linguistic inventions, as well as inventions from the natural world (animals, objects, substances, names, etc.) Creating was the opposite of finding, while inventing seemed to offer something that was less complex in between. In 'The Sixth Day' (*Natural Histories*), the creative activity of the gods is described comically, as a parody, which required a high level of inventiveness.

Levi did not deny creativity but felt that the creative process was only a part of the productive process (see the ironic story 'Creative Work' in *Flaw of Form*, and 'The Fugitive' in *Lilith and Other Stories*). Creation, in his view, was subject to stochastic rules and could not be reproduced. He did not reject creativity, just as he did not exclude the possibility of miraculous events taking place in a scientific environment. That is, he did not deny the existence of natural, or artificial, processes whose causes or workings are unknown and could therefore never be the object of manipulation. Levi provided three examples of this in the article 'Reproducing Miracles', in *Stories and Essays* where he criticized the theory of miracles.

Levi thought that artistic creativity existed but that it should never be relied on. Like Calvino, Levi tended to think that creation was a subset of invention, a short-cut that avoided the intermediate passages: 'if it works, it works' (Calvino 1985). Innovation, to Levi's mind, was never the result of teamwork, but only of an individual, as he explained in an article on the Nobel Prize winner Salvador Luria ('Bacteria Roulette' in *Stories and Essays*) where he stressed the random nature of scientific discovery. Without the mind of an individual, who is able to grasp the leap forward of the discovery, there can be no invention: 'often all you need is the intuition of a moment to solve a centuries-old problem that powerful minds have been worn out attempting to solve.' Levi had a similar view of literary activity, which he considered very close to scientific activity. Results might vary from one to a hundred according to timing and context, and there were no precise rules in either.

What Levi rejected outright was the idea that inspiration could explain the success of a literary work. In his view, what we call inspiration was simply that which we cannot explain. If the timing and the context of an experiment are not predictable, however, 'one can prepare spiritually and physically in order to be predisposed towards making an invention,' as Ghersi's *New Industrial Recipe Book* taught us, Levi once said with his usual irony (*Conversations*). Similarly, Levi once described narrative invention as a flight where one never touches ground ('Writing a Novel' in *Other People's Trades*).

The relationship between invention and creation in Levi's work cannot be reduced to a mere opposition: it is more complex. Perhaps Levi's greatest literary invention was, as Bartezzaghi put it, 'the invention of himself as a centaur, half-narrator and half-narrated, a victim transmuted, already at the time of the events that took place in Auschwitz, into a witness, with an objectified memory' (1997). Invention does not mean creating something from nothing; it is, in an etymological sense, a discovery of something that already existed: a discovery. Levi's *inventio*, a solid rhetorical structure, 'delved into the deposits of his memory and experience, and, at the same time, plummeted the depths of his linguistic and lexical skills' (Bartezzaghi 1997). The real issue for Levi as a writer was thus having something to say.

One of Levi's passions in his writing was to imagine new technological inventions and observe the effect they had on the people who experimented with them. In the short story, 'The Mnemagogs' which Levi wrote in 1947 soon after his return from Auschwitz, the protagonist invented a technique for producing smells which, in their turn, evoked memories. This technique was pretty basic when compared to the Mimete, the machine that was able to fabricate objects that was the focus of two stories from the 1960s, 'Order at a Good Price' and 'Some Applications of the Mimete', published together with 'The Mnemagogs' in *Natural Histories*. One of the characters managed to duplicate his wife with the machine, and ultimately created a replica of himself.

'The Versifier', a story in the form of a dialogue later turned into a radio play, was about a machine for writing verse that a poet had acquired from an insistent salesman so that he could produce poems on commission more efficiently. Levi's stories about technical inventions often included the figure of a salesman. A typical example was Mr Simpson, an employee of the American company Natca. In *The Periodic Table*, there is a detailed description of the sales techniques employed by these characters which is almost a study of *Homo commercialis*.

Another machine, or technological invention, was described in the story 'Sleeping Beauty in the Refrigerator: A Winter's Tale' (*Natural Histories*). A beautiful young girl was placed under hibernation by a German inventor and then defrosted by her heirs at fixed intervals. In the opposition between heat and cold was an allusion to the girl's erotic value, a 'treasure' held hostage by the family that owned her. At the end of the story, she escaped with the help of a young man who was in love with her, relinquishing her eternal youth but finally freeing herself of her technological prison.

Nearly all the stories in *Natural Histories* focused on inventions that alter the behaviour of those who use them in one way or another. Five of these stories made up a mini-cycle devoted to Mr Simpson and Natca inventions, including the Mimete, the Calometer measuring beauty, the Minibrain, forcing insects to perform preset tasks, the VIP-Scan, and—more surprising still—the Torec, or Total Recorder, a virtual-reality helmet that recreated everything from the flight of an eagle to a football game, experiences under extreme conditions or an amorous encounter. The helmet functioned with a pre-recorded tape. Some reproduced experiences recorded from reality: the blue band indicating artistic experiences, sacrifice, life-saving, among other things; the yellow band recreating mystic and religious experience. Others, and in particular tapes with a black band, were experiences created *ex novo*, synthesizing images, sensations and sounds in the same way as music is mixed by a sound engineer.

'Retirement Package', published in 1966 and included in *Natural Histories*, predicted what was to become virtual reality, as the critic Elémire Zolla noted in an article in *Corriere della Sera* on 1 June 1993, entitled 'The Miracle of Primo Levi: Prophet of Virtual Reality'. In the story, the author also reflected on the ethics and legitimacy of experiencing virtual reality, while throwing in several troubling observations with the apparent nonchalance he adopted in almost all of his science fiction stories.

Flaw of Form, Levi's second collection of short stories published in 1971, also featured a few technological inventions. These included, among others, the protective shell in 'Protection', the reference to genetic manipulation in 'The Synthetics', and the device regulating sexual activity in 'Red Lights'. Two inventions in particular stand out. The first was the Knall, in the story by the same name, a toy which had the power to kill at close range that became a craze, electrifying a population stultified by technology with clandestine duels in public places. The second, again giving the title to the story, was the Psychophant, a creation that was able to diagnose the personality of whoever placed their hands on it by materializing objects reflecting their inner desires (a subtle allusion to psychoanalysis, and a parody of parlour games). The story 'With the Best Intentions' also predicted the future, imagining a single 'Network' that superseded the telephone exchange, and behaved as if it had a mind of its own, to the extent that its creators had no power over what it did.

Levi's passion for technical inventions stemmed from his interest in science and technology, but also from his idea of science fiction: real facts that he developed with a hefty dose of irony by imagining the effects on the behaviour of individuals.

Creation/Evolution

In the story, 'The Sixth Day' (*Natural Histories*), the story of the creation of mankind was cast as being the work of a team of divine experts seated around a boardroom table in a pseudo-company. These minor divinities, each specializing in a different discipline (anatomy, economics, psychology, water, thermodynamics, chemistry and mechanics), discussed what form, and which special features, to endow humans with. Levi humorously wove do-it-yourself techniques, creation theory and Darwinian evolution into the act of creation. At the end of the story, the news that the supreme god had acted on his own and created man from clay reached the boardroom: the Bible had won over science. Aside from the literary *divertissement* in this story, Levi was clearly interested in the question of the origins of life. As a technician, he rejected the label of 'scientist'. He firmly believed that creative activity was actually composition, or bricolage, from a given number of elements and according to precise laws. Invention prevailed over creation. The theme of creation was also important in the Jewish myth of the Golem, linked to the ancient Jewish tradition of the Kabbalah, which Levi used in his Mittel-European inspired story 'The Servant' (*Flaw of Form*). The Old Testament version of the creation was resolved by Levi in a letter cipher: 'magic' being itself a combination.

In *The Search for Roots*, Darwin figured among Levi's favourite authors. He appreciated Darwin's idea that nature was not anthropocentric, although humans possessed the intellectual tools to decipher creation. Levi's comments on the passage he chose to include in his personal anthology made this very clear:

> Darwin's work is filled with a deeply serious religiousness, the sober joy of a man who extracts order from chaos, who rejoices at the mysterious parallels between his own reason and the universe, and who sees in the universe a great design. [. . .] By denying a position of privilege for mankind in the act of creation, his intellectual courage has reinstated the dignity of all men.

Curiously, many of Levi's stories would appear to pay homage to Lamarck's theories rather than to Darwin's. The theory of acquired characteristics brought about through adaptation to the environment being passed down to the offspring, perhaps, was a more effective narrative springboard (offering, for example, the possibility for comedy) than undiluted Darwinism.

PORTRAIT OF A CHEMIST (1952)

This photo was taken at the SIVA factory where Levi was working in 1952. Next to Levi, there is Giovanna Balzaretti, a fellow chemist he met at university in the 1930s. Levi's biographer, Carole Angier, wrote that Gianna (as Levi called her) had been called by Levi to work in the varnish factory when he first started there. He had met her by chance on the tram in Turin and had been looking for an assistant. Giovanna was well-qualified for the job, with a second degree in pharmacology. Levi must have realized she was an ideal candidate. The two former students from the Turin Chemistry Faculty developed a resin that enjoyed great commercial success: it was called PVF. The striking thing about this image is Levi's posture. His sleeves are rolled up, revealing his arms, including the one with the number tattooed on it in Auschwitz. Giovanna is standing straight next to him, looking elegant in her white lab coat, her hand in a pocket. Levi is looking away from the photographer, and his lab coat looks rumpled, especially compared to Giovanna's. Levi looks sad. This was the time when he was transitioning from writing his early books to building his identity as a professional chemist. They are difficult, but fruitful, years. In other photos taken of Levi at the SIVA factory, he is more relaxed, less posed. In many of the pictures he is smiling, and gesticulating freely. Giovanni Tesio remembers that one of the last times he saw Levi, at the end of 1986, while preparing a long interview for an 'authorized biography', Levi hugged him as he was leaving the house. It was an unusual gesture for Levi, and it struck Tesio.

The Periodic Table

A Book about Chemistry

Levi had probably been thinking about writing a book about chemistry since at least 1963, when he handed in his manuscript of *The Truce* to Einaudi. Winning the Campiello Prize had galvanized him, to the extent that in July 1963 he stated in an interview for the Roman evening daily *Paese Sera*, conducted by Adolfo Chiesa, and to the Einaudi editor Ernesto Ferrero, that 'We know everything about miners, thieves, "ragazzi di vita", and prostitutes, but we know almost nothing about chemists: nobody has ever written about them. And yet the art of the chemist has some fascinating features that deserve to be better known [. . .] I am tempted in fact to write some stories about my profession.'

The idea must have been in his mind for a long time, given that in a 1961 review of a book on chemistry by Fabrizio De Sanctis, published in *Il Ponte*, Levi expressed his enthusiasm for this 'person who is so influential in the technical world of today'. It was hard, however, for Levi to make headway with the project, and it took a long time to materialize. While for his first two books about the Lager experience Levi not only possessed a great deal of material but also, more importantly, a general framework—the Lager itself and the journey home—his book on chemistry and chemists lacked an overarching structure.

Ideally two themes needed to be interwoven in this new project: chemistry, and work. In the mid-1960s, he had not yet conceived how to work these two together. Three years after stating his intention to write about chemists, Levi confessed in an interview that he had tried, unsuccessfully, to write about the issue of work: 'I tried to write some stories about my life in the factory. They're the worst. No, I'll never succeed' (p. 2845). Levi was in a pessimistic vein, as he had not yet found an organizing principle for his stories. In the same interview he added:

> It's the other world that is realized in my books. The world that includes my experiences as a young man, the racial discrimination, my attempts not to be different from my schoolmates, and then my discovery of the Jewish tradition (Judaism as opposed to fascism, as freedom is to terror, because I also discovered that many principles of freedom are found within the substance of the purest Jewish tradition), and the partisan war, and, finally, the Lager and having written about this monstrous distortion of what is human (Fadini 1996, partially cited in *Notes on the Texts*, p. 2845).

Levi was attempting to explain to his interviewer the split between all his various identities (chemist and writer, Italian and Jew, witness and author) and why *Natural Histories* had represented a kind of vacation from his writing about the Lager experience.

When one reads these interviews today, it feels as if Levi had already found the key to how to write his new book, but this was not the case. For one thing, there was a superimposition—almost an interference—between his desire to write about chemistry and his more general concern with the issue of work. He was only able to separate the two themes at a later stage, when he opted for writing one book of stories predominantly about chemistry and another (*The Wrench*) mainly about work, while maintaining elements of both in each.

As time passed, in fact, he began to think about how he could write about his life as a chemist, and about the profession that had sustained, challenged and satisfied him since 1946. That his autobiography would become the central theme of *The Periodic Table* had not yet become apparent, but little by little his autobiography was beginning to emerge as a unifying principle. Considering how methodical Levi was in his writing, it is always surprising to discover just how sudden and unexpected were his illuminations regarding the underlying pattern of his work. Since he was first and foremost a writer of short stories, his work was constructed piece by piece, without necessarily having in mind a framework. It is very likely that in this case too Levi had a 'eureka moment', like those 'points of intuitions' he described as inspiration for *Natural Histories*.

In order to trace the genesis of *The Periodic Table*, however, it is necessary to take a step back. This is all the more important given that *The Periodic Table* was a turning point in Levi's literary career, accrediting him for the first time as a successful fiction writer, both in the eyes of the public and his own. It was no chance that in 1976, after *The Periodic Table* came out, Levi was finally able to retire from his job at the Silva chemical factory in Settimo Torinese, as he had told his German translator he had wished to do since the 1960s (although he went on consulting for the company until 1978).

Levi began to feel more optimistic about his writing in 1963, owing to a temporary reprieve in his work as a writer of witness narratives. After winning the Campiello Prize, Levi told the journalist Enzo Fabiani that he was done with writing about the Lager experience: 'I've said everything there is to say.' When asked whether he would go on writing, Levi answered:

> Yes, because I have more fun writing than I do being a chemist. However, there is another aspiration to be cultivated in secret. That is, to find a point where the two worlds meet, and convey to readers the significance of scientific research. There are numerous fascinating sources, but not much is ever written about what goes on inside a lab. It would be no less than reproducing in a modern form the earliest, most mysterious, emotions of mankind: that moment of uncertainty, whether or not you kill the buffalo, whether or not you find what you are seeking. There's a whole narrative tradition built on things that

happen to doctors or factory workers, but there is nothing about the spiritual adventures of a chemist (Fabiani 1963).

Levi had not yet realized that the chemist he would be writing about was himself. Perhaps he had, but he still needed to take another step and find the organizing principle for the pieces of the mosaic. He would only find the framework once he realized that the pieces were as autobiographical as the chapters that made up *If This Is a Man* and *The Truce*, and that the narrative voice was the same: Primo Levi himself. This time, it was Levi the chemist not Levi the deportee speaking, although his 'secret companion' as he later called him, would always be there and would never leave his side. Back in 1963, Levi may still have had in mind an epic narrative, as in the story 'Bear Meat' that Calvino in his 1961 letter to Levi considered only partially successful ('the attempt at a Conradian mountain-climbing epic appeals to all my sympathies, but for now it remains an intention', p. 2846). Thus, the idea for *The Periodic Table* did not really begin to take shape until 1966–1968.

A letter to his Croatian translator, Mladen Machiedo, who wrote to ask him what he was working on at the time, confirmed this hypothesis. Levi answered that he was writing his fourth book, and this was not *Flaw of Form* (which would come out three years later, in 1971) but another project:

> I have started. It is going to be a book about my experience as a chemist. Aside from this, I have little else to say. The first story describes my youthful love for chemistry, or rather for alchemy: chemistry feels too obvious, unveiled, lacking in mystery. [...] I've also written a story about the atom. In general people find it boring, while chemists love it, which is not a good sign in itself. All scientists one way or another have had adventures, even if they have never discovered anything. It's like hunting. You go hunting, shoot at something, and either you kill the animal, or it runs away, or maybe the animal kills you (Machiedo 1969).

The hunting metaphor may have had the function of deflecting evil as Levi often used it when talking about *The Periodic Table*, but it also conveys the epic, adventurous quality he deeply desired for his new book. Two stories can easily be identified in his letter to Machiedo. One is 'Carbon', which he later said he had first conceived in prison in Aosta after he had been captured by the Fascist militia, but which was dated 1970 in the typescript he presented to Einaudi. The other was most probably 'Hydrogen', the second story in the collection that initiated the autobiographical account.

It was in 1968 that Levi accepted that one aspect of the book's organizing principle would be autobiography. It is hard to say whether he had already identified Mendeleev's Periodic Table as the other. The fact that he had already written some of the stories did not mean he already knew how the book would pan out. In a 1971 letter to Piero Bianucci answering some of his questions, Levi wrote: 'As far as my work today as a fiction writer is concerned, at the moment it is reduced to very little, almost nothing. I'm thinking about finding a link, a contamination if you will, between my two different activities (as a chemist and as a writer). For now, though, the meagre result is about twenty pages at the bottom of my drawer which are waiting for better times.' What did Levi mean by 'contamination'? He was perhaps looking for a way to transform his work as a chemist into a work of fiction. It was the right thing to do, since, after the deportation, it was the next best stock of stories he had at his disposal. *The Periodic Table* provided precisely this opportunity for contamination, making the book—as Calvino saw it—also about 'the experience of the writer'.

It is likely that the 'twenty pages at the bottom of the drawer' were the two stories Levi wrote to his Croatian translator about, in addition to some other material. The typescript handed in to Einaudi dated the last draft of most of the chapters between 1973 and 1974, which means that Levi had finally found an organizing principle and the book was put together in under two years. Levi incorporated into his project two older stories about work that he had kept in his drawer: 'Maria and the Circle', first published in the socialist daily *L'Italia Socialista* on 19 September 1948, which became 'Titanium'; and 'Night Shift', published by the Turin edition of the communist daily *l'Unità* on 31 August 1950, which became 'Sulfur'. 'Sulfur' may well be the story Levi was alluding to when he said to Fadini that he had never been successful in writing about factory life; nonetheless he decided to recycle it once he had established that the periodic table of chemical elements would be the narrative key of his book. He had to change the element, however, from Bicarbonate to Sulphur, showing once again the extent to which Levi was prepared to re-cycle his work and never waste anything.

Another story, 'Cerium', whose date of composition is unknown, was almost definitely recycled from an earlier idea, as testified in a note to himself in the typescript of the 1958 edition of *If This Is a Man*. In a presentation of *The Periodic Table* in 1975, Levi said:

> I did not put that episode in *If This Is a Man* so as not to con-taminate it, because the episode is cheerful. Cheerful [. . .] well, the background isn't cheerful, but it's the story of a victory, of an audacious and risky undertaking, carried to its con-clusion. And so, it would have been jarring within that other context, which is, rather, a context of defeats, a context of tra-gedies, a dramatic context (p. 2846).

When updating the chapter, 'The Last One' he had added the anec-dote about Alberto's trading, but not the episode of trafficking in 'Cerium'. This would imply that the story had already been sketched out when he was working on *If This Is a Man*.

Once the autobiographical principle had been established, the pieces of the mosaic began to fit together into the second unifying framework, which was the 'Table of Elements'. This happened over 1971 and 1972. Then things began to speed up: the list of possible stories (which Levi had mentioned as early as 1966 in his interview with

Fadini) began to take shape within the framework of his professional life as a chemist before and after his deportation to Monowitz. None of this would have been possible if he had not already written *The Truce* and the stories in *Natural Histories*. The structure of *The Truce*, based on the chronological sequence of Levi's return to Turin, together with the narrative freedom afforded him by the fantasy stories in *Natural Histories* (written at the same time as he was working on his first two works of witness narrative), clearly provided a strong foundation for Levi's new venture. Levi finally felt he was authorized to be a real writer, and that he was allowed to write about the parts of his life that were not linked to the Lager experience. The chemist whose vocation, early experiences and professional activities he wanted to write about was himself. It was not such a huge shift from his previous position—centimetres, millimetres even—but it took him years to get there. Levi was a slow writer, but as soon as he hit upon the right formula—and in this case it was actually formulas he was writing about, chemical formulas—he worked extremely fast. This was all the more necessary as his job afforded him little free time. By 1973, many of the stories that would be included in the book were ready. He had written 10. It would take another year to complete the project and write the stories that were still missing. There followed a painstaking period of editing, as the type-script he handed in to Einaudi shows.

As Scarpa pointed out (2015), in the 1966 interview with Fadini one can recognize 'Argon', 'Zinc', 'Gold' and 'Potassium'. 'Carbon' was published in *Uomini e Libri*, a journal he had links to, in 1972. 'Iron' was an adapted version of the story 'Bear Meat', which he had already shown to Calvino. 'Gold', on the other hand, was published in *Il Mondo* without the first four pages describing his life in Milan, which in the version published in *The Periodic Table* served to link it with 'Potassium'. Levi had finally managed to square the circle by opting for the structure of an autobiography with four interwoven components. The first of these was his being a chemist by profession. Then there were the 1938

Racial Laws that, as he himself pointed out, turned him into a Jew. A third was his personal struggle against Fascism and his own history of political and civic engagement. This, in its turn, became the fourth component: a lens through which to read the history of his native city, Turin, and of Italy in general, over a period of 30 or 40 years. These four components were then distributed according to the overlying scheme of Mendeleev's Periodic Table, a poster of which had been hanging in the lecture hall where he had studied as a student.

When the critic Lorenzo Mondo asked him during a television interview where the title came from, Levi said it was

> that poster hanging in the main lecture hall of the Chemistry Institute representing the Periodic Table discovered by the Russian Chemist, Mendeleev. The chemist had realized that when he ranked elements according to their progressive atomic weight he obtained correspondences that mystified him. He did not understand at the time, but these correspondences have now been explained. He had found an order that had been missing before. As often happens in our profession, things happen and then one sees the pattern. Suddenly. It is just like when you turn a light on: before it is dark and then suddenly there is light. After Mendeleev, it was discovered that matter has an order, it is not disordered. This leads one to suppose that the entire universe is ordered, not disordered. That was why I liked the ambiguous title. It may not mean much to many readers, but I chose it as an ordering principle for my stories' (Poli and Calcagno, 1992).

The epic quality Calvino had written about in his letter in response to the stories in *Natural Histories* had finally found its way into Levi's work. The stories in *The Periodic Table* were low key, everyday epic, not high flying—a style which was perfectly suited to the author's character.

Calvino's Letter and 'Argon'

In 1974, the collection was almost complete. In July that year, Levi wrote to his German friend, Hety Schmitt-Maas, that he was finishing the book, using the summer period to work on what he called his 'chemistry stories'. He also informed her that 'Hydrogen', 'Gold' and 'Arsenic' had been published in magazines, although the only certain publication was 'Gold' in *Il Mondo*. Of the others there is no trace. In November, Calvino—who was *de facto* Levi's editor at Einaudi—received the latest version of the stories and wrote his first impressions in a letter to Levi (Calvino 2000). It would seem from the letter that the stories mentioned there ('Iron', 'Phosphorous', 'Nitrogen', Uranium', 'Silver' and 'Vanadium') had been the most recent, as he calls them 'new stories'. The typescript of the edited version was in fact dated 1974. Calvino had previously received other stories, including the two he mentioned in brackets in his letter ('Lead' and 'Mercury'), which Levi claimed he had written before his deportation. The truth was that he had written them in the 1960s, as he later confessed in an interview with Giovanni Tesio (Levi 2016). It is likely, as in 'Carbon', that the ideas for the story had been initially conceived when he was very young and reworked much later so that they could be included in this collection. They may also have been part of a previous project for a collection that had been planned but never executed, and then recycled in *The Periodic Table* with titles referring to the chemical elements.

Calvino commented that 'Carbon' 'symbolized the experience of the writer', an intuition that Levi appreciated. The story also contained an explicit reference to the writer Raymond Queneau with the term 'micro-story'. This derived from Levi's reading of Queneau, as well as from an original idea conceived while he was in the Lager that he had confided to Pikolo, as Levi recalled in a letter written in the 1940s. Calvino focused in his letter on 'Argon'. He disagreed with the idea of placing the story at the beginning of the collection: 'I still have reservations about the fact that it's at the beginning (in spite of its value as a prologue), because it's the only chapter in which the chemical element is metaphorical' (p. 2848). He initially suggested moving the story to the middle of the book '(For example: return from deportation; finding that the family has survived; reflection on the meaning of family continuity)' but ultimately conceded that the organizing principle of the Periodic Table would be disturbed: 'But if the chapters are in order by atomic weight (with exceptions, I think) I won't say anything else' (p. 2848). And yet, the order of the stories was not necessarily according to atomic weight, since in Mendeleev's Periodic Table the elements follow a stochastic order, on many levels and in various arrangements. Two stories, 'Cerium' and 'Uranium', moreover, were included in the category of the Lanthanides.

In Levi's final typescript he kept 'Argon' at the beginning of the collection, despite Calvino's misgivings. It is uncertain when the story was written. It was probably one of the oldest stories, which underwent many different revisions over the years. An editor told Cavaglion (Cavaglion 1991) that he had received a typed copy of 'Argon' in the early 70s. The story was the result of a great deal of research into the Jewish Piedmontese dialect, and of those lists of words which revealed Levi's passion for linguistic variations; a passion that runs through his work and featured in many of the articles that were then published in *Other People's Trades*. In 1976, after *The Periodic Table* was published, Levi sent the glossary of expressions he had reconstructed with the help of his friends and family to Armand Lunel, an expert in the Jewish Provencal dialect (Cavaglion 2008). Later he told a student that 'Argon'—or at least an outline of the story—had already been written in 1946 (Zargani, 2007). Again, Levi had recycled a previously existing text and incorporated it into his new autobiographical work.

Judging from his additions and corrections to the typescript in Cavaglion's possession, for a total of four pages, it would seem that Levi had transformed what was originally an article, written in order to share his philological musings with a wider public, into a chapter of his autobiography. The last two and a half pages of the story about his father and his paternal grandmother were additions to the earlier typescript. This passage created a natural link to 'My Grandfather's Shop', later included in *Other People's Trades* but first published in *La Stampa* in August, 1984. By the same token, the tone and subject matter of the story 'Guncotton Stockings' (published by *La Stampa* in June 1984, and then collected in *Other People's Trades*) might well have been a chapter in *The Periodic Table*. Both of these pieces may well have already existed as raw material and then been discarded for the book; alternatively, they may have already been conceived as 'narrative ideas' and not written until later. Comparing the typescript to the final published version of the story, the typescript gave a Latin citation next to the title from Ovid's *Tristia* (Quem legis, ut noris, or 'Know who you are reading', IV, 10, 2), which was then cut.

Levi's multiple narrative styles, voices and tones, as well as the centaur-like spirits that coexisted within him, were harmoniously woven together in *The Periodic Table*. They ranged from an essay on linguistics, which resounded with articles in *Other People's Trades*, such as 'Argon', to fantasy stories that recalled those in *Natural Histories* (mostly 'Carbon', but also 'Lead' and 'Mercury'); from stories that anticipated those later collected in *Lilith and Other Stories*, to 'Vanadium', whose story would later be told in *The Drowned and the Saved*. *The Periodic Table* is certainly Levi's most variegated book of stories. At the same time, it is also the most amalgamated, as Calvino had detected. It was a sort of summation of Levi's narrative breadth, transitioning from an epic tone to pure humour, from autobiographical detail to erudite divagation. This extreme, almost bizarre, variegation was successful owing to its construction and composition. Rather than being, as he had originally planned, a book about the 'adventures of chemists', it turned into a book about his adventures as a chemist. It was transformed into an autobiography, almost a memoir, and yet there were continuous shifts in perspective, direction and narrative point of view which eluded the overarching framework of the life of Primo Levi the chemist. The auto-biographical novel made up of stories melded scientific subject matter with themes that were humanistic. Adventures in the profession were seen through the lens of the adventures of a man, in the wider context of his country, Italy, in a troubled period of history. But there were also the adventures of the Jewish people in contemporary history in Europe. It was no doubt his most successful book, which finally turned him into a fully-fledged writer, recognized as such not only by his readers but also by critics. There was also a spike in Levi's foreign—especially American—readership after the book was translated in 1984 and published by Schocken Books with a dust-jacket blurb by Saul Bellow which decreed its instant success: 'After a few pages I immersed myself in *The Periodic Table* gladly and gratefully. There is nothing superfluous here, everything this book contains is essential. It is wonderfully pure' (p. 2798).

THE TYPESCRIPT

The typescript of *The Periodic Table* was preserved in the Einaudi archive (now in the Turin State Archive, Folder n. 1053, File n. 3009). It comprises 195 numbered typed pages as well as two pages labelled 'bis' (double). The chapters are all typed, on different sheets of paper, with strips of typed paper sellotaped onto the previous text where passages had been added. Some of the sheets are photocopies of typed pages. There are numerous revisions, edits and cancellations, showing that Levi continued to hone the text to the last, as he had done with all his previous books.

The Yiddish proverb in the epigraph ('Ibergekumeneh tsores iz gut tsu dertsailen'. (It's good to tell past troubles') was not in the typescript. It must have been added while Levi was correcting the proofs. 'Argon' shows the most revisions, with a number of sellotaped paper strips, and different versions of the story typed with different line spacing. There is no date. 'Hydrogen', on the other hand, is a photocopy of a previous typescript, and again there is no final date. A couple of sentences were cut from 'Zinc', one of which contained the hunting metaphor Levi had mentioned in the interview ('killing the bison, running away and perhaps being charged'). This shows that even when Levi was answering questions in an interview, he used a register based on words he had already written, which means that many of the expressions he used in his interviews were significant. The last revision of the typescript of the story is dated 3 December 1972. 'Iron' was finally revised on 15 April 1974. The first few lines of 'Potassium' were cut in the published version of the story. In the typescript, the story started with the lines: 'I passed my exams with high marks, but it wasn't important. I only cared indirectly, I would probably get a good degree, but then what would I do with it? 'Then', meaning 'after', but 'after' what? It was January 1941 [. . .]'. Another passage was also eliminated: 'Piedmont was our real fatherland, the one in which we recognized ourselves. *Our fathers and ancestors, wise patriarchs smelling of tobacco, nearly all merchants of silk, spoke as their mother tongue an extraordinary piedmont epic woven with corrupted Hebrew terms.*' The passage in italics had been cancelled because it had already been used in a previous version of 'Argon'. A few lines later the name of Gobetti was taken out of the list of famous Piedmont anti-Fascists. The typescript has several paper strips with revisions taped over the original. The final revision was dated 4 February 1973. The text of 'Nickel' underwent heavy revision, with several paper strips taped onto the typed pages, on the back of one of which there were some scribbled notes: 'talk more about *If This Is a Man*', a number indicating the length of the story in terms of the total number of characters, and a name, Diogene. It was dated 1 May 1973. The final draft of 'Lead' was dated September 30, 1973. The typescript of 'Mercury' has a map hand drawn by Levi and was dated 6 January 1974. 'Phosphorous' was finally revised, according to the typescript, on May 1, 1974; 'Gold' on 26 May 1973; 'Cerium' was dated both 17 December

1972 and 31 December 1972. The typescript of 'Chromium' replaced a longer passage with the final, shorter version typed on a strip of paper:

> Along with the liberating relief that belongs to the veteran who tells his story, I felt in writing a complex, intense new pleasure, similar to that of the student who penetrates the solemn order of differential calculus. It was exhilarating to seek and find, or create, the right word, that is, fitting, concise, and strong; to draw things out of memory and describe them with the greatest rigor and the least mass. Paradoxically, my baggage of atrocious memories became a wealth, a seed; it seemed to me that, as I wrote, I was growing like a plant' (p. 878).

The final draft was dated 18 November 1973. 'Sulfur', which had already been published, has two different dates: 31 August 1950 and 20 July 1973. 'Titanium', an old story published a decade earlier, was simply dated 1947. Revision of 'Arsenic' was completed on 10 August 1973; 'Nitrogen' was signed off with the words 'Pietra Ligure, 5–7 August 1974; 'Tin' was dated 16 April 1972; 'Uranium', 30 June 1974; 'Silver', again 'Pietra Ligure', 14–19 August and the name Ceirato was changed to Cerrato; 'Vanadium' was dated 15 September 1974; 'Carbon' simply '1970'.

Most of the stories (14 out of 21) were thus dated between 1973 and 1974. Only three chapters were from 1972, the year Levi started putting the book together in its final form. Thus, the book could be said to have started with 'Chromium' in November 1972 and ended with 'Vanadium' in September 1974, although the order in which Levi wrote the stories was not reflected in the final order of the chapters in the book. 'Vanadium', about Levi's interactions with Docktor Muller was the last story, chronologically speaking, and was probably the most difficult to write, even though the episode was from an earlier time (Belpoliti 2015).

The paper strips—taped on top of one another, half unstuck or completely detached owing to the tape losing its sticking function—show the extent to which Levi worked on his writing piece by piece. He would add or correct more than he would take away: single words, a few lines, or whole passages. The technique was the same when he republished *If This Is a Man* in 1958, heavily revising the 1947 text. The additions did not alter the original text; they completed it. Levi's changes, especially those where he rewrote the beginnings of the stories, often sharpened the openings and made them more memorable.

THE BOOK

The contract Levi signed with Einaudi was dated 10 October 1974, a month before Calvino sent him his letter of approval ('Dear Primo, I've looked at the new draft of *The Periodic Table* and it seems to me it's going very well' [p. 2847]). The book came out as the second volume of the new series 'Supercoralli'. The dust-jacket illustration was *Waterfall*, an etching by Escher, an artist Calvino also admired and chose for the cover of his *Cosmicomics*. The editorial copy was written by Ernesto Ferrero, summarizing the main themes of the collection while touching on Levi's work more in general. After commenting that 'Levi's vocation as writer of witness narratives has not been exhausted by his remarkable books *If This Is a Man* and *The Truce*', he went on to write that 'At first sight the book may appear to be "the autobiography of a chemist".' Here Ferrero picked up a theme close to Calvino's heart: it was also the 'history of a generation' that grew up in the years of Fascism and became adults during the war; that took part in the partisan struggle, suffered deportation and then had to find their way in post-war society. In Ferrero's words again, it was 'an exemplary story of a man who, with the solid foundations of his profession as a chemist, teaches himself to understand the physical and the animal world, to take a stand, and to measure himself with unforgiving irony and self-irony.' In the last lines of the blurb, Ferrero upended his thesis: 'Or perhaps the book can be read as an apology: his relentless challenge against inert or malevolent matter as a metaphor, like Conrad's, for our existence, for its opacity, out of which strange failures or unexpected successes may emerge.' This summed up Levi's everyday epic perfectly.

The Periodic Table won the Prato Literary Prize in 1975 and the Camerino Prize for literature about mountains in 1982 for the story 'Iron'. The book was not immediately successful, however. In 1982 it was reprinted in the series 'Nuovi Coralli' (n. 331) and four reprints followed over the next 10 years with a total of 25,000 copies sold. There were two paperback editions (Einaudi Tascabile n. 203) in 1994 and 1995, which included the text of a 1986 interview with Philip Roth. By 1995, 10 years after Levi's death, a total of 100,000 copies had been printed. A school edition was published in 1979 in the 'Readings for Middle Schools' series, with an introduction by Natalia Ginzburg, who had favourably reviewed the book when it first came out. The school edition also included a detailed set of notes written by Levi himself. Four editions of this book were printed up to 1990, the fourth consisting of 3,000 copies. A further 120,468 copies were printed between 1998 and 2015.

As with the previous school editions of his books, Levi cut a few episodes or phrases he thought may be unsuited to young readers. Most of his notes were technical or scientific, explaining the chemistry; some were historical, and others acknowledged the sources of his citations in the text. These notes confirm that Levi's literary references had shifted from Dante to Manzoni, and that the author knowingly, and increasingly humorously, played with intertextuality. Between 1979 and 1988, three editions were printed with a total of 23,000 copies.

'VANADIUM' AND THE GREY DOCTOR MÜLLER

The penultimate story in *The Periodic Table* bears the title 'Vanadium', a chemical element listed in Mendeleev's Table with the atomic number 23. This element is rare, malleable and hard, three qualities that recur in the story. The subject is again the concentration camp—more specifically, one of the chemists who worked in the Buna laboratory. In the fictional narrative, the character is called Dr Müller; his real name was Ferdinand Meyer.

The first part of the story describes a chemical issue, involving a paint, whose peculiarity is that it lacks the requisites necessary for it to work. In these pages Levi deploys all his skills as an experienced chemist and a paint specialist, but also as a writer. A German firm sends to the SIVA company of Settimo Torinese, where Levi is employed as technical manager, a consignment of defective resin. This leads to an exchange of letters between the company—in the person of Levi himself—and W., 'the big, respectable German concern', an offshoot of the chemical firm I. G. Farben, which was broken up by the Allies after the war. I. G. Farben, as is well-known, used labour from the Monowitz concentration camp where the young Jewish deportee was being held.

After the problem of the defect in the resin has been explained, enter Dr L. Müller, who suggests a solution: vanadium naphthenate, an additive which would make the paint usable, by removing the defect which prevents it from drying satisfactorily (Levi compares the result to 'a miserable kind of flypaper'). During the exchange of letters, it suddenly dawns on Levi that Dr Müller is a chemist who had worked in the Buna laboratory in Monowitz-Auschwitz. The revealing detail is a linguistic slip: a spelling mistake in the German word 'Naphthenat', which is written as 'Naptenat'. This is a crucial clue. Levi remembers that Müller, 'in the unforgotten laboratory full of cold, hope and fear', used to say 'Beta-Naptylamin' instead of 'Beta-Naphthylamin', omitting the 'h's, as his correspondent has done with 'Naphthenat'.

There follows a flashback. Levi takes us back to the Buna laboratory and describes his meeting with Müller. These are two pages in typical Levi style, a perfect blend of narrative and reflection. Then we come back to the present day, or rather to 1967, as we learn two pages later, where the story of the rediscovery of Müller unfolds. Levi, still not entirely sure that Müller is the man he had met, contacts a representative at the firm W. to request some information about the German chemist: his age and physical appearance, and what he had done during the war. As expected, this was the Müller he knew. Levi describes his violent excitement at the discovery, but adds that he is not out for revenge; he is no Count of Monte Cristo; he merely wishes to redress the balance.

This is the first time, since *If This Is a Man* was published in Germany in 1961, that Levi has come face to face, albeit through correspondence, with a German who was in Auschwitz. This particular German was not a member of the SS, but he had still collaborated in the project of the Third Reich. Müller, we learn, 'had shown pity, or even just a rudiment of professional solidarity' (p. 930). Levi recalls that he had talked to him as one chemist to another, and that he had allowed him to shave, and even given him a pair of leather shoes. Addressing him with the formal 'Sie', Müller had asked him: 'Why do you look so troubled?'. But the young Italian deportee, who thought in German at the time, had concluded: 'Der Mann hat keine Ahnung'—the man has no idea (p. 930). He manages to discover his address, writes him a letter and sends it, enclosing a copy of the German edition of *If This Is a Man*. The story continues with a double-layered correspondence: on one hand, an official dialogue between the two firms on the subject of vanadium, the chemical element which justifies the story's inclusion in *The Periodic Table*; on the other, a private correspondence between the former chemist at the Buna factory and the ex-deportee. Three letters follow: Müller's reply to Levi, Levi's reply to Müller, and Müller's second reply to Levi. There is a fourth letter, which Levi starts to write but never finishes—or at least never sends—because his German correspondent unexpectedly dies. Levi fills in the gap of the last letter in the story.

There is another, untold story, interwoven with this story in *The Periodic Table*. As Levi's biographer Carole Angier pointed out in *The Double Bond* (2002), the correspondence between the two men in fact took a somewhat different course, and, as in some of his other books, Levi has 'filled out' the story, so that the published version is a mixture of truth and fiction. The reason behind this is not merely Levi's natural reticence and tact—he changed the names of the firm and of Müller himself so that they wouldn't be recognized—but also his desire to create a narrative that was clear and effective in literary terms. Once again, he proved himself to be a good writer, and for this reason, as Mario Barenghi has argued in a recent study (2013), a valuable witness. The two roles are inextricably linked.

Barenghi analyses how Levi used fiction to make his testimony more effective. In Levi's case, as in that of other witnesses, truthfulness is not the only criterion in creating a retrospective account. The problem with the extermination camps is that an account cannot preserve the same form as an event which is intrinsically formless, and impossible to document. What is important, Barenghi points out, is the moral value of the experience, which never lies in the here and now (or rather in the there and then). Levi's literary work is valuable precisely because of the process of construction of meaning, which moves from experience and develops over an unpredictable period of time through the work of memory. In other words, Levi's work is exemplary because it is produced by a narrative strategy founded on a precise economy of memory. In short, in Barenghi's view, he is a great witness because he is a great writer; the two sides of the same coin are in fact one and the same.

Barenghi's essay is detailed and complex, despite its brevity; it is based on a definition of the concepts of memory and recollection. We believe Levi, he argues, because of his style, because of the morality of his writing, and also because of the form of his testimony. Levi's aim, as he states in the opening lines of *If This Is a Man*, is not to supply new, lurid details, but to reflect on humankind. His research is into human beings in general. It is the work of a writer and a great moralist in the classical sense.

How, then, should we judge the story 'Vanadium'? With the help of the correspondence between Levi and Müller-Meyer, we can try to reconstruct what really happened. It wasn't in fact Levi himself who identified Müller-Meyer, but a third person, not mentioned in the story, who played an important role in Levi's relationship with Germany: his friend, Hety Schmitt-Maass. Hety was a correspondent of Levi's from 1966 to 1981. She introduced him to the works of Jean Améry, and it was she who discovered Müller-Meyer's address. In one of Levi's first letters to her, in late 1966, he asks for information about some people who had worked in the Buna laboratory: Dr Pannwitz, Dr Probst, Dr Hagen and Dr Meyer the engineer. 'They all worked in the polymerisation department at Buna-Monowitz. I mentioned Pannwitz in my book; Meyer was particularly kind to me and my colleagues.' Hety had married a chemist who worked in Ludwigshafen, I. G. Farben's model factory, of which the Buna factory was a clone. She had met another chemist, Reinhard Heidebroek, who had spent some time at Auschwitz, working there with his wife. Returning from the camp after one of these periods, he had reported to his colleagues and friends that it was a concentration camp. It should be added that Hety was the daughter of a socialist, anti-Nazi pedagogue who was persecuted and interned in Dachau in July 1944. In a letter to Müller-Meyer in April 1967, Hety informed him of her family's fate under the Nazi regime. She sent a copy of this letter to Levi, which helped him appreciate the situation in Germany and created an even closer relationship between the two friends.

Hety was the one who, having got hold of Müller-Meyer's address through her ex-husband, from whom she had separated many years earlier, wrote a letter in January 1967 to the Buna chemist and sent him a copy of the German translation of *If This Is a Man*. Hety had taken upon herself, as she writes to Müller-Meyer, the task of delving into 'a past that no one has gotten over', using the contacts that she had established with Hermann Langbein, an ex-deportee and the author of several books, Améry and Levi himself. In her letter to Müller-Meyer, she explained her links to the Ludwigshafen chemists, and urged him to write to Levi. Five days later, Levi wrote to Hety and told her the story of the razor and the shoes, which reappeared almost word for word in 'Vanadium' eight years later. He commented on the case of Heidebroek as a typical example of a man who was neither a Nazi nor a bad man but had obeyed the orders he was given. He reminded her how these people later justified themselves by claiming that they had gone to Auschwitz to prevent true Nazis being sent there. That justification is credible, Levi tells Hety, only on one condition—that the person who made the claim can prove that they did something concrete, however trivial, at their own personal risk, to support the victims and defy the authorities. This was the key issue in Levi's view: blind obedience to authority, which is both the strength and the weakness of the German people.

On 2 March 1967, Müller—or Ferdinand Meyer—replied to Hety, thanking her for sending her Levi's book and for putting them in contact, and assuring her that he will write to Levi. He did so that day. The letter was amiable; he discussed the hell of Auschwitz and expressed his delight that Levi has survived. He listed Levi's companions and asked about the Breslau physicist Dr Goldbaum, who is not mentioned in *If This Is a Man* but who features in a later short story included in *Moments of Reprieve*. Thus, the first part of 'Vanadium' is complete fiction. In his letter, the former Buna chemist told Levi that he now worked for BSF in Ludwigshafen—the 'W.' of the short story. If he really had been engaged in correspondence with Levi about a consignment of resin, there would have been no need for him to tell him this: his interlocutor would have known it, since they would already have exchanged several letters as representatives of the two firms. Evidently, Levi wanted to keep Hety out of things, but he also created a little mystery, solved by investigative deduction, which works very well in the overall economy of the story. Angier is right in saying that Levi broke through the fictional barrier here, but perhaps at that moment and in that respect, he didn't like to admit it openly.

Later that day, Meyer wrote a second letter to Hety Schitt-Maass about one of Améry's books, *Intellettuale a Auschwitz* (*At the Mind's Limits: Contemplations by a Survivor on Auschwitz and Its Realities*), which she had either given him to read or recommended to him, and asks her to pass on his thoughts on the book to Améry, with whom Hety is in touch. That same day, Levi too wrote her a letter in which he discussed various personal matters and concluded by thanking her for giving him Meyer's address, and for sending Meyer his book. Ten days later, on 12 March, Levi replied to Meyer. As he explains in 'Vanadium', he decided to do so in Italian, as his German is incorrect. He told Meyer that he knew very little German aside from what he learnt at Auschwitz. He didn't know whether his interlocutor understood French or English, either. The reason why he expressed himself in his own language is typical of Levi: 'The letter I am about to write will require clarity and precision'—qualities attainable, it would appear, only in Italian. The tone of the letter is not hostile, but neither is it friendly. As Levi confesses in 'Vanadium', he cannot hide his 'violent excitement'. While professing to have pleasant memories of the Buna chemist, and wishing, as his interlocutor requested, to achieve a *Bewältigung* of the past, he did not conceal his hesitation: for the first time he found himself communicating with someone who had been on the other side of the barricade, though he understood that Meyer had been on that side against his will. He agreed to the idea of meeting him—indeed he considered it indispensable—and suggested some possible dates, but it is clear that this is not exactly what he wanted. Meyer answered his questions regarding Levi's fellow laboratory workers: he didn't know anything about Brackier and Kandel, while Goldbaum, he writes, had died of hunger and cold during the evacuation from Auschwitz to Buchenwald. Levi then gave a brief account of his own life from Auschwitz up to the present, including his adventures after the liberation, which he had described in *The Truce*. Then he asked some brief, peremptory questions of his own. What was Pannwitz like? Was he still alive? Had the management of I. G. Farben been reluctant to take workers from the concentration camp? Had they thought they were helping the prisoners by doing this? Had the prisoners' work been useful, useless, or even detrimental? What did he know of the 'bunkers' of Birkenau? Why did he know his name? Were they not simply numbers? He asked Meyer what he remembered about Levi himself. He reminded him of the episode of the razor and the leather shoes, and says he had had the impression that he was dealing with a man who felt pity, and perhaps shame. After the vaguely inquisitorial tone of this passage, the conclusion of the letter is more conciliatory: 'please don't feel obliged to reply.' Levi asked Meyer for a copy of his notes on the period and ended his letter with a sentence expressing his underlying conviction, despite his agitation: 'I am delighted to be able to communicate with you; for my part, I look upon this meeting between us, though for the moment it is only an epistolary one, as an unexpected and extraordinary gift of destiny, and I am sure that only good can come of it.' The following day he sent copies of the letters to Hety.

In 'Vanadium', Levi summarizes this letter, and adds that he doesn't feel like a representative of the people who had died in Auschwitz, any more than he sees Müller as a representative of their executioners. He excludes the friend–enemy dichotomy here, comparing it to the clash between the Horatii and the Curiatii, with which he feels no affinity. He also makes an observation about his own character: he is not of an argumentative disposition; he finds an adversary distracting; he is more interested in the person as a human being, and is perhaps all too inclined to believe his interlocutor; indignation and judgement come only later, when he is 'on the stairs' (p. 933), when such reactions are no longer any use. In truth, a judgement does emerge from the letter, and it is neither absolutory nor condemnatory.

Meyer's reply is not publicly available, but Levi summarizes it in 'Vanadium'. Levi makes an unusual observation which puts the whole story on a different level.

> It was not what I had been expecting. It wasn't a model letter, a paradigm. At this point, if my story were invented, I would have been able to introduce only two types of letter: one humble, warm, Christian, from a redeemed German; one vile, arrogant, icy, from a stubborn Nazi. Now, this story is not invented, and reality is always more complex than invention: rougher, less combed, less rounded. Rarely does it lie on a flat surface (p. 933).

A further aspect of Levi's personality—and of his view of the concentration camp—comes into play here. While balancing his story between reality and invention, he is faced in this letter with the kind of person he will later place in the 'grey zone'. By the end of his account of Meyer's lengthy reply to his questions, he states that the German chemist was 'Neither wicked nor heroic: with the rhetoric and the lies, in good or bad faith, filtered out, he remained a typically grey human specimen, one of the not few one-eyed men in the kingdom of the blind.' Meyer is not a distant example, like that of Chaim Rumkowski, on whom Levi will dwell in *The Drowned and the Saved*, but a very close one. The issue concerns Levi directly. Reality is on an inclined plane, and now he finds himself having to negotiate it, judging the chemist even though he had had friendly looks, words and gestures for him in the hell of Auschwitz. It is not an easy task.

Levi begins his discussion of the letter with a visual detail: the photograph that Meyer had enclosed with it—an image that 'startled me': 'The face was that face: aged, and yet ennobled by a clever photographer, I felt it high above me uttering those words of casual and momentary compassion: 'Why do you look so troubled?' (p. 933). He then goes on to outline the contents of the letter, where Meyer gives an account of his experiences from when he joined the National Socialist German Students' League and the Sturmabteilung to his arrival in Auschwitz as a chemist—an account that attempts to absolve himself from the crimes of Nazism, even though he had been a supporter. He expresses shame and indignation, but Levi is disinclined to believe him, or at any rate to justify him. Ultimately Meyer doesn't accept any responsibility. Levi comes to the conclusion that he had constructed a convenient past for himself, albeit in good faith. Meyer answers Levi's questions about I. G. Farben with a 'crazy' opinion: that the giant Buna-Monowitz factory complex with the intention of 'protecting the Jews and helping them to survive' (p. 935). He also claims 'he had never learned of any unit that seemed designed for the killing of the Jews' (p. 935). At the end of the letter, Meyer requests a meeting with Levi, either in Germany or on the Riviera. After summarizing the letter, Levi tries to draw some conclusions; his observations move from Dr Meyer to himself. He seems to be moving in and out of fictional narrative—trying to find a point of equilibrium between the way he feels while telling the story, albeit with its literary invention, and the element of reality which entails writing about it, remembering, and trying to understand. Nothing is simple in Levi's fiction, precisely because of this mixture of literary creation and testimony. Similarly, nothing is simple in Levi himself as the author is both narrator and protagonist of the story.

In the last two pages of the story, he reveals his feelings: 'I didn't love him, and didn't wish to see him, and yet I felt a certain measure of respect for him: it's not easy to be one-eyed' (p. 936). There is an indirect reference to a medieval proverb ('Blessed is the one-eyed person in the land of the blind'), and perhaps also an allusion to a short story by H. G. Wells, 'The Country of the Blind': 'He wasn't a coward or deaf or a cynic, he hadn't adapted, he drew up his accounts with the past and the accounts didn't balance: he tried to balance them, and maybe he cheated a little. Could one ask much more of a former SA?' (p. 936). He recalls that in his first letter Meyer had used a German word, *Bewältigung*, which suggests the idea of 'getting over' the past—a euphemism much used in post-war Germany—or 'redemption from Nazism' (p. 936). 'And yet this escape into clichés was better than the florid obtuseness of other Germans: his efforts at overcoming were clumsy, slightly ridiculous, irritating, and sad, yet decent. And hadn't he procured for me a pair of shoes?' (p. 936)

Levi sketches out a draft reply, listing the main points at the end of the story:

> I thanked him for having brought me into the laboratory; I declared myself ready to forgive my enemies and maybe even to love them, but only when they showed sure signs of repentance—that is, when they ceased to be enemies. In the opposite case, of the enemy who remains such, who persists in his desire to create suffering, certainly he should not be forgiven: one can try to redeem him, one can (one must!) discuss with him, but it is our duty to judge him, not forgive him (p. 937).

The inclined plane tips even further when Levi 'discreetly cited' the case of two Germans in the Buna factory who had made concrete gestures 'on our behalf', which were distinctly more courageous than what Meyer claimed to have done. He concludes,

> I admitted that not everyone is born a hero, and that a world in which all were like him, that is, honest and defenceless, would be tolerable, but that is an unreal world. In the real world, armies exist, they build Auschwitz, and the honest and defenceless smooth the way for them. Therefore, every German must answer for Auschwitz, indeed, every man; and after Auschwitz we are not permitted to be helpless (p. 937).

He did not mention the planned meeting on the Riviera. The very same evening, Müller-Meyer phones him at his home in Turin, and in a laboured but excited voice announces that in six weeks he will come and see him in Finale Ligure. Eight days later, Levi hears from Meyer's wife that her husband has suddenly died at the age of 60. However, in Levi's correspondence with Hety, there is a letter from him to Meyer, written in French and dated 13 May, 1967; it covers some of the topics and even contains some of the sentences of the draft letter he summarizes in 'Vanadium'. The tone is more conciliatory and it is clear that Levi's feelings are complex. He describes the amphibious nature that Auschwitz has produced in him: he has the privilege, but also faces the dangers, of living two lives. The concentration camp has left him with a dual identity—that of writer and chemist: 'While continuing to work as a chemist, I found myself gradually assuming the role of a man of letters (which I am not).' This occupation takes up much of his time, as he tells his correspondent, and that is why he is late in replying. But there is also another reason: he finds himself in a dilemma. He feels—he explains— torn between his opinion of Nazi Germany on the one hand and his tentatively affectionate attitude towards post-war Germany on the other; torn between his opinion of Germans in general on the one hand, and his judgement of Germans—as individual people—on the other. What is more, in the case of Meyer, he is torn between respect and gratitude on the one hand, and doubt that this can help him come to terms with the past on the other. This idea of an amphibious, dual, centaur-like nature is sanctioned by a key issue in Levi: twin battles he feels must be fought. On the one hand, a battle against inertia, bad conscience and injustice in others; on the other, a battle against the same faults in himself. He makes the same points about cultivating a relationship with the 'enemy' that are summarized in 'Vanadium', stating that he had not approved of Eichmann's hanging but that it had been right to capture him and put him on trial, since German and Austrian justice had allowed him to live in peace. He then cited two examples of Germans who had taken positive action in the Buna factory and paid a price for it. One was a member of the Polymerisationsabteilung, called Grober, who had taken bread to a Dutch Jew, and then had suddenly disappeared in November 1944, probably sent to the Russian front. The other was Stawinoga, who had taken Levi into a bunker with him during an air raid and had come to blows with a German 'Green Triangle'—an episode which Levi later described. He also mentions Sina Rasiniko, one of the Ukrainian girls in the laboratory. Is this letter the one that followed the draft, the draft he was writing before Meyer's sudden death? Why did he send it to Hety? We don't know the answer to either of these questions. At any rate, he ends the letter by thanking his correspondent for taking him into his laboratory, and thereby saving his life—Meyer had claimed credit for this in one of his letters. The conclusion is affectionate: Levi promises that they will meet, and ends with the words 'I shake your hand very warmly.'

In another letter from Levi's correspondence with Hety, she describes her own meeting with Hermann Langbein and Dr Meyer. In her opinion, their attitude is that of people who continue to refuse to see reality; Meyer displays a certain embarrassment when asked questions about what happened in Auschwitz. Levi replies to Hety on 17 June 1967, commenting on her account. This was the time of the war in Israel, and Levi is concerned and distressed, confessing to her that he felt shame—the same shame that stems from Auschwitz—towards his children, for having fathered them in a world perpetually on the brink of war. These feelings were later replaced by relief at the Israelis' military success, though he is critical of the state of Israel. But that is another story.

In the letters that follow, Meyer's name crop ups again, though not as often as in their previous correspondence. Levi, however, is not the only person who communicates with Meyer. In September 1967, the German chemist, who had taken up philosophy in recent years, writes a long commentary on Améry's *Intellettuale a Auschwitz*; he sends it to Hety, who duly sends it on to Améry. The author's reply to Meyer is polite but terse, and criticizes Levi. In his view, the author of *If This Is a Man* is more inclined to be forgiving because he is an Italian and did not have the same experience of imprisonment as Améry. Améry is of German origin. To emphasize his meaning, he uses a metaphor: there is a great difference between the owner of a tavern forbidding entry to a stranger and his forbidding it to one of the regulars.

Several years later, in 1976, Hety translates 'Vanadium' into German in three weekends, with the help of an Italian friend. Levi had sent it to her and asked for her opinion: will the Meyer family be hurt when they read it? Hety replies on 20 February, 1976 that they probably would, but it is unlikely that they will do so even after it has been translated. She adds that she was surprised to see how critical Levi was of Müller-Meyer—far more critical than she had been aware of at the time of their correspondence. 'Didn't I listen to you carefully enough?' Hety wonders, struck by her Italian friend's sternness. She recalls an occasion when they met in Germany, where Levi had been visiting at the time, and they telephoned Meyer; she had the impression that Levi enjoyed the conversation, even though afterwards he confessed that he was frightened of meeting Meyer. She thought he feared that he would burst into tears when he saw him. Now she understands something: what had seemed like fear at the time was in fact perhaps something else, something quite different. What that something was, she doesn't say.

But let us return to the time of Meyer's death, which Levi discusses in a letter to Hety in January 1968. He says that he is sad about it, but he also confesses that he had followed the German chemist's attempts to exorcize the past with a kind of impatience, without any real desire to help him. But now it is over. In a later letter, Hety tells him that Meyer died on 13 December, probably from a heart attack. When she heard the news, she had immediately thought of the meeting with Levi that would never take place: what a pity, she writes; we wasted a unique opportunity, for one should never postpone things if one is in a position to help somebody. She asks Levi if he regrets asking Meyer to wait until spring before meeting him again—and here a detail emerges which we don't find in 'Vanadium'—it would seem that Levi and Meyer had actually met. Hety writes that Meyer had wanted *another* meeting with Levi. But did such a meeting really take place, or is she referring to their phone call—which was at least a direct conversation, without the mediation of writing? Perhaps. But if Primo Levi did communicate with Meyer at least once through a medium other than writing, and did speak to him, at least on the telephone, that did not happen with Dr Müller in *The Periodic Table*. Here, in fiction, Levi's rejection of the enemy's advances is inflexible, like the chemical element vanadium, which is rare and malleable, but also hard. Is literature, as an invention of reality, more realistic than reality itself?

LEMMAS

Science

Levi never called himself a 'scientist'. He defined himself as a 'technician' because, in his view, chemistry was based on applied technique rather than on science. And yet scientific culture played an important role in his intellectual and moral formation, as he told Tullio Regge in his interview, in *Conversations*. Levi saw science as a stimulus for his activity as a writer, as both a formidable source of inspiration and a rich seam of primary material. It is thus hard to separate Levi as a scientist (or technician) from Levi as a writer and poet; he was a hybrid product of the two different spheres. The idea of science that Levi transmitted in his writing and in his interviews and conversations was that it required the mixing together of different ingredients. One could thus claim, as Mario Porro has done, that Levi's aim was to unite scientific and humanistic culture, so often separate, in an encyclopaedic project, in the hope that he could find a way through the labyrinth, or create order out of the chaos of the life he was living (Porro 1997). Science and literature had a cognitive element in common, in Levi's view: a chemist works with his hands but still needs theories, or models, from which to deduce consequences; when these are applied, they find confirmation or rejection through direct experience.

Porro also commented that Levi distrusted philosophy, believing that the fundamental issues—the problems of matter and the forces that regulated it—had already been spelt out by the pre-Socratics, whom he considered the greatest philosophers in human history. Levi's scientific culture was based on positivism, and was acquired through his father's influence, his reading and his university training in Turin. He was an avid reader of Darwin and Lombroso, and was part of a cultural circle in Turin made up of positivist physiologists who believed in the 'science of matter' rather than in 'knowledge of form'. It is not by chance that aesthetics play such

244

a limited role in Levi's work and that art hardly ever featured in his cultural references or daily experience. Underlying his scientific culture there was a basic belief in naturalism, as Levi made clear in many of the articles collected in *Other People's Trades*. As Porro put it, naturalism meant, for Levi, adopting the method of observation, modelled on that in use in a laboratory. In Levi's approach, the place where the experiment took place was a laboratory—even the Lager was a laboratory conducting experiments in biology.

In order to appreciate the function of science in Levi's work, it is therefore essential to set science and literature side by side, bearing in mind the intrinsic logic of the two crafts (chemist and writer). Both involve assembling and disassembling, putting things together and taking them apart, following a series of steps (a scientist in a laboratory is an artisan in the same way a writer is, at least from a technical point of view). It is important to remember that writing was not, in Levi's view, strictly speaking a trade. It was, rather, a production, or a transformation, as he claimed in *The Wrench*: anyone who writes transforms their own experience into a form that is accessible and acceptable to the reader.

Parallels between science and literature are so common that it is hard not to imagine they share a method. Matter presupposes impurity, as we learn from *The Periodic Table* which praises imperfection. Levi would not consider himself a pure scientist, but he was able to appreciate the impurity of alchemy, which was not only the earliest form of chemistry but also an opportunity to contaminate or purify matter throughout time. As Porro reminds us, the epistemology of chemistry was essentially a science of similarity and dissimilarity. We could stretch this idea further and say that Levi's epistemology was that of mixing elements together, lauding blending.

Following Gaston Bachelard's indications, one could consider Levi's imagination to be 'material': on a horizontal axis, one could place the theme of metamorphosis, seen as a sign of natural vitality, a place for transformation; on a vertical axis, one could position the theme of biological depth, of a possible return to the inheritance of acquired characteristics through evolution, but also the potential upswing towards reason (sublimation, as a chemical procedure, to which Levi often referred).

Images of flight were frequent in his works: both angelic ('Angelic Butterfly', 'The Great Mutation') and through space. Porro suggests considering the theme of Levi's roots (*The Search for Roots*) as a plunge into the depths, a walk through an Inferno, or an initiation ceremony measuring a man's strength (as in Job, Conrad and Melville's work which he anthologized).

It is clear that it is extremely difficult to draw a line between science and the humanities. The struggle against mute matter is what forged mankind. Application, which for Levi was the same as technique, was the middle point between the two cultures. Underlying Levi's worldview was a competitive, Darwinian idea of existence. This did not presuppose an outright apology of conflict, but conflict did play a role. Both writers and scientists attempt to transform dark matter into light, but a successful transformation is by no means certain.

Freedom is central to both writers and scientists: freedom as the result of effort, of working on oneself and on others by means of one's 'products'. Freedom was precisely what was missing in the Lager. Every form of liberty had been abolished, and the biological predispositions of humankind (such as language and communication) had been denied. Levi was attracted to biology and biochemistry (the chemistry of the human body), and was passionately interested in genetics, spotting a possible link with linguistics—another of his passions. In any case, science for Levi presupposed, or implied, studying human beings, seeking some kind of rationality or order both in matter and in society. Levi was well-aware of the instability of this order. He knew it was temporary and random, but he never ceased looking for it. Writing was, for Levi, establishing order.

The theme of disorder was key in many of his stories, where monsters, deviations or 'Flaw of Form' loom. These stories reveal Levi's humanist bent, his project for reconstructing humanity. This was what Levi took away from his experience of the Lager, where science and technology played such an important role in the genocide. *If Not Now, When?* ends with a new life coming into being on the same day as the atomic bomb was dropped on Hiroshima. The history of science was connected to the history of technology, in Levi's view. Despite his personal tragedy, Levi's message was one of hope regarding the future of science and technology, showing again his deeply humanist roots. Science and technology were not separate disciplines, each with its own laws; they were both governed by human beings, in whose hands lay the destiny of humanity.

Chemistry

Levi enrolled in the Science Faculty of Turin University in 1937; in 1938, the Fascist government emanated Racial Laws prohibited Jews from attending school, but allowing those already enrolled in college to complete their studies. Levi described his college experience in *The Periodic Table* and in *Conversations*: his work in the chemistry lab turned out to be the most formative.

Levi graduated in 1941 summa cum laude, but he was not allowed to attend his dissertation viva as he had hoped owing to the Racial Laws. The official title of his dissertation, tutored by Giacomo Ponzo, was *The Walden Inversion*. However, he would later claim (in the chapter 'Chemistry Examination' in *If This Is a Man*, among other places) that his real thesis was another physics experiment which he wrote up under the supervision of Alfredo Pochettino entitled, 'The Dielectric Behavior of the Ternary Mix $C6H6=CHCl3=C6H5$'. Levi also wrote about this double dissertation in his 1984 article 'Asymmetry of Life'.

Chemistry was the fulcrum not only of Levi's life but also of his life's work. It was thanks to chemistry, as he repeated constantly, both in writing and in conversations, that he survived the concentration camp. After passing a chemistry exam, he was sent to the chemistry Kommando and spent the last two months of his imprisonment working at the Buna chemical plant at the core of the Monowitz-Auschwitz Lager.

On returning to Italy, Levi started working as a chemist at the DUCO factory in Avigliana. He later attempted working as a freelancer and then entered the Silva resin and paint factory, where he would work from 1947 to 1975, starting out as a lab technician, rising to director of production, and ending his career as general director of the plant.

Chemistry became part of Levi's literary effort with the publication of *The Periodic Table* in 1975, the same year that Levi resigned as general director (continuing as a consultant until 1978). Many of Levi's articles and short stories revolve around the work of a chemist. It also played an important role in *The Wrench* (1978), which was based on a conversation between a chemist and a crane operator. Among the articles, 'Ex Chemist' was significantly placed early in the collection, *Other People's Trades*. References to chemistry as an activity with its own initiation rites and its own specific language abounded in the collection, in particular in the articles 'The Language of Chemists' (I and II), and in 'The Sign of a Chemist'.

A university professor of chemistry, and an informed critic of Levi's works, Gianlorenzo Marino, conducted a survey of Levi's output, working from the editions published between 1987 and 1990 in the Einaudi series 'Biblioteca dell'Orsa'. His search words included the elements, inorganic compounds, minerals, technical terms from organic chemistry, laboratory equipment, the names of chemists and physicists. In addition to the 21 elements of Mendeleev's Table that Levi used as titles for the chapters of his book, *The Periodic Table*, Marino found 58 other elements mentioned by Levi over a total of 377 citations (including four elements in his poems).

Levi was well-aware of the influence of his training in chemistry on his linguistic and lexical choices. In *Conversations,* he claimed that low-level chemistry ('almost like cooking') had provided him in particular with a 'vast assortment of metaphors'.

> I find I am richer than other writer colleagues because for me words like 'light' or 'dark', 'heavy' or 'light', or 'azure' have a wider and more concrete range of meanings. For me, azure is not only the colour of the sky; I have five or six azures I can choose from [. . .] I thus have an inventory of primary material at my disposal, of 'mosaic tiles' to write with, that is greater than the stock of words a writer with no technical training has. In addition, I have developed the habit of writing compactly, avoiding the superfluous. The precision and concision people say are the feature of my writing are the result of my trade as a chemist. Likewise, my habit of objectivity, not allowing myself to be deceived by appearances (*Conversations*).

In *The Search for Roots*, Levi wrote that a book he read in his youth, Sir William Bragg's *Architecture of Things*, influenced his decision to study chemistry at university. Bragg persuaded him to trust the ancient atomists rather than follow those who saw matter as being infinitely divisible. Levi's scientific training was mostly in chemistry and physics, but he was also deeply interested in biology and natural science. Again, in *The Search for Roots*, Levi translated and briefly commented on a passage taken from Ludwig Gattermann's *Manual of Organic Chemistry*, published in Berlin in 1939—the same book that he later found in the hands of Doktor Pannwitz during the absurd chemistry exam he was forced to take in the Lager. As well as being a stimulus for studying German, a language that would prove essential for his survival in Auschwitz, the book represented for Levi 'the words of a father'. In Gatterman, he found 'the authority of a man who teaches things because he knows them, and he knows them because he has experienced them.' In Porro's definition of chemistry as the science of similarities and dissimilarities (1997), Gattermann urged Levi to distrust the almost equal, approximations, surrogates or patches.

Chemistry in *The Periodic Table* presented itself as a living, demiurgic science that instilled one with a sense of the importance of rigor, industriousness and survival, and that solved puzzles and identified the culprit in detective thrillers. Levi's view of his trade brings to mind alchemy: the science of transformations and creation of matter. Levi often recalled that the origins of chemistry lay in alchemy in his works. The image he gave of his prime trade was certainly epic, but in a minor, daily sense of the word. In *The Periodic Table*, he wrote about chemistry as being a solitary activity, on foot, unarmed, within reach—that is, closer to the endeavours of nineteenth-century pioneers, or of the great inventors who worked in solitude, than to chemists working in huge modern laboratories. Levi stayed faithful to the idea of chemistry as a trade, and was convinced that real discoveries were always the result of an individual's endeavours. His materialism also originated in chemistry: not so much chemistry that decomposed elements as chemistry seen as a 'constructive science of matter, where form and substance are dynamic, the fruit of a game of forces, the momentary consolidation of a process of deformation' (Porro 1997).

Mendeleev's Table was more than just a framework for Levi's *The Periodic Table*. It represented a time in the history of chemistry when experimental science was transformed into written science. Levi always claimed he was interested in the parallels between written formulas and what took place in the test tube, how practical experiments were codified into the written word. Thus, the links between science and literature, and between chemistry and fiction, were not unfounded. There was a definite similarity in their thrust. Moreover, chemistry was key to a central issue in Levi's work: impurity. In *The Periodic Table*, Levi linked the two aspects of his life—chemist and writer—to his Judaism, which he perceived as a potential rather than as an identity, as an element of possible mutation or transformation rather than as a fixed idea of himself. One could ultimately claim that for Levi chemistry was the language of matter, and in this sense a 'literature of life'.

Paint

One of Levi's first publications was a technical article published in a Milan-based specialized journal, 'Pitture & Vernici' (Paints and Varnishes) in November 1946. Some of the unique features of Levi's writing were already present in this article: concision, clarity and precision. Another early piece was a playful poem written on resigning in 1947 from the DUCO plant, which circulated among Levi's friends and family but was not published until much later. A third piece written from the point of view of an 'expert in paint', as Levi called himself, was written with a colleague, Carlo Molino, as an encyclopaedia entry in the early 1970s (perhaps 1972). Although the entry was co-authored, it is interesting to compare and contrast its style to the 1946 piece. Levi often claimed, with a certain coquettishness, mixed with his usual irony and self-denigration, that the model of writing that inspired him was a 'weekly report' from a lab or a factory.

Symmetry/Asymmetry

Levi's graduating dissertation focused on asymmetry. It was a survey, rather than a laboratory experiment, leading Levi in *If This Is a Man* to set the record right and state that his real thesis was experimental (*Measure-*

ments of Dielectric Constants). The theme of the dissertation, however, would turn out to be significant in his writing, where there are numerous references to symmetry and asymmetry. In particular, the characters that shadowed the author-narrator: Alberto in *If This Is a Man;* Cesare in *The Truce*; Emilio in *The Periodic Table*, even Faussone in *The Wrench*, and several other figures in the short stories. These characters have always been interpreted as 'doubles', on the basis of hints scattered throughout his works by Levi himself. Quoting Heine, a few lines of whose work he translated and included in *At an Uncertain Hour*, Levi pointed at the figure of a 'pallid companion' following him like a shadow.

Levi was fascinated by asymmetry, and returned to the topic of his dissertation, at the suggestion of Tullio Regge, in an article for the journal *Prometeo* ('The Asymmetry of Life', 1984). In it Levi reflected on the fact that 'all the main actors of the living world (proteins, cellulose, sugars, DNA) are asymmetrical. Right-left asymmetry is intrinsic to life; it coincides with life; it is unfailingly present in all organisms, from viruses to lichens and oak trees, from fish to man. This fact is neither obvious nor unimportant; it challenged the curiosity of three generations of chemists and biologists and it gave rise to two big questions' (p. 2658, *Uncollected Stories and Essays*). Levi revealed his interest in open forms while analysing various hypotheses linked to asymmetry, concluding that, 'the asymmetry we are talking about is fragile. It is, however, unfailingly present in living matter, where it may be an evolutionary necessity to prevent spatial 'errors' (p. 2662).

Levi was attracted to symmetric forms, such as those reproduced in 'Azote' (*The Periodic Table*), or a building that he considered beautiful because it was symmetrical. But he was also drawn to asymmetry, such as in Timoteo's reversed mirrors in 'The Builder of Mirrors' (*Stories and Essays*). The theme of symmetry was also present in the 1960s story 'Order at a Good Price', and in 'Versamine' (both in *Natural Histories*) where versamines were benzoyl derivatives that contained asymmetric spiro nuclei that converted pain into pleasure. In 'Heading West' (*Flaw of Form*), Levi used the idea of symmetry to explain the behaviour of lemmings, while in 'Self-Control' (*Lilith and Other Stories*), the protagonist had an evident problem with symmetry. What seemed to attract Levi was the phenomenon explored in 'The Mirror Maker': asymmetric symmetries, or enantiomorphism.

Mountain Walking

Levi spoke at length about his passion for mountain walking in a conversation with Alberto Papuzzi published in the *Rivista della Montagna* (Mountain Review) in 1984. Levi described some of his clambers to the peaks in the Gran Paradiso National Park, and about the rock climbing 'gyms' around Turin (Picchi del Pagliaio, Denti di Cumiana, Rocca Patanua, Pio Sbarua). One of the stories forming the chapter 'Iron' in *The Periodic Table* was about mountain climbing. Levi was the protagonist together with Sandro Delmastro, a fellow student at Turin University, who was one of the first resistance fighters in the Piedmont group to be killed. Levi's interests in chemistry, nature and anti-Fascism were melded into a small-scale epic culminating in a climb and a night spent on the mountain. The chapter was rewritten from a previous, longer version, 'Bear Meat', which had been published by *Il Mondo* in 1961. It was Levi's first epic of human adventure, inspired by Melville, Conrad, Kipling and London), and an early foundation for later stories, with a different tone and narrative intention, collected in *The Wrench*. In his interview with Papuzzi, Levi explained that mountains and anti-Fascism were inseparable; both an 'absurd form of rebellion'. He made his ideology of the mountains very clear: 'the idea of measuring ourselves against extremes had been handed down to us; it was essential to do one's utmost.' Mountain walking represented the freedom to make mistakes, and signified becoming masters of one's own destiny.

After Italy signed an armistice with the Allied Forces on 8 September 1943, turning German troops still occupying the north of Italy into enemies rather than allies, Levi took refuge in the mountains in Valle d'Aosta. He fought briefly as a partisan, but was then captured. In later conversations, and in his work, Levi often said that his experience of extreme fatigue when mountain walking had prepared him for Auschwitz. He even claimed it was one of the things that saved him.

Another story devoted to the theme of mountain climbing—or rather to a climb of Mount Disgrazia with his friend Silvio Ortona that never actually took place—was 'Weekend' (*Lilith and Other Stories*), first published in *La Stampa*. The story referred to a period when Levi lived in Milan after graduating. In the chapter 'The Canto of Ulysses', there is another mention of Levi's mountains: 'And the mountains when one sees them in the distance . . . the mountains . . . oh, Pikolo, Pikolo, say something, speak, don't let me think of my mountains, which would appear in the evening dusk as I returned by train from Milan to Turin!' (*If This Is a Man*, p. 108) which was also an explicit reference to Manzoni's 'farewell to the mountains' in *The Betrothed.*

PORTRAIT OF THE FAMILY (1963)

In 1963, *The Truce* won the Campiello Prize, his first recognition of his talent as an author. Although the book was a sequel to *If This Is a Man*, the main body of the book was the story of an adventurous journey filled with picaresque episodes. It was just under 20 years since his return from Auschwitz-Monowitz, and only five years since his first book was re-published by Einaudi. Levi was an established chemist who wrote books, as well as being a witness of the concentration camps, of course. Newspapers and television channels vied to interview him; he featured on the small screen in a cultural programme called *Approdo*. This image appeared in an extremely popular weekly magazine called *Gente* (People). For the first time he was portrayed with his wife, Lucia, and his two children, Lucia and Renzo. This was the first and last time his family appeared in public.

Primo married Lucia Morpurgo, who was a teacher, in 1947, the year he first published *If This Is a Man*. He referred to her in a joyful tone in one of the first poems he wrote when he got back from the camp. She saved him. In 1948, Lisa was born, followed by Renzo in 1957. The family is surrounding Primo, who is sitting at his typewriter, a sheet of paper ready to go, the book shelf behind him filled with tidily stacked volumes. It is a perfect portrait of a writer with his family. Levi is wearing a coat and tie and he is turning towards his wife, speaking to her, as she stands behind him. His hand is raised, while Lucia's head is slightly bowed. She is smiling, as if she is agreeing with what he is saying, the smile sealing their understanding. Lisa's arms are folded as she looks towards her father, while Renzo is tucked in between his parents and is staring at the sheet of paper as if he is reading. There are a few objects on the table: a pen holder, a metal file, a glass ashtray. This moment of happiness captured by the camera is perfectly in line with the popular magazine it appeared in. It is a women's magazine, for housewives and ladies who do not work. The lives and troubles of celebrities are the magazine's mainstay: singers, actors, the former royal family. This portrait reflects the image of a writer who is not a writer (although Levi only adopted this formula later on). He is a successful chemist, if there is such a thing. He had started working at the Silva factory, which specialized in paints, in 1948; he became technical manager in 1950, and general manager in 1962. He never stopped thinking about becoming a full-time writer, however. He wrote about his desire to retire in order to devote more time to his writing to his German translator, Heinz Riedt. There is an air of normality, consonance, and happiness in this photograph. The image is designed to be reassuring for readers, even though the books Levi had published were not in the least reassuring. The idea of 'normality' was a recurrent one in Levi's life, and he never rejected normality as an ideal. Rather, he clung to it. The photograph published in *Gente* communicates an idea that writers are not necessarily eccentric or non-conformist. Levi was 'a normal man with a good memory', the caption read.

The Wrench

BOOKS IN PAIRS

Having found the key to writing *The Periodic Table*, the solution for the other book Levi had been planning to write became clear. Levi was well aware that the two books were twins. In an interview, he stated 'My books come in twos: first the two books about the Lager, then two books of short stories. *The Periodic Table* is an only child for now. I'm planning to create a sibling, more chemistry stories but about organic chemistry this time. The title is already there, *Double Bind*; the book isn't' (Poli 1976a). The gestation of the book was to be quite long, however. He wrote a few pages in a school notebook, just like the one he used to write *The Truce* in, a basic skeleton of the book in note form as well as the first few lines: 'Z had lived in sin for 15 years and he knew it, but his sin was exterior, impalpable, and compensated by a full and vigorous professional life.' Gabriella Poli, who had read Levi's notes, summarized the plot thus:

> Z. was a chemist, and owned a small, artisanal factory that pro-
> duced fake tortoise-shell objects such as combs, spoons and
> spectacle frames. The problem was that Z. was an environment-
> alist (his factory was poisoning the water and the ground soil
> with its toxic waste products). He was tormented by remorse
> and found it very hard to deal with his guilt. The first story in
> *Double Bind*, which was evidently autobiographical, never saw
> the light of day, despite its atmosphere of suspense and success-
> ful structure—or rather, it did but Z.'s remorse and sense of
> guilt were cut. This ended up in a book that Levi had not yet
> conceived (Poli and Calcagno 1992).

Inhabitants of Settimo Torinese, where the Silva chemical factory was based, remember the waste products flowing into a ditch during the 60s and 70s, where the water changed colour continuously. The pollution, and Z.'s guilty complex, were thus based on facts. The title was set aside, only to be recycled 10 years later for another book that was never finished.

The environmentalist story was followed by another story that would soon become *The Wrench*: 'The logical continuation of my book of short stories *The Periodic Table* was obviously a book about organic chemistry. I already had a title in mind, *Double Bind*, which was an allusive title. But then this book didn't go anywhere because I poured most of the material into *The Wrench*' (Boeri 1983). This statement shows once again the extent to which Levi was willing to recycle his material between different projects. This was because, however different the material was, the 'drawer' from which Levi pulled it out was always the same: his life, his experience, and his reading reinterpreted in the light of the two vital aspects of his existence.

Only two of the chapters which made up *The Wrench* had previously appeared in print, published as short stories by *La Stampa*. Since his resignation as director of the Silva chemical factory in 1975, Levi clearly enjoyed more free time to devote himself to his writing. Even though he continued to work part time until the end of 1977, he was increasingly able to be the full-time writer he had dreamt of becoming as far back as 1959, or even earlier when he had just finished *If This Is a Man*.

The Wrench was published a year and a half after ' "With Malice Aforethought" ' came out in the Turin daily in March 1977. This was probably the time Levi took to write the whole book. In an interview with Giuseppe Grassano for the introduction to his second monography (1981), Levi declared that he wrote *The Wrench* 'with extreme facility.' 'I still have the manuscript which I typed directly with hardly a correction. It felt very easy to write that way, as if I were freeing myself of the obligations of a literary writer. It felt as if I were recording what someone was telling me on a tape recorder,' he told Grassano. Levi called *The Wrench* a novel, but it was in fact, like all his other works, a collection of single, short stories, each of which could have existed in their own right. Once again, brevity was an important feature of his fiction writing.

The rigger Faussone, the protagonist of the book, thus made his first appearance in *La Stampa* (3 March 1977), in the story that would then be transformed into the first chapter of *The Wrench*. Levi described Faussone as being 'about thirty-five years old, tall, slender, nearly bald, tanned, always clean-shaven. He has a serious face, fairly rigid and not particularly expressive.' In the short story published in *La Stampa*, he spoke the Turinese dialect of the San Paolo quarter, while in the book he is depicted as being provincial with a 'limited vocabulary' full of 'platitudes.' He boasted a family tree that probably gave Levi the opportunity to inlay further stories about Faussone's family, stories which he may have heard over the years talking to workers at the Silva chemical factory, or with other people he came into contact with during the course of his professional life. Faussone was depicted as a strategist and diplomat, hustler, acrobat, philologist and hot-head.

In the transition from short story to chapter, the rigger Faussone's Piedmontese dialect underwent a few modifications, becoming more demotic, and Italianized, as linguists have pointed out. The word 'intrigo', for example, was edited to become 'trigo', 'ciao' to Ciau', 'night' to 'nàit'. These are very small changes. Levi's linguistic inventiveness, tone and internal structure are already in place in the short story that first came out in the newspaper. Later changes included adjusting the figure of the narrator-listener and connecting the story to the other chapters in the book with minimal internal references, exploiting to the full the opportunities offered by the rigger-speaker and chemist-listener-narrator duo. These two parts are the real novelty of the book, which derived from Levi's natural quality of being a good listener.

The other story that had previously come out in *La Stampa* on 12 June 1977, and then, in a very similar form, became the eleventh chapter of the book, was called 'The Conic Couple'. There were only two significant additions: a passage that connects the chapter to the one preceding it, and the detail of the sick cat ('gatto ramito' in dialect).

HISTORY OF THE BOOK

In November 1977, Levi wrote to his German correspondent Hety Schmitt-Maas, who features in *The Drowned and the Saved*, to tell her that as of 1 September he would be a 'free man' after resigning from what he called his almost 30-year 'corvée' (duty). He informed her that he was currently engaged in writing a series of stories that he had heard from a 'rigger' who had travelled all over the world for his work. Levi explained the genesis of the book in several different interviews. It was supposed to be called 'Vile Mechanic' with an evident reference to Manzoni, 'but my editor convinced me not to use that title' (Gerosa 1981). In the typescript, 10 or so possible titles for the book were listed. 'The actual act of conception for the book took place in Togliattigrad, where I travelled for a matter of paints and where I didn't actually meet Tino Faussone, as he doesn't really exist, but at least 12 types who were similar to him. They were technicians from the FIAT factory and other companies in the filière who were down there to help build the Zigulì factory' (Poli 1979). Levi travelled to Togliattigrad in 1972 and 1973. In other interviews, he stated that Faussone told his stories in that city. However, the episode in 'Anchovies II', for example, took place in April 1970, when Levi went to Moscow to settle a controversy concerning the quality of an enamelled wire that had been delivered to a Soviet factory, as he wrote to Hety in June of that year.

The first impulse to write the first chapter of the book—although Levi was not entirely aware that this was the case, as he confessed in an interview—was when he heard the story of the 'malice', or evil spell, which he later included in ' "With Malice Aforethought" '. The original story was not set in Saudi Arabia, as it is in the chapter, but in Lombardy. Levi first heard it from a friend of the ethno-musicologist Roberto Leydi. An interviewer who asked him why he chose the title *The Wrench* were told by Levi that he liked the sound of it, and there was no other reason (Manzini 1978). In conversation with Francesco Poli, Levi told him that while he was on his trip to Togliattigrad, the 'idea came to him of writing a story where the narrator was a witness'. He put this idea into practice using a narrative mechanism that he was very familiar with, having adopted it in his first two Lager books, *If This Is a Man* and *The Truce*. It is this mechanism, in fact, that links *The Wrench* to these early works, as well as its adoption of a spoken register—a form of oral narration that Levi used throughout his writing life and in nearly all his works—that derives from relating lived experience. Some of the settings and narrative techniques Levi adopted in this 'novel' resembled Nikolai Leskov's *The Enchanted Wanderer*, translated into Italian by Tommaso Landolfi and published by Einaudi in the 'Nuova Universale' series in 1967 and which Levi may well have read.

When *The Wrench* came out, the subject matter of the book led to numerous interviews, during which Levi provided an abundance of information about its genesis. In one of these, he claimed that the idea for the book came to him after the first short story was published in *La Stampa*. 'There was enough blood, skin and bones in the figure of Faussone,' he claimed, 'to flesh out a whole book' (Poli 1979). Once again, Levi showed how a book could be conceived as a result of a flash of intuition, or a piece of writing that already existed. The second chapter, 'Cloister', was based on the author's own experience in the Silva factory, as Levi explained in other interviews (Boeri 1983). It is quite easy to imagine this episode as part of *The Periodic Table*, if there had been such an element as 'acetic acid'. The stories related in *The Wrench* were collected by Levi over the course of his life as a chemist, during his work trips, or told to him by his friends. The way Levi appropriates other people's stories is very interesting.

Talking about 'Argon', the story about Levi's Jewish heritage that opened *The Periodic Table*, Levi once said,

I often meet friends who say, 'How strange, your grandfather would say the same things as my grandfather.' Well, they are in fact the same person, as when I was compiling the chapter they were referring to, the first chapter of *The Periodic Table*, I had to dip into our collective memory, not only my family's but also that of many other families, in order to gather together this collection of bizarre sayings (Bocca 1985).

Other stories were derived from Levi's readings, from novels or scientific articles. Levi often turned to his friend Roberto Vacca for information, writing or telephoning him to check some technical detail or other. The story 'The Bridge' was inspired by a technical manual, 'a wonderful book about bridges that I considered essential reading as much as *The Divine Comedy*' (Grassano 1981). Only one of the stories, Poli has told us, was completely invented, but we do not know which (Poli 1979). As with his other books, the typescript Levi handed in to Einaudi included a handwritten date of completion at the end of each chapter. Seven chapters were written in 1977, between March and December, and five others were completed by August 1978.

In other interviews after the book came out, Levi stressed that Faussone and his adventures were the fruits of his imagination. While, in the past, he said, he only told authentic stories, 'in this book I have become a forger' (Di Rienzo 1979). With *The Periodic Table* and *The Wrench*, Levi had become a fully-fledged writer, the identity that had been so wrapped up in his experience as a witness was left aside, giving way to a new identity which he touched on in *The Wrench* itself. In his presentation of *Natural Histories*, Levi confessed to feeling like Tiresias, a figure who had direct experience of duality, being both man and woman (although in this case Levi spoke of the duality of sin and fraud). At this point in his career, Levi's duality was no longer just between being a chemist and being a writer, between 'two cultures' as it was expressed at the time. It was also between being a witness and being a writer, especially as his public identity since the 1970s had become that of witness par excellence. There was one aspect that linked his identity as a witness to the Piedmontese rigger's story, and that is spoken register and oral narrative style. Whenever Levi talked to critics or journalists about *The Wrench*, this was what he always said. 'The book is a literary venture, of course, but there is a basis of truth. The language Faussone speaks was actually spoken by a similarly well-travelled technician from the Piedmont region. The book is not a forgery, it is not a fraud. It is rather a restoration. People's speech patterns are full of incredible resources and enchanting metaphors. Why shouldn't we write them down?' (Di Rienzo, 197).

Levi appears to be fully aware at this point in his literary career of this additional duality: the spoken and written nature of his narrative style, the 'writing down' of ordinary people's speech, which he had always done since *If This Is a Man*. A critic once observed that Faussone's stories sound as if they had been recorded and then transcribed. Levi answered:

> I deliberately made these stories sound as if they were recorded. It's not that I planned it, but I wanted to write a book that was not literary, or that was even anti-literary, with as few hints of a literary register as I could possibly get away with. This is why the language my protagonist speaks is essentially written in a spoken register, and in particular, the language of his trade. It is evident that in this respect it is very different from the language we normally expect to find in books. That is precisely why I chose it. It was a subtle polemic against myself, against my tendency to write in an erudite, elegant, polished style, which is essentially very distant from everyday life (Arian Levi 1979).

In this interesting explanation, Levi shows how aware he was of the differences between *The Wrench* and *If This Is a Man*, but also of the extent to which his anti-literary instinct was an essential force behind his narrative style. Over the years, Levi had experimented with various narrative devices, from an aulic, high register to a spoken, low register. And yet the language in *The Wrench* was not merely a reproduction of natural speech; it was, rather, an actual transcription.

The linguist Gian Luigi Beccaria, who annotated a paperback edition with Levi's assistance, has pointed out that the originality of the book lies in its language, in the Piedmontese Italian of turners, riggers, fixers and electricians. The language Levi invented for Faussone was a complete novelty, even compared with the spoken registers used by Piedmontese contemporaries such as Beppe Fenoglio and Cesare Pavese who both used a higher register, or a rural variation, of the Piedmontese dialect. Levi's language was the concrete Italian spoken by people in the city, placed in a context of invention but still very real. The book would be a perfect manual for studying regional or popular Italian terms and expressions (Beccaria 1983). Moreover, as Beccaria has also stressed, it is also a text book of specialist technical terms in the context of factories and companies, as well as of a remarkable repertoire of vernacular expressions (his annotated edition brings many of these to life). Levi did not provide translations of dialect terms into Italian (which other fiction writers, such as Lucio Mastronardi, did at the time); nor did he write Italian 'contaminated by smatterings of dialect thrown in here and there'. His language was 'conceived' in dialect, and his dialect 'was modulated by playing with syntax rather than with words or expressions'. The syntax, was 'deliberately poor and repetitive, or, reflecting the dialect, it was highly disconnected' (Beccaria 1983)

The Typescript

The manuscript Levi handed in to his publisher was made up of photocopies of his typed pages, which are now housed in the Einaudi archive in Turin (now the Turin State Archive, Folder n. 1054, File n. 3013). There were 163 pages. The first thing that strikes one is the handwritten list of potential titles for the book, on a photocopied sheet placed at the beginning of the manuscript. At the top of the list was the title A *regola d'Arte* (Perfection) written in red with an indication of the series in which it would be published (Supercoralli Nuova serie), rather than *Vile Mechanic*, which was the title Levi said he had originally intended for the book.

The page is divided into two columns. On the right there is the list of proposals for titles: *Piè d'opera* (*On the Job*), *Vile meccanico* (*Vile Mechanic*), *In bolla d'aria* (*In a Bubble*), *La chiave a stella* (*The Wrench*), *Il passo del gatto* (*The Cat's Footstep*), *Tiresia e il serpent* (*Tiresias and the Snake*), *Grigio Ferro* (*Gray Iron*), *A regola d'arte* (*Perfection*), *Faussone il montatore* (*Faussone the Rigger*). Choosing the right title for a book is vitally important. Each and every one of these offered a different interpretation of the book. In addition to the Manzoni reference contained in *Vile Mechanic*, several of the titles alluded to the theme of work (*Piè d'opera, A regola d'arte, In bolla d'aria*, as well as the title that was eventually selected, *La chiave a stella* (*The Wrench*). The title *Il passo del gatto* alludes to the movement of cranes on building sites, but also to Levi's favourite animal. *Grigio Ferro* also contained a reference to work, or rather to work materials, and includes the adjective 'grey' that Levi was already thinking about with regard to *The Gray Zone*. Moreover, grey is the dominant colour throughout Levi's *oeuvre* (Belpoliti 2015). The title *Faussone il montatore* foregrounds the protagonist, while *Tiresia e i serpenti* was inspired by a passage in a story that sheds light on the dual nature of the narrator-listener and makes an elliptical reference to his links with Auschwitz.

In the left column Levi listed the number of pages for each chapter and wrote the approximate number of words next to each of these: the total was 158 pages and 60,000 words. The Conrad quote that Levi chose for the end of the book was also written on this sheet, with the editor's indication to place it 'under the general heading'. Some acknowledgements are also noted by hand ('I thank I. N., G. I., Rob. V., Ciagne, T. A., G G Gazzone', although the last name is hard to read) but these would never make their way into the published book.

The typescript was as always quite heavily edited, with cancellations, re-phrasing, new passages typed over the old, with strips of paper stuck on top of the original, but the pages that were handed in were, as we have said, photocopies.

The dates of completion for the various chapters were indicated thus: 'Cloister', 29/8/78; 'The Sassy Girl' 19/9/78 (with a phrase cancelled in the fourth paragraph after 'practical example': 'you need to leave time for the stories to gel'); 'Tiresias' 3/11/77 (with a long passage added running from 'it's easier to tell whether a piece of metalwork is on the air bubble than a written page' to 'At this point I noticed that Faussone, despite the wine . . . ' which talks about the responsibilities of a writer which are much lighter than those of a rigger or someone who makes 'scaffolding in a mining tunnel'. And is a long meditation on the act of writing itself). 'Offshore' was dated 24/1177; 'Metalwork', 13/12/77 (an additional typed sheet of paper stapled onto the previous sheet provided a new version of a passage); 'Wine and Water', started writing 1/6/78, finished writing 19/6; 'The Bridge', 29/12/77; 'Without Time', 2/5/78; 'The Bevel Gear', 1/4/77; 'Anchovies I', 'commenced 24/6'; 'The Aunts', 22/5; 'Anchovies II', 8/8/78.

LEMMAS

Work

Deportees in the camps were condemned to forced labour, which, in Levi's view, could not properly be called 'work': it was too close to the labour of animals, it was too tiring, and it could lead to death by exhaustion. There were, however, some inmates who worked to the best of their abilities. One example was Lorenzo, the surly mason from the Piedmont region, who worked as a 'volunteer civilian worker' in the Buna plant. In 'The Return of Lorenzo' (*Lilith and Other Stories*), Levi described how Lorenzo saved his life by bringing him stolen soup from the civilian camp out of 'pure altruism' (p. 1405). Work 'possessed him to the point that it hindered human relations' (p. 1403). Once he had returned to Italy, however, he became 'mortally weary, a weariness from which there was no recovering', and ended up 'rejecting life' despite Levi's attempts to get him into a hospital in Turin. Lorenzo's work ethic showed that, even when forced, work could be a precious gift. Lorenzo unwittingly represented both sides: oppression (a biblical curse), and liberation; but Levi rejected the idea that only the latter can save mankind from the former. Levi's ideal was that of *Homo faber*, humans constructing themselves and the world through their work. Levi's early reading of Conrad introduced Levi to the work epic, inextricably linked to a sense of adventure, challenges, and of course the possibility of making mistakes—Faussone's main theme. In Faussone's worldview, work gives you the chance to make mistakes, and errors give you the experience that will help you mature.

The Wrench was almost entirely devoted to the theme of work. The book not only described it, but also revealed some of its secrets. One example was the idea of 'malice', or the tricks people use to complete a job without making mistakes. Levi compared the work of a crane rigger to that of a chemist (the Narrator to whom Faussone told his stories was a chemist) and to that of a writer. The Narrator transcribed Faussone's words, but also made it clear that riggers, chemists and writers were all working with construction. Levi wrote that 'love of one's work (a privilege enjoyed, unfortunately, only by a few) is the best, most concrete approximation of happiness on earth—but most people don't realize this' (p. 1023). Yet, 'love or, conversely, hatred of work is a personal matter, which depends greatly on the individual's own history and less than one might think on the industrial structures within which the work takes place' (p. 1024). This phrase became part of a wider debate in 1979, triggered by an article published in the far-left daily *Lotta Continua* by Tommaso Di Ciaula, who was a writer and factory worker. Di Ciaula criticized Faussone's love of work in itself, claiming that a factory worker felt 'condemned' to work.

The theme of work was present in all of Levi's work, directly or indirectly: *The Periodic Table* and *The Drowned and the Saved* both contained Levi's reflections on the subject, and one story in particular in *Other People's Trades*—the title itself revealing the importance of work—focused on the theme ('Thirty Hours Aboard the *Castoro 6*'). One of Levi's hobby horses was the idea of 'specifications', the features that the products of our work must have, or the criteria assigned *a priori* to these products, which Levi often described ironically, constructing whole stories from some of these specifications ('Our Fine Specifications' and 'The Sixth Day'). There was some overlapping in Levi's mind, in fact, between work and play: both brought about pleasure.

Levi adopted the concept of 'trades' with insistence. In his interview with Philip Roth (*Man Saved from his Trade*) he claimed he would never have survived Auschwitz without his 'trade' as a chemist (he never used the word 'profession'). A trade required the use of one's hands as well as one's skill. Levi's ideal of a tradesman was of course Libertino Faussone, nicknamed Tino, the protagonist of *The Wrench*, and a perfect example of *Homo faber*. Writing was a trade, or at least it was when the product was socially useful. Levi always claimed it was wrong to write for oneself. One was entirely free to do so, of course, but, in his view, it was not a trade if one did.

Hands

In *Conversations*, recalling his university training and laboratory experience, Levi talked about the importance of returning to an appreciation of manual activity, which Fascist education, with its emphasis on Gentile's philosophy, had neglected. Levi often referred to hands in his work, especially in *The Wrench* where the crane rigger Faussone, the protagonist, afforded him the opportunity to develop his passion for Darwin. Not by chance, monkeys played an emblematic role in the book. Faussone was compared to a cat, owing to his continuous balancing acts, and to a monkey, owing to his manual dexterity.

Hands, together with eyes and noses were the organs required for his work as a chemist producing paints and varnishes (as several chapters of *The Periodic Table* state). Paola Velabrega conducted a survey of references to hands in Levi's work in relation to his various trades and passions (chemistry, writing, climbing, etc.), which she presented in the article 'Hand/Brain' (Velabrega XXXX). She concluded that hands in Levi's work were essential not only for implementing ideas, but also for generating them. The very act of writing required the movement of hands to make thoughts material. Handwriting was for Levi the apex of evolutionary development for humans, because through writing memory, the act of witnessing, and thus history came into being. The past took on a strong ethical significance for Levi: preserving memory was a guarantee of values.

Levi was well-aware of Darwin's research into the importance of hands in the evolutionary process. Velabrega cited a 1920s edition of *The Origin of the Species* in this regard: 'Man would never have been able to acquire its present position as dominator of the world without the use of hands, which are so marvellously suited to operate obeying his will'. In addition, Levi must surely have read a 1977 Einaudi edition of André Leroi-Gourhan, *Gesture and Speech*, where hands were key.

Of the dozens of references to hands in Levi's work one could cite 'The Mark of the Chemist' in *Other People's Trades*, where the chemist's hands are indelibly marked by a 'professional stain' obtained when the conical glass joints broke 'in the palm of our working hand' (p. 2205). Another article, '*"Leggere la Vita"*' (again in *Other People's Trades*), discussed a locution meaning to denigrate someone that could be considered 'reading someone's life on his hand the way palm readers do' (p. 2068). Levi tended to prefer the palm to the back of the hand since it was with the palm that humans did all their everyday work.

Another aspect that Levi paid great attention to was the language of gestures, with the natural capacity of hands to communicate states of mind, feelings and social status. It would almost seem that Levi was more interested in hands than in faces, although he did at times describe his character's faces in some detail, almost as if they were hands that he could read. Hands were also tools for playing games, as with the juggler in the Lager (*Lilith*), and in the slapping game (*Other People's Trades*). Velabrega noted that in his adolescence Levi read a lot of Conan Doyle's Sherlock Holmes mysteries, where hands, thumbs and nails are carefully observed alongside jackets and shoes. Levi cited the English detective in the story 'Lilith'.

Among the inventions in Levi's fantastic and science-fiction stories was the Psychophant, a machine that was set in motion by placing a hand on a tray. Objects materialized which then interpreted your innermost desires. Levi also invented a rebus puzzle on his computer which he sent to the newspaper games editor. Giampaolo Dossena revealed the solution in his 1988 book, *La zia era assassinata* (Aunt was Assassinated): the clue to the word 'Camp' was 'gelid neglected hands'. As Velabrega showed in her article, the theme of hands rapidly moved on to the theme of the Lager.

Charles Darwin

While visiting Faussone's aunts ('The Aunts' in *The Wrench*), the narrator/author recalled 'long-ago readings of Darwin, of the craftsman's hand that, making tools and bending matter, rescues the human brain from indolence, and to this day guides, stimulates and pulls it forward, as a dog does with his blind master' (p. 1097). Darwin had a great influence on Levi as a young man, and in his personal anthology, *The Search for Roots*, Darwin figured as one of the most important players in the 'salvation of understanding'. Levi quoted the 1924 edition of *The Origin of the Species*, which was probably in his father's library, together with works by Marx and Lombroso—a library Levi described in great detail in *Conver-sations* and in numerous other interviews.

Through his reading of Darwin, Levi developed the idea—which was to be so essential in *If This Is a Man*—that humans were basically animals. The anthropology of Levi's first book was Darwinian: human behaviour was dictated by biology. Levi's scientific training also played a role, of course, leading to his analogies between human behaviour and chemical elements. In the article written after the Apollo 8 flight, 'The Moon and Man' (*Stories and Essays*), Levi again referred to the Darwinian idea that

> Man, the naked ape, a terrestrial animal descended from a long line of terrestrial or marine creatures, every one of his organs shaped by the restricted environment that is Earth's lower atmos-phere, can be removed from that atmosphere without dying [. . .] Human matter (or rather animal matter), besides being adaptable in an evolutionary sense—on a scale of millions of years and at the cost of the incalculable sacrifice of less fit variations—is adaptable here and now, on a scale of days and hours [. . .] We are unique, sturdy, versatile animals, motivated by atavistic impulses, and by reason, and, at the same time, by a 'creative force' as a result of which if an undertaking, whether good or bad, can be achieved, it cannot be put aside but must be achieved (p. 2337).

In *The Search for Roots*, Levi cited Darwin in an attempt to answer the question: Why are animals beautiful? Levi admired Darwin's response because of the 'composed beauty of his strenuously tight reasoning' and because

> Darwin's work is filled with a deeply serious religiousness, the sober joy of a man who extracts order from chaos, who rejoices at the mysterious parallels between his own reason and the universe, and who sees in the universe a great design. [. . .] By denying a position of privilege for mankind in the act of creation, his intellec-tual courage has reinstated the dignity of all men.

Darwin was the diametric opposite of Rabelais, in Levi's view. He represented order against disorder, intellectual sobriety compared to the French writer's unhinged joy. These two sides were both present in Levi, who identified in Darwin the most mature form of scientific reflection (Darwin was also a writer), and in Rabelais the undeniable liberty of writing, imagination that cannot be subjected to any preconceived rule (as a doctor, and therefore, in his way, a scientist). As a young man, Levi probably read Darwin together with Marx and other utopian socialists influenced by Marx. His idea of hands being the noblest part of the human body was not only Darwinian but probably also Marxist.

Claude Lévi-Strauss

In 1983–84, Levi and his sister, Anna Maria, translated two of Lévi-Strauss' books for Einaudi: *The Way of the Masks* and *The View from Afar* (only Primo was acknowledged in the publications). Levi had always been interested in anthropology and ethnology, and had most likely read Lévi-Strauss' 1950 UNESCO publication, *The Race Question* (an Italian edition of which Einaudi published in 1967). There is evidence of the influence of Lévi-Strauss in a great deal of Levi's work, especially in a conference paper entitled 'Racial Intolerance' that Levi gave in Turin in 1979. *The Drowned and the Saved* refers specifically to the chapter 'The Anthropologist and the Human Condition' of *A View from Afar*. When the French edition of *The Wrench* came out, Lévi-Strauss wrote the blurb: 'I read it with great pleasure because I love books about work above all. From this point of view Lévi is a great anthropologist. Moreover, the book is very funny.'

On 17 January 1984, after completing the translation of *A View from Afar* (eventually published in May that year), Levi wrote a letter in French to Lévi-Strauss (Mengoni 2015). In his typical self-effacing manner, Levi opened his letter with the phrase, 'Monsieur, I don't know if you know me . . . ' and went on to explain that he had translated two of Lévi-Strauss' books into Italian which he had been fascinated by, and admitting that he had been previously unaware of his methodology (the structural analysis of myths). Levi then commented that he had been particularly struck by Chapter 22, 'A Belated Word about the Creative Child', and stated that

Lévi-Strauss' pedagogical approach mirrored his own, which he had outlined in *The Wrench*. For this reason, Levi added, he was enclosing a copy of the book and suggested reading in particular the chapters 'Tiresias' and 'Metalwork' as examples of the creative use of factory jargon. Levi then went on to comment in some detail Chapter 14, 'Pythagoras in America' which focused on the bean myth of the Missouri Pawnee tribe, comparing it to some Greek myths. Levi described a regional tradition whereby Epiphany cakes were baked with one black and one white bean thrown into the mix: those who found the white bean were considered lucky, while those who happened upon the black one would have bad luck and have to atone for it in some way. The Italian word for bean, 'fava', Levi informed Lévi-Strauss was also a vulgar term indicating the tip of the penis. Lévi-Strauss responded with a short letter on 25 January, telling him there was a similar tradition in France, and suggesting that Levi add a translator's note to the text describing the tradition and outlining the ambivalence of the term, which, the anthropologist pointed out, was already present in Greek and Roman thought. Levi responded on 3 July with a letter accompanying copies of his translation of *A View from Afar* together with the English editions of *If This Is a Man* and *The Truce* and announcing a new edition of *If This Is a Man* to be published by Julliard. On 23 July, the correspondence resumed, with a letter from Lévi-Strauss in which he stated not only that he had read the two books and been very moved by them, but also that he was confused by the idea that such a great author should waste time translating his work rather than writing his own. Lévi-Strauss commented on the humility and wealth of detail in *If This Is a Man*, while remarking that in *The Truce* he had been struck by the difference between novelists and memorialists. While the latter, in his view, generally focused on the most significant moments ('temps forts') Levi had concentrated on marginal aspects ('les periodes de marge'), which Lévi-Strauss considered no less important for understanding a historical period.

Aside from this exchange of letters, the author of *If This Is a Man* and the structural anthropologist had a great deal in common. Not only did they share their roots in Judaism and the Enlightenment, they were also both critical and deeply sceptical, as well as being secular and agnostic in their education and family traditions. Another factor they had in common was writing. In addition to anthropology, Lévi-Strauss was a writer. As a young man, he started writing a thriller, but never completed it. His most important book, *Tristes Tropiques* (1955), also translated as *A World on the Wane*, was a literary work, influenced by Chateaubriand. Both were long neglected by literary critics who did not consider them writers: Levi was too much of a witness, and Lévi-Strauss too much of an anthropologist. Distance as a vital ingredient of the ethics of a 'view from afar' was another idea they shared. Their reflections on human nature followed Freud's *The Future of an Illusion* (1927) and *Civilization and its Discontents* (1930), which clearly influenced both their work. Whether Levi read Freud before or after he came back from the Lager, a few of his books were anyway in his father's library. For all these reasons, as the Einaudi commissioning editors had shrewdly imagined, Levi's curiosity for language and for anthropology made him an ideal translator of Lévi-Strauss' work.

Few critics grasped the importance of Primo Levi's literary qualities to begin with, even though readers immediately appreciated his capacity for communicating, as well as his ability to send a clear, direct message. Pier Vincenzo Mengaldo (1990) was the first critic to tackle Levi's language and writing style, analysing and exploring aspects such as precision, clarity, and transparency. He stressed in particular Levi's taste for brevity and linguistic economy, paring language down to the essential. He also discussed Levi's predilection for parataxis, or asymptotic-paratactical sentence structures, as well as for repetition.

There are two layers to Levi's prose. On one hand, his aulic style is based on adverbial locutions derived from his schooling (it is the language of the Classical Lyceum, as well as the 'artistic prose' of writers from D'Annunzio to the Rondisti), incorporating 'traditional' elements and classical stylistic devices. On the other, Levi deliberately and insistently adopts scientific and technological terms to innovate his language (*Conversations*).

Aulic language, Mengaldo writes, is the 'basso continuo' of Levi's prose, in particular when he describes picaresque events or characters, to which he gives an unexpected air of solemnity. He adopts the same technique in *If This Is a Man*, when he touches on serious or complex issues. For Levi, Dante is the writer of all writers, a model that provides him with the stylistic devices and images he needs to describe the characters in his variegated world (particularly in his first two books). Classicism is such an important element of Levi's writing, that it has at times become its object (such as in the short story, '*Quaestio de Centauris*'). It is the intersection between classicism and technical and specialist languages ('The Language of Chemists', to which Levi dedicated two essays in *Other People's Trades*) that is at the root of Levi's pastiche. This most original element of Levi's prose is often used to express humour.

Mengaldo calls Levi's style 'multiple pastiche'. On one level, Levi parodies the same scientific reports and technical references he adopts to innovate his style. On another, his parodies range from biblical to mythological parody, or from lyrical parody (Ungaretti Baudelaire) to rehashing a sport's article or news item. Levi's irony is applied not only to people and their masks, but also to their 'products', first and foremost their linguistic products. The main target of Levi's humour, apart from the animal nature of his protagonists, is language itself.

Pastiche is a form of intellectual exercise, a way for the omnivorous reader in Levi to re-fashion the language and modes of expression he has come into contact with throughout his life. These include the language of Classical Lyceum, of Chemistry, of the Lager, of the paint factory, Piedmontese dialect, Jewish Piedmontese dialect, classical and twentieth-century poetry, the language of journalism, the idioms of bureaucracy and white-collar workers, the language of politicians, and so on (examples of narrative-linguistic pastiche can be found in the short stories '"Dear Mama"', 'Sisters of the Swamp', 'A Will', 'Dialogue Between a Poet and a Doctor', in *Lilith and Other Stories*). Another aspect is Levi's use of jargon and specialist language from textile merchants, information manuals, chemists, specialized and technical workers, Piedmontese Jews, etc. What piques Levi's interest most, besides the way words are used and their meaning, is their inventiveness. The most spontaneously innovative of his books in this respect is *The Wrench*, which showcases the numerous dialectal and technical imports that form the linguistic fabric of the novel.

Mengaldo summarizes other operational aspects of Levi's language in his study. Levi re-assigns or re-purposes a precise scientific or specialized meaning to commonly used words and expressions. In addition, Mengaldo points out, Levi's tendency to use a language with a high level of technical or scientific specialization often leads to portmanteaus and other word combinations (compounds, derivational prefixes or suffixes). Adopting technical terms, Mengaldo comments, allows Levi to articulate the meaning of the referent in a specific, multifaceted and innovative way. Similarly, Levi uses bureaucratic language, mimicking bureaucratic forms or formats, to mock bureaucracy itself (pastiche).

Levi's irony is metalinguistic. It serves to tone down the tone of the discourse, express perplexity and cast doubt on science and technology itself. Levi's irony is not only critical; it is also playful. The writer is the one who is having the most fun. Mengaldo reveals a contradictory element in Levi's use of oxymorons (including oxymorons with three elements), which would appear to contrast with the considered clarity of his prose.

This deployment of oxymorons is the greatest homage that Levi's rationality can pay to complexity, chaos, and contradiction. Oxymorons, as Mengaldo points out, are a compromise between two opposing forces, where clarity both resists and yields to its own necessary obscurity. At the core of Levi's language there is an unresolved knot, which readers perceive clearly and Levi exemplifies in the rhetorical figure of the oxymoron that rejects and confirms, confirms and rejects. It is a linguistic symptom of the split the author has often spoken about over the course of his life.

It is important to distinguish between Levi's narrative prose and his non-fiction, between a newspaper article or essay and one of his pastiches, although there are many passages in his work where these elements overlap. In *The Drowned and the Saved*, an example of discursive prose, his different approaches converge in a fortunate synthesis: discursive and probabilistic essay writing (typical of a scientist) blends with fiction; bearing witness combines with a reflective, knowledge-based element (Manzoni is Levi's model in this book; not just Manzoni the writer, but also Manzoni the theoretician and moralist).

Mengaldo sees the main characteristics of Levi's writing as being a strong taste for the spoken word; a lively sense of the social nature of language (the fall of the Tower of Babel is, for Levi, the most destructive myth); verbal playfulness; a taste for the signifier that would appear to be in contrast with the parsimony and sobriety of his prose; and a conception of life as theatre. More than one critic (Mengaldo and Segre, among others) have commented on the use of the historical present in *If This Is a Man*, together with its satellite forms such as the future, the present conditional and past indicative (Mengaldo 1990). Segre commented in particular on how the present tense appears to record experience as in a diary (Segre 1996). David Bidussa (1997) underscored the significance of the present tense and its corresponding idea of time, over and above any stylistic considerations. The peculiarity of *If This Is a Man* is the fact that the same situation is repeated in infinity. Bidussa has linked this temporal aspect to the gnomic present—a verb in the present tense used to express a general truth without reference to time —which is the structure adopted in proverbs (all of Levi's books in one way or another make use of this form of popular knowledge); but also to the eternal present of collective memorization. For Levi, the time-frame for bearing witness is immobility. It is the here and now, not in the sense of an eternal present, as in the circular time of myths, but in the sense that time is stuck.

The language of *If This Is a Man*, which we may consider 'classical' today, sounded out of tune for readers in the 1940s, who were looking for 'contemporary' forms. It is highly likely that the classical-humanist background (the 'basso continuo') of the book, the explicit and implicit references to Dante—the poet who was hallowed by the Italian education system in a nationalist and even fascist function (Boitani 1992)—felt out of date to post-war readers. Levi's language contained too many references to a cultural universe that was perceived as remote, if not extraneous: put simply, it was outdated. Most Italian literary writers at the time sought a 'realist', or neorealist, language to narrate the events of the war, the Resistance, and above all the new social reality of Italy, that had been so long obscured by Fascist rhetoric and propaganda;

a language that was born directly from life experience, or at least had found a way to communicate this experience in words.

What to us today may seem to be the only possible—or at least the most convincing—way to write about the abomination of the Lager (an aulic style, 'high' tone, classical stylistic devices, a rhetoric of narration borrowed from the Latin classics, figurative narrative and the moral force of reflection) might have appeared irrelevant in the new cultural and literary climate in 1947. Pavese's rejection of *If This Is A Man* on behalf of Einaudi, claiming it was better to wait before publishing the book—a view that Natalia Ginzburg agreed with—may well have had something to do with this linguistic 'prejudice'. Levi worked with a language that had been discarded by others, a language that was considered 'old'.

Levi stated on several occasions that if he had not been a chemist, he would have liked to have been a linguist. His work is a testament to his passion for words, their origin, meaning, use and 'abuse' (including that particular form of abuse represented by language games). Further examples are his cultured and curious linguistic digressions in *Other People's Trades* (about 10 of the essays are on the subject of language) and in many of his *Uncollected Stories and Essays*. *If This Is a Man* and *The Truce* are also filled with aspects of linguistic interest, some of which Levi himself stressed in his notes for the school editions of the two works.

Levi's focus is not only on human language, but also on natural language, in particular the language of animals (bees and insects). His linguistic passion stems from his curiosity, but also from the value of language for communicating among different peoples and nations (especially as a result of the Auschwitz experience), and from the playful aspect that is powerfully present in language and in particular in linguistic games. By becoming a writer, Levi, at least in part, satisfied his vocation to be a linguist.

The Search for Roots

In 1980, Giulio Bollati asked several writers from the Einaudi stable to create a personal anthology of books they would recommend to young readers. These anthologies would be published in the 'Readings for Middle Schools' series which had been very successful over the previous decade and made writers such as Calvino, Levi, Rigoni Stern and Sciascia famous. Bollati asked Primo Levi, Italo Calvino and Paolo Volponi, among others, to put together an anthology that represented a highly personal choice of readings, thus creating a portrait of the author.

The contract for *Antologia Personale* (Personal Anthology), as the book was originally titled (later becoming the subtitle), was signed in June 1980, with a deadline at the end of that year. By early autumn, with the help of his editor, Guido Davico Bonino, Levi had completed his anthology and handed it in to Bollati with a letter, now in the Einaudi archive. The letter was intended—at least by the author—as a Preface. The opening of the letter was in fact corrected from 'Dear Bollati' to 'Dear Publisher'.

Turin, September 2, 1980

Dear Publisher,

When Giulio Bollati proposed publishing a personal anthology I accepted right away because the idea spoke to my natural narcissism. I have worked on the project with pleasure, but as I proceeded with my selection, alongside gratification, more subtle sensations came over me. I will try to define these here.

I realized that this personal anthology is by no means exhaustive. No writer can be completely defined by the readings that have flowed into his bloodstream. My complete self is not contained in the authors and readings that follow, nor in those that I was not able to include. There have been other heavier inputs in my life. My outputs as a writer have certainly been influenced by what I have read, but my direct experience has been a far greater influence. This anthology is therefore incomplete, and we must not ask too much of it.

Nevertheless, I felt more exposed selecting these readings than I ever have writing my books. I have never undergone psychotherapy, nor have I ever had surgery, but this project felt like the equivalent. I felt as if my guts had been opened, or rather, as if I were opening them up myself, like Mohammed in the ninth circle of the Inferno in Gustav Doré's illustration. I have not left an explicit confession, but any nosy reader will notice things in my choices and in my omissions. Following the trail of Hansel and Gretel's breadcrumbs, if they think the challenge is worth it, they will be able to penetrate my guts and examine the ecosystem in operation there: saprophytes, day and night birds, worms, orchids, climbing plants, butterflies, crickets and spores. Just like Alcofribas in Pantagruel's mouth in the passage I selected for this anthology—and yet, I swear that when I was choosing it, I didn't realize how pertinent it was. I must have a trace of Es after all. In sum, you asked me to strip myself bare, and I have done so with all the seriousness and lack of shame I could summon up.

The order of the readings corresponds to the order in which I happened to read them, with the glaring exception of the first. The diagram that opens the anthology suggests four possible itineraries to follow in the readings.

Thank you for your proposal. I hope that at least some readers will find nourishment in the food that has nourished me.

Yours,

Primo Levi

Giulio Bollati and Carlo Carena decided that the anthology Levi had presented was unsuitable for the school series. Accordingly, on 27 November that year, Giulio Einaudi wrote Levi a letter, reminding him that the original aim of the project was to present suitable readings for middle-school students and proposing a possible solution to the problem.

> I saw, and I know, that the readings that you chose are 'more advanced' than the ones we would normally present to young people of this age. I think that the originality of your anthology, however, merits a solution which is a lesser evil. That is, we should publish an annotated version—an idea that had been considered in the original project—except that the Notes on the Texts should be entrusted to a person we have complete faith in, with the consent and the supervision of the author.

Less than a week later, the publishers found another destination for Levi's Personal Anthology—they decided to publish it as a book for 'adults', and then follow it up later with an annotated 'young adult' version. In a letter dated 8 December, Levi expressed his pleasure at the solution and suggested 'a different, wider ranging preface-justification' for the adult edition. 'I plan to hand it in soon,' Levi promised. 'As far as the notes for the middle-school version go,' he added, 'I agree they would be useful but I would very happily leave the task to somebody you trust, because I have some other meat on the fire right now.' The new contract, in the prestigious series, 'Gli Struzzi', was dated 9 December 1980. Levi handed in the typescript in March 1981.

The 'meat' Levi had 'on the fire' was the short-story collection, *Lilith and Other Stories*, the contract for which he signed in September 1981. The collection was published in October that year, but what was really keeping Levi busy was the novel that would later be called *If Not Now, When?* which he had already started researching and writing in 1980 (the contract for this book was signed in February 1982, with a March 1983 deadline).

In an interview she gave after her first novel came out, Rosellina Balbi pointed out that Levi's 'reading itinerary' in his anthology, which started with the Book of Job, was similar to that of the protagonist of Levi's first book, *If This Is a Man*: 'his itinerary starts with oppression and injustice, and after a more or less clear course that raises his awareness, it ends up with salvation.' (Balbi 1982). This observation once again shows the extensive links in Levi's literary work, with every piece being nourished by the next, or even by those that were written years before.

THE PREFACE

The Preface for the 'adult' anthology was based on the one he had written for the middle-school edition but was wider-reaching, richer and more complex. In fact, it constitutes one of the most important and significant texts in Levi's intellectual autobiography. It focused on a definition of *hybridism*, a concept that Levi considered important in his path as a writer, a path that he said he had mapped by 'harvesting, retrospectively and in good faith, which would bring to light the possible traces of what has been read on what has been written'. Levi called the book a 'second level' piece of work. This was an excellent definition for a literary autobiography written while redesigning a map of past and future work. Levi used the metaphor of the creatures that inhabited his guts (in the final version, the differences with the creatures mentioned in his letter to Bollati were significant: worms or orchids no longer featured). He then defined his perception of time as 'elastic', like sparrows' and squirrels' sense of time, and when he talked about how he felt denuded by writing his personal anthology, he referred to a detail of an etching by Gustav Doré of a scene from Dante's *Inferno*, one of his favourite references.

Above all, however, he expressed his awareness that while working by day he had produced 'a nocturnal, visceral and for the most part unconscious piece of work', to the extent that he repeated in this context a phrase he had used in various interviews and public speeches: 'I must possess a bit of Es after all.' This was the closest Levi—who was an avid reader of Freud and his psychopathology of everyday life—ever got to psychoanalysing himself. The 'roots' of the title referred to the parts of himself that lived underground, the most complex and troublesome parts. Levi declared that he felt disarmed when dealing with this side of his research, and stressed the blatant asymmetry of his relationship to the writers whose books he has read, such as Rabelais 'to whom I have stayed faithful for forty years without resembling him in any way and without knowing precisely why.' It was reading *Pantagruel* that first revealed to him the complexity of what he had done by compiling his personal anthology.

Levi's Preface was at once a splendid commentary on the selected texts and a legend to his map. He summarized the possible analogies among the authors and indicated four main paths to follow when reading the texts. These paths partly coincided with and partly diverged from the diagram given at the beginning of the book, but they provided an explanation of the commonalities and variations among his choices of texts. Levi also attempted to explain why he had not included certain other texts, justifying these exclusions by citing circumstances, actual impediments or simply personal idiosyncrasies towards some authors. When Tesio asked Levi in an interview whether he was deliberately concealing the influence of some of these authors in his work, he answered:

> In my intentions the anthology was supposed to be specific. I deliberately excluded names that are (or should be) the heritage

of every reader such as Dante, Leopardo, Manzoni, Flaubert, etc. If I had included them it would have been as if, under the heading 'Distinguishing Features' on my Identity Card I had written 'two eyes'. In other words, I omitted the works that have said something to everybody, or at least to all the Italian writers of my generation (Tesio 1981).

The image Levi chose to describe his way of reading and rereading the same books throughout his life was once again that of an animal, a woodworm in this case: 'I must confess that I prefer the sure choice, making a hole and then boring my way inside for years, like wood-worms when they found a piece of wood they really like.' When an interviewer asked him whether it was true that the anthology started out as a shelf of favourite books, Levi answered,

Yes, that's true. The shelf pre-exists the idea of the anthology. I have always made a habit of keeping the books I consider important, important to me that is, on one shelf of my book-case. I have also always had the habit of underlining significant passages in pencil, not only formative readings, but also surprising ones. This shelf in some way represents my cultural horizon, which is both vast and imprecise because I myself am a hybrid, half-chemist–half-writer—or, if you prefer, first chemist then writer. On the other hand, relationships between human beings and books aren't always lived out in the open, some of the links are subterranean and obscure (Einaudi newsletter 1981).

The concept of the shelf of books is vital for understanding the genesis of Levi's work and the numerous direct or indirect citations contained there (intertextuality in all its various forms, from parody to disguise, from pastiche to caricature). *The Search for Roots* thus provides a rich seam of information for understanding Levi's references, both from the texts he included and those he did not.

Levi habitually pondered everything he did, including of course the anthology project. It did not escape his notice, in fact, that the very idea of an anthology—which was not a selection of his own pieces but other authors—had a funereal quality, as if he were writing his own epitaph. He this attempted to lighten things up with a quote from Friedrich Schiller commenting on Lewis Carroll's *The Hunting of the Snark*: 'The dead no longer change and do not push other roots, they thus have the right to criticism.'

Another important feature of the anthology is that the selections were not placed in any historical order. The choices, rather, reflect the order in which Levi came across the authors and first started reading them, except that his taste for creating hybrids cross-pollinated some of the roots. Levi gave in to 'the temptation of contrast, bringing trans-century dialogues to life'. Nevertheless, Levi wrote, Job—in whom Levi identified, or at least identified a part of himself, the part that was 'degraded to laboratory animal'—was the first selection in recognition of his primogeniture.

The diagram placed at the beginning of the book indicating the four main paths to follow when reading is similar in many ways to the diagram of the Lemmas that Levi provided for the Einaudi Encyclopaedia published in 1977 (but already under construction in house in 1974, [Bertonem 1994]). Levi had already used this form of 'writing', which was a way of summing things up with words and signs together. The sphere or ellipse, as Calvino called it in an important review of the anthology, drawn by the author, looks more like a planar map ('suggesting four possible paths to follow through several authors in the field') than a drawing of a vectoral path. Levi drew these lines by hand, these meridians of a globe of resistance to pain, but he did not draw the parallels, leaving the reader to link the authors horizontally, including those writers such as Homer, Gatterman, Russell, Parini, Mann, Brown, Swift, Melville, D'Arrigo and Langbein, which were not included in the map.

The four paths indicated in the diagram—two for sufferance and self-testing and two for salvation ('laughing' and 'understanding') were not merely a key for reading an encyclopaedia of fragments of contemporary life. They also had an ethical and gnoseological value because they indicated the paths Levi himself followed in his life, between the figure of Job, the just man who suffered unjustly—the individual *par excellence* in Levi's ethics—and the solitude of the universe illustrated in the image of black holes:

> The misery of man has another face, one imprinted with nobility; maybe we exist by chance, perhaps we are the sole instance of intelligence in the universe, certainly, we are immeasurably small, weak and alone, but if the human mind has conceived Black Holes, and dares to speculate on what happened in the first moments of creation, why should it not know how to conquer fear, poverty and grief? (*The Search for Roots*)

Black holes are thus not a metaphor for disappearance (he used the term in an article, 'The Black Hole of Auschwitz', seven years later): they are a hypothesis created by the human mind for explaining astrophysical events. Astrophysics, Levi once wrote enthusiastically, was 'the greatest cultural revolution'.

Calvino, in his review of the anthology entitled *The Fours Paths of Primo Levi* (1981) called the work an encyclopaedia. Levi gave his riposte to this definition in an interview, suggesting a link between his 'encyclopaedia' for the self-taught (those who learnt through 'indiscriminate reading', as he put it in his Preface) and Flaubert's two encyclopaedic copy clerks, Bouvard and Pécuchet.

> Oh yes, Flaubert. The relationship is apparent. Flaubert's is nihilistic. It can be summed up by saying that there is no culture. Or rather, there is culture but it is not accessible to Bouvard and Pécuchet. Culture is aristocratic. Flaubert is an upside-down *Encyclopédie*. The *Encyclopédie* declared that everyone could

know everything, while Flaubert claimed that the men on the street cannot know anything. My intention, by contrast, is clearly optimistic. It was born from the desire to get people to participate in the idea that the world of books has its own weight and materiality, and that one can strike up a relationship, a friendship or even kinship with the protagonists of books. One can fall in love with a woman in a novel, or with a man, of course. In this sense, an example that comes to mind is Hermann Hesse's Journey to the East, where the author is on a pilgrimage with literary figures from the books in his library and the books he has read (Einaudi newsletter, 1981).

THE TYPESCRIPT

Levi gave the anthology to his publisher with the selected passages in the form of photocopies made from the books in his possession, as he indicated at the beginning of each piece, under the title he decided himself for each chapter. Where there was no existing translation, Levi translated the passage himself. He translated a text dated 1911, *The War of Fire*, and a passage taken from a Chemistry Manual by Gatterman, a detail from the American Society for Testing Materials, and simply annotated *Horcynus Orca* by D'Arrigo, as well as a poem by Belli.

The dates of the texts included in the anthology refer to books in Levi's possession with publication dates as far back as 1924, with an edition of Darwin's *The Voyage of the Beagle*, that does not acknowledge the translator, which might have belonged to Levi's father. Several others dated back to the 1930s, from books which must also have come from his father's library, although many of his books were lost during the war. Among the books from his youth was one that was very important in his formation as a writer, *Concerning the Nature of Things: Six Lectures Delivered at the Royal Institution*, by Sir William Bragg, which had been given to Primo by his father. Another was an Italian translation, probably a first edition in Italian of Swift's *Gulliver's Travels*, with no indication of the publisher or translator. Most of the other selections were taken from books Levi had bought and read in the 1960s and 70s. The passage from Roger Vercel, taken from the book Levi was reading in the infirmary the night the Germans left the concentration camp, was called *Remorques* (1935), and was translated by a friend called Vera Levin Drisdo, a secretary at Einaudi, who also translated Bulgakov's *The Master and Margarita* and many other books Einaudi titles. She was a Russian polyglot who had been saved by an Italian soldier after the 8 September 1943 armistice.

The anthology was published in the series 'I Struzzi' (n. 240) with an Escher etching, *Sphere Spiral*, as the dust-jacket illustration, an artist already used for the jacket illustration of *The Periodic Table*. The image was chosen as a counterpart to Levi's diagram. The dust-jacket blurb cited part of Levi's Preface. Two editions were printed, the first in 1981 and the second in 1987, for a total of 18,000 copies. Ten years after Levi's death, it was brought out in paperback, as with his other books, under the series 'Einaudi Tascabile'. Further editions added 15,474 copies between 1997 and 2015 to the total number of copies sold.

The anthology was not included in the newly translated *The Complete Works of Primo Levi*, published by W. W. Norton in 2015. It was considered a minor work with little significance, as if the fact that it was not Levi's own work detracted from its importance. And yet, Levi was an author who frequently cited the works of others and often appropriated them as his own.

LEMMAS

Alessandro Manzoni

Alongside Dante and Leopardi, Manzoni is the author that figures most often in Levi's opus, predominantly with his most famous work, *The Betrothed*, a set-text in post-unification Italian education. The novel is cited in *If This Is a Man*, more as reminiscences of images or situations than as lexical attributions; Levi's mechanical memory of Dante's verses is in fact much stronger. An example pointed out by Tesio is in the chapter 'The Events of the Summer', when the prisoners chew chicory and chamomile, but there is also a hint of Manzoni in the most Dantesque chapter of the book, 'The Canto of Ulysses'. The phrase 'don't let me think of my mountains, which would appear in the evening dusk as I returned by train from Milan to Turin!' (p. 108), recalls Manzoni's famous 'farewell to the mountains'. For Levi, those mountains are the symbol of his homeland. We find the same image in *The Drowned and the Saved*, in the chapter 'Stereotypes', where Levi comments on the concept of 'patria' (homeland) with an analogy from *The Betrothed*. He recalls that, for Lucia Mondella, 'the *patria* is visibly identified with the 'jagged peaks' of her mountains rising from the waters of Lake Como' (p. 2532).

Levi cites Manzoni most frequently when he is grappling with topics such as human gestures and oppression. In the essay 'Renzo's Fist' (*Other People's Trades*), Levi comments negatively on the gestures Manzoni's characters make, saying he finds them 'at the limit of the credible' (p. 2088). Levi is already interested in gestures in *If This Is a Man*. This is particularly evident in his description of the Kapo in 'Chemistry Kommando', Alex, with his threatening fists, and at the end of the chapter, 'Chemistry Examination', where he describes a contemptuous gesture which provoked so many reactions in German readers, as Levi later recounted. In 'Renzo's Fist', Levi shows how careful his rereading of *The Betrothed* is. He has often said he is more of a rereader than a reader of new books (though this is only partially true).

Rereading the episode where Renzo meets the monatti (corpse-carriers during the plague), Levi compares them to the devils of Malebolge 'with a group philosophy and a group ethics' (p. 2087). He thus establishes a direct link between Dante's image, Manzoni and the Lager, since in *The Drowned and the Saved*, members of the Sonderkommando are compared to corpse-carriers. To explain the psychology of the 'crows' in the crematorium, Levi cites the episode in *The Betrothed* of the little girl Cilia, who died of the plague. Another important reference in 'Renzo's Fist' is the episode of Agnese's capons, a 'precautionary gift' to Dr Azzeccagarbugli from his future son-in-law. Levi was struck by Agnese's outburst, when she gasps, 'Poor things!' which, in his words, 'bears the seal of literary and psychological genius: it is a compendium of that tangle of piety, tolerance and cynicism that is so typically Italian' (p. 2089). Agnese, Levi concludes, has 'performed a transference and has glimpsed [. . .] a symbolic value' (p. 2089) between the capons and herself, Lucia and Renzo: the three of them are the 'poor things'.

In a 2006 article 'Chiaro/Oscuro', Domenico Scarpa calls attention to a link between this citation from Manzoni and Belli's poem 'Se more', which Levi chose for his anthology, *The Search for Roots*. It is interesting to see how Levi touches on one of the main themes in *The Betrothed* and, at least in part, in many of Manzoni's works: a theme we might call 'Italian ideology'. Although he describes this ideology precisely, he never examines it in depth, perhaps because he is too busy interpreting a typical feature of the German character, Masslosigkeit (lack of measure), which he analyses in the chapter 'Letter to the Germans' (*The Drowned and the Saved*). Levi sees the cynicism, tolerance and piety of Italians—aspects which he mentions in various interviews when he talks about his stay in the Italian transit camp at Fòssoli—as benevolent when compared with the excesses of the Germans.

Manzoni is key in Levi's last book, where he analyses the theme of oppression at great depth and with acute perceptiveness. In 'The Gray Zone', the central chapter of *The Drowned and the Saved*, Levi cites

Chapter 2 of *The Betrothed*, where Manzoni expresses his view of the relationship between oppressor and oppressed: 'The troublemakers, the oppressors, all those who do harm of any sort to others, are guilty not only of the evil they do but also of the perversion of their victims' minds' (p. 2436). Levi's parallel is with what he calls the 'grey zone': that undefined area where the SS forced prisoners to work as their collaborators, the culminating example being the Sonderkommando, or special squad, who guided prisoners to the gas chambers, stripped the corpses, and put them in the crematoria.

Levi develops the theme of personal responsibility along the same lines as Manzoni's pietas (which is more Jansenist than Catholic). He also analyses the idea that evil corrupts its victims, challenging the victim/torturer dialectic that attempted to make victims and executioners co-responsible. As 'The Gray Zone' demonstrates, the idea of co-responsibility should be analysed in combination with the idea of the perverting influence of evil on its victims. Manzoni provides Levi with an interpretative key to address this complex topic.

There are several other passages where Levi mentions Manzoni. In his notes to the school edition of *The Truce*, for example, Levi associated his 'truce' to Renzo Tramaglino returning home and finding his untended garden run over with weeds (a reference to the relationship between chaos and order), and joins Ulysses in embodying the figure of the veteran returning home. In an article from the 1960s, collected in *Other People's Trades* with the title '*Tartarin of Tarascon*', Levi mentions the love that writers feel for their negative characters and cites Manzoni's fondness for Griso. In 'Novels Dictated by Crickets' in the same collection, Levi refers to the appearance of the 'bravos' as Manzoni describes them: their aggressively coloured uniforms are for him an ethological example of aggressiveness. Levi quotes Manzoni's Perpetua at the beginning of the chapter 'Tin' in *The Periodic Table* when she says, 'It's a bad thing to be born poor'; in 'Silver', he refers to the first lansquenet to die of the plague, as an example of evidence that should not be ignored. These passages remind us that literature is for Levi a continuous source of quotations and examples from which he can draw whenever he wants to cite a commonplace or use an analogy. He is highly skilled in using popular wisdom, reframing what has already been said and recurring to proverbs or clichés, as 'Leggere la Vita' in *Other People's Trades* shows. In Levi, who is perhaps more connected to direct experience than any other writer in Italian post-war literature, and who is one of the few authors who cannot be said to have been generated by the 'yawning of a book', intertextuality and metatextuality are always present.

Dante Alighieri

If This Is a Man is strongly permeated by Dante's presence: on a lexical level, with its numerous references to *The Divine Comedy*, but also on a structural level, since Levi's journey down into the depths of the *anus mundi* is a reprise of Dante's first canticle, *Inferno*. Moreover, many of the figures of the torturers, in particular in the first chapters, are modelled, at least on a literary level, on Dante's stereotypes.

The first figure that appears is Charon, at the end of the first chapter, embodied by a German soldier who asks prisoners if they have any money or watches they will no longer need. Immediately afterwards, faced with the inexplicability of the Lager, the author quotes two verses from the Canto XXI of *Inferno*, where the devils of Malebolge turn to the condemned soul as it arrives in Hell.

Tesio, urged by Levi, spotted one of Levi's many borrowings from Dante in the chapter 'Ka-Be': the phrase 'mi inducessi' is from *Inferno* XXX:89. Similarly, there is an explicit reference to Canto XXIV:92–93 in the chapter 'October 1944'. These covert and overt references testify to a time when many *terzine* from the *Divine Comedy* (and often the whole of the *Inferno*) were routinely learnt by heart in Italian schools, sometimes as early as elementary school. Dante was, for ideological reasons apart from anything else, a shared heritage among Italian schoolchildren. *The Inferno* was a cognitive paradigm on which many events of individual and collective life were modelled by analogy. One of these was the concept of 'counterpoint' (*Inferno* XXVIII:142) that links guilt to punishment in the chapter 'Beyond Good and Evil'.

The chapter title, 'The Drowned and the Saved', for example, is taken from Dante's *Inferno* IV:62–63 and *Inferno* XX:1–3 (Mondo 1995). Similarly, the description of the SS guard barking at the prisoners as they arrive, is modelled on the figure of the guard-dog Cerberus in *Inferno* VI:13–15. Likewise, Levi's description of Doktor Pannwitz in 'Chemistry Examination' contains a reference to Minos. The chapter, 'The Canto of Ulysses' is explicitly dedicated to Dante and one of his characters, Ulysses (*Inferno* XXVI), with whom Levi seems to identify. In this chapter, Levi tries to recall the lines in *The Divine Comedy* dedicated to Ulysses in order to teach Italian to Pikolo, his partner in delivering the midday gruel to the chemistry Kommando. Levi's memory fails him, and this failure is compounded by the difficulty of translating the lines into French, the language of his interlocutor.

This translation exercise, made worse by the lacunae in his memory, led Levi to reflect, perhaps for the first time, on a few analogies between Ulysses' condition and that of the prisoners in the Lager. As Piero Boitani points out (1992), Levi radically shifts both the interpretation of Dante's Ulysses proposed in Italian schools under Fascism ('a model of the heroic destiny of the lineage'), as well as the traditional reading of European and Italian romanticism ('Levi annihilates the orthodox and traditional critical reading of the *terzine*'). Ulysses dared to challenge divine dictates for the sake of knowledge. This is why he became, as Levi wrote in his notes to the school edition, 'a modern hero' who represents all the anguish and daring of Dante's time, as well as ours. Levi's new interpretation centres in particular on the anachronism of 'as pleased as Other'. Dante's 'Other' stands for God (it is anachronistic because Ulysses was a pagan hero but nonetheless speaks as if he were a Christian believer). The parallel that Levi establishes implicitly in the chapter (and later explicitly in his notes to the school edition) is between Ulysses, whose ship was sunk by God's will, and the fate of the Auschwitz prisoners. Paradoxically, they were both 'punished': Ulysses for breaking the barriers of tradition, the prisoners because they dared to oppose an overwhelming force, which was then the fascist order in Europe.

There is 'something else', another aspect of Levi's interpretation, 'something gigantic that I myself have only just seen, in a flash of intuition, perhaps the reason for our fate, for our being here today . . . '. (p. 109), which Levi comments on in his notes to the school edition. Among the various roots of German anti-Semitism, and therefore of the Lager system, he pointed out, there was a deep hatred and fear of the intellectual sharpness of European Jews. The young Levi and Pikolo identified with Ulysses' companions, recognizing that they were both representatives and heirs of that great tradition. Boitani puts forward the idea that what actually flashed through Levi's mind at the time, as he struggled to express the meaning of Dante's *terzine*, was that of a God who was perhaps happy for the fate of the Jewish people. The different interpretation that Levi provided many years later normalizes and perhaps hides that terrible thought, although it is hard to believe in Levi as a theologian, given the deep-seated secularism he shows throughout the book, particularly in the episode of Kuhn's prayer in 'October 1944' ('If I were God . . . ').

That Dante is a reference point for much of Levi's work is also confirmed in *The Truce*, where we find at least three explicit quotations, all three from the *Inferno*. The first refers to Mordo Nahum (*Inferno* XXVII:123); the second recalls the figure of Capaneo (a story with the same name, the first draft of which was written at the same time as *The Truce*, is dedicated to him in *Lilith and Other Stories*); the third in the penultimate chapter where, taking up the image of the journey—this time towards freedom—he speaks of the 'proud company' (*Inferno* XXII:14–15). There are also quotations from Dante in *Natural Histories*, notably in the short story, 'Angelic Butterfly', which cites a line from *Purgatory* Canto X:125 with a typical image of metamorphosis. There are references to *Purgatory* in two of the essays collected in *Other People's Trades*: when Levi cites Psalm 119, which Dante quotes in 'Signs on Stone', and when he describes an image of Arachne that accompanies an illustrated edition of the second Canto by Gustav Doré in 'Fear of Spiders'. In an essay in *Stories and Essays* on flying ('Man in Flight'), Levi refers to the episode of Geryon in *Inferno* XVII:116–17, where Dante experiments with gliding and makes a 'magical descent over the Malebolgias' (p. 2385).

These later references are erudite citations that no longer evoke the fear and condemnation that loomed in Levi's earlier works. Dante is a guide for Levi, a figure who was able to go through the experience of hell without relinquishing his curiosity and thirst for knowledge. At the same time, he is a paradigm of encyclopaedic knowledge that is not an end in itself; it is imbued with moral and ethical significance. This is the way Levi presents the knowledge of human behaviour that he acquired from the Auschwitz adventure. Levi's interpretation of Dante is a perfect reversal of the way the poet was presented in Fascist rhetoric. Behind many of his implicit quotations, however, there remain the signs that he read Dante through D'Annunzio, as well as—and this is a counter-remedy—through Gozzano.

Dante provides Levi with a model of psychological knowledge in his Lager-Inferno, to the extent that Levi's character portraits (in particular in the chapter 'The Drowned and the Saved') resemble Dante's descriptions of the condemned. Both show great precision in their character sketches, use few words to depict only what is essential, skilfully identify their character traits and attribute greatness even to the reprobates among the condemned. In short, Dante is a master of exemplariness; he is an *exemplum*. In Levi's last book, *The Drowned and the Saved*, he returns once again to the *Inferno*. In the chapter, 'The Intellectual in Auschwitz', Levi describes rereading 'The Canto of Ulysses' from *If This Is a Man*. On the first page of the chapter 'Stereotypes', Levi cites Francesca (*Inferno* V:121–23), who tells Dante 'there is no greater pain /than to remember happy times/ in misery', and goes on to create a parallel with the Yiddish saying he also used to preface *The Periodic Table*, 'It's good to tell past troubles' (p. 2521). (Levi quotes the same saying in the chapter 'Potassium' in *The Periodic Table*, a book that contains many other images from *Inferno*).

Poetry is often the 'matrix' of Levi's prose. There are three references to Dante that Levi made explicit in the notes included in the poetry collection, *At an Uncertain Hour*. The first is a poem written shortly after his return from Auschwitz, 'February 25, 1944' which cites *Inferno* III:57; the other in a poem 'Brown Swarm', written on 13 August 1980, which takes an image from *Purgatory* XXVI:34. It is no coincidence that this poem renews the painful memory of the Lager; he wrote it as he was starting to write *The Drowned and the Saved*. The third is the only explicit reference that is taken from *La Vita Nuova* (XXVI) rather than *Divine Comedy*. It can be found in the poem 'Another Monday', which is about the sadness of having to return to work at the beginning of the week. At the end of the poem 'Minos snarls horrifically/ from the megaphones of Porta Nuova' (p. 1892). The reference to Dante through Minos is also present in 'Chrome' (*The Periodic Table*). The only reference to Dante's *Paradise* (V:81)—perhaps not by chance—is contained in 'Iron': 'the Jew who "in your midst does not mock you"' (p. 785).

Alberto Cavaglion (2012) has hypothesized that Levi studied Dante's *Divine Comedy* with Giovanni Andrea Scartazzini's commentary, dated 1874–1882. The ninth edition was published by Hoepli in Milan in 1929, with Scartazzini's commentary revisited by Giuseppe Vandelli and a critical essay provided by the Italian Dante Society.

Giacomo Leopardi

At high school, Levi read Leopardi assiduously, alongside Dante and Manzoni; they were three of the literary classics in Italian education. In a 1963 interview with Pier Maria Paoletti ('I am a chemist, a writer by chance'), he says Leopardi's works, together with Foscolo's, have been 'stuck' in his memory since high school. In a much later interview with Aurelio Andreoli in 1981 ('For Primo Levi this is a different way of saying I'), he explains that Leopardi is not a favourite because of the poet's pessimistic vision. He did not include him in his personal anthology alongside Dante, because Leopardi belongs to his personal sphere ('I deny being a great reader of classics and novels', *Nuova Società*, 1981).

Nonetheless, Levi cites Leopardi openly in many of his works. Examples include a significant article published in 1983 by the Sondrio Banca Popolare, whose title, 'The Brute Power', is taken from a Leopardi poem that Levi quotes in a foreword ('To Himself'); and an essay, '"The Most Joyous Creatures in the World"' (*Other People's Trades*), where Leopardi's philosophical dialogue *In Praise of Birds* is the starting point of an ethological reflection on the behaviour of birds. Levi sees the core theme of Leopardi's prose as being perfect adherence to moral inspiration: 'These pages are firm and lucid, still valid, and their power comes from the constant, but unstated, comparison with the misery of the human condition, with our essential lack of freedom, symbolized by our earthbound nature' (p. 2200). Leopardi is a master of style and thought, a ruthless investigator of the human condition, therefore a moralist, as well as a natural philosopher. Both these aspects come together in Levi: morality goes hand in hand with a materialist philosophy, to the extent that for him Lucretius and Leopardi are on the same wavelength.

In a short story ('Dialogue Between a Poet and a Doctor', in *Lilith and Other Stories*), Levi imagines a dialogue, in the manner of Leopardi, between a young poet—an anguished Leopardi—and a doctor, who is part-family doctor and part-psychologist. Parodying Leopardi's 'Moral Operettas' and poems, Levi builds a pastiche: the poet's philosophy is transformed into a report of an individual illness. The story presents an element of schoolboy humour and reveals not only his deep knowledge of Leopardi's philosophical ruminations, but also a sense of identification with the poet. First published in *La Stampa*, Levi later added a passage on the young poet's relationship with women. At the end of the story, the poet crumples the doctor's prescription in his hand and throws it in the gutter.

Answering questions about translating Kafka's *The Trial*, Levi quotes two lines from Leopardi's poem 'Saturday night in the Village', creating a link between Kafka and Leopardi with an affective short-circuit ('An Aggression Named Franz Kafka'). In another conversation, on the topic of his relationship with Judaism, Levi says that in the absence of God, he has adopted Leopardi's point of view, since the poet accuses nature of deceiving his children with false promises of good that he knows he cannot keep ('Me and God'). A quote from Leopardi's 'The Calm After the Storm' ('Surcease from suffering / Is happiness for us') opens the chapter 'Shame' in *The Drowned and the Saved*, the book which contains the greatest number of quotations from other authors, and is a reliable, though not exhaustive, catalogue of his extensive literary knowledge. Levi writes, 'the pessimist Leopardi was stretching the truth in this description: he proved to be an optimist despite himself. In most cases, the hour of liberation was neither joyous nor exhilarating. It usually struck against a tragic backdrop of destruction, slaughter, and suffering' (p. 2457).

It is in the poems, especially those dedicated to animals, however that the presence of Leopardi—the poet-philosopher, a radical critic of anthropocentrism—is felt most keenly, alongside Darwin. The critic, Massimo Raffaeli quotes Leopardi's famous poem 'Broom' in this regard: 'Nature has no more love or care for the seed of man than for the ants: and if the destruction of one is rarer than that of the other, it's for no other reason than that mankind is less rich in offspring.'

Charles Baudelaire

In the penultimate letter Levi sent to the German translator of *If This Is a Man*, as he was finishing up his revisions in May 1960, Levi feels he needs to explain the provenance of the expression 'shameful disorder' (*infame tumulto*). This phrase appears in 'The Story of Ten Days', in the first line of the diary entry for 27 January that ends the book. The line reads, 'Dawn. On the floor, the shameful disorder of skin and bones, the Sómogyi thing' (p. 165). He explains to his correspondent that the word *infame* is a more or less unconscious theft from Baudelaire,

> *Au détour d'un sentier une charogne infâme*'. A shocked corpse, without any sign of piety from others, 'a Sómogyi thing', is more than *ebärmlich*; it is foul, scandalous, cries out to heaven; it is a stain of shame on God, on the Germans, on us, on everyone. We need a stronger word: *schändlich*. As for the word *tumulto*, I deliberately adopted the word outside its normal usage to capture the image of that hideous vision of broken limbs, which have found no peace even in death. Here, too, it would take something less obvious than *Haufe*.

The idea of a 'more or less unconscious theft', with its inherent self-irony is also significant. In his commentary on *If This Is a Man*, Cavaglion (2012) uncovers a series of references to Baudelaire. In the poem 'Shemà' that Levi uses as a preface to his book, there is an echo of Baudelaire's appeal '*Au Lecteur*' (To the Reader) used as a preface to his *Les Fleurs du Mal*. There are other passages in the book where Cavaglion glimpses these 'thefts', in the form of echoes or cryptic quotes, to the extent that the critic speaks of a Baudelairian Dante, or rather, of Dante Baudelaire. The reference is to Baudelaire's '*Au Lecteur*', but also to 'Dance Macabre'. Cavaglion also posits that references to both Dante and Baudelaire, with whom Levi created such dense intertextuality, were gradually eradicated—starting with Baudelaire—as Levi worked on his revisions for the 1958 Einaudi edition. That is, the edition we read today.

The hypothesis Cavaglion puts forward is that Levi was constructing a new image of himself as a writer, which required him to discard his previous literary aesthetic in order to take on the role of the writer-chemist. Cavaglion comments on his adoption of a stereotypical profile of the scientist-writer, and describes how Levi made a last-ditch attempt to change this at the end of his life, without, in Cavaglion's opinion, succeeding. The hypothesis highlights Levi's first and last works as being at the extremities of a fiction/non-fiction spectrum, overshadowing all the fiction he wrote in between.

When Levi pointed out the calque on Baudelaire to his German translator, the very fact that he wrote about it testifies to his desire to achieve an incisive yet literary style at a salient point in the book. References to Baudelaire and Dostoevsky were gradually revised and excluded because they represented the literary background of the former high-school student, who remained a curious and omnivorous reader from 1947 to 1958. Later, the awareness of his role as a writer shifted to his other main source of material: his work as a chemist. The letters that Levi wrote through the 1960s and 70s—to his translators, to his interlocutors, to Hety, with whom he also discussed his concentration-camp experience—show clearly how his work as a chemist gave Levi a double layer. He does not hesitate to call himself an 'amphibian', a person who frequents two kingdoms: land and sea. It is not always easy, however, to distinguish between his marine and terrestrial nature—to stick with his metaphor. On returning to Turin after surviving the Lager, his lexical, literary, cognitive and even ethical heritage was the result of his education: Dante, the Old Testament, classical mythology, the Gospels, Latin authors. Baudelaire is certainly among this group but, as the letter to the German translator shows, his presence is not as immediately obvious as Dante's, and is undoubtedly more hidden and 'unconscious'.

That a change is underway in his personality as an author is indicated by another letter to Riedt, dated 31 December 1959. After explaining that the last lines of the poem 'Shemà' (from which the title *If This Is a Man* is taken), are not taken from the foundational prayer of the Jews, 'Shema Yisrael' (Hear, O Israel), although they are biblical in tone—perhaps an unconscious plagiarism of some prophet—he suggests the translator replaces the poem with another one written in 1945. He does not say which, but it seems he sent it with the letter, writing that it is a poem 'which today I much prefer to the first one, because it is less obviously linked to the theme of the book, and therefore (it seems to me) sounds more freely allusive. If it is possible to translate it effectively, I would be glad see it in the other's place; I leave you and the publisher free to choose'. Riedt does not agree and leaves 'Shemà' as the preface. While Levi appears to be remarkably consistent, he is in fact, like most authors, a writer in the making. Although he constantly returns and continues to return to his experience of the Lager, he undergoes a series of transformations and changes in literary identity within the basic continuum of his style and personality. The presence of Baudelaire in his work, and then his absence, is a significant indicator.

François Rabelais

Undoubtedly *Gargantua and Pantagruel* is an important reference point for Levi, from which he has often drawn inspiration for details (the reference to the latrines of the Russian camp in *The Truce*, to give just one example, certainly comes from Rabelais). Levi loves, first and foremost, Rabelais' inventive skill, his whimsy and his idea that man is free rather than predestined, that he is his own maker (Levi uses the expression *faber sui* from an article published in *Il Giorno* in 1964, later published in *Other People's Trades* as 'François Rabelais'). Rabelais, writes Levi, feels 'close to us as a model, in his cheerfully curious spirit, his jovial scepticism, his faith in tomorrow and in man; and again, for the way he writes, so alien to categories and rules' (p. 2029). This ability to disregard categories and rules was what Levi appreciated about Rabelais in the 1960s: his 'writing however you like', as he defines it, referring to Sterne and Joyce too, 'without doctrines or precepts, pursuing the thread of imagination exactly as it unspools, by spontaneous demand, different and surprising at each turn, like a carnival parade' (p. 2029.). This way of writing is what Levi admired, being himself both free (his imagination is inventive and loose) and rigorous, striving to write in an everyday style, working more on a lexical than syntactic plane, privileging brevity and concision over overt expression or elaborate form.

Perhaps this is why Rabelais is a model for him; certainly for the joy that Levi perceived in his prose, given that, 'It would be hard to find a single melancholy page in his entire body of work, and yet Rabelais was familiar with human misery; he is silent about it because, a good doctor even when he writes, he refuses to accept it, his impulse is to heal it' (p. 2029). The therapeutic effect of writing, most of all on those who use writing as a therapeutic tool, is one of the aspects that Levi emphasizes most often in his interviews, starting with his experience of writing *If This Is a Man*.

In the short story 'In the Park' (*Flaw of Form*), there is a discussion among the immortal characters where Rabelais is quoted. Similarly, in 'Our Fine Specifications' in the same collection, one of the characters, Di Salvo, suggests Renaudo read Rabelais' *Decretals* where he will find 'Our Fine Specifications' (the whole story is inspired by the passage from Rabelais). Di Salvo advises his colleague to consider Rabelais' work 'an indispensable manual for every modern man' (p. 671).

In *The Search for Roots*, Rabelais is placed before two authors who are dear to Levi: Porta and Belli, examples of multilingualism that even Levi, although he didn't belong to the 'expressionist line' of Italian literature, has experienced in some of his books. Rabelais is summed up in the motto: 'Better to write about rice than about crime'. In his short presentation text to the three passages from *Gargantua and Pantagruel* he chose to anthologize, Levi reiterates, with identical words, the concepts expressed almost 20 years earlier in his article in *Il Giorno*: the idea that there is a relationship between Rabelais' incoherent and capricious way of narrating and the joy that flows from his pages. The book most imbued with Rabelais' spirit is undoubtedly *The Truce*.

Art

Henri, one of the 'saved' in *If This Is a Man*, 'has the delicate and subtly androgynous body and face of Sodoma's St. Sebastian' (p. 93). Levi's reference—pictorial or artistic citations are rare in his work—is to a painting now in the Uffizi Gallery in Florence by the artist Giovanni Antonio Bazzi, known simply as *Il Sodoma*. There are several references to Gustave Doré, whose illustrations for Dante's *Divine Comedy* he appreciated, in *The Search for Roots*, and elsewhere. In 'Fear of Spiders' (*Other People's Trades*), Levi describes a 'negligible phobia' he developed from an 'engraving by Gustave Doré illustrating 'Arachne' in Canto XII of *Purgatory*, with which I collided as a child' (p. 2147). Further references to art can be found in the short story 'Angelic Butterfly' (*Natural Histories*), where Leeb's long manuscript contains a chapter 'concerned with the iconography of angels and devils, from Sumeri to Melozzo of Forlí, and from Cimabue to Rouault' (p. 443). Similarly, the protagonists of the story 'Sleeping Beauty in the Refrigerator: A Winter's Tale' have paintings by Renoir, Picasso and Caravaggio hanging on their walls, while the 'apparatus' in the story 'The Measure of Beauty' (*Natural Histories*) is calibrated according to Sebastiano del Piombo's painting, *Fantesca*. In *Lilith and Other Stories,* the whole article, 'The Valley of Guerrino', is devoted to the fresco painter, Guerrino. Nonetheless, it cannot be said that art or the description of works of art play a decisive role in either Levi's fiction or non-fiction. True to his classical education, Levi does not attach great importance to this aspect of culture and human expression; rather, his aesthetics are directed towards the 'world of forms'— be they natural or artificial, insects or technological objects. This demonstrates that his attention to beauty is closely linked to his scientific interests; for Levi, and perhaps for many technologists and scientists, even a chemistry formula can be beautiful to behold.

The Bible

Explicit quotes from, or references to, the Bible are a constant in Levi's work. There are quotes from Exodus (*If This Is a Man*), Ecclesiastes (*Natural Histories*), Genesis and Leviticus (*Leviticus*), as well as a host of biblical figures, such as Moses, Samson and Delilah, Solomon, Jacob, Cain and the Snake (the most common biblical reference in his work). Levi also cites specific episodes: Babel (*If This Is a Man*), the Last Judgment (*The Drowned and the Saved*) and the Garden of Eden (*If Not Now, When?*). His references are not always from the Jewish Old Testament. Some are from the Christian tradition, through Dante—the literary figure with the greatest influence on Levi's culture—who introduced him to the Christian world, on the one hand, and pagan mythology on the other. Classical Greece was filtered through Dante and Homer, both obligatory reading in Levi's classical high school. Levi cites many heroes from classical mythology, such as the Christianized Ulysses in *If This Is a Man*; Tiresias, Hercules, Prometheus and Medusa (in *The Drowned and the Saved*); Circes and Tantalus, to name a few. The Old Testament is cited specifically in 'Argon' (*The Periodic Table*), an account of his Jewish ancestry, and in *If Not Now, When?* where Levi explores Eastern-European Jewish traditions, the Talmud and Jewish proverbs. Both of these are rereadings of the Bible that Levi undertook while writing the novel. The figure of the Golem is mentioned in 'The Servant' (*Flaw of Form*) and 'Lilith' (*Lilith and Other Stories*), based on Jewish legends which also inspired a 1965 poem with the same title. There is a direct reference to Jewish ritual and tradition, which Levi rediscovered at Auschwitz, in the two poems: 'Shemà' and 'Passover'. Both poems are interwoven with Old Testament references, revealing a re-emergence of the education he received as a young man.

Pain

In 'Against Pain' (*Other People's Trades*), Levi explains why animals must be respected: not because they are God's gift to man, as theologians know, or because they are at man's service, as others say,

> but because a rule engraved within us, and acknowledged by all religions and codes of law, requires that we avoid creating pain, either in humans or in any other creature capable of feeling it. 'All is mystery except our pain.' The layman has few certainties, but the first is this: it is acceptable to suffer (or to cause suffering) only if doing so prevents greater suffering (p. 2059).

Levi doesn't think that the life of a crow or a cricket is worth as much as human life, and he is doubtful that an insect can perceive pain the same way humans do, but he admits 'birds probably feel pain and mammals definitely do' (p. 2059). The task of all humans, in Levi's view, is 'to reduce as much as possible the tremendous volume of this 'substance' that poisons every life, pain in all its forms' (p. 2059). The article is a clear example of Levi's ethics, inspired by Kant, which fit his character perfectly.

The theme of pain returns to other places in Levi's work, in particular in *If This Is a Man* and, in the chapter 'Useless Violence' in *The Drowned and the Saved*. In a 1984 poem, 'Pious', Levi makes an allusion to the well-known lines by Carducci (*t'amo pio bove*) when the poet describes a bull's life of daily violence. The bull is far from being a literary animal. In fact, Levi writes, 'Pious bull my ass. Pious under duress, / Pious against my will, pious against nature' (p. 1975). He is an object of man's violence: 'Oy gevalt! Unheard–of violence / The violence of making me nonviolent' (pp. 1975–76).

As Porro observed (1997), in Levi's work, reason can never be a contributing factor in rebuilding humankind, since there is no certainty that reason will triumph or that its products will not be poisoned fruits. Paradoxically, pain is what the recreation of the world may depend on. This concept is explored in a short story, 'A Will' (*Lilith and Other Stories*), where an old tooth-puller leaves a letter and a 'holographic will' to his son, who is destined to follow in his footsteps. Levi playfully but punctually parodies an ancient text, and enunciates his theory of pain. 'Experience will also teach you that pain, though perhaps not the only information of the senses that can be doubted, is certainly the least dubious' (p. 1488). Citing Descartes ironically ('that French sage whose name escapes me' [p. 1488]), the tooth-puller reminds his son that the certainty of existence should have been based precisely on pain and not on methodical doubt: 'In fact, often those who think aren't sure they're thinking, their thought wavers between awareness and dream, it slips between their fingers, refuses to be grasped and fixed on the page in the form of words. But those who suffer, yes, those who suffer have no doubts, those who suffer are, alas, always certain, certain they are suffering and *ergo* exist' (p. 1488).

This concept is completely secular. There is not a hint of theology in Levi's work, let alone a 'theology of evil'; pain is seen as a physiological fact. Levi is a materialist—we could call him a Leopardian materialist—who considers pain as a source of knowledge.

Happiness/Unhappiness

'Sooner or later in life we all discover that perfect happiness is unrealizable, but few of us pause to consider the opposite: that so, too, is perfect unhappiness' (p. 13). These words appear in the chapter 'The Journey' in *If This Is a Man*, a reflection just before the departure of the freight train that will transport the Jews from the Fòssoli transit camp to Auschwitz. It is a moral reflection that Levi then goes on to substantiate by stating that our 'human condition is hostile to everything infinite', and then listing 'the obstacles preventing the realization of both these extreme states': our 'inadequate knowledge of the future' (hope or uncertainty about tomorrow); 'the certainty of death' (a limit on joy but also on sorrow); 'our material cares' that, while 'poisoning every lasting happiness', nevertheless 'assiduously distract us from our misfortunes' (p. 13). Reflections of this kind appear elsewhere in Levi's work. His sources are Stoic philosophy, Scepticism, Montaigne, Leopardi and Pascal's *Thoughts*.

Levi returns to the idea of unhappiness—the subject of his most intense moral reflection throughout his work—in the chapter of *If This Is a Man* which Levi called, not by chance, 'A Good Day':

> For human nature is such that sorrows and sufferings simultaneously endured do not add up to a whole in our consciousness but hide, the lesser behind the greater, according to a definite law of perspective. This is providential and allows us to survive in the camp. And this is the reason that so often in free life one hears it said that man is never content. In fact, it is a question not of a human incapacity for a state of absolute happiness but of an ever-insufficient knowledge of the complex nature of the state of unhappiness; so that the single name of its major cause is given to all its causes, which are numerous and arranged hierarchically. And

when this most immediate cause of unhappiness comes to an end, we are painfully surprised to see that behind it lies another one, and in reality, a whole series of other ones (p. 70).

Levi reveals a high degree of psychological sensitivity, considering that Levi was a young man when he wrote *If This Is a Man*. There is certainly in his nature a habit of introspection, a source of his psychological reflections, which is combined with his close observation of other people's behaviour. Of all the characters portrayed in his first book, Elias, the deranged dwarf endowed with bestial vigour and perhaps insanity, is unique in being described by Levi as 'a happy individual'. Levi returns to the topic of happiness and unhappiness in *If Not Now, When?* in Mendel's reflections on Leonid and Linde, namely, within a relationship of desire, love and envy. It is also present in Levi's poems, in a more figurative way, without the piercing analysis that appears in *If This Is a Man*.

Envy

Levi explains in 'To Translate and Being Translated' (*Other People's Trades*) how the Italian word *invidia* 'has a more specialized meaning than the French *envie*, which can also mean desire, and than the Latin *invidia*, which also incorporates hatred and aversion, as is attested b by the Italian adjective *inviso* (abhorrent)' (p. 2119). The family of words, Levi posits, originally referred to the idea of 'looking poorly upon' 'to see badly', both in the sense 'causing harm by looking, that is, casting an evil eye, and in the sense of feeling uneasy when looking at a person who is hateful to us, and of whom we say (but only in Italian) that *non possiamo vederla* (literally, "we can't see him", meaning "we can't stand him")' (p. 2119). Levi mentions the term in an article on the difficulty of translating from one language to another, but he uses the word 'envy' often in his work. This may well indicate that it is an emotion that both attracts and repels Levi but which he considers a significant feature of human behaviour, to the extent that he dedicates a passage to it in his personal anthology, *The Search for Roots*.

The first time that the term appears is in *If This Is a Man*, when Levi describes the reactions to the news that he has been included in the small number of those who will work in the Buna chemical laboratory: 'Many comrades congratulate us; Alberto first of all, with genuine joy, and not a trace of envy. Alberto holds nothing against my good fortune, and is really pleased, both because' (p. 132). For Levi, in the Lager envy is opposed to friendship; it is its exact opposite. Envy produces unhappiness not only for oneself, but also for others; the greatest example is Hitler who in the Appendix is presented as 'a failed painter and failed architect, [who] pours out onto the Jews the resentment and envy of frustration' (p. 137). Envy also generates evil in Mendel, whose name means 'consoler' in *If Not Now, When?* He envies Leonid for his youth and precipitous love, and yet he is ashamed of it.

The passage from Bertrand Russell's *The Conquest of Happiness* that Levi included in his personal anthology is all about envy. For Russell, envy is the greatest obstacle to achieving happiness. In his view, after anxiety it is one of the strongest causes of unhappiness and one of the most deeply rooted and universal human passions. The extract also contains one of Levi's rare reflections on education. In general, his work does not seem to provide any pedagogical guidelines. On the basis of the philosopher and logician's words, Levi gives some indications as to how to cure envy: for saints, the answer is altruism; for ordinary men, envy is an obstacle to achieving happiness. The only appropriate remedy, he concludes, is mental discipline, and the habit of not indulging in useless thoughts. Russell's suggestions are well suited to Levi's stoicism; in both there is in fact the idea that social mechanisms are nothing more than projections of the psychological mechanisms of individuals. In Russell's view, envy is linked to the social mechanism that is competition: instability in the social order of the modern world, alongside the doctrines of democracy and socialism, have greatly extended the field of envy, meaning that envy occupies a singularly important place in our age.

Hermann Langbein

Born in Austria, Hermann Langbein, the famous historian of the camps, fought in the Spanish Civil War before being made a prisoner in Dachau, Auschwitz and Neuengamme, where he was a member of the secret self-defence organization. A convinced communist, he left the party in 1956 after the Soviet occupation of Hungary. It was not until 1972 that he wrote *Menschen in Auschwitz* (*People in Auschwitz*) which Levi tried several times to have translated into Italian. The book was rejected by Einaudi and finally published by Mursia in 1984, with a foreword by Levi (*Uncollected Stories and Essays*).

Levi had been in contact with Langbein since the 1960s, when the Austrian historian played an important role in the international organization of former deportees (as also emerges from Myriam Anissimov's biography, *Primo Levi: Tragedy of an Optimist* [1999], which refers to their correspondence). In his foreword, Levi explains the significant role Langbein played in the extermination camp, where he was interned as a 'political prisoner': secretary of one of the most powerful officers in the camp and at the same time member of the clandestine committee. After his release, Langbein had access to the records of the trials against Nazi criminals. What interested Levi was the depth and breadth of Langbein's research, and the fact that he was the only historian in the post-war period who devoted so much attention to understanding how 'man can go that far', concluding,

> Those who bear the greatest responsibility are Menschen, too; they are made of the same raw material we are, and it did not require a great effort or real coercion to make them into cold-blooded assassins of millions of other Menschen. A few years of perverse indoctrination and Dr Goebbels' propaganda were sufficient. With some exceptions, they were not sadistic monsters; they were people like us, trapped by the regime because of their pettiness, ignorance, or ambition (p. 2672).

Levi's foreword was written before the book came out in Italy, and it anticipates some the themes he would go on to explore in 'The Gray Zone' (*The Drowned and the Saved*). Langbein's analysis applies not only to

Nazism but also to every totalitarian society. In 1981, Levi translated a passage from *People in Auschwitz* to include in his personal anthology: Levi explains that the book was close to his heart and that he wished he had written it, but had been unable to because his horizons were too narrow in the Lager. In his correspondence with Hety, Langbein is mentioned several times, a sign that there was a close, continuous relationship over time between Levi's German correspondent and the Auschwitz historian.

Mario Rigoni Stern

The writers Levi felt closest to, owing to their similarity, common experience and sensitivity, were Fulvio Tomizza, Nuto Revelli and Mario Rigoni Stern, author of *The Sergeant in the Snow* (1953), a pictorial dialectal *anabasis*, as Vittorini defined it. Levi paid attention to Stern's work throughout his life, and included a passage from one of his books, *The Story of Tonle*, in his personal anthology, *The Search for Roots*, which he introduced with loving words. Levi points out that the fact that Stern exists is nothing short of miraculous, first and foremost because of his own miraculous survival. Fate led him to fight all the wars of his time, and he emerged unscathed and uncorrupted from the French, Albanian and Russian fronts, and from the Nazi Lager. For Levi, Stern was a great example of how literature can be linked to language and territory; a life experience filtered through memory.

As Stern himself recounted in an article published the day after his friend's suicide in *La Stampa* (a newspaper they both contributed to), 'La Medusa non ci ha petriti' ('Medusa has not turned us to stone', 14 April 1987), the two writers often met in Turin and Levi once visited Stern in Asiago, where he lived. Their friendship dates back to the 1960s, when Einaudi published Stern's novel, *Il bosco degli urogalli* (1962), and Levi wrote him a letter. In his article, Stern—who, like Levi, was not a professional writer —cited a 'private' poem Levi had sent him in 1984: 'To Mario and Nuto / I have two brothers with a lot of life on their shoulders, / Born in the shadow of the mountains. / They learned indignation / In the snow of a faraway country, / And they wrote books that were not useless. / Like me, they tolerated the sight / Of Medusa, who did not petrify them. / They did not let themselves be petrified / By the slow snowfall of the days.'

Levi dedicated the short story 'Mutiny' (*Flaw of Form*) to Stern. Clotilde, the protagonist, is an adolescent, who lives in the woods and talks to plants and animals. The article, 'Fossil Words' (*Other People's Trades*), opens with a disquisition on Stern's use of the word 'baita' ('shelter, refuge, salvation, home' p. 2212) in *The Sergeant in the Snow*.

PORTRAIT OF LEVI SMOKING AND DEBATING (1978)

This is a very unusual image of Levi. He is voluptuously inhaling the smoke from his cigarette, his palm resting on his cheek, his eyes half-closed. The photograph was taken by Giuseppe Varchetta in 1979, when Levi was at the Milan communist party festival, the Festa dell'Unità, presenting Paolo Volponi's book *Romanzo e Lavoro*. He has just published *The Wrench* (1978), and three years have gone by since *The Periodic Table*. He no longer works at the SIVA factory, having finally retired. He has grown his beard, which gives him an air of the wise man, or the prophet—although Levi would have hated the idea. He did not like prophets. The grey hair, beard and receding hair line all lend him gravity. In other photos from the same presentation, Levi is wearing his glasses, or is holding a can of beer and a plastic glass. His gestures are measured, contained. It is as if he has undergone a physical mutation compared to the photos of him as a chemist taken over the previous decade, or the family figure published in *Gente*. Other photos from this period portray him speaking in public, his glasses pushed up onto his head, his cigarette held between his index and middle fingers. He is just beginning to look like the man he became many years later, the image we have of him in the last years before his death. He no longer wears the striped sports jackets he wore in the 1960s, captured in a 1966 photograph by Pieralberto Marché, the theatre director and actor that staged *If This Is a Man*. He is now a retired chemist, and no longer sticks a pen into the pocket of his sports jacket, a sign at the time that you were a professional man. The double, centaur-like identity (chemist and writer, witness and writer) he spoke to journalists about after *The Truce* was published is beginning to fade. He now speaks as a writer and uses material from many walks of life in his writing. He has turned into an

313

engaged intellectual. He contributes pieces to newspapers about current affairs and politics, from Kappler's escape to Aldo Moro's kidnapping and death. His presence at the Festa dell'Unità was a mark of this new role.

Lilith and Other Stories

THE COLLECTION

In early 1981, Levi decided to publish a new collection of short stories. In the spring-file where he kept his manuscripts, there were many pieces that had been published over the previous decade in journals and newspapers, especially *La Stampa*, with whom Levi had collaborated more intensely. This was not the first book Levi put together by collecting short-fiction pieces. *Natural Histories* and *Flaw of Form* followed the same pattern. And yet, Levi's attitude towards this new collection was different. By this time, he felt more confident, more truly a writer. The contract signed with Einaudi bears the date 19 September 1981, less than a year after he had accepted Einaudi's proposal to publish a personal anthology of the books that had most influenced his work.

In 1978, Levi had finally retired from the SIVA chemical works and had devoted himself to writing full time. These were his most prolific years, during which he also planned the books he would write in the future. For *Lilith and Other Stories,* he gathered 38 pieces, dividing them into three sections: 'Present Perfect' with 12 stories, 'Future Anterior' with 15 and 'Present Indicative' with 9. In this division, the present-perfect tense indicated that, in Levi's view, the past never really passed, was still in some way present and would continue to loom over the future. Not by chance, the second group of stories was collected under the title 'Future Anterior', and the present-indicative tense does not appear until the third set of stories, last in the time sequence.

The two collections, *Lilith and Other Stories* and *Other People's Trades*, where Levi gathered his essays, were conceived together and are inter-connected, confirming the hypothesis that they were 'twins', as Levi suggested that *The Periodic Table* and *The Wrench* had been. The stories in *Lilith and Other Stories* were published in the years between 1973 and 1981, while the essays in *Other People's Trades* appeared between 1976 and 1985 (with a few exceptions that were published in the 1970s). However, as far as publication dates are concerned, nearly all the stories had come out in print between August 1977 and September 1980, during which time Levi had also published several poems and articles. There was a period between April and November 1978—just after publishing *The Wrench*—when Levi only published stories in *La Stampa*. This was probably when Levi decided to compile a collection. Putting together the stories for *Lilith*, Levi excluded only two from before 1981, 'The Interview' and 'Made for Each Other'. These two stories were later included in the collection *Stories and Essays*, a double-sided book published by *La Stampa* in 1986.

It is interesting to observe that the section entitled 'Present Perfect' and devoted to the Lager experience, contained stories written between 1975 and 1980 (most of them between 1977 and 1979), that is, before the project for *The Drowned and the Saved* was conceived. Over these years, the writer's 'mechanical memory'—as he defined it—produced further variations on the theme of the Lager. Names and episodes from his 'Auschwitz adventure' which had not found a setting in previous books worked their way back into these stories. There are only two exceptions to this rule: 'Capaneus' and 'A Disciple', were re-editions of two texts written much earlier, in 1959 and 1961, respectively. Their narrative style betrays the fact that they belong more properly to the atmosphere of *The Truce* ('A Disciple', in fact, appears in the notebook manuscript of *The Truce*), or even to that of *If This Is a Man*. On the last page of the 1947 edition of *If This Is a Man*, published by De Silva and then handed over to Einaudi as a draft manuscript for a new edition, there is a penned annotation: 'Capaneo'. This shows that a plan to write a story after the publication of *If This Is a Man* already existed in the late 1940s or at most the early 1950s.

Years later, in his Preface to *Moments of Reprieve* (1986), the US edition collecting his stories and other pieces from *Stories and Essays*

(1986), Levi explained how these short stories—marginal 'states of grace' as he called them—were born in a different spirit from *If This Is a Man*. They were conceived from a desire to represent strange, bizarre human figures and episodes. These characters demanded—some more imperiously than others—that he remembered what happened, and that he left a trace of their existence in his writing. Clearly Levi chose to adopt a different narrative tone for his attempts to salvage these memories. There is more pleasure in the telling of the story, and less asperity—a feature which Levi had always recognized as one of his traits in that period of his life, both as a man and as a writer. It finally felt to him as though the terrible truth of the Lager were behind him in that period, although it was later to reappear in his last book *The Drowned and the Saved* as a kind of re-appraisal. These stories were not witness accounts but, rather, stories of individuals, stories of moments of respite, rest, or reprieve during the harsh life of the camp. There were also stories of salvation ('Cesare', 'Avrom' and 'Gioele') he had heard told or read. The word 'Reprieve' in the title indicated a suspension of the death penalty. They are stories, not personal accounts, he stated in his Preface.

Whenever he was asked why he had gone back to writing about the Lager experience decades after the early testimonies, Levi would answer that in *If This Is a Man* he had tried to write the most important and most difficult things. The book was a witness statement, in a legal sense: an indictment. This was why, he would explain, certain episodes or subjects felt marginal at the time, 'an octave lower', and he only came around to writing about them much later (Bravo and Cereja 1987). Moreover, the stories in 'Past Perfect' show a greater attention on Levi's part to Eastern European Jewish tradition which—except for a few figures—was almost entirely absent in his first two books. This was also true for the poem 'Ostjuden', written in February 1946 on his return to Italy, and dedicated to the Eastern European Jews he had met in the camp, some of whose names and trades Levi had given in *If This Is a Man*.

In the decades that had gone by since publishing his first book, the writer had both the time and the means to reflect on his encounter with the Yiddish communities in the camps, and he would go on to talk about these encounters in many interviews after 1982. He had also read and researched their culture and civilization, elements of which find their way into the stories in this collection, to the extent that one could consider them a link between the two books on the Lager experience and the novel *If Not Now, When?* as he himself suggested in an interview on the new collection *Lilith and Other Stories* in 1980 (Romano 1981). Similarly, they could be seen as a preamble to *The Drowned and the Saved*, although the tone and the subject matter are completely different.

It was not by chance that the last piece in the first section of this collection was the story 'The King of the Jews', a narrative essay written in 1977 that later found its way in a different version into 'The Gray Zone', the theoretical core of *The Drowned and the Saved*. The title alluded to Jesus's death in a historical context and the story is, in some ways, a reflection on the function of a surrogate and his relationship with power. The story first appeared in *La Stampa* on 20 November 1977, but was already in the writer's mind at least two years before. Levi had written to his cousin Anna Yona about his idea for a story and asked her for reading material on Chaim Rumkowski, the protagonist of the story. Another point to bear in mind is that Levi gave the title 'Present Perfect' to what he considered 'moments of reprieve' in his experience of the Lager.

The story 'Capaneus' had been published in November 1959 by the literary journal *Il Ponte*. The first version had an interesting beginning: 'Me. You know me. It could be that down there, in those zebra rags, my beard even more unkempt than usual, my head shaved, I looked very different from now. This has no importance. The basis is the same.' Levi later cut this incipit in a new version published in *La Stampa* on 28 May 1978, editing out all references to himself (that is, to the author of *If This Is a Man*), although a year after Einaudi had republished the book it was pretty evident who he was talking about (Scarpa 2015). The edited lines, moreover, show how Levi had been trying—at least in the period when he was writing *The Truce*—to find a narrative tone that reflected the informal register of his early writing, adopting a 'spoken' tone. His literary models in this case included Joseph Conrad who was referenced at the end of *The Wrench*. Rewriting 'Capaneus' 20 years later, Levi changed the name of one of the story's protagonists and made the tone more impersonal while maintaining his signature 'oral' register. Readers encountering the story in *La Stampa* would automatically have identified the narrator's voice as that of the Auschwitz survivor, author of *If This Is a Man* and *The Truce*. This of course changed the dynamic. Levi's changes to the story were additions to the original text, which he kept almost as it was. He also made the Dante reference in the title—Capaneo was a figure in Canto XIV of Dante's *Inferno*—explicit in the later version, where it was implicit in the original. The later newspaper edition, furthermore, made erudite references to Villon and Rabelais, and cited *Edda*, as well as giving the protagonist Rappoport a Latin phrase to say.

In his rewriting of the story 'A Disciple', re-published in *La Stampa* on 1 June 1975, Levi added some text in order to better define the figure of Bandi, and cut a few references such as the Prague cabaret and the chorus of a song. He also changed the beginning and the end of the story. Where Bandi had said 'Meine erste Organisierung' ('The first thing that I've organized') as he handed him a radish, Levi changed the text to the more lyrical 'I've learnt. It's for you: it's the first thing I've stolen.'

The essay-like quality of some of the stories (nearly all of them, in some way or other, have the tone of an essay) is also worth mentioning. In particular, 'The Story of Avrom' (1976) is a summary (an art in which Levi excels, in both stories and essays) of a 1984 preface that Levi would go on to write for Marek Herman's *Diary of a Jewish Boy During the Second World War*, having presumably seen the book in manuscript form. 'Tired of Fictions', which came out in 1978, was another story rewritten from a book that Levi prefaced in 1973. The story that gave its name to the collection, 'Lilith', was presented in *La Stampa* not as a story—not even as a 'Sunday Story'—but, rather, as a 'Melancholy Story' (the same title as a poem written in 1965). With the exception of these two 'essay-stories', 'The King of the Jews' and the two stories about Lorenzo and Cesare's return to Italy, there are only seven set in the Lager.

One must add to this body of work on the Lager experience, after *If This Is a Man*, the three pieces collected in *Stories and Essays* and of course 'The Last Christmas of the War', published privately in 1984 and later by the journal *Triangolo Rosso* (but present in *Moments of Reprieve*, 1986).

The second section of *Lilith and Other Stories* bore the title 'Future Anterior', a grammatical tense that indicates a 'future in the past'. Thus, two of the three sections conjugate in the past. Answering a student who asked him how to interpret the 'science fiction' elements of his work, meaning their atmosphere of dreams and visions, Levi declared, with his usual sense of humour:

> I wouldn't take the stories in the section of *Lilith*, 'Future Anterior', too seriously. They are stories I wrote with a different stimulus each time. I would also like to say this: I think a book, or a story, has more value the more interpretations you can make of it, so all possible interpretations are correct. In fact, the more interpretations a story can offer, the more ambiguous that story is. I'd like to insist on that word, 'ambiguous'. A story must be ambiguous, otherwise it's just an account. So, every-thing has value: rationality has value, the world of science fic-tion has value, and the sensation of dreams has value. Some of these stories, I must confess, are actual dreams, dreams in the strictest sense of the word, nocturnal dreams. Dreams have been interpreted, we know they contain many different things; they contain things left over from the day, but they also contain profound traces of the personality of the person who is dream-ing. These stories are dreams that I have elaborated as well as I could so that I could give them a form that I could transmit, and that readers could use' (Costantini and Togni 1990).

Most of the stories, as we mentioned earlier, were published between 1977 and 1978, some with different titles in *La Stampa*, or in the weekly literary supplement *Tuttolibri*. 'Gladiators', which Levi discussed with high-school students in Pesaro, was published in the journal *L'Automobile*, while the 1973 story, 'Tantalum', came out in

Il Mondo. The subject matter and the title—Tantalum is a chemical element—mean the story belongs to *The Periodic Table*, although the fantasy element of the story most likely persuaded Levi not to include it in the later book. Levi made a few corrections to the newspaper or journal texts before adding them to his collection, such as in 'Dialogue Between a Poet and a Doctor', which originally came out in a weekly column of *La Stampa* where he often published both essays and stories.

The title of the third section, 'Present Indicative', refers to current situations that are 'indicative' of the times. This final section contains stories which have similarly strong links with *The Periodic Table*. 'The Molecule's Defiance', for example, is in fact a chapter of the book, while 'Weekend' is a chapter of Levi's autobiography before deportation, and 'Decoding' is a story about contemporary racism. There are also links with *The Wrench*. 'The Soul and the Engineers' could well have had Faussone as a protagonist—it was probably a story Levi had heard. Other stories bear no relation to Levi's other works. 'The Sorcerers', for example, is really an ethnographic story, with a narrative style Levi later developed in *Flaw of Form*. 'Guests' too could well have been a story of partisan warfare that Levi had heard and then written down. The story could also have been derived from old memories; they are reminiscent of Calvino's partisan stories but cruder and more imaginative. There are several references to Calvino in this collection as a whole, with deliberate allusions to his work, such as in 'A Tranquil Star' which was originally published in the journal *L'Astronomia*. 'Brief Dream' and 'The Girl in the Book' are two story-digressions, echoes of a genre that was popular in the cultural pages of newspapers in the 1950s and 60s.

THE TYPESCRIPT

The typescript comprises photocopies of the stories and an index where the original title of the volume is indicated as *The First Wife*. Later, 'Lorenzo's Return', the only story that had not previously appeared in a journal or newspaper, was added to the index. It is thought that Levi saved the story for a collection—rather than publishing it in a newspaper with a far wider circulation—out of decency. He wanted to reserve the story—of the man who saved his life at Monowitz and then let himself die—for a smaller circle of readers (Scarpa 2015). There are also some corrections written directly onto the typescript that was handed over to Einaudi for publication. In 'Capaneus', the name Lonzana is changed to Valerio in the first line. The title 'Inside the Lager with Lilith', which had appeared in *La Stampa*, was corrected simply to 'Lilith'. In 'The Story of Avrom', the words 'central parish' were changed to 'Parish of St Maximus.' At the beginning of 'The King of the Jews', Levi changed the words 'to Auschwitz' to 'On my return from Auschwitz,' and the image of the coin that was printed alongside the story in *La Stampa* was added to the type-script. 'Gladiators', on the other hand, was an original manuscript, typed directly onto the back of sheets publicizing new books released by Rizzoli (1 April 1976) which happened to include Ken Kesey's *One Flew Over the Cuckoo's Nest*. There is a small hand-written addition to the text (given here in italics): 'He was mad with rage and continued, *through the empty frame of the windshield*, to pound the head of the driver.' The original title of the piece was 'Bread and Circus'. In 'Dialogue Between a Poet and a Doctor', there is a small correction (given here in italics): 'He wanted to punish the woman *for the pain she had caused*'. In 'Tantalum', Levi wrote that the piece had been published by *Il Mondo* on 27 December 1973, and that it had probably been re-published in *Pittura e Vernici* in April 1979. Levi cut the name Cassola in 'Brief Dream' and noted by hand: 'a science fiction novel.'

THE BOOK

The collection was published by Einaudi in October 1981 in their lit-erature series 'Nuovi Coralli' (n. 320). The title was chosen by Giulio Einaudi. The cover featured a detail of the stained-glass window designed by Marc Chagall for the Jerusalem Hadassah Medical Center. The author wrote the dust-jacket blurb:

> These stories, written between 1975 and 1981, deal with differ-ent subjects and have different tones. I have tried to group them

together, and forcing the boundaries every now and then I have created a first group of stories which pick up the themes of *If This Is a Man* and *The Truce*; a second group that follows on from *Flaw of Form* and *Natural Histories*; and a third group whose protagonists are flesh and blood characters. My hope is that each story fulfils its function, which is simply to concentrate into a few pages, and transmit to the reader, a vivid memory, a state of mind, or just an idea. There are happy stories and sad ones, because our days are both happy and sad. As far as I know, there are neither hidden messages nor fundamental prophesies—if a reader were to find any, it's their gain.

From 1981 to 1994, there were two reprints of the book, and 21,000 copies sold. Later the collection was re-published alongside the two previous books of short stories.

Lilith and Other Stories was Levi's third book of collected stories. Writing to a literary critic, Levi stated:

A book, just like any other human enterprise, comes about as a result of a cost/benefit analysis. In publishing a collection of stories, the risk for the author is to be considered soft; for readers to feel they have wasted money and time. The benefit (or rather the hope of a benefit) is to save from annihilation some stories that I, as an author, have enjoyed writing, and others that people close to me and whose judgement I trust have liked. Anyway, why should a collection of short stories be less noble, or softer, than a novel? This is a prejudice that I believe started in the heads of booksellers. As a reader, for example, I happily choose short stories because I feel they are more spontaneous. I could cite several authors who, by general consensus, have been more successful in their short story writing than in their novels. The first to come to mind are Maupassant, Cortázar, Singer, and, of course, Boccaccio' (Tesio 1981).

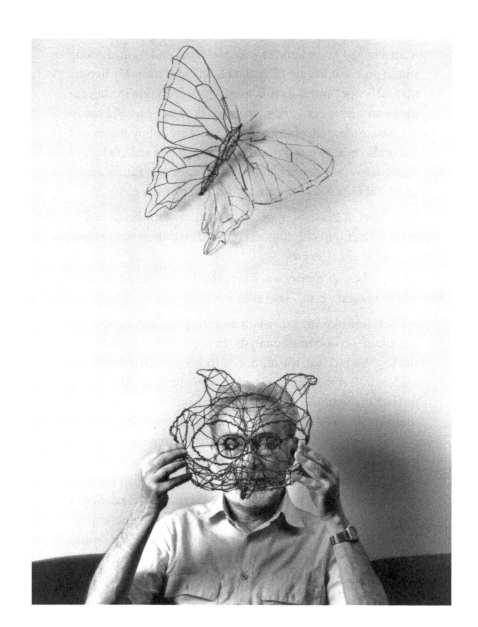

PORTRAIT WITH AN OWL MASK (1986)

In 1986, Mario Monge went to Levi's house to take some photographs. It must have been in the summer, maybe June, as Levi is wearing a short-sleeved shirt. The photographer took shots of Levi in various poses and performing different actions. In some of these, he is holding the insulated copper-wire sculptures he enjoyed creating. This was an unusual passion, which he first developed when he was working at the SIVA factory. His colleagues remember him collecting the copper-wire discards from production material—the wire they experimented the varnishes by coating. He would take the wire home and create crocodiles, kangaroos, ants, owls, butterflies, seagulls, penguins, insects and many other creatures. When Philip Roth interviewed him for the *New York Review of Books* in 1986, he saw these mysterious sculptures, and thought they looked like 'a Jew playing his own nose'.

When he had finished twisting the wire into animal sculptures, he would give some to friends and keep others at home. In Monge's photograph, there is a butterfly on the wall behind him—perhaps the protagonist of the story in *Natural Histories*, or the butterfly sheet that flies away from the poet in another story, or even one of the inhabitants of an ecosystem that has flourished in his gut, as described in *The Search for Roots*. The animals sculpted out of insulated copper wire are the same animals that Levi wrote about in his stories. They make up a little zoo, or bestiary.

Animals and beasts are the positive and negative poles of Levi's poetic and imaginative universe. Every living creature, in Levi's view, had a double identity, or—as a chemist would put it—a double value. In this portrait, Levi is holding one of his creations: the head of an owl he has created with his own capable hands. The copper-wire sculptures are two-dimensional, but the wire creates a sense of volume which projects a third dimension. Like a pencil drawing, it circumscribes space with its fine line and closes it in without saturating the space. They look so light because they are both outlines and three-dimensional figures.

Levi identified with owls. He drew one on his Mac, and the cover of the first edition of *Other People's Trades* featured three stylized owls in a vertical column. Monge took several shots: in one, Levi holds the owl to his side; in this one, he is holding the creature in front of his face as if it were a mask. The copper-wire sculpture hides part of the writer's face, or, rather, it creates a new face. Observing the image, the foreground/background changes from the owl to Levi and back again. The owl mask is on his face but does not cover it. It shows two natures in one: human and animal. The last chapter of his most important last book, *The Drowned and the Saved*, talks about human animals. This photograph of Monge's shows that Levi was well aware of his two sides.

LEMMAS: Levi's Alphabet of Animals

Alfil

In the story 'Lead', a chapter of *The Periodic Table* (a story Levi claimed to have written before the war, together with 'Mercury', with its theme of the 'union of opposites, the 'two-backed beast' and the hermaphrodite alchemist linked to the story *Lilith*), the protagonist Rodmund from the island of Thiuda was a metal hunter specialized in lead. In the course of his travels, he boarded a cargo ship where: 'The crew chief came from Crete and was a great liar: he told of a country inhabited by men called Big Ears, who have ears so large that in winter they wrap up in them to sleep, and animals with tails in front who are called Alfil and understand the language of men.' Rodmund had met other sailors who had spoken to him about

> a big island called Icnusa, the island of metals. About this island they told the strangest stories: that it was inhabited by giants, but that the horses, the oxen, and even the rabbits and chickens were tiny; that the women were in command and went to war, while the men watched the animals and spun wool; that these giants ate men, and especially foreigners; that it was a land of prostitution, where the husbands exchanged wives, and even the animals coupled randomly, wolves with cats, bears with cows; that pregnancy lasted only three days, then the women gave birth and immediately said to the child, 'Get up, bring me the scissors and a light, so I can cut the cord.' (p. 827)

Redmund laughed these stories off, and countered:

> When I return and talk about the countries where I've been, I, too, enjoy inventing oddities, and here they tell fantastic things about my country: for example, that our buffalo don't have knees, and

327

that to kill them all you have to do is saw at the base of the tree that they're leaning against at night to rest—under their weight, the tree breaks, and they fall flat and can't get up (p. 827).

The fantastical stories collected by the metal hunter meld together themes from medieval bestiaries, such as the *Liber Mostrorum* edited by Corrado Bologna and published in 1977, and creatures created by Swift. Levi's keen interest in the relationship between micro and macro, revealed in all of Levi's imaginary creatures, was evident in the almost fairy tale 'Bridge Builders' (*Lilith and Other Stories*) where a giantess was set against to a miniscule man who persisted in his attempts to build bridges (the same trade as Faussone, the rigger in *The Wrench*).

Anchovies

With vinegar, lemon, tomato, soaked in brine, or drenched in olive oil—this is how the indirect protagonists of the chapters 'Anchovies I' and 'II' (*The Wrench*) were presented. Anchovies were not really given the full status of fish; rather, they were considered a basic food source. From the depths of the sea to our table, a product of the fishing industry, food for survival. In 'Anchovies I', samples of anchovies from all over the world were shipped in great quantities into the paint factory where Levi was to perform 'anchovy resistance tests' (p. 1089) on the varnish he was designing for the inside of paint cans. In 'Anchovies II', while Levi continued to struggle with the viscosity of the varnish, he introduced a subplot concerning fruit flies and their fatal attraction to acetic acid—almost as an illustration of both industrial history and scientific cause and effect—along the same lines as a similar description in *The Periodic Table*:

> And I once had a bad experience with fruit flies. I'm not sure whether you know this, but scientists love fruit flies because they have very large chromosomes; in fact, it seems that almost everything we know today about heredity, biologists learnt from the bodies of these flies, crossbreeding them with one another in every possible manner, shredding them, injecting them, starving them, and giving them strange things to eat—so, you see, showing off

can often lead to trouble. Drosophila, as they're called, are beautiful, with red eyes, they're just three millimetres long, and they don't harm anyone—in fact, maybe against their will, they've done us a lot of good (p. 1109).

Again, Levi revealed himself as an omnivorous reader of science.

Animalcules

Observation, normal in babies and children, was a habit that Levi continued into adulthood. As he described in 'The Invisible World' (*Other People's Trades*):

> One day, my father, who was an expert habitué of all the used bookstalls along Via Cernaia, brought home a slim, elegantly bound volume for me; it had been printed in London in 1846, and the title, at once modest and pretentious, was *Thoughts on Animalcules; or A Glimpse of the Invisible World Revealed by the Microscope*, by Gideon Algernon Mantell, Esq., LL.D., F.R.S. (Gentleman, Doctor of Laws, and Fellow of the Royal Society) (p. 2194).

The book was a revelation to the 15-year-old Levi, leading him to undertake a path of enquiry into that which was not visible to the human eye, the pullulating world of the inhabitants of a drop of water or immediately under the surface of a piece of material. This path was the diametric opposite of astronomy, seeking multiple forms of life in the infinitely small rather than in the infinitely large. Not by chance, telescopes and microscopes were significant in Levi's life and, metaphorically, in his work. Levi's passion for the infinitesimal was important because, like most scientists, he had a predilection for zooming in, which was often mistaken for a love of exactitude, but which was in fact a maniacal attention to detail. Levi also wrote about invisibility in *The Wrench*, where the narrator explained to Faussone the difference between organic and inorganic chemistry (as he did in the comparison with the elephant in 'Anchovies I'). Under the microscope borrowed from his father—an engineer interested in Lombroso's theories and spiritualism—Levi placed, among other things, skeins of hair, the skin from his thumb pads and flies. He described the vortices and paramecia in great detail, 30 years after the article published in *La Stampa* where he gave an example of scientific writing worthy of Galvani and Spallanzani (whose names appeared in 'Casa Galvani', a poem on experimenting with frogs also published in *La Stampa*).

Ants

The image Levi adopted to describe how *If This Is a Man* came into being was that of the termite hill. The image not only conjures up the idea of overcrowding in a collective space—the Lager—but also the very nature of an agglomeration (*The Periodic Table*). If he had called it an anthill, it would have expressed an idea of hard work in a context of order. The image of a termite hill transmitted by Maeterlinck in *The Life of Termites*, was hellish, like Huxley's *Brave New World*. Termites, with their destructive nature that demolishes everything in their path, represented the negative side of insect life. Ants represented a more positive view (isoptera as opposed to hymenoptera), although Levi's idea of ants remained ambivalent.

Ants brought prisoners in concentration camps to Levi's mind, as his 1980 poem, 'Brown Swarm' (*Collected Poems*), made clear with its image from Dante's *Purgatory* (XXVI:34). The poem opens with the rhetorical question, 'Who could have chosen a more ridiculous route?' which does not anticipate the devastating finale. After describing the ants' absurd and tireless 'little errands' across the tram lines, building a city within a city, Levi repeats the Dantesque image of the 'brown swarm' (two sets of sinners on the terrace of Lust walking in opposite directions to purge their excessive desires) in three lines that abruptly change the tone of the poem into an invective—further marked by a line break: 'Not thinking of /I don't want to write it, I don't want to write about this swarm / I don't want to write about any brown swarm' (p. 1934).

In other works, ants were more simply an image of Levi himself, such as in the ironic story 'Full Employment' (*Natural Histories*), where ants collaborated with Mr Simpson, who kept their colonies well fed as long as they stayed away from his house (almost the reverse of Calvino's

'*Argentine Ant*' in *Cosmicomics*). Another example was the 1986 story in the form of an interview, published in the nature magazine *Airone* and later collected in *Stories and Essays*. In 'The Ant's Wedding', the queen ant told the story of her half-hour courtship, her wedding flight, her fertilization and her husband's demise soon after. The queen ant invited humans to follow her example, establishing a clear division of labour, where reproduction was left to the queen to turn the 'tap' on and release sperm from the sac on her abdomen, releasing fertilized (female) eggs or shutting off the duct for unfertilized (male) eggs:

> As for your system, believe me, we have never understood it. I mean, the honeymoon is fine, but then what do you need all those repeat performances for? All productive hours frittered away. You'll see, in time you, too, will get to that point, just as you managed to achieve the division of labour: for the working classes fecundity is nothing but waste and demagoguery. You, too, should delegate it, you have kings and queens, or even just presidents; leave it to them, the workers should be working. And why so many men? That fifty-fifty of yours is obsolete, let me tell you; it's no accident that our regime has existed for a hundred and fifty million years, and yours not even a million. And ours has been tested, it's been stable since the Mesozoic, whereas you change yours every twenty years at best (p. 2308).

Animals gave the prudish writer the excuse to talk about sexuality, although only from a biological point of view. He wrote ironically about human behaviour while relativizing it against animal behaviour. Levi poked fun mostly at the link that humans make between sentiment and sexuality, which appeared bizarre when seen from the point of view of animals. Levi found the capacity of social animals such as ants, bees, and squirrels to 'think about tomorrow' to be 'exquisitely human', making them 'not imprudent concerning the future' ('A Bottle of Sunshine', *Stories and Essays*, p. 2367).

Atoúla/Nacani

In 'Children of the Wind' (*Lilith and Other Stories*), Levi described the unique species inhabiting one of the two Wind Islands:

> On Mahui, [. . .] it's possible for someone armed with patience and endowed with good vision to spot some atoúla, or, more often, one of their females, a nacunu. Apart from the well-known cases of certain domestic animals, this is perhaps the only animal species in which the male and female are designated by different names, but that fact is explained by the clear sexual dimorphism which characterizes them, and is certainly unique among mammals (p. 1459–60).

These invented creatures were rodents:

> The atoúla—the males—are up to half a meter long and weigh from five to eight kilos. They have grey or brown fur, a very short tail, a pointed nose equipped with black vibrissae, and short triangular ears; their stomach is bare, rosy, lightly covered by a sparse down, which, as we will see, is not without evolutionary significance. The females are somewhat heavier, and longer and more robust than the males; their movements are quicker and more confident, and, according to the reports of Malay hunters, their senses are more developed—above all, the olfactory. Their coat is entirely different: the nacunu, in all seasons, wear a flamboyant livery of glossy black, marked by four tawny stripes, two on each side, which run from the snout along the sides and join near the tail, which is long and thick and shades from tawny to orange, bright red, or purple according to the animal's age (p. 1460).

The reversal of male and female characteristics in these creatures, compared to humans, of course, was visible in the male species' laziness but, most significantly in terms of their two names, in the absence of 'coupling'. Levi described in some detail how fertilization took place:

> Coupling does not exist among the atoúla. In the season of love, which lasts from September to November, and thus coincides with the driest period, the males climb at sunrise to the top of the

plateaus, and sometimes even the highest trees, competing to gain the most elevated positions. There they stay, without eating or drinking, for the whole day: they turn their backs to the wind and into the wind discharge their semen. This consists of a thin liquid, which in the warm, dry air evaporates quickly, and is spread by the wind in the form of a cloud of fine dust: every grain of this dust is sperm.' When the scientist-narrator explained how he had collected samples of the sperm on glass plates, he found: 'the sperm of the atoúla are different from those of all other animal species, and resemble, rather, the grains of pollen of anemophilous plants. They don't have a caudal filament; they are covered instead by tiny branching, tangled hairs, so that they can be carried by the wind for remarkable distances' (p. 1460)

—yet another case of hybrid animal-plants. Further details of the strange dissemination dance followed:

During the discharge of the sperm the atoúla don't move; sitting upright on their haunches, their front paws folded, they are shaken by a slight tremor whose function may be to accelerate the evaporation of the seminal fluid from the hairless surface of the stomach. When the wind changes suddenly (a frequent occurrence in those latitudes), you get the singular spectacle of innumerable atoúla, each one erect on its elevation, all simultaneously orienting themselves in the new direction, like the weathervanes that used to be placed on rooftops. They appear intent and tense, and do not react to stimuli: such behaviour is explicable only if one recalls that these animals are not threatened by any predator, which otherwise would easily get the better of them (p. 1462)

Their gestation was only 35 days, while 'birth and lactation have no notable features' (p. 1462). Levi's scientific tract—this story is no less—was again focused on the mechanisms of sexuality. The irony with which he tackled the subject showed how Levi, like so many other scientists and observers before him, was fascinated by the biology of reproduction and by Freud's intuition that there was a relationship between sexuality and curiosity.

Bees

Levi professed a particular interest in 'social' insects such as ants, bees and termites, owing no doubt to his extensive reading in the field of entomology. He might have read J. H Fabre's works on hymenoptera and beetles, as well as the three books by Belgian symbolist poet Maurice Maeterlinck that made him famous (*The Life of the Bee* [1901]; *The Life of Termites* [1926]; *The Life of the Ant* [1930]), and, of course, Karl von Frisch's 1927 book *The Dancing Bees*, one chapter of which was cited and briefly summarized in 'Full Employment' (*Natural Histories*). In this story, the Natca employee Mr Simpson had invented a pan pipe that could communicate with animals and make mutually advantageous arrangements with them. As the narrator-author explained, with non-gregarious animals the instrument was less successful.

Bees and other social insects interested Levi because they represented a form of collective life that followed rigid rules, strict hierarchies and class or caste divisions—in the same way that life in the Lager was organized. In *The Drowned and the Saved*, Levi commented that it was highly likely that a certain level of domination of some men over others was inscribed in the genetic heritage of social insects. In the article 'Aldous Huxley', later collected in *Other People's Trades*, Levi reviewed the deeply ironic and pessimistic utopia depicted in *Brave New World* positively (irony and pessimism being traits Huxley shared with Levi). The new order excluded destabilizing passions in favour of well-being and absolute peace—a constitution, Levi observed, that had been 'chosen millions of years ago by ants and termites, and never amended since then' (p. 2022). Freedom always implies risk, Levi never tired of repeating: the possibility of falling prey to the evillest consequences such as war or social conflict. However, as Levi explained, this was the price to pay for the form of evolution man had carved out for himself throughout history, and what distinguishes man from social animals.

Many of the stories in *Natural Histories* and *Flaw of Form* highlight the double risk to which humans are exposed. Becoming an insect means being reduced to the level of an animal. Insects pass on their genetic code without any variation, and angels are nothing but worms (neither of them,

Levi pointed out, possessed anuses). Social insects were evidence for those who believed that natural selection was an essential feature of the animal kingdom. Von Frisch claimed that natural selection was no longer efficient in humans, unlike in the insect world where he still deemed it effective. One could imagine that Levi's article 'Beetles' (*Other People's Trades*) was a response to Von Frisch's claim. In Levi's Appendix to *If This Is a Man*, he also referred to beekeeping. Charles (the same character that featured in 'The Story of Ten Days') had returned to his house in the Vosges hills, where he was a beekeeper and teacher. Stern, who symbolized a balanced relationship with nature and with his native environment, was also an apiarist. In an article written after Levi's death, Stern recalled a visit to Levi in Asiago where the two writers talked about beehives.

Beetles

Levi, unlike most readers, correctly identified the monstrous bug into which the protagonist of Kafka's *Metamorphosis*, was transformed. Most critics interpreted the creature as being a giant roach, but in 'Beetles' (*Other People's Trades*) Levi correctly noted that 'Kafka knew what he was doing in his atrocious hallucination, where the traveling salesman Gregor Samsa, 'waking one morning from uneasy dreams,' finds he has been changed into an enormous beetle, so inhuman that no member of his family can tolerate his presence' (p. 2187).

Another writer (and passionate lepidopterist) to identify the bug was Vladimir Nabokov, who even dared defy Kafka's prohibition to make a drawing of it. In the chapter 'The Beetle and the Butterfly' in *Lectures on Literature* (1980), Nabokov commented wryly: 'Next question: what insect? Commentators say cockroach, which of course does not make sense. A cockroach is an insect that is flat in shape with large legs, and Gregor is anything but flat: he is convex on both sides, belly and back, and his legs are small. He approaches a cockroach in only one respect: his coloration is brown.'

Levi probably first read Kafka's story in German, where, as Nabokov observed, the charwoman referred to the bug as a Mistkafer, or dung-beetle: 'It is obvious that the good woman is adding the epithet only to be friendly. He is not, technically, a dung beetle. He is merely a big beetle. (I must add that neither Gregor nor Kafka saw that beetle any too clearly).'

Levi and Nabokov shared a passion for butterflies and beetles (to whom he devoted a whole chapter in *Other People's Trades*), and for tennis. In 'The Irritable Chess Players' (*Other People's Trades*), Levi compared chess to writing poems and to tennis in as much as these activities were, in his view, solitary: 'Perhaps it is no surprise that tennis players, for example, who play alone or at most in pairs, are more irascible and neurotic than soccer players or bicyclists, who compete in teams' (p. 2155). Nabokov was a poet and played chess as a young man, publishing a book of poems and chess problems. In exile in Germany, in fact, he earned his living as a tennis coach.

Levi demonstrated a keen interest in insects throughout his work, describing their distinguishing features and using their correct names. In *Other People's Trades*, as we have said, he devoted a whole chapter to beetles. He was fascinated by their structure, which he described in detail, highlighting the correspondence between their form and their function and outlining the evolutionary purpose of their wings, which he (unlike Nabokov) correctly called 'elytra'. Levi mentioned the 'beautiful *cetoniae* (so beloved of Gozzano' [p. 2185]), 'sacred dung-beetles', click beetles, and fireflies (which are also the subject of two of his poems). He described the incredible strength of a beetle if swallowed: 'it will not follow the tactics of Jonah swallowed by the whale or Pinocchio and Geppetto in the belly of the Terrible Dogfish, but, with the strength of its forelegs, meant for burrowing, will simply dig an exit through the body of the predator' (p. 2186). Levi did not examine the Egyptian or Christian symbolism of beetles, however. He believed that humans identified more easily with social insects such as ants and bees, the industriousness of spiders, or the beauty of butterflies, while there was little connection between men and beetles. This was one reason why beetles are considered alien or monstrous, and why, perhaps, Kafka chose this bug in his 'atrocious hallucination' ('an awkward, ungainly insect, reviled by everyone'—Levi, in his essay 'Translating Kafka' [*Stories and Essays*, p. 2349]). Levi concluded that essay ironically, claiming that 'from the day they take over the world, many millions of years will have to pass before a beetle particularly beloved of God completes his calculations and finds, written on a piece of paper in letters of fire, that energy is equal to mass multiplied by the speed of light squared' (p. 2188).

In *The Wrench*, Faussone told the story of going round and round in a snow storm in Alaska, like roaches (*boie panetere* was Piedmont dialect for insects that burrow in flour or bread). Roaches were infamously linked to Rudolf Höss, Commander of Auschwitz who had the brilliant idea, Levi wrote, of using Zyklon B, a common anti-roach pesticide, to kill Jews ('Introduction to The Commander of Auschwitz'). In *The Search for Roots*, Levi also referred to beetles in 'The Measure of All Things' as an example of a 'standard' from the American Society for Testing Materials, citing a method for testing the resistance of adhesive materials to beetles. If anyone tried to follow the specifications and construct a testing machine of this kind would produce something akin to Michel Carrouges' idea of the 'bachelor machine' he had imagined Kafka creating in his story *The Penal Colony*.

Birds

There is one place in Levi's work in particular where birds flock together: in his poetry. Here Levi's taxonomy of ornithology reached its peak, with seagulls, crows, eagles, nightingales, sparrows, blackbirds, parrots and owls crowding the poems. In places, the references were symbolic; in others, they were literary, following an Italian tradition championed by Leopardi and Montale. They represented cheerfulness—even hilarity; at the same time, they could evoke the darkest of thoughts. Levi wrote two poems about crows as messengers of death in the 1940s and 50s, and one to a seagull, represented as an environmentalist, in the 70s. Birds also featured in his other works, of course. In particular in *If Not Now, When?* where they were a part of the landscape and the soundtrack (animals and birds were portrayed as being an inherent part of nature, rather than as the symbolic presences they played in other works).

Another reference was to the children at Birkenau defined as 'birds of passage', or in *The Truce*, where Levi compared the two Jewish girls the narrator and Cesare had met on their journey home to two birds in the sky, without a care for tomorrow.

An article published in *Other People's Trades* was about birds: '"The Most Joyous Creatures in the World"'. It was based on an operetta by Leopardi called *In Praise of Birds*, but interpreted in terms of animal behaviour. 'After decades of intensive and widely popularized studies of animal behaviour, the impression one comes away with is singular and vaguely alienating' (p. 2199) Levi wrote, citing animal behaviourist Konrad on the nature of birdsong as a territorial claim to state that, 'To attribute such feelings as gaiety, boredom, and happiness to animals (with the possible exception of dogs and certain monkeys) is acceptable only in the context of poetry—otherwise it's arbitrary and greatly misleading' (p. 2200–01). As an illustration that birdsong was not necessarily an expression of joy, as Leopardi had interpreted it, Levi took owls (birds of prey), cuckoos (whose behaviour 'by the light of our human morality seems to have been dictated by a twisted cunning'), and migratory starlings, which he had observed in his hometown, in piazza Carlo Felice and in Corso Turati where they had gathered in large numbers after abandoning the countryside (the same phenomenon had taken place in London in 1914). Here is his description:

> At dawn they set out in serried regiments 'to go to work,' that is, to the fields outside the industrial belt; they come home at sunset, in gigantic flocks of thousands of individual birds, followed by scattered stragglers. Viewed from a distance, these flocks seem like clouds of smoke; then, suddenly, they display astonishing manoeuvres, the cloud becomes a long ribbon, then a cone, then a sphere; at last, it spreads out again and, like an enormous arrow, points straight for its nightly shelter. Who commands that army? And how does he give his orders? (p. 2202).

The article first came out in *La Stampa* on 27 November 1983, two years after a similar piece published in *la Repubblica* by Calvino ('The Starling Invasion', 3 December 1981) and later published with changes in *Palomar* (1983). Calvino's article contains similar observations and a longer, more articulated description of the cloud of starlings with its various graphic metamorphoses.

Buck

Null Achtzehn, the Muselmänn from *If This Is a Man*, reminded Levi of Jack London's sled-dog Buck. Levi often referred to Jack London, and in particular to Buck, the protagonist of *Call of the Wild*, in his work (see, for example, the chapter 'Offshore' in *The Wrench*, set in Alaska). In 'Cerium' (*The Periodic Table*), Levi compared himself directly to the dog: 'I was reliving, I a respectable university graduate, the involution-evolution of a famous respectable dog, a Victorian and Darwinian dog who is deported and becomes a thief in order to live in his "Lager" of the Klondike, the great Buck, of *Call of the Wild*' (p. 867). The comparison is quite obvious: thievery and cunning could contribute to survival.

Levi reviewed Gianni Celati's Italian translation of *Call of the Wild* (*Buck dei lupi*, 1987) in *La Stampa*. There were, indeed, several parallels between Levi's experience and Buck's. They both started life in a protected environment (a big Victorian house for Buck, and a relatively wealthy family home in Turin for Levi); both were captured by their persecutors with a trick (a garden hand sells Buck for money, while Levi was denounced by a spy who pretended to be a friend); they were both transported by a goods train and segregated; violence awaited both on their arrival, making them both no more than animals. In addition, they were both trained to accept violence (for Buck, the first day was a 'nightmare', surrounded by 'savages', while Levi felt he had been thrown into a primordial world), and both subjected to the hierarchies of domination. Music accompanied both (the orchestra playing as prisoners filed into Auschwitz, and the eskimo dogs barking a tune as Buck joined the camp). In terms of approach, both stories were narrated with a focus on animal instinct, where the rules of a pack were surprisingly similar to those in place in a concentration camp. In his review of the book, Levi outlined these parallels, but then distanced himself, presenting Buck as a commander—perhaps even a Kapo.

Being reduced to a dog-like state of bestiality, an image which Levi often used in *If This Is a Man*, was a regression (and therefore an 'involution') to a pre-human state of animal-hood, while for Buck the experience was without doubt an 'evolution'. For both Buck and Levi, however, work was a last refuge, the only alternative to servitude, which is how Levi interpreted Buck's work pulling the sled. In London's story, the dogs were described as being passive and indifferent when they were off duty, but as soon as they were reigned into the sled they suddenly came to life. In comparing the Lager to Klondike, Levi referred to Solzhenitsyn's *One Day in the Life of Ivan Denisovich*: work was a kind of 'intoxication' or addiction, to the point that dogs who were taken off sled-duty abandoned themselves to death.

Work was a central theme for Levi, with many different facets. It could be ennobling, but it could also be destructive and even toxic. Work could be fun, but it was also a commitment. When describing the inventiveness of his work as a chemist, for example, Levi spoke of a quality that was commonly cited by animal behaviourists: 'insight' ('Ex-Chemist' in *Other People's Trades*).

Jack London was, in Levi's view, an animal behaviourist at heart, but he also criticized the ending of *Call of the Wild* in his review because he thought that Buck's gratitude to his savior, Thornton, was excessive: the domineering animal had been tamed too easily. Levi did not agree with Celati's comment that the story was an example of 'old-fashioned mythical narration'. Only the final part of the story, where Buck was transformed into a ghost dog, heading a pack of wolves who became fearsome nocturnal predators, was mythical in Levi's view, while Celati was convinced that the entire thrust of the story was mythical. Their difference of opinion was dictated by their differing views of society, and of what makes individuals behave the way they do within their social groups.

In Celati's opinion, in accordance with Nietzsche, London was tackling the issue of the impotence of individuals in an increasingly mass society. *Call of the Wild*, in this framework, represented the triumph of wilderness over civilization. An individual, either randomly or by choice, could escape homologation and triumph over the one-size-fits-all rules of society. In Celati's own fiction, individuals rejecting society were incarnated, first, by a madman, then by a child, a rebellious adolescent, a dimwit, an illiterate, and finally, a man on the street.

For Levi, by contrast, the involution–evolution dialectic took place within the individual (Buck was a victim and a persecutor, a deportee and a Kapo). As he pointed out in *If This Is a Man*, society in itself is neither good nor bad; it depends on the circumstances. Civil society can easily—and often does—provide the means to reign in the savage force of individuals before this leads to disastrous consequences. Concentration camps were the result of a distortion that became the rule, just as the use and abuse of sled dogs was the result of the gold rush. Levi's ethical code oscillated between his faith in reason and his distrust of it. He admired the primordial strength of some individuals, just as he was by Buck, whose ambiguity is well-known. Levi concluded his review with his usual irony and scepticisms: the wild ghost dog who goes every year on a pilgrimage to pay homage to his owner's grave, he felt, was just a little 'too human'.

Butterflies

Butterflies were part of the ecosystem in Levi's gut 'that hosts what one cannot suspect', as Levi declared at the beginning of *The Search for Roots*, together with 'saprophytes, diurnal and nocturnal birds, climbers, crickets and moulds'. One of the first butterflies to appear in Levi's work was 'Angelic Butterfly', in the short story with the same name first published in *Il Mondo* in 1962 and then collected in *Natural Histories*. The name was a reference to Dante's *Purgatory* (X:124–26): 'do you not know that we are worms and born to form the angelic butterfly that soars, without defences, to confront His judgement?' On the terrace purging pride, the pilgrim sees shapes bent under the weight of huge boulders, reminding the proud sinners that men on earth are, as Sapegno annotated in his commentary, 'defective and transitory forms': just as a worm that forms a cocoon dies giving birth to a winged butterfly, so when men die their soul is released and rises naked and undefended to the supreme judge.

The butterfly image recalls the pre-Christian myths of the Psyche, where the spiritual soul is of the same nature as angels. In Levi's story, a Nazi scientist, Professor Leeb, conducted an experiment in metamorphosis with a group of human volunteers. Rather than transforming his subjects into higher creatures (angelic butterflies), however, the result of the experiment was an 'involution': by feeding them in a certain way, the humans were transformed into horrific birds.

In the chapter 'Vacation' in *The Truce*, a mutation took place when the narrator came across Flora, a fellow prisoner in Buna who had been a prostitute there. Meeting her again, Levi felt transformed in her presence: 'Compared with those ghosts, my self of Buna, the woman of memory and her reincarnation, I felt changed, intensely "other", like a butterfly before a caterpillar' (p. 356). There was another butterfly in 'Mercury' (*The Periodic Table*). As four women on the island are shared out among the crew in exchange for jars of mercury, the narrator was attracted by a 'small thin girl' with grey eyes: 'she made a cheerful, light impression, like a tickle, and I imagined I was capturing her in flight, like a butterfly' (p. 840).

As well as being symbols of Psyche, butterflies were also emblems of light-spiritedness and inconstancy for Levi. In a 1984 poem collected in *At an Uncertain Hour*, 'A Profession', the narrating voice says that 'lines will buzz around you, like drunk moths; One comes near the flame, you grab it' (p. 1963). Again, in 'The Fugitive' (*Lilith and Other Stories*), the poet/office worker who only had five or six flashes of inspiration in his life had 'the awareness of having a poem in his mind, ready to be caught in flight and fixed on a page like a butterfly'(p. 1463). In the story, the sheet of paper on which the unique poem had been written kept on disappearing, becoming finally a kind of insect:

> He took a magnifying glass and saw that it was so. Tiny hairs were sticking out from the page, corresponding to attributes of the letters on the other side. In particular, the extremities stuck out, the legs of the *d*'s and the *p*'s, and, above all, the little legs of the *n*'s and the *m*'s; for example, behind the title 'Annunciation', the eight legs of the four *n*'s could be clearly seen (p. 1466).

The theme of metamorphosis, and the ambivalence of butterflies (day and night creatures, sleeping in their chrysalises or flying with their new wings) recurred often in Levi's work. In the 1980 poem 'Heart of Wood', about a horse-chestnut tree on his street, under whose bark 'hang desiccated / Chrysalises that will never be / butterflies'—a failed metamorphosis. The most noteworthy story featuring butterflies was the 1981 piece in *Other People's Trades* called 'Butterflies', where Levi described an exhibition of butterflies at the Turin Museum of Natural History, revealing his admiration for the insect world, which was, in his view, more varied than that of birds and mammals because of their continuous transformations. They 'run, fly, leap, and swim [. . .] amassing the skills of the weaver, the potter, the miner, the murderer with his poisons, the trapper, and the wet nurse' (p. 2141). Levi asked the rhetorical question: 'Why are butterflies beautiful?', answering 'Certainly not, as Darwin's adversaries insisted, to give pleasure to humans [. . .] butterflies existed at least a hundred million years before the first human being. I believe that our very concept of beauty, which is necessarily relative and cultural, has been modelled over the centuries on butterflies, as well as on stars, mountains, and the sea.' And yet, 'examining a butterfly's head under the microscope: for most observers, admiration gives way to horror and disgust [. . .] But the fascination of butterflies is not merely a product of colour and symmetry: deeper factors contribute as well. We wouldn't find them so beautiful if they weren't able to fly, or if they flew as straight and alertly as bees, or if they could sting.' The mystery of their metamorphosis, in addition, took on 'the value of a poorly deciphered message, a symbol, and a sign' (p. 2142). Gozzano studied butterflies, Levi pointed out, and Dante wrote about caterpillars: 'Just as butterflies are beautiful by definition, and serve as our standard of beauty, similarly caterpillars ('entòmata in difetto,' Dante called them, 'like . . . unto insects undeveloped') are ugly by definition.' Levi reminded his readers that 'The strange name that the butterfly has in English harks back to an ancient northern belief that a butterfly is a sprite that steals butter and milk, or turns them sour' and ended the article by talking about a 'rare butterfly, a brown-and-violet-winged Nymphalis antiopa', landing on Hermann Hesse's hand: 'The furtive visit of a butterfly, which Hermann Hesse describes on the last page of his diary, is an ambivalent annunciation, with the flavour of a serene foreshadowing of death' (p. 2143).

Cats

Cats are the most cited animals in Levi's work (according to Jane Nystedt they are mentioned 69 times), and are one of the most interesting creatures for animal behaviourists, producing observations on their nature, as well as metaphors and generally positive views. In various articles and conversations, and in particular in 'Novels Dictated by Crickets' (*Other People's Trades*) Levi recalled Huxley's famous instructions to a young aspiring writer: 'purchase a pair of cats, observe them, and describe them [. . .] animals, and especially mammals, and domestic animals in particular, are like us, but "with the lid off". Their behaviour is similar to what ours would be if we were free of inhibitions' (p. 2075). In general, the people Levi admired, or characters he described positively in his work, had feline characteristics. The ambiguous character Henri, for example, in *If This Is a Man*, is described as being able to run and jump like a cat. Similarly, the Russian military nurse in *The Truce*, Marya Fyodorovna, was like a forest cat, 'with oblique, wild eyes, a short nose with flared nostrils, and agile, silent movements' (p. 260). Even the rogue Cesare, returning from his eternal trafficking or amorous (and sexual) adventures was described as looking like a cat after a tremendous rooftop battle. The elusive Sandro in 'Iron' (*The Periodic Table*), was 'made like a cat, a creature you could live with for years without ever being allowed to get under its sacred skin' (p. 786). In the same chapter, Levi told the story of Sandro's mutt who had come too close to a litter of kittens without understanding the mother cat's aggressive 'signs', and had ended up with a 'permanent trauma' (p. 788)—a reference where two animals are cited together.

Faussone also possessed feline qualities: he was agile, fast-moving and had quick reflexes:

> men are made like cats, and I'm sorry to bring up cats again, it's only on account of the profession. If they don't know what to do with their time, if they don't have any mice to chase after, then they scratch each other, they escape onto the roof, or maybe they climb up a tree and start meowing because they can't get back down (p. 1081).

In *The Wrench,* cats come up quite frequently. In one striking image, a Russian inspector had the face of someone with a poor digestion: 'he looked like a cat, yes, one of those cats that develop the unfortunate habit of eating lizards, after which they stop growing, become melancholic, don't lick their fur, and instead of meowing go hhhh' (p. 1079).

Cats and mice are often depicted together, their struggle seen as an example of the eternal hunt. The image of cat and mouse is never dramatic; it is as if they are a natural, indissoluble couple, their opposition sanctioned by literature, rhymes, and proverbs (as in *If Not Now, When?*). Levi confessed in *The Periodic Table* that he had had very little contact with animals as a child: 'Except for some country cat in remotest childhood, I had never touched an animal' (p. 852). Cats were domestic animals, but still elusive. Levi saw himself as being a cat in the house where he lived all his life and would die ('My House' in *Other People's Trades*): 'It's not easy for me to talk about my relationship with my house: perhaps that relationship is catlike in nature; like cats I enjoy physical comfort, but I can also do without it, and I would be able to adapt pretty well to an uncomfortable place to live, as I have many times in the past' (p. 2018). His computer was like a cat: 'When I've satisfied its hunger, it buzzes quietly, purring like a contented cat' (p. 2237). There was also a kitten playing with the pages of Solmi's translation of Queneau that Levi and Calvino were editing in Rhèmes-Notre-Dame: 'every now and then he tried to turn the pages' (*Calvino: Queneau e le Scienze*, 1985).

Like many other writers, Levi preferred cats to dogs, identifying with them. He appreciated their gentle, detached, inoffensive, and seemingly benevolent manner but knew they were always ready to defend themselves if they were attacked. Cats are emblems of wisdom. Unlike dogs, they do not obey orders and cannot be reduced to slavery. Furthermore, cats were observant, a quality which Levi certainly admired. Their sense of balance and wile was the stuff of legends, where cats always got what they wanted, and in some cases were even seen as being clairvoyant, like snakes but with more positive connotations.

Centaurs

Written in 1960 and published in *Il Mondo* in 1961, the short story '*Quaestio de centauris*' was highly significant, not only owing to its form—with its various narrative planes and mythological divagations—but also because the image of the centaur itself is significant for Levi, who often claimed he identified with it. 'The Sixth Day' (*Natural Histories*), possibly the first piece of writing after Levi returned from the Lager, features a centaur. In his earliest interviews, in fact, Levi described himself as a centaur or a hybrid: half-chemist, half-writer; half-chemist, half-deportee. Over the course of time he would add two other dichotomies: half-Jewish, half-Italian; half-man of science and half-writer of fiction. In a 1966 interview, he went as far as to say that these divisions produced a degree of paranoia.

Levi's centaur-like identity featured a great deal in the interviews he gave in the 1980s, thus becoming a recurrent theme throughout his life as a person and as a writer. The first split Levi recognized was between being an author who was well-known for two serious books on the Lager experience, and the man penning short, jokey pieces that had no connection whatsoever with his witness literature. The truth is that there is not a single page of Levi's opus that is not in some way related to the triggering event that turned him into a writer: his deportation to Auschwitz.

The image of the centaur for Levi did not only represent a split in his work as a writer. It was also a split in human nature, a fundamental element of the Lager experience. In Greek myths, centaurs represented union or division between humans and animals within a figure that is half-horse, half-man. Trachi, the centaur in '*Quaestio de Centauris*' was an emblem of the unstable union between instinct and reason. The story was a story of creation—a new world born from the flood—as well as a description of the narrator's youth. It was the story of an initiation and the story of an impossibility (expressed in the Latin title).

The story opened emblematically with a gift from the narrator's father: the 260-year-old centaur Trachi had been passed down into the young boy's hands, initiating a long friendship. It goes on to tell the story of Trachi's taming of the boy, his version of how centaurs are generated and the destruction of life after the flood. Levi reworked a Jewish myth in this story, blending it with elements of Greek mythology, creating a hybrid version of events that was at the same time a 'personal' explanation for the origin of life. The part of the creation story that was neither Greek nor Jewish, but clearly hybrid, was evident in the details regarding the fact that there were no unclean animals saved on the ark (unlike the biblical version). The centaurs' traditions were born with a 'Noah-like inventor and saviour, whom they call Cutnofeset'. In his Ark 'only the archetypal animals, the key species, were saved: man but not the monkey; the horse but not the donkey or the wild ass; the rooster and the crow but not the vulture or the hoopoe or the gyrfalcon' (p. 511). These animals came about after the flood, from a 'a deep layer of warm mud' that covered the earth. 'Now, this mud, which harboured in its decay all the enzymes from what had perished in the flood, was extraordinarily fertile' (p. 511).

The idea that mud and clay were the origin of life was recurrent in Levi's work, both in his mythological stories (for example, 'The Sixth Day') and in his scientific articles (for example, a 1987 review entitled 'Adam's Clay'). It was linked to the theme of impurity (developed in particular in *The Periodic Table*), which, in its turn, was connected to the theme of symmetry. The myth narrated by Trachi to his young disciple was that of a 'wild, ecstatic fecundity in which the entire universe felt love, so much so that it nearly returned to chaos' (*The Periodic Table*). It was a time when all the elements 'fornicated' with one another, and produced hybrids:

> This second creation was the true Creation; because, according to what is passed down among the centaurs, there is no other way to explain certain analogies, certain convergences observed by all. Why is the dolphin similar to the fish, and yet gives birth and nurses its offspring? Because it's the child of a tuna fish and a cow. Where do the delicate colours of butterflies and their ability to fly come from? They are the children of a flower and a fly. And tortoises are the children of a frog and a rock. And bats of an owl and a mouse. And conchs of a snail and a polished pebble. And hippopotami of a horse and a river. And vultures of a worm and an owl (p. 512).

All these creatures were the hybrid products of the animal, vegetable and mineral kingdoms. The myth of panspermia (which Levi also mentioned in a story called 'Disphylaxis', collected in *Lilith and Other Stories*, where the hybrid is female) explained the origins of all living forms, even extinct monsters such as dragons, chimeras, harpies, minotaurs and giants.

Centaurs were the result of the 'profligate son' Cam's love for a Thessalian mare, taking the best features from both and thus creating their double identity. Centaurs did not inherit the herbivorous nature of horses. Rather, they took on 'the red blindness of the bloody and forbidden spasm, the moment of human-feral fullness in which they were conceived'. The inverse union between stallions and women was very rare, but when they do take place 'her two natures, however, inversely assembled. The creatures have the head, neck, and front feet of a horse, but their back and stomach are those of a human female, and the hind legs are human' (p. 513). Levi explained the problems they faced with feeding in great detail, almost scientifically: 'Even if centaurs are limited to a strictly vegetarian diet by their predominantly equine constitution, it must be remembered that they have a torso and head like a man's: this structure obliges them to introduce through a small human mouth the considerable quantity of grass, straw, or grain, necessary to the sustenance of their large bodies' (p. 514). Moreover, centaurs were especially sensitive to 'every germination, animal, human, or vegetable, as a wave of joy running through their veins' and were also able to perceive 'on a precordial level, and in the form of anxiety and tremulous tension, every desire and every sexual encounter that occurs in their vicinity' (p. 515).

The story continued as a love story, between Trachi and the only woman in the vicinity, Teresa (a name that harks back to Ugo Foscolo, giving the story a flavour similar to his 'Ortis'), who was also the object of the narrator's desire. Things ended tragically: once Trachi realized his young friend and Teresa were a couple, his feral nature came to the fore. He broke off all contact with humans and disappeared back to the land of his origin, not without first having violent sexual relations with a number of mares. The finale had all the trappings of a Roman myth with the sighting of a 'man riding a dolphin' (another hybrid) who then sunk into the depths off the coast of Corfu as soon as he saw the ship.

Years later, in a chapter of *The Periodic Table* devoted to the Jewish origins of his family ('Argon'), Levi commented on his use of the centaur as a metaphor for the human condition: 'man is a centaur, a tangle of flesh and mind, of divine breath and dust' (p. 760). It was the Hebrew people, in Levi's view, that embodied the human condition in general, that were centaurs because 'The Hebrew people, after the dispersal, lived this conflict long and painfully, and drew from it not only its wisdom but its laughter, which is missing from the Bible and the Prophets' (Ibid).

Creation

Levi was fascinated by the origins of life, and like many other writers interested in science, he played with the theme. He was convinced that invention was more important than creation, that 'creation' was ultimately little more than a construction, a do-it-yourself combination of a given set of elements.

His first reference to primordial chaos was in *The Truce*, with reference to the first day after the concentration camp was liberated by the Russians:

> a high wind blew over the face of the Earth: the world around us seemed to have returned to a primal Chaos, and was swarming with deformed, defective, abnormal human examples; and each of them was tossing about, in blind or deliberate motion, anxiously searching for his own place, his own sphere, as the cosmogonies of the ancients say, poetically, of the particles of the four elements (p. 235).

The erudite reference to the 'cosmogonies of the ancients' was to pre-Socratic philosophy. In '*Quaestio de Centauris*' (*Natural Histories*), a Second Creation of a mythical, hybrid creature—a re-creation in both senses—was described as coming out of a 'deep layer of warm mud' (p. 511), while in 'The Sixth Day', commissioned by the Italian state radio RAI in the early 1960s, the creation of the world took place following the decisions of a group of experts around a table in a board room of a quasi-divine agency. Rather than creating the world from nothing, the divinity considered evolutionary theory and evaluated, in an almost Darwinian fashion, the pros and cons of each free act. In the story, the possible forms for those who were to be created, according to the science of matter and psychology, were surveyed one by one in an ironic but scientific approach. Molluscs were considered and then rejected, as were reptiles. Water-based or land-based forms were then surveyed, and making a choice between mammals and birds was recommended, with the form of a centaur, half-man, half-animal, featuring at one point. Finally, the news reached the boardroom that the experts' opinion had been set aside in favour of a greater god, who had decided that men should be formed from 'seven measures of clay, and that they mixed it with river water and sea water' (p. 550). Creation had won out over evolution; the Bible trumped science as 'the female Man was created from one of his ribs' (p. 551).

In a story from Levi's following collection, dedicated to Calvino, Levi ran through the whole evolutionary process, from the aquatic stage, to birds, to reptiles and mammals, and to the 'birth' of eyes and hands ('His Own Maker', *Flaw of Form*). The creation myth was an important part of Jewish culture, which began to influence Levi's work more profoundly from the 1960s owing to his reading and his reflections, as he confessed in many of his interviews. The Golem myth, which Levi worked into a few essays and stories, was a creation myth. One example was 'The Servant' (*Flaw of Form*), which Daniella Ansallem has commented on in an essay on the stories contained in *Lilith and Other Stories* (*Golem and Jewish Myths in Levi*) In Levi's work, Jewish creationism is presented as a close relative of evolutionary construction (the Golem was linked to the Kabballah and the combination of Hebrew letters): the aim was to achieve a 'magic' result from a limited set of possibilities, combining different letters to produce different words, and to produce life itself. In this respect, Levi's linking of different combinations and word games to Judaism made him similar to George Perec, another Jew for whom Judaism was more important as an identity than as a religion.

Levi included Darwin in his personal anthology, *The Search for Roots*. Evolution was for Levi a decided turn against an anthropocentric view of the world: butterflies were not beautiful in order to please human beings— their beauty was an evolutionary fact. In Darwin's theory, humans were not at the centre of the world, but they possessed the means for explaining it.

In his review of Cairns-Smith's book, *Seven Clues to the Origin of Life* (1986), which was published in February 1987 in *La Stampa* (now in *Uncollected Stories and Essays* as 'Adam's Clay'), Levi had the opportunity to go back to one of his favourite themes: that mud, or clay, could have been an intermediate step towards organic life. This theme resolved the conflict between his study of chemistry and his interest in alchemy, between his interest in creationism and his militant espousal of Darwinism. Levi had a clear inclination for alchemy; *The Periodic Table* should probably be recast as a study in the art. The Russian scientist who discovered (or invented) the periodic table, Mendeleev, was in fact both a chemist and a spiritist (*On Spiritism*), while Jewish culture was imbued with elements of alchemy (Scholem, Alchemy and Kabballah). It is hard to say to what extent these elements filtered into Levi's intellectual formation, but it is clear that his cultural sensitivity as a curious and avid reader was stimulated by the many strange books in his father's library, where scientific tomes were shelved side by side with books by Lombroso and Mosso.

Levi was anything but a scientist's scientist. He loved cultural hybrids and philosophical games, and appreciated contamination and impurity, even intellectually. His review of Cairns-Smith's book on the origins of life made this very clear when he wrote that 'The origin of life on Earth is not a problem like any other; it's the one problem over which all scientists, and not just biologists, have racked their brains since the beginning of science' (p. 2760). After stating that 'the accepted answer came from the classics and Aristotle: life originates by means of spontaneous generation from corrupt matter' (an idea he later used in a short story), and describing how modern science with the 'electron microscope' had proved the opposite, Levi concluded that 'unless we wish to resort to supernatural hypotheses—some spontaneous generation must have occurred' (p. 2761). Cairns-Smith's book provided an answer: 'Primitive life, proto-life, would be based not on carbon but on clay silicates: yes, that same clay used by God the Father to make the first man' (p. 2762).

Crows

At dawn on 21 January 1945, 'we saw the plain deserted and lifeless, white as far as the eye could see under the flight of the crows, deathly sad' (p. 155). Four days later 'The number of crows had increased considerably and everyone knew why' (p. 163). These lines are from 'The Story of Ten Days' (*If This Is a Man*), where Levi told the story of the Germans' escape from the concentration camp. The crows were there because of the enormous number of unburied corpses.

Crows in *Genesis* were perspicacious; Noah chose a crow to leave the ark after 40 days to see if the flooding had gone down. In both cases, the Bible and in Levi's first novel, crows were messengers of a change of state. They were also, however, unclean animals that could not be ingested, like eagles, kites, vultures, owls and falcons. In animal symbolism, crows herald tragedy or death, which is how we find them in Levi's two poems, 'Song of the Crow I' and 'Song of the Crow II'. The first poem was written at the same time as 'The Story of Ten Days'. It provides a detail not included in the repugnant description of the Lager in the chapter. The crow was a messenger from very far bringing 'bad news'. It had crossed the mountain and flown through low cloud to 'To find your window' and become a corrupting influence 'To sit in your heart each evening.' The poet heard the crow giving this message while it was 'obscenely dancing Outside the window, on the snow.' Then suddenly, 'he stopped, he stared malevolent. Etched a cross on the ground with his beak, And spread his black wings' (p. 1886). The description, which was both naturalistic and symbolic, marked the landscape of death that the escaping SS soldiers left behind them at Monowitz.

In the second poem, written in 1953, the crow was again a messenger chasing the poet—to whom he speaks adopting the intimate 'tu' form in Italian—'to the ends of the earth' with its 'little black shadow' 'Till what was prophesied has been accomplished, Until your strength disintegrates, Until you too end Not with a bang but in silence' (pp. 1903–04).

Of all the animals in Levi's bestiary, crows have the heaviest symbolism, both because of the terrible reminder of the episode in the Lager and because of its connotations. Crows are characters in Levi's work with their own voice.

Delta

A piece called 'The TV Fans from Delta Cep.' (originally published in *L'Astronomia* in April 1986, but then included in *Uncollected Stories and Essays*) was written in the form of a letter to Piero Bianucci, editor-in-chief of *La Stampa* and popular author of science books and TV programme. The writer was a fan from the 'eighth planet of Delta Cepheid' (p. 2728) whose sun was the Cepheid of Cepheus. The text never actually declared whether the inhabitants of this planet were 'animals' or 'plants', but described them thus:

> The men here don't have beards—in fact, they don't even have heads. Our men are ten or twelve centimeters long and look like your asparagus, and when we want to be inseminated, we put them under our armpits for two or three minutes, as you do with thermometers when you take your temperature. We have ten armpits: we are all built with binary symmetry, so that our width is the golden section of our radius [. . .] Males cost from twenty to fifty thousand lire depending on their age and condition, and they don't bother us much. [. . .] our temperature varies, around −20°C in winter, 110°C in summer—but we'll become friends anyway (p. 2727).

When it was very hot the inhabitants burrowed underground for half an hour to protect themselves. The letter writer also claimed she had won a prize as a short-story writer: 'Three years ago I even won a prize. It was for a very sexy short story, about a girl who had bought a male with her first paycheck and then she fell for him and didn't want to exchange him or have him pulped. I wrote it in 2.36 seconds. We do everything pretty quickly' (p. 2728) The piece concluded with a request from the recipient for the formulas of several of the products she had seen advertised on TV: 'please send me the formula for your most important: (a) anti-fermentatives; (b) anti-parasitics; (c) anti-conceptions;* (d) anti-aesthetics; (e) anti-Semitics; (f) antipyretics; (g) antiquarians; (h) antihelminthics; (i) antiphons; (j) antitheses; (k) antelopes' (p. 2728).

Designers

As Faussone said (*The Wrench*), designers come in all kinds:

> there is the elephant designer, the guy always has to be correct; he doesn't care about elegance or economy, he just doesn't want any trouble, so he will use for of something when one will do. [. . .] There's the parrot designer who, instead of working out the plans himself, cribs from someone else—the way you do in school—without realising that everyone is laughing at him behind his back. There's the snail designer, meaning the bureaucratic type, who goes very, very slowly, and as soon as you give him a nudge he jumps back and hides in his shell, which is made out of rules and regulations [. . .] Finally there's the butterfly designer [. . .] And it's the most dangerous type, because they're young and bold, and they're always trying to trick you; [. . .] They only care about what's new and what's beautiful, without realizing that, if a work is well designed, it's beautiful automatically' (p. 1059).

The butterfly designer, in Faussone's view, was responsible for the near collapse of the bridge that gives the name to the chapter.

Dogs

Dogs feature throughout Levi's work. According to Nystedt, who conducted a word search of his opus, the word 'dog' appears 147 times, outranking 'horse' (144), 'cat' (69), 'rabbit' (51), 'hen' (48), 'louse' (44), 'chicken' (27), 'butterfly' (41), 'snake' (39) and 'ant' (36). Dogs were perhaps the animals that most brought to Levi's mind his experience in the Lager and the concentration-camp environment in general. The first thing Levi heard when the goods-train shutters were opened for the transported prisoners arriving in Auschwitz were 'outlandish orders in that barbaric barking of Germans in command' (p. 15). Dogs were identified with the oppressors, not only in Levi's mind. Most writers of holocaust witness literature, as Daniela Amsallem noted (*Le symbolisme du chien: Primo Levi et la littérature juive après la Shoah*) featured dogs obsessively (see, for example, Yoram Kaniuk and Elie Wiesel).

Incomprehensible, shouted orders followed 'the tradition of the 'drill,' the harsh military practice, a Prussian legacy, immortalized by Büchner in Woyzeck' as Levi put it in *The Drowned and the Saved* (p. 2494). These orders were almost always accompanied by the sound of barking, 'which seems to give vent to a centuries-old rage' (p. 15). The image that Levi seemed to be referring to was that of Cerberus, the terrifying three-headed dog with snakes rising from his head and neck that Canto VI of Dante's *Inferno* 'howls through his triple throats like a mad dog' (VI:14). It was, of course, a literary image but there was always a subtext in Levi's work adding extra layers to the established connotations of the animal—in this case, dogs as guardians of the gates of Hell according to an ancient tradition, with negative connotations. Levi rarely identified with dogs as he did with other animals; when he did, it signified that humans had been reduced to a state of brutality through force rather than having undergone a metamorphosis by choice.

In *If This Is a Man*, dogs represented a final step before pure degradation (as Resnyk commented, 'Si j'avey une chien, je ne le chasse pas dehors' [p. 66]). Dogs were themselves a form of degradation: the herculean Elias, with his 'bestial vigour' had a 'small hooked paw' (p. 91) rather than a hand, and the final humiliation was guards; they also watched over your inner thoughts ('the pain of remembering, the old fierce anguish of feeling myself a man again, which attacks me like a dog the moment my consciousness comes out of the darkness' [p. 135]). Dogs were by no means imaginary presences in the Lager. The Germans trained dogs to tear prisoners apart (Appendix to *If This Is a Man*). A dog's bark was the epitome of the voice of an animal, the lowest level of the Babel Tower, where the grotesque voices speaking confounded languages were considered 'animal'.

Subjection through sound was one important part of the destruction of the prisoners' humanity experimented in the Lager. Air-raid sirens were defined in 'Cerium' (*The Periodic Table*) as an elaboration of

an evil musician, who had put into it fury and lament, the wolf's howl at the moon and the typhoon's breath; the horn of Astolfo must have had such a sound. It caused panic, not only because it was announcing bombs but also because of its intrinsic horror, like the wail of a wounded beast that reaches as far as the horizon (p. 870).

Dogs were also a symbol of obedience. In *The Drowned and the Saved*, Pavlov's dog was mentioned as an example of a conditioned response, although Levi commented that memory also produced a mechanical reaction. When the roll-call in the soup kitchen was called, it 'worked like the bell that conditioned Pavlov's dogs: it provoked an instantaneous secretion of saliva' (p. 2477). In 'Phosphorous' (*The Periodic Table*), the librarian guarded the books like a 'barnyard dog', a definition that came up often in Levi's work: 'The librarian, whom I had never seen before, guarded the library like a barnyard dog, one of those poor dogs that are deliberately made vicious by means of a chain and hunger' (p. 849). The image of the barnyard dog was common in Italian literature, underlining its atavistic relationship with farming communities. Dogs were working animals, unlike cats, who were elegant but untameable. Sciascia, for example, in *The Day of the Owl*, described a chained dog, Bargello, which became the object of a philological reflection on the part of Captain Bellodi (Sciascia and Levi shared a passion for the etymology and variety of meanings of words).

Levi's negative view of servant dogs placed him in opposition with the animal behaviourist Konrad Lorenz, who preferred dogs to cats and celebrated canine obedience (*Man Meets Dog*, 1950). The image of lapping like a dog was extended, in *The Drowned and the Saved*, to one of the Jewish warriors who were selected by Gedeon (Judges 7,5), excluding those who lapped up water from the river like dogs or who kneel down to drink. He chose only those who drank by bringing cupped hands up to their mouth. Dogs do not have hands; they use their mouth to bark and to eat, to bite and to take hold of things. In Levi's view, this was savage rather than noble. Not by chance, as a true Darwinian, he appeared to prefer the monkey in *The Wrench*.

In *The Truce*, dogs took on a slightly different meaning. They were portrayed as being less brutal than wolves, which represent pure ferocity. Writing about the character Mordo Nahum, Levi cited Hobbes' famous phrase 'Man is a wolf to man', showing there were, in Levi's mind, three players: man, dog and wolf. Dogs were in the middle, expressing ferocity but only when they were commanded or trained to do so. Dogs were ruthless, but never as much as wolves. Wolves, on the other hand, in their pure ferocity, preserved an aura of nobility (absolutes, for Levi, were always charged with ambivalence, attracting and repelling at the same time). An example of this intermediate form of brutality, or feral attitude, towards others was Buck, in London's *Call of the Wild*.

The character known as 'the Greek' in *The Truce* was a 'lone wolf, eternally at war with everyone' (p. 277), which endowed him with a certain nobility, although Levi went on to describe him as 'old before his time, enclosed in the circle of his bleak ambition' (p. 277). Cesare was the exact opposite, even though he cultivated solitary adventures he was playful. 'For Cesare 'work' was at times an unpleasant necessity, at times an amusing opportunity for encounters, and not a cold obsession, or a Lucifer-like affirmation of himself' (p. 277). Only humans, or animals that resemble them, play games.

Dogs were thus an image of individual subjection to a superior law, deprived of personal liberty, just like the Nazi prison guards who obeyed orders from above. Being deprived of liberty was one of Levi's main themes, based on ancient tradition: 'what matters to me is to live free, not to have a collar like a dog' ('Gold', *The Periodic Table*, p. 865). Dogs do not enjoy variations, stochastic or procured elements that create novelty; their behaviour is absolutely predictable. In this sense, they can be associated with insects who similarly thrive on repetition, although dogs are essentially individual, not social, animals such as bees or ants. Dogs are like people deprived of a social context or the games that society requires of its citizens. Dogs were mentioned in 'Versamine' as guinea pigs for an experiment, but also as anti-dogs—a dog that has been stripped of his natural code of behaviour owing to the substances he had been administered. Levi's anti-dog was not ferocious like a wolf but a little mutt.

Another story in *Natural Histories*, 'Full Employment', talked about communication between humans and dogs. Levi denied that there was a man–dog language, although he admitted there was a certain level of mutual understanding. The topic of animal language resurfaced in 'On

Obscure Writing', one of his most symptomatic pieces collected in *Other People's Trades.*

If Not Now, When? was the only book of Levi's where animals were led back to their own sphere, part of the sights and sounds of the landscape, in a form of more or less balanced cohabitation between humans and their environment. In this novel, animals were just animals. Dogs, for example, did not represent pure brutalization—they were simply dogs. In an article on smells ('The Language of Odors', *Other People's Trades*), animals were described in terms of ethology, as examples of a trait—their sense of smell—that contributed to their natural selection through the ages. In this case, Levi admitted that dogs were superior to humans, citing Virginia Woolf's dog, Flush, and G. K. Chesterton's Quoodle, before citing the far smaller range of doors the human nose can smell. Levi concluded the article by describing the power of doors to evoke memories. After his second visit to Auschwitz in 1982, the 'odor of Poland [. . .] released by the fossil coal used to heat homes, struck me like a sledgehammer' (p. 2234). Levi thus revisited an idea he had first written about in 'The Mnemagogs' (probably in 1946), a short story where an old doctor keeps odours in little glass cases to remind him of the important moments of his life. It is no chance that Levi's sense of smell was linked to his experience of Auschwitz. The writer did not state it directly, but the experience left a trace of the hound in him: a mnemonic sense of smell.

Dolphin

The narrator/listener in *The Wrench* was stopped at a Russian airport because he had a book on dolphins with him. On interrogation as to whether he was a specialist in the field, the narrator answered that he was just a curious chemist. Dolphins recurred here and there in Levi's work, at times as mythological animals, at others as the objects of his readings about animal behaviour and language. In 'Let's See What Has Come True' (*Uncollected Stories and Essays*), an article published in *Tuttolibri* in 1982, Levi included in his list for the year 1970 'Language of Cetaceans': 'As far as we know, the investigations stopped after Lilly's early results with dolphins. They have an intelligence comparable to that of dogs, and a language that seems quite evolved; but I don't think it has been deciphered yet' (p. 2592). It makes one wonder whether Levi read Gregory Bateson's books deciphering the language of cetaceans.

Dromedary

If Levi had had the time, it is likely that he would have published a dialogue with a dromedary in the nature magazine *Airone* as he had done with other animals that featured in his poems. He did write one poem (in November 1986) called 'The Dromedary', in which the animal listed his modest qualities and called himself 'ugly'. His saving graces were that he could feed himself on his hump and live on very little. 'There's no servant who's without his kingdom. Mine is desolation; It is boundless' (p. 2004). Is it possible that Levi identified with this animal?

Elephants

There was one poem on elephants in Levi's collection ('The Elephant', 1984), which was about Hannibal's heroic and 'absurd' traverse of the Alps with his army on elephants. The poem told the elephant's story in the first person: 'You want my story? It's briefly told. A shrewd Indian nursed and tamed me, An Egyptian shackled me and sold me, A Phoenician dressed me in Armor And set a tower on my rump'. For Levi, again, elephants were an emblem of servitude (a role often occupied by donkeys in his work). The elephant in the poem was buried under avalanches in the Alps where he had slipped on ice and fallen, unable to get up. His refrain throughout the poem, and his 'dying trumpet blast' was 'Absurd, absurd' (p. 1969).

Ethology

Levi often described himself as an observer, at times going as far as comparing himself to a Kibitzer, a Yiddish term for spectator (often in the context of card games). Levi's primary source, aside from his flights of fantasy, was his close observation. From the start, the young Levi, witness and narrator of *If This Is a Man*, had a sharp eye for detail and an incredible capacity for reading behaviour and character though people's gestures, words and postures. The meanings of these minimal signs were later expanded in his reflections and his writing, with the result that his opus leaves us with a complex grid of intertextuality. Observation was a skill that Levi needed as a chemist: to be able to recognize a process 'at a glance' and only later use intelligence and the 'words of the Father' (referring to the textbook Levi cited in *The Search for Roots*) to conceptualize it. *If This Is a Man* was the first of Levi's 'ethological' books, but not the last: he applied his knowledge and skill in the field of animal behaviour in everything he wrote, including his short stories and newspaper articles. In his Appendix to *If This Is a Man*, written 30 years later, made the zoological significance of the Lager experience explicit, thus implicitly accepting his function as an ethologist in the 'gigantic biological and social experiment', as he called it in the chapter *The Drowned and the Saved* (p. 82).

In the short story, 'The Measure of Beauty' (*Natural Histories*), the narrator, who was clearly Levi himself, loved spying: 'I have always loved this activity, seeing without being seen, especially from an elevated position' (p. 501) and his hero was 'Peeping Tom, who preferred to die rather than give up peering at Lady Godiva through the slats of venetian blinds' (p. 501). The sexual part of the story of Peeping Tom was omitted, as was the blindness caused by his spying (Freud wrote about the Lady Godiva legend in an article on temporary blindness as a symptom of sexual conflict and on voyeurism more in general). The narrator explained his passion thus: 'Spying on other people, regardless of what they are doing or about to do, and of any ultimate discovery, gives me a profound sensation of power and gratification, perhaps an atavistic memory of the extended periods of waiting endured by our hunter ancestors, reproducing the vital emotions of chase and ambush' (p. 501).

Observation was not a secondary activity for Levi as a writer. His skill as an observer was at the root of his becoming a writer—it was intrinsically linked to his being a chemist, a trade in which he was required to trigger and observe reactions and then write a weekly report on them. Levi often said that this professional habit was what made him a writer. His skill as an observer also stood him in good stead for finding clues. Some of his short stories are constructed like thrillers—Levi would scatter clues here and there to slow down the solution of the mystery, with the result that some critics and superficial readers felt the story was too mechanical.

The historian Carlo Ginzburg wrote about the links between hunting and the art of narration, which, he claimed, were both based on induction ('Morelli, Freud, and Sherlock Holmes: Clues and Scientific Method' in *The Sign of Three: Dupin, Holmes, Pierce* [1984]). Levi used the scientific method of induction a great deal, but tempered it with deduction. The narrator of the 'termite-hill' that was Auschwitz focused on a single clue—a character, say—to build up his narrative. The art of a storyteller, like that of a chemist, was far from abstract. It was based on practice and on 'the words of the Father', and could be passed on to others through direct experience. Calvino's review of Ginzburg's book ('Ears, Hunters, and Gossips', *la Repubblica* [1980]) would equally apply to Levi.

In several interviews, Levi talked about the experimental nature of the Lager: a closed society with no social activity boiled down to pure hierarchy. Levi often focused on this concept. When people arrived in the concentration camp, they thought they would find kin, not rivals or enemies in the struggle for survival. In some conversations, Levi stated that he regretted not having been able to grasp the various hierarchies that structured the camp on arrival. Many of the portraits in *If This Is a Man* were based on the characters' behaviour or more generally on their personality; they were presented as individual examples of more general traits. For example, the engineer Alfred L. The chapter 'The Drowned and the Saved', 'shows among other things how empty is the myth of original equality among men' (p. 88).

Levi's passion for observing human animals was also expressed in the story of Cesare's adventures in *The Truce*, where the narrator became a spectator of his friend's swindles. Levi, as a narrator, was a detached observer, but as an animal behaviourist, he applied his moral system to the behaviour of his subject. Models that come to mind, which Levi must have read at school, were Montaigne and Machiavelli. Like them, Levi was pessimistic about human behaviour; he had no illusions, but always expressed his point of view freely, with no 'charitable' interpretations.

In *The Wrench*, Levi's ethology turned to the world of work. In Claude Lévi-Strauss' review, he stated that Levi was a great ethnographer. Three stories in *Flaw of Form* reflect his skill in that field. The first is 'Observed from a Distance', where cities and other forms of conglomerations on earth are viewed, and reported on, from afar (recalling Calvino's *Invisible Cities*, although Calvino wrote it later, in 1972). The other two are 'Recuenco: The Nourisher' and 'Recuenco: The Rafter', where—in a typical mechanism for science fiction—the same episode was played out from two opposing but symmetric points of view, one mythically bucolic, the other cynically technological. 'The Sorcerers' (*Lilith and Other Stories*) was inspired by Levi's readings in anthropology and written as an ethnographic account, while cruelly parodying western anthropological culture. Another example was in 'Uranium' (*The Periodic Table*) where Levi described 'the strategies and tactics of the rep':

> in terms of sexual courtship. In both cases there is a relationship between two; a courtship or a negotiation among three would be unthinkable. In both cases, you note at the start a sort of dance or ritualized opening, in which the buyer accepts the seller only if he keeps strictly to the traditional ceremony; if that happens, the buyer joins the dance, and if the pleasure is mutual they achieve coupling, and that is the purchase, with both partners visibly satisfied. Cases of unilateral violence are rare; not coincidentally, they are often described in terms borrowed from the sexual sphere (p. 912).

In this case, as in the descriptions from the Lager, the ethological material stemmed from Levi's direct experience. Levi had a reflective personality, and writing was for him an act of pure reflection. Another example of ethology concerning everyday life (social anthropology has nowadays almost entirely replaced sociology as a discipline, and Levi set the trend) was his close attention to the desk sizes of public employees, where a bigger desk was 'a coded expression of the measure of their power' ('Uranium', p. 914), or again his observation of reciprocal influences in couples ('Aunts', *The Wrench*) that led to a wider consideration on the division of gender roles in the animal kingdom. Levi was not only an ethologist of human behaviour—he was also a master of generalizations by analogy (Lorenz demonstrated the importance of this methodology in his article 'Analogy as a Source of Knowledge' [1985]). In 'Novels Dictated by Crickets' (*Other People's Trades*), Levi reminded his readers that

> the science of ethology has come into being and rapidly attained maturity, showing us that animals are different one from another and from us, that every animal species follows laws of its own, and that these laws, to the extent that we are able to understand them, are in close accord with evolutionary theories—which is to say, they favour the preservation of the species, though not always that of the individual (p. 2075).

The conflictual relationship between individuals and species was one of the central questions in Levi's ethics. It was also a contradictory issue because as a scientist Levi was well aware that the law of large numbers was dominant in nature. Levi was also a firm believer in Darwin's theories. However, his intellectual formation, the liberal-socialist ambient in which he was brought up, in addition to his Jewish culture, gave Levi a bias towards constructing an individual ethical framework. This framework is evident in particular whenever Levi wrote or spoke about the capacity for invention or innovation, which he strongly believed belonged to the individual and not to the species or to the collective. Levi considered culture and ethics two different tools (where work was the synthesis of the two) for moderating the domination of the collective over individuals, or individuals over the collective. Perhaps this was why he felt such a great attraction for adventure, explorers and writers of adventure stories, where challenging experiences (like his own) fortify individuals. Joseph Conrad and Jack London, both ethologists in their way, represented, in Levi's view, the seminal conflict between nature and the individual, between preserving the species and survival of the individual. Buck in *Call of the Wild* embodies precisely this dialectic.

Levi warned his readers about the dangers of reading human behaviour in purely animal terms, or seeking animal characteristics in humans at any cost. It was a risk that Levi himself took; when he fell into the trap, his writing was at its crudest and most lucid. It was not the most scientific, but it was certainly the most loaded with moral passion. In 'Novels Dictated by Crickets', Levi cited Desmond Morris' *The Naked Ape*: 'I think that not all human actions can be interpreted in these terms, and that the method doesn't take us very far. Socrates, Newton, Bach, and Leopardi were not naked apes' (p. 2076). If these famous people were to find themselves in a concentration camp as guinea pigs in the 'great biological experiment' conducted by the Nazis, who knows whether they wouldn't have become animals?

In *The Drowned and the Saved*, Levi reached the bitter conclusion that the history of the Lager experience had been written mostly by those who had not plummeted its depths, himself included:

> The ones who did never returned, or if they did their capacity for observation was paralysed by pain and incomprehension. On the other hand, the vantage point of the 'privileged' witnesses was certainly better, if only because it was situated higher and therefore looked out over a broader horizon; but it, too, was falsified, to a greater or lesser extent, by privilege itself (p. 2416).

As an ethologist, Levi possessed, in his way, the pathos of distance (which was one of the peculiarities of his friend, Calvino). He had an additional advantage in that, when he described the Lager, it was from two different viewpoints—as an observer, and as the subject of his observation. These two viewpoints, as has often been noted, corresponded to two different stages of his life and two different time frames, whereas a true ethologist can only be an external observer of the animal being studied.

Flies

Levi thought flies were stupid, flitting unpredictably here and there with no purpose. He wrote a poem ('The Fly', 1986), perhaps after a short stay in a 'sanitary hospital', where a fly spoke in the first person about its ability to get everywhere: 'No locked doors for me: There's always a window, A crack, a keyhole' (p. 2003). This fly played the same role as the crows in the two poems written in the decade after his return from Auschwitz, as a messenger of death: 'I'm the last to kiss the lips / Of the dying and the soon to die. I'm important. / My monotonous Buzzing, irritating, meaning-less, / Repeats the one message of the world / To those who cross this threshold. I am mistress here: / The only one who's free, unhampered, healthy' (p. 2003). Compared to the two crow poems, the tone of 'The Fly' was more disenchanted, bitter, and resigned, with less invective. The fly on the hospital wall had discreetly normalized death, turning it into a natural, inevitable event.

Giraffes

Giraffes have a hidden quality that appears to attract writers. The first time Calvino's Mr Palomar appeared in the columns of *Corriere della Sera* (1 August 1975), was in a short story called 'The Giraffe Race', set in the Vincennes Zoo, a reduced version of which was then included in *Palomar* (Calvino 1983). Mr Palomar-Calvino, at the zoo with his daughter, observed a giraffe running, and described his strange lumbering step as if it had a mechanism constructed of a collection of heterogeneous parts. There was ultimately, however, Calvino stated, 'a natural grace that emerges from those ungraceful movements' (Calvino 1985, p. 80). Calvino's aim was to find harmony in an unharmonious world, 'a unifying element' which, Mr Palomar explained to his daughter, came from the 'spots on the hide, arranged in irregular but homogeneous patterns: they agree, like a precise graphic equivalent, with the animal's segmented movements' (p. 80).

In Levi's story, 'The Giraffe in the Zoo' (*Uncollected Stories and Essays*), first published in 1987 by the nature magazine *Airone*, the giraffe being interviewed by a journalist was a male specimen (as were all the animals in Levi's imaginary zoo, except the spider). The journalist was taken by the matter of how the giraffe's legs could support so much pressure, and asked his subject whether he suffered from hypertension, varicose veins or inter-nal haemorrhages. The giraffe was unfailingly polite, despite a little initial nervousness, and patiently explained that 'our four legs have natural, built-in elastic hose. I must tell you, they are extremely comfortable. Veins and arteries don't get exhausted, even if the pressure is what you've calculated, and they are made of an excellent material that doesn't wear out; in fact, it renews itself over time' (p. 2773). He also described, with anatomical precision, the difficulties they face when drinking, owing to the length of their necks and legs. The piece was almost an encyclopaedia entry—in the form of a dialogue—on the anatomical peculiarities of giraffes. In the story, the journalist decided to write the giraffe's final comment down into his notebook. The passage is worth quoting it in full, so that it can be compared with Calvino's piece:

> In spite of their structure, which is so different from that of all other quadrupeds, when giraffes run they are extraordinarily elegant. Their pace is between a gallop and a dance. The four legs leave the ground almost simultaneously while the neck balances the majestic rhythm of their gait. It appears slow but is very fast: it recalls the sailing of a ship, and betrays not the least effort. The vast body sways naturally, tipping inward when the animal changes course. Observing it, I realized how great is their need for the freedom of large spaces, and how cruel to confine them within the meshes of a fence. And yet the specimen that I interviewed was born here, in captivity, ignorant of the unspoiled splendour of the savanna; but he carries its primeval nobility within himself (pp. 2773–4).

Levi's description was as spare and precise as ever, but it was also poetical. His ethical conclusion—that it was wrong to keep such a noble animal in a confined space—regarded the animal but also reflected on himself, without anthropomorphizing the giraffe, however. By contrast, the animals Calvino described through the medium of Mr Palomar were nearly always projections of the state of mind—confused, perplexed or troubled—of the protagonist. Animals were distant from humans for Calvino because he didn't feel one bit like an animal. One wonders why the two writers were so fascinated by giraffes? The image of graceful movement brought about by the unusual and apparently unharmonious mechanism of their legs was a way to underline the discomfort humans still felt at their adoption of an upright stance, which freed the hands for grasping and the face for gesturing and talking (Levi and Calvino were both avid readers of André Leroi-Gourhan). The theme of movement and running appeared in several of Levi's stories and articles, including, for example, 'A Long Duel' (an auto-biographical tale included in *Other People's Trades*) which ends with a running race.

Goosander

'Goosandering' with girls watching you from below, was the expression Faussone used in his account of his first experience of cable-wiring, sus-pended 20 metres above ground. The narrator in *The Wrench* stopped his account: 'I had to interrupt the narrative here because of this "goosander-ing". The locution was familiar to me—"goosandering" means more or less "displaying bravado" or "showboating"—but I hoped that Faussone might explain the origin of the word to me, or at least clarify what a goosander is' (p. 1068). With his usual scientific precision and curiosity, Levi/narrator went on to explain: 'Later on, for my own purposes, I did some research, and found out that the goosander is the common merganser, a species of duck with beautiful plumage, which is now exceedingly rare in Italy; but no hunter could confirm for me that its behaviour was peculiar enough to jus-tify this metaphor, which is still widely used' (p. 1068). The central nar-rative of the chapter 'Without Time' was Faussone's account of a love affair that ended badly. At the end of the chapter was another animal, an old, mangy ibex, who was 'sick' and 'ugly', scraping the door of the shelter where the couple was staying with its horns. Faussone tried to find mean-ing in the episode, a moral of the story: 'What does all of this mean? It was a signal, as if by scratching the metal with its horns the ibex wanted to tell us something. Here I had thought that the girl and I were at the start of something, but really we were at the end' (p. 1076). *The Wrench* was all about the work of humans, but it also featured many animals, who often played a symbolic role: snakes, monkeys, spiders, cats, elephants, anchovies, etc. Of all Levi's works, this was the most Darwinian, praising hands as tools of human progress. Perhaps for this reason Faussone, the solitary, roaming protagonist of the book, was surrounded any animal-metaphors, animal-colleagues, animal-symbols and animal-objects.

Hens

According to Nystedt the word 'hen' or the expression 'little hen' appears 48 times in Levi's works. There is no doubt that hens have always played an important role in domestic life; for centuries, they were the most common backyard animal in Europe. This is the way hens are depicted in Levi's 'Russian' books, *The Truce and If Not Now, When?* There were in fact only two incidents featuring hens that bare worthy of note (or three, if you count an autobiographical episode in 'The Need for Fear' in *Other People's Trades*). The first was in a chapter in *The Truce* entitled 'A Little Hen', which was a kind of incunabula of the stories and novels that would follow. The incident involved Primo, Cesare and their companions trying to communicate the concept of 'chicken' to the Russians, an attempt that failed miserably given the language barrier. Resorting to ribald mimicry and repeating 'cockaday' had no effect as 'the interpretation of the chicken's sound is highly artificial' (p. 328). The solution, which was equally artificial, was found in a drawing: 'I drew a chicken in the dirt, complete with all its attributes, including—out of an excessive zeal for specifics—an egg behind.' The answer to the quiz was Kura, Kuritsa!' (p. 329).

The other episode saw Levi and his wife taking a tour of farms to gather chicken manure in the chapter 'Nitrogen' (*The Periodic Table*). They were attempting to collect uric acid from the pollina, or chicken manure, for a client that wanted it to manufacture cosmetics. Levi and his wife discovered the stuff was not given away and was sold 'at a high price' (p. 902), and emerged from the experience worse for wear. Like Renzo's capons in *The Betrothed*, hens are generally trussed up, sold to the highest bidder.

Horses

Horses are one of the most common animals in Levi's work, and they are generally depicted in a positive light. In *If This Is a Man,* however, they are associated to the figure of the 'Muselmänn', the type of prisoner who is too stupid to spare himself and works himself to death. A similar image of forced labour can be found in a poem written in 1946, while Levi was working on his first novel. 'Monday' (*At an Uncertain Hour*) depicts a cart-horse as 'locked between two poles. / It can't even look askance. / Its whole life is plodding.' Levi goes on to compare the sadness of the cart-horse to the sad life of a man: 'And a man? Isn't a man sad? / If he lives alone for long / if he thinks time is over / a man's a sad thing too' (p. 1890). In this last verse, there is a clear echo of the title of Levi's first novel, with the result that horses become a metaphor for the sufferance of mankind so typical of nineteenth-century poetry.

In another episode from Levi's lager experience, recounted in the chapter 'The Cantor and the Veteran' (*Lilith and Other Stories*), describes the public washing of Vladek, a spectacle organized by Otto, the head of the barrack and one of the 30 founding fathers of Auschwitz. Vladek was put in one of the soup vats carried outside and 'washed personally, as you might wash a horse, scrubbing him from head to toe first with a brush and then with rags for cleaning the floor.' At the beginning of *The Truce*, by contrast, the Russian soldiers on horseback provided an image that was both triumphant and tragic; they were the first real people the prisoners had seen since their liberation. 'They seemed to us miraculously physical and real, suspended (the road was higher than the camp) on their enormous horses between the grey of the snow and the grey of the sky' (p. 216). The reference here was to the chivalrous ideal of shining knights in Armor.

Horses inhabit the huge spaces dominated by the Russians, both in *The Truce* and in *If Not Now, When?* Often seized as war booty by Russian soldiers, horses travelled wearily across the same desolate plains as the prisoners and became a much-coveted source of sustenance. Horses were also a metaphor for strength and power, incarnated by the old Avesani, the Moor of Venice, and in this sense, they were out of place in the Lager stories (dogs were to horses what the Lager was to the journey in *The Truce*). In *If Not Now, When?* a broad-backed draft horse, fondly adopted by Pavel, took on the features of a secondary character in the novel, but came to a sad end. As if in a Western, the horse was made to climb up into a train carriage and later refused to get off. In their furious attempts to coax him out, the horse was crippled and the former prisoners were forced to slaughter him on the spot. Horses were not only a physical presence. They were, most importantly, a means of transport, equivalent to a train or a truck. In a chapter of *The Periodic Table*, horses were described in cinematic terms, emitting steam from their nostrils like the horses in Eisenstein's films.

Inventing an Animal

In an article on inventing animals, Levi imagined animals that could exist, or that were possible in nature, such as centaurs or chimera. The writer had engaged in this activity since writing the short story '*Quaestio de Centauris*', where in order to re-invent a hybrid animal that already existed, he rewrote its family tree. Levi cited a book by P. J. Farmer, a work of science fiction, where the author invented an additional organ to solve the problem of centaurs' difficulty in breathing. In a spirit akin to Raymond Queneau's workshop of potential literature (Oulipo), Levi attempted to invent animals that worked; his preference was for 'scientific realism' (or science-fiction). Borges, in his textbook of fantastic zoology, created some highly original animals, but none of them adopts the incredibly innovative solutions produced by ticks, fleas or tapeworms. The funniest part of the article, which is an exposition on the art of invention, in the Latin sense of the word, is when animals invented by students in middle school in Turin are described. These include the executioner, the lymph dinosaur, the gigantic neck, the Monstrumgaricos, the Cocò and the Cibercus. In these brief descriptions of every animal invented by the schoolchildren Levi showed incredible expertise in creating thumbnail sketches of the animals.

Inspiration

Huxley was convinced that animals provided the raw material for writers. A clear example of this can be found in Aesop's fables, but also more recently in magazines such as *Nature* or *Scientific American*, or in Lorenz's works, where the seeds of writing are sown. Levi's writing is linked to a double vocation: one imposed by chance (the Lager), the other sought since childhood (the animal world). One might even posit that his trade as a chemist, the declared source of many of his books, was a subspecies of the discipline of the naturalist. In Levi's case, a naturalist who treated chemical elements as if they were animals, and animals as if they were chemical elements. Levi claimed, in the chapter 'Novels Dictated by Crickets' (*Other People's Trades*) that 'a writer need only choose, he can overlook the truths set forth by scientists—it is enough for him to draw liberally on this universe of metaphors. It is precisely by leaving the human island that he will find every human trait multiplied hundredfold, a forest of prefabricated hyperboles' (p. 2076).

His best stories about animals were actually Elseviers, artistic pieces written for newspapers, of which he was a master. In his articles for *La Stampa*, Levi excelled in giving a form to the unformed, mysterious, stochastic or random. The short pieces in *Other People's Trades* are a perfect continuation of Levi's work in *If This Is a Man*, although on a different level and from a different point of view, 'from afar' as Lévi-Strauss would put it. In his pieces about animals (and even in his articles about those bizarre, rational, mysterious things which are words), Levi reveals himself as a portrait artist, or rather, as a miniaturist working on a tiny scale to construct small descriptive or argumentative masterpieces based on the same principle that he had already experimented in his first narrative work, *If This Is a Man*.

Kangaroos

The kangaroo's name was Innaminka, and, although it was not clear at the beginning of the story, he was a male of the species. He had been invited to a buffet dinner, where he felt uncomfortable owing both to his shape and to the food that was served. In the 1977 short story 'Buffet Dinner' (*Uncollected Stories and Essays*), the kangaroo represented anyone who feels out of place, among people they don't know, often an object of derision. He was approached by superficial young women, was unable to find a place to relieve himself and ended up nibbling at the leaves of the same ficus tree where he had urinated. At one point in the story, a woman

> sat down on a small armchair beside him and started talking to him sweetly [. . .] Since he, too, was unhappy, he felt sympathetic toward the woman, and for the first time that evening he stopped wishing that the reception would soon be over; instead he hoped that the woman would continue to caress him [. . .] This however was not to be. The woman continued to caress him, but with increasing distraction, paying no attention to his shivers of pleasure, and continuing all the while to complain about certain human troubles of hers.'

In the end, a man dragged her away after saying 'something very unpleasant and brutal to her' and the woman followed, without giving the kangaroo so much as a 'farewell glance' (p. 1228). The scene is reminiscent of certain scenes in 1960s Italian cinema, from Fellini to Antonioni. The kangaroo in the story was an example of an animal metamorphosis generated by a blend of feeling extraneous—the kangaroo's body—and the desire for relationships—the woman's monologue. The story ends with the kangaroo escaping from the dinner party with 'long, happy, elastic leaps' (p. 1228).

Lemmings

These rodents, together with the village elder of the Amazonia Arunde tribe, are the undoubted protagonists of 'Heading West', one of the short stories collected in *Flaw of Form*. Lemmings are small. soft-furred mammals that live in colonies, typically in Arctic tundras. Their peculiarity, studied by historians and geographers for many centuries, is that their population fluctuations are chaotic, causing them to seek outside their natural habitats. The result of these mass migrations is often seen as mass suicide. In Levi's story, the lemmings march in columns in a state of excitement until they have exhausted their physical and psychological energy and abandon themselves to death. The two naturalists, Anna and Walter, witness and diligently attempt to explain 'a swelling beneath the torrent of those innumerable, small desperate creatures who were running toward death [. . .] Toward the marshland and the sea just beyond' (p. 595). The biological phenomenon that provokes the mass suicide ultimately escapes them.

The story is a reflection on the meaning of life, and why animals or humans struggle to stay alive. The quest for explanations leads the two researchers to conduct a survey of an Amazonian tribe that succumbs to death. However, the conclusion is a Catch-22 situation. Having identified a potential antidote, the members of the tribe refuse to take it, while Walter is suffocated by herds of lemmings as he tries to nebulize them with his chemical formula. Levi explores once again the theme of symmetry: 'the most common defence—and the least ignoble—is the one that exploits our fundamental ignorance of the future. And, you see, even here there is symmetry: this uncertainty is the same one that makes life insupportable to . . . To the lemmings. For everyone else, the will to live is something profound and confusing' (p. 590). In Levi's view, then, life requires asymmetry in order to be lived tolerably.

Lichen

Cladonia Rapida was a parasite endemic to automobiles, 'a highly specialised lichen whose unique and requisite substrate is made up of the interior and exterior structures of automobiles' (p. 447) whose name was derived from one of the most common lichens eaten by reindeer. The short story entitled 'Cladonia Rapida' (Natural Histories) was written in the form of a scientific report, including statistics and percentages. It plays on words commonly used in the context of cars, a classic example of Levi's parody.

Man

The expression Levi used when describing men being reduced to the condition of animals was 'bestialization'. Similarly, the word 'beast' recurs obsessively throughout his work, not only in the context of the Lager. One example is in the curious story, 'The Beast in the Temple' (*Lilith and Other Stories*) which repeats the same paradigm with a couple of interesting variants: an external observer—the narrating voice of a tourist—and an optical illusion created by the columns of the temple, which the author decided to reproduce in a drawing. The suggestion is a reversal of point of view is called for, from the narrator to the narrated beast, and vice versa. All readers need to do is switch their gaze from the gaps to the columns and back again.

In *The Drowned and the Saved*, Levi stated that men were not beasts, but could easily be transformed into animals depending on the situation. In his 1976 Appendix to the School Edition of *If This Is a Man*, exploring the issue of the hatred of Jews ('improperly called anti-Semitism'), Levi referred to the zoological phenomenon:

> animals belonging to different groups of a single species manifest signs of intolerance toward one another. This happens even among domestic animals: we know that a hen from one hen-house, introduced into another, is pecked for several days, as a sign of rejection. The same happens among rats and bees and, in general, all species of social animals. Now, man is certainly a social animal (Aristotle confirmed it), but we would be in trouble if all the zoological urges that survive in man were tolerated! Human laws are useful precisely for this: to restrain animal impulses (p. 184).

This passage is highly significant because nowhere else in his work does Levi explain directly what human laws are based on. Social morals are, in any case, established by rules; they are effective only inasmuch as their aim relates to values which are not intrinsic. That is, they are not natural laws; they are dictated by the process of civilization. In Levi's view, which is essentially pessimistic, the most important moral quality is moderation, which civilization has imposed on mankind. It could be claimed that his pessimism lies in his Jewish roots, shared by Freud, the father of psychoanalysis, who reflected on the destiny of humanity in the 1930s. Although Levi was not an adept of psychoanalysis, there are areas he shared with Freud, especially in his return to Judaism. Yosef Hayim Yerushalmi (1996) has suggested that they have in common an ambivalence towards their historical context and their Jewish roots.

Another parallel can be drawn with the anthropologist, Claude Lévi-Strauss, whose work Levi knew in-depth, having translated it into Italian. They shared other features: their Jewish roots, their deep scepticism and the fact that they were both highly literary writers that were unrecognized as such. Take for example the passage from the chapter 'The Anthropologist and the Human Condition' in *The View from Afar*:

> Culture is neither natural nor artificial. It stems from neither genetics nor rational thought, for it is made up of rules of conduct, which were not invented and whose function is generally not understood by the people who obey them. Some of these rules are residues of traditions acquired in the different types of social structure through which, in the course of a very long history, each human group has passed. Other rules have been consciously accepted or modified for the sake of a specific goal. Yet there is no doubt that, between the instincts inherited from our genotype and the rules inspired by reason, the mass of unconscious rules remains more important and more effective; because reason itself, as Durkheim and Mauss understood, is a product rather than a cause of cultural evolution (Lévi-Strauss 1985, p. 34).

In a conference in 1979 in Turin on racism, Levi dealt with some of the crucial issues in the relationship between humans and animals. While accepting that there are different human races ('there is no debate'), Levi went on to explain how racial prejudice was a feature of the animal kingdom rather than that of humans. He thought it was typical of wild animals, and especially fierce animals, for two reasons: first, because it could also be found in social animals, and second, because there was no remedy. In the same talk, Levi described the division in castes of hymenoptera, ants and bees and the need for hierarchy in domestic animals such as hens.

With reference to Lorenz's book *On Aggression*, which examined the 'so-called evil' of aggressive rats to explain the biological basis of racism, which in his view had no place in human culture (there is an echo of Lévi-Strauss here, with reference to his book *Race and Culture* which Levi must have read). There is however a gap between Levi's examination of animal behaviour and his survey of racism in Europe in the twentieth century. The problem of how the Nazis succeeded in reducing people to animals remained. In Levi's Appendix to *If This Is a Man*, he cautions against finding a biological explanation for the atrocities, comprehending the Nazis words and deeds, and thus somehow justifying them: 'they are words and deeds that are not human but, rather, counter-human, without historical precedent, barely comparable to the cruellest events of the biological struggle for existence' (p. 190). Levi admits that war could possibly have an element of the biological struggle, but 'Auschwitz has nothing to do with war; it is not an episode of war, it is not an extreme form of war. War is an everlasting terrible fact: it is deplorable but it is in us, it has a rationality, we "comprehend" it' (p. 190).

In conclusion, it is worth citing two passages from Levi's works, because Levi is not a thinker, but a writer who thinks and there is a significant difference between the two. The first is from *The Truce*. Recently freed, the former prisoners hadn't eaten for 24 hours, and sat on the floor of the train car: 'I had bitter thoughts: that nature rarely grants compensation, and neither does human society, being timid and slow to diverge from natures gross schemes; and such an achievement would represent, in the history of human thought, the ability to see in nature not a model to follow but a shapeless block to carve, or an enemy to fight' (p. 239). The second is in the same chapter, 'The Greek', which is full of moral considerations (not by chance it is the first chapter of the book written when Levy was returning to writing fiction at the end of the 1950s):

> Moral codes, all of them, are rigid by definition: they do not admit nuances, or compromises, or mutual contamination. They are accepted or rejected entirely. This is one of the main reasons that man is a herd animal, and more or less consciously seeks proximity not to his neighbour in general but only to one who shares his deep convictions (or his lack of such convictions) (p. 245).

Metamorphosis

Levi was very interested in changes of state, in a mythological or zoological context. In one of his so-called science-fiction stories, 'Angelic Butterfly', published in 1962 and later collected in *Natural Histories*, a Nazi scientist attempts to develop the morphological potential of humans. However, rather than obtaining an angelic butterfly, his experiments with different feeding regimes produced birds that looked like vultures. Metamorphosis was not only a dream cultivated by myths and religion; it was also, as Levi insisted, keenly sought by science (religion and science are the twin dreams of humanity). Metamorphosis in plants and animals is an established fact, and it is no chance that animals that transform excite Levi's curiosity the most: insects, fish, amphibians, crustaceans, molluscs, jellyfish, corals and butterflies, a species Levi wrote about in an article called 'Butterflies' (*Other People's Trades*). Levi himself underwent a change of state, metamorphosis—although the writer never uses this word—when he was deported to Auschwitz. The theme of amphibians, or centaurs, the idea of being composed of two natures is a recurrent one in Levi's writing and conversations. While the idea of hybridism stresses the aspect of blending, or impurity, which creates innovation through the exchange of genetic or cultural heritage, metamorphosis is a radical change in state, scratch that. It was this radical change that fascinated Levi in particular.

Another example of metamorphosis was narrated in the short story 'His Own Maker' (*Flaw of Form*), which described the evolution of living species from an aquatic form of life to becoming human. Phylogenesis and ontogenesis cross paths and recur in various stories, as Levi was susceptible to the theories of Haeckel on the ontogenesis of organisms. A poem written by Levi in 1980, 'Autobiography', draws a parallel to the story. It was inspired by a fragment of Empedocles, which describes a marine organism being transformed into a crab, a dinosaur, a toad, a woodlouse, a deer, a cricket, a salamander, a scorpion, a unicorn, an asp and an ass, until it became a dancing girl, and finally the philosopher himself, who bore 'strange signs' of his past mutations on his body.

Another interesting example of metamorphosis, which is more literary than scientific, is the last chapter of *The Periodic Table*, dedicated to

Calvino and resembling Calvino's short stories. In 'Carbon', Levi tells the story of a carbon atom that never changes despite becoming a part of many different organisms throughout time, until it enters a cell which 'belongs to a brain, and this is my brain, of me who writes, and the cell in question, and in it the atom in question, is assigned to my writing' (p. 946). In the early 1980s, Levi returned to the theme of the metamorphosis of an angel. In his story 'The Great Mutation' (*Stories and Essays*), Isabella grows wings and feels she must learn to fly. The wings continue to grow but the girl's father is so disturbed that he amputates them.

Moles

Levi's bestiary can be divided into animals that love open spaces and those that hide away or dig themselves into burrows. There are more of the latter than of the former. Levi seemed to identify with animals that hide and often transformed himself into one of them (becoming an animal as in Kafka). The theme of the hideaway or burrow triggered in Levi a whole series of considerations and caused him to write one of his most significant pieces, 'My House', the first article collected in *Other People's Trades*. 'I believe that I exemplify an extreme case of sedentary life comparable to that of some molluscs, such as limpets' (p. 2015). The old mole in the poem by the same name, written in 1982, opens with an explanation as to why the mole 'chose to live alone and in the dark' (p. 1950). The mole's life underground is protected, 'where I never feel the cold or heat / or wind or rain or day or night or snow' (p. 1950). The mole is blind but his eyes are no longer any use underground, where he lives nearly all the time except when the new moon excites him and 'sometimes then I entertain myself / emerging suddenly to scare the dogs' (p. 1950).

Like many other animals in Levi's work, moles have a double existence, in prose and in poetry. Levi dedicated an article to them in *Airone* entitled 'Nose to Nose: A Date with Love in the Dark' (*Uncollected Stories and Essays*). Levi interviews a male mole in this short piece who is erudite and wise. He knows the value of his fur, one of the few that can be stroked both ways owing to the fact that moles have to be able to move backwards in their tunnels. His hearing is 10 times sharper than human hearing, and love is the result of their sense of smell. Moles only mate for two weeks a year, always underground; their mutual quest is an exhilarating adventure in Levi's view. The interviewer asks the mole whether he never wishes he could explore the world above ground. The mole answers that that is the stuff of youth, group adventures with other young moles. Finally, Levi recycles the same episode that closes the poem. The title 'Old Mole' cites *Hamlet* (Act I, 5: 'Well said, old mole'), with a distant echo of Marx ('Well burrowed, old mole' in *The Eighteenth Brumaire of Louis Bonaparte*), as well as a clear reference to Kafka's unfinished story, 'The Burrow', published posthumously in 1931.

Monkeys

The Wrench is a book where one keys feature heavily. One chapter, 'The Helper', has a monkey as its protagonist. Faussone himself has something of the monkey about him, owing to his profession as a rigger that requires him to climb up onto cranes, pylons and bridges in a reverse process compared to the evolution of man from trees to the earth. Faussone is monkey-like in his skill at handling materials, but his elegance, and his ability to keep his balance suspended mid-air on beams and narrow bridges, is more feline. While Levi commented on the miracle of manual dexterity, Faussone quipped that having four hands like a monkey would be very useful in his line of work.

Levi's praise of hands can be found in the chapter devoted to Faussone's two aunts, whom the narrator (Levi's alter ego) compared to two little animals in the cage of their apartment. The description is filled with detailed physiognomic and behavioural observations, where a guide dog for the blind, a bird on a branch and a lion in a cage figured as metaphors for Faussone himself. The passage about hands reads thus: 'they brought to mind long ago readings of Darwin, of the craftsman's hand that, making tools and bending matter, rescues the human brain from indolence, and still to this day guides, stimulates, and pulls it forward, as a dog does with his blind master' (p. 1097). This is why the monkey's help in Chapter 3 lends the book an evolutionary flavour, with human skill and labour as its culmination. In *The Wrench* work and play are closely linked, and yet, at the end of the day, considering not only its amusing and stimu-latingly aspects but also the fatigue and repetition, and ultimately risk, work is considered more important than play, and work is what distinguishes men from animals. The other thing that distinguishes men from animals is their motivation; motivation is what singled Faussone's ability from that of the monkey climbing with him: 'he didn't have a derrick to build [. . .] the whole thing was a game' (p. 980). Faussone found in the monkey a com-panion, a friend that hurt the most to leave: 'everyone knows that the great-est friends of animals—those who best understand them and are best understood by them—are loners' (p. 976). Levi's description of the gradual approach between the man and the monkey details the rituals of mutual discovery, including deciphering signs. In the end, the adventurous monkey caused a disaster on the truss, and ran away, never to show his face again. Faussone would have liked to have taken him home, 'making quite a pres-ent for my aunts' (p. 982) but was ultimately saved from doing so.

Monsters

The subject was central in Levi's work. He considered himself a hybrid composed of two different parts. Throughout his work there are strange, multi-formed animals: women-swans, men-insects, men-fish, men-mammals, anti-dogs, ladybird figures, men-beasts, men-birds and many others. And yet these animals are never monstrous. Monsters do not really figure in Levi's universe. In fact, even the term bestiary is probably inexact. In Levi's view, every man or woman was partly animal; for every man woman there was potentially an animal that could be linked to them. After Auschwitz, mankind was hybrid, humanity had explored its interior and exterior limits. Levi considered people to be hybrid because biology, zoology and animal behaviourism remind us that humans are a slightly more evolved form of animals.

Mice

Mice are everywhere, in Levi's short stories and in his novels. They can be terrifying ('The Need for Fear' in *Other People's Trades*), or they might preach sermons, like the mouse in the 1983 poem who climbs up onto a shelf and addresses the poet, quoting Plutarch, Nietzsche and Dante, 'that I mustn't waste time, / blah, blah, that time is growing short, /that wasted time won't come again, / that time is money, / and that he who has time shouldn't wait for time / because life is short and art is long' (p. 1955). This mouse is definitely a literary mouse, a town mouse, unlike the field mice that appear in tragic moments, in the midst of garbage, death and misery. In the poem, the imaginary mouse is rejected by the poet: 'if he's a mouse then let him preach to mice' (p. 1955).

Neoteny

'Neoteny, that's what this mess is called, when an animal breeds while still in the larval stage' (p. 442), the Colonel in 'Angelic Butterfly' explained to his allies who had been seeking out Professor Leeb and who had returned with the guano of a strange animal. In biology, neoteny is when an adult animal preserves a young body or some characteristics of their youth. The Colonel cites the axolotl, a 'little monster', which is actually a salamander, an amphibian beast that achieves sexual maturity without undergoing metamorphosis. It lives in the lakes of Mexican plateaus and is often used in biological research.

Many of the strange animals cited by Levi, including single celled organisms, shared this characteristic—they were used in experiments. This meant that their names appeared more frequently in the scientific journals Levi read voraciously and recycled in his fiction. The Colonel explained the phenomenon thus: 'it's as if a caterpillar—no, to be more precise, a female caterpillar—mated with another caterpillar, became impregnated then laid its eggs before developing into a butterfly. And from these eggs, naturally, more caterpillars were born. Why bother, then, becoming a butterfly Western mark why bother becoming "the perfect insect" when it can be avoided?' (p. 442).

In his research on metamorphosis, the Nazi scientist, Professor Leeb, appeared to have found a way to exploit the potential human capacity for neoteny. The experiments he had been authorized to conduct aimed to create a future for men as angels. Once again, the story was based on a two-way metamorphosis involving both involution and evolution. Worms and angels were at two ends of a tight thread, as Nietzsche might have put it, with humans in the middle. The failure of the experiment showed that the only possible destiny for mankind was involution: the angelic stage could not be achieved, while regression to an animal state was always possible. Angels became vultures. In this short story there is also one of Levi's rare references to art: Melozzo da Forlì's angels and Georges Roualt's images of fallen man.

Oysters

The meleagrina, or pearl oyster, Levi commented in a footnote to the poem entitled 'Meleagrina', is 'a different species from the common edible oyster' (p. 1960). The specimen in the poem speaks directly to the 'hot-blood' humans harvesting it, asking what they 'know of these soft limbs of mine / beyond their taste?' (p. 1960). Levi had already used the theme of contracting and expanding, of protective shells, when talking about his attitude to his house, which he described as that of a limpet. 'I'm more like you than you think, / condemned to secrete secrete / tears mother-of-pearl and pearl / like you, if a shard should harm my mantle / I repair it day by day in silence' (p. 1960).

The beginning of the poem that follows, 'The Snail' (both written in 1983), also opens with a rhetorical question. The snail, like the oyster, is protected by 'its shell of deeming limestone / denying the world and deny-ing itself to it' (p. 1961). However, in this poem, the mollusc is on the move rather than sedentary, albeit in no hurry. Levi describes with the precision of an entomologist the trail the snail leaves behind him on the meadow 'drenched in dew' (p. 1961). Levi departs from his habitual pessimism when he describes the snail finding 'its boy/girl mate / And fearfully / Throbbing tense outside its shell it / tastes / The shy delight of double love' for of course Levi would not forget that snails are hermaphrodites.

Another sedentary insect Levi describes is the lac insect, described in *Domum Servavit* (*Other People's Trades*), from whose secretions sealing wax is made.

The male and female of the creature in question begin their lives in the form of reddish larvae, barely visible to the naked eye; in countless swarms, they lazily explore the twigs of certain exotic trees until they find a break in the bark sufficient to allow them to insert their proboscises deep into the succulent wood beneath: at this point, they're taken care of, set for life, without a care, but, by the same token, without an experience, and emotion, or a sensation. Their number is vast, millions of individuals on a single tree, and in fact the term 'lac', used in all languages to describe the substance they secrete, comes from an ancient Sanskrit word that means 'a hundred thousand' (p. 2082).

On reaching maturity, the females lose their legs and remain in one place, continuing to secrete resin, while the male 'resolves to undertake a single fleeting enterprise: [. . .] He leaves his prison and fertilizes a number of females, without direct contact, by utilizing the aperture designed for the purpose; then he dies' (p. 2083). Levi makes a direct reference to the 'exemplary Roman matron of antiquity, *domum servavit, lanam fecit*: she lived at home, spinning wool, or, in our case, exuding resin' (p. 2083). Although Levi claims that to attempt to draw a human moral from the behaviour of the animals is a 'senseless bad habit', he concludes, with Aesop, 'that the price of guaranteed prosperity can be high, and that early retirement can be fatal' (p. 2083.).

Parasites

'Among animals, it is the parasites that we should especially admire for the originality of the inventions inscribed in their anatomy, their physiology, and their habits. We do not admire them, however, because they are distasteful or harmful; still, once we get over that preconception realm opens out before our eyes in which, truly, reality surpasses imagination' ('The Leap of the Flea', p. 2113 in *Other People's Trades*).

Tapeworms are the parasites Levi admires the most: 'devoid of brain, digestive tract, and locomotor apparatus, [it] produces in the course of its adult life many millions of eggs. This enormous compensatory fecundity serves to inform us that a tapeworm's infant mortality is extremely high and that a larva's likelihood of enjoying a career is on the order of magnitude of one in a million' (p. 2115). One of the most interesting short stories in *Natural Histories* was about tapeworms ('Man's Friend'). The story is a fine example of how Levi melds together information from many different fields of knowledge, with a large dose of irony. It is written as if it were an encyclopaedia entry combining the disciplines of biology, linguistics, history of art and philology. The scientists who unlocked the key of the tapeworm's epithelial cells, and therefore of their 'verses' or 'interjectionals' were Serrurier Flory (perhaps inspired by Paul Flory, Nobel Prize–winning chemist for his micro-molecular studies in the early twentieth century, and Bernard W. Losurdo (possibly based on Antonino Lo Surdo, an Italian physicist who experimented with the effect of an electric field on the spectrum of gas emissions). The short story in the form of an essay plays on the idea of metalanguage, a language of forms, which would allow humans to decipher the verses of 'man's friend', the tapeworm. The protagonist is a Professor of Assyrian studies who is used to decrypting abstruse oriental texts. He succeeds in deciphering the mosaic of cells and breaking their code, finding rhythm and meaning there. The final section of the story reveals 'the new and thrilling frontier of emotional relationships between the parasite and the host' (p. 463). The deciphered texts parody a religious appeal to a higher being ('Oh powerful one') and resemble similar literary games played by another Jewish writer, George Perec who often parodied scientific or ethnographic research.

Levi's interests in parasites is significant in that the writer is not only interested in the complexity of their mechanisms and anatomy. What fascinates him the most is their ability to live off their host without causing the host to die. As researchers have often pointed out, parasites are an example of an inverse hunter–prey relationship because parasites are much smaller than their hosts. 'The old-school human parasite had to be intelligent, because he lacked the appropriate instincts: for him, parasitism was a choice, and he was obliged to invent his own artifices.' By contrast, the animal parasite is 'all instinct, totally programmed, and its brain is minimal or entirely lacking' (p. 2114). Levi was also interested in the economic lessons to be learnt from the animal kingdom.

In both *If This Is a Man* and *The Truce*, parasites are seen in a completely different light. The ever-present lice, for example, are part and parcel of the struggle for survival for human beings and parasites alike. On one wall of the washhouse 'an enormous white, red, and black louse stands out, with the caption "Eine Laus, dein Tod" (A louse is your death), and the inspired distich: [. . .] After the latrine, before you eat, wash your hands, don't forget' (p. 36). Levi initially thought these warnings were 'pure examples of the Teutonic sense of humour', but later realized it was an important 'instrument of moral survival' (p. 36). Checking for lice was an obsession in the lager, and marked the rhythm of the prisoners' day: 'only the return March, the roll call, and the check for lice will separate us from our rest' (p. 127). The gas used in the extermination chambers was originally used as a disinfectant against parasites.

In *The Truce*, the situation is reversed. Rather than a Kapo inspecting the prisoners, the check takes place in Leonardo's clinic in Katowice. Levi is the one performing the daily inspection for lice on concentration-camp survivors and returning soldiers, becoming an expert in the field. The type of lice he found most commonly had a red spot on its back which, 'observed under strong enough magnification, would reveal itself to be formed by a tiny hammer and sickle' according to a joke that was 'tirelessly repeated by our clients' (p. 265). In this territory controlled by the Russians, Levi studies the hierarchy of the parasite army: lice are 'the infantry, whereas fleas are the artillery, mosquitoes the air force, bedbugs the parachutists, and cockroaches the sappers' (p. 265). As Levi reminds his readers ironically at the end of a short piece called 'A Wartime Pipette' (*Stories and Essays*), 'lice are not very likeable creatures, but they have no racial prejudices' (p. 2294). Again, Levi shows his sympathy for parasites whose elemental structure does not require them to make ideological distinctions, like the flea who does not distinguish between rich and poor (*Other People's Trades*). After describing the 'diabolical' leap of the flea in scientific detail, Levi reveals his usual scepticism: 'there may be readers who wonder what the purpose of such research might be: a religious soul might reply that the harmony of creation is mirrored even in a flea; a secular spirit would prefer to point out that the question is beside the point'

(p. 2117). Levi's agnosticism is corroborated by an irrepressible quality: his curiosity, which is much-loved parasites and insects do not possess.

A final example of human parasite is the short-story interview, 'Live from Our Intestine: *Escherichia Coli*' (*Uncollected Stories and Essays*) first published in *Airone* in February 1987. Like the other short-story interviews published in his column 'The Imaginary Zoo', the piece is an amusing debate on the destiny of the bacteria present in the intestine and faeces of the host body. Escherichia coli bacteria are the cause of many infections, as well as being used in molecular biology experiments today, as the journalist in the interview explains. The bacteria, in its turn, describes what they and humans have in common: 'In essence you are ciliates, too: all your mucous membranes are ciliated' (p. 2766).

Seagulls

At the end of the 1970s, seagulls reached Settimo Torinese, having come up river along the Po, year after year. Levi described their itinerary from the Adriatic Sea, past cities and 'mounds of tar and leftover polyethylene', having 'forgotten backwash and salt water' in the poem 'The Gulls of Settimo'. These birds are for Levi an emblem of the natural world losing its memory of itself: 'Past forgotten, they pick over our waste' (p. 1924).

Another of Levi's short story-interviews, published in 1987 in *Airone* as part of his column 'The Imaginary Zoo', is entitled 'The Seagull of Chiavasso'. A herring gull tells the journalist the story of how he came to settle near the garbage dump in Chiavasso rather than in his natural habitat, diving for mullets in the sea. The interview adopts an ironic tone, at times is even comic, but there is also a deeper pessimism. The journalist is of course a representative of the race that produces garbage and waste, but closes the interview with the hope that one day the rivers will be cleaned up and 'even the sea will go back to the way it was' (p. 2270). The seagull on the other hand is worried for the future, 'the next generation scares me; there's no restraint any more' (p. 2270).

Serpents and Worms

Henri, one of the 'saved' in Auschwitz (*If This Is a Man*) was 'inhumanly sly and incomprehensible, like the Serpent in Genesis' (p. 95). The serpents of mythology were significant in Levi's work; he considered them partly responsible for his transformation into a hybrid creature: a Centaur, half-chemist and half-writer. In *The Wrench*, Levi wrote:

> A long time ago I, too, had stumbled into the middle of a fight between gods; I, too, had come across snakes in my path, and that encounter altered my condition, giving me the strange power of words; and since then appearing as a chemist before the eyes of the world, yet feeling the blood of a writer in my veins, I felt as if I had two souls in my body, which is one too many (p. 997).

The reference was to Tiresias, who came across a male and a female snake intertwined on his path and, after separating them with his stick, found he had been transformed into a woman. Seven years later, he stumbled upon the two snakes again, and separated them, thus regaining his male identity. Levi, or at least the narrator of the novel, confessed to feeling a little like Tiresias himself, especially in his observation skills, given that distinguishing a male from a female python is no easy task. Tiresias was able to experience living as both genders, and received from the gods (Jove) the gift of seeing the future as compensation for losing his sight at the hands of Juno. Faussone, too, came across two snakes making love on his path in Turkey, not too far from Greece, but he left them well alone.

In the short story, 'The Sixth Day' (*Natural Histories*) when the work in progress of the creation is underway, and the characters debate what form to give 'so-called man', Arimane suggested that of the serpent. 'It is strong and cunning: "the most cunning of Earth's creatures," it has been called by the highest judge. Its structure is of an exceptional simplicity and elegance, and it would be a shame not to perfect it further' (p. 544). An essay called 'Hatching the Cobra' (*Stories and Essays*) used the cobra as a metaphor for the 'danger undeniably inherent in any new scientific knowledge' and concludes with an exhortation: 'don't hide behind the hypocrisy of neutral science: you know enough to be able to assess whether a dove or a cobra or a chimera or perhaps nothing at all will emerge from the egg that you are hatching' (p. 2407). In 'Nitrogen' (*The Periodic Table*), Levi and his wife go to an exhibit of snakes in Turin to collect uric acid from a python, only to find that their dung 'is sold at the weight of gold' and the owners had 'permanent, exclusive contracts with the big pharmaceutical companies' (p. 903).

In the short piece 'Made for Each Other' (*Stories and Essays*), Plato and his girlfriend, Surfa, came together like two snakes, albeit in only two dimensions: 'as they went on talking Plato felt his profile being deliciously redrawn, so that one side of it ended up reproducing, in negative and with precision, the corresponding side of the girl: they were made for each other' (p. 2272). The essay 'The Need for Fear' explored irrational fears, in particular of snakes. Levi started his list with *forficula*, the subject of a belief so deeply rooted in our collective memory ('that if you are not careful they'll crawl into your ear') that they are called earwigs in English. He then went on to examine the fear of bats, and rats (with a reference to Orwell's novel *1984*). However, the greatest phobia was against snakes, although, as Levi noted, 'The flesh-and-blood snake, like any other animal, is impervious to issues of morality: it's neither good nor evil, it eats and is eaten.' (p. 2245). Levi described, again in scientific detail, their 'diverse array of ingenious and specific inventions' including a 'thermal eye' sensitive to infrared rays, 'that is, to heat emitted by birds and mammals'; a dis-articulated jaw; and a double syringe in the venomous species. And yet, it was the 'literary serpent' that fascinated Levi in particular, from 'the very first pages of Genesis' (p. 2246). At the very beginning of *If This Is a Man*, when Levi describes the scene inside the train car, the image evokes the idea that men and women had been reduced to the state of worms or human larvae: 'someone would light the mournful little flame of a candle, to reveal the secure swarming of a confused and indistinguishable human mass, sluggish and aching, rising here and there in sudden convulsions and immediately collapsing again in exhaustion' (p. 14). In Genesis 3:14, God cursed the serpent: 'on your belly you shall go and you shall eat dust all the days of your life', while worms—smaller versions of snakes—grow in putrid flesh.

In 'The Need for Fear', Levi explained that 'The serpent is the beast by definition, and it contains nothing that is human: significantly, the Italian word for snake, *biscia*, is nothing other than a variant on the Latin and Italian *bestia*, ("beast") (p. 2246). He then went on to cite Dante who identified snakes with thieves because they 'slither silently and creep into men's houses by night; in the seventh circle of hell, thieves and serpents endlessly turn into one another' (p. 2246). Finally, Levi listed the number of times snakes appeared in La Fontaine's fables: only three times, 'in marginal and vaguely allusive roles', compared to the wolf (fifteen times), the lion (seventeen times) and the fox (nineteen times), 'they are all intensely humanized, both in their vices and in their virtues' (p. 2246). The only positive snake in literature that Levi was able to identify was Kipling's python Kaa, who is 'wise, cautious [. . .] a friend to Mowgli, but a distant one: a cold-blooded friend [. . .] of whom he must always be wary' (p. 2246). The article ends with a personal memory when Levi crushed a small snake underfoot thinking it was a viper.

Spiders

In *If This Is a Man*, while the prisoners are waiting to do their chemistry examination with Doktor Pannwitz, they are told to wait in silence. Waiting for the men means resting: 'we are always happy to wait; we are capable of waiting for hours with the complete dull-witted inertia of spiders in old webs' (p. 99). In *The Truce*, Hurbinek, the boy prisoner who didn't speak, Kaspar Hauser of the Lager, Kleine Kiepura as he was known, was described as having grown 'too fast and awkwardly: very long arms and legs stuck out from his short, stocky upper body, like a spider's' (p. 229). Hurbinek was the first character to be described by Levi as a spider, followed in *The Truce* by the accountant Rovi, the self-appointed camp chief in Katowice. Levi gives an almost detached description of the man, revealing his entomological interest in human behaviour:

> Witnessing the behaviour of a man who acts not according to reason but according to his own deep impulses is a spectacle of great interest, similar to that enjoyed by the naturalist who studies the activities of an animal with complex instincts. Rovi had won his post by acting with the same atavistic spontaneity with which the spider constructs its web, since, like the spider without a web, Rovi couldn't survive without a position (p. 259).

The description has a strong moral basis, the animal being a metaphor for the man. Since the 1970s, Levi's increasing interest in entomology, his reading and research, led him to moderate his tendency to anthropomorphize animals. He never forgot, however, that his point of view was influenced by the fact that he belonged to the family of primates.

Spiders are among those animals Levi considered ambivalent, and it was the only one Levi actually disliked. In *The Periodic Table*, Giulia, his classmate, asked Levi to get a spider off her desk. In doing so, the author compares himself, in one of the many allusions to Greek mythology, to 'Hercules before the Hydra of Lerner', a snake that has mythological links with centaurs. Levi also admired spiders for their ability to build spiders webs. Like Faussone, they were endowed with a built-in trade. In fact, the rigger compared himself to a spider when he was building a suspended bridge in India ('The Bridge' in *The Wrench*).

However, spiders were also an image of death for Levi. In 'Fear of Spiders' (*Other People's Trades*), he wrote about an experience he had as a child in the country: 'I was on the verge of sleep when I heard a ticking sound. I turned on the light, and there was the monster: black, all legs, descending toward the night stand with the hesitant yet inexorable gait of Death' (p. 2144). This article on fear of spiders is one of the most interesting pieces devoted to animals because the writer described his repulsion and disgust, and appeared to confirm the psychoanalytic idea that spiders are enemy-mothers. In a previous piece on how observing animal behaviour could be useful for a novelist, 'Novels Dictated by Crickets' (*Other People's Trades*), Levi explored the sexual habits of spiders and 'the fact that many female spiders devour the male, immediately following or, in some cases, even during the sex act' (p. 2078). In 'Fear of Spiders', Levi reminded his readers (and himself) that 'we cannot subject animals to moral judgements [. . .] How much less right do we have to export our human moral judgements to animals as distant from us as the arthropods' (p. 2145). Levi appeared to deny the validity of the various psychological reasons he listed for hating spiders, but he didn't reject them outright. On the contrary, he evaluated each explanation carefully, even considering 'a psychologist of the subconscious' in his examination of his own repulsion.

'Spiders' fuzziness supposedly has a sexual meaning, and the disgust that we experience therefore points to an unrecognized rejection of sex on our part: that is how we express it, and, by the same token, this is how we will seek to free ourselves of it' (p. 2146).

Levi's 'personal and negligible phobia' was caused by an engraving by Gustave Doré illustrating 'Arachne' in Canto XII of *Purgatory* which he came upon as a child. This was an image of an incomplete metamorphosis: Arachne was 'already half-spider' and she is 'politically depicted backward, with her buxom breasts where you would expect to see her back, while from her back six gnarled, hairy, painful legs have issued: six, which with the desperately flailing arms make eight. Kneeling before the newborn monster, Dante seems to be contemplating its pudenda, half-disgusted, half-voyeur' (p. 2148).

Levi wrote a poem called 'Arachne' in 1981 (*At an Uncertain Hour*) where the spider speaks in the first person, describing her torn web and her plans for building a new one: 'I've got long patients /and a little mind, / eight legs and a hundred eyes, but a thousand spinning teats, / and don't like fasting, / I like flies and males'. She intends to wait, 'hiding in her hole' and 'wait for a male to come / suspicious but drunk with desire' (p. 1941).

All these images and citations culminated in Levi's last 'Imaginary Zoo' short story-interview for *Airone* published in 1987, 'Love on the Web'. The last part of this comic piece was devoted to the female spiders 'conjugal behaviour' (p. 2776) and her cannibalism, a taboo often present in animal stories. Cannibalism is never declared as a theme in Levi's work, but especially in the first two books it is hinted at in the braying dogs and in the reduction of the prisoners to an animal state. In 'Love on the Web', Levi describes the female spider devouring her husband after fecundation, but also provides examples of systems adopted by males to avoid being devoured, which include diversions like dancing or 'kidnapping females as soon as they hatch' (p. 2777).

Yet another spider is the one cited by Levi remembering Calvino on the occasion of his translation of Queneau's *The Song of Styrene* (Calvino, Queneau, and the Sciences). In this address, Levi recalled the title of Calvino's most famous work, *The Path to the Spiders' Nest*, where spiders make a nest instead of weaving a web. The young protagonist of the novel, Pin, dislikes both spiders and fireflies, hairy insects who remind him of women, beautiful from afar but disgusting from close up. In contrast, Levi loved fireflies, and Levi played with the Italian word for firefly (*lucciola*) and for light (*luce*) when writing about his wife Lucia. In his 1986 article, 'The Spider's Secret' (*Uncollected Stories and Essays*), Levi compared his trade in the production of paints to the ability of the spider to solidify their thread. In this article, Levi provided an important autobiographical detail: that in his 'lower level' 'memories of paint or replacing those of Auschwitz. I notice it in my dreams, from which the Lager has disappeared by now, but in which more and more frequently I am confronted by a paint-related problem that I can't solve' (p. 2735).

Squirrels

Squirrels were one of Levi's 'linguistic animals' that he wrote about because he was interested in their etymology. Although Levi always considered the name, origin, etymology, and meaning of the animals he wrote about, this is one of the few examples of a purely linguistic interest. The article in *Other People's Trades*, entitled 'The Squirrel', opens with Levi's two aunts calling a friend of his 'Prùn', Piedmont dialect for squirrel. Levi traces the origin of the noun back to the Latin *pronus*: 'the illusion is unmistakable: a squirrel's back is never level. When the creature is standing on all fours, it is "prone" (inclined) toward the ground' (p. 2105). Going back even further, Levi finds the Greek name *skìouros*, a compound of 'shadow' and 'tail', owing to 'a common belief that on hot days a squirrel would take shelter from the sun in the shade of its tail' (p. 2105). After examining other forms of the name in various European languages, Levi recalls a squirrel he ran into many years before in a biochemistry lab. The squirrel was on a treadmill, 'forced to walk endlessly on the treadmill to keep from being dragged. In that laboratory, scientists were performing experiments on sleep [. . .] The squirrel was exhausted.' Levi took pity on the animal he compared to galley slaves, or forced labourers, and switched off the motor: 'the squirrel fell asleep on the spot' (p. 2107).

Tadpoles

In the story 'Frogs on the Moon' (*Stories and Essays*), Levi described his adventures in what he called 'the country interlude' that lasted for 'the entire school vacation'. In these three months Levi would become a naturalist, exploring 'humble grasses and flowers' (p. 2296), birds, bugs, spiders, ants and dragonflies. His favourite spot was a stream, home to 'nimble green beetles' and, most important of all, hundreds of tadpoles. Even as a child, it would seem, Levi made close observations: the trout settled on the right bank far away from the Sunday fishermen, while 'the tadpoles had settled on the left side in order to stay away from the trout' (p. 2296).

In the article, Levi comments that tadpoles were 'chimeras, impossible beasts all head and tail' and that 'there metamorphosis [. . .] Really was an extraordinary spectacle [. . .] The tadpole's tale would swell into a small knob, near its route. The knob grew, and in two or three days two webbed feet emerged' (p. 2297). The young Levi took the tadpoles home in a small basin to start with, but observing that the walls of the basin were too steep for the tadpoles to climb, he then put wooden boards in the water, but most of them died. He concludes that 'a completely understandable instinct, the same one that drove us to the moon, drives the tadpoles to leave the expanse of water where the transformation took place. It doesn't matter where they go—anyplace but that one' (p. 2298).

The 'giant leap' onto the moon was the object of two articles Levi wrote at the end of the 1960s, in particular, 'The Moon and Man' in *Stories and Essays*. Like tadpoles, the desire to reach other planets, in Levi's view, was a purely animal instinct.

> Human matter (or rather animal matter), besides being adaptable in an evolutionary sense—on a scale of millions of years and at the cost of the incalculable sacrifice of less fit variations—is adaptable here and now, on a scale of days and hours: we all saw the astronauts on TV, floating in space like fish in water, learning new equilibriums and new reflexes, never realized, or realizable, on the ground. Therefore, man is strong not only because he became so, from the time, a million years ago, when from among the many

weapons nature offered animals he chose the brain: man is strong in and of himself, he is stronger than he thought possible, he is made of a substance that is fragile only in appearance, he was mysteriously designed with enormous, unsuspected margins of safety. We are unique, sturdy, versatile animals, motivated by atavistic impulses, and by reason, and, at the same time, by her 'creative force' as a result of which if an undertaking, whether good or bad can be achieved, it cannot be put aside but must be achieved (p. 2337).

Levi's optimism regarding both mankind and science was at its peak in this period. It would later wane, as the writer became more perplexed and pessimistic, but he was never a catastrophist. It is interesting to compare the thesis proposed in this article to Levi's observations regarding human capacity for animal behaviour in the concentration camps. One helps revitalize the other.

Traces

Levi, like many of his characters, observed and followed traces, signs, marks, or trails. His article, 'Signs on Stone' (*Other People's Trades*), is about mineral traces in flagstones and a perfect example of his trademark exploration of the world around him in a quest for traces to interpret or decipher. Of all the 'creatures' Levi has ever contemplated, perhaps the most challenging is the first book he ever wrote, *If This Is a Man*, which he himself described as 'a book of modest dimensions but like a nomadic creature, it has left behind a long and tangled trail for 40 years now (*The Drowned and the Saved*, p. 2535). As the critic Cavaglion has remarked, there are traces of Levi's first book in all of the books that followed; some are evident, others are hidden. Cavaglion indicated several articles, stories or anecdotes relating to Levi's lager experience. The image of a book as a creature is very striking, as if the subject of the Lager were somehow ungraspable, and un-domesticated: a wild beast inhabiting Levi's day, leaving traces in his nocturnal, infernal or subconscious life. The beast not only chases the protagonist, as in every fable or fairy tale; it is also being chased, and it leaves a long trail behind it. Every hunter is himself prey, and every prey is also a hunter.

Vilmy

Vilmy was an imaginary animal, half-dog half-cat described in the story: 'it had big blue eyes and long lashes, pointed, twitching, nearly transparent years that culminated in two peculiar tufts of light fur, and along hairless pink tail' ('Vilmy', in *Natural Histories*, p. 638). Vilmy milk was addictive because the quantities of N-phenyl oxytocin present in low quantities in the milk of all mammals, which creates an emotional bond and dependency between mother and child, is 20 times higher in the Vilmy. Their expressions are 'human-like' but 'with a touch of fox-like cunning.' The specimen described in the story has legs that 'ended in for coarse little hands with opposable thumbs, brown on top and pink inside' (p. 640). She was also fascinated by clocks and the ticking. The codependency created by Vilmy milk created a desire that was

> oppressive, savage, and idiotic desire, and hopeless, because with a woman you can speak, at least to yourself; even if she is far away, if she is not yours, or is no longer yours, you hope at least to speak to her, you hope for love, for reunion; it may be a vain hope, but it's not insane, it has a conceivable gratification. This instead does not. It's a desire that damns you because it has no gratification. You can't even find it in your imagination. It's pure desire, without end. The milk is pleasant, it's sweet, but you guzzle it and you're just as before. And even their presence, touching them, caressing them, it's nothing, less than nothing, a whetting of one's desire, nothing else (p. 641).

Like Levi's other imaginary, or real, animals, Vilmy gives desire a shape: Vilmy is a metaphor for desire itself.

LEVI, THE ECOLOGIST

Born in 1919, the year of the Spanish Flu, Primo Levi went on to write about the epidemics that swept through the extermination camps, particularly in his first two books, *If This Is a Man* and *The Truce*. Perhaps it was precisely because of his experience of bad sanitation in the Lager, in addition to his work as a chemist, that the writer was so interested in ecological issues. In a short story, 'Best is Water' (*Flaw of Form*), there is a young chemist named Boero whose job was to verify the value of the coefficient of viscosity in distilled water. Boero discovered that his measurements did not match those established in Landolt's Tables; the water had congealed. A few days later, 'The water of the Sangone was viscous from its sources to its confluence with the Po' (p. 2910). The anomaly gradually expanded to all rivers and watercourses, with the result that, within a few months, all the tall trees in the contaminated areas had died, replaced by weeds and shrubs. It was then the turn of human organisms, who grew sluggish and then began to get sick and die.

Out of 20 stories in the collection, at least 8 deal with ecological catastrophes of one kind or other. The jacket copy stated that human beings at the time were behaving like people who believe they are navigating a calm river when the banks suddenly disappear, the water becomes a whirlpool and they hear the sound of a waterfall: 'All the indices are soaring: world population, DDT in penguin fat, carbon dioxide in the atmosphere, lead in our veins', with the result that, while half of the world awaits the benefits of technology, the other half is living on scorched lunar ground, poisoned by waste products accumulated in just a few decades. Levi was a witness of the Jewish extermination, the writer of *The Truce*, the chemist of *The Periodic Table* and the narrator of *If Not Now, When?* but he was also an ecologist proposing a new environmental approach. This is a side of Levi that has not yet been fully explored. In 1979, presenting a book by a fellow chemist, Luciano Caglioti (*The Two Faces of Chemistry*), Levi wondered if the time had finally come to put an end, if not to consumption, at least to the waste and the artificially created needs that caused air, water and soil pollution.

Flaw of Form is a collection with many short stories about the environment, written by a chemist who had read Rachael Carson's *Silent Spring* (published in Italy in 1963), the environmental scientist's denunciation of the indiscriminate use of insecticides, as well as the biologist, Parul R. Ehrlic's book, *The Population Bomb*. In his environmental stories, Levi describes the collapse of Planet Earth as a result of the imbalances in the biosphere. In 1983, he returned to the subject in an essay, 'The Brute Power', published in the *Banca Popolare di Sondrio* newsletter, where he contrasted entropy with homeostasis, a mechanism for self-regulation and self-preservation. 'If not the universe, at least this planet is governed by a force that is not invincible but perverse, that prefers disorder to order, jumble to purity, a tangle to parallelism, rust to iron, a pile to a wall, and stupidity to reason' (p. 2629). The balance between entropy and homeostasis, in Levi's view, is extremely unstable, especially in the historical and political sphere. 'Our current malaise originates in this: we no longer perceive restraining forces, homeostasis, and feedback loops. The world seems to be moving forward toward an unspecified catastrophe and we can only hope that its progress is slow.'

If his first collection of short stories, *Natural Histories*, published in 1966, Levi focused on environmental issues, but the stories were filled with optimism. As Porro observed, this optimism was probably the result of the economic boom, while only five years later, in *Flaw of Form*, Levi raised an alarm through his short stories. In 1970, Levi read an issue of *Scientific American* where biologists and economists explored the idea of a biosphere—an interdependence of the global system—a concept that was later formulated by James Lovelock, also a chemist, in *Gaia* (1979). At the time, the term 'Anthropocene', formulated in 2000 by another Nobel Prize-winning chemist, Paul Crutzen, was not yet in circulation, but in the issue of *Scientific American* that Levi read, there was already a hint of the dangers of an alteration of biological and geochemical balances triggered by human action.

One of the issues that most interested Levi—at the time he was director of the SIVA paint factory in Settimo Torinese—was overpopulation, a topic which he linked to the more ethical and philosophical question of pain. Several articles and short stories about the animal world explore this question. The short story 'Heading West' is an example. Two biologists, Anna and Walter, are engaged in a study of lemmings, who leap to their death for mysterious reasons, and an Amazon tribe, the Arunde, who refuse all painkillers and often commit suicide. Levi comments, 'Humanity has had its back turned to nature for a while now; it's made up of individuals and puts all its efforts into the survival of the individual, into prolonging life, and into vanquishing death and pain' (p. 591).

Levi developed these themes in further articles and stories published in magazines and newspapers on both the animal and plant worlds. In 'Mutiny', another story in *Flaw of Form*, which was dedicated to his friend, Mario Rigoni Stern, the protagonist, Clotilde, talks to plants and they answer. Levi's environmental ethics distinguished between the behaviour of scientists and technicians; Levi placed himself in the latter category. In the 1980s, he proposed the idea of an oath for both groups, similar to the Hippocratic oath for doctors. In a 1982 interview for the Italian adult-entertainment magazine, *Playmen*, for example, Levi stated that as a matter of urgency, a code of ethics for physicists, chemists and biologists should be published.

In a 1987 short story in Levi's 'Imaginary Zoo', 'Live from Our Intenstine: *Escherichia Coli*'—one of his last stories—a bacterium present in the human intestine, E. coli, is interviewed by a journalist. E. Coli warns the journalist, 'Be careful: if an epidemic should break out, you'll be the ones to suffer, but so will we, who live in peace in your precious bowels' (p. 2765). Levi adds ironically that the epidemic could be deadly for humans, whereas the bacteria 'in the long run [. . .] would learn to adapt and survive even in the intestine of a cockroach or an oyster, but it would take time and effort and a good number of victims' (p. 2765).

PORTRAIT WITH A PERSONAL COMPUTER (1986)

Primo Levi at the computer. Mario Monge took the picture against the light, capturing a dark profile of the author in silhouette. Levi's glasses are visible, the outline of his chin, his beard trimmed short, his nose and his hairline. You can just see his hands, typing at the keyboard. The luminous centre of the photograph is the screen of the computer, which is facing slightly to the right, towards the photographer. One can just read a few lines of a poem that Levi was writing. 'Soldier'. One can see the date: 25 June 1986.

25/6/86

SOLDIER

My feet are encrusted in mud
My head and my heart empty,
My fingers cramping
on the loaded rifle.
I do not know this country,
This putrid air is my enemy
All around the night and enemies
Are flattened out in ditches.
If I see them I will shoot,
They will do the same.
We will never know why
We would never see each other in the face
In war every man is alone
But my mother is the moon . . .

Which Levi do we see in this photograph? Certainly not the former deportee, or the witness. The chemist? Perhaps. A man familiar with technology. Probably. Levi has always revendicated his role as a technician rather than as a scientist. He worked with paint, and thus manipulated molecules, working with both his head and his hands. The computer makes this clear. It was unusual among Italian writers who were mostly from the Humanist tradition, with the exception of Gadda. Levi was perhaps one of the first Italian authors to use a computer. He wrote about it in *La Stampa* in an article entitled 'Personal Golem' (later collected in *Other People's Trades* as 'The Scribe').

In September 1984, he bought himself a Word Processor, 'that is, a device for writing that every time you reach the end of the line automatically goes to the next, and allows you to insert, erase, and change words and even whole sentences instantaneously' (p. 2235). Levi owned a typewriter, perhaps more than one, on which he wrote his first books on returning from the Lager. He later moved onto an electric typewriter, which appears in several photos dating from the 1970s. He moved on to the word processor because, as he stated in 'The Scribe', 'electronic time rushes along' (p. 2235). This article describing his approach to the new technology shows how pleased he was; it was the pleasure of a neophyte: 'my gadget is a luxury, it's fun, it's even exciting' (p. 2235). Levi compares the program disc of the computer to the legend of the Golem, the inert 'rabbi-magician created from clay'. One day, he received a 'scroll of parchment upon which a verse from the Torah was written' in his mouth, which gave him life, until it was removed from his mouth again. What we see in the photograph in silhouette sitting in front of the technological Golem, is an old man. Monge has captured this duality, and this was perhaps why he accentuated the contrast between the darkness of Levi's profile and the luminosity of the computer screen. In 'The Scribe', Levi confessed that his first reaction to the gadget was anxiety, and 'the writer's age-old fear' that his words 'might be stolen or flushed down a sewer' (p. 2237).

In January 1995, in an article called 'Can Poetry Get Along with the Computer', Levi concluded that:

> the computer seems to me to be an excellent tool for clear and distinct tasks. Poetry isn't one of them: it is fluid, oblique, continuous, surrounded by halos and shadows. It is no accident that, while poems have been written for thousands of years, no definition has yet been formulated, no 'list of specifications' has been universally accepted. In short: poetry is compatible with the computer, but has little to gain from it and nothing to fear (p. 2694).

If Not Now, When?

A DRAWER FULL OF UNUSED IDEAS

In interviews Levi often spoke about having a drawer full of unused ideas that he would dip into throughout his life. In this container were at least two episodes used in *If Not Now, When?* The first was the story of the new car that was hitched onto the train in Munich, taking him and other deportees, refugees and decommissioned soldiers back to Italy. Levi had already told the story of this 1945 episode in *The Truce*. In the new car was a group of highly determined Zionist Jews—boys and girls from all over Eastern Europe—on their way to Israel: 'They felt immensely free and strong, masters of the world and of their destiny.' (From 'Iasi to the Line', *The Truce, Complete Works* I). The second episode was dated 1972, when his friend Emilio Vita Finzi told him about a group of Jewish partisans who had fought Nazi forces in Eastern Europe whom he had come across in the Jewish Assistance offices in via Unione, Milan,

In fact, the germ of the novel was already present in 1966, just after publishing *Natural Histories*. When asked by a journalist from *Il Giorno* whether he was planning on writing some new stories or a book, in a written answer Levi stated: 'Nothing for now, but I am tempted to write about an amazing story, a true story, of another return, another path of salvation across war-torn Europe. People have told me this story, and it is so full of adventures and necessities, tragedies and surprises, that it would be a pity if it were not written. However, I need some tranquillity, and lots of time.' Vita Finzi's account may have taken place before 1972, or perhaps Levi had heard the same story from another source previously.

In one of the rare interviews he gave in 1981 after publishing *Lilith and Other Stories*, Levi revealed that he was working on a novel, the longest he had ever written. 'The subject is historical, set in the Second World War. I started it a year ago, but I'll not say anything else as I am not sure I'll ever reach the end' (Romano 1981). The plan for the book was interwoven with a project Levi had been thinking about since 1979—perhaps even earlier—with a certain clarity of vision. 'I had started a series of essays on the Lager, an analysis of my experience from a standpoint of 40 years later. I had already written three or four of these essays but . . . ' (Dal Buono 1982). Levi temporarily abandoned this project in order to throw himself into writing *If Not Now, When?* He did not stop writing newspaper articles and essays, however. In 1980, he published 24 pieces, six of which were short stories and four poems. In 1982, he published 14 pieces, none of which were short stories, and only one poem, proving that his work on the novel occupied him full time and was a source of pleasure and joy. He was reading, researching and writing intensely.

When he had finished writing the novel, he told his German translator, Barbara Kleiner, in an interview, that there had been two core ideas that had inspired the book: the Munich episode he described in *The Truce,* and Vita Finzi's account. In the same interview, he remembered events from 15 years before, in 1966, perhaps triggered by the publication of *The Truce* and the story of the young Zionists.

> The second impulse came from a story told to me by a friend, a Jew from Turin, who had fled to Switzerland during the war. After returning to Milan he started working in a centre that gave assistance to, and found jobs and houses for, all the Jewish refugees who had come to Italy. Among these tens of thousands of refugees, he noticed a close group of young men and women who refused to be labelled as refugees, choosing rather the title of 'combatants'. They insisted on this status and put the centre in Milan in an awkward situation. I noted down this story and

left it for 15 years in my drawer. Then I got the idea that if I put these two episodes together, I could make a novel out of them. Before starting I did a great deal of research in the archives. That was when I bumped into a little book [published in Italy] and written in Yiddish that tells a similar story to mine. It was the story of a group of Jews who had fought in the Pripyat marshes and then came to Italy where they had attempted to write a kind of collective diary. Many episodes in *If Not Now, When?* were taken from this diary (Kleiner 1986).

The two episodes were therefore fused into one, especially since the young partisans at the end of the novel appear to want to settle in Milan ('This is a good place to start living'), unlike the boys and girls in the new car described in *The Truce* who aimed to emigrate to Israel. The diary Levi cited in his interview with Kleiner was written in Yiddish by M. Kaganovich and published in Buenos Aires in 1956. In another interview, Levi stated that he had found the book in Paris in the Bibliothèque Nationale and that he had translated it with great difficulty 'in order to appreciate how one can reason, think, and write in Yiddish' (Pacchioni 1982).

There was perhaps a third event that generated the idea of the novel. This was the debate that broke out in Israel in 1979 about the way Jews reacted passively to their extermination. In an interview entitled 'Itinerary of a Jewish Writer' (1982), Levi mused, 'Did Jews really let themselves be led to slaughter without resisting? If they did, why? If they didn't, how many resisted, when, and where?' There is another possible reference, if not a source of inspiration. This was the TV series, *Holocaust*, with the Berlin-based Weiss family at its core. Josef, the protagonist's son, was a Jewish doctor of Polish origins who avoided deportation by fleeing to fight with Jewish partisans in the Ukraine. Levi had watched *Holocaust* and read the book it was based on, and had reviewed both.

Levi had never been as thorough and fully documented as he was for this novel in any of the eight books he had written until that time. He even provided a bibliographic comment at the end of *If Not Now, When?*, which was unusual for a novel: 'My aim was not to write a true story, but rather to reconstruct a plausible though imaginary itinerary for one of these groups. Most of the events I describe actually took place, though not necessarily in the places and at the times I frame them in.' It was almost the opposite of what most writers in the Italian tradition since Manzoni had always done: that is, invent an original manuscript that serves as a basis for a fantastic story, keep the setting as realistic as possible and make real references to documents of the time. This novel was the product of invention—he insisted on this repeatedly—but it was firmly rooted in a historical context which almost entirely overlapped with his experience—to the extent that parallels between *The Truce* and *If Not Now, When?* have often been drawn.

In an interview with Rosellina Balbi, Levi confided that he had cut one important passage from the beginning of the book:

> The actors are ready, or nearly ready. Their profiles are still veiled, they still haven't emerged from the indistinct universe of things that do not yet exist but would already like to exist. They start to stir, weakly at first, grey against a background of grey. They speak softly, or perhaps they are not speaking at all, they are agitating and moaning like newly born puppies. They are waiting, expecting to go on stage but scared at the same time (Balbi 1982).

It was a way to exorcize the fact that he was becoming a novelist, and that he had crossed the line between being a writer of witness statements and a writer of fiction. Levi declared to his cousin, Giovanni Levi, as well as to friends, that he finally felt like a novelist after writing this novel. In his interview with Balbi, in fact, he explained how he had come to appreciate the strange nature of fiction characters while he was writing *If Not Now, When?* Each of them is made of paper, drawn in black and white, and lives on the page. And yet one can fall in love with them, hate them, in short, create an emotional attachment to them. This is also true for characters created by other writers. Once life has been breathed into these characters one establishes a unique relationship with them—at least that's what happens with me—a relationship of reciprocity and collaboration.

Balbi asked: 'So you cannot be sure that your characters don't urge you, persuade you, even force you, to get them back onto the stage?' Levi answered: 'No, I cannot exclude that possibility. In short, I don't know. What is sure is that they keep on circling me. I think everything will depend on their desire to come to life.' These themes also come up in two short stories in *Flaw of Form*: 'Creative Work' and 'In the Park'. They show Levi's desire for literary invention at the same time that they reveal a guilty complex.

As far as the 'autonomous' existence of his characters are concerned, Levi said he had had more than one argument with his wife, and even with himself, about allowing Leonid, the young, tormented Russian former paratrooper, to die.

Dov was also going to die but I had to resuscitate him at the last minute because I felt guilty. Killing off a character is a crime. I'm not exaggerating. It's not like killing a person, but the experience is not that different. There are also traces of my obsession with characters in 'The Park' (*Flaw of Form*). All the literary characters in the story are no more than ink and paper, but in their own way they have a bodily form. It is hard to place them into a philosophical category; they are certainly not mammals because they reproduce themselves in their own way. You, as an author, feel endowed with boundless power: you can do whatever you want to a character, kill it, make it beautiful, omnipotent, or perverse, you can make it suffer or feel pleasure. This was a relatively new experience for me, this feeling of infantile omnipotence. It is true, children create their own universe where they can do what they want, and from this point of view writing is a form of regression (Pacchioni 1982).

In his interviews, Levi pauses with gusto to comment on each of the characters in his book, starting with Mendel whose name stands for Menachem the 'consoler', with whom Levi admitted he identified himself (Balbi 1982). Then there is Gedale who actually existed:

> A poet, not a musician. His real story coincides with that of his character. He too hid in a convent and then eventually fled, encouraged by a nun, and from that moment on became a partisan in real life. Today he lives in Israel, and is the President of the Israeli Author's Association. I have no idea whether he has read the book or ever reacted to his portrayal (Monticelli 1982).

Leonid, on the other hand,

> was born dead; he had too much death already inside him. He tries to escape his destiny by falling in love with Line, but when Line dies, he wishes for, and ultimately finds, death. He too is based on a person I met in real life [. . .] Line is diabolic, she courts love but does not fall in love herself, an almost biblical figure. It is not by chance that when Mendel thinks of her, he lists all the great seductresses in the Bible (Mancinelli 1982).

In the same conversation, Levi defines Gedale as a figure of 'youth and adventure'. In one of the first drafts, there was a character named Nikita Khrushchev, the future leader of the Communist Party in the Soviet Union. The episode described in fact took place, as the character was in real life the head of the Ukrainian Partisan movement. In later drafts, as Tesio has shown, Khrushchev was removed.

For the first time in Levi's work, women characters play an important role in *If Not Now, When?* Interviewed about Rokhele Bianca and her relationship with Isidor, from which a child was born, Levi said these characters were completely invented, only distantly related to literary figures. She was one of those women taken out of the ghetto with no experience whatsoever whose lives are totally turned around, in all their innocence, by the turbines of war. I'm glad, though, that you thought she was a portrait of a real person. It means that I've succeeded in tricking at least one of my readers. In depicting the figure of Rokhele Bianca I really didn't have a physically existent model before my eyes or in my mind. What I did have were indirect models: the women in Ashkenazi Jewish literature who are the undisputed leaders of their households (Pappalardo La Rosa, 1982).

The only female character who did in fact exist, as Levi told Roberto Vacca (Vacca, 1982) is Polina, the girl pilot.

After winning the Viareggio Book Award in July, and the Campiello Prize in September, and following the book's success with readers, the Italian press began to pay attention to Levi. He generously conceded several interviews at the time, and *If Not Now, When?* finally granted him recognition as a famous literary author. By contrast to critics in the not-so-distant past, nobody denied he was a novelist, and interviewers no longer mentioned his profession as a chemist (or ex-chemist, as he had retired in 1975). Literary critics, who had been slow to do so, now accepted him as a fully fledged author. They no longer spoke of his books as 'testimonials', and he was no longer considered simply a witness of the Lager experience or of the extermination of the Jews.

Levi gave interviewers a great deal of information regarding the documents that constituted his sources, on which he had worked for almost a year before starting the novel. He also went into great detail in the bibliographic references he cited in the final note. He mentions Turgenev's descriptions, as well as Chagall's photographs and pictures (Calcagno 1982). In an interview with his German translator, he cites an episode inspired by reading Darwin's *Voyage of the Beagle*: the bell-ringer who 'marked the hours by firing his hunting rifle into the air:

one, two, three, four shots' (Kleiner 1986). Asked about the visual aspects of the novel, he talks mostly about the influence of the Bible and popular traditions, especially the proverbs and idioms in Yiddish culture that constitute the linguistic and cultural foundation of the novel. He reminded his interviewer, however, that he himself did not speak the language: 'I was obliged to reproduce a language that was not mine, so it was natural for me to dip into expressions from Italian dialect' (Calcagno 1982). Levi also wrote an article for *La Stampa* on the experience of writing *If Not Now, When?* which is a form of confession regarding the creative process ('Writing a Novel', in *Other People's Trades*).

A 'FIRST TIME'

'*If Not Now, When?* has been called a 'novel' but . . .' an interviewer commented to Levi. 'The idea was all mine,' Levi answered. 'When Einaudi asked me how to present the book I said, "Call it a novel." I think that is legitimate' (Pappalardo La Rosa 1982). On another occasion, the book was called, quite rightly, 'a story full of adventure, a western' (Vacca 1982). The novel was printed in the 'Supercoralli' series where Einaudi published all their most important, potentially successful novels. The jacket illustration was a reproduction of a painting by Igor Grabar, *March Snow* (1904), of a woman balancing two buckets of snow on her shoulders. The image was selected by Giulio Einaudi after a brief discussion with Levi, who did not initially agree with the choice but then gave in. The dust-jacket blurb described it as an 'epic novel' and said it provided a new perspective on Eastern European Judaism. After a brief plot summary, the novel was called 'Levi's first fully fledged novel'. On the back cover was an emblematic phrase from the book: 'In the snow and mud they had found a new freedom unknown to their fathers.'

The title, as Levi explained in his note, 'was suggested to me by some words that I found in the *Pirkei Avot* (Ethics of the Fathers), a collection of the sayings of famous rabbis that was edited in the second century AD and is part of the Talmud.' This collection had been attributed to an imaginary figure of a Jewish song-writer, Martin Fontasch. The refrains in the novel were written by Levi, who manipulated and rewrote the text in an original poetic pastiche, as he had done with the poems he published in newspapers that were then collected in *At an Uncertain Hour* (*The Complete Works of Primo Levi* III). In his conversations with his German translator, he stressed some aspects of the rhythm of these verses, showing, as he did with Heinz Franz during the translation of *If This Is a Man*, that he was fully aware of the value of rhythm and of the linguistic challenges of translating his work.

> I too would go for the second version of the hymn, but with one reservation: it is obvious that in the Italian, which is supposed to be a translation from Yiddish, the rhythm is lost. In many verses I 'broke' it deliberately. But German is much closer to Yiddish, and so I think a certain metric uniformity should be preserved so that the words can actually be sung. The text, I think, tends towards hendecasyllables, though it is not strictly adhered to, given the condition the supposed author was in when he wrote them (Letter, 14 November 1984).

The book contract is dated 17 February 1982. The manuscript was handed in on 30 March and the novel came out in April. By the end of the year, four editions had been printed, for a total of 110,000 copies. Sales were boosted by the unprecedented double victory of the two most important literary prizes that same year—the Viareggio and the Campiello. A new paperback edition was printed in 1992 in the 'Einaudi Tascabile' series (n.96) which underwent four reprints in four years for a total of 45,000 copies. Just under 50,000 further copies were printed in the years that followed. The novel was prefaced by a map showing the legs of the journey the protagonists had taken, just like its 'twin' *The Truce*. The map is, similarly, essential when reading the book.

THE TYPESCRIPT

The manuscript that Levi handed in to Einaudi, preserved in the Einaudi archive (now in the State Archive in Turin, File 1056, Folder 3022), was made up of 316 typed pages. Among the first 159 pages of yellowing paper, one can see additional sheets of whiter paper with revisions and rewrites of passages of text. There are also several strips of lighter paper stuck onto various sheets of the original typescript. In addition, there are numerous handwritten corrections, where Levi used white-out for his edits. Levi did not retype the whole manuscript. He made partial changes, rewriting passages or single pages as he went along. Some of the pages were punched for a file holder and were numbered differently. Levi also made handwritten notes on the back of other sheets, as if he wanted to check the correct order of the events he was narrating in the novel. He crossed text out with a black pen, stuck white strips onto previously typed text and wrote in pen on top. He also stapled the last three sheets together, the ones with a bibliography of his research for the book, and wrote the date, 7 February 1982, on the top sheet (which was not included in the printed version). Finally, he noted the final word count in pen: '118,000 words'. Levi edited the manuscript at least twice, and noted the dates on the top, right corner of the sheets. The first edit probably took place while he was writing the novel; the second was a full revision. Why did Levi continuously date his manuscripts as he was working on them? One explanation may be that it was a habit born from his professional activity as a chemist, where, as Levi himself claimed, his weekly reports became the basis for his creative writing. It is as if he were writing a professional record of his writing activity, in order to keep track of what he did when. Another possible interpretation that needs to be explored is that dating his work reveals the complexity of his relationship with time. Time spent writing was time detracted or re-assigned from other activities, work or family duties. What kind of time was Levi keeping in his manuscripts? There is no answer to this question as yet.

The novel was clearly heavily edited, with many variations and cuts. Focusing on the edits on the first page of the novel (first pages are significant for all authors, but in particular for Levi), we can see that the passage that was later cut, cited in the interview with Rosellina Balbi, is longer and has been modified quite starkly. Here it is:

The theatre is ready; it stretches from the Sciti Plain to the little alleyways of old Milan. The time range is more limited, covering little over two years, but they are years that weigh heavily, years in which the scales were tipped, and the nature of the world as it is now was delineated, for better or for worse. The characters' profiles are still veiled, they still haven't emerged from the indistinct universe of things that do not yet exist but would already like to exist. They start to stir, weakly at first, grey against a background of grey. They speak softly, or perhaps they are not speaking at all, they are agitating and moaning like newly born puppies. They are waiting, expecting to go on stage but scared at the same time. They are pathetic and irritating, these unborn, or not-yet-born characters in a book that has not yet been written. 18 January 1981.

There are other passages crossed out in the first three pages of the book. In the initial dialogue between Mendel and Leonid, after Mendel says 'I fixed rifles, too', Levi cut the line where Mendel boasted that, when he was a child, he 'made gun-powder out of ground beechwood charcoal and saltpetre from the stables'. Further on, when Mendel asks Leonid where he got his packs of salt, a long passage was excised:

Things happen when you come from a long way away. You walk, by night and sometimes by day. You meet people, good and bad. You talk, maybe not that much because you don't know who you are talking to. There is trade. Trade never dies. Summer came and I no longer needed my woollen army corset, that's where I got the salt. There are places where they have salt, places where they have tobacco, and others still where they have nothing. You walk and walk and without knowing where you're headed, without knowing where you want to live not even if you want to live, only where you do not want to live. You walk and walk, living day to day, doing a bit of trade, and you even learn something, though there are certain questions nobody has the answer to. Nobody knows what will happen tomorrow or in a year, and this is normal. But nobody knows what happened yesterday or a year ago, and this is strange. It's strange living like this, you feel you are going wild.

On the side of the page was the date: 20/1/81. The galley-proofs were dated 'Turin, 11 December–20 January 1981'. As Levi declared to Giulio Nascimbeni in an interview, 1981 was indeed a happy year.

A RETURN TO JEWISH ROOTS?

Over the course of his life, Levi's approach to his Jewish heritage ranged from an early detachment, to an acceptance of his cultural roots, and later to a lively interest. This culminated in the publication of *If Not Now, When?* in 1992, when his sense of his own Jewish identity became interwoven with his relationship with Israel.

There was never any doubt that Levi was a Jewish writer, although his Jewishness was not a determining feature of his identity—at least, not the first and foremost feature. He repeated on numerous occasions that before being deported to Auschwitz he had simply been a young member of the Turin bourgeoisie. It was only after the Racial Laws of 1938 that his Jewish identity came to the fore, and after the experience of the Lager he embraced it more fully. In a 1982 speech at a conference on Jewish literature at the Rockefeller Foundation, Levi started by saying that in Italy and abroad he was considered a 'Jewish writer': 'I only started to accept this completely in more recent years and quite late in my career as a writer.' The speech was published in 1984 in the *Israeli Monthly Review* with the title 'Itinerary of a Jewish Writer'. This was a reconstruction of his development as a writer in the light of his Jewish identity and its interplay with his role as a witness: what he saw as his duty to repay a debt for his companions who had died in his place. Levi's testimony in *If This Is a Man* is based on the condition of humanity as a whole, not on that of being Jewish, unlike other Jewish holocaust writers. In fact, as we have noted, the term 'Holocaust' or 'Shoah' is never adopted by Levi. The novelist was included in the list of holocaust authors only after his death.

From his earliest writings in the 1940s and 50s, Levi always defined himself as a political prisoner rather than a Jewish one. He also claimed to speak on behalf of all deportees in general, and in particular those who were deported owing to the fact that they were Jewish rather than as a result of a political choice. Levi was concerned not to restrict the issue of deportation to the 'Jewish Question'. In his view, the deportation of the Jews was the lowest point in the barbarity that swept across Europe during the Second World War. This concern is particularly visible in the autobiographical sections of *The Periodic Table*, where Levi deals for the first time with the overall history of his education and identity.

In the 1960s and 70s, Levi seemed to be more interested in stressing his identity as an Italian, rather than Jewish, author. In the interviews he gave after the publication of his books, the theme of his Jewish identity was not a recurrent one. Interviewers focused rather on his double life as a writer and a chemist, and addressed him as a witness of Nazi horror rather than as a Jewish deportee. Interest in Jewish philosophical, religious and literary traditions increased progressively at the end of the 1970s in Italy, alongside a curiosity towards Middle European culture, the Great Vienna and Eastern European Jewish traditions. In that period, German or Yiddish writers began to be translated into Italian, corresponding to Levi's rediscovery of his first encounter with Yiddish culture 30 years before in the Lager (although in his 1965 poem 'Lilith' he already hinted at a Jewish sensibility).

In 1977, Claudio Magris explained in his Preface to a reprint of *Far from Where*, a book dedicated to Eastern European Jewish traditions, that this increasing interest in Jewish culture was the result of a new perception of the fragmentation of totality and a nostalgia for fullness, the absence of a centre of values and the search for a different condition that might salvage certain aspects of collective living. The cultural climate of those years re-evaluated Jewish culture, and took it on as an emblem of the modern and postmodern condition. Levi was re-attracted to Judaism, and especially to the Ashkenazy traditions that he had come across in the Lager. This rekindled interest was revealed in some of the stories published in *La Stampa* and then collected in *Lilith and Other Stories*, which are ideally linked to *If Not Now, When?* In the title story, and in 'Our Seal', 'The Cantor and the Veteran', the influence of the Jewish literature he had been reading was clear. There was the same voice in *If Not Now, When?*

In this novel, Levi undertook a translation of a passage in Yiddish, a language he didn't speak but studied in great depth, as well as of other texts in the Yiddish cultural tradition. He was fully aware that the Ashkenazy traditions were different to his own, given that the Italian Judaism—as he explained in 'Argon' (*The Periodic Table*)—were deeply enmeshed with the history of Italy. Especially during the Risorgimento, bourgeois and intellectual Jews took an active part in the movement, and considered it a struggle for their own emancipation. In 1848, under pressure from the Piedmont Jews who were close to the Savoy court, King Carlo Alberto issued a decree giving full political citizenship rights to Jews in the Savoy kingdom.

Levi described Jewish culture in the Piedmont in three articles later collected in *Other People's Trades*: 'Ritual and Laughter', 'The Best Merchandise' and 'My Grandfather's Shop', which was more autobio-graphical. Cavaglion in *Notizie de Argon* (2006) commented on Piedmont's Jewish culture and on Levi's genealogy. Levi rejected the idea of Jewish identity as racial. In his view, one is Jewish only in a cultural and religious sense. Levi was enrolled in the Turin Jewish Community register, but did not go to Synagogue. He never renounced his cultural Jewish identity, and from the early 1980s he started to cultivate it with great pride, stating in interviews that he felt three-quarters Italian and one-quarter Jewish, but that the one quarter part was very important to him. In an interview with Raffaella Manzini and Brunetto Salvarani, for the religious journal *Qol* (1986), Levi declared: 'Judaism is for me a tradition and a culture, and I am interested in both aspects. I think I would be interested even if I weren't Jewish'.

When *If Not Now, When?* came out in 1982, Israeli troops had just occupied Lebanon. Levi's signature was at the top of the petition of democratic intellectuals who felt clarification was needed concerning the meaning of Judaism. Levi again stressed his identity as an assimilated Jew, and talked of his discovery of the Ashkenazy branch of his religion in his youth, traces of which would later emerge in the Jewish Piedmont dialect adopted in 'Argon'. When Fiona Diwan (1982) asked Levi to what extent his narrative style could be considered 'Jewish', claiming that 'Jewish stories are always structured as stories within stories', Levi said he didn't think the narrative of *If Not Now, When?* was Jewish. He claimed the four themes of the novel—memory, *pietas*, the journey and 'inside' storytelling—were not intrinsically Jewish but, rather, belonged to all cultures. He did agree with his interviewer, however, that the themes of '*pietas*, memory, and journeys in the case of Jews were loaded with a legacy of suffering, with a past drenched in pain. Jewish memory is a painful memory, the memory of a chain of tragic events lost in the folds of history but ever alive'.

After commenting on Claudio Magris's work (1971), Paola Valabrega (1982) analysed *If Not Now, When?* by tracing the elements of Central European Jewish culture there. She cited in particular Levi's poems, written in February 1946 on his return from Auschwitz: 'Ostjuden', dedicated to the Jews he had met in the Lager on the theme of the devastation of their culture. The theme of *pietas*, which would recur in the 1970s and in *If Not Now, When?* was already present in the poem. Valabrega showed that the themes of diaspora and exile were already present in *The Truce*, even though the hero that most incarnated the *nostos* was of course Ulysses. Another interesting comment regarded Levi's family lexicon: 'Like some Jewish writers, Levi identifies family language with the tenderness of stories set in the past: anecdotes, stories, memories sent down from generation to generation surrounded by an aura of legend' (Valabrega 1982).

If Not Now, When? paid close attention to the minutiae of the *shtetl* in the tradition of Jewish authors, such as Sholem Aleichem whom Levi included in his personal anthology, *The Search for Roots*. What appeared to interest Levi in his Jewish characters—including those he invented in the novel—was the fact that they were 'lacerated', as he wrote regarding Tewje, one of Aleichem's protagonists. It was the double identity every Jew had always been forced to take on, a split that divided the world and was similarly felt by the author. That was precisely what Levi felt, as though he were split into two identities. On the one hand, these identities divided his personality, but on the other there is no doubt that they were a source of enrichment, a fact that was perhaps only fully perceived after his death. The novel told the story of this split, even though, in the end, the characters in the book decided to stay in Italy rather than emigrate to Israel.

Another issue that Levi cared deeply about was the possibility of writing an epic novel. It was reading Magris, as well as other authors he cited, such as Aleichem, Roth and the Singer brothers, that he realized that Eastern European Jewish literature was the last epic literature in twentieth-century European culture. Magris has said that he once suggested, in a meeting of Einaudi consultants, that Levi should translate some of these authors, but he never did.

In 1987, after Levi's death, a long conversation with Stefano Jesarum on the Jewish condition was published (1987). Levi talked about the Jewish culture he was brought up in, the figure of his father, and again described himself as a 'returning Jew'. In another interview with Risa Sodi on Auschwitz and Judaism (1987), he spoke ironically of his experience of American Judaism. After the English translation of *If Not Now, When?* was published in the US, American Jews were critical of the Eastern European setting of the book. One particularly polemical review was published in the American Jewish journal *Commentary*, which had previously published translations of some of his stories. Levi wrote a letter to the editor of the journal ('Letter to the Editor of *Commentary*', in *Uncollected Stories and Essays*) providing a detailed reconstruction of his experience and some reflections on an issue that was highly debated among Jews internationally in the 1970s. That is, the accusation that Eastern European Jews had been incapable of reacting to racial persecution and the Nazi 'final solution'.

After *If Not Now, When?* came out, Levi wrote more frequently about Jewish matters. He published a piece on the Warsaw revolt ('The Daring People of the Ghetto', 1983); Foreword to *Jews in Turin*, the exhibition catalogue for the centenary of the Turin synagogue, in 1984; a presentation of a book on Eastern European Jews in 1985; and many other articles. At the end of his foreword for the Turin synagogue, Levi concluded bitterly:

> For every human group, there is a critical mass below which stability ceases: it is at that point that things become more and more diluted until they are silently and painlessly dissolved. Our community, unless something we cannot predict takes place, seems to be on this path. What we would like to do with this exhibition is show our Turin friends and our children that we have filial piety, who we are and where we are from (p. 2682).

Another article, 'The Hard Path to Liberty', later published by Guido Lopez, revealed the complex relationship Levi had with Italian Judaism. It was the transcription of a speech Levi had prepared for the annual meeting of the Italian Jewish Community, postponed after the

Israeli occupation of Lebanon in 1982 which Levi publicly denounced. After undergoing several variations, the article became a part of the introduction to *The Drowned and the Saved*.

LEMMAS

Israel

At the end of the return journey narrated in *The Truce*, Levi realized that a new car had been hooked onto theirs in Munich.

> At the tail end of the train, travelling with us toward Italy, was a new car, crowded with young Jews, boys and girls from all the countries of Eastern Europe. None of them looked more than twenty, but they were extremely determined and confident; they were young Zionists, they were going to Israel, taking any route they could and by any means they could [. . .]. They felt immensely free and strong, masters of the world and of their destiny (p. 395).

A similar encounter was described in *If Not Now, When?*, where Gedale's band of partisans bumped into a Palestinian Brigade affiliated to the British Army who explained why Italy might be 'a good place to start living' (p. 1854).

Unlike the many Jewish survivors of the concentration camps, including Italian Jews, who decided to emigrate to Palestine after the war, Levi went back to his home city, Turin. Levi explained that his decision was determined by the fact that his family had survived the war, his house was still intact and he had plenty of job opportunities as a chemist. He had always felt more Italian than Jewish, and had never planned to emigrate to the Promised Land. In an interview, Levi said he had come across Zionist propaganda as a young man, but had never been particularly taken by the movement. Nonetheless, Levi was profoundly attached to the State of Israel and followed internal developments closely, corresponding closely with many friends who had elected to move there.

In 1967, in a speech at an event sponsored by the Jewish community in the Turin Synagogue, included in *Uncollected Stories and Essays*, Levi defended Israel's existence: 'Everyone should remember that the generation that created Israel consists almost entirely of people who escaped the massacre of Judaism in Europe' (p. 1183). He warned against intransigence in any religion, including Israel's, and stressed the values of peace and tolerance above all others. Finally, he developed an argument to which he would return in later interviews and speeches: that 'man for man' Israel is made up of Europeans and therefore has European roots. After the Six Day War in June 1967, Levi wrote to his dear friend, Hety, describing his state of mind. He was relieved that Israel had not been destroyed, which would have been a tragedy in his view, but was also disappointed that Israel had not yet fulfilled its promise to become a model nation (a land of justice, equality and labour). By contrast, he was critical of Italian left-wing newspapers that praised Nasser as a champion of democracy and socialism. On returning from a trip to Israel in April 1968, Levi wrote an enthusiastic article on his encounters there, reversing his previous assessment. 'Encounters in Kibbutzim' (*Uncollected Stories and Essays*) stated that 'Israel is not Europe: though heir to all the currents of European thought, Israel visibly lacks that historical sediment that makes Europe one, from Gibraltar to the Urals, and constitutes the framework of all its urban conglomerates [. . .] Israel is still a country of pioneers, especially in the kibbutzim' (p. 1185).

Throughout his life, Levi oscillated between taking a positive view of the country's absence of roots, and a strong conviction that Israel should do more to reconnect with the European roots of its founding fathers. In his more critical periods, he accused Israel of becoming no different to any other Middle Eastern country. In 1969, to the consternation of his community—his biographer Carole Angier recalled—Levi signed a petition protesting against Israel's policies promoted by a group of left-wing Turin intellectuals.

In June 1982, Israeli troops invaded and occupied part of Lebanon in an operation called 'Peace in Galilee'. On this occasion, too, Levi signed an appeal to the Israeli government, asking them to withdraw their troops. Levi's participation in the appeal caused a great deal of controversy, but Levi continued to defend his point of view in a series of interviews that condemned Menachem Begin's policies as 'fascist'. Levi was torn between his ties with Israel and his disapproval of the acts of its governing class. In his conversations, first with Giampaolo Pansa and, two years later, with Gad Lerner, Levi further honed a concept he had already expressed in the past. In his view, Israel was not the centre of Judaism; the diaspora was. The Italian Jewish community was highly critical of this approach, and considered Levi a 'traitor' for signing the appeal. Levi described the sensation as being like an interior civil war: in his guts. Nonetheless, he insisted that criticizing the policies of Israeli governments was not anti-Semitic; it was, rather, a statement of the freedom of expression that was the mark of western democracies. Levi published another important article *in La Stampa* on 24 June 1982, expressing his critical point of view once again, despite the criticism of his community ('Who Has Courage in Jerusalem?' later included in *Uncollected Stories and Essays*).

Anti-Semitism

One of the most frequent questions students asked Levi regarded the Nazi's hatred for Jews. As early as June 1961, in his questionnaire for the magazine *Illustrated History*, Levi interpreted anti-Semitism as a form of intolerance that is intrinsic in humans but has a zoological explanation. Two pieces are particularly important in this regard. The first is the 1976 Appendix to the School Edition of *If This Is a Man*; the second, a 1978 conference address entitled 'Racial Intolerance'.

In the Appendix, Levi wrote: 'Now, man is certainly a social animal (Aristotle confirmed it), but we would be in trouble if all the zoological urges that survive in man were tolerated! Human laws are useful precisely for this: to restrain animal impulses' (p. 184). Levi explained the universal phenomenon of intolerance, of which anti-Semitism is an example, in his view. He started with 'the establishment of Christianity as a state religion,' and went on to examine in particular detail the history of German anti-Semitism, concluding: 'we can therefore state that anti-Semitism is a specific case of intolerance; that for centuries it had a mainly religious character; that in the Third Reich it was exacerbated by the nationalistic and militaristic propensity of the German people, and by the peculiar "differentness" of the Jewish people' (p. 189). Levi had always claimed that this 'differentness' was based on historical and cultural factors, rather than on race. At the end of his long disquisition on the subject he was still not satisfied: 'Yet I have to admit that these generally accepted explanations do not satisfy me: they are reductive, not commensurate, not proportional to the facts to be explained. In rereading the accounts of Nazism, from its murky beginnings to its violent end, I can't escape the impression of a general atmosphere of unrestrained madness that seems to me unique in history' (p. 189). It was the personality of Adolf Hitler that constituted the problem. In the pages that followed, Levi explored the idea of charismatic leaders, who became the material executors of the extermination, and their followers. Levi concluded that perhaps the phenomenon cannot be comprehended: 'Perhaps what happened cannot be comprehended, or, rather, shouldn't be comprehended, because to comprehend is almost to justify' (p. 190).

Levi always tried to extend his analysis of anti-Semitism to similar manifestations of intolerance that had led to mass killings over the course of history, as well as in more recent times. In 'Racial Intolerance', Levi examined the many facets of Jewish identity, its history, geography and specific culture, and further developed his observations regarding animal behaviour. His main source for these observations was Konrad Lorenz (cited several times in *Other People's Trades*, and considered the inspiration for some of the animal stories in *Natural Histories* and *Flaw of Form*).

Kafka

It was the publisher, Giulio Einaudi, who commissioned Levi to translate Kafka's *The Trial* for his new series, 'Writers Translated by Writers'. When he had completed the job, Levi confessed he had suffered a great deal translating the book, owing both to the language and to the circumstances described there, to the point that he actually felt 'conflict'. The translation was very successful. Critics commented on the book as if it had been written by Levi, and he was invited to give a series of interviews on translating Kafka. In one of these conversations, Levi was asked whether there were any parallels between Kafka's work from 1883 to 1924 and the persecution of the Jews. Did Kafka's *The Trial* foresee the mass extermination that was to come?

In Levi's view, Kafka had an animal-like sixth sense. He was 'a harbinger, as if he had possessed that mysterious sensibility which enables some creatures to predict earthquakes' (p. 2614) or like a mole who moves underground and ignores the problems above ground. Kafka and Levi shared many features: they were both Jewish, and both employees—Kafka by a big insurance company; they both approached writing as a 'second job'. Yet, Levi firmly rejected the claim that they were similar.

In his article, 'Translating Kafka' as well as in his 'Note on Kafka's *The Trial*', and in another short article he wrote on the subject entitled 'A Mysterious Sensibility', Levi denies any 'affinity with Kafka' (p. 2348).

> In my writing, for better or for worse, knowingly or not, I have always tended toward a transition from obscurity to clarity, rather like a filter pump, sucking in turbid water and turning it out purified, even sterile (I think Pirandello said this, I don't recall where). Kafka takes the opposite approach: he endlessly unravels hallucinations that he draws from incredibly deep layers, and never filters them. The reader feels them teeming with germs and spores; they are full of burning significance, but he is never helped to tear the curtain or go around it to see what it conceals. Kafka never touches down, he never consents to give you the end of Ariadne's thread (p. 2348).

To whatever extent Levi listed their differences, there were still a few things the two writers had in common, aside from their subtle humour (though Levi denies Max Brod's idea of laughter: 'I don't really believe in the laughter that Brod speaks of: maybe Kafka laughed while telling stories to his friends, sitting around a table in the beer hall, since people are not always consistent, but he certainly didn't laugh when he was writing' (p. 2349).

One similarity was the way animals featured in their writing. Deleuze and Guattari (*Kafka: Towards a Minor Literature*, 1975) examined, for example, the role of dogs in Kafka, where not only did dogs become men but also men became dogs. Animals, in the critics' view, were a means to escape an unmanageable situation. Animals were the protagonists of

Kafka's stories even when they were not explicitly considered as such; they represented a symbolic essence of the author's aggression, linked to an idea of freedom. Levi also used animals in this way. As well as reflecting the very real risk of regression, they also represented freedom from ties. They were a primal force. While Levi feared Kafkian metamorphosis, the continuous cycle of animal to human back to animal represented, for Deleuze and Guattari, a static, immobile journey that can only be appreciated in terms of intensity. Animals show humans how to escape and where to escape to—a route humans are not equipped to find on their own (see, in this regard, Levi's 1977 story 'Buffet Dinner').

It is interesting to see that the two French critics linked the animal theme to that of travel. They are, in fact, two different forms of 'deterritorialization', or relative deterritorialization, as Deleuze and Guattari put it, given that going back to the starting point, returning home, is what defines a journey. In 'My House', Levi described himself, especially when he was at home, as being sedentary, like a limpet: 'After a brief larval stage, in which they swim freely, limpets fasten onto wave-pounded rocks, secrete a shell, and then never move again for the rest of their lives' (p. 2015). His journey to Auschwitz was his personal deterritorialization, throwing him into the chaos of the Lager, where he was transformed into a dog, forced to undergo an animal metamorphosis. Auschwitz marked an ambivalent change of state in Levi, who was transformed from being an innocuous limpet to being an aggressive animal, barking and lapping up his food. It was at the same time the source of his gift, a magic wand, a metamorphosis that gave him a new sensibility and transformed him into a writer. It is as if he were unable to separate himself from an animal metamorphosis, as if he were chained to this destiny. Deleuze and Guattari's idea that in Kafka an animal metaphor was neither a metaphor, a symbol, or an allegory, nor an error, a curse or a punishment, could well be applied to Levi. In their view, it was an 'intensity card', a creative form of escape that means nothing other than itself.

Another theme the two writers shared was eating and speaking (or writing). Deleuze and Guattari wrote at length about Kafka's problems with the German language, using Klaus Wagenbach's observations. They described his German as being that of a nomad, gypsy or immigrant. This was another deterritorialization, this time of Kafka's mouth, the mouth of the narrator: 'the mouth, tongue, and teeth find their primitive territoriality in food. In giving themselves over to the articulation of sounds, the mouth, tongue, and teeth deterritorialize. Thus, there is a certain disjunction between eating and speaking, and even more, despite all appearances, between eating and writing' (Deleuze and Guattari 1975). It is certainly possible to write while you are eating, the critics pointed out; in fact, it is easier than speaking while you are eating. However, in their view, writing transforms words into things that can compete with food more easily than speaking does. This observation can be applied to Levi, for whom orality was all-important. 'Return, eat, tell' were Levi's imperatives. Return home from the Lager, satisfy the terrible hunger he had suffered, tell the story of what had happened. All three of these were attempts at deterritorialization, in Deleuze and Guattari's terms, but they failed because, even though Levi survived the inferno of Auschwitz, he remained a nomad (a deportee), all his life. Hence his insistence on his house, on being sedentary: despite all appearances, he never completely regained his composure. Levi's recurrent dream of returning home, telling his story and not being believed—the story being so impossible that even Levi found it hard to believe—was described in *If This Is a Man*: his physical need to tell his story was on the same level as his need to eat (dreams of eating and dreams of speaking alternated among prisoners). The urge to write *If This Is a Man* was born from this need, and indeed the story began in the Buna chemical laboratory.

Speaking, and above all, writing, were equivalent to fasting in Deleuze and Guattari's view. As with Kafka, the tongue compensates its deterritorialization with respect to food with a reterritorialization of sense. When it ceases being an organ of sense it becomes a tool of sense. It is possible to interpret Levi's oral style of storytelling (in written stories too) as a desperate attempt to confer meaning on the incomprehensible meaninglessness of his deportation. Levi bears no guilt, and for this reason he always rejected the idea of forgiveness. One can recognize in him the 'minor use' of that majority tongue Deleuze described (1996). This was precisely the opposite of those critics who claimed that Levi's Italian, formed in the classical lyceum where the Latin and Italian literary tradition was upheld, was a 'majority' tongue. This claim denied Levi the prerogative of being—like other great writers—a foreigner in his own language. It is not by chance that the language critics now praise in Levi was not recognized at the time. Levi worked with a babel of tongues discarded by others, 'old' tongues.

Still another trait the two writers had in common was their Jewish roots. George Steiner, in *No Passion Spent* (1998) commented that *The Trial* belonged to the literary genre of commentary because it did not reflect only itself but also incorporated elements of exegesis and rabbinical hermeneutics. Jewish tradition is iconoclastic towards mimesis, or, more in general, towards the semantics of representation used to create an aesthetic experience by means of fiction. The proliferation of secondary and tertiary discourse—commentaries on commentaries—in the Jewish diaspora lends credence to Steiner's thesis. Kafka had to make the difficult choice: either give up writing 'invented' stories, or incorporate a commentary on his narrative, even though the latter would still constitute a transgression (especially, in Steiner's view, in the case of his short stories). There was a similar dilemma on a different plane. Even before he was deported to Auschwitz, Levi had a strong urge to write, but when he came home, it felt blasphemous to become a writer, even though he already was one to all effects. He was destined to be a witness; that was his Law. A witness could write in a literary style, but he still had to be a witness. Like Kafka, as a Jew, Levi had to submit to censure, or go against a prohibition. Thus, when he published his first short stories (which he defined as science fiction or games, two variations of the topic that obsessed him) they were under a pseudonym. 'Fiction' created a problem for him because fiction in literature implied falsehood, and this was precisely what his Law did not allow. Like Kafka, Levi had to go against a prohibition in order to give space to the epic, lyrical, or fictional impulses that were his lifeblood as a writer.

Levi recognized this infraction in Kafka's *The Trial*, which, as Walter Benjamin put it, was the crisis of the 'pure transmissibility of truth': 'From the first sentence, you are plunged into the nightmare of the unknowable, on every page confronted with haunting passages. K. is followed and persecuted by alien presences, by tiresome busybodies who spy on him from near and far, and in front of whom he feels stripped naked' (p. 2634). This was Kafka's drama, expressed by means of an opposition between the language of love that he aspired to, and the grammar of a man who had fallen from grace which manifested itself, according to Steiner, through the code of law.

In Levi's 'Note on Kafka's *The Trial*', he wrote about his difficulty untangling the text, 'Often, during this work of translation, I felt a collision, a conflict, an immodest temptation to untangle in my own way the knots in the text: in short, to correct, to tamper with the choice of words, to super-impose my writing style on Kafka's' (p. 2635). His urge was to rewrite the book. It was not just the evocation of the unjust and senseless trial that Levi was subjected to when he was deported to Auschwitz, thus discovering he was a Jew, that triggered a reaction in him (as many interviewers have insisted). It was, rather, finding the unresolved issue of his own identity as a writer in Kafka's work. The sense of oppression that translating *The Trial* gave him was a reminder of a broken prohibition: becoming a writer despite Auschwitz.

At an Uncertain Hour
(Collected Poems)

Primo Levi wrote poems all his life, at least since he was in high school, if not before. These early poems were mostly goliardic in spirit: comic verses or satirical poems about friends or teachers. Later, in the years he worked full time as a chemist, he composed occasional verse, mostly parodies on his colleagues' retirements or resignations. One of the first verses Levi considered a full-blown poem was called 'Crescenzago', written before his capture by the Fascist militia and his subsequent deportation. The first poem to make its way to print, however, was 'Buna'. The Biella-based journal, *L'amico del popolo* (Friend of the People) affiliated with the Italian Communist Party and edited by Silvio Ortona, published the poem in its 22 June 1946 issue, and later printed extracts of the book Levi had written on returning from Auschwitz. It was not until 1970, however, that Levi collected 23 poems in a private edition and circulated the volume among his friends.

In 1975, Vanni Scheiwiller published 27 of Levi's poems in a collection entitled *L'Osteria di Brema* (The Bremen Inn), all except one of which had already circulated in the earlier private edition. Finally, as late as 1984, Garzanti published the collection *At an Uncertain Hour*, which contained these previously published poems, together with Levi's translations of other poets. This was the first, almost complete collection of poems written by one of the greatest twentieth-century writers in Italy. After this collection, Levi continued to publish poems in *La Stampa*, and went on writing them until the very last days of his life. In

431

a photograph taken in 1986 by Mario Monge, in fact, Levi is at his computer, and on the screen, one can see the first few lines of the poem 'The Soldier'.

Levi's earliest published poem was thus 'Crescenzago', which he composed in February 1943 when he was in Milan before being captured and deported. As he described in *The Periodic Table*, as soon as he got back to Turin at the end of 1945, as well as writing bits and pieces of what was to become *If This Is a Man*, he also wrote poems. This is what he said in 'Chromium' (p. 876): 'I wrote short, bloody poems, I told my story giddily, speaking and writing, so that little by little a book was born.' The fact that the poems and the testimonies that would later become a book were conceived and written at the same time is a vital element for understanding Levi's work as a whole, both his fiction and his non-fiction. It is therefore important to place the lines of poetry he wrote in 1946, but did not publish until 1970, side by side with the pages of his first book, *If This Is a Man*.

SHORT, BLOODY POEMS

'Buna' was dated 28 December 1945, and was composed two months before 'The Story of Ten Days', which was written in February 1946. The next group of poems, composed between 3–11 January 1946—'Singing', 'February 25, 1944', 'Song of the Crow I', 'Shemà' and 'Get Up'—contained the nucleus of some of the themes later developed in *If This Is a Man*. *Singing* was inspired by an episode that took place in the Lager. One line of the poem was used in other works, including the presentation of *If This Is a Man* that was published in the journal *L'Italia che Scrive* in 1947: 'Not martyrs, infamous, or saints.' The word 'drowned', which became highly significant in Levi's experience, as well as in his public and private lexicon, first appeared in the poem 'February 25, 1944', the title and the date referring to a specific day during his imprisonment at the Fòssoli transit camp. The crow who brings bad news to the poet in

'Song of the Crow I' was mirrored at the end of 'The Story of Ten Days', where Levi describes the period between the hasty retreat of the German Army and the arrival of the Russian Troops. 'Shemà', dated 10 January 1946, was the poem that became famous as the Foreword to *If This Is a Man*. It first came out with the title 'Salmo' in the pages that were published as a preview in *L'amico del popolo* in 1947. 'Get Up', dated 11 January 1946, was included as a preface to *The Truce*, published 16 years after the first edition of *If This Is a Man*, in 1963.

Italo Rosato (1997) identified several cross-references between Levi's poems and his narrative fiction. The poem 'Buna', for example, was cited in the early pages of the chapter *The Drowned and the Saved*, and on the last page of the chapter 'Kraus'; 'Singing' appears in the final pages of 'Die Drei Leute vom Labor', and in the chapter 'Chromium' in *The Periodic Table*; the lines 'I've come from very far away / To bring bad news' and 'To bring you the sad news / To take the joy from your sleep' from 'Song of the Crow I' are re-used in the closing pages of the chapter 'Ka-Be'; 'Get Up' is published at the end of the chapter 'Our Nights'; 'Sunset at Fòssoli' is cited at the beginning of the first chapter, 'Journey'. These are just some of the references.

A second group of poems, written between 17 January and 28 June 1946, were composed over the same period that Levi was writing the first draft of most of the chapters of *If This Is a Man*. This group differs from the other in tone and in subject matter. The poems could almost be said to be a counterpoint to the testimony of the Lager experience Levi was engaged in writing at the same time. The poem 'Monday', and the later 'Another Monday' in a completely different timbre, alluded to a happy time in his life, as Levi explained years later to his Croatian translator, Mladen Machiedo.

'Another Monday' came about in a happy moment of my life. On returning home from the concentration camp I had gone through a few hard months, owing to trauma, solitude, and also to the lack of work and money. Then in a few days I found a job at the Montecatini works in Avigliana, and a girlfriend, who became my wife. The poem recalls my departure from the station of Porta Nuova for Avigliana, on a freezing Monday at dawn, which was nothing like that other desperate departure of the first 'Monday' (the other poem). It was a happy departure. I felt I could hear in the raucous megaphones of the station the thundering voice of Minos sitting in the second circle of hell (*Inferno* V:4) deciding who would end up in heaven and who would not. It was, rather, a parody of the Universal Judgement (22 June 1970).

'Monday', the sadder of the two poems, contained three lines that recalled the famous lines in 'Shemà' in the use of the conditional ('If he lives . . . If he thinks') and in the universal use of the word 'man'. The four poems written in 1946 were also different in tone to the 'short, bloody poems' written earlier. They were more meditative, especially 'Ostjuden' and 'Sunset at Fòssoli' which were written on the same day—7 February 1946—and adopted the same 'high' register as *If This Is a Man*. The poem that followed, 'February 11, 1946', clearly dedicated to his wife, was not included in the 1975 Scheiwiller edition, but was published in the 1984 definitive collection. There is a certain symmetry with the other poem using a date as a title, 'February 25, 1944', where the poet also addressed a woman. The culmination of this change in tone was the poem 'Avigliana', a love poem, dated 28 June 1946, in which he converses from a distance with his girlfriend and future wife, Lucia Morpurgo.

It has been noted that Levi only wrote eight poems between 1949 and 1965, and these eight poems were written more or less contemporaneously with Levi's drafts of *The Truce* and the stories collected in *Natural Histories*. Levi abandoned poetry writing while he was working on these new works of fiction, as he did at other times over his career as a writer. This should lead us to reflect on the parallels between his poetry writing and his fiction writing.

Levi's poems were often conceived as a result of a re-evocation of an experience in the concentration camp, or of themes linked to that experience. In this sense, they could almost be said to anticipate the later stories or reflections in his fiction. This would explain the concentration of poems written between 1979, when Levi started working on *The Drowned and the Saved*, and 1985 when he finished the first draft. *Flaw of Form*, published in 1974, cited a few lines from *There Were a Hundred* as an epigraph dated 1 March 1959.

The last group of poems, written between 1949 and 1965, all revolved around the theme of the Lager and came out before *Natural Histories*, which was prefaced not by a poem of his own but by a citation from Rabelais's *Gargantua and Pantagruel*. The poem 'Lilith', which anticipated some of the themes later used in the story by the same name, closed the group of poems published in 1970. In the later collection, *L'Ostello di Brema* (The Beer Hall in Bremen) four more poems were added, written between 1970 and 1974.

Before the book came out under the Scheiwiller imprint, Levi wrote a letter to Giulio Einaudi to explain why he had 'defected' to another house the same year as *The Periodic Table* was published.

Dear Publisher, at highly irregular intervals, and since I was very young, I have brought thirty or so poems into this world. Several years ago, I spoke to your editors and they informed me that Einaudi would not publish them owing to the size and the subject matter of the collection. Scheiwiller, who came across the poems by chance, has now given me the opportunity to print them. I am writing to inform you of this decision, given the clause that is contained in the contract that ties us both. Thanking you in advance, and cordial greetings, Yours, Primo Levi.

This short letter shows that Levi took an active interest in his poetry and proves that he had already planned to collect his poems and publish them years before. The title of the collection was a line taken from his poem 'Arrival', inspired by a poem by Heine which mentions the Bremen beer hall where 'a man who's come to port' would be happy to sit. It suggests a moment of truce, or temporary calm, since 'He doesn't fear or hope or wait / But stares intently at the setting sun.'

It was not until 1978, however, that *La Stampa* started publishing Levi's poems in its cultural pages. The first was 'Gold and Hatred'—later the title was changed to 'Huayna Capac'—followed by 'The Girl of Pompeii'. Both of these poems marked a new trend, where the narrative voice in the poem belonged to historical figures or to animals. These masks would them become a significant element of his last poems. Before Levi published his own poems in the Turin newspaper, several poems translated from English and German came out between 1976 and 1977 in the literary supplement *Tuttolibri*. These were later included in the collection *At an Uncertain Hour*. Levi wrote that they were 'musical rather than philological' versions of the originals.

Coleridge, *The Ancient Mariner* and the Title

The title *At an Uncertain Hour* was taken from Coleridge's *The Rime of the Ancient Mariner*, which Levi cited at the beginning of the poem 'The Survivor', dedicated to 'B.V.' (Bruno Vasari): 'Since then, at an uncertain hour . . . ' Until recently, it was thought that Levi had come across the poem in Beppe Fenoglio's translation, published by Einaudi in 1964. This translation had already been published in 1955 in the literary journal *Itinerario*, but there was a previously existing edition of Coleridge's work that Levi could well have come across. This had been translated by Mario Praz, published in 1925, and then re-reprinted in 1947. In addition, Maria Luisa Cervini translated an anthology of Coleridge's poems and essays that was published by Utet in 1931, that circulated widely and was later reprinted in 1960. Further translations of the poem include those by Terza and Nancioni that came out in 1889. These would have been harder to find but could well have been picked up in one of the second-hand book stalls along the River Po that Levi's father used to go to. Before the 1960s, however, Levi would never have been compared—as he would later be—to The Ancient Mariner himself: 'who grabs the wedding guest on the way to the wedding, to inflict on him the story of evil' ('Chromium', p. 876).

In a letter sent to the sociologist, writer and poet, Kurt Heinrich Wolff, in May 1965, it becomes clear that Levi had read Coleridge in English, since he suggests the title 'Upon a Painted Ocean' for the English translation of *The Truce*, rather than the previously suggested *The Reawakening* (Luzzato and Scarpa 2011). The line he had used as the title of his poetry collection, *At an Uncertain Hour*, was reused in 1986 as an epigraph to *The Drowned and the Saved*. In an interview with Sodi, Levi remembers how shocked he was when he was when he first read *The Ancient Mariner*: 'I had just got back from the concentration camp, and I too behaved exactly like him' (1987).

The Coleridge quote appears in two passages in Levi's work. Apart from the autobiographical story already cited, 'Chromium', there is a passage from the 1966 'Note on the Dramatized Version of *If This Is a Man*' where Levi writes: 'I became like the Ancient Mariner in Coleridge's ballad, who grabs the wedding guests on the street to inflict on them his sinister story of evil and ghosts. In a few days I had repeated my stories dozens of times, to my friends, enemies and strangers' (p. 1173). The Ancient Mariner is also one of the characters that figure in the short story 'In the Park' (in *Flaw of Form*): the fellow with 'eyes like coals, skin like leather, and his shirt unbuttoned, who doesn't drink and doesn't pay, doesn't sing, doesn't pay attention to the others, and says things that no one is listening to, is the Ancient Mariner' (p. 682). This was the character who would then play the role of the narrative voice— almost as if he were a double of Levi's—in all of his poems until 1964 ('Arrival' and 'Lilith'). Half way through the 1960s, this became the image Levi relied on to convey himself. In other words, the spectre that haunts Levi's poetry from 1946 to 1965 increasingly resembled the figure conjured up by Coleridge, and that is how he appeared on several different occasions in Levi's work.

THE GARZANTI EDITION

In the later Garzanti edition, Levi placed the poems in chronological order and dated each according to when they were written (which did not always correspond to when they were published in *La Stampa*, as the bibliography of Levi's *Complete Works* demonstrates). As Levi stated in his letter to Einaudi, he had originally sent his new, bigger collection of poems—with 40 additional pieces—to his own publisher before looking elsewhere. When he received no reply, he went to Garzanti, which published them in 1984 in the 'Poesie' series. This was the second book of poetry Levi published outside Einaudi.

Garzanti published three editions altogether, including the 1984 collection, with a total of 7,000 copies sold.

Levi wrote the dust-jacket blurb himself; later, when the book was re-reprinted, his presentation was used as a Preface. It was a commentary on his own work, in which he stated his conviction that in the history of humanity poetry was born before prose and that this was also true in his personal history. 'At irregular intervals' he had written poems, and he went on to claim that the urge to do so was 'written in our DNA'. This suggestion of a biological necessity for writing poetry reveals a core element of his thinking. Levi proposed readers enjoy his poems on a non-aesthetic level, as he himself claimed that they were 'excellent'. He places them within the overall framework of his Opus: 'I can only assure possible readers that in rare moments [. . .] single stimuluses have taken on a certain spontaneously natural form that my irrational half continues to consider unnatural.' Poetry, in Levi's view, was more suited than prose for 'transmitting an idea or an image'. This comment sheds light on Levi's consideration of his own prose.

In 1985, *At an Uncertain Hour* won the 35th National Giosué Carducci Poetry Competition in Pietrasanta, and the Abetone Prize in Pistoia. In a letter to the critic Gina Lagorio, Levi commented on the Carducci prize, 'No prize has ever given me such pleasure because I didn't expect it. Clearly, the publishing adultery I have committed has brought me luck' (28 July 1985).

VARIATIONS

There were very few changes made to the poems between the 1970 private edition and the Scheiwiller collection. The only significant ones were the elimination of a line in 'Song of the Crow II': 'Not with death / Before death', and of three lines at the beginning of 'The Dark Stars' immediately after the first line, 'No one should sing again of love or war', a cut which changes the interpretation of the poem.

In the Garzanti edition, however, the author made several alterations. He added biographical notes and additional information for the reader at the bottom of the poems that had already been published, including literary references, citations, or calques in the titles or bodies of the poems, or simply an indication of what inspired him to write them. These notes form an additional commentary on his own work that recall the annotations Levi made to the school editions of *If This Is a Man* and *The Truce*.

Levi's poetry relied on a great number of literary sources and used numerous borrowings and hidden citations. The Bible, in particular Deuteronomy, and Wisdom Literature were important sources. The first time 'Shemà' was published in *L'amico del popolo*, in fact, the title was 'Salmo', a fundamental Jewish prayer: *Shemà Israel*, or 'Listen to Israel'. Commenting on this poem, Levi once said it was his 'blasphemous interpretation of a Yiddish prayer' (Monticelli 1982). Other authors Levi often cited were Dante, T. S. Eliot, Catullus, Villon, Shakespeare, Coleridge, Heine, Rilke, in addition to scientific literature, as he stated in *The Search for Roots*. There were also historical sources, newspaper articles, the poetry of the Resistance, and the poets Éluard, Aragon, Carducci, Gozzano and even Pascoli. Poems written after 1965 tended more towards parodies, although 'Crescenzago' already clearly reflected this aspect. Domenico Scarpa noted that the first line was a remake of a popular Neapolitan song by Salvatore Di Giacomo, whose music was written by Francesco Paolo Tosto, 'A Marechiare ce sta na fenestra' (2015).

When Levi prepared the poems previously printed in *La Stampa* for publication in the Garzanti collection, he made several edits. In the poem 'Huayna Capac', for example, he altered a few words. 'Annunciation', originally published in the archery magazine, *L'Almanacco dell'arciere* in 1980, on the other hand, was completely reworked in order to make the tone a little more classical. There were corrections made to the fourth and third from last lines of 'Unfinished Business': 'You'll find the book in my drawer / Under a green cloth' was changed to 'You'll find its outline in my drawer / Down below, with the unfinished business.' Similarly, in 'The Work', the 'dog barking at a concert' was once a 'soothsayer'; in 'Nachtwache', the line 'Others tossing sleepless with desire' substituted 'turning restlessly looking for trouble'; in 'The Snail' the words 'its moderate liberty' were cut. In the poem '2000', the final version published in the Garzanti edition kept only five lines out of the original ten, and one of these five was placed in a different order (the original 10 line version appears in Alberto Sinigaglia's *Vent'anni al Duemila* (1982). Except for this final example, all the other changes are small edits. In one case only, it seems, Levi cut out a personal reference.

A careful reading of Levi's poetic opus, however, reveals further material for reflection. One element that is particularly striking is the fact that Levi dated each poem. This appears to have been dictated by a desire for precision but was also a need to provide a chronological framework for his poetry, and to link the poems to various events in his life. The dating of the chapters in Levi's most important works of fiction was done for the same reasons: to present his writing as auto-biographical, both to himself and to others.

There were three poems found after Levi's death, that—if the dating is accurate—Levi chose not to include in the Garzanti edition. These were 'The Decathlete', published on 4 September 1984 in *La Stampa*; 'To the Muse', dated 5 September 1982; and 'Casa Galvani', composed on 3 May 1984. 'To the Muse', in particular, is a meditation on the act of writing poetry and on the poet's absence of inspiration at that moment ('Why do you visit me so rarely?').

Italo Rosato (1997) has commented that in Levi's poetry, 'closed metric forms are passed over, even though many lines are regular. When greater expressivity is required, the rhythm is accelerated, slowed down or broken. Emphasis on certain semantic transitions deflagrates whatever metric regularity there may have been.'

TRANSLATIONS

The fact that ten 'translations' of poems—from Heine's *Book of Songs*, in particular, but also from Kipling and from an anonymous seventeenth-century Scottish ballad—were included in the Garzanti collection, is interesting. These translations had already appeared in the literary supplement of *La Stampa* (*Tuttolibri* 1976). As Levi himself commented, these were not translations so much as re-elaborations of the original texts—a practice that Levi also applied to his own poetry, as his notes to the individual poems show. In the section devoted to the translated poems in the book, Levi wrote: 'These translations were intended to be more musical than philological, and more of a *divertissement* than a professional job.'

This kind of under-statement was typical of all of Levi's observations on his own poetry. He said that he was 'not accustomed to the label of poet, I feel like an actor playing the wrong part,' and quipped, 'you cannot call somebody who writes an average of one poem a year a poet' (Audino 1984). And yet, Levi's poetry, and all of his reflections on poetry in general contained in *Other People's Trades* and *Uncollected Short Stories and Essays* revealed a deep interest in the intricate relationship between invention and re-invention.

Franco Fortini (1997), claimed that Levi's poetry was the product of a narrative necessity, but that this also worked the other way around. In his view, in Levi's prose there was a constant tension towards poetry, both in its form and in its expression. The link between them, he claimed, lay in the need for a narrative pretext, almost an expedient. In Cesare Segre's opinion, 'poetry is the quintessence of an author's work, but with something extra: that is, it reveals his persuasive, exhortative or warning side. Levi, who was generally sober in his judgements, and so loth to preach, pushed himself further in his poems, as if the artificiality of the form were a counterweight to the solemnity of language' (Introduction to *Opere Complete* II, 1988).

The 'artificial'—almost mannered, though never mannerist—nature of poetic form made Levi's poetry very different from other post-war neorealist poets, even though they shared with Levi the desire to communicate extraordinary life experiences (Rosato 1997). Neorealist poets attempted to meld formal structures with a spoken register, thus closing the gap between literature and real life. Levi's poetry, by contrast, aimed for a more formal register, 'almost as stuffy as an old Classics teacher', as Fortini once said. biblical references, literary parodies, hidden citations, borrowings from nineteenth-century models such as Carducci, re-elaborations of Dante and Latin poetry, make Levi's poetry an exception in post-war Italian poetry rather than the rule. Some critics even claim they are not really poetry. Fortini felt that Levi's poems expressed 'the part of the subject that is in the shade,' and that the closer they got to that dark core, the less formally successful they were as poems. Other critics have disagreed with this.

The poems covered many different subjects. In addition to those written after getting home, which were about his experience in the concentration camp, there were poems inspired by scientific literature (the image of 'black holes' was present in many of his works, including the article about Holocaust denial in *The Search for Roots* where he talked about the 'black hole of Auschwitz') and others featuring historical figures, animals, and plants.

After the 1970s, the autobiographical elements of Levi's poetry became less distinct; this was when he began to assume the mask of a historical figure, or of an animal or a vegetable. Rosato called this approach 'transcendental autobiography', whereby the mask allows the poet to transcend his anguish and actually express it. Greppi, on the other hand, claimed that the poems were forms of exorcism, 'the final and most recondite opportunity to consolidate a defence system' (1995). Rosato observed that, while in his prose Levi's images and subjects belonged to the semantic field of building activities and scientific endeavour (connecting, measuring, weighing, constructing, etc.), in his poems he used terms which alluded to impurity, organic material, and pathology. Fortini indicated Borges as one of the sources of Levi's poetry, owing to its 'demonstrative pace', and Pavese's *Lavorare Stanca* as another, because of its narrative development. Massimo Raffaelli (1998) pointed to the Carducci of *Barbarian Odes* as a source, as well as Quasimodo's Greek and Latin translations, and, of course, the poets Levi himself cited in his annotations to the Garzanti edition of *At an Uncertain Hour*.

As far as metrics were concerned, Raffaelli commented that 'the perfect coincidence of syntax and metrics, of a complete sentence and a hendecasyllable line, were typical of Levi's entire poetic production (1998). Levi often adopted the rhetorical figures of anaphora and chiasmus, expressing accumulation and repetition, which are also present in the Bible (Levi's cited whole lines of biblical verse in his poems). He also exploited the epigraphic element in order to give his poems an air of solemnity. Levi would always reject the role of prophet. He used to say he did not appreciate prophets either in society or in politics, and yet his poems were peppered with prophetic warnings and invectives, in addition to references to the Books of the Bible, as if he were writing according to a medieval canon.

Levi wrote an article on rhyme ('Rhyme on the Counterattack' in *Stories and Essays*), and another on the relationship between mankind and computers, in addition to two stories about the act of composing poetry and the various fantasies that surround poets ('The Versifier', in *Natural Histories*, and 'The Fugitive', in *Lilith and Other Stories*). His poems also played with language. One example of this was 'First Atlas', published in 1980 and included in the Garzanti edition of *Collected Poems*.

POETRY AND COMPUTERS

In January 1985, an interview with Levi was published in an IT magazine. Asked whether poetry was compatible with computers, Levi said personal computers had changed things for the better:

> The computer seems to me to be an excellent tool for clear and distinct tasks. Poetry isn't one of them: it is fluid, oblique, continuous, surrounded by halos and shadows. It is no accident that, while poems have been written for thousands of years, no definition has yet been formulated, no 'list of specifications' has been universally accepted. In short: poetry is compatible with the computer, but has little to gain from it and nothing to fear ('Can Poetry Get Along with the Computer?' in *Uncollected Stories and Essays*, p. 2694).

The photographer, Mario Monge, who went to Levi's house to take some portraits of him in June 1986, caught the author at his computer with the screen lit up. He was writing a poem, or at least he was posing as if he had been writing one. In the photograph, you can see Levi's silhouette, and the lines of an unpublished poem he had already written:

25/6/86

SOLDIER

My feet are encrusted in mud
My head and my heart empty,
My fingers cramping
on the loaded rifle.
I do not know this country,
This putrid air is my enemy
All around the night and enemies
Are flattened out in ditches.
If I see them I will shoot,
They will do the same.
We will never know why
We would never see each other in the face
In war every man is alone
But my mother is the moon . . .

The poem in the photograph stopped here, the continuation was probably on the next screen page.

Other People's Trades

The first piece in the book of articles and essays *Other People's Trades* was called 'My House', published in *Architect's Digest* (AD) in 1982. It was not a random choice, given that the story represented Levi's house in a metaphorical sense: the house of knowledge. The collection contained pieces on the topics and issues that most interested Levi, as a chemist and as an author, and most of all as a curious human being. The articles ranged from linguistics and poetry, to science and technology, touching on subjects as diverse as odours, lunar travel, children's games and insects. Levi wrote about anything that interested him, certainly since the 1970s, but even before that time. *Other People's Trades* is a book of Elseviers; at least, that is how his publisher classified the collection. In the author's file kept in the editors' office, where note was kept of all the books for which Levi was under contract with Einaudi, the title *Other People's Trades* was in brackets preceded by the word Elseviers. When the time came to sign the contract in December 1984, the title was written in capital letters. The book was, in fact, a collection of articles published mostly in *La Stampa* on a wide variety of subjects.

In Italian newspaper jargon, the word Elsevier indicates the leading article on the cultural page of, usually on the subjects of literature, art or history. Since the early nineteenth century, and even more so at the beginning of the twentieth, the cultural page was always the third page of the paper, whereas now it tends to be in the middle, either as a pull-out central page or a literary supplement. The name derives from the Dutch publishing house Elsevier that designed the distinct, elegant typeface used by printers for newspaper cultural pages. The leading

446

cultural article was not usually linked to news in the publishing or newspaper world. Rather, it would start with an idea and develop it into an essay which was supposed to be a blend of analysis and digression. Famous writers of Elseviers in Italian newspapers were Emilio Cecchi and the poet, Eugenio Montale.

The pieces Levi published between 1976 and 1984 in the Turin daily, where he had become a close collaborator, were Elseviers, and as such were printed in their rightful position: page three, left column, with a two or three-line title, separated from the text by small graphic symbols such as stars, for example. Nearly all the pieces selected by Levi to appear in the book that would be called *Other People's Trades* had appeared on the third page of *La Stampa* as Elseviers, the earliest being 'On Obscure Writing' (11 December 1976). The only exceptions were book reviews or reports, or when an article was prompted by an event in the news. 'The Irritable Chess Players', for example, bore a caption stating that the chess match was still underway. In this case, the article was published in a different position, lower down on the page.

When selecting which pieces to include in the collection, Levi left out the articles that did not have the features of an Elsevier: those that were linked to a specific event or topics that did not fit with the other pieces. In fact, there were not that many exclusions, as one can see in *Uncollected Stories and Essays*. It was almost as if Levi had written all his newspaper articles on a specific wave-length so that all the pieces published in *La Stampa* would fall within a pre-established band of oscillation between a more encyclopaedic and a more narrative style. Articles and essays on the topic of the Lager and deportation experience were excluded, as were those that discussed events in the Second World War or the extermination of the Jews. Nevertheless, these subjects were mentioned on the sidelines of some of the articles that were included, such as 'The Language of Odors', which dealt with the senses. One article, 'The Quiet Town of Auschwitz', was originally included in the typescript but Levi left it aside, and it was later included in *Stories and Essays*.

The result was that this collection of articles and essays was unique in Levi's whole Opus because it was entirely 'positive', with no dark areas or shadows. The only other book that was similarly 'positive' in character was *The Wrench*, which could be considered a twin to *Other People's Trades* owing to the features they have in common: curiosity, encyclopaedic knowledge, zoology, a cult for a well-executed job but also for a moral. In one of the few reviews written about this unusual book, Calvino wrote that Levi's articles were always 'based on observation.' *Other People's Trades* was the least reviewed and perhaps least read of Levi's works, at least in the decade after it came out, despite the fact that it dealt with contemporary culture, cutting-edge science and the complexity and crisis of classical rationality. From 1977 to 1981, Einaudi published a 14-volume encyclopaedia edited by Ruggiero Romano using key-words as its organizational principle. Scientists, philosophers, historians and epistemologists—many of whom were also Einaudi authors—took part in this cultural project, whose purpose was to take stock of the known world. Although Levi was not one of these, he would not have been immune to the climate of cultural regeneration taking place at the time. Einaudi's trademark con-mingling of literature and science, philosophy and technical knowledge aimed to create a gateway to cultural truth, among other things. A drawing that Levi made of the paths that readers should follow when dipping into his personal anthology *The Search for Roots*, which was published at the beginning of the book, was most likely modelled on the key-word principle of the Einaudi Encyclopaedia. There are clear links in terms of topics and interests, as well as authors, between this book of Elseviers and Levi's anthology. Together they form a map of current knowledge, almost a personal encyclopaedia.

The peculiarity of Levi's Elseviers lies in their privileged view point as well as their encyclopaedic nature. They never contain empty notions. While Cecchi's Elseviers were always highly visual, and Montale's were a diary of his ideas and reflections, Levi's, Calvino claimed, were spurred by micro-observations, which were always 'alert and detailed', and whose focus was the observation of detail. This was true to the extent that they were often presented as detective stories with a case to solve. Most writers of Elseviers believed that it was important to make some kind of moral point in their articles, but Levi transformed this idea of a moral into a practical suggestion or a specific attitude, owing in part to his scientific training. In his Elseviers, he tended to present himself as a chemist, and often made references to his profession, underlining the fact that he was anything but literary.

The collection opens with a Preface which is an explicit declaration of Levi's poetics, similar in tone to his Preface to *The Search for Roots*. Levi presented himself as someone who kept himself 'clear of crowds', who had always pursued his own 'isolated way' and was caught in a double bind: 'too much of a chemist, and a chemist for too long, ever to feel myself a genuine man of letters; too caught up in the landscape, parti-colored, tragic, or strange, to feel like a chemist in every fiber of my being' (p. 2012). With these words, he was certainly attempting to distance himself from his profession, but it was more of a statement of the fact that there were always three identities at work in his writing: witness, writer and chemist. In any case, in Levi's view, even though his path was 'serpentine', he continued to build for himself a 'a jumbled, gap-filled, know-it-all culture'—again a typical understatement.

Another significant element of the 'Premise', which was also true for his other works, was his attempt to be transversal, to 'explore the transverse bonds that knit together the worlds of nature and culture; I have frequently set foot on bridges that join (or ought to join) scientific culture with literary culture, crossing a crevasse that has always struck me as absurd.' The theme of two cultures, and the absurd demarcation line that separated scientific from humanistic culture, was a central issue in Levi's literary and scientific interests (Porro 2009). The title came from Levi's admission that his articles were incursions into other people's trades:

They are 'field invasions', incursions into other people's professions,[1] poaching in private hunting reserves, raids into the boundless territories of zoology, astronomy, and linguistics: sciences that I've never studied in any systematic manner, and which therefore cast upon me the enduring spell of an unrequited, unconsummated love, exciting my impulses to be a voyeur and a busy body.

THE HISTORY

Levi's 'Premise' was dated 16 January 1985. The same month, Levi handed in to Einaudi the manuscript. It was a bundle of photocopies and newspaper cuttings on which Levi had written and crossed out lines in pen. The first article in the collection was the emblematic choice of 'My House', which was a declaration of immobility—'I have always lived (with involuntary interruptions) in the house where I was born' (p. 2015)—at the same time as being an exercise in memory (the house as a memory-building technique) and a statement of his 'limpet-like nature'. 'My House' was written in 1982, but Levi decided to place it before a 1965 article on Aldous Huxley that was published in *Il Giorno*. In its turn, this article preceded another one written in 1980 and published in the journal *Noi Chimici* ('Ex Chemist'), and a 1964 piece on Rabelais, which was the oldest article in the collection, originally published in *Il Giorno*. Up to the 1976 article, 'On Obscure Writing', the order of the articles was not chronological in terms of when they were written. From that piece onwards, they were placed in the same order in which they were published, except for 'Fossil Words', published in January 1985, which was the last Elsevier to come out in *La Stampa* before 'The Eclipse of the Prophets' was published.

---

1 The translator here uses the word 'profession' to translate the Italian *mestiere*. perhaps unaware of the reference to the title, where the Italian *mestiere* was translated as 'trade'.

There are 19 articles with an autobiographical bent (the majority), although Levi does not necessarily dwell on the family's Jewish heritage. The city of Turin features in seven articles, especially memorable being 'Signs on Stone'. There are smatterings of science and technology throughout the articles, but 11 of them are devoted to a specific scientific or technological subject. Chemistry is less of a recurrent theme than in other books, and Levi dwells less than usual on the topic of labour. Eccentricity seems to be a prevalent factor in Levi's choice, giving the feeling that he is borrowing from 'other people's trades', such as zoology, ethology and entomology. There are 11 pieces on animals and 8 on games. The selection of literature covered is similarly eccentric, providing, together with the anthology *The Search for Roots*, a useful catalogue of the books Levi read.

Levi's increasingly intense collaboration with *La Stampa* in 1979, and his prolific production of Elseviers alternated with short stories for the newspaper, lead one to suppose that, after publishing his collected stories in *Lilith and Other Stories,* Levi was thinking of doing the same thing with his articles. From April 1978, in fact, Levi was writing one Elsevier a month.

Some of the autobiographical pieces, such as 'Guncotton Stockings', 'The Skull and the Orchid', 'My Grandfather's Shop' and 'A Long Duel', recall chapters in *The Periodic Table*. 'The Long Duel', a story from his adolescence, was first published in *La Stampa* in August 1984. Levi rewrote the piece for the collection in his typical fashion, adding passages to the original text while leaving the order of the narrative unchanged. He also added almost three pages to the story, including the slapping episode that did not figure in the newspaper version.

THE TYPESCRIPT

Levi delivered his bundle of photocopies annotated in pen, with the addition of a few pages typed directly onto the back of sheets of paper he had already used. The article 'The Scribe', on personal computers, was typed on a computer which he had just started using at that time. The article that was edited most heavily from newspaper to book was 'Congested Air'. Levi added a great number of lines, thus integrating the original piece with examples to illustrate his theory of language. He also made several changes to the text. Several other articles were also edited: 'About Obscure Writing' (where the reference to Pellico was added); 'Novels Dictated by Crickets' (where the example of Don Bartolo was included), 'The Leap of the Flea'; 'The Children's International' (with a new passage of nearly half a page on 'the cry of truce or time out' and another on the English translation of a counting game); 'The Force of Amber' (with its added reference to the boy who fell into the well, an event that was covered in the news); 'Ritual and Laughter', and finally 'The Eclipse of the Prophets' (where Levi added a citation from *If This Is a Man*). 'The Eclipse of the Prophets' was the only article in the whole collection that was published on the front page of *La Stampa*, and yet Levi placed it at the end of his collection. In 'Aldous Huxley', on the other hand, Levi cut a passage from the newspaper version. 'Thirty Hours Aboard the *Castoro 6*' was not the article that had come out in *La Stampa* under the title 'Captain Nemo's Guest'; it was, rather, based on a story that came out four years later called 'Men of Multiform Ingeniousness' in a book published by *Ecos*, a journal produced by Eni, the Italian energy conglomerate (Ecos Stories). Although the two pieces are on the same subject and have many elements in common, the piece included in *Other People's Trades* has a greater narrative thrust while the other is more journalistic. 'On Obscure Writing', published in *La Stampa* on 11 December 1976, triggered a polemical response from Giorgio Manganelli on 3 January in the Milan daily, *Corriere della Sera* (Manganelli 1994). Levi then answered Manganelli's sharp critique in a letter which was published in the Letters page, sparking an exchange that placed two differing worldviews and ideas about literature in opposition. Critics later commented on the fact that 'light and dark' were an essential binary opposition in Levi's work as a whole (Scarpa 1997).

The Book

The collection went to print in February 1985 in the series 'Gli Struzzi' (n. 292). The jacket design, depicting three identical owls in different shades of blue and grey, was credited as being 'by Primo Levi using an Apple Macintosh computer'. In the copy he signed and gave to Gina Lagorio, Levi wrote that the owl was his self-portrait. The dust-jacket blurb Levi almost certainly had a hand in, or approved, stated that the experience of the Nazi concentration camp was 'a distant and indefinite background against which different topics stand out'. The book is defined as 'a summation of the eccentric experiences and reflections of one of the least conformist of writers, and perhaps, beyond the author's intentions, a brief, but truthful autobiography'. The book won the Aquilieia Prize in 1985. Two editions came out between 1985 and 1987 for a total of 14,000 copies. In 1998, a further 22,000 copies were printed. This was the least successful of Levi's books in terms of sales.

LEMMAS

Encyclopaedias

The incredible range of Levi's interests (from chemistry, biology, and animal behaviour to philosophy and literature), in addition to his twin professions as chemist and writer, gave Levi an encyclopaedic nature. *The Search for Roots* was a testimony to his multifaceted knowledge, including readings from fields as far apart as religion (Book of Job), natural history (Darwin), anthropology (Marco Polo), technology (Vercel), poetry (Porta, Celan), linguistics (Belli), psychology of the individual and of society (Melville, Russell), adventure (Conrad, Melville), science (Thorne), among others. *Other People's Trades* was another showcase for his vast range of knowledge, revealing at the same time his fascination with observing the social and natural world at a micro level, and for collecting seemingly random objects and memories. And yet, Levi was not an encyclopaedist in the traditional sense, that is, he was not a proponent of 'circular knowledge'. Although he would appear to have been an heir to the inventive taxonomies of medieval encyclopaedias, and certainly cultivated a passion for technical details—like the tables in Diderot or D'Alembert's encyclopaedias—he was actually more of an 'encyclopaedist of fragments', as Calvino phrased it so well in his review of *The Search for Roots* in the daily *la Repubblica* ('Levi's Four Paths', 11 June 1981). In Calvino's view, referring both to Queneau and Levi, contemporary encyclopaedias could no longer rely on a universal framework or language embracing all branches of knowledge. In the contemporary world, no single system 'could hold up'. Rather than a circle of knowledge, there was 'a vortex of fragments'. Levi and Calvino shared an 'encyclopaedic obstinacy'—'a need to hold together, in a precarious equilibrium, all the heterogeneous and centrifugal acquisitions that constitute the entire treasure chest of our dubious knowledge'.

Levi's enlightened intelligence was motivated by curiosity rather than by reason. After Auschwitz, he was well aware of its limits and had experienced, first hand, its fallibility.

Computers

In September 1984, Levi bought a personal computer, or 'word processor' as he called it initially. A few months later, he published an article called 'Personal Golem' in *La Stampa* about his gadget (later renamed 'The Scribe' and collected in *Other People's Trades*. Levi's attitude towards the machine was not the typical reaction of the 'austere generation of humanists' (p. 2236); it was, rather, that of a scientist who worked habitually with machines and technical aides and was curious about the advantages his new Mac could offer. In the article, he hints at the possibility that a computer, like the Versifier in his short story, might write and correct texts of its own accord, which would mean losing 'the philologist's noble joy of painstakingly reconstructing, through a succession of erasures and corrections, the path that led Leopardi to the perfection of 'L'Infinito' (p. 2238). Levi discovered he could play chess on the computer—and wrote 'The Hidden Player' in October 1984 (*Stories and Essays*)—as well as draw. In fact, Levi designed the cover of *Other People's Trades* on his Mac. In 1985, he returned to the topic of computers in 'Can Poetry Get Along with Computers?' (*Uncollected Stories and Essays*), an article that attempted to answer the question that had been posed by an IT magazine, *Genius*, in an ironic reflection on the relationship between people and machines. In his 'Post Scriptum', Levi referred obliquely again to the invented machine of his story 'The Versifier': 'if I ever witness the birth of a machine for writing poetry that guarantees an output of reasonable quality and quantity and is not too expensive—I will buy one' (p. 2694). In his *Dialogue with Tullio Regge* (1984), Levi spoke a great deal about his early experiences with computers and about the negative attitude of the liberal arts towards the technical world.

Food Preservation

On 14 January 1981 Levi gave a conference on the subject of food pres-
ervation at the Turin Open University, introduced by old friend Silvio Ortona.
Levi had retired from his job as a chemist and devoted himself full-time to
writing. He was in the process of writing *If Not Now, When?*, a book which
was to do a great deal to establish his reputation as a writer, and yet he
accepted the invitation to speak to a group of mature students on a subject
he had been interested in many years before. In the 1970s, in fact, the
historian, Ruggiero Romano, had commissioned Levi to write a chapter in
a children's encyclopaedia published by Fabbri in Milan. The chapter was
to be on Baron Justus von Liebig, the inventor of stock cubes made from
meat extract.

Ian Thomson summarized Levi's lecture in his biography (Levi 2003).
Preceded by a concert of classical music, the lecture was recorded on
tape, and while not complete and of poor quality, it is still possible to hear
it today. Levi's voice is firm, his tone is steady and his arguments are clearly
laid out. When Levi spoke in public, he was always precise and coherent.
The fact that Levi stopped every now and then makes one think there was
a typed script, or written notes of some kind, that he was consulting.
Although retired, it was definitely Levi the chemist speaking, with his habit
of observing things from a distance, and attempting to classify what he
saw according to unexpected parameters. He also revealed his interest in
anthropology, as he did when he described the black market in operation
at Auschwitz, the price and commercial value of the scarce resources in
the hands of the prisoners in 'This Side of Good and Evil' (*If This Is a Man*).
Moreover, he called upon his talent as a linguist, as a historian of objects,
and as a sociologist of everyday life, that was revealed in so many articles
collected in *Other People's Trades*. For Levi, classifying meant thinking,
attempting to create order, however temporary or contingent, in the chaos
of the world.

Levi's lecture was typical. He pointed out that not only humans had a
problem with preserving food—animals did too. In order to preserve, he
explained, you need somewhere to stockpile your food. A prime example

of natural food preservers were bees, among his favourite animals. Bees had invented honey, a long-lasting foodstuff with no water in it. Levi outlined four different systems for preserving food that humans had discovered over the course of their history: drying, smoking, salting and freezing. He examined each of these systems, showing his usual propensity to analyse both structures and their internal articulations, or the relationship between the different parts of a system. Levi showed how the four systems were interlinked, and how they were all present in the natural world. Techniques developed by humans were simply particular cases—often highly ingenious—of methods that already existed. This idea, that nature was the source of everything, from matter to thinking, was a cornerstone of Levi's implicit epistemology. One of his most important methodologies was observation of real life. At one point in the lecture, when he was talking about smoking food, he commented that 'humanity has been poisoned by theories for many centuries' and that these theories were like a screen between the observer and the phenomena being observed. Our ancestors, who were hunters, were not encumbered by these theories, Levi pointed out, stressing the need for practical applications, but also for 'just reason'.

His presentation of Baron von Liebig was a case in point. A grocer's son, he fell in love with chemistry at a young age, inventing practical systems, many of which were still in use. However, as Levi pointed out with regret mixed with pride, chemistry was increasingly in the hands of machines. Levi's tendency to pay attention to detail has theoretical consequences, incarnated by the figure of von Liebig who invented a tool to refrigerate liquids in the laboratory. And yet, the Baron was famous not so much for his chemical breakthroughs, as for a food product: stock cubes derived from meat extract. The fact that in most Italians' minds stock cubes brought to mind the stickers used to advertise them, Levi commented, was an example of a product and its marketing being discovered at the same time. The Baron was called in by industrialists to find a way to preserve food as a military imperative. The Liebig extract was the immediate result of the existence of huge armies, navies and other military units, that needed great quantities of meat for long periods of time. It was by no means a product of peace. The meat broth was not very nutritious. Levi's intellectual irony and scepticism was at work in this lecture when he commented on food that was considered to be healthy because it was marketed as being healthy. He went on to list the common misperceptions in chemistry, such as the fact that phosphorus helped your intelligence, or that cholesterol was triggered by the food you ate rather than by the human body.

Just as he dismantled the arguments supporting racism or racial prejudice, Levi demolished contemporary food myths, and offered a small catalogue of negative and positive prejudices, both old and new. 'There is only one truth,' he pointed out, 'and it cannot be changed every five years.' Levi finished his lecture by asking his mature students some questions about their food habits.

Italo Calvino

> We don't choose our relatives but we do choose our friends and travelling companions. I was bound to Italo Calvino by a subtle yet deep tie. We were almost the same age, and, having both emerged from the defining experience of the resistance, were first recognized as writers at the same time, in the same (for us memorable) review by Arrigo Cajumi, in these columns, which paired his *Path to the Spider's Nest* with my *If This Is a Man*. We were both naturally shy, and never spoke at length: it wasn't necessary. A hint, a brief reference to our respective 'works in progress,' and the understanding was immediate (p. 2701).

Levi wrote this in his article, 'With the Key of Science', published in *La Stampa* the day after Calvino's death. Calvino was very important for Levi, not only as a fellow writer, but also as an intellectual foil. Calvino reviewed Levi's first book for the left-wing daily *l'Unità* (6 May 1948) and was probably the person to write the dust-jacket blurb for the 1958 Einaudi edition of *If This Is a Man*. From then on, Levi submitted all of his writing to Calvino for comments.

In 1961, Calvino read the short stories that were to form the collection *Natural Histories*. He immediately realized that there was something intellectually and stylistically new in Levi's work, describing it as 'science fiction, or rather biological fiction' (p. 2837), and adding that 'they assume a common culture notably different from the one assumed by so much of Italian literature' (p. 2838). In 1963, it was again Calvino, together with other editors at Einaudi, who decided to publish *The Truce* in a fiction series, and to write the jacket blurb where he recognized the epic and picaresque elements of the book, although he didn't sign it.

In Levi's obituary of Calvino, he stated that 'to me he was like a brother, more than that, like an older brother, although he was four years younger' (p. 2702). He did not state however the extent to which Calvino was indebted to Levi, in particular with regard to his short-story collection, *Cosmicomics*. One could well call them 'biological fictions' like Levi's *Natural Histories* which Calvino read before writing his own. In the letter Calvino wrote to Levi in 1961, he commented on his 'fantasy mechanism, which takes off from a scientific-genetic starting point' which 'has a power of suggestion that's intellectual but also poetic' (p. 2837). This mechanism could well be said to apply to Calvino's *Cosmicomics.*

In an interview, published in 1968 in Croatian, Levi acknowledged that Calvino may have been inspired by his story 'The Sixth Day' (Machiedo 1968). In 1970, Levi dedicated the short story, 'His Own Maker'—a sort of Cosmicomic—to Calvino. The two writers borrowed constantly from each other. Cesare Cases pointed out an echo of Calvino's 1957 novel *The Baron in the Trees* at the end of 'Carbon', the final chapter in *The Periodic Table*, while Pier Vincenzo Mengaldo linked a passage from Chapter 5 of *The Watcher* to the end of *The Truce* (both books came out in 1963). In Levi's story, 'The Park' (*Flaw of Form*), which featured Pin among the figures made famous by their authors, there was a deliberate reference to Calvino's work. Similarly, in the story, 'Brief Dream' (*Lilith and Other Stories*) Levi appeared to have drawn on a short story by Calvino that featured trains ('The Adventure of a Soldier'). In 1974, Calvino, who had moved to Paris, gave the go-ahead for publication of *The Periodic Table*. He suggested organizing the chapters differently in a letter dated October 1974, and three years later wrote the unsigned jacket blurb for *The Wrench*.

An important moment in their relationship was when they revised Sergio Solmi's translation of Queneau's *A Pocket Cosmogony* together. Calvino mentioned their collaboration twice in his introduction to the 1982 Einaudi edition of the book entitled *A Little Guide to the Little Cosmogony*, while Levi recalled it in his 1985 article dedicated to Calvino, as well as in a presentation of another translation of Queneau's work in 1986 ('Calvino, Queneau, and the Sciences' in *Uncollected Stories and Essays*). In the 1980s, in two separate reviews—*The Search for Roots* (1981) and *Other People's Trades* (1985)—Calvino focused on Levi's encyclopaedic approach, commenting on his curiosity and his tendency to investigate words and things. Calvino was the first critic to spot Levi's passion both for animal behaviour and for language, going as far as describing his work as 'zoological glottology' or 'an ethology of language'. A further crossover from that time was an article Calvino wrote about why people write (published in *la Repubblica*, 31 March–1 April 1985), where he cited a piece by Levi on the same subject ('Why Do We Write?' in *Other People's Trades*).

In 1985, Calvino asked Levi to help him translate a poem by Queneau, *The Song of Styrene*, which was one of the last things he worked on before dying in September that year. In Levi's obituary, he commented: 'We had other ties as well. With two scientists for parents, Italo, alone in the Italian environment, had an appetite for science' (p. 2703), going on to confess that 'we discussed and shared vague and ambitious projects for a mediating and revealing literature, straddling the 'two cultures', sharing in both' (p. 2703). Levi and Calvino were tied by their appetite for science, but they also had their differences. As Porro (1997) pointed out, while Levi relied predominantly on 'the science of matter', Calvino acknowledged 'knowledge of form'. The author of *Time and the Hunter* was influenced by the structuralists, enjoying narrative games, game theory and Leibnitz. Levi, on the other hand, preferred mixing elements into hybrids. The difference between these two views of science could be summed up by the opposition between hands and eyes; between Calvino's gaze from a distance (Belpoliti 1996) and Levi's direct action using the tools of his two trades (Valabrega 1997). Moreover, Levi's naturalism, compared to Calvino's, was within the realm of a humanist world view, as one can see in many of the articles published in *Other People's Trades*.

Another interesting parallel between the two writers was their relationship with animals (see Calvino's piece, 'The Goats Are Watching Us', published in 1946 in *l'Unita*). They are both materialists, in the pre-Socratic sense of the term. While Levi's formation was in the nineteenth-century scientific tradition (Levi read both Darwin and Lombroso in his youth), Calvino was more influenced by the Enlightenment, with its eighteenth-century empirical materialism. Calvino's vision did not place humans at the centre of his universe, while Levi, who was more practical, believed in his profession as a chemist, and considered humans to be central. To be human was for him a vital criterion for judging reality, as he declared in the title of his first book (*If This Is a Man?*).

Finally, memory was also an important topic for both writers. For Levi, it was an essential part of his thinking, in particular in *The Drowned and the Saved* (1986). In the last years of his life, Calvino was planning an autobiography, where the theme of memory played an essential role. He never completed the project, and the autobiography was published posthumously.

Aldous Huxley

One of the first articles that Levi wrote in 1965 in *Il Giorno* was about the British writer, Aldous Huxley ('Aldous Huxley' in *Other People's Trades*) whose work Levi read and reread. One of his favourites, together with *Brave New World*, was *Point Counter Point*. Levi appreciated Huxley the novelist rather than Huxley the pacifist, mystic, sociologist or historian of religions. He was particularly interested in the dystopia Huxley presented in *Brave New World* and he summarized the plot in this article. Levi often quoted Huxley when stating that novelists should be zoologists.

Paul Celan

In an article published in *La Stampa* in December 1976, later included with the name 'About Obscure Writing' in *Other People's Trades*, Levi cited his contemporary Paul Celan, 'a German Jew who miraculously survived the German slaughter' (p. 2065), who later committed suicide in Paris, as did Trakl, another indecipherable German-speaking poet. Their poetry was a perfect example of obscurity, in Levi's view: 'their shared fate leads us to think of the obscurity of their poetics as a sort of pre-suicide, a will-not-to-exist, a flight from the world, ultimately crowned by a yearned-for death' (p. 2064). Celan's obscurity, in particular, was 'truly a reflection of the obscurity of his own and his generation's fate. [. . .] It sucks us in, in the same way that a whirlpool does, but at the same time it defrauds us of something that ought to have been said but wasn't, and therefore it frustrates us and keeps us distant (p. 2064). Levi's assessment of Celan's poetry was trenchant:

> it is not a communication, it is not a language, or at most it's a dark and truncated language, the language, in fact, of someone about to die, and alone, as we are all alone at the point of death. But because we are not alone when we are alive, we should not write as if we were. We have a responsibility, as long as we are alive: we must answer for what we write, word for word, and ensure that every word hits its target (p. 2065).

However, five years later, while Levi was gathering material to include in *The Search for Roots*, he decided to anthologize Celan's 'Fugue of Death' in a recent Italian translation. Levi claimed he had succeeded in penetrating the meaning of very few of his poems, but 'Fugue of Death'—which Celan himself repudiated—was an exception which he carried within himself like a graft. The poem, with its reference to 'the Black milk of morning' and its description of the contrast between Germany, his fatherland, and Margareta's 'golden hair', might well have been written by Levi.

Turin

The first piece in *Other People's Trades* is called simply 'My House'. It opens with these lines:

> I have always lived (with involuntary interruptions) in the house where I was born: the way I live was not, therefore, the result of a choice. I believe that I exemplify an extreme case of sedentary life, comparable to that of some mollusks, such as limpets. After a brief larval stage, in which they swim freely, limpets fasten on to wave-pounded rocks, secrete a shell, and then never move again for the rest of their lives (p. 2015).

Levi's rock was his apartment on Corso Re Umberto, or more in general the city of Turin, specifically the centre of Turin that Levi described in several different pieces (in *Other People's Trades* alone, 'Signs on Stone' and 'My Grandfather's Shop') that recreated the sounds and objects of his youth. Levi had a preference for pre-war Turin, the city he remembered from his adolescence before it was dramatically brought to an end by his deportation. He described the ancient city, before the streets were widened under Fascism, where his grandfather and ancestors lived and plied their trades, as well as the Turin University science faculty and chemistry lab after the war in *The Periodic Table*. In *The Wrench*, Faussone told stories of episodes that took place in Turin, and described the apartment of his two aunts. In addition, Levi talked about his city, its customs, its dialect (Piedmontese rather than Torinese), and the problems created by immigration from the south of Italy in the 1960s, in many interviews.

In an interview with Giovanni Tesio (1989), Levi talked about the two views he had of Turin: the first while he was being transported to the Fòssoli transit camp; the second on his return from Auschwitz—almost as if the terrible experience in the Lager had been an intermission between the two cityscapes. The view of Turin as he was leaving was of February sunset, a dark sky behind the imposing Mole Antonelliana. When he returned to his hometown, it was morning. He arrived at Porta Nuova, and found the place damaged by bombs and by the insurrection. When Tesio asked him what parts of the city he was most attached to, Levi answered that they all featured in his books: the area around his apartment, his high school, his faculty, the Valentino Castle, via Po, the old via Roma, and the road from Turin to Settimo and back that he took for 20 years to go to work at the SIVA varnish factory. In *If This Is a Man*, Levi's homesickness for his city-centre apartment is tangible.

Clarity/Obscurity

In the 1970s, several intellectuals—Franco Fortini, Natalia Ginzburg and Goffredo Parise, among others—participated in an ongoing debate in the Italian dailies about writing clearly so that readers can understand. Levi contributed with an article, which was almost a treatise on literary ethics, published in *La Stampa* in December 1976, and later included with the title 'About Obscure Writing' in *Other People's Trades*. Levi stated that 'perfectly clear writing' could not exist because it

> demands perfectly knowledgeable and completely mindful writer, and that does not correspond to reality. We are all made up of ego and id [. . .] And so we are condemned to drag along with us, from cradle to grave, doppelgänger, a mute and faceless brother, who is nonetheless partly responsible for our actions, and therefore for our pages, too (p. 2062).

Levi questioned the claim that 'the only authentic form of writing is that which 'comes from the heart,' (p. 2062) claiming that 'the purpose of writing is to communicate, to transmit information or feelings from mind to mind, from place to place, and from time to time. Someone who is understood by no one transmits nothing, is only a voice crying in the wilderness' (p. 2062). Levi cited other obscure writers, including Ezra Pound, and the poets, Georg Trakl and Paul Celan. In his view, shouting, crying inarticulately or moaning belong to the animal world or to the world of incommunicability.

Communicating clearly was an ideal that Levi pursued in his books and articles, focusing in particular on the importance of clarity in this article. As a counterpoint to clarity in writing, there was, of course the subject matter of the books Levi wrote about his experience in Auschwitz. This implied digging into the obscure recesses of the human spirit in a quest to explain the behaviour not only of the people who planned and built concentration camps but also of those who actively collaborated in running them. Obscurity was what Levi made it his mission to deal with, abstaining all the while from moral judgement, in *The Drowned and the Saved*, and especially in 'The Gray Zone'. The opposition between clarity and obscurity was the lodestar that guided Levi on his intellectual and personal path—a path which finally led him to commit suicide. Domenico Scarpa (1997) traced Levi's complex position regarding this conflict through the readings he suggested and included in *The Search for Roots*. There was an asymmetric symmetry between the two sides of Levi's personality—the clear and the obscure—and the two sides did not always fit together well.

Uncollected Stories and Essays

HISTORY OF THE BOOK

In 1986, Editrice La Stampa, the newspaper's publishing wing, asked Levi if they could collect some of the articles and short stories that they had already published into a book in order to distribute it with the newspaper. The collection stayed under this imprint for several years. Today, many of these short stories can be found in the posthumous collection *Last Christmas of the War* (2000), and most of the articles in *The Complete Works* or in *Asymmetry and Life* (2002).

Levi wrote a Preface, as he did for *Other People's Trades*, where he stressed that his 'pieces' spanning 25 years 'reflect an intrinsic libertinism'. He begged the reader 'not to go looking for messages', because he distrusted 'the type of human being' who claimed to be 'the prophet, the oracle, the seer.' He insisted that he was, by contrast, 'an ordinary man with a good memory who fell into a vortex, who came out of it more by good fortune than by virtue, and who since that time has had a certain curiosity about vortexes, large and small, metaphoric and material' (p. 2261).

Curiosity is the abiding feature of all of these pieces, written over a quarter of a century of 'almost absolute fidelity to *La Stampa* starting in 1960 (p. 2261). Levi sent 'The Commander of Auschwitz' to the newspaper, which decided to publish the piece, as editorial notes from the time show, even though he did not become an established contributor until 1975. Another piece that was written in the 1960s was 'Apollo 8' (1968).

Levi divided the collection into two sections, giving the title to the book. In the first section, the fantasy and memory stories are collected in chronological order of publication in the newspaper. Many of these could easily have been included in the first section of *Lilith and Other Stories*, since they were additional tiles of the Lager mosaic. However, unlike the earlier stories, these were set outside the concentration camp, or were triggered by memories after the events, so that their reflective component is stronger than their narrative force. They included 'The Quiet Town of Auschwitz', 'A "Mystery" in the Lager', 'The Machine Gun Under the Bed' and 'A Wartime Pipette', which was perhaps the closest to being a short story of them all. The tone of the two stories, 'The Mirror Maker' and 'The Man Who Squeezed Through Walls' was more similar to the tradition of mysterious, persuasive stories of the Orient, less technological or 'biological fiction' (as Calvino called it) than the stories in the first two collections.

The articles in the second section covered a wide range of subjects and tone. At least half of them were pieces that Levi did not include in *Other People's Trades*, partly because of their heterogenous and bizarre nature. Others were mostly Elseviers, especially the ones after 'A Bottle of Sunshine'. Five of the pieces were originally published in a Sunday column called 'Seven Days', which was printed on page five of the newspaper from around 1977. These articles were usually short pieces written by famous collaborators of the paper such as Sciascia, Consolo and Ceronetti, as well as Levi himself. This was an attempt to give new energy to the Elsevier format by linking the content more closely to events in the news. Levi's rubric was called 'Customs', alternating short apologues and opinion pieces. Some of these ended up in *Other People's Trades* and *Lilith and Other Stories*, but most were finally collected in this book.

THE BOOK

Uncollected Stories and Essays was published in the series 'Page Three' that collected pieces written by influential collaborators of *La Stampa*.

There were three editions: the first in November 1986, with 5,000 copies; the second with 8,000 copies. The book, illustrated with 10 drawings by Emanuele Luzzati, was distributed together with the newspaper and was not for sale on the open market. Levi wanted to call it *The Mirror Maker*, which was then taken up in the English translation. The book of *Uncollected Stories and Essays* also contained two poems that had not been included in *At an Uncertain Hour*: 'To My Friends', first published on 31 December 1985, and 'The Thaw', dated 3 April 1985. In addition, Levi re-introduced five short stories taken from *Lilith and Other Stories* ('Disphylaxis', 'Bridge Builders', 'The Molecule's Defiance', 'In Due Time' and 'The Soul and the Engineers').

A third edition, that came out in May 1997, included the poem 'A Valley', which had been originally published in *La Stampa* on 10 February 1985, as well as 'Five Natural Interviews': 'The Mole' (17 November 1986); 'Escherichia Coli' (17 November 1986); 'The Seagull' (14 January 1987); 'The Giraffe' (1 February 1987); and 'The Spider' (26 February 1987). These had all appeared in *Airone* between November 1986 and May 1987.

LEMMAS

Editor and Translator

As well as being one of their most important authors, Levi collaborated with Einaudi as a translator and editor. He started consulting for their science series, directed by Paolo Boringhieri, in June 1952. His contract stipulated that he would work exclusively for the Turin publisher, translating, revising, proofreading, advising and editing the publisher's newsletter (*Notiziario Einaudi*). The salary was to be paid monthly as an advance on his royalties.

In the following years, Levi revised Schmidt and Marties' *Principle of High-Polymer Theory and Practice*, together with a treatise on the bio-chemical and public-health aspects of food by Giulio Buogo, which was supposed to come out in the series 'Piccola Biblioteca Scientifico-Lettarario' but which was never published. He took part in some of the summer residential meetings in Rhêmes, a town in the mountain area of Aosta, where Einaudi consultants and authors brainstormed ideas and projects. From 1963 until his death, he received reading copies of books from Einaudi so that he could form an opinion on their suitability for pub-lication. To start with, these were mostly books about the Lagers, but after 1980 he was also involved in decisions regarding books on industrial-labour relations, and, more in general, non-fiction. He was rarely consulted regarding fiction submissions. Levi tried in vain to persuade Einaudi to translate and publish two books that he was particularly keen on: Eugen Kogon's 1946 *Der SS-Staat* (*The SS State: The System of German Concen-tration Camps*), and, more importantly, Hermann Langbein's *People in Auschwitz*, which had come out in Germany in 1972.

Ultimately, however, he was not involved in many publishing decisions. The Einaudi archives, which contain his letters to the publishers and his index cards, document a total of 11. The first was in 1966, with a letter written to Ponchirol. In the 1970s, he was asked for an opinion on Annie Lauran's 1975 collection of oral witness statements made by concentration- camp survivors (*Le casquette d'Hitler ou le temps de l'oubli*), which he suggested rejecting. In 1980 he was consulted on two books: Martin Gilbert's *A History of the Holocaust*, and a manuscript submitted by Paolo Barbaro, a history of labour that Einaudi perhaps thought had some affinity with *The Wrench*. For both, Levi's verdict was negative. Two books were sent to Levi for an opinion in 1983 and 1985 respectively, both about the holocaust. The first was a collection of papers from a 1982 conference published by Gallimard le Seuil (*L'Allemagne Nazie et le genocide Juif*); the second, a book by Yves Béon, who survived the Lager where V2 bombs were built (*Planet Dora*, 1985). The archives contain detailed reports from Levi on the contents and context of both. In 1983, he received a manuscript about the adventures of an engineer, but did not recommend publishing it. In the same year, Levi proposed Margaret Buber-Neumann's 1949 book, *Under Two Dictators: Prisoner Under Hitler and Stalin*, which Einaudi rejected and which was later picked up by the Bologna publisher, Il Mulino. He also rejected Margarete Glass Larsson's *I Want to Speak: The Tragedy and Banality of Survival in Terezin and Auschwitz*.

Levi's most interesting report was on a book of scientific essays written by one of the great twentieth-century authors—who had trained as an engineer—Carlo Emilio Gadda. Levi critiqued them as 'prolix, diligent, but flat and didactic, boring'. Especially the essay on lignite, he commented, 'feels like it's plagiarized, and written on commission'. Levi insisted that the essays held little technical interest, and that some of them were not Gadda's original contributions as the writing was not typical of Gadda's style. He admitted, however, that they might contribute to updating the economic history of the country. Levi's report was well written, sharp, and, at times appeared to jokingly imitate Gadda. He criticized some of Gadda's technical conclusions, and questioned his claim that an engine can be run on ammonium. His recommendation was not to publish, hypothesizing very few readers. This showed that Levi paid some interest to sales figures as well as to the value of the book in its own right.

In the last years of his life, Giulio Einaudi and his colleagues tried to persuade Levi to participate more fully in the life of the publishing house.

He offered Levi an office in via Biancamano, round the corner from his home in Corso Re Umberto. This proximity explains why the correspondence between Levi and Einaudi, unlike that of many other authors, was so limited. In 1987, shortly before Levi's death, Einaudi had started re-publishing all of Levi's works in the series 'Biblioteca dell'Orsa' edited by Paolo Fossati and Giulio Bollati, with Levi's collaboration. In view of this, Levi started to work on a biographical profile, or chronology, which he never finished. The three volumes of the collected works came out in 1987 (*Autobiographical Works*), 1988 (*Novels and Poems*), and 1990 (*Uncollected Stories and Essays*), with prefaces by Cesare Cases, Cesare Segre and Pier Vincenzo Mangaldo respectively.

In 1997, on the 10th anniversary of his death, Einaudi, on the basis of a proposal by Ernesto Ferrero and Paolo Fossati, launched the two-volume edition of the *Opere Complete*, edited by Marco Belpoliti, with an Introduction by Daniele Del Guidice. The *Complete Works* included for the first time 480 pages of previously unpublished material shared between the two volumes (*Pagine Sparse I and II*), together with notes on the texts describing the development of each work. The works were arranged chronologically for the first time. In the same year, *Primo Levi: Conversazioni e interviste*, a book containing a selection of interviews, edited by Marco Belpoliti, was published, as well as *Primo Levi: Un' Antologia della Critica*, edited by Ernesto Ferrero, containing previously published essays on Levi's life and work.

The most challenging translation Levi completed was Henry Gilman's *Organic Chemistry*, in collaboration with Giorgio Anglesio. This was a four-volume manual totalling 3,652 pages, which were translated into Italian between 1951 and 1959. Three volumes were published by the newly established house, Boringhieri, in 1956, 1957 and 1960. Levi did not work on any translations between 1960 and 1975, as he was probably kept busy by his day job as a chemist and by his evening and weekend activity of writing. It was only when he retired from the Silva factory that he started translating again, accepting proposals from Einaudi, and presenting proposals to Adelphi, where Luciano Foà (who had been secretary-general at Einaudi when *If This Is a Man* was published) was now working.

In August 1975, Levi wrote to Foà: 'I have recently been detaching myself from my activity as a chemistry, and I now have more free time. I'm planning to devote only a part of it to creative writing; for the rest, I'd like to dedicate myself to something interesting to translate.' In the same letter, Levi proposed translating Jacques Presser's *The Night of the Girondists*. The proposal was accepted and Levi's translation, alongside a preface and chronology, was published in May 1976. He translated some of Heine's poems from the Book of Songs that same year in *Tuttolibri*, which were later included in his 1984 collection *At an Uncertain Hour*. In 1975, again, Levi translated Mary Douglas' book *Natural Symbols*, which was published in the 'Piccola Biblioteca Einaudi' series in 1979. The book must have interested Levi in its own right, as it focused on the relationship between societal codes and individual behaviour. In 1981, Levi's personal anthology, *The Search for Roots*, was published. The anthology featured several of his own translations: Joseph Henry Rosny's *The Quest for Fire*, a text from the manual of organic chemistry, a piece translated from the by Ludwig Gattermann, another from the English, a passage from *People in Auschwitz*, and a 'translation' from the Roman dialect of the poet Belli.

In 1982, after *If Not Now, When?* was published, Levi was asked by Giulio Einaudi to translate Kafka's *The Trial* for the new series 'Writers translated by other writers'. The job was extremely challenging, not only linguistically but also psychologically, as he confessed in an interview and in 'Translating Kafka'. In his translator's note, Levi explained why he had chosen a middle course between Alberto Spaini's 1933 interpretative translation and Giorgio Zampa's 1973 parallel text translation: 'I made a determined effort to balance faithfulness to the text with the flow of expression.' The other choices Levi made in his translation have been analysed by Sandra Bosco Coletsos in a 1985 article ('La Traduzione di Der Prozess di Franz Kafka'), who considered Levi's version 'softer' than the original. Between 1983 and 1984, Levi translated two books by Claude Lévi-Strauss with his sister, who did not sign her work. *The Way of the Masks* and *A View from Afar* were published by Einaudi in 1985 and 1984, respectively.

Levi reflected on the art of translating, and on his reactions to his works being translated, in a piece that came out in *La Stampa* entitled

'Translating and Being Translated' (*Other People's Trades*). He concluded that when a translator 'manages to find, or even invent, the solution to a problem, he feels "like a god", without, however, having to bear the burden of responsibility that weighs on the author's back [. . .] the joys and labours of translating are to those of creative writing as those of grandparents are to those of parents' (p. 2123). He made a similar claim in his 1975 letter to Luciano Foà, where he said he would divide his time between creative writing and translating. Nonetheless, Levi was convinced that translating required creativity, which he amply demonstrated in his translation of *The Trial*.

Artist

Visiting Levi in Turin for an interview, Philip Roth describes the 'playful constructions skilfully twisted into shape by Levi himself out of insulated copper wire' (*London Review of Books*, 23 October 1986). Levi tells Roth that the wire is 'coated with the varnish developed for that purpose in his own laboratory' at the SIVA chemical factory, where he worked until a decade earlier.

> There is a big wire butterfly, a wire owl, a tiny wire bug and, high on the wall behind the desk, are two of the largest constructions: one the wire figure of a bird-warrior armed with a knitting needle,' Roth continues. When he couldn't work out what this figure represented, he asked Levi if 'the man playing his nose' was a Jew. 'Yes, yes,' he said, laughing, 'a Jew, of course.'

Today (until January, 2020), these handmade animals and funny characters created from Levi's imagination are in the *Wunderkammer* of the Galleria d'Arte Moderna (GAM) in Turin in an exhibition entitled *Figura*, curated by Guido Vaglio and Fabio Levi and designed by Gianfranco Cavaglià. It is truly a 'chamber of wonders', because those who know nothing of Levi's passion will be surprised to see the owl and the butterfly Roth saw in Levi's apartment, as well as a spider, shark, turtle, seagull, kangaroo, hedgehog, basilisk and centaur, and other human figures. Some animals are missing from the exhibition, given that Levi gave many of his creations away to friends and relatives. The figures are a testament to Levi's activity as a bricoleur—a word made famous by Claude Lévi-Strauss, two of whose books Levi translated. A bricoleur, or 'handyman' is someone who reuses whatever scrap materials are at hand, adapting their project to the characteristics of the material available, or giving objects or materials a new function. In a way, Levi was a bricoleur all his life. He reused the experience of the Lager—an experience he certainly did not seek out—to become a writer, an ambition he had before he was deported. He also constantly reworked his knowledge as a chemist, and other life experiences, into his books.

Rereading his work today, now that his literary qualities are recognized over and above his role as a witness bearer, and now that we know that it was the Lager experience that turned him into a writer, it becomes clear that he used both his head and his hands, just as he did when he constructed his animals and characters. The copper-wire figures, in fact, resemble his biological fantasy stories, being both invented and real, visionary and real. Roth offers a key to interpreting these figures, which are reminiscent in some ways of Jean Dubuffet's 'art brut', and in others of childhood games, when he writes, 'Of all the intellectually-gifted artists of this century—and Levi's uniqueness is that he is even more the artist-chemist than the chemist-writer—he may well be the most thoroughly adapted to the totality of the life around him' (*London Review of Books*, 23 October 1986)

The animal figures provide us with an insight into who this twentieth-century Jewish chemist-artist from Turin, whose first book was an account of his experience as a prisoner in a Nazi extermination camp, was. He was an artist, not in the modern sense of the term, but in the classical one: a craftsman, a 'handyman', a man who considered adaptability one of the most important features of his life and work. At the same time, as Roth writes, he was an intellectual—a word which is in disuse today. The concept is closely linked to the child-like passion we can glimpse in his copper-wire models. In fact, his curiosity was insatiable: he was interested in everything, eager to experience everything, endowed with a sense of wonder that, as his cousin Stefano Levi Della Torre once said, was revealed in his smile. A further key to his complex personality may lie in his passion for games, an important aspect of the writer that has not yet been fully explored, with the exception of an essay by Stefano Bartezzaghi dedicated to the writer-game player. The constructions exhibited in the GAM *Wunderkammer*, most of which were created between 1955 and 1975, are tangible evidence of this passion. Levi loved word games above all, but he was also an amateur linguist, enjoyed children's games and pursued strange and bizarre subjects to write about.

In the central display case of the exhibition, there are some sheets taken from his notebooks, which show Levi's experimentation with shapes and numbers. Levi's fascination for form is one feature that combines various elements of his passion for games and bricolage: mathematical formulas, computer drawings, three-dimensional solids, soap bubbles and minimal surfaces. His copper-wire constructions, housed under Cavaglià's white pinnacles, are a perfect expression of his interest in form. Primo Levi is truly polyhedric: there are more faces in the shade—still to be explored—than those that have already been illuminated.

PORTRAIT OF A RETIRED CHEMIST (c.1986)

Levi is back in the chemistry lab, wearing a work apron. He retired years ago, but he has decided to pose for the photographer, Bernard Gotfryd, in his old lab. His gaze is intense, but sad. He looks tired. His right hand is resting on his left wrist—the same pose he had struck in other photos taken in the lab—and he is leaning with his left elbow on the counter. The picture was taken in 1985 or 1986; the frames of his spectacles were the same as the ones in the Mario Monge photographs. He has visibly aged. In previous photos there was always the same stubborn energy that transpired from his writing, blended with the wisdom and thought-fulness that often appeared to restrain the force of his personality. For at least a decade, Levi has been fighting bouts of depression. Has age finally caught up with him, even though he was never really youthful. In 1982, an interviewer for *Stampa Sera* asked him outright: 'You are retiring at 60, and with retirement comes all that empty time. Is useless-ness really a synonym of age?' Levi answered: 'Me? Old? In absolute, I suppose I am. My date of birth, short-sightedness, grey hair, grown-up children, all point to the fact.' The week before, he quipped, someone had even stood up for him on the tram. And yet, he insisted, he didn't feel old. He hadn't lost his curiosity for the world around him, his interest in people or his taste for competition, games or solving enigmas. Calvino once commented that he had leapt from youth directly to old age, bypassing the phase of adulthood. One could not say the same for Levi. There was always a child lurking behind the semblance of a middle-class adult. As he stated in the interview, he likes competing, playing games and solving enigmas. He still loves nature, the same nature he observed and described in his earliest childhood and adolescent experiments in the written word. This photograph shows the child's other side: the gravity of age, which goes well with the wisdom a man of his age has acquired. Primo Levi, in fact, was always wise in his way. Perhaps too wise.

The Drowned and the Saved

HOW THE BOOK WAS CONCEIVED

Levi's original choice for the title of *If This Is a Man* was 'The Drowned and the Saved', but in the end it became the title of the most significant chapters in the book, where the core of his theory regarding the two categories of prisoners was laid out. The theme that was so central to the last book Levi published in his lifetime was thus a very old one. It was conceived with his first book and featured in *The Truce*. The ninth chapter of *If This Is a Man*, in fact, gave four examples (Schepschel, Alfred L., Elias and Henri) of the 'privileged prisoners' who belonged to the category of the 'saved'; that is, those who collaborated in one way or another with the camp authorities.

The Drowned and the Saved explored many of the issues that Levi had been grappling with throughout his life. These included the themes of memory, gratuitous violence, shame analysed in the early pages of *The Truce*. The idea of the 'grey area', the thorny question of camp collaborators, was the subject of many articles written in the 1970s and was first touched upon in the 1947 edition of *If This Is a Man* where he described the situation of political prisoners and Jewish collaborators who became Kapos in order to survive the camp. There was also the relationship with German readers to consider. Since 1962, when the German translation of *If This Is a Man* was published, many Germans had continued to write to Levi. This phenomenon persuaded him to propose a book containing his answers to these letters to Einaudi. The proposal was not accepted, as Einaudi felt there was too little material to work on. Cesare Cases, author of the first review of the 1947 edition of *If This a Man*, and a staunch supporter of Levi's work, was one of the board members who rejected the idea. Levi finally recycled what he called 'the German project' into the final chapter of The *Drowned and the Saved*.

The genesis of Levi's last book was thus both complex and intricate, and incorporated numerous aspects of his life work. After all, it revisited after 40 years those very 'aspects of the human mind' that Levi had predicted back in 1947 would 'furnish documentation for a detached study' (Preface to *If This Is a Man*, p. 5). However, the topics Levi covered are not as important in understanding its genesis as the fact that Levi conceived the project from the start as a book, envisaging its structure, chapters, sections and internal references.

So, when did the idea for this book come about? In an interview with Giorgina Arian Levi, soon after *The Wrench* was published in 1978, Levi talked about his plan for his next book:

> I have an idea concerning the Lager that tempts me and that I feel could be quite topical today. That is, to revisit the Lager experience after 35 years, to see it with my own eyes, with the eyes of someone who is indifferent, with the eyes of a young person today who has no inkling of these things, even with the eyes of the enemy. I think a good sociological study could come out of it. Other people have already tried to do it, but I think I have something of my own to say. I would like to stake my position on the question of ambiguity. I realize it's a difficult topic and that it has already been dealt with, and handled pretty crudely, like Cavani's film Night Porter. But the theme of the relationship between victims and their executioners is worth looking into further, exploring all its nuances. Above all, the naïve interpretation that there were on one side the executioners, who were pure, unaffected by doubts about their methods, and on the other victims who were sanctified by their role as victims must be rejected at all costs. This was never the case. The human machine, the human animal is more complex.

There were intermediate stages. Those who have been called executioners were not pure executioners; they took on the role as executioners for some reason. I would like to explain these reasons in my next book (Arian Levi 1979).

It is evident that Levi already had a clear picture of what the central idea of the book would be in 1979: he aimed to review his past experience with new eyes. The main theme was to be 'ambiguity', a theme which he had already sketched out in the chapter 'The Drowned and the Saved' in *If This Is a Man and* decided it was vital ('the ambiguous life of the Lager', p. 82). Other important topics were to be the relationship between victims and their executioners, and the sanctification of victims—topics he had written about back in 1955 in an article called 'The Deported. Anniversary', published in a Turin periodical, where he discussed the fact that executioners had a 'human nature'. At that point they were still just a project Levi had in mind, but these themes did finally work their way into *The Drowned and the Saved.*

The year 1979 was also the year that Levi wrote articles assiduously attacking French revisionism, especially the Franco-British Holocaust denier Robert Faurisson. He wrote, among other articles, a front-page editorial for *Corriere della Sera* entitled 'But We Were There' (3 January 1979), and a review of a book on the San Saba rice fields with the title 'A Lager at Italy's Gates' (19 January 1979). In total, he wrote 11 articles and one short story, published in several newspapers and journals between January and August that year, all of which discussed concentration camps and the extermination of the Jews. Two years before, in February 1977, he had written a short piece for *La Stampa* called 'Movies and Swastikas', on the victim-executioner relationship, as a critical reaction to the 'phalanx of Nazi-porn movies' (p. 1229) spawned by Liliana Cavani's film, *Night Porter.*

THE NIGHT OF THE GIRONDISTS

In order to reconstruct the genesis of *The Drowned and the Saved*, or at least of the chapter 'The Gray Zone', one must go back four years to the end of 1975, when Levi translated Jacques Presser's *The Night of the Girondists* for Adelphi. Levi had read the book (originally published in Dutch in 1957 and the following year in English as *Breaking Point*) and presented a proposal for an Italian edition to Einaudi, who rejected it (Belpoliti 2015). At that point, Levi took the proposal to Luciano Foà, who had once worked at Einaudi—where he had backed re-publication of *If This Is a Man*—and had then founded Adelphi in 1962 with financial support from Roberto Olivetti. Levi completed his translation in 1976. He wrote about the experience to Gabriella Poli, a journalist at *La Stampa*:

> The whole time I was assailed by violent emotions. Westerbork was the camp built by the Dutch for Jews who had fled Poland. Under Nazi occupation, it was made into a transit camp for deportations from Eastern Europe. As I translated the book, I relived my experience at Auschwitz. Writing the Foreword cost me a great deal of effort. But it is high time we deal with these thorny issues. The area between victims and executioners is a grey one, it is not a desert (Poli and Calcagno 1992).

In his foreword, while indirectly citing Liliana Cavani's film, Levi declared:

> There are many signs that the time has come to explore the space that separates the victims from the executioners, and to do so with a lighter hand, with a less murky spirit, than has been the case, for example, in some recent popular films. Only a Manichean rhetoric can assert that that space is empty; it is not, it is scattered with vile, miserable, or pathetic characters (who occasionally possess all three qualities at once) and it is indispensable that we know them if we want to know the

human species, if we want to know how to defend our souls when a similar trial returns' (*Uncollected Stories and Essays*, p. 1222).

It is highly likely that the idea of writing an essay on this idea of a 'band of grey'—the term 'band' was borrowed from geography— came about as a result of this close encounter with Georg Cohn, the protagonist of the book Levi was translating, in the same months he was engaged in the task.

In October 1986, 11 years later. Levi received a prize for *The Drowned and the Saved* which was called 'Witness of the Times' in Acqui Terme. In his acceptance speech, Levi stated that the book had had a long gestation: 'I started writing it as early as 1975; then I stopped; then I started again; then I started making changes, and so on. The book was a response to signs I was able to perceive all around me' (Colombo 1987).

APPENDIX TO *IF THIS IS A MAN*

In this speech, Levi was almost certainly referring to another piece of writing from that period, before he started out on the translation and foreword to Presser's book. This was, of course, the Appendix to the School Edition of *If This Is a Man*, which gave him the opportunity to return to the subject of concentration camps 20 years after writing the book. Originally written in 1972, the Appendix was not published until 1975, as a letter from Einaudi communicating that the Appendix would only be added to later editions shows. It is now an integral part of all editions of the book. The Appendix was written 'in order to answer the questions that were repeatedly addressed to me by student readers' (p. 167). The concept of the 'grey area' is not directly tackled, but some of his responses show that Levi was mulling over the matter at the time, and that there were many unresolved issues that he felt needed addressing. Some of these were to re-emerge years later. There was a connection between the Appendix and the chapters that made up *The Drowned and the Saved*, however. It is well known that Levi would work on single chapters, short stories or articles, even when he had no idea what form the final product would take. If it is true that the question of the 'grey area' was the original nucleus of the book he had in mind, as he told Arian Levi, then it is clear that the other chapters took shape later, or already existed in some cases, such as the 'Letter to the Germans'. They would not be included in the book until Levi had decided what the overall structure would be. Once all the material was in place, Levi started the task of constructing the book, assembling all the pieces, adding block after block to the original foundation, the first inspiration.

Levi suggested adding his Appendix to the School Edition of *If This Is a Man* to the German translation when it came out in 1979, but the editors felt it was too 'scholastic' and was not suitable for a work of literature of this calibre and did not include it. Levi told his friend, Hety Schmitt-Maas, in a letter dated July 1979, commenting that it was his intention to dig further into some of the more pertinent issues and seek out more details in the future. This would become his plan, with a precise target. He told Hety that he was thinking of a new book but that it had not yet taken shape. It would be a set of short stories on the Lager experience, each accompanied by an essay. In August, he asked Hety to put him in contact with Reinhard Heidebroek, a young chemist who had been at Buna, whom he later wrote about as Mertens in 'The Quiet Town of Auschwitz' (*Stories and Essays*). Hety wrote to Heidebroek's wife with Levi's request, and told her Levi was working on a new book about Auschwitz.

CHAIM RUMKOWSKI AND 'THE GRAY ZONE'

In November 1977, Levi published a piece in *La Stampa* that he had finished writing a month before. The article was entitled 'The King of the Jews' and was about Rumkowski, president of the Lodz Ghetto who had so keenly collaborated with the Nazis in eliminating the Jewish population of that city. With a real-life example, Levi explored for the first time the theme that he had originally set out in the Foreword to *The Night of the Girondists* the year before. The piece was based on an article by Solomon F. Bloom that came out in the December 1948 issue of the journal *Commentary*; Levi had written to his cousin Anna Yona asking for a photocopy. Four years later, 'The King of the Jews' was published as part of the collection *Lilith and Other Stories*, with seven stories on the Lager experience, and Levi's idea of writing essays for each story seemed to have vanished. With several changes, this story became the final episode of the chapter 'The Gray Zone' in *The Drowned and the Saved*. It contained, for the first time, the phrase 'broad band of grey consciences', which then became the expression 'grey area'.

In 1984, Levi published another foreword, this time to Hermann Langbein's book, *People in Auschwitz*. He had originally received it from the author in 1972, so it is quite likely he had written his comment years earlier. In it, Levi further explored the issue he had been grappling with for many years, and proved he was already gaining a grasp of its complexity: the responsibility borne by the whole camp hierarchy from the top 'down to the grey zone of the Kapos and the prisoners who were given a rank and authority' (*Uncollected Stories and Essays*, p. 2674).

In an interview with Giuseppe Grassano in 1978, a portion of which was published three years later (1981), Levi claimed he had in mind— or rather sitting 'in his gut, or in his belly'—something that was 'hard to digest, linked to the theme of *Night Porter*. That is, revisiting the Lager experience 35 years on.' Once again, Levi was thinking about that 'grey area' of ambiguity. Levi went on to tell his interviewer that he had published several stories in *La Stampa* on a subject he had begun to tackle in *If This Is a Man* and *The Truce*. He cited an episode from Manzoni's *The Betrothed*, where Renzo Ramaglino threatens Don Abbondio with a knife. In his view 'Don Rodrigo was responsible for even the smallest oppressions visited on his victims'. He also referred to Pontecorvo's film *Kapò*, concluding that 'if you claim you can distinguish black from white it means you don't know human beings. It's a mistake and can only be tolerated only in official celebrations.' The theme of the 'grey area' was beginning to take shape, but it had not yet been developed into what it would become in the chapter 'The Gray Zone'.

In early October 1979, Levi's plan seemed to have come to a halt. He wrote to Hety (cited with her initials in the chapter 'Letters from Germans'), telling her that his plan to 'revisit' the subject of the Lager was still just that. It was not that he did not have the time, he insisted, but that he lacked the courage. He told her that he was reading a great deal around the subject, however, including *Anus Mondi* by Wiesław Kielar, who was one of the first arrivals in Auschwitz and who ended up spending a full five years there. Levi commented that the book was interesting but 'suspicious' because Kielar had been one of the privileged *Prominents* in the camp. Levi did not actually use the expression 'gray zone' in this letter, though it was clearly what he was alluding to. In 1979, Levi wrote again to Hety to tell her that after six months' toil, there was not much to show for the planned book on the Lager experience; he had only managed to write a Preface and an Index. As a form of alibi, and perhaps as self-flagellation, Levi sent a flurry of articles, short stories and poems to *La Stampa*. Nevertheless, he continued gathering material for his planned book, reading, among other things, Eric Fromm's *The Anatomy of Human Destructiveness*.

In November 1979, Levi told the booksellers' newsletter, *Informatore Librario*, that he would soon be going back to writing about the Lager experience, despite the fact that, after *The Truce* was published in 1963, he had officially declared he would never return to the subject again. In an interview for *Vogue* with Enrico Arosio after *Other People's Trades* had come out, Levi mentioned two projects. One, he said, was closer to completion. It was 'a book of essays on the sociology of the incarcerated, an old project that I have temporarily abandoned. I've already written six of the essays: they are about memory in captivity, how social relationships develop, what happens to language. I hope to finish it by next year' (Arosio 1985). In the end, there were eight chapters. It is evident from this interview that Levi harboured a certain degree of ambivalence regarding this project. He realized it was a complex subject, and that it would force him to tackle issues that had been unresolved for decades—perhaps since his return home in 1945.

With some degree of approximation, it is possible to identify the six chapters Levi described to Arosio. These were 'The Memory of the Offense', 'The Gray Zone', 'Shame', 'Communication', 'Useless Violence' and 'Stereotypes'. 'The Intellectual in Auschwitz' and 'Letters from Germans' were probably written last, together with the Conclusion. As we have seen, 'Letters from Germans' already existed, at least as a project and as a first draft, as early as 1961. Levi worked on *The Drowned and the Saved*, on and off, for almost 10 years, having written, collected and published in the meantime *The Wrench, Lilith and Other Stories* and *Other People's Trades*, and having spent two years working intensely on *If Not Now, When?* This leads one to think that the book has long trail behind it (Levi used the expression 'trail' in *The Periodic Table* in 1975), going back as far as his very first book, and, in particular, the chapter 'The Drowned and the Saved'.

THE TITLE

As Giorgio Calcagno recalls in an interview with Levi, the original title of his first book was supposed to be *The Drowned and the Saved*, taken from the chapter with the same name. Bearing in mind that the literal translation of the Italian title would be 'The Submerged and the Saved', Calcagno suggested, almost certainly prompted by Levi, that it could have been derived from a *terzina* in Dante's *Inferno*: 'Of a new pain behoves me to make verses / And give material to the twentieth canto / Of the first song, which is of the *submerged*' (*Inferno* XX:1–3). Other critics, such as Lorenzo Mondo, have cited other possible sources in Dante: 'And thou must know, that earlier than these / Never were any human spirits *saved*' (*Inferno* IV:62–63), and Canto VI, which Levi was well-versed in, often citing the figure of the guard dog Cerberus ('Cerberus, monster cruel and uncouth / With his three gullets like a dog is barking/ Over the people that are there *submerged*', *Inferno* VI:13–15).

The title was left in a drawer for 30 years. In the meantime, Levi's popularity both at home and abroad had surged, and critics had finally realized he was a force to reckon with. Many readers and critics were struck by the fact that he was going back to the subject of the Lager experience after so many years and despite the fact that, since at least 1975 with the success of *The Periodic Table*, he had finally established his reputation as a writer. The fact of the matter is that if one follows his career closely, taking into account his stories, poems and newspaper articles, it is very clear that Levi never stopped working on the subject of the Lager. Nonetheless, in the interviews he gave after *The Drowned and the Saved*, he was repeatedly asked this question: Why have you gone back to the subjects of memory and reflection on Auschwitz? As if his very identity as a writer were not intrinsically linked to his role as a writer of witness memoirs.

THE BOOK

The essays contained in *The Drowned and the Saved* were written at different times. Part of 'The Gray Zone', as we have seen, was based on a 1977 article about Rumkowski which first came out in *La Stampa*. It was then published in *Lilith and Other Stories* and later re-edited (Belpoliti 2015). Among the previously published pieces included in the book, this was the oldest, with the exception perhaps of a shorter version of 'Letters from Germans'. The preface, dated June 1982, on the other hand, had been written as an address to the 1982 Jewish

Community Congress and was only published in the *Complete Works* after his death. The address and the text which was eventually published as a Preface to *The Drowned and the Saved* were different in several ways. As always, Levi edited his work carefully. In the case of 'The Gray Zone' for example, he left the central section almost untouched, and made significant changes to the beginning and the end; in the Preface, by contrast, he edited the central section more heavily. The chapter 'The Memory of the Offense' had previously appeared with the title 'The Lager and Memory' in a collection of essays edited by Massimo Martini called *The Trauma of the Deportation* (Mondadori, 1983). This too had previously been presented as an address to the 1983 Turin conference entitled 'The Duty of Bearing Witness', whose proceedings were published by the Piedmont Regional Council. Levi added three passages to the conference paper, in addition to the final paragraph, which links it to the rest of the book.

We can confirm from a letter he wrote to his close friend, Bianca Guidetti Serra on March 19, 1980 ('Dear Bianca, this is supposed to be the first chapter of the book people suppose I am writing') that Levi had already finished the chapter 'The Gray Zone', which he included in his letter. The manuscript had been written on a typewriter, not a computer, and was dated 24 December 1979. It was significantly different to the version that was published in *The Drowned and the Saved*. Without comparing the two texts in detail, given that there are numerous small changes, it is interesting to see how Levi worked on the longest and most complex chapter in the whole book. The sheets he sent to Bianca had clearly been typed at different times, and alternated different line spacings, as if he had been working at a collage of passages that had been written previously and then corrected and completed in order to create a finished product. Despite the many additional corrections in the passage from typescript to galley proof, the version Levi sent to his friend was essentially complete. What is so fascinating is that the constant variations (such as the phrase 'But our need to divide the field between "us" and "them" is so strong—perhaps for reasons rooted in our origins as social animals—that this one scheme, the friend-enemy dichotomy, prevails over all others' [p. 2430], which was previously expressed as 'The need to divide the field is so strong—perhaps for biological reasons—that . . . ') did not alter the text in any significant way. Levi worked with the rigorous attention of an etcher with his engraving tool, cutting and smoothing his text. He added the incision 'regardless of the label attached to him' to the phrase 'For the camp leadership, the new arrival was by definition an adversary—regardless of the label attached to him—and had to be destroyed immediately' (p. 2432); he cut the word 'Michelangelo' from the phrase 'to re-enact the gesture of Christ on Judgment Day'; he took the tattoos out of the list of 'sinister rituals' on arrival at the camp, leaving 'the immediate kicks and punches, often to the face; the riot of orders shouted with real or simulated rage; complete denuding; the shaving of the head; the ragged clothing' (p. 2432).

The added details or refined ideas in his edits evidence the extent to which time had sharpened Levi's memory. For example, the historian of Mauthausen, Hans Maršálek, was not actually named until the final version. Again, the percentage of Jews, which he had given as 95 was corrected to 90–95 per cent. Still again, an explanation was provided as to why there were so few Russian prisoners of war at Auschwitz in brackets '(for the most part, they were exterminated immediately after capture, machine-gunned on the edge of enormous common graves' [p. 2442]).' In some places, Levi added whole paragraphs. There were few syntactic changes made to the 1980 (or slightly previous) manuscript before going to print; however, there were also very few sentences that were entirely rewritten or cut in order to be replaced by other sentences written using a different construction. Similarly, Levi hardly ever altered the structure of his sentences, except for changes to single words. This shows that he had already reached a formal stylistic balance in the typescript, which he basically maintained right the way through to publication in *The Drowned and the Saved*, even though he constantly corrected the text in many different places in small ways ('one or the other' becomes 'both'). In the first chapter, 'The Memory of the Offense', a strip of paper was glued onto the last page of the manuscript, where Levi had added one of the most important passages in the entire book: the final paragraph starting with 'An apology is in order' to the end of the chapter 'untainted by the drifting I have described' (p. 2429). The final sentence in 'Letters from Germans', where Levi described his friendship with Hety, was also added on a glued strip of paper, which corrected and honed the sentence he had originally used to close the chapter.

In an interview, Levi said he had written *The Wrench* on his typewriter, almost without corrections, as if it had been dictated to him. 'The Gray Zone', by contrast, presented itself as tormented, especially from a conceptual point of view. All the author's corrections and alterations reveal his desire to clarify his argument or modulate a statement in order somehow to make a wider point.

When Levi handed in his manuscript of 112 pages to Einaudi it was a complete piece of work. He had retyped all the chapters on his Macintosh computer, which he had only recently bought, and had used for the final drafts of the book. The dot-matrix printout was typical of the time, printed on tractor-feed paper (now housed in the Turin State Archive, Folder n.1057, File n. 3026). Some chapters were dated according to when their last draft took place): 'The Gray Zone', 20 June 1985; 'Communication', 17 August 1985; 'The Intellectual at Auschwitz', 13 September 1985 as a starting date and 22 September as a finishing date; 'Stereotypes', started 17 October 1985, completed 24 November 1985; 'Letters from Germans', 28 December 1985; 'Conclusion', 3 January 1986.

The book was published by Einaudi, as no. 305 in the 'Struzzi' Collection, with a detail of the Hans Memling's *Last Judgement* (housed in the National Museum in Gdańsk) on the cover. Under the jacket illustration, there were four abstract nouns with the determinate article required in Italian: 'I delitti, i castighi, le pene, le impunità' (crimes, punishments, torments, impunity). These were taken out in the next edition. Robert Gordon pointed out that the subtitle of the book was derived from Cesare Beccaria. Levi's contract with Einaudi bears the date 14 February 1986, and the book was published mid-year. Eight editions were printed over the next four years, with a total of 71,000 copies. Seven paperback editions followed in the Einaudi 'Tascabile' series (n. 59) with commentaries by, Giovanni Raboni, Paolo Flores D'Arcais, and Levi himself, with 58,000 copies sold between 1991 and 1996, bringing the total sales to 129,000 copies. In the years that followed, 150,000 more copies were printed, revealing a growing interest in Levi's last piece of work. In 1986, *The Drowned and the Saved* received the Marotta Prize and the Acqui Terme Prize dedicated to 'Witnesses of Our Time'.

LEMMAS

'The Gray Zone'

'The Gray Zone', perhaps the most important chapter in *The Drowned and the Saved*, explored the 'Manichean tendency to shun nuance and complexity and to reduce the river of human events to conflicts, and conflicts to duels, us and them' (p. 2430). Returning to an argument he had already posited in *If This Is a Man*, Levi explained that when they were in the concentration camps, the enemy not only surrounded the prisoners, it also inhabited them. In his view, it was impossible to reduce the reality of the Lager 'to two blocs, victims and persecutors [. . .] 'us' on the inside and the enemy on the outside, separated by a sharp geographic border' (p. 2431). In this chapter, Levi described the 'sinister rituals' that accompanied entry into the camps and demonstrated how the lack of allies, even in fellow deportees, deliberately transformed the experience into a 'covert and constant struggle' to obtain privileges that were essential for survival (Levi described some of these privileges in 'The Drowned and the Saved' in *If This Is a Man*). The 'category of inmate-functionaries is both its framework and its most disturbing feature. This category is a grey zone, with undefined contours, which both separates and connects the two opposing camps of masters and servants. It has an incredibly complicated internal structure, and harbours just enough to confound our need to judge' (p. 2435).

'The Gray Zone' was essentially a treatise on the psychology and anthropology of imprisonment, but, at the same time, Levi reminded his readers that these rules could also be applied to everyday life, 'Wherever power is exercised by the few, or by one man alone, against the many' (p. 2435). A prison camp was simply a 'laboratory' for the exercise of power. Levi borrowed from scientific research in animal behaviour to describe human behaviour in the camps, avoiding moral judgement and clearly indicating where responsibility lay:

Before discussing one by one the motives that drove some prisoners to collaborate, to varying degrees, with the camp authorities, however, we should forcefully assert the imprudence of rushing to moral judgement in human cases such as these. It should be clear that the greatest fault lies with the system, the very structure of the totalitarian state. The criminal complicity of individual collaborators, great and small (never friendly, never transparent!), is always difficult to evaluate (p. 2436).

And yet, as Levi pointed out, the tendency was universal: 'The rise of the privileged—not only in the camps but in all human society—is a disturbing but inevitable phenomenon. The only places where you don't find them are utopias' (p. 2436). Moreover, 'privilege is born and proliferates, even against the will of power. But power normally tolerates and encourages it' (p. 2436).

As he had already made very clear in *If This Is a Man*, the Lager was a 'laboratory', and the grey zone within it had an incredibly complex structure. Levi stressed two aspects. First, that 'the smaller the area of power the greater the need for outside assistance' (p. 2435) and second, that 'the harsher the oppression, the more widespread among the oppressed is the willingness to collaborate with power' (p. 2435). Citing Manzoni's *The Betrothed* ('The troublemakers, the oppressors, all those who do harm of any sort to others, are guilty not only of the evil they do but also of the perversion of their victims' minds'), Levi attempted to argue that individual complicity should not be judged by those who have never been subjected to similar conditions of coercion.

As promised, Levi examined one by one the 'collaborators' within the camp, from the Kapos leading the work squads and barrack chiefs to the lower level functionaries, analysing their behaviour according to his belief that 'a certain measure of man's domination of man is probably inscribed in our genetic heritage as herd animals' (p. 2438). His readings in animal behaviour helped Levi analyse the grey zone and were an essential tool in his quest for a rational explanation of human behaviour under extreme conditions. Two cases were fleshed out with greater detail in the chapter, backed up with witness statements, depositions, and other reports written after the camps were liberated: the Sonderkommandos, prisoners who directly operated the crematoriums, and Chaim Rumkowski, the head of the Lodz Ghetto in Poland (to whom he had already dedicated a short story in *Lilith and Other Stories*). Levi's conclusion at the end of the chapter was drastic. Like Rumkowski, 'we, too, are so blinded by power and prestige that we forget our basic fragility. We make our deals with power, willingly or not, forgetting that we are all in the ghetto, that the ghetto is walled in, that outside the wall are the lords of death, and that not far away the train is waiting' (p. 2456).

One of the issues that Levi was anxious to explore in this chapter was the relationship between brutality and compassion. In Levi's view, these two extremes could coexist within the same person, given that people were neither coherent nor monolithic. Compassion was an unknown quantity, with no inherent logic. The truth was that 'There is no proportionality between the compassion we feel and the dimensions of the sorrow that gives rise to compassion. A single Anne Frank arouses more emotion than the myriad others who suffered like her but whose images have remained in the shadows' (p. 2446). Levi's secular morality rejected the idea of sanctity (his 1946 poem 'Singing' stated 'Not martyrs, infamous, or saints'):

> Maybe saints are the only ones who have been granted the terrible gift of compassion toward the many. What remains for the gravediggers, the Sonderkommandos, and all of us, in the best of cases, is the occasional feeling of compassion toward the individual, the Mitmensch, our fellow man: the flesh-and-blood human being who stands before us, within reach of our providentially myopic senses (p. 2446).

The Night of the Girondists

In August 1975, Levi wrote to his friend Luciano Foà, to propose translating and publishing the Dutch writer Jacques Presser's book, *The Night of the Girondists*. Levi did not speak Dutch, as he had confessed in his short story 'A "Mystery" in the Lager', and yet he was convinced he would be in a position to translate it.

Luciano Foà, as secretary-general of Einaudi, had pushed for re-publication of *If This Is a Man* in 1958. Levi might well have spoken to his editor at Einaudi before turning to Foà, but Foà was the man who had published Anne Frank's diary in 1954 and had encouraged publication of Levi's first book. After a brief exchange of letters, a contract was agreed and drawn up, giving Levi the go ahead for the translation in September.

The book came out the next year, with a foreword by the translator. This foreword was significant because it was the first time that Levi had written explicitly about the grey zone, the undefined area between victims and their persecutors. The significant passage reads thus: 'There are many signs that the time has come to explore the space that separates the victims from the executioners, and to do so with a lighter hand, with a less murky spirit, than has been the case, for example, in some recent popular films' (p. 1222). The film Levi was alluding to was Liliana Cavani's *Night Porter*, which he would later criticize explicitly in 'The Gray Zone'.

Presser was an extremely well-read Dutch historian, and a Jew, whose wife, Deborah Appel, was arrested in 1943 and deported, first to the Westerbork transit camp, and then to Sobibor, the extermination camp where she died. Before the war he had taught in the Jewish Lycée in Amsterdam, but he was forced into hiding until the armistice. In 1949, he wrote a biography of Napoleon, and in 1950 he was commissioned by the government to write an account of the persecution of Jews during the Second World War. *The Night of the Girondists* was not, therefore, an account of a personal experience in the camps but, rather, the result of compiling a vast number of documents and witness statements that Presser had collected in the course of this undertaking. Presser also wrote detective stories.

The first edition of the book was in 1957, as a favour for guests at 'Book Week' events. It won a prize and was later reprinted by Muelenhoff. After 1963, as de Waart has shown (2014), it was translated into seven languages. The first translation was into English, published by *Breaking Point* in 1958, followed by a German edition (Rowohlt, 1959). The book enjoyed brief popularity but then sank into oblivion. However, Presser published another book on the extermination of Dutch Jews in 1965 (*Extermination*), which brought him back into the limelight.

Levi worked on his translation from between the end of 1975 and early 1976, confessing to Gabriella Poli and Giorgio Calcagno that the experience produced violent emotions in him: 'Translating I relived Auschwitz. Writing the Foreword also cost me a great deal. It is time, however, to deal with these burning topics. The gap between victims and their persecutors is a grey zone, it is not a desert' (Poli and Calcagno 1992). Levi's foreword made at least three of his motives for wanting the book to be read in Italian very clear. First, he thought the novel told the tragic story of the deportations almost as if it were a truthful account, with 'the character of a document' (p. 1220). Second, it told the story of an 'identity crisis' of a Western Jew. Finally, it told the story of a Jew who had collaborated with the Nazis.

The protagonist of the novel was a thinly veiled alter ego of the author: Jacques Suasso Henrique was a history teacher at the Jewish Lycée, like Jacques Presser. He was an assimilated Jew (like Levi) and despised cowardice in Jews. At school, he had taught his students about the 21 deputies of the Gironde that were guillotined on 31 October 1783, during the French Revolution. Later, one of his students provided him with the opportunity to become the head of the Jewish security forces at the Westerbork transit camp. Suasso thus avoided deportation, but at the transit camp he came across Cohn, a collaborator, and Jeremiah Hirsch, a Jew who urged him to reflect on his Jewish identity. Every week, a train set off from Westerbork to deliver its cargo of Dutch Jews to certain death, while the security forces had the power to choose which prisoners would be transported next. When it was Hirsch's turn, Suasso had an argument with Cohn and ended up slapping him, receiving, in punishment, an order to present himself for the following week's transport. The novel was Suasso's diary of that week waiting for his final journey, with continuous flashbacks to his life in Amsterdam.

In his foreword, Levi examined the significant aspects of the book. By means of the character 'Rabbi' Hirsch, Presser illustrated how many assimilated Jews found deliverance (a 'path to salvation', [p. 1221]) in the religion of their fathers. The novel also described 'Jewish self-hatred (another aspect of the identity crisis)' which, Levi claimed, gave rise to the 'many anti-Semitic Jews in Western Europe' (p. 1221). Levi pointed out that people like Cohn, who collaborated with the Nazis in order to survive the war, were almost invisible in normal conditions: 'Similar individuals have existed, and certainly still exist among us in a virtual state. In normal conditions they are not recognizable (Cohn wanted to be a banker), but merciless persecution develops them and brings them to light and to power' (p. 1221). Power, as Levi would later state in *The Drowned and the Saved*, was what transformed them.

Another aspect Levi developed in his foreword, from an idea that he had already explored back in 1955 in his article 'The Deported. Anniversary' (*Uncollected Stories and Essays*), was that the death of so many victims was not 'glorious' or 'honourable'. He wrote:

> It's naive, absurd, and historically false to claim that a demonic system like National Socialism sanctifies its victims; on the contrary, it degrades them and dirties them, assimilates them, and all the more willing they are, clean, lacking political or moral backbone. Cohn is detestable, monstrous, and should be punished, but his wrong is the reflection of another, much more serious and general fault (p. 1221).

Levi again referenced Manzoni when he talked about 'the contagion of evil'. 'Should Cohn be judged?' Levi answered his own question:

> Well, the opinion of this book is that Cohn should be judged. His speech on the 'sinking ship' is specious, and so is his claim (how many times have we heard it!): 'If I didn't do it, someone worse than me would'. One must refuse; one always can, in any case, perhaps following the path of Miss Wolfson. He who does not refuse (but one must refuse from the beginning, not put one's hand in the machine) ends up yielding to the temptation of passing to the other side, where he will find, at best, an illusory gratification and a destructive salvation (p. 1221).

Nevertheless, aware that there was always a spectrum of culpability, as he declared nine years later in *The Drowned and the Saved*, Levi was at pains to point out that,

> Cohn is guilty, but there is an extenuating circumstance. The general consciousness that we should not give in when confronted by

violence but resist is a current notion, not of that time but of the period that followed. The imperative of resistance developed with the resistance and with the global tragedy of the Second World War; before that, it was the precious patrimony of a few (p. 1223).

After reading Presser's book, Levi stated, 'today those who want to understand can understand, and I think that this book can help' (p. 1223).

How did Levi discover the book? In the foreword, he claimed he 'came across this story by accident, many years ago; I read it and reread it many times, and it stayed with me' (p. 1220). The phrase 'by accident' is significant, given the reaction the book caused. Until recently it was not known exactly when Levi 'came across' the book. However, a newly unearthed letter Levi wrote to Hetty on 30 April 1967 gives us a clue. In the letter, Levi informed Hetty that he had received the book directly from Presser's German publisher, Rowohlt, who asked him to read it and compare it to Jean-François Steiner's *Treblinka*. Levi told his friend that he was interested in the 'alarming subject of Jewish (or Norwegian, Italian, French, Ukrainian, or, why not? German) collaboration with the Nazis.' Levi wrote the letter in English. He added that he did not know Presser personally, but that he hoped to meet him with Saul Bellow and André Schwartz-Bart at a conference for Jewish writers planned for November of the following year, which he hoped to attend ('if everything works out'). The meeting never took place.

According to Levi's biographer, Ian Thomson (2003), Ruth Orthel, who had interviewed him for a documentary she was making, gave Levi the original Dutch edition of the book, although Orthel subsequently denied this. Another hypothesis for the source of the book was Philo Bregstein, a friend of Presser's, but he too denied giving Levi a copy. What is certain is that the Italian edition of the book included a Preface and a Chronology by Philo Bregstein (originally written in Dutch) which was missing from the other translations, including the German edition. Who translated Bregstein's contribution from the Dutch?

Levi had been familiar with the book for at least a decade before he suggested translating it. He was also, of course, familiar with the subject of Jewish collaboration with the Nazis. He was a witness to it, and the subject was also highly debated in Europe and in the United States after the Eichmann trial, and, in particular, after Hannah Arendt's reports on the trial and her book, *The Banality of Evil*, translated into Italian in 1964. Could one reasonably claim, then, that Levi first started to explore the subject of the grey zone as early as 1964? We know that he had not come up with the expression yet, and that it was an idea that would naturally take shape gradually over time, but it would seem almost certain that Levi was already beginning to think about the issue at this time.

Finally, since Levi did not speak Dutch, what language did Levi translate the book from? The Dutch critic, Raniero Speelman, in a conference on translations of Levi in the Netherlands (2005), referred to a letter from Levi responding to a letter from the owner of the Bonardi bookshop in Amsterdam, Marina Warner. Levi wrote: 'No, other than Presser, I have not translated anything else from Dutch. It was a solitary tour de force.' Is it possible that Levi translated the book from the Dutch edition?

Two critics have attempted to answer this question: Lina Insana, an American critic, in *Arduous Tasks: Primo Levi, Translation, and the Transmission of Holocaust Testimony* (2009), and Bert de Waal in *Da de nacht der Girondijnen a La notte dei Girondini* (2014). Being Dutch and speaking German, de Waal compared the Dutch and German editions with Levi's translation into Italian. From Levi's letter to Hetty we know that he had received a German edition of the book. De Waal excluded the fact that Levi might have used the English translation, and compared parallel passages of the three other versions, noting that Levi had at times misinterpreted some of the German (which was relatively faithful to the Dutch). Insana added that a phrase from Levi's translation was derived from the title of a book by Gitta Sereny on Franz Stangl, the commandant of Treblinka: *Into That Darkness*. The book was published in Italy in 1975 by Adelphi, and had come out in English the year before. According to Insana, Levi's translation of Presser accentuated the moral responsibility of the protagonist, and marked the witness element of the book compared to the Dutch text. She believed Levi used the German edition as a basis for his translation into English.

De Waal analysed the changes Levi made, compared to the Dutch or the German. Even when these were minimal, they showed that Levi's translation was a writerly translation, with partial rewrites of the original. He did not agree with Insana on the accentuation of the protagonist's internal moral conflict. The Dutch critic commented that Levi's translation of Kafka's *The Trial*, which came out several years later also for Einaudi, made significant changes and reformulated some of the source text. De Waal pointed out Levi's reticence in some parts of Presser's novel, especially in scenes where sex was portrayed as being an important way to survive in the camp. This was an aspect of the grey zone that Levi did not write much about (except for veiled allusions in *The Drowned and the Saved* in *If This Is a Man*, where the young Henri was compared to Saint Sebastian of Sodom for his body and face that were 'subtly androgynous' [p. 93]), partly because his experience was in a men's camp.

Jean Améry

In December 1978, on hearing that the Austrian philosopher, Jean Améry, had committed suicide, Levi wrote an article in *La Stampa* entitled 'Jean Améry, the Philosopher-Suicide' (*Uncollected Stories and Essays*). The article opened stating that 'The dreadful episode of the People's Temple, the collective suicide of nine hundred followers of a mystic-satanic sect, is incomprehensible' (p. 1262). Examining once again the notion of incomprehensibility, he noted:

> After all, every human action contains a hard core of incomprehensibility: if it weren't so, we would be able to foresee what our neighbour will do. This doesn't happen, and maybe it's for the better. Understanding the reasons for a suicide is particularly difficult, since, in general, the victim himself isn't conscious of them, or provides himself and others with explanations that are intentionally or unintentionally distorted (p. 1262).

Levi went on to summarize the salient points of his life: Jean Améry was a 'new name' that the assimilated Jew adopted to show that the Hans Meyer that once was had lost his identity at Auschwitz-Monowitz, where he had been interned and tortured. Citing from his best-known work, *At the Mind's Limits* (in Améry 1980), Levi came to the conclusion that 'Whoever has succumbed to torture can no longer feel at home in the world. The shame of destruction cannot be erased. Trust in the world, which already collapsed in part at the first blow, and in the end, under torture, fully, will not be regained' (p. 1263). In a chapter of *The Drowned and the Saved* that was dedicated to Améry entitled 'The Intellectual at Auschwitz', Levi developed the theme further and revealed that he had had an exchange of letters with Améry using his friend Hety as his go-between.

It was Hety, in fact, who introduced Levi to Améry's works when she sent him first a review and then a copy of his book. The correspondence between Levi and Améry started out in Italian, then turned to French, English, and, finally, German. Hety would correct Levi's letters and send them back to him. In December 1966, Levi wrote to Hety after receiving the book she had sent him. *Jenseits von Schuld und Sühne: Bewäitigungsversüche eines Überwältigten* (Beyond Guilt and Atonement: Attempt to Overcome a Defeat) came out in 1966 and was immediately translated into Italian as *Intellettuale a Auschwitz* (Améry 1987). He asked Hety whether Améry's work had been published in French, as he knew he was living in Belgium at the time, and commented on Améry's review of Jean-François Steiner's *Treblinka* that Hety had sent him, which tackled the differences between Nazi Lagers and Soviet ('Communist') Gulags. Over the next year, Hety kept Levi up to date with Améry's latest work and his appearances on television. Hety informed Levi that she had met Améry and his wife Lizzi. In a letter dated August 1967, Levi told Hety that he agreed with Améry on many topics but was unable to follow his 'metaphysical elucubrations' about being Jewish. For Levi, the fact of being Jewish was actually 'quite simple'. Levi received more work by Améry from Hety in 1968. First, Preface to the *Future: Culture in a Consumer Society*, published in 1964, and then *Über Das Altern: Revolte und Resignation*, which was later translated into Italian by Bollati Boringhieri (*Rivolta e rassegnazione: sull'invecchiare*, 1988). Hety kept Levi abreast of her correspondence with Améry, and commented on the differences between Améry,

Levi and Langbein. In Hety's view, Levi was the only one of the three who had not become hardened and resentful over the years.

Ten years later, in 1978, Levi wrote to Hety asking her what she knew about Améry's suicide. Given that the philosopher was little known in Italy, there was very little information on his death in the newspapers. He had not yet written the article for *La Stampa* that would come out in December, but he started reading and rereading Améry's work, finding there 'the lucid desperation of a man wounded to the core, and deprived of his roots.' Levi concluded that, having been tortured once, Améry would be tortured for life, and thus his suicide was comprehensible, while suicides are 'generally mysterious'. Hety told Levi that Améry had been depressed and had once attempted suicide by taking an overdose but had been saved by his wife. He had undergone a cure, but had never really recovered, and had been disappointed by the cool reception of his work. He had felt like a failure as a writer, and was further tried by bad reviews, a rejection letter from a publisher for his book on Charles Bovary and another from an important newspaper for an article he had proposed. Améry's wife, Hety explained, had been thinking about sending him to a sanatorium, but while she was out of the house Améry had killed himself.

The Intellectual in Auschwitz was an opportunity for Levi, seven years after Améry's death, to deal with the Austrian philosopher's survival story and to polemicize for the first time with his ideas. After summarizing Améry's life experience, Levi compared and contrasted himself with Améry, citing three major differences between the two. The first regarded their Jewish identity, which Améry experienced as a destiny that he was fated to rail against. The second, which was an essential difference, was the 'endless death' of torture. Améry wrote about his experience in *At the Mind's Limits*, and Levi focused in particular on Améry's statement that being an intellectual at Auschwitz was not 'useful', and could actually be harmful. He did not remember Améry in his block, but Levi felt that his definition of intellectual was too narrow. For Levi, one could be an intellectual if one was a naturalist, mathematician or philosopher of science, not just in the liberal arts. He adopted an expression of Lidia Rolfi's, who was also a 'lucky' survivor of Auschwitz, and stated 'for me the Lager was a university; it taught us to look around ourselves and take the measure of men' (p. 2514). The third difference was the subject of labour, in particular manual labour, which Levi never considered diminishing, as Améry did (intellectuals were 'tormented by an acute sense of humiliation and destitution'). Levi concluded: 'Unlike Améry and others, however, I felt only moderately humiliated by manual labour: obviously I was not yet "intellectual" enough' (p. 2508). Levi's philosophy inspired by Conrad that men are forged by adverse circumstances and by exploring their limits was in stark contrast to Améry's ('Moreover, dignity could be found in even the most exhausting manual labor, and a person could adapt, maybe by recognizing in it a rough asceticism or, depending on one's temperament, a Conradian measuring of oneself, a patrolling of one's own borders' [p. 2509]) On a linguistic level, moreover, Levi rebutted Améry's claim that he was 'pained by the mutilated language' of the camp. After all, he was a German speaker, so 'His suffering, if I may, was more spiritual than physical. He suffered because he was a German speaker, because he was a philologist who loved his language: the way a sculptor would suffer to see one of his statues defaced or mutilated' (p. 2509). Finally, Levi commented on Améry's theory that giving a 'blow for a blow' gave one dignity in the camp. Levi claimed he was 'intrinsically unable' to do so, owing to his character and his education.

The moral considerations of the two Auschwitz survivors were thus very different. Améry was in constant conflict with his ambient and had a competitive view of life in the concentration camp, while Levi's 'vision of the world was different from and complementary to' his counterpart's. For him, 'The business of living is the best defence against death, and not only in the camps' (p. 2520). Levi's descriptions of life in the camps were detailed and often humorous accounts of the tactics and strategies employed to survive. Levi's epic was not based on the theme of conflict with the enemy or with the other. It was founded, rather, on his personal experience of Auschwitz, which threw all of his moral convictions into disarray and forced him to elaborate a theory of the Lager as a vast-scale biological and social experiment, where humans at times were obliged to behave as animals. Levi thus accepted, or rather did not hide, the negative effect on humanity of the experiment. He also refrained from considering Auschwitz as being the 'ground zero' of human experience, after which its ethics can only improve.

Améry's pessimism stemmed from his humanist education, from the failure of the 'Geist', or Spirit of German idealism. In Levi's view, culture was not lost at Auschwitz. On the contrary, his culture had brought him advantage. His scientific culture was at the basis of his trade as a chemist, as was his naturalism: 'I know, this "naturalistic" attitude doesn't come only or necessarily from chemistry, but for me it came from chemistry. It hardly seems cynical to say so' (p. 2514). Scientific culture gave him the tools to look around and make close observations. Chemistry was a 'legacy of mental habits' (p. 2514). Moreover, Levi was not, like Améry, a 'political combatant', even though he had been arrested as a partisan. He claimed he was ignorant of the forces of history that Améry, the 'demeaned scholar' aspired to understand. More importantly, he was a non-believer. Améry, too, Levi admitted, had been agnostic, but Levi, unlike Améry, never tried to find an explanation of any kind, not even in 'transcendental justice' (p. 2518).

Their images of death were also in contrast.

> Améry observes that the intellectual (the 'young' intellectual, I would specify, such as he and I were at the time of our capture and imprisonment) derived an odourless, decorous, literary image of death from his readings. Here I translate 'into Italian' his observations as a German philologist, who was obliged to quote the *'mehr Licht!'* of Goethe, *Death in Venice*, and *Tristan*. For us Italians death is the second term of the binomial 'love and death' (p. 2520).

And yet, Levi concluded, for him death was as far from this as possible:

> Death in Auschwitz was trivial, bureaucratic, and commonplace. It wasn't commented on, it wasn't 'comforted by tears' (Foscolo). In the face of death, of inurement to death, the border between education and lack of education disappeared (p. 2520).

Hannah Arendt

On 11 April 1961, Adolf Eichmann, one of those chiefly responsible for the extermination of the Jews, was put on trial in Jerusalem. Israeli secret agents had abducted him the year before in Argentina, after which he was transported to Israel in order to undergo trial. This was a key moment in the construction of international consensus concerning the terrible events that had taken place during the Second World War; it was also a historic moment for the Jewish communities of the diaspora. On 4 April that year, the Florentine journal *Il Ponte* published an insert containing an article by Levi on Eichmann, which was the transcript of a speech Levi had given in February in Turin at a conference on Auschwitz and other concentration camps. In June 1960, Levi gave a deposition on the deportations which was added to the records of the trial of Eichmann. The article published by *Il Ponte* reminded readers that one of the prerogatives of Nazism was to corrupt people's consciences. The Nazis, he commented, had been able to find traitors and collaborationists in every country they occupied, creating or restoring an atmosphere of ambiguous consensus, or open terror, necessary for implementing their terrible plans.

Concentration camps were 'places of corruption', as well as of torment and death. This consideration anticipated a theme Levi would go on to develop over the following two decades, remarking as he did in the article that there were Jewish collaborators in the Polish ghettos just as there were in the concentration camps. Many of the camp functionaries, in fact, were prisoners; the majority of these were Jewish. The core of the article regarded the violation, distortion and brutalization of human conscience. Concentration camps, in Levi's view, demonstrated like no other place how feeble human conscience was, and how easy it was to subvert and submerge it. What the Germans did in the Lager was to humiliate, degrade and reduce men to the level of their guts, using methods such as transport by cattle car, the yellow star pinned to their breasts, the tattooed numbers, the ill-fitting clothes, the shoes you couldn't walk in, the daily march of the bedraggled men before the impromptu band. Many of these images emerged during the trial of Eichmann, and Levi used an expression that would later return in *The Drowned and the Saved*: 'the contagion of evil'.

At the same time as Levi was reflecting on these themes which became part of his deposition and contributed to the case for the prosecution of Eichmann, the American philosopher with German origins, Hannah Arendt, had been sent by the *New Yorker* to cover the trial. Arendt's dispatches from Jerusalem, which were collected and published in 1963 in the book, *Eichmann in Jerusalem: A Report on the Banality of Evil* triggered heated debate among American intellectuals, in particular among the Jews of the Diaspora. The controversy created by Arendt's philosophical musings focused on two issues.

The first can be summarized by the formula Arendt herself coined to express her findings: the 'word-and-thought-defying banality of evil' (1977, p. 252) With this expression, Arendt posited that Eichmann did not represent absolute evil; in her view, Eichmann was 'so normal [. . .] that he posed a challenge for legal judgement' (p. 48). His conscience was an empty container that didn't have its own language but was a vehicle for middle-class respectability. The second regarded a subject that Levi had already written about but which Arendt was not necessarily familiar with, although other scholars such as Raul Hilberg most certainly was. This was the complicity of Jews with the Nazi regime (Arendt used the word 'collaborationism' twice in her book). The expression 'the banality of evil', in Arendt's mind, was intended to indicate that Nazi criminals were not great in any way, and that there was no greatness in the evil perpetrated by those who had planned and implemented the extermination of the Jews. Arendt wanted to say that Eichmann did not have the features of a devil; his evil was not superhuman but perfectly human.

Levi had written about this in his 1955 article 'The Deported. Anniversary', where he commented 'we are men, we belong to the same human family that our executioners belong to' (p. 1128). However, it was the matter of Jewish collaboration with the Nazis, raised by Arendt, that fanned the flames of the debate in the United States after the book was published, with the Jewish community united against her. Levi did not give his opinion on the subject in his article, as he did not consider himself either a historian or a scholar but, rather, a witness who preferred to talk about only the things he experienced in the first person. It was only later, as he researched the subject more deeply, that he would refine his point of view, although he never abandoned the role of witness.

In his 1976 Appendix to the School Edition of *If This Is a Man*, Levi described the staff at the concentration camp as being 'diligent men who carried out inhuman orders, (who) were not born torturers, were not (with few exceptions) monsters: they were ordinary men' (p. 191). He then added, 'monsters exist but they are too few to be truly dangerous; more dangerous are the common men the bureaucrats ready to believe and to obey without question, like Eichmann' (p. 191). This passage reveals that Levi had probably read Arendt's book, although he had already broached some of these questions in the 1950s. In fact, the first seeds were already sown in 1946 in the chapter 'The Drowned and the Saved' in *If This Is a Man*.

Levi never directly referenced Arendt in his work, not even in *The Drowned and the Saved*. The only time he ever mentioned her was in an April 1979 interview with Giorgio Segre, which came out in the Jewish journal *Ha-Tikwa*. In one of the last questions, Levi was invited to comment on the relationship between the oppressors and the oppressed in concentration camps. Levi's response was cautious. He would not develop the thesis of the 'grey zone' for another seven years, and confessed to his interviewer that his ideas on the subject were not clear. Whenever the subject of Jewish persecution comes up, the tendency is to simplify. As Levi saw it, human beings are animals that prefer simplicity over complexity. And yet, he concluded, things are not simple; they are rather complicated. Levi used the word 'complicated' often in *The Drowned and the Saved* to indicate that none of the systems were binary: 'the hybrid category inmate-functionaries [. . .] Is a grey zone, with undefined contours, which both separates and connects the two opposing camps of masters and servants. It has an incredibly complicated internal structure, and harbours just enough to confound our need to judge' (p. 2534).

In the interview with Segre, Levi cited Arendt, claiming that her idea of the 'banality of evil' followed the same lines as his conviction that circumstances were far more important than human nature. 'We are not talking about monsters here. I never saw even one monster. They were people just like us that behaved in a certain way because there was Nazism and

Fascism in Germany. If Nazism or Fascism returned, in whatever country, there would be people, like us, that would behave in the same way.' Levi also tackled the controversial question of the complicity of Jewish Councils with their Nazi persecutors. Responding to the young Israelis who claimed they would never collaborate, he added, 'It's true. They would not do it. But if they had been born 40 years before they would have. They would have behaved exactly like the deported Jews behaved then; in fact, exactly like the deported Russians, or the deported Italians.'

In his 1984 foreword to the Italian translation of Hermann Langbein's *People in Auschwitz* (originally entitled *Menschen in Auschwitz*), Levi remarked that 'those who bear the greatest responsibility are Menschen, too' (p. 2673), picking up the key word in Langbein's title, *Menschen*—meaning 'human being'—which also featured in the title of his own first book *If This Is a Man*.

> They are made of the same raw material we are and it did not require a great effort or real coercion to make them into cold-blooded assassins of millions of other *Menschen*. A few years of perverse indoctrination and Dr Goebbels's propaganda were sufficient. With some exceptions, they were not sadistic monsters; they were people like us, trapped by the regime because of their pettiness, ignorance, or ambition (p. 2673).

Clearly, Levi's approach mirrored Arendt's expression about Eichmann and, more in general, about the Nazi criminals. Where they differed, on the other hand, was in what Simona Forti (2012) called the 'Dostoyevsky paradigm' whereby power, and consequently Nazism, had a demoniacal quality, and where absolute power was incarnated in certain human beings.

In his exploration of the 'grey zone', Levi was attempting to define something far more complicated than Arendt's 'banality of evil'. Since he could not 're-enact the gesture of Christ on judgement day: overhear go the righteous, over there the wicked' (p. 2431), Levi posed a more radical question having experienced life in the concentration camp himself. The chapter 'The Gray Zone' opened with the question, 'Have we survivors succeeded in understanding and making other people understand our experience?' Levi went on to state, as he had done in his 1979 interview, that 'what we commonly mean by the verb "to understand" coincides with "to simplify": without a profound simplification, the world around us would be an endless and undefined tangle that defies our ability to find our bearings and decide our actions' (p. 2430). Levi made a conscious decision to hold together understanding and the complexity of reality. He did not want to simplify, and was not satisfied with the traditional 'friend–enemy dichotomy' propagated in Carl Schmitt's works. The expression 'grey zone' addressed the grey area between victims and persecutors, or as Forti put it with reference to Arendt, the 'normality of evil'.

In her book, *The New Demons*, Forti analysed the commonalities among Levi, Arendt and another Jewish writer, Elias Canetti, especially in his 1960 book *Crowds and Power*, and in his 1962 essay 'Power and Survival'. Canetti's view was that survival was the central tenet of power. In *The Drowned and the Saved*, and in particular in 'The Gray Zone', Levi analysed the micro-physics of power inside the barbed-wire fence of the concentration camp, showing how the main aim of every prisoner was, in fact, to survive at any cost. Precisely because he had experienced the dominion of the camp in person, Levi, unlike Arendt, was able to illustrate how the will to preserve personal privilege was essential to survival. In the camps there were not only the SS guards and the Kapos. 'We ordinary prisoners were surrounded by swarms of low-level functionaries. They formed a picturesque menagerie of sweepers, vat washers, night watchman, bed smoothers, [. . .] lice and scabies inspectors, messengers, interpreters, and assistance to assistance' (p. 2436). In a context of this kind, power was like a drug, and it took hold more effectively in places where obedience and reverence were required.

Forti pointed out that in *The Drowned and the Saved*, 'In a few concise lines, Primo Levi managed to express the "truth" about the relationship between power and evil that twentieth-century philosophers have never ceased looking for' (2012).

There are at least two areas where Levi's analysis was more perceptive than Arendt's. First, Levi's insistence that there could not be an easy dichotomy between victims and persecutors, and that it was important to recognize a spectrum of involvement in the prisoners themselves. Being a victim, Levi reminded us, did not necessarily mean being absolutely innocent, as many of his examples showed. Second, and closer to home, by introducing the concept of the grey zone and thus of the spectrum between victims and their persecutors, Levi exposed himself to the risk of becoming an intrinsic part of the endemic evil of the Lager environment. Several episodes in the book illustrated this risk, including, in the chapter 'Shame', where 'egotism' led the protagonist to drink all the available water without sharing it with his friend Daniele (p. 2465).

The feature that Chaim Rumkowski and the Sonderkommandos had in common was the determination to survive as long as possible, using any means, at any cost. Levi gave the first precise account of this survival instinct in *If This a Man* when he listed the four categories of those who were 'saved'. By the time Levi wrote his last book, *The Drowned and the Saved*, he had developed a more complex and radical approach. He concluded, in fact, that death was not an absolute in the concentration-camp experience; life was. Forti commented that this was the most significant difference between Arendt's 'analogy of evil' and Levi's 'grey area'. Without recourse to philosophy or theory, Levi reversed the previously undisputed equation between evil and the desire for death (Forti 2012). The struggle for survival in the gigantic biological and social experiment of the Lager, in fact, was such that the prisoners were so thirsty for life and 'blinded by power' that they 'forgot their basic fragility' (p. 2456) and the essential truth that death was what defined life. Forti concluded that Levi demonstrated, more effectively than Arendt, that the desire to get the most out of life had become a supreme value.

There was one other aspect that made Levi unique, even compared to Arendt who had used philosophical tools to perform an in-depth analysis of the subject of evil and how the Nazis transformed it into an absolute. This unique aspect was Levi's attitude to sitting in judgement. While he made it perfectly clear that persecutors and victims were never on the same level, and that persecutors should be punished, Levi took a more problematic approach. Any form of judgement, in his view, was by definition complicated, and needed to take into account 'the infernal environment into which they had been abruptly plunged' (p. 2440). It was 'illogical to expect from them—and rhetorical and fails to claim that everyone always practiced—the behaviour we expect of saints and Stoic philosophers' (p. 2440). Of course, the Sonderkommandos, 'special squads' assigned to operate the crematoriums, represented 'an extreme case of collaboration' but Levi could not accept the idea that they were privileged just because 'for a few months they got enough to eat'. After a long meditation on the impossibility of making a case against them, Levi concluded: 'each individual is an object so complex that it is useless to try to predict behaviour common especially in extreme situations; we cannot even predict our own behaviour. This is why I ask that the history of the "crematorium crows" be pondered with compassion and rigour, but that any judgement of them be suspended' (p. 2449). For the same reason, Levi said he was 'paralysed' before the case of Chaim Rumkowski, and adopted the Latin term *impotentia judicandi* to describe his paralysis.

Another feature that distinguished Levi from Arendt was the idea of offence. In the first chapter of *The Truce*, Levi described the prisoners' state of mind after being liberated from Auschwitz in January 1945 and identified why 'the marks of the offence would remain in us forever'.

> No one would ever grasp better than us the incurable nature of the offence, which spreads like an infection. It is foolish to think that it can be abolished by human justice. It is an inexhaustible source of evil: it breaks the body and soul of those who are drowned, extinguishes them and makes them abject; rises again as infamy in the oppressors, is perpetuated as hatred in the survivors, and springs up in 1000 ways, against the very will of all, as a first for revenge, as moral breakdown, as negation, as weariness, as resignation (p. 217).

The marks of the offence, Levi recognized, would never be erased, not even by human justice: 'the condition of victimhood does not exclude guilt, which is often objectively serious, but I do not know the human court that could be delegated to take its measure' (p. 2436).

The controversy surrounding Arendt's book on the Eichmann trial caused Gershom Scholem, a scholar of Jewish mysticism and friend of Walter Benjamin, to initiate a correspondence with Arendt whom he respected and liked. Scholem was outraged by Arendt's claim that Jewish Councils were complicit with the Nazis and concluded that nobody could predict how they would behave under the same circumstances. He told Arendt that many of the functionaries in the camp were forced to take terrible decisions in circumstances that could never be reconstructed or reproduced. In his view, it would be presumptuous to judge them having not been present at the time.

Unlike Arendt, Levi did not absolve nor condemn either the persecutors or the victims. What he did do was attempt to understand, at the cost of making his analysis more complicated. He was able to do this because he had been present at the time.

Bruno Bettelheim

A psychoanalyst and child psychotherapist, born in Vienna in 1903, Bettelheim was captured after the Anschluss in 1938 and sent first to Dachau and then to Buchenwald. He was released in 1939 and emigrated to the United States, where he published several articles on his experience in the concentration camps. In 1960, he published *The Informed Heart: Autonomy in a Mass*, a more articulated analysis of his Lager experience.

Levi was always critical of Bettelheim's psychological interpretations. In the chapter *'Shame' (The Drowned and the Saved)*, he expressed the matter directly:

> I do not believe that psychoanalysts—who have delved into our tangles with professional rapacity—are competent' to explain the impulse of survivors to bear witness. 'Their interpretations, even those of someone who, like Bruno Bettelheim, lived through the ordeal of the Lager, seem approximate and simplistic, as if the theorems of plane geography were being applied to spherical triangles (p. 2469).

On another occasion, in a conversation with Anna Bravo and Federico Cereja which contributed to research on the deportation conducted by the Piedmont chapter of the Association of Former Deportees, and published posthumously in 1984, Levi talked more freely about Bettelheim's theories.

When one interviewer told him how concentration-camp survivors generally rejected Bettelheim's ideas, Levi said he was of the same opinion. In his view, Bettelheim over-relied on psychological categories, and attempted to explain the prisoners' reactions using the concept of regression to infancy, while he himself felt that the concentration camp had produced the opposite effect, forcing him to become an adult (Levi cited Lidia Rolfi in saying that the Lager was his university).

When his interviewer objected that perhaps this was true for a small minority, while the majority of prisoners might have been reduced to a state of regressive infancy by food and sleep deprivation, forced labour and camp conditions, Levi denied this was the case. He had observed his fellow prisoners closely, and his curiosity and anthropological interest had been sharpened while he was held in the concentration camp. Levi also thought that Bettelheim's view that Anne Frank's family did not try to escape, but, rather, settled into their daily habits and closed their eyes to the imminent danger of Nazism, was ungenerous.

In another interview with Risa Sodi, recorded soon before his death, Levi again criticized Bettelheim. When Sodi asked him why he was so hostile to psychoanalysis, Levi rebutted that the concept of regression could be valid for some people, for him the opposite was true. Levi's interpretation of The Informed Heart was relatively narrow, because its central theme was not the forced infantilization of prisoners, but, rather, the possibility of maintaining a state of inner freedom under extreme conditions. Bettelheim presented a detailed analysis of prisoners' reactions to their life in the Lager, using data collected personally, as well as witness statements and research conducted after the war. He concentrated on what induced prisoners to accept the mechanisms of camp life to the point where they identified with the Nazis, a fact which was incomprehensible to those who had not experienced it. Bettelheim's enquiry, using the tools of psychoanalysis, explored the dynamics that led to what Levi defined as the 'grey zone'. While Bettelheim delved deeper into psychological mechanisms, especially those of the prisoners who managed in various ways to survive, Levi was more interested in the idea of individual responsibility, focusing on the power of the unjust to pervert the just.

Bettelheim was convinced that the crux of the matter was the loss of freedom of choice, even when this choice meant accepting death. A striking example in his book was the story of the Jewish ballet dancer, who was forced by a guard to dance while she was queueing for the gas chamber. In Bettelheim's interpretation, dancing helped the woman reclaim her humanity; galvanized, she turned on the SS guard and shot him with his service rifle. Levi rejected this idea of a heroic morality, positing instead that there were an infinite number of gradations between black and white, between good and evil. Under no circumstances did Levi accept judgement over individual choices in a regime of coercion and absolute dominion. There was one chapter in Bettelheim's book defending the actions of prisoners. Entitled ' Individual and Mass Behavior in Extreme Situations', the chapter contains a penetrating analysis of how prisoners who survived concentration camps had almost definitely renounced their inner freedom in order to save their lives. Levi claimed the opposite was true—survival was a Darwinian struggle.

Levi and Bettelheim also disagreed on the responsibilities of the Germans. Bettelheim attempted to explain the subservience of Germans by analysing the mechanisms of the Nazi totalitarian state. Levi, on the other hand, stressed the personal responsibility of those who did not speak out and ended up being complicit with the extermination of millions of men, women, and children. In *The Informed Heart*, Bettelheim talked about the common occurrence of suicides in the Lager, while Levi in many interviews stated that suicides were rare, and that, by contrast, many nervous conditions actually disappeared after imprisonment in the camps. Bettelheim committed suicide in 1990.

His main aim was not only to shed light on what took place in the camps but also to show how the mechanisms in place in those extreme conditions were not unique to Nazi concentration camps. Rather, they were possible in any mass society where similar mechanisms could restrict individual autonomy. Levi was not convinced that this was true. While Levi focused on anthropological issues such as human nature and aspects of morality, Bettelheim was more interested in the psychology of individuals and finding explanations for individual behaviour. Bettelheim cited the autobiography of the Jewish Hungarian doctor, Nyiszli, to whom Levi also referred in 'The Gray Zone'. Bettelheim noted with pride that Nyiszli (one of the very few surviving witnesses of the Sonderkommandos who had conducted experiments on human guinea pigs alongside the notorious Dr Mengele), did not allow the moral consequences of his activities to get in the way of his profession. He also commented on how modern society paid more attention to technical skill than to the uses that this skill can be put to, to the detriment of mankind and freedom.

Levi's attitude towards technology was again precisely the opposite, given that, as he often reminded his interlocutors, his profession as a chemist saved him. In his view, technology was not dangerous. In fact, it was a tool of progress, even though he recognized, especially towards the end of his life, that an indiscriminate use of science and technology could be dangerous. In an interview on the 'sinister power of science', Levi went so far as to propose conscientious objection for scientists and technologists who work in the military sector.

Sigmund Freud

In an interview with Levi, Sodi asked him about his attitude towards psychoanalysis. Levi said he was not in favour of psychoanalysis, but that he had read and appreciated the works of Sigmund Freud, who was, in his view, a great writer and poet, as well as being extremely perspicacious. Levi must have read *The Interpretation of Dreams* and *The Psychopathology of Everyday Life*, both of which he cited in an interview regarding the choice of his pseudonym, Damiano Malabaila (the name meant 'bad wet nurse', which Levi called a 'Freudian slip'). He might well have also read *The Future of an Illusion,* as he cited Freud's ideas about religion, as well as *Moses and Monotheism*, attracted by its Jewish theme. In the context of turn-of-the-century Turin, and of Levi's family circle, Freud's ideas probably circulated by word of mouth, rather than through his works, even though Levi's father could read German. It was not until the 1940s, in fact, that Freud's works were published in Italian. Levi, on the other hand, might have read (or reread) his works in German.

Levi made many references to dreams in his work, while rejecting psychoanalysis as a technique for understanding individuals. Levi preferred to apply Freud's theories to culture. There were some indirect references to Freud in *The Drowned and the Saved*, in particular in the chapter 'Shame', which explored the concept and mechanisms of anguish. However, Levi's Freud was a hybrid, blended with classical moralists and Leopardi's philosophical approach. This hybrid approach was an example of how Levi was not interested in adopting any one theory when analysing a problem. He preferred using a variety of cultural influences to reinforce his arguments, which were based in part on his personal experience, and in part on rational analysis. The truth is that Levi adopted the rationalism of Freud, of Leopardi and of other poet-philosophers, and blended it with his own. The closest Levi got to appropriating Freud's ideas was in his Preface to his personal anthology, *The Search for Roots*, where he confessed to having an 'Id', and in 'To a Young Reader' (*Other People's Trades*) where he advises young readers and writers: 'Don't be afraid of mistreating your it by muzzling it. There is no real danger of that; 'the tenant on the floor below' will always find a way of making himself heard, because to write is to strip oneself naked—even the sparest writer strips himself bare' (p. 2242).

Variam Shalamov

The short-story collection, *The Kolyma Tales,* edited by Piero Sinatti, was first published in Italy in 1976 by Savelli. *Tuttolibri*, the literary insert of *La Stampa*, asked Levi to write a review, with the idea that a survivor of a Nazi concentration camp would be well placed to comment on a book of stories about the Soviet Gulags. The review was published as 'From Stalin's Lagers' in *Uncollected Stories and Essays*. After stating that 'one can't but harbour respect for someone who has served, whatever the reason, seventeen years of deportation', Levi went on to describe the 30 stories contained in the book. He stressed the fact that the Soviet Lagers (he never used the term Gulag) were a model for 'all subsequent concentration-camp regimes' and that they 'cast their shadow, unfortunately, on all the deficiencies, uncertainties, inertia, and silence of today's Soviet Union' (p. 1212). However, regarding the stories in the collection—a fraction of the stories written by Shalamov—Levi's review was quite negative. In his view, 'Stalinist terror and isolationism also transmit their paralyzing infection to their witnesses and their opponents' with the result that men like Shalamov 'deserve our respect anyway' but 'their stature is inferior to that of their peers who battled Hitler's terror, all who today denounce the crimes committed by Western civilization in Asia and Africa' (p. 1212) One reason for his negative judgement was political: 'their political development appears limited and crude' (p. 1212). Levi was also critical of the author, whose despair, he believed, led him to no longer believe in anything:

> he hopes for nothing more than the end of his suffering; he has no star to aspire to. His despair, otherwise dignified and contained, does not end with liberation; it is the mute despair of someone who feels annihilated and no longer believes in anything, of some-one who during decades of useless suffering has exhausted every political reason, indeed, every reason, to live (p. 1212).

Moreover, 'the label of 'political prisoners' is affixed to them more or less at random, with the dual purpose of disseminating terror and recruit-ing free labour, and the pair it with Russian resignation (Tyutchev's "infinite patience") but without pride (p. 1212). And yet, 'paradoxically, the weak-ness of these stories [. . .] strengthens their documentary value. They seem to say: 'Here, read and see what the Lager reduced me to' (p. 1212). Levi went on to criticize the translation and, more in general, the literary value, of the stories.

Gustav Sterling, who published *A World Apart*: *The Journal of a Gulag Survivor* in 1951, questioned Levi's negative view of Shalamov in a 1999 interview, which was intended to be used as a preface to the Italian addi-tion published by Einaudi, but which was then rejected. Herling accused Levi of underestimating, or even denying, the horrors of the Soviet Gulags. Herling's theory was that Levi, like all the Italian Left—especially the Communist Party—did not appreciate Shalamov because they were unable to admit that the Soviets administered concentration camps. The theory was unfounded, because Levi was never enrolled in the Communist Party, was often openly critical of the Party and always defined himself as a socialist partisan of the Justice and Liberty movement. Moreover, Herling's assumption got in the way of two other important issues, which he appeared to ignore. The first was 'political': for Levi a 'political' response to the Stalinists terror (or to Hitler) was crucial. One could also express the concept in another way. Rather than 'political', one could say 'rational'. All Levi's readers—including Herling, who was a great fan—know how important rationality was for him. Levi's culture was born of the Enlightenment. However perplexed and doubtful he was, he always wanted to understand and help others understand, both for himself and for his readers. It is clear that Shalamov's Russian spirit was very distant from this rationalist (even scientific) approach. The Enlightenment, with the exception of very rare cases, did not take root in Slavic countries, as Shalamov's stories show. In fact, like much of Russian fiction, their interest lies precisely in that despair that Levi abhorred.

Levi was not always enlightened, however. In his review of Shalamov's short-story collection, the burden of duty in being rational was made very clear. What he could not accept in the Russian writer was his nihilism, and the absence of hope reflected in the stories. 'Mute despair' was what gave Shalamov the strength to write fiction, but he failed actively or 'positively' to combat Stalinism. In Levi's view, he simply struggled to survive in the Gulag, where he defended himself tooth and nail, and where he was ruthless in his judgement of himself and of others. He did not appear to have had any *pietas*, which is perhaps what made him a great writer, aside from the Chekhov-like tone of his stories.

As a reviewer of Shalamov's stories, Levi was first and foremost a witness and survivor himself, who placed great emphasis on the stunting of 'political development' resulting from Stalinist terror and isolationism. He did not criticize Solzhenitsyn in the same way, however. Is it possible that Levi thought Solzhenitsyn was more of a writer and less of a witness? What we do know is that Shalamov, who was unpredictable and irascible (he has also been called a timid idealist), had decided not to write about his Gulag experience. He had been tired and sick, and was under constant KGB surveillance in the retirement clinic where he was staying. He certainly had no desire to go back to prison in the Kolyma region and lose the small benefits he had acquired. This was in stark contrast, as many critics have pointed out, to the cynicism displayed by the narrator of his stories set in Stalin's 'white crematorium'.

Levi gave a political slant to his interpretation of Shalamov's works, not because he wanted to denounce the mystification of his stories—he often repeated that the witness account was truthful and worthy of respect—but to prove how 'half a century of forced disinformation can wear down the opposition more effectively than the much fiercer and more efficient Hitlerian terror, which did not have the time or the means to sever the age-old cultural bonds that tied Germany to the rest of Europe. The same political asphyxiation that debased socialism in the Soviet Union has debased its very opponents' (p. 1213). Levi did not ignore the existence of the Soviet Gulags; he wrote about them throughout the 1950s and 60s.

As Herling's book pointed out, Levi's and Shalamov's approach to political action—and politics as a whole—was very different. Herling appeared to ignore, or underestimate, Levi's need not to put Lagers and Gulags on the same level. This was not for theological reasons. Unlike other contemporary Jewish writers and thinkers, who claim that the genocide of the Jews was a unique, and unrepeatable event, Levi was a scientist, not a philosopher of history or a theologist. The issue that he grappled with was how could the Germans allow Hitler to commit the genocide against the Jews? Levi wavered between one explanation which regarded the German 'spirit' (is there such a thing as a collective character?) and another based on biology, or animal behaviour, but he was increasingly aware that he was treading on uncertain, slippery ground. Levi came up with many different hypotheses over the course of his life, but it was in his masterpiece of political and intellectual honesty, *The Drowned and the Saved*, that he set out the reasons why equating Nazi and Soviet concentration camps did not help him get to the bottom of the thorny issue of the specific context of Germany, and also impeded a clear examination of the Russian and Soviet context. For example, Levi wondered to what extent Soviet gulags were the legacy of Tsarism. Levi did not believe in evil, or, rather, evil was not a valid explanation for what took place. For an enlightened positivist like him, even though Nazism appeared to be a mani-festation of evil, the concept was not sufficient to explain it.

For Herling, on the other hand, the main issue—and his obsession as a writer—was the presence of evil in the camps which he had been unable to explain because he was not religious. Herling was not interested in for-mulating historic judgement, or in delving into the political rationale for the Soviet, or Nazi, regime. For him it was impossible to imagine socialism without Gulags, and this is where Levi and Herling were diametrically opposed. As Levi often answered to his readers, who asked repeatedly over the 1950s and the 60s why he only wrote about the Nazi Lagers and not the Soviet Gulags—he had been a witness not a judge. This was why he only wrote about what he had seen and experienced in the first person. In his interview on Shalamov, Herling claimed that left-wing intellectuals—including Levi—were convinced that Soviet communism was better than Marxism, owing to the fact that its roots lay in the enlightenment and in political rationalism. Nothing that Levi wrote reflects this assumption. In his view, the discriminating factors were the planning of the extermination, the use of technology (the gas Chambers) and the idea that a regime can decide to destroy an entire population by means of wide-ranging power and large-scale technology. All these factors, as Levi often wrote and said, could equally be applied to the Soviet Gulags.

LEVI, BELLOW AND THE KING OF THE JEWS

On 20 November 1977, *La Stampa* published a short piece by Primo Levi at the bottom of a page in its Arts and Culture section. Entitled 'The King of the Jews', it was accompanied by an illustration of both sides of an aluminium alloy coin, one side of which was emblazoned with the Star of David. What followed was an autobiographical account. Levi had come across the coin at Auschwitz after the liberation of the Monowitz camp. From that small object, kept as a lucky charm first in a purse, then later in a drawer, the writer tells the story of the man who minted the coin: Chaim Rumkowski, a Jewish industrialist whose business had failed and who had been named as the head of the ghetto of Lodz, occupied by the Germans in 1940. He had been seen as a sort of uncrowned king of the ghetto. Exhausted and hungry, however, he was an obvious target for elimination—not before being put to work in the textile mills of the city, producing the canvas needed by the German Army, however. Both executioner and victim, this character was used as an example of the 'grey zone' by Levi in his last book, *The Drowned and the Saved* (1986), which defined the area between black and white, between victims and perpetrators. In the piece Levi described the insane megalomania of this character; the way Rumkowski took on the role of king and absolute ruler, complete with a court and bards, in the camp.

The story printed in the Turin newspaper did not refer to the 'grey zone', which only later became a vivid image: 'a broad band of grey consciences that stands between the potentates of evil and the pure victims' (p. 1415). Levi had already introduced the concept a year earlier in his Preface to Jacques Presser's, *De Nacht der Girondijnen* (The Night of the Girondists), which he himself had translated for Adelphi. The expressions and formulas used to refer to the 'grey zone' were even more precise and detailed than those used in the story dedicated to Rumkowski. However, Levi found the personality of the head of the Lodz Ghetto, who minted coins and printed postage stamps just like a sovereign, far more interesting: he was fascinated by the man's ambiguous relationship with power. Rumkowski was a Jewish persecutor of the Jews who ended up in the gas chamber. Levi told the story in great detail, albeit succinctly. After being published in the newspaper, the story was reused twice: first in a short story collected in *Lilith and Other Stories*, published in 1981, and then in the chapter 'The Gray Zone' in *The Drowned and the Saved*.

The short story that came out in the collection in 1981 is identical to the one that appeared in *La Stampa*. Levi positioned it at the end of the 'Present Perfect' section, a group of 12 short stories about the concentration camps and Nazi persecution, some of which date back to the 1950s. The story underwent several changes in *The Drowned and the Saved*, however. Notably, the image of the coin used in both *La Stampa* and *Moments of Reprieve* was left out, ridding the story of any autobiographical slant. Not only were there numerous changes in the choice of words, but the opening was also revised. The additional text was used to connect the story of Rumkowski to other places where Levi addressed the 'fundamental theme of human ambiguity fatally provoked by oppression' (p. 2449). In the first few lines, the author warned readers that this was a story already told elsewhere, and added a reference to Gabriele D'Annunzio, presenting Rumkowski as an imitator of the dictators of the day (Mussolini and Hitler). Levi referred to the idea of a necessary hero and adopted a style to suit it, such as when the dean of Lodz imitates Mussolini and Hitler's pseudo-conversations with their crowds of supporters. At another point, Levi added a quick reflection on the relationship between failure and the ability to obtain moral force through the experience of defeat and personal ruin—twice Rumkowski had failed as an industrialist. Levi also considered the struggle between power-groups when political regimes collapse citing two examples: the ministers of

Salò, and Hitler's court. In this way, Levi added historical and psychological background concerning the internal dynamics of power.

Levi made further small alterations to the text which were more judgemental towards Rumkowski and other Jews in what would later be called the 'grey zone', phrases that recall the Preface to *The Night of the Girondists*. Why did Levi write about Rumkowski again so many years after returning from Auschwitz? It was undoubtedly his desire to define the 'grey zone' more fully that led him do pick up the story once again. Moreover, Levi had recently found out various things that allowed him to reconstruct at least part of the story, 'which is fascinating and sinister' (p. 2449). It was not a sudden illumination which impelled him to gather additional information on Rumkowski; it was, rather, a slow but identifiable process which, at least from 1975, was sometimes documented. This process culminated in the final draft of the chapter in *The Drowned and the Saved* on the 'grey zone', traces of which go back to the mid-50s and early 60s.

In a piece from 1955 entitled 'The Deported. Anniversary', written for the tenth anniversary of the end of the Second World War and the return of the deportees from the concentration and extermination camps, Levi wrote explicitly that the perpetrators belonged to the same human family as that of the victims. They were not characters from a distant world, not abnormal. He stressed that they themselves were just like the deported men, women and children. In another text from 1961, 'Testifying about Eichmann', he explored the contaminating effect of evil, in reference to the Sonderkommando, the ravens of the crematorium. These commandos were made up of Jews who participated in the extermination of other Jews in the gas chambers in order to prolong their own lives, even by a few months. Their stories, alongside that of Rumkowski, would find their way into the chapter 'The Gray Zone' in *The Drowned and the Saved*. The concept of contamination is closely linked to Levi's approach to the figure of Rumkowski, to his relationship with power and his two-facedness.

In a letter sent to his friend Luciana Nissim in 1979—who had been deported to Auschwitz along with her husband, the economist Franco Momigliano, and Levi—Levi explained why this theme was so important to him. The letter contained a photocopy of the piece that had appeared in *La Stampa*, so Levi must have previously told Luciana and Franco the story of Rumkowski. Luciana was not the only person with whom he shared the experience of his deportation to Auschwitz. As a trained doctor, after returning from Auschwitz, Luciana worked as a paediatrician at the Olivetti factory. She then underwent psychoanalysis first with Franco Fornari, and later with Cesare Musatti, in order to train as a psychoanalyst herself. Levi had been in close contact with her from the early 60s, and the story of Rumkowski, the first completed piece of the grey-zone triptych, is close to two of his key issues: the involvement of victims in the power strategies of the perpetrators and the contagion of evil. Luciana had survived the camp owing to her profession as a physician, but after publishing her eye-witness account *Memories from the House of the Dead* (the title was taken from Dostoyevsky), she remained silent for a long time.

In a long essay titled 'Variazioni Rumkowski: sulle piste della zona grigia' (Rumkowski Variations: Tracking the Grey Zone), Martina Mengoni documented the sources from which Levi drew the information for his story. Three books were particularly influential: *The Final Solution* by Gerald Reitlinger, published in 1953 (published in Italian by Il Saggiatore in 1962); *Bréviaire de la haine. Le troisième Reich et les Juifs* by Léon Poliakov which came out in 1951 (published by Einaudi in Italy with the title *Il nazismo e lo sterminio degli Ebrei* in 1955); and *The Destruction of the European Jews* by Raul Hilberg, published in 1961 (but which did not come out in Italian until 1995 with Einaudi). Levi must have known Poliakov's book as it was translated by his sister Anna Maria and was published in the essay series, 'Saggi'. Three years later, in 1958, the new expanded edition of *If This Is a Man* was published in the same series.

Mengoni quoted an article that appeared in the American magazine *Commentary* in December 1948, written by Solomon F. Bloom, entitled 'Dictator of the Lodz Ghetto. The Strange History of Mordechai Chaim Rumkowski'. This text would become the main source for the parts devoted to Rumkowski in the books by Reitlinger and Poliakov, being the first report of the affair to appear outside Poland. Details of this article, Mengoni pointed out, fit Levi's description of Rumkowski perfectly, especially his fate (Levi referred to a verse composed in honour of Rumkowski by one of his court poets, cited in *Commentary*).

The author speculates that Levi may have read the piece in the French translation which had first appeared in the journal *Les Temps Modernes* in 1949. The literary journal was distributed in Italy, and particularly in Turin, whereas *Commentary* was more difficult to find. In any case, Levi had been aware of the existence of this article since the 50s, as it was mentioned in a note in Anna Maria's translation of Poliakov's work (the title of Bloom's article was translated into Italian). Whether Levi actually read Bloom's article in *Commentary* has not been established, but details of the story had already been revealed in the other books mentioned. Levi was an avid reader and may have gotten hold of Bloom's article at a later date when he wrote the story published in *La Stampa*. Mengoni suggested a further source: a story by a Polish writer, Adolf Rudnicki, 'The Merchant of Lodz', included in the volume *I topi* (The Mice) published by Mondadori in 1967, where a historical and psychological profile of Rumkowski is outlined. Levi may well have read it, since other details are similar to those reported by Rudnicki.

There is another possible indirect source not mentioned by Mengoni which is also very interesting. It could have attracted Levi's attention to the figure of Rumkowski, and led him to write a story about the coin he had picked up at Auschwitz. Unlike the authors mentioned above, with the exception of perhaps Poliakov, due to his importance in the study of Nazism, Saul Bellow is very well-known, even notorious. It is highly unlikely that his works would have been unknown to a reader as curious as Levi. The American novelist won the Nobel Prize in 1976. Rumkowski appears in one of his best-known novels, *Mr Sammler's Planet*, a book that contributed to his fame. The novel was published in the US in February 1970 and Feltrinelli brought out the Italian translation a year later.

Mr Sammler's Planet was Bellow's seventh novel, published six years after his masterpiece, *Herzog* (1964). The protagonist, Arthur Sammler, was a Polish Jew, just over 70 years old, who had lived in New York for 20 years, but still felt like a 'foreigner'. As we soon learn, Sammler had escaped a Nazi massacre buried under a pile of corpses, and lost an eye. He then went on to fight the Nazis, and remembered killing a German soldier in a flashback (this detail reminds us of Levi's *If Not Now, When?* written in 1982, which tells the story of a band of Jewish partisans, but it might just be a coincidence).

Sammler was a journalist, and had lived in London in the 1930s, where he had met H. G. Wells. Caught out by the outbreak of war in Poland, where his wife had gone to help settle her father's estate, he was rescued by a graveyard caretaker, where he hid in a tomb and was fed pieces of stale bread. Emerging unscathed from the war, Sammler ended up in a refugee camp, from where he was saved by a wealthy cousin, Elya Gruner, who took him to America and looked after him. Elya, to whom Sammler was emotionally attached, was about to die. The whole story, including the various flashbacks, takes place over three days, and includes some of the things that happened to the protagonist in New York, with the Six Day War in Israel in the background.

'And you and Ussher had such conversations about that crazy old fellow—King Rumkowski. The man from Lodz ... What do you think?' (p. 13). Mr Sammler did not answer right away. Instead he dwelt on the theme of the 'banality of evil' in a complex, often contradictory, commentary: agreeing with Arendt at times and arguing with her at others ('The idea of making the century's great crime look dull is not banal' [p. 13]). *Bellow: A Biography* (2002), by James Atlas, informs us that Bellow was highly critical of Arendt, and had come to hate her, having met her in person.

According to Atlas, *Mr Sammler's Planet* is a book full of philosophical musings, a long meditation disguised as a novel. Through the character of the Holocaust survivor who had fled to the US, various aspects of American society are examined, including the student protests at the beginning of the book. Sammler was yet another incarnation of the American intellectual who was in conflict with the culture of his day, adversarial and lost. The figure of Rumkowski, who hovers within the novel, however, never became central.

From conversations with American relatives in the novel, we learn that Sammler would be ready to write an article on the Dean of Lodz. The idea came to him when he was summoned as a witness at the Eichmann trial but did not go—hence the theme of the 'banality of evil'. What prevented him from writing further about the character of Rumkowski, however, was another project that had kept him busy over the years—a book about H. G. Wells. This is what persuaded Shula, Sammler's daughter, to steal a manuscript about life on the moon by the Indian scientist, Dr Lal, in the mistaken belief that she could help her father research a book on Wells. The manuscript was returned to its rightful owner after a few adventures, and in the final part of the novel Sammler finds himself in conversation with the Indian scientist, a man of great culture, who had imagined transferring mankind to the Moon.

This was the most extensive reference to Rumkowski. The speech, more like a monologue, revolved around philosophical themes. Sammler quoted Brecht and De Sade among others, until he revealed to Lal that he had been warped by the experience of Nazi massacre and the events that followed. What haunted him, he said, now that he found himself living in the bustling city of New York, was the role that each of us chose to play back then. Rumkowski's role as 'the mad Jewish King of Lodz' (p. 190) was foremost in his mind. Sammler told Lal the story of the King. The information Sammler gives the scientist closely resembled the details included by Levi in the story that appeared in *La Stampa* (for example: in

Mr Sammler's Planet he was a director of an orphanage, whereas Levi wrote that he was a director of Jewish charitable institutions').

Bellow's style was obviously different. In Bellow's version, the story was truncated, coming out in short spurts. However, the point of view was quite clear: Rumkowski was 'a man with a bit to play, like so many modern individuals' (p. 190). Over a full page, Sammler described the situation in the Lodz Ghetto. There were other details suggesting that Bellow may have consulted the same sources as Levi, in particular the article in *Commentary*, a journal Bellow had contributed to. There was also, of course, the fact that Jewish American intellectual circles considered the topic highly relevant.

Bellow concentrated on the theatrics of Rumkowski's recitation, that of the tragic clown, *Ubu Roi*, which, according to Mr Sammler, was much admired by Germans. The explanation of the Dean of Lodz's role provided by the protagonist of the novel was too vague for the Indian scientist. Bellow was exploring the issue of the relationship of Jews to their community, which comes up in many of his works. One of the main themes of the novel—which expressed Saul Bellow's conservative, even reactionary, traits—was precisely Sammler's living contradiction in New York, as a Polish Jew and as an American citizen. American Society was, in Bellow's view, full of contradictions, neuroses, excesses, and superficiality.

Sammler told Lal that he was intrigued by Rumkowski. In fact, he wanted to understand what the true stature of a human being is:

> I am not speaking only of moral demand upon the imagination to produce a human figure of adequate stature. What is the true stature of a human being? This, Dr. Lal, was what I meant by speaking of the killers' delight in abasement in parody—in Rumkowski, King of the rags and shit, Rumkowski, ruler of corpses. And this is what preoccupies me with the theatricality of the Rumkowski episode (p. 190).

Bellow's point of view was only apparently different from Levi's, as we can see at the end of 'The Gray Zone' in *The Drowned and the Saved*. Bellow was interested in the relationship between what the Dean of Lodz thought of himself and the part he played for the Nazis. Levi introduced a similar Shakespearean theme at the end of 'The Gray Zone', where he defined Rumkowski as a 'symbolic emblematic figure' (p. 2455), just as Bellow had stated that Mr Sammler was symbolic.

> In this strip of half-consciences Rumkowski, a symbolic, emblematic figure, should be placed. It is hard to know whether he should be at the top or the bottom. He alone could say, if he could speak to us—lying, perhaps, as he may always have lied, even to himself. Yet he would help us to understand all the same, the way every defendant helps his judge, even when he doesn't want to, even when he is lying, because man's capacity to play a role is not unlimited (p. 2455).

The theme of performance is very significant for Levi.

Mengoni stressed that what unites Levi and Rudnicki, one of his sources, is that they both sketched Rumkowski. Their obsession was with what was visible, or, rather, what Rumkowski thought of himself, how he saw himself, how he saw the choices he made. Rudnicki placed greater emphasis on the importance of the rhetoric of the work of Rumkowski. On the first page of his essay-story, 'The Merchant of Lodz', Rudnicki spoke expressly of acting: 'Hitler was not terrible, the town pharmacist who recognized the Hitler in himself, and acted it out in an everyday role was terrible' (quoted from Leopold Buczkowski, director of a cabaret in Warsaw).

Levi went a step further than both the Polish writer and Bellow, because he looked at the story from another point of view—its possible relevance. Having said that the ability of a man to act was not unlimited, he wrote: 'None of this is enough, however, to explain the sense of urgency and menace that emanates from this story' (p. 2455). He is interested in understanding how we can recognize ourselves in Rumkowski, since we see ourselves reflected in him, 'His ambiguity is ours, the innate ambiguity of hybrids kneaded out of clay and spirit. His fever is ours, the fever of Western civilization that "descends into hell with trumpets and drums"' (p. 2455). The expression is taken from Alfred Döblin's *Berlin Alexanderplatz*.

Levi ended his reflection on Rumkowski with a quote from Shakespeare outlining the folly of the proud man. It is when Isabella, the protagonist in *Measure for Measure*, describes the condition of those who find themselves in the same position as the Dean of Lodz, when their authority is precarious, their judgement is full of errors, and their weakness inherent. Like an angry ape, they then 'make the angels weep'. Levi's is a portrait of an insane man, dazzled by power and prestige, to the extent that he 'forget(s) our essential fragility' (p. 2455) Rumkowski had made a deal with power, but Levi included himself and his readers in this observation, 'Like Rumkowski, we, too, are so blinded by power and prestige that we forget our basic fragility. We make our deals with power, willingly or not, forgetting that we are all in the ghetto, that the ghetto is walled in, that outside the wall are the lords of death, and that not far away the train is waiting' (p. 2455) It is no coincidence that the grammatical subject of the last sentence of the essay is 'we'. Levi did not remove himself from the picture. He was completely inside it, unlike Sammler in Bellow's novel.

However, as Philip Roth pointed out, in *Mr. Sammler's Planet*, it is not clear which came first: Bellow's denunciation of American society in the 60s, or the story of the survivor of the Holocaust? The two themes were melded in the novel, and, more generally, in Bellow's fiction, from the 1940s, when *The Victim* (1947) came out—with his the first reference to the Nazi massacre in Europe, up to *The Bellarosa Connection* (1989), where the subject is dealt with at greater length than in *Mr. Sammler's Planet*.

At the centre of the narrative of *The Bellarosa Connection* is Harry Fonstein, another Polish Jew, who escaped the clutches of the Gestapo and the SS through a series of events throughout Europe, thanks to Billy Rose, a rich Broadway producer from America, who is the promoter and financier of a clandestine network called 'Operation Bellarosa'. He arrived in America, transiting through Cuba, thanks to his marriage to an American woman called Sorella. Fonstein became wealthy owing both to his astuteness and his wife's practical intelligence. Fonstein, the Jew from Galicia, wanted to thank Billy Rose and talk to him only briefly, but the producer avoided any contact. Fonstein never speaks in the novel directly. The narrator is another character, who is also a Jew, and the founder of the Mnemosyne Institute, where he became rich teaching memory techniques. Bellow's story revolves around two focal points: first, the relationship between memory and oblivion; second, the identity of Jewish American survivors, and more generally of Jews who did not have first-hand experience of the extermination carried out by the Germans during the Second World War (a theme which was also present in *Mr. Sammler's Planet*).

Levi and Bellow do not appear to have many things in common, apart from their Jewish origin. There is of course Bellow's blurb on the dust jacket of the American edition of *The Periodic Table* (written at the insistence of the translator, Raymond Rosenthal), which contributed to the popularity of Levi in the US. Then there is a reference to a meeting between the two writers, which wasn't the warmest, during Levi's American tour. But it is precisely in relation to *The Bellarosa Connection* that Bellow quoted the Italian writer in a letter addressed to Cynthia Ozick at the end of the 1980s, on the publication of her book, *The Messiah of Stockholm*.

The Jewish American Ozick, was accused by a reviewer, Robert Alter, of not addressing the subject of the Holocaust. In his letter, Bellow reflects on the fact that American Jewish writers have not dealt with what was, in fact, the central event of their times: the extermination of the Jews of Europe, a term that Bellow preferred to the word 'Holocaust', more commonly used today. It is an autobiographical personal reflection, which reflects on the situation in the 1940s and the books that Bellow wrote back then. With reference to the extermination, he wrote: 'only a few Jews . . . (like Primo Levi) were able to comprehend it all.'

Curiously, at the end of the letter to Ozick, Bellow also quoted Shakespeare, using an expression from Macbeth ('metaphysical aid'). As Mengoni pointed out, Shakespeare's words, which Levi cited when he wrote about Rumkowski in both versions, is a potential key to interpreting Rumkowski. They speak of the fragility of man, but also of his ridiculous appearance, an absurdity mixed with tragedy which then produces tragicomedy. Can we consider Levi a tragicomic writer? Or rather, was he at least aware of the tragicomic aspect of the extermination? The idea that this could be either comic or ridiculous might be surprising were it not for the musicologist, Massimo Mila. When Levi died, Mila wrote in *La Stampa* that Levi was a humorist, who was attentive to the ridiculous side of man's behaviour. Levi's first book, *If This Is a Man*, contains rare but very pronounced present comic moments, as far back as in 1958. The same is true for *The Truce* (1963).

It was Levi's sense of duty that allowed him to write about tragic events in a comic vein. Comedy is evident in many of the stories collected in *Lilith and Other Stories*, where the story 'The King of the Jews' can be found. The tragicomic aspect of Rumkowski's story—the man's silly antics and the reference to the passage from *Measure for Measure*—was of interest to both Bellow and Levi. Who knows if it was Bellow's insistence on the tragicomic that led Levi to read the newly translated *Mr. Sammler's Planet*, come across Rumkowski again, and convince himself to pull the old coin out of the drawer, and tell the story of the terrible and tragic-comic Dean of Lodz? It is a hypothesis not to be brushed aside.

LEMMAS

Colour

In his *Dialogue with Tullio Regge*, Levi claimed that as a chemist he had always worked with at least five or six shades of blue. However, at least in his first two books, *If This Is a Man* and *The Truce*, the dominant colour is grey, which is not a colour in itself but, rather, a spectrum of intermediate shades between black and white. In Levi's work, colour was often used metaphorically, representing a state of mind or casting a particular light on psychological situations. More rarely, colour was used symbolically. In his last book, *The Drowned and the Saved*, Levi used the adjective grey to define the 'zone' between black and white where there were different shades or degrees of responsibility for actions that took place within the concentration camp. Massimo Bucciantini pointed out that grey was not a synonym for passive in Levi's system; passivity corresponded to the colour white. White was undifferentiated anguish while grey was the colour that represented specimens of humanity who were determined to survive and were willing to do anything in order to succeed.

Poland was grey, as was the concentration camp itself, where everything was grey including the prisoners, who saw the dawn light as being as grey as the 'future [that] stood out before us, grey and inarticulate' (p. 111). The adjective 'grey' was used to describe a state of mind, or the landscape surrounding the Lager which clearly influenced the prisoners' mood. Writing years after his experience, in *If This Is a Man*, Levi described the bread served in the camp as being 'a slab of grey bread' (p. 60).

In *The Truce*, grey was the colour that expressed the psychological connotations of the landscape, which was 'between the grey of the snow and the grey of the sky' (p. 216). This was how Levi described the fields outside Auschwitz after liberation; it was, after all, in the middle of the freezing Polish winter. During Levi's journey back to Italy, as the seasons slowly changed, the palette of colours became more varied, though there were never very many.

As a result of his scientific training, Levi knew that colours were a matter of perception: he knew that light was what produced colour, and he also knew that when he was looking at fields in the winter, the colour grey was the result of the absence of light. The Buna camp, in *If This Is a Man*, was 'desperately and essentially opaque and grey' (p. 68), since, as he recalled in his conversations, in the Polish winter sunlight is a rare thing. In *If This Is a Man*, Levi used a palette of 26 colours, from yellow to green, and blue to brown. In *The Truce*, there were 39, including red, purple, green and brown, and the changing colours of the forests were a dominant theme over the course of Levi's long journey through the Ukraine and Belarus. In other books, Levi used the colour grey to define a person who was not particularly interesting, or, in *The Periodic Table*, to describe metals or other substances in his personal periodic table, or to describe the grey or white dust that clung to the bodies of the prisoners. In his poetry, grey had a negative connotation; the 'grey companion' in 'Buna', for example.

Many of the colours Levi used were composite: grey-green, or green-grey, the blue-black of cadmium, a white-and-blue banner, the reddish-brown of a girl's hair, emerald green, verdigris, blue-green. Black, which is not strictly speaking a colour, but which is the opposite of white, was present in both *If This Is a Man* and *The Truce*, where it was used to describe the colour of the prisoners' clothes, beards and hair. In *If Not Now, When?*, the sky was described as looking black. However, as Levi slowly moved on to writing about subjects other than his Lager experience, the colour black lost its purely negative connotations and became simply a part of the author's palette of colours. In his early works, based on his experience in the concentration camps, the mud was black, and the earth in many of the Eastern European countries Levi travelled through on his long journey home was black, as were the berets of the Jewish Partisans Levi met on the train. In *The Periodic Table*, there was black enamel and 'lampblack' and a 'shiny black mirror' (p. 887). Uniforms were black as were the swastikas, the same colour as coal or soot. In *Lilith and other Stories*, a drawing of 'sinister black sun' (p. 1443) featured in the story 'Dizzying Heat'. The drawing was made by Ettore, a writer of palindromes, who had 'lost the thread some time ago' (p. 1443), although the black sun was nothing to do with depression, but, rather, an allusion to the state of mind of anyone engaged in creative work. In Levi's work, if depression were to have a colour it would not be the black of the classical or mediaeval tradition—it would be grey.

The colour white, at the end of the spectrum of light, was the colour of the sky and the sun ('cold, white, and distant') in *If This Is a Man*. The smoke from the crematoria chimneys was white, as was the snow, of course. Snow was a constant in Levi's landscapes, where it was either a neutral presence, or, in some of the short stories, even reassuring and pleasant, but only when it was found far away from Poland or Auschwitz. In *If Not Now, When?*, white was an essential component of Levi's description of the landscape. In *The Truce*, a composite of white and blue produced 'pale blue'. More in general, white was the colour of the temporal and spatial limbo Levi found himself in after being freed from the camps and before returning home. In 'Titanium' (*The Periodic Table*), the white paint used to paint a cupboard is 'so white' because 'it's Titanium' (p. 889). In 'Uranium', Levi described the surface of the metal as 'silvery white' (p. 916). Men's clothes in the camp were blue-and-white striped, while the women's were generally dark smock-like dresses. In *If Not Now, When?*, the whites of the eyes of the Uzbek chess player challenging Leonid were described as being 'of such a pure white that they verged on pale blue' (p. 1572). This description showed how Levi, the writer-chemist, was fascinated by nuances of colour and by changes from one colour to another. This fascination was also reflected in his descriptions of dawns and sunsets, where colours changed from red to violet to grey to silver. Violet and pink also made a rare appearance in Levi's descriptions of cloth. In addition to describing the colour of the sky, Levi also described the colour of the surface of water: 'dark blue overhead, emerald green in the east, and violet with wide orange stripes in the west' (p. 679). This was one of the most vivid descriptions in his entire Opus, appearing in a short story collected in *Flaw of Form*. In *If Not Now, When?*, the epic thrust of the novel led Levi to indulge in more colourful descriptions, in the manner of novelists he appreciated such as Manzoni or nineteenth-century Russian writers. Orange and brown were dashes of colour added here and there, and the colour blue was often contaminated, as in *If This Is a Man*, to 'bluish', the colour of the tattooed numbers under the skin.

Levi never spent too many words on descriptions of landscapes; his rapid sketches were also relatively lacking in colour. Levi used the colour red, recognized culturally as the primary colour *par excellence*, to describe hair colour, building bricks and landscapes: the reddish brown of conifers, but also the sun (described as white in Auschwitz, as we have seen). Skin, and blood, but especially facial expressions were red in Levi's descriptions. A face that turned red was an outward sign of shame, a sentiment that in his short stories and in the novel *If Not Now, When?* did not necessarily have negative associations but, rather, connoted a universal state of mind, in both men and women. Of course, the books chronicling the Lager experience were the exception. Finally, the triangle political prisoners were forced to wear was red.

The most common colour in Levi's works was green, the colour of nature by definition, but there was very little of it in and around the Lager. Levi created many different composite greens in his author's palette: verdigris, green-black, green-gold, the colours of trees, fields, mountains and rivers. Chemical components also went from light green to dark shades of green-black. After the first two books, and especially in the short stories and in his autobiographical *The Periodic Table*, green was associated increasingly with brown, a colour which was present in *If This Is a Man*, and in Levi's poems. With a probable reference to Dante's *Purgatory* (XXVI:34), Levi used the expression 'brown swarm' as a title for a poem on termites. Nazi uniforms were also brown. Levi used a startling emerald twice in his opus, once to describe the setting sun—where there was also violet and orange—and once for mushrooms.

Blue was a much rarer colour, even though in European cultural tradition over the previous two centuries it had enjoyed enormous popularity owing to its evocative power, psychological strength and appearance of depth. In Levi, there were the two shades of Prussian blue and super-blue in chemistry. There were also the faded 'blugins'—the foreign expression 'blue jeans' as it sounded in Faussone's mouth—of the girl in the chapter 'The Sassy Girl' in *The Wrench*.

The most negative colour in Levi's palette, not through any deliberate choice on his part, was yellow. Yellow was the colour of ill-health ('we have swollen, yellow faces', p. 136), which was one of the main features of the Lager experience described in Levi's first two books, although in *The Truce* there were dashes of yellow that were not associated with sickness. The yellow star, as Michel Pastoureau pointed out, marked Jews as well as prisoners taken from lunatic asylums, prostitutes and, more in general, the dregs of society.

Levi extended the meaning of colours from simple adjectives to metaphors, but even in this respect he was parsimonious, never squandering a colour in his precise descriptions.

Memory

In a 1986 short story remembering a fellow chemist who died in the Lager whom Levi had forgotten for years, Levi described himself as the brother of a character from a Borges story: 'At times, though only as far as Auschwitz is concerned, I feel like a brother of Ireneo Funes, "the memorious" (*el memorioso*) described by Borges: the man who remembered every leaf of every tree that he had seen, and who said, "I have more memories in myself alone than all men have had since the world was a world."' ('A "Mystery" in the Lager', p. 2317). This was an example of the 'mechanical memory' that Levi claimed all prisoners developed in the chapter 'Communication' (*The Drowned and the Saved*, p. 2482), and which, as he stated in 'Vanadio' (*The Periodic Table*) created 'pathologically precise memories' (p. 929).

Stefano Bartezzaghi pointed out that Levi alternated two ancient ideas of memory analysed by Harald Weinrich. The first was that of the wax tablet, where impressions can be etched and recorded, which appeared in *If This Is a Man, Flaw of Form* and *The Drowned and the Saved*. The second was that of a storage container, a warehouse, a suitcase, a mine or a wardrobe, to which Levi referred in *The Periodic Table, Uncollected Stories and*

Essays and *The Drowned and the Saved* (Bartezzaghi 1997). Levi's approach to memory was complex. The very fact of writing *If This Is a Man* was subject to a vital question: should the Lager be remembered or should the memory of such a terrible experience be erased forever? The answer Levi gave in the Appendix to the 1976 edition of the book was: 'remembering is a duty' (p. 179). More in general, Levi believed that no experience, even the most traumatic, is completely without meaning. In his view, every experience was a building block of personal knowledge. The roots of Levi's memoirs lie in this conviction. Writing was a way to fathom the depths of memory, analyse the past, and build up a rational view of what has taken place. He did not believe that everything could be explained, and yet he never gave up looking for reasons. He tried to narrow the margins of the inexplicable, such as when in the Appendix he attempted to explain anti-Semitism. The Lagers were 'not an accident, and unforeseeable historical event. The Nazi lagers were the apex, the Crown of European fascism, its most monstrous manifestation' (p. 179), a system which could be replicated in Africa, Asia, Cambodia or Vietnam.

Levi's enquiry into the role of memory was particularly far-reaching in *The Drowned and the Saved*. The first chapter, 'The Memory of the Offense', opens with the statement that 'Human memory is a wonderful but fallible instrument' (p. 2420). Levi analysed the way memories tend to change over the years in both victims and oppressors, listing the psychological mechanisms that falsify memory on both sides including trauma, 'the interference of other, 'competing' memories; abnormal states of consciousness; suppression; repression' (p. 2420). In this analysis, Levi appeared to pay homage to several of Freud's theories. He went on to examine the 'slow decay' that takes place even in normal conditions when the forces of nature reduce 'order to disorder, youth to old age, and extinguishes life in death' (p. 2420). However, he pointed out that 'a memory that is recollected too often, and expressed in the form of a story, tends to harden into a stereotype, a tried-and-true formula, crystallized, perfected, adorned, that installs itself in the place of the raw memory and grows at its expense' (p. 2420).

The first part of the chapter was focused on the conscious or unconscious manipulation of memory—typical of dictatorial regimes—that was evident in the 'confessions, depositions, and admissions' of the oppressors. This manipulation reached its apex in the figure of Hitler, with his continuous 'flight from reality' (p. 2427), which Levi compared to those of gamblers: 'like all gamblers, he had constructed a scenario spun superstitious lies that he ended up believing with the same fanatical faith he demanded from every German' (p. 2427). The second part of the chapter was devoted to what Levi called 'the drifting of memory' which he observed 'among the much larger ranks of the victims, where it is obviously unintentional' (p. 2427). In these cases, 'those who suffer an injustice or an offence have no need to concoct lies to absolve themselves of the guilt they do not feel [. . .] But this does not mean that their memories have not been altered as well' (p. 2427). Levi gave the example of a close friend he had in Auschwitz, Alberto D., whose relatives after his death constructed and alternative reality because they could not bear the truth of what had happened to him. At the end of the chapter, Levi included himself in the category of drifting memory: 'an apology is in order. This book, too, is steeped in memory, and in fact a distant memory. So it draws on a questionable source and has to be protected from itself. Consequently, it contains more reflections than memories; it dwells more readily on the state of things today than on a retrospective account' (p. 2429). This was an extraordinary example of intellectual honesty, considering that memoirists usually declare that what they have written is absolutely true.

Bartezzaghi has also commented that there appears to be a double level of memory in Levi's work: voluntary, and involuntary. Voluntary memory was linked to the episodes at Auschwitz, and was painful; involuntary memory, on the other hand, resurfaced in sleep and in dreams. In *The Truce*, Levi clearly stated that memory prolonged pain, but, at the same time, opened up potential for a story (in the sense of a painful gift): 'we passed the rest of the night singing and dancing, telling one another our past adventures and recalling our lost companions: since mankind is not permitted to experience joys untarnished' (p. 370). Levi cited Yiddish proverb in the frontispiece of *The Periodic Table* (and again in *If Not Now, When?*): 'it's good to tell past troubles.' There was another eloquent example of these two levels of memory— voluntary and involuntary—in the short story 'The Mnemagogs', which, not by chance, this story was written just after returning from Auschwitz as an unintentional counter-melody to *If This Is a Man*. Montesanto's 'memory-evokers' were glass bottles containing odours that evoked sensations, events, places or people from the past. Prisoners in the concentration camp were visited by memories even when they were in a momentary truce, such as in the infirmary, where the sound of the band playing as prisoners marched in and out of the gates left an indelible mark. Levi often stated that this band music was his most persistent memory.

The chapter 'The Canto of Ulysses' in *If This Is a Man*, provided a vivid example of Levi's struggle to retain a memory from before Auschwitz. While he was attempting to recite the lines of Canto XXVI from Dante's *Inferno* to Jean, 'the Pikolo of our Kommando' (p. 103), Levi realized that there was a 'hole in my memory' and that, however much he struggled to retain fragments, he could no longer remember the poem. The importance of memory was, moreover, one of the principles of Judaism, which Levi was beginning to explore in the concentration camp: 'thou shalt not forget' was a commandment repeated by the prophets. Memory was also viewed by Levi as a discipline; it was one aspect of the art of rhetoric that had once been cultivated by the ancient masters and had later fallen into disuse.

Oblivion, the opposite of memory, was also an important theme in Levi's work. Writing was a cycle: memory led to the act of writing, which, in its turn, led to freedom from the oppression of memory (writing as salvation), and, finally, to oblivion. The cycle was not completely innocuous, of course, since memory is an essential part of the narrative, and when it is made objective it has even more capacity to be destructive. As Bartezzaghi commented, memory in Levi's work served the function of expressing what was impossible to put into words, especially in dreams where the memory if the morning reveille ('Wstawać') lingered in prisoners' minds for years after their liberation.

It could be said that Levi became a prisoner of his own sense of duty to remember, and that he was a victim of repetition—the general principle behind the actualization of memory. Maurice Halbwachs, the French philosopher who died at Buchenwald, developed the concept of collective memory. He claimed that not only memory, but also oblivion, was a social phenomenon: memory survived through communication within a group; if the group ceased to exist, there was oblivion. In his view, there was a certain conflict between history and memory, inasmuch as history perceives differences and discontinuity, while memory sees similarities and continuity. This was why, in Yosef Hayim Yerushalmi's view, Jewish culture does not possess a historiography in the same way as other cultures do, having always privileged memory over history.

Levi's greatest preoccupation, evident from his later writing on the theme of 'negationism', was that the generation that had experienced concentration-camp life directly would die out and be forgotten. 'The Memory of the Offense' should, in his view, be passed on through the generations. Levi was highly aware of the trajectory he had followed throughout his life, from bearing witness to political engagement and concrete action, followed by retirement from active life when he became increasingly aware of the need to pass on his memories. His recognition of the complexity of his role was unique among the great memorialists of the twentieth century. He repeatedly warned his readers of the dangers of oblivion on the one hand, and of the power of distortion of memory on the other demonstrating, once again, the profound dualism of his personality as a writer and thinker. Adopting a distinction made by Tzvetan Todorov, Levi's memory was 'exemplary', rather than 'literal'. That is, it was based on a quest for justice and was incarnated in anonymous laws, whereas 'literal memory' was a simple reproduction of the past, all the harder to forget if the past was painful. Literal memory created an undifferentiated and often sacralised— and therefore sterile—idea of the past.

Humour

In an article published a few days after Levi's tragic death, the critic Massimo Mila wrote: 'This may sound over-stated, but if I had to sum up the author in one word, I would call him a humourist.' Levi's humour was particularly evident in his short stories—where his capacity to perceive the comic side, without becoming aggressive, or even seemingly amused, was given full rein—but there are many examples throughout his fiction. The German Charon carrying prisoners into Auschwitz on his truck at the beginning of *If This Is a Man* is a case in point, as is the description of Alberto's stealing in the darkest chapter of the book, 'The Last One'. Levi's sharp and thoughtful observations give his humourism his unique quality. *The Truce*, and many other of his books, are full of these witty descriptions. Take, for example, 'Argon' in *The Periodic Table*. Added to this was a deep, and often indulgent, human sympathy. Levi often took on the point of view of 'the other', and his frequent animal characters were away to express his spontaneous empathy. Humour was also the way Levi avoided judgement of his characters or of the events he narrated. It was what allowed him to draw consequences first and foremost for himself, and permitted him to develop morality without ever becoming moralistic. Moreover, humour lent strength to his dialogues and was at the core of the implicit theatricality of his writing. Levi's modesty (Mila used the word 'introverted'), and his sense of humour—a distinctly human characteristic—were two qualities he shared with Alessandro Manzoni, one of his literary 'fathers'. They were also the sources of his *pietas*, so evident in *If This Is a Man*, *The Drowned and the Saved*, and *The Truce* (especially in the chapter *The Dreamers*). Levi's *pietas* did not have a religious connotation; it was based on his experience plummeting the depths of the human spirit, and on his profound thinking. His evaluation of the world around him was at the same time perplexed and amused. He had the ability to be constantly surprised by things ('astonishment' and 'wonder' were constants in his writing), and yet he never renounced his capacity for judgement ('responsibility' was a key concept for him). He was able to participate in the unhappiness of others. Levi's humanism was also his personal antidote to the tricks that destiny played on his life, the 'roulette' of chance as he called it.

Calvino, Levi and Black Holes

In April 1975, the Italian edition of *Scientific American* (*Le Scienze*) published the translation of an article on black holes, by Kip S. Thorne, entitled 'The Search for Black Holes.' The magazine was very popular in Italy, and two of its keenest readers were the writers Italo Calvino and Primo Levi. In

September, Calvino wrote a piece about black holes for his regular column for *Corriere della Sera*, commenting that all the friends of his alter ego Mr Palomar had been talking about nothing but black holes for the past few weeks, and going on to summarize the scientific article very effectively, adding his own philosophical and anthropological reflections on the place of mankind in the universe.

The topic had been a favourite of Calvino's since the 1940s, and had made an appearance in many of his books, especially in *Cosmicomics*. The shifting paradigm, in Calvino's view, was the passage from explosion to implosion; from theories positing the universe in expansion, to those claiming the universe was contracting or disappearing. Calvino must have read a book published by Einaudi in 1965 called *Teorie cosmologiche rivali* (Rival Theories of the Universe) which presented various arguments in the form of a debate among scientists. In the same period, Italian society was in turmoil. Mr Palomar, the protagonist of Calvino's column, observed that images of emptiness were taking the place of images of fullness, darkness was behind light, and absence determined presence. One month later, Calvino went back to the subject in an article in the same column entitled 'A tidal wave in the Pacific'. The opportunity was presented by a letter to the newspaper from the astronomer Margherita Hack contesting Calvino's science. Palomar-Calvino answered citing another *Scientific American* article by Roger Penrose on black holes published four years earlier.

Calvino was particularly struck by Hack's accusation that he had been taken in by images. For somebody who thinks in images, and who is constantly hunting for images at the furthest boundaries of possibility, Calvino wrote (as himself rather than as Mr Palomar), the charge was a serious one. It was as if he had come up against a sign forbidding hunting in a forest (science) that for him was hunting reserve. He then added consideration regarding method: thinking in images, he commented, functions according to a mechanism of analogy, and can be reduced to very simple oppositions such as inside or outside, full and empty, light and darkness, high and low, et cetera. It may well be, he concluded, that these analogies follow the same paths as today's science, accompanying them for a short while.

Levi had read the same article by Thorne, and he must have kept the cutting, because six years later, in 1981, he cited it in his personal anthology *The Search for Roots*. Black holes were the central theme in the anthology: in the ellipse-shaped diagram Levi placed at the beginning of the book they were one of the poles, labelled JOB at the top and BLACK HOLES at the bottom. The four arrows, which are the four meridians of the diagram, or the four possible pathways through which to read the works anthologized by Levi followed, converge towards the printed words BLACK HOLES, indicating the pathways of 'salvation through laughter' and 'salvation through understanding', and passing on the way 'man suffering unjustly' and 'the stature of man'.

In presenting the extract from Thorne's article, Levi explained why he had included the piece in his anthology. His interpretation of black holes was very different to Calvino's. In the first paragraph, Levi commented on the cultural Revolution underway owing to the work of astrophysicists. There were new celestial monsters before which the profane could only repress unprecedented shivers, be silent and think. He concluded by reminding his readers that the interplanetary expeditions of recent years had confirmed that there were no other forms of life similar to ours in the solar system. This conclusion introduced the phrase that led to the second paragraph, which was twice as long as the first: 'We are alone'. This vivid expression became the title for the last piece in the anthology, sounding more like a moral and psychological consideration than a scientific one.

While life on earth was increasingly complex, discoveries in the universe beyond had upped the ante: 'Every year that passes, while earthly matters grow ever more convoluted, the challenge of the cosmos grows keener and more bitter: the heavens are not simple, but neither are they impermeable to our minds—they are waiting to be deciphered.' In this brief presentation to Kip S. Thorne's article, Levi expressed his attitude to his own life at that precise moment in time. It was the early 1980s, when Levi was writing the essays that went on to make up *The Drowned and the Saved*, and when he was writing more poetry than usual. His conclusion was that 'maybe we exist by chance, perhaps we are the sole instance of intelligence in the universe, certainly, we are immeasurably small, weak and alone, but if the human mind has conceived Black Holes, and dares to speculate on what happened in the first moments of creation, why should it not know how to conquer fear, poverty and grief?'

Some critics have interpreted this observation as proof of Levi's deep-rooted pessimism; others, of a newfound doubt in the values of the enlightenment. This was not the case. His view of the world, of mankind and here of the universe was always moderately pessimistic and moderately enlightened. His attitude, accentuated as he got older, had always been one of well-tempered scepticism. In his later years, he may have given the impression that this scepticism had become pessimism. His view of science, moreover, had always been given to entropy; in his reflections on the world there was a clear idea that there was progressively more disorder.

In 1983, Levi published an article called 'The Brute Power' in a journal published by the Sondrio Banca Popolare where he wrote: 'if not the universe, at least this planet is governed by a force that is not invincible but perverse, that prefers disorder to order, jumble to purity, a tangle to parallelism, rust to iron, a pile to a wall, and stupidity to reason' (p. 2630). Levi indicated a force that was able to buck this trend, to which Levi ascribed a moral quality: a self-regulating mechanism called homeostasis, a word derived from Ancient Greek that indicated the tendency of living organisms to achieve equilibrium and go on to maintain their status quo, even when external conditions change. Levi knew the process well, as it was present in chemistry, and, in particular, in thermodynamics. 'This quality, of self-preservation against the brute power of degradation and death, is typical of living matter and its more or less crude imitations, and it is called homeostasis. It enables us to resist the thousands of changes, internal and external, that threaten to break our balance with the environment.' In homeostasis it is possible to regain a balance by means of a 'feedback loop', which Levi explored in this article describing at length James Watt's invention of the centrifugal governor that ensured a constant speed for the new steam trains. Levi went on to apply the concept of homeostasis to politics, concluding, in a distinctly pessimistic tone that appears to contradict the cautious optimism of his presentation of 'We Are Alone':

It has been the dream of politicians of all eras to devise tools for homeostasis that would enable them to maintain the health, or at least the survival, of the regime they believe in [. . .] Our current malaise originates in this: we no longer perceive restraining forces, homeostasis, and feedback loops. The world seems to be moving forward toward an unspecified catastrophe and we can only hope that its progress is slow (p. 2633).

Calvino's riposte to Margherita Hack entitled 'A Tidal Wave in the Pacific', described the US Navy ship, the Wateree, being beached by a 20-metre-high tidal wave, stranded miles from land but kept upright by its keel. The crew, as described in Willard Bascom's *Waves and Beaches: The Dynamics of the Ocean Surface* cited by Calvino in his article in *Corriere della Sera*, continued to carry out their duties as if they were still at sea, adapting to their new situation. Without necessarily drawing a moral from this account, Mr Palomar wonders whether something similar might not have taken place in the distant past, sea creatures thrust onto land by a tidal wave or some other catastrophe and quickly learning to survive there. The approach of Calvino's persistently perplexed character, Mr Palomar, was to apply himself with extreme precision to a limited area of existence and observe what happened under his gaze, starting with things that appeared to be completely insignificant.

In a previous article, which was really a short story, later included as the first story in *Palomar*, the character used the technique to observe a sea wave. However, the result was far from interesting; if anything, it was a failure. Levi's observation technique described in 'The Brute Power' was similar. In fact, in *If This Is a Man* Levi had already developed a method and approach based on attention to the smallest details, which were then analysed in a wider framework. It was a kind of model where observation of minutiae, interest in insignificant events, visual, auditory or linguistic details allowed the author to come up with broader statements and reflections. He put the same technique to work in a wider and more articulated context, and within a better-defined conceptual framework, in the book he was working on at the time of writing this article: *The Drowned and the Saved*.

Calvino's defence against Hack's accusation that he had become a 'hunter of images' revealed the difference between his observation technique and Levi's. Might Levi have been similarly accused of being a 'hunter of images'? Two years after publishing 'The Brute Power', accompanying a photography exhibition on Nazi concentration camps, Levi wrote a piece on the power of images which was later published in the ANED journal, *Triangolo Rosso*, with the title 'Why Revisit These Images?' Levi wrote: 'It seems to me that these images confirm what information theory says: an image "tells" twenty, a hundred times as much as a written page of the same size. Moreover, it is accessible to all, even to the illiterate and to the foreigner; it's the best Esperanto' (p. 2695). Despite this claim, however, he did not generally cultivate an interest in images in the same way Calvino did, especially in the 1950s when he went hunting for them in the forest of scientific images in order to glean ideas for his stories and novels.

Levi's view of images was framed, rather, in terms of the 'theory of information'; in other words, in quantitative terms. He did not use Calvino's analogy technique, which allowed him to transform visual images into written words. Not that Levi did not use analogies. He did, but he never really trusted them. He preferred metaphors—such as animals—as a tool for activating literary fantasy, and he used them often in his prose and his poetry. His use of elements in *The Periodic Table* was also metaphoric, as Carlo Ginzburg quite rightly noted. Levi preferred inventing objects of mechanisms outright, using his scientific imagination. Or rather, he invented 'things' which he then used as a basis for creating technical details that were coherent with the invention, giving the narrative credibility. An example of this technique were the stories involving Mr Simpson in *Natural Histories*. His was a parallel science, a parallel botanics, a parallel physics, a parallel technology, not, like Calvino's, purely literary imagination.

Calvino was working on the cosmology of 'Mr Palomar's observatory' when Levi's presentation of Thorne's *Black Holes* came out in 1975. His theories can be linked to a December 1974 article by an astronomer from Harvard, David Layzer, on the 'cold' variant of the Big Bang Theory, published in *Scientific American*. Calvino's article in *Corriere della Sera* on the subject was divided into different sections, each with a subtitle. The section on his theory of the universe was headlined 'The Latest News about Time', which summarizes Layzer's *Scientific American* piece on the reversibility of irreversibility of time and on the entropic themes of order and disorder. The section that followed was called 'The Collector of Universes', where Calvino explained Mr Palomar's approach, which was more sensitive to the suggestions of plastic images than to philosophical implications. Calvino was struck in particular by an illustration in Layzer's article depicting four different probabilities of four phases in the evolution of the time system. Images attracted Calvino-Palomar more than theories. Was the same true of Levi? It would not appear so, at least not in the same form and intensity as they did in Calvino's case. Calvino concluded his article by commenting that Mr Palomar had decided to start another collection, this time of images. He had no idea why he was attracted to them, Calvino wrote, but he was convinced that they could signify many different things.

In May 1980, just one year before *The Search for Roots* came out, containing the article 'We Are Alone', Calvino published a review titled 'No, We Are Not Alone' in the Rome daily *la Repubblica* to which he had recently begun to contribute. The headline was most likely written by the editorial staff, but it was not inappropriate, as Calvino explained in the first line of the article, which cited Jacques Monod's popular classic *Chance and Necessity* (1970). Calvino summarized Monot's position: old alliances had been broken and humans were well- aware that they were alone in the indifferent immensity of the universe where they had evolved by chance. Levi had come across the work of Monot—a professor of cellular genetics, and had received the Nobel Prize for Physiology or Medicine in 1960—in the Italian translation of *Chance and Necessity* published by Mondadori (though he may have read them in French) and in two other translations published by Einaudi (*The Logic of the Living*, 1971, and Francois Jacob's *Evolution and Tinkering*, 1976).

Calvino's review was not of Monot's book, however. It examined Ilya Prigogine and Isabelle Stengers' *The New Alliance: Metamorphosis of Science*, which was published in France in 1978 and translated into Italian by Einaudi in 1981. Prigogine was born in Moscow in 1917, two years before Levi. He naturalized as a Belgian and received the Nobel Prize in

1977. In his review, Calvino noted that Prigogine and Stengers did not correct Monot's premises—they altered his prospects. 'Irreversibility is a source of order, a creator or order'. In Calvino's view, Prigogine and Stengers had reversed the view of thermodynamics as being based on the ineluctable death of the universe as a result of the triumph of entropy, and on the degradation of every energy into heat with no return. This view was the opposite of Levi's, who suggested that homeostasis was an element of self-preservation against this degradation. Calvino was struck by the optimism of Prigogine and Stenger's book. He concluded the review by describe their interpretation of Newton's separation of the human world from the physical world, citing a review of the same book in *Le Monde* by the French epistemologist Michel Serres.

Had Calvino modified the view of the universe in expansion that he presented in some of his *Cosmicomics*, substituting it with an idea of its implosion? Domenico Scarpa has suggested that in the last few years of his life, in the newspaper column he then published as *Palomar* (1983), Calvino started to withdraw from the world and became more introverted, segregating his own shell, as he put it years before in 'The Spiral', a cosmicomic story with a strong autobiographical element. In his view, in *Mr. Palomar*, Calvino had imagined a character that embodied a negative aspect, a personification of a Black Hole, as he put it. His original name had been Mr Mohole, taken from the name of a drilling project, just as Palomar had been the name of an astronomy observatory.

In a dialogue published posthumously, which was supposed to launch a new series of story-essays on the expansion/implosion arguments but which never took off, Calvino considered the tension between the two conflicting views of the universe. While preparing his review of Prigogine's work, Calvino must have explored the positive elements of anti-entropy, or negative entropy as Michel Serres defined it. Serres was convinced that literature was what stood in the way of entropy and dissipation because it showed a capacity for creative organization. Scarpa has pointed out that Calvino identified the structural anthropologist, Claude Lévi-Strauss, as being a bulwark against entropy, but it was Serres who played a greater role in shaping Calvino's views, especially in his later years when he was writing *Under the Jaguar Sun*, the book which planned to express itself through five senses. Literature was thus seen as an island of order in a sea of disorder.

Prigogine's point was that dissipative structures organize disorder continuously, but in a temporary fashion. Literature, as many essays in Calvino's collection, *The Uses of Literature*, showed, has precisely this capacity for negative entropy. The character of Mr Mohole, who was never fully developed, was intended to express his own relationship with the world he cultivated in his lifetime a world based on renunciation, as Scarpa pointed out (2006), where he never allowed himself to be effusive, autobiographical, objective, superfluous or daring. He was a paragon of a secular intellectual from the regions of Liguria and Piedmont, if one were to give the description a regional slant. Mr Mohole was supposed to represent a personification of a black hole, as we already said. And yet, Calvino's review of Prigogine and Stenger's book provided a glimpse of something new, a change of pace accompanied by the possibility, cultivated in his final years, of writing an autobiography, revealed in the posthumous publication of *The Road to San Giovanni*.

As for Levi, his position was different—or rather, similar, but only up to a certain point, at least as far as black holes are concerned. For one thing, Levi did not create a 'new alliance' between the human and the natural world in order to cope with entropy, disorder or degradation of energy. He was faithful to the nineteenth-century scientific view of entropy, expressed by Clausius in 1865, and identified the solution in homeostasis, as he showed in 'The Brute Power'. Was this a cultural bias, or just part of his character? As Calvino revealed in the interplay between Palomar and Mohole, character definitely played a role, as did life experience. In order to understand Levi's interpretation of black holes, we need to go back to 1975.

One of the most immediate results of Thorne's article was the poem 'The Dark Stars' published in his first collection. In *At an Uncertain Hour*, he gave his source as being '*Scientific American*, December 1974.' A dark star is a theoretical star that has a surface escape velocity that equals or exceeds the speed of light and yet the poem was dated 30 November

1974, before Thorne's article was published in the magazine. This incongruence was noted by Lorenzo Marchese, who had conducted some research on Levi's correspondence with Vanni Scheiwiller and discovered that Levi backdated the poem in order to place the poem 'Farewell' at the end of the collection, which he thought more appropriate.

'The Dark Stars' (p. 1915) was written on 30 November 1974; Levi always noted the date his poems were composed. For this reason, the poem is entirely relevant to the matter of black holes. The opening is categorical: 'No one should sing again of love or war'. This statement was followed by a blank line, in response to the command that no one sing. The poem continued in a desolate tone, reformulating Thorne's article in dry, yet desperate terms: 'The order the cosmos took its name from has been dissolved; The heavenly legions are a snarl of monsters, The universe besieges us, blind, violent, and strange. The sky is scattered with horrible dead suns, Dense sediment of shattered atoms.' Levi concluded: 'Only despairing heaviness emanates from them, Not energy, not messages, not particles, not light; Light itself falls back, broken by its own weight.'

Levi did not use the expression 'black hole' either in the title or in the body of the poem. He preferred the traditional term 'dark stars, and the poem has a classical tone, despite its being constelled with scientific terms that had become normal lexical items such as energy, messages, particles, and atoms. The final two lines were the darkest: 'And all of us human seed we live and die for nothing, And the heavens perpetually roil in vain' (p. 1916). The first of these two lines echoes the poem 'Shemà', which opens If This Is a Man ('Who dies by a yes or a no'). Scarpa, while admitting that the poem was a declaration of solitude for a man in the cosmos, felt the poem showed a desperation that contradicted itself, especially when compared with Levi's presentation of Thorne's article in The Search for Roots. Levi's work often contemplated contradictions, and thematic or even psychological oxymorons. The very first of these was the invective expressed in the poem 'Shemà' taken alongside Levi's statement that If This Is a Man was a 'a detached study of certain aspects of the human mind'. Levi's presentation of Thorne's article contradicted the poem 'The Dark Stars'.

There were always two different tensions in Levi's life and work which never found a solution: between desperation and optimism, and between black humour and positivity. Levi expressed these binary oppositions in the figure of the centaur in the early 1960s, a figure which lay at the heart of personality as a man and as a writer from the very start of his career in *If This Is a Man*, if not before. There was the Levi that lifted his gaze up to the skies, out towards the universe, and stated that the order of the cosmos was not what it was for the Ancients; it was no longer immobile and fated, nor was it stable. The 'cosmos' of the poem was no longer a word that could be used lightly, since what Leo Spitzer called 'the harmony of the world'—an ordered universe creating music, as imagined by the classical and medieval world—had been 'dissolved'. There was no more order. Looking up, Levi saw a 'blind, violent, and strange' universe. These words were perfect for describing his own universe in the concentration camp. The last words of the poem, in fact, were 'in vain'.

The article of Thorne's that Levi selected for his personal anthology presented a more optimistic view of black holes, and yet the poem is its counterpart. They are the twin valves of a mollusc named Primo Levi; they are the upswing and downswing of an oscillation; they are opposing, yet complimentary poles of the same personality. As Levi himself often pointed out, poetry was the part of his personality that lay in the shadows, an expression of his deepest anxieties and obsessions held within a literary shell that was highly traditional. Many of his poems erupted from a dark well, and contain their own cyclic negativity, coming to the writer in bursts. Tracing the chronology of his poems, in fact, it is possible to see how most of them were written in two distinct periods: first, on his return from the Lager, in 1946 (14 poems were written that year); second between 1979 and 1980 (when he wrote 9). According to his biographer, Carole Angier, these periods were the darkest and most depressed of his life.

On the subject of the poem inspired by black holes, Scarpa has commented that Levi wrote 'The Dark Stars' with his nerves tensed up and his eyes wide open, creating lines with strong joints and elastic muscles. In the critic's view, Levi's poems were didascalic rather than lyrical. Lying within his explanatory style, in fact, there lurked the dark magma of his psyche, the Id that Levi confessed to having in the Preface to *The Search for Roots*. This book, which was published much later than most of his poems, was the perfect companion to his poems precisely because it is an anthology, which, as he wrote in the preface, allowed him to strip off some of the layers he hid behind and reveal himself for what he was. The three adjectives used in 'The Dark Stars'—'blind, violent, and strange'— were used both in the poem and in the piece included in his personal anthology, as Scarpa noted. The only difference was that the word 'blind' was replaced by 'hostile' in his introduction to Thorne's article, a minimum adjustment considering this was prose and the other was poetry.

The expression 'black hole' appeared in another article published by Levi in *La Stampa* 12 years after writing 'The Dark Stars: The Black Hole of Auschwitz' (22 January 1987). The headline was probably written by the editorial staff, but the expression was also used in the body of the article. The article was not actually about the main camp of Auschwitz; it was about Treblinka and Chelmno, where the elimination of the Jews took place immediately on arrival, without the distraction of the selections: 'neither labour camps nor concentration camps, they were black holes for men, women, and children whose only crime was to be Jewish, places where people got off the trains only to enter the gas chambers, and from which no one came back alive'. In this metaphorical sense, a black hole was a way of expressing 'something' where there is 'nothing', not even a ray of light.

Having started out as a cosmic image, an element of astronomy, black holes for Levi the witness bearer were transformed into a metaphor for the extermination of German Jews. The context of the article was the revision-ism underway in Germany that compared the Nazi concentration camps to Soviet gulags. Levi accused German revisionists such as Nolte and Hillgruber, of 'trivializing' the slaughter of the Jews and denying its unique-ness: 'We, the Germans, during the Second World War, simply followed a horrible but by now established practice: an "Asian" practice made up of slaughters, mass deportations, merciless exile to hostile regions, torture, family separations. Our only innovation was technological: we invented the gas chambers' (p. 2752). The article was short, and added little to what he had written on other occasions, and later, in *The Drowned and the*

Saved, about the 'historic singularity' of the Nazi camps, built with a technological final solution—the gas chambers—for eliminating millions of Jews. It is relevant because in this article Levi shifted the term 'black holes' from a scientific, cosmological context to a historical one, after the precedent of the poem 'The Dark Stars'. There was a difference however. In the poem, the black hole appeared to be high over the poet's head; in this article, by contrast, it seemed to be opening up the ground under his feet and pulling the whole of European history down with it. Primo Levi, for all his passion for science, and for articles published by *Scientific American*, was suspended between these two spaces where 'Light itself falls back, broken by its own weight, And all of us human seed we live and die for nothing' (p. 2752).

Suicide

The writer, Ferdinando Camon, travelled to Turin several times between 1982 and 1986 to record a long interview with Primo Levi (1989). Their last conversation took place in Turin in May 1986, just under a year before Levi's death. The interview focused on the issues of guilt, sin and evil, and the responsibilities of the German people. Towards the end of the interview, Camon commented to Levi that he always seemed to be ironic and understanding, that he smiled a great deal, and that his nature revealed a love of life, both before and after the violent trauma. Levi agreed, but confessed that he had had several depressive episodes since, although he said he was not sure that they could all be traced back to the initial trauma as each episode had its own label, different every time.

In the many interviews Levi gave throughout his life, he rarely spoke openly about his psychological state, and hardly ever about his depression. There were also very few explicit references to depression in his work; any direct or indirect allusions he made to his mood always referred to the past. For example, in the chapter 'Phosphorus' (*The Periodic Table*), Levi wrote about his feelings for Giulia, a colleague and previous classmate in the mysterious chemical factory outside Milan, owned and run by the Swiss 'Commendatore'. He alluded to his frustration at not being able to declare his feelings for women in general, and Giulia in particular: 'my incapacity to get close to a woman was a sentence without appeal, and would accompany me to my death, restricting me to a life poisoned by envy and abstract desires, sterile and without purpose' (p. 855).

Levi's depression was more evident in his poems, particularly in those written immediately after his return to Turin between December 1945 and 7 February 1946. This was probably post-traumatic depression after his experience in the concentration camp, but there were other factors too, which led to the 'episodes' he mentioned to Camon in his interview. In general, the poems collected in *At an Uncertain Hour*, and others later included in the *Collected Poems*, corresponded to certain moments in his life and were mirrors of his dark side. They had been composed at an 'uncertain hour', as the title suggested.

In his correspondence with Hety between 1966 and 1981, when Hetty died unexpectedly, there are a couple of letters where Levi describes the depression gripping him. In a letter dated August 1971, for example, he wrote that his job at the factory was wearing him down and causing him grief, compounded by a sensation that he had no future as a writer. He confessed to his dear friend that reading the papers every day was depressing, as all he found there was bad news, crises, crimes and the threat of an even darker future. In the letter, Levi asked himself what the roots of the depression that he felt he was drowning in were, and even hinted at the need for medical help, but he was unable to provide an answer. He wondered whether Auschwitz was behind it all, but then decided against this hypothesis. The roots of his deep anxiety were atavistic, he decided, perhaps inherent in his identity with Jewish culture, as Jews were always worried about their future. He had been under the protective wings of Federico Accati, the owner of the SIVA factory, since his return from Auschwitz, but he now felt that the reassurance of working there was coming to an end. Moreover, he felt his literary success had been short-lived, and was anguished by his uncertain future. In this same period, Levi wrote an impassioned letter to his friend, fellow concentration-camp survivor, and doctor, Leonardo De Benedetti, describing his state of mind. In December that year, things appeared to be looking up, and Levi announced that he felt ready to go on a work trip to the Soviet Union. He wrote to Hety and said he was ashamed of his previous letter, but also commented on how the depression had felt at the time (he used the expression 'verstimmung'—discord, or lack of harmony).

This was not his last depressive episode, however. The final episode took place 16 years later, at the end of 1986, when Levi threw himself down the stairwell of his apartment building in Turin. As Giovanni Falaschi commented in an article (2001), few of his friends ever cast doubt on the fact that this had been a voluntary act. It is still hard to believe, however, that the person that Camon had described as being sweet, calm, self-ironic, lucid and deeply rational had been able to take his own life. During the interview, Levi had asked Camon whether it was his presence or what he had written that gave him the impression of his placid nature. Camon had reassured him that it was mainly his presence, but that his works confirmed the impression in that his writing was full of fantasy, allegory, metaphor and life. Levi did not contradict this description, and the interview veered on to other questions. They never returned to the topic of his depression.

Another Auschwitz survivor and suicide, the Austrian essayist Jean Améry, wrote *On Suicide: A Discourse on Voluntary Death* (1999), first published in German in 1976. He wrote it after unsuccessfully attempting suicide, and defined suicide as being a 'Freitod'—a 'free death'. There is no evidence that Levi read the book, but it is highly likely. Levi had been very keen on translating his most influential book, published in German in 1966, known in English as *At The Mind's Limits: Contemplations by a Survivor on Auschwitz and Its Realities*, but never did so. In 1978, after Améry's death, Levi published an article commemorating his life and work in *La Stampa* entitled 'An Intellectual in Auschwitz'.

Levi stressed two aspects that were interlinked: on the one hand, human behaviour was unpredictable and fundamentally free; on the other, not everything could be explained. A suicide never really knows why he wants to take his own life, and if he attempts to explain it, the reasons are not necessarily the real ones. In Levi's case, there are two possible explanations for his suicide. The first is that his desire to end his life was linked to his deportation and a sense of guilt for having survived, coupled with the shame of being tainted by the experience. The second is that Levi suffered from depression even before he was sent to Auschwitz; if anything, his period in the concentration camp was a period of reprieve from depression. Levi often described his time at the Monowitz camp, the forced labour, the endless danger, as being an experience in Technicolor, while the rest of his life was essentially black and white. Both explanations are probably true. The reasons for his voluntary act were inextricably linked and contaminated one another throughout his life, feeding Levi's depression to the point of no return, leaving his friends, family and acquaintances in shocked disbelief.

The list of reasons for throwing himself down the stairwell of his own apartment block on 11 April 1987, was long: negationism, waning faith in witness literature, the fear of failing as a writer and the fear of not being able to write anything good in the future, to name just a few.

The poems Levi wrote in the last years of his life, in addition to the early poems, reveal some of these reasons, and more besides. The February 1984 poem, 'The Survivor', the first line of which gave the title to the collection citing Coleridge's The Ancient Mariner, describes the agony of seeing the ghosts of his comrades' faces. In 'Brown Swarm', written four years before, the swarm of ants was transformed in his mind into his own brown swarm of prisoners that he didn't want to talk about. In the cantata, 'Unfinished Business', written in July 1981, Levi metaphorically resigned from life, with its 'unfinished work'. Almost all his poems contain some kind of premonition or testify in some way to his anguished state of mind, including those where he identified himself with an animal and provided the voice for their monologues.

Giovanni Falaschi explored the many facets of Levi's suicide, attempting to provide a reason, or explanation for the depressive crisis that led up to it. He did not find a root cause (if ever there was one), to use the expression Levi used in his August 1971 letter to Hety. Levi had intuitively decided that the reasons for his depression went far back in time and that his experience at Auschwitz, and, above all, on returning from Auschwitz, were a kind of trigger. One important aspect of Falaschi's research was his interpretation of Levi's dreams and their links to the poems. Levi often recounted dreams in his works, particularly in *If This Is a Man* and *The Truce*. When he was at Monowitz, he would dream of escaping; when he returned, by contrast, he would find himself dreaming of being back inside. *The Truce* ended with the famous dream of returning to the Lager. 'The Survivor', a vital poem for understanding the links between Levi's Auschwitz experience and his episodes of depression, features the word 'dreams.' The poem was written in the third person— *he* sees the faces of his comrades. They are twice dead: they were the living dead while they were in the Lager, 'grey with cement dust' and they were also the dead returning to pay him a visit, 'Dyed by death in their restless sleep: At night they grind their jaws'. In the last six lines the voice shifts to the first person, and direct speech: 'Back, away from here, drowned people, Go. I haven't stolen anyone's place, I haven't usurped the bread of anyone, No one died for me. No one. Go back to your haze. It's not my fault if I live and breathe. And eat and drink and sleep and put on clothes' (p. 1965). Subject pronouns are very significant in Levi's work, revealing the plurality of subjects in his poetry and fiction, and testifying to a split in the subjectivity of the writer and his voice.

In another poem, 'February 25, 1944', written in January 1946, and inspired by Dante and T. S. Eliot's *Wasteland*, Levi's profound depression is clearly depicted. The constant shift between 'I' and 'we', indicating a common fate ('We who were already drowned') addressing a female 'you' ('beyond death destroyed you' [p. 1885]). This poem was one of the only places where Levi placed himself—that is, his poetic, narrative self—in the category of 'the drowned'.

Returning to the subject of the relationship between Levi's poetry and his dreams, Falaschi observed that the uncertain hour that gave the collection its title was the hour that dreams appeared: poems appeared to him implacably, with the same tenacity as those recurrent dreams of being in the Lager or fearing returning there. Dreams are depicted in this way in 'The Survivor', and in 1946, with the poem 'Get Up' that was cited at the beginning of *The Truce*, where the first three lines described the 'dense and violent dreams' he had 'in the savage nights' (p. 1889). Falaschi remarked that the citation in 'The Survivor' from Coleridge's *Ancient*

Mariner ('This heart within me burns') which was shifted to the third person ('his heart within him burns') had already been used 40 years earlier in 'Get Up', where Levi had written 'Our hearts broke in our breasts' (p. 1889). This intertextuality shows an emotional and literary continuity over the course of Levi's writing life, with a reference to Coleridge appearing as early as 1946. In general, there are several themes that Levi returned to obsessively throughout his life, but these are probably the symptoms rather than the causes of his depression. The classical structure of poetry, and the opportunity to cite other poets and sources, made this literary form an ideal cauldron-container for the molten matter Levi needed to pour into it. He also recycled many lines from his poetry in his prose, especially in *The Drowned and the Saved*, which was perhaps the most anguished of his works.

Falaschi's article suggested two possible triggers for Levi's suicide. One was the fear that he would no longer be able to write. Many critics, following Levi's own clear and persistent indications, have stress how therapeutic the act of writing was for Levi (Segre 1996). Writing meant communicating. At one point in the interview, Camon commented that Levi had obviously found the incommunicability of the Lager experience painful. Levi confirmed this, stating that he was by nature a talker. If someone gagged him, he said, he would die. When Camon asked whether this was a common experience, Levi answered that the others did die, without necessarily knowing that incommunicability was the reason.

The ability to speak was a basic survival mechanism for Levi, and, more in general, for every prisoner. It was not only the ability to speak German, the language of the Lager; it was, in Falaschi's view, the purely expressive function of words. If you cannot tell your story, you die. One could also add that speaking, like eating, takes place through the mouth. Similarly, eating and storytelling are closely linked. For Levi, writing was an antidote for the poison that had been injected into his veins during his imprisonment.

One of the nightmares that caused Levi most anguish was described in *If This Is a Man*: Levi returned home to his family and friends and attempted to tell them about his experience in the Lager, but nobody listened.

It is an intense pleasure, physical, inexpressible, to be at home, among friendly people, and to have so many things to recount, but I can't help noticing that my listeners do not follow me. In fact, they are completely indifferent: they speak confusedly among themselves of other things, as if I were not there. My sister looks at me, gets up, and goes away without a word (p. 57).

Falaschi pointed out that Levi neglected to mention his mother, both in this dream and in the one he recounted in *The Truce*. He suggested that there were two reasons for this absence. First, that the figure of his mother was linked to his mother tongue, while in the Lager he only spoke German or Yiddish, even though his mother tongue, the Italian he learnt and cultivated at home and at school, was the language that the expressed himself in when he returned. Second, his sister's betrayal was a subconscious symbol of the absence of fraternal sentiment in the Lager. The greatest shock for Levi was that there were no friends or companions in the camp, even among his fellow deportees. The linguistic confusion in the Lager—a veritable Babel of languages—was a further element that made communication almost impossible. Despite all these difficulties, however, and despite the recurrent nightmare of not being heard, Levi did manage to tell the story of his experience.

In his final months, the idea that he would no longer be able to write became an obsession. He began to feel that he no longer possessed the necessary tools, and told his friends, acquaintances and colleagues that this was the case. His publisher, Giulio Einaudi, paid him a visit in early 1987 and asked him if he would take on the honorary role of president of the company. Levi rejected his offer, and told Einaudi he did not feel up to it, given his state of mind. On his return to the office, Einaudi told his colleagues that Levi was deeply depressed, and was suffering from writer's block, even though he had been working on a new book right up until almost the end of 1986. The new project was a series of letters written to a woman friend, filled with stories of his life and anecdotes linked to everyday chemistry (such as why an egg becomes hard-boiled). He also returned to his graduate dissertation on the Walden Inversion, and talked about episodes in his past. There were six complete chapters ready by December 1986, but in early January 1987 Levi was unable to continue.

In his conversation with Camon, Levi gave an example of this type of block, or depressive crisis, which he called 'stupid'. The trigger was a foot operation, which made him feel old all of a sudden, as it took more than two months for the incision to heal. During his convalescence, a cloud of depression enveloped him. In commenting on this with Camon, Levi denied that these episodes were linked in any way with his experience in the concentration- camp. Falaschi observed that there was a significant passage in the chapter 'Ka-Be' in *If This Is a Man* about a foot problem. The episode took place in early 1944 at Monowitz, when a group of prisoners were required to transport heavy iron supports from the railway to the camp. Levi was paired up with Null Achtzehn, who stumbled and dropped the support on Levi's foot: 'The corner of the piece of iron has cut the top of my left foot' (p. 42). Feet and shoes were essential for survival in the Lager, and even outside, as the Greek made clear in *The Truce* after their liberation from the camp when they needed to find shelter and food. Levi did not necessarily see the connection with the wounded foot that had him admitted to the infirmary so many years before; perhaps he had repressed it. Falaschi, however, claimed that the episode may have reverberated with him, and made the relapse into depression more alarming. No one will ever know whether this was the case or not, but what we do know for sure is that the Lager experience continued to rear its head throughout his life. Falaschi described the Auschwitz experience as being like a 'basso-continuo' accompanying him at all times.

The Drowned and the Saved is another work that contributes to the debate. The book appeared to have been written with surprisingly little internal conflict, despite the complex issues he tackled there (the grey zone), and the difficulties of his past and present life that he was relating. However, it expressed deep anguish—after his suicide, of course, it was impossible to perceive the work in any other way—combined with intellectual honesty, which was the feature noted when it was published in 1986. A few months later, Levi took his own life, which led many to think that the book was his last will and testament, and leading them to hunt for its hidden message.

Tesio was one of the critics to be interviewed immediately after Levi's death (*la Repubblica*, 12–13 April 1987). An expert in Levi' works, he had been visiting Levi on a regular basis for several months, recording their conversations in order to research and write an 'authorized biography', but Levi had put a stop to their meetings owing to his depression. In the interview, he declared that they had established a relationship of 'friendly, almost psychoanalytical venting.' Tesio described how Levi kept on going back to a memory of a fellow prisoner in the Lager, and how painful this digging back into the past had been for him: 'going back to that experience was painful, and it tired him immensely.' In his statement to the Milan daily *Corriere della Sera* (12 April 1986), Tesio was even more explicit: 'There were some moments of the past that Levi kept going back to, as if he were discovering things, or situations, that he had never before shed light on. Other moments he wouldn't explore. He would mention something then immediately pull back.' When asked whether in Tesio's view there was anything in particular from Levi's past that scared or disturbed him, the critic answered:

> More than one thing. Levi seemed to be reliving these moments more painfully than ever before. I can't be more precise. I don't feel I am authorized. One thing I can say is that he was tormented by the memory of a companion in the Lager. It was as if he were just now shouldering the guilt for not having been able to save him, or for not having been able to alleviate his pain at the time.

Falaschi has attempted to find out who this companion was, whose memory pained Levi to such an extent and who perhaps contributed to Levi's final crisis. Who generated such a deep sense of guilt, or shame, in Levi's psyche? He suggested three possibilities after searching through his witness statements and all the names of his fellow prisoners in his books. The first was Rene, the robust young man who stood just in front of Primo in the line for the selections, and who was 'chosen' to go to the gas chambers—perhaps owing to an exchange of identification cards—thus saving Primo. The second was Daniele, the companion with whom he refused to share his water, while he did share it with Alberto, described in *The Drowned and the Saved*, who survived the camps and who made Levi feel deeply ashamed every time he met him. The third was Alberto Dellavolta, with whom he had a symbiotic relationship, who died on the march while being transferred from Auschwitz, while Levi was fortunate enough to have caught scarlet fever and was recovered in the infirmary, Ka-Be. However, he ultimately decided it was none of these but, rather, a woman, a female 'comrade', as his biography might indicate, who would be more likely to have inspired these kinds of feelings. Tesio gave up the name: it was Vanda Maestro.

The conditions Levi was living in at the time of his suicide were far from positive. He had two old, sick people in need of assistance in the house with him, and his psychological defences were very low. In this context, he found himself contemplating a painful memory that he had buried so deeply that he had almost forgotten it. There were traces of this memory in his work, but first let us go back to Vanda Maestro.

Vanda was born in the same year as Levi, in 1919. They had a great deal in common: they had known each other since high school, she was Jewish, from Turin and graduated in chemistry. They shared a friend, Luciana Nissim, who was also Jewish and a doctor. The story of this trio was told in the chapter 'Gold' in *The Periodic Table,* which was Levi's most autobiographical book, containing a 'digest' of his life, and many secrets, which he entrusted to his readers in his inimically dry style. The three joined a motley array of partisans in the mountains, but were recognized as Jewish, arrested by officers from the Republic of Salò and sent to the transit camp at Fòssoli together, before being deported together to Auschwitz. They met Franco Sacerdoti and Mr and Mrs De Benedetti at Fòssoli, and soon friendship turned to love. Franco and Luciana became a couple, as did Primo and Vanda. Levi makes the briefest of mentions of this in *If This Is a Man*, when he described the railway car they found themselves in on their way to Auschwitz:

> Next to me, crushed, like me, body against body for the whole journey, there had been a woman. We had been acquainted for many years, and the misfortune had struck us together, but we knew little of one another. Now, in the hour of decision, we said to each other things that are not said among the living. We said farewell and it was short; everybody said farewell to life through his neighbour. We had no more fear (p. 15).

Vanda Maestro has been an object of conjecture for Levi's biographers. The psychoanalyst, Luciana Nissim, who survived Auschwitz as a doctor, and who published one of the earliest witness accounts in 1946 on her return (Memories from the House of the Dead), described Vanda being sent almost immediately to the gas chambers. At the end of the chapter in *The Truce* called 'The Big Camp', Levi related how he heard the news of Vanda's death from the Croatian Jewish partisan, Olga: 'Vanda had been gassed, fully conscious, in the month of October; she herself, Olga, had obtained two sleeping pills for her, but they were not enough.' (p. 233). Levi spoke to her, as we have seen, in the poem 'February 25, 1944', which he wrote on his return to Turin: 'I'd like to believe something beyond, Beyond death destroyed you. I'd like to be able to say the fierceness With which we wanted then, We who were already drowned, To be able someday to walk again together Free under the sun' (p. 1885). The second-person singular address in Italian was in the feminine form.

Vanda was also present in two passages from the chapter 'Chrome' (*The Periodic Table*), although she was not named specifically. The first was when he described the agony of the first few months after his return home:

> I had been back from prison for three months, and I found life hard. The things I had seen and suffered burned inside me; I felt closer to the dead than to the living, and guilty for being a man, because men had built Auschwitz, and Auschwitz had swallowed up millions of human beings, many of them my friends, and a woman who was dear to me (p. 876).

The second was two pages later when the woman who would become his wife was introduced, although, again, out of some sort of modesty, Lucia was not named: 'Within a few hours we knew that we belonged to each other, not for a meeting but for a lifetime, as in fact it has been. Within a few hours I felt new and full of new powers, washed clean and cured of the long illness, finally ready to enter life with joy and strength.' It was in this optimistic context that Vanda was finally exorcized: 'likewise, the world around me was suddenly cured, and the name and face of the woman who had descended to hell with me and had not returned were exorcised'

(p. 878). The cryptic reference to Dante ('the face') revealed Levi's anguish for Vanda's death, an anguish that had overwhelmed him until meeting a woman in the flesh and blood that he knew would be a 'meeting for a lifetime' exorcized it. The use of the word 'exorcism' implied the presence of a curse, an irrational malefice that required a miracle of a sort, a mysterious beneficial force, to heal it.

A further reference to Vanda was in a 1953 commemorative piece that was published anonymously but that Falaschi has correctly attributed to Levi. Levi described Vanda's far-ranging knowledge and psychological insight, and hinted at the sensibilities they shared. Levi commented that one could sense in her a current of underlying pain that she consciously embraced but kept under the surface, commanding instant respect from all those who met her.

Falaschi attempted to reinterpret Tesio's remarks about the 'comrade' Levi felt such terrible remorse about at the end of his life for not being able to save and not being able to alleviate his infernal pain at the time. The remarks did not appear to refer to Vanda because they were separated on arrival in Auschwitz. Levi joined the men in the line for forced labour, and Vanda, together with Luciana, her friend, were sent away with the women. Falaschi concluded that Levi's sense of guilt was not related to a specific instance in the real world, but, rather, to an inner demon that had emerged from his state of depression.

In the months leading up to his suicide, Levi's biographers have identified a few salient circumstances that might have contributed to his state of mind. His long conversations with Tesio certainly must have stirred up some uncomfortable memories, considering that Levi interrupted his sessions with his interviewer. He was also forced to undergo prostate surgery, in preparation for which, as his biographers have observed, Levi had suspended his anti-depressants. He mentioned this detail to David Mendel, who was a doctor and a friend as well as being Jewish and a fan of his writing. However, when Levi resumed his conversations with Tesio, Angier confirms, Levi was back on his medication. He had suspended work at the end of 1986 on a book that was to be called *Double Bind*, about a love affair between an old chemist and a married woman with children, conducted by means of letters relating various episodes of his past. In a letter dated 15 October 1986, but actually written on 26 October, Levi wrote about his lifelong difficulties with women, love and sex. The letter matched the autobiographical tone of *The Periodic Table* perfectly, although the device of letter-writing within the narrative afforded Levi the opportunity to be more direct and less reticent about his affective and sentimental life. Bringing his work on the book to a halt heightened his fear that he would no longer be able to write, and deepened his depression further.

On 10 April 1987, Levi called Tesio and asked to resume their conversations. The next day, he killed himself. Falaschi was ultimately unable to find a reason for the suicide. There were, however, two triggering factors that biographers agree on: first, survivor guilt (why me and not another?), and second, his re-emerging memories of his 'comrade' Vanda Maestro, both the woman he was in love with at the time of her death, and one of those who 'drowned' in the Lager.

Unlike Améry, who wrote a fascinating, fast-paced, convincing but unilateral apology of suicide, Levi stated in his lifetime that 'Understanding the reasons for a suicide is particularly difficult, since, in general, the victim himself isn't conscious of them, or provides himself and others with explanations that are intentionally or unintentionally distorted' (p. 1262). As Levi confided to Camon, the reasons for his repeated bouts of depression from 1946 to the end of his life were probably atavistic, in the distant past, or even in the stars. As he wrote in his piece 'My House': 'I have always lived (with involuntary interruptions) in the house where I was born: the way I live was not, therefore, the result of a choice' (p. 2014). Sixty-seven years after his birth there, he threw himself down the stairwell of that same building.

LEVI'S HALL AND STAIRWELL (c.1987)

This is the entrance hall of Corso Re Umberto 75, the building where Levi lived all his life. In the background, the stairwell, where Primo Levi's inert body lay on 11 April 1987. The apartment building was typical of the Turin middle class: a porter's lodge, wooden frames around the doors, antique letter boxes, a marble-tiled floor with geometric patterns. It was like so many of the buildings on the avenue which led towards the centre of Turin without actually getting there. The city's bourgeoisie lived in the neighbourhood—professionals and artisans—renowned for their discretion, considered elsewhere reserve. This discretion was the result of generation after generation passing on knowledge, moderation and serenity. In other words, wisdom.

Turin was once a capital city. Its own Savoy royalty stripped the city of its birthright after Unification When the capital was moved to Florence, there was uncharacteristic fury among the Turinese; there were even some deaths. However, once Rome was finally settled on as the capital of a newly unified Italy, Turin went back to its old routines. Levi was deeply rooted in this culture, symbolized by his house in Corso Re Umberto. Nearly all the buildings along this avenue were painted grey, with art-nouveau decorations, such as friezes depicting fauns and other mythological figures on their facades. Levi's was stone-clad at street level, finished with a cornice of dark red bricks, which over the years had lost their lustre.

In the early 1980s, Levi wrote a short piece about his apartment—not the stairs or the hallways specifically, but the apartment on the other side of a dark wooden door he called home. Both taking stock of his life, and paying homage to the place that had provided him with a shell for so many years, 'My House' begins: 'I have always lived (with involuntary interruptions) in the house where I was born: the way I live was not, therefore, the result of a choice. I believe that I exemplify an extreme case of sedentary life, comparable to that of some mollusks, such as limpets' (p. 2014). While declaring that he had lived there his entire life, and that this had not been a free choice on his part, he stated that the house was a shell, a container that had always protected and shielded him. Aside from a year in Milan, which he wrote about in *The Periodic Table*, the period he spent at Auschwitz which we know about from his witness writing, and a few business trips here and there, he lived in this apartment for 67 years.

Cavaglion commented that shells were an obsessive metaphor for Levi: shell, armour, niche or nest expressed the same concept, which he used throughout his work, starting with *If This Is a Man*. In the chapter 'Our Nights', he wrote: 'Man's capacity to dig a niche for himself, to secrete a shell, to build around himself a tenuous barrier of defence, even in apparently desperate circumstances, is astonishing and deserves serious study' (p. 53). The image was identical—not by chance—to the one at the beginning of 'My House'.

Levi's habitual modesty makes the understated description of his house, which was his parents' before him, typical of his personal style and of the class he belonged to: 'What distinguishes my house is how undistinguished it is' (p. 2015). Nothing ever changed: neither the furnishings nor the habits of its inhabitants. On the front door,

> where for twenty years a horseshoe that had been found by my uncle Corrado hung (in those days, you could still find horseshoes in Corso Re Umberto), an amulet that I couldn't say whether or not it had properly exercised its protective force; and where for another twenty years there dangled from a nail a large key whose purpose everyone had long forgotten but which no one dared to throw away (p. 2017).

Levi described in detail the hiding places, nests inside the nest where he would secrete himself as a child. Despite the transformations over the years,

> the apartment where I live has preserved its anonymous and impersonal appearance: or at least, that's how it looks to us who live in it. But it's well-known that people are poor judges of everything that concerns them, of their own personalities, their own virtues and defects, even their own voices and faces; others, perhaps, might see it as deeply symptomatic of my family's reclusive tendencies (p. 2018).

Levi never required more from his home: 'Certainly, I have never consciously demanded from my home anything more than to satisfy my primary needs: space, warmth, comfort, silence, privacy' (p. 2018).

That 11 April, Levi threw himself down the stairwell, inside his own 'shell' of a home. His body was discovered at the bottom of the staircase that spiralled up to the third floor where he lived. To the right of the photograph, just past the letter boxes, there is a brass plaque on the wall in art-nouveau capital letters: 'NO BEGGING' it says.

FURTHER READING

The bibliography on the life and works of Primo Levi has grown considerably in the last decade, both in Italy and abroad. In particular, many articles, books and conference proceedings have been published in English-speaking countries following W. W. Norton's publication of *The Complete Works of Primo Levi*, edited by Ann Goldstein (New York and London, 2015). The Centro Internazionale di Studi su Primo Levi website (www. primolevi.it) is kept up to date with everything regarding Levi, including translations of his books. In the following sections, you will find suggestions for further reading, divided into the areas covered in this book.

WORKS

References to Primo Levi's works are for the two-volume 1997 Einaudi edition, edited by Marco Belpoliti, with an introduction by D. Del Giudice. A new edition of the *Opere* was published by Einaudi in 2016, which includes texts that had been rediscovered in the meantime. There is also a new volume of interviews integrating and expanding on *Conversations and Interviews 1963–1987* (edited by M. Belpoliti; Turin: Einaudi, 1997). In 1987, Einaudi began publishing the Works of Primo Levi in the series 'Biblioteca dell'Orsa'. Three volumes were published until 1992, with the works arranged in thematic rather than chronological order. The 1997 edition, in the 'Nuova Universale' Einaudi series, is arranged in chronological order and contains 480 pages of Levi's works, as well as *The Search for Roots* and 170 pages of Notes. An identical reprint in four volumes was distributed by the Italian daily, *La*

Repubblica, in January 2009. Finally, in 2016, the new edition of the *Opere complete* was published by Einaudi, edited by Marco Belpoliti. In 2017, the third volume came out, which contains a wide, almost complete selection of Primo Levi's conversations and interviews, again edited by Marco Belpoliti (Title is *Opera complete III*). This volume contains some important tools: a bibliography of Primo Levi from 1937 to 2018, and an index of names contained in his works edited by the International Center for Primo Levi Studies, and in particular by Domenico Scarpa and Daniela Muraca. Regarding the dissemination of Levi's works in the world, there are an ever-increasing number of studies, translations, and new editions. *La manutenzione della memoria. Diffusione e conoscenza di Primo Levi nei paesi europei* (edited by G. Tesio; Turin: Centro Studi Piemontesi, 2005) collects the papers presented at a 2003 conference, and *Primo Levi à l'œuvre: la réception de l'œuvre de Primo Levi dans le monde* (edited by P. Mesnard and Y. Thanassekos; Paris: Kimé, 2008), presents the proceedings of a conference held in 2006. More information on this subject, with a list of translated books, can be found in the online bibliography of the Centro Internazionale di Studi Primo Levi, Turin.

LIFE

The first biographical study of Levi came out in 1992, five years after his death. It was written by Gabriella Poli and Giorgio Calcagno, two journalists from *La Stampa*, who had followed the writer's literary activity closely: *Echi di una voce perduta. Incontri, interviste e conversazioni con Primo Levi* (Milan: Mursia, 1992). The biography delves into both the biographical and literary aspects of Levi's life and is still a crucial contribution on both fronts. Myriam Anissimov published the first biography of the writer, first in French, in 1996, and then in Italian three years later: *Primo Levi o la tragedia di un ottimista* (Milan: Baldini & Castoldi, 1999). However, while amassing a great deal of information about Levi, the biography contains many inaccuracies, if not outright errors (see Domenico Scarpa's, 'Un Levi improbabile' in *La Rivista dei Libri*, April 1997). In 2002, two extensive biographies were published: Carole Angier's *The Double Bond* (New York: Farrah, Strauss and Giroux, 2002) translated into Italian as *Il doppio legame. Vita di Primo Levi* (Milan: Mondadori, 2004) and Ian Thomson's *Primo Levi* (London: Hutchinson, 2002, later translated into Italian by Utet). Both reconstruct Levi's life, ancestors, family and environment and contain a considerable amount of first-hand information about Levi's personal life. Angier's book is an indispensable tool, and stands out for its focus on the relationship between his life and works, highlighting the close connections between the two. She has a talent for interpretating the texts and a marked literary inclination both in her narration and in her search for details of Levi's life. Thomson's biography follows events in the author's life more closely but he possesses an uncommon ability to investigate unpublished details and details. Philippe Mesnard was the first to publish a biography in images (*Primo Levi. Una vita per immagini*; Venice: Marsilio, 2008), which is a fascinating visual document. He also wrote a literary biography of the author *Le passage d'un témoin* (Paris: Fayard, 2011), which outlines both biographical and literary events. Ernesto Ferrero wrote a profile of Levi centred on his life and works, *Primo Levi* (Turin: Einaudi, 2007), which is a good introduction to his life. For younger readers, Frediano Sessi's book, *Primo Levi; l'uomo, il testimone, lo scrittore* (Trieste: Einaudi Ragazzi, 2013) is also a good introduction. Giovanni Tesio has spoken on several occasions about the biography he never wrote: 'A proposito di una biografia mancata' (in *Primo Levi: memoria e invenzione*, edited by G. Ioli; San Salvatore Monferrato: Edizioni della Biennale 'Piemonte e Letteratura', 1995). He gave an account of his recorded conversations with Levi in a subsequent volume published by Interlinea editore: *Primo Levi ancora qualcosa da dire* (2018). Pietro Scarnera's graphic novel *Una stella tranquilla. Ritratto sentimentale di Primo Levi* (Bologna: Comma 22, 2013), is interesting. The debate on Levi's partisan activities has recently been reopened: *Primo Levi testimone e scrittore di storia* (edited by P. Momigliano Levi and R. Gorris; Flroence: Giuntina, 1999), and in particular the essays by Stuart Woolf in *Il senso della storia per Primo Levi* and by Paolo Momigliano Levi, 'L'esperienza della Resistenza nella vita e nell'opera di Primo Levi' (in *Primo Levi testimone e scrittore di storia*, 1999). On the same topic: Frediano Sessi, *Il lungo viaggio di Primo Levi* (Venice: Marsilio, 2013) and Sergio Luzzatto, *Partigià* (Milan: Mondadori, 2013), brilliant historical essays that have triggered a broad discussion in Italy and abroad. On Levi's participation in the National Association of Former Political Deportees in Nazi Camps, see, *Primo Levi per L'ANED. L'ANED per Primo Levi* (edited by A. Cavaglion; Milan: Franco Angeli, 1997), which collects Levi's contributions alongside numerous witness statements from former deportees. Two volumes of Levi's photographic and documentary portraits came out in 2019: *Album Levi*, edited by R. Mori and D. Scarpa (Turin: Einaudi, 2017). See also, M. Belpoliti, *Photo Levi* (Turin: Acquario, 2021). A reconstruction of Levi's journey home from Auschwitz to Turin in the form of a parallel journey can be found in M. Belpoliti's *La prova* (Milan: Guanda, 2017), which can be read in tandem with a film directed by Davide Ferrario with a screenplay by M. Belpoliti, *La strada di Levi* (DVD; Chiarelettere, 2007).

CRITICAL STUDIES

The first comprehensive critical contribution to appear was *Invito alla lettura di Primo Levi* by Fiora Vincenti (Milan: Mursia, 1973), later updated by Mario Miccinesi. This volume benefited from the supervision of Levi himself, in particular regarding the circumstances in which he wrote his books and the bibliographical information. In 1981, Giuseppe Grassano published a monograph (*Primo Levi*, Firenze: La Nuova Italia, 1981), which was seen as the reference study for the work of this author for many years. in 1997, M. Belpoliti published a short profile of Levi (*Primo Levi*, Milan: Bruno Mondadori, 1997), much of which is now included in this book. In 2000, Edoardo Bianchini published a new monograph (*Invito alla lettura di Primo Levi*, Milan: Mursia, 2000) that analyses Levi's works, themes and motives and examines critical studies on Levi. In the same year, a study by three young authors, Fabio Moliterni, Roberto Ciccarelli and Alessandro Lattanzio, came out: *Primo Levi. L'a-topia letteraria. Il pensiero narrativo. La scrittura e l'assurdo* (Naples: Liguori, 2000). Enrico Mattioda wrote an extensive monograph on Primo Levi (*Primo Levi*, Rome: Salerno Editrice, 2011) that stands out for its originality and attention to new aspects of his work. Particularly interesting chapters are: 'Il brutto potere' and 'Tra le pieghe del male'. *Primo Levi's Ordinary Virtues* by Robert Gordon (Oxford: OUP, 2001) is one of the best essays ever on Levi's work as a whole, and on his human and intellectual standing. It is highly recommended for the originality of its approach. Françoise Carasso re-published *Primo Levi. La scelta della chiarezza* (Turin: Einaudi, 2009), which was originally published in 1997 before the new edition of the *Opere*. Among the volumes published abroad we would like to mention: Risa Sodi, *A Dante of our Time. Primo Levi and Auschwitz* (New York: Peter Lang, 1990) and Mirna Cicioni, *Primo Levi. Bridge of Knowledge* (Oxford-Washington: Berg, 1995). The various writings of Gian Paolo Biasin are recommended, in particular: 'Il ghetto e il treno: sul discorso morale di Primo Levi' [*L'asino d'oro* 2(4) (1991): 129–141]. On food, see 'If This is a Man: Il nostro pane-Brot-Broid-chleb-pain-lechem-kenyér quotidiano' (in *I sapori della modernità*; Bologna: Il Mulino, 1991). Also, 'Contagio' (*Riga* 13 [1997]; special issue on Primo Levi, edited by M. Belpoliti).

An important monographic volume for the breadth and variety of its contributions is the special issue of the journal *Riga—Primo Levi*, edited by Belpoliti and published in 1997, with the following dictionary entries: M. Belpoliti, 'Animali'; G. Bertone, 'Antologia'; A. Cavaglion, 'Asymmetries'; D. Scarpa, 'Chiaro/oscuro'; G. P. Biasin, 'Contagio'; S. Bartezzaghi, 'Cosmichimiche'; R. Gordon, 'Etica'; F. Sessi, 'Finzione'; P. Pauletto, 'Frontiere'; M. Lollini, 'Golem'; D. Amsallem, 'Illuminismo'; S. Nerzi, 'Iterazioni'; P. Valabrega, 'Mano/Cervello'; M. Raffaeli, 'Memoria/Memorie'; D. Giglioli, 'Narratore'; L. Grazioli, 'Necessità'; I. Rosato, 'Poesia'; E. Affinati, 'Responsibilità'; M. Porro, 'Scienze'; F. M. Cataluccio, 'Sopravvissuti'; L. Scarlini, 'Teatro'; M. Sebregondi, 'Triangulazioni'; D. Bidussa, 'Veris'; M. J. Calvo Montoro, 'Visitatori'. The issue also includes an anthology of reviews and articles on Levi's books (Calvino, Fonzi, Raboni, Magris, Mengaldo, Fortini, Rigoni Stern, Steiner, etc.). For an introduction to Levi's work, we recommend *Primo Levi: un'antologia della critica* (edited by E. Ferrero; Turin: Einaudi, 1997), which contains numerous essays that have appeared elsewhere. These include: Cavaglion, 'Il termitaio'; G. Grassano, 'Note sui racconti fantastici'; S. Levi Della Torre, 'L'eredità di Primo Levi'; P. Valabrega, 'Primo Levi e la tradizione ebraico-orientale'; D. Meghnagi, 'La vicenda ebraica'; N. Bobbio, 'Primo Levi perché'; M. Mila, 'Il sapiente con la chiave a stella'; G. Einaudi, 'Primo Levi e la Casa editrice Einaudi'. In 2016, it was republished by Marcos y Marcos with new essays and additions as well as the proceedings of a conference on the animal behaviourist and anthropological aspect of Levi's works. Two collections of conference proceedings are also useful: *Primo Levi come testimone* (edited by P. Frassica, Fiesole: Casalini Libri, 1990) and *Primo Levi: memoria e invenzione* (1995). The proceedings of the conference *Primo Levi. Il presente del passato*, edited by A. Cavaglion (Milan: Franco Angeli, 1991), contain contributions by F. Fortini, R. Pierantoni and others. S. Levi Della Torre edited a special issue of *La Rassegna mensile di Israel* dedicated to Levi [56(2–3) (May–December 1989)]. The book by various authors, *Primo Levi, il mestiere di raccontare il dovere di ricordare* (edited by A. Neiger; Fossombrone: Metauro Edizioni, 1998) contains contributions by A. M. Carpi on *The Truce*, F. Sessi on 'Truth and Fiction', A. Neiger on Levi and Améry and E. Rutigliano on Levi and Canetti. Enrico Mattioda edited the conference proceedings *Al di qua del bene e del male. La visione del mondo di Primo Levi* (Milan: Franco Angeli, 2000) with some important essays. Among the many collective volumes, or conference proceedings, published in English, it is worth mentioning: *Reason and Light: Essay on Primo Levi*, edited by S. R. Tarrow (Cornell University, Ithaca, 1990); in French, the third issue of *Narrativa* of the Centre de Récherches Italiennes of the Université Paris X Nanterre (January 1993) edited by M. H. Caspar with various essays on poetry, the body, and memory. *Shoah, mémoire et écriture: Primo Levi et le dialogue des savoir* (Paris–Montréal: L'Harmattan, 1997) is edited by Giuseppina Santagostino, the author of several previous essays on Levi, science fiction and the body. Robert Gordon edited the collective volume *Primo Levi* (Cambridge: Cambridge University Press, 2007) containing essays on language, Turin and science. *Voci dal mondo per Primo Levi* (Florence: Firenze University Press, 2007), edited by Luigi Dei, contains essays on Levi and Judaism. Enrico Palandri's *Primo Levi* (Mondadori Education, 2011) is worth noting. Finally, one of the most original contributions to our knowledge of Levi is *Lezioni Levi*, 10 lectures previously published separately by Einaudi but later collected into a single volume edited by F. Levi and D. Scarpa and published by Mondadori in 2019.

LEVI AS WITNESS

For a long time, Levi's contribution as a witness was considered more important than his literary output, which was only recognized later. We recommend starting with Daniele Del Giudice's *Introduzione a Opere,*

Vol. 1 (Turin: Einaudi, 1997), reprinted in the new edition of *Opere complete, Vol. 1* (Turin: Einaudi 2016). Another useful reference is *Primo Levi. Il presente del passato* (1991), containing the proceedings of the ANED conference with contributions by B. Vasari, S. Miniussi, N. Bobbio, L. Rolfi, G. Tedeschi, F. Faruffi, C. Pavone and R. Levi Montalcini. A revealing interview by Anna Bravo and Federico Cereja, *Intervista a Primo Levi, ex deportato* (Turin: Einaudi, 2011) is included in *Opere complete, Vol. 3* (Turin: Einaudi, 2017). Massimo Lollini shed new light on this aspect of Levi's work in his essay 'Il caso Primo Levi e il problema della testimonianza' [*Il piccolo Hans* 72 (Winter 1991): 193–210]. He further developed this exploration in a more recent essay, 'Il diario di dieci giorni di Primo Levi' (in *Memorie, diari, confessioni*, edited by A. Fassò; Bologna: il Mulino, 2007). Further reading should include Thomas Klinkert's 'Problemi semiotici della scrittura nei testi del dopolager: Primo Levi e Jorge Semprún', as well as Walter Geerts', 'Primo Levi e i due testi del testimone', which focuses on the *Report on Auschwitz*. Both can be found in *Telling the Lager: Deportation and Autobiographical Discourse* (edited by M. Bandella; Frankfurt am Main: Peter Lang, 2005). In reviewing *The Drowned and the Saved*, George Steiner ('Accounts of Torture') drew some interesting conclusions [see *Primo Levi*, edited by M. Belpoliti, *Riga* 13 (1997)]. Jan De Volder discusses this in 'Writing and Surviving' in the issue of *La Rassegna mensile di Israel* dedicated to Levi [56(2–3) (May–December 1989)]. See also Anna Bravo and Federico Cereja, *Una misura onesta* (Milan: Franco Angeli, 1993), which explores deportation witness narratives. A key essay on the theme of bearing witness in general is Carlo Ginzburg's 'Unus testis. Lo sterminio degli ebrei e il principio di realtà' (1990), which was later reprinted in *Il filo e le tracce. Vero falso finto* (Milan: Feltrinelli, 2006). On the topic of autobiography in Levi, see: Gianluca Cinelli, 'Il paradosso della testimonianza' (in *Ermeneutica e scrittura autobiografica*; Milan: Edizioni Unicopli, 2008), and the chapter on Levi by Anna Maria Mariani in *Sull'autobiografia contemporanea* (Rome:

Carocci, 2012). We would also like to point out Mario Baenghi's *Lezione Levi, Perché crediamo a Primo Levi* (Turin: Einaudi, 2013), which links Levi's writing in order to bear witness to his later literary production.

IF THIS IS A MAN

The 1947 edition of *If This is a Man* edited by De Silva was not in print for long. It was not made available again until it was included in *Opere complete, Vol. 1* (2016). Regarding the 1958 version, the book everyone reads, we recommend the annotated edition edited by Alberto Cavaglion, published by Einaudi in 2012 under the aegis of the Centro Internazionale di Studi su Primo Levi in Turin. It contains an extensive set of notes as a commentary on the text as well as indexes compiled by Daniela Muraca. Also useful is the school edition with notes by Giovanni Tesio (Milan: Einaudi Scuola, 1997), in addition to an annotated edition by Stefano Levi Della Torre published by UTET. Levi collaborated to produce an annotated edition for schools with his own notes in the series 'Letture per la scuola media' (Turin: Einaudi, 1973). The dramatic version by Pieralberto Marché and Primo Levi was published by Einaudi in 1966 in the series, 'Collezione di teatro'. The text of the radio edition is currently unpublished. 'Rapporto sull'organizzazione igienico-sanitaria del Campo di concentramento degli Ebrei di Monowitz (Auschwitz–Alta Slesia)' by Leonardo De Benedetti and Primo Levi that Alberto Cavaglion saved from oblivion can now be read together with other texts by Levi in *Così fu Auschwitz. Testimonianze 1945–1986*, edited by F. Levi and D. Scarpa (Turin: Einaudi, 2015). With an introduction and an extensive apparatus of notes by the two editors, it allows us to follow the evolution of Levi's witness statements from 1945 onwards by means of previously unpublished texts. Fabio Levi's Introduction to the special edition prepared by the Centro Internazionale di Studi su Primo Levi in Turin (Turin: Einaudi, 2014) is also worthy of note, as is Robert Gordon's Introduction to the English edition of the *Auschwitz Report* (London: Verso, 2006), one of the first in-depth studies on the extermination camps. Also noteworthy is the philological edition edited by Matteo Fadini, *Su un avantesto di 'Se questo è un uomo'*, which includes a new edition of the 1946 *Report* in *Filologia Italiana* 5 (2008) and an essay by Fadini that reconstructs the history of the text. Philippe Mesnard edited a French edition of the *Report* (*Rapport sur Auschwitz*; Paris: Kimé, 2005), with a long introduction. On Levi's statements regarding Einaudi's rejection of his first book, see *Conversazioni e interviste 1963–1987* (edited by M. Belpoliti; Turin: Einaudi, 1997) and in particular the third volume of *Opere complete* (2017), where you will also find further bibliographical references and citations of the interviews in which Levi comments on the rejection. For those who want to explore the differences between the 1947 and 1958 editions, the study by Giovanni Tesio, *Su alcune aggiunte e varianti di 'Se questo è un uomo'* in *Studi Piemontesi* (November 1977), is the best place to start. Tesio was able to consult Levi's manuscript notebook that contained additions and corrections to the 1947 edition, including parts that were not used in the 1958 edition. Letters written by Levi in 1946 while he was writing his first book can be found in Jean Samuel and Jean-Marc Dreyfus', *Mi chiamava Pikolo* (Milan: Frassinelli, 2008); the book also contains a photograph of the first page of the chapter 'Il canto di Ulisse' that Levi sent to Jean. A commentary on the variants between the 1947 and 1958 editions can be found in M. Belpoliti, 'Levi di carta' in *il Verri* 65 (October 2017). In 1993, Alberto Cavaglion published an essay, *Primo Levi e 'Se questo è un uomo'* (Turin: Loescher, 1993) with some interesting contributions for interpreting *If This is a Man*. The essay was later expanded into a book published by Carocci: *Primo Levi: guida a 'Se questo è un uomo'* (Rome, 2021). Another notable contribution is Cesare Segre's, *'Se questo è un uomo' di Primo Levi* (in *Letteratura italiana. Le Opere, Vol. 4: Il Novecento, La ricerca letteraria*; Turin: Einaudi, 1996). We also recommend *Primo Levi* (Paris: Ellipses, 2000) by Daniela Amsallem, a superlative expert on

Levi. The following year, she published *Primo Levi au miroir de son œuvre* (Lyon: Éditions du Cosmogone, 2001), a far-reaching and in-depth study of his entire *oeuvre* as well as a guide to the book, *Si c'est un homme* (Ellipses, Paris, 2001). In order to place the 1947 edition of *If This is a Man* in the context of the postwar period and the various witness statements on the deportation and the extermination camps that began to come out at the time, Robert Gordon's contribution, *Scolpitelo nei cuori. L'Olocausto nella cultura italiana (1944–2010)* (Turin: Bollati Boringhieri, 2013), is essential reading. Chiara Volpato and Alberta Contarello, 'Psicologia sociale e situazioni estreme: Relazioni interpersonali e intergruppi in "Se questo è un uomo" di Primo Levi" ' [*Quaderni di psicologia* 20 (1999)] present a psychological reading of the book, while a psychological analysis of the dreams recounted in the book, according to Gregory Bateson's theory, can be found in the chapter dedicated to memory in Pietro Barbetta's *Figure della relazione* (Pisa: Edizioni ETS, 2007).

IS *IF THIS IS A MAN* REALLY 'A DETACHED STUDY'?

Mario Barenghi was among the first to note the possible dual interpretation offered by the poem that opens *If This is a Man*, and the definition 'a detached study on some aspects of the human mind' is his. Essential reading on the subject includes his books, *La visione del mondo di Primo Levi* (2000); *Tre morti, tre alberi. Primo Levi e il senso della testimonianza* (a paper presented at the conference 'Primo Levi et la chimie des mots', Luxembourg, 30 November 2011). We also recommend his book *Perché crediamo a Primo Levi* (2013).

THE DEPORTED, THE LAGER, MUSELMÄNN

In a 1983 interview with Anna Bravo and Federico Cereja, *Intervista a Primo Levi, ex deportato* (2011), which was first published in a magazine, Levi talks about the world of the Lager, daily actions, habits, and customs and the relationships between prisoners. The conversations collected in *Conversazioni e interviste 1963–1987* (1997) in the 'Lager' section are now included in the third volume of *Opere complete* (2017). These provide a great deal of additional information. Levi speaks at length about his experience of the Lager in his Appendix to *If This is a Man*, originally written for the 1973 school edition and now included in all commercial editions. His handwritten notes to the 1973 school edition are particularly revealing. Giorgio Agamben grappled with the question of the Muselmänn and of the witness in *Quel che resta di Auschwitz: l'archivio e il testimone* (*Homo Sacer 3*) (Turin: Bollati Boringhieri, 1998), a book which sparked lively debate when it came out. For more information, see the article by Stefano Levi Della Torre, 'Il sopravvissuto, il mussulmano e il testimone', included in the Italian edition of *The Drowned and the Saved*, with an introduction by D. Bidussa (Turin: Einaudi, 2003). Similar issues are addressed by Federica Sossi in *Nel crepaccio del tempo. Testimoniare la Shoah* (Milan: Marcos y Marcos, 1997). We recommend in particular the chapters 'Primo Levi: con gli occhi legati al suolo' and 'Jean Améry: il tempo sospeso'.

PROPER NAMES

Alberto Cavaglion, like other commentators on Levi, has drawn attention to the proper names of the people mentioned in *If This is a Man: In Così fu Auschwitz* (2015) which includes the first texts written by Levi upon his return from the Lager: lists of deportees with names, surnames and their occupations.

HOLOCAUST

An interesting study dedicated to the origin of the word is Vera Sullam Calimani's, *I nomi dello sterminio* (Turin: Einaudi, 2001), republished by Marietti in 2018. The book reconstructs the history of the expression and how Primo, Elie Wiesel and other witnesses of the Shoah related to it.

TIME

There are now many studies dedicated to the concept of time in Levi: Domenico Scarpa discusses time in 'Chiaro/oscuro' with reference to the use of verb tenses in *If This is a Man*, as does David Bidussa more broadly in 'Verbi'. Both essays are collected in *Primo Levi* (*Riga* 13 [1997]). We also suggest reading Davide Bidussa's essay, 'Tempo storico e tempo cronologico nella scrittura di Primo Levi' in *Al di qua del bene e del male. La visione del mondo di Primo Levi* (2000).

I/WE

Two linguists, Nunzio La Fauci and Liana Tronci, addressed the topic of We/Us in *If This is a Man* in *Noi-Nous-Nosotros*, proceedings of the 19–20 October 2012 Zurich conference, edited by M. C. Janner, M. Della Costanza and P. Sutermeister. The topic was further expanded in the paper, 'Se questo è un uomo: chimica della quarta e prima persona' in *Prisma Levi* (edited by H. Necker; Pisa: Edizioni ETS, 2015), one of the most important studies on grammatical subjects in *If This is a Man*. This study is complemented by Pier Vincenzo Mengaldo's essay, 'Lingua e scrittura in Levi', first published in 1990, and now included in *Primo Levi: un'antologia della critica* (1997), which also contains other ideas on the same theme. Another interesting essay by Sophie Nezri-Dufour is 'Iterazioni' (in *Riga* 13 [1997]). One of the first to point out the distinction was Alberto Cavaglion in 'Un modo diverso di dire io' (in *Ebrei senza saperlo*; Naples: L'Ancora del Mediterraneo, 2002).

DEPOSITIONS

In *Così fu Auschwitz* (2015), you will find the depositions Levi wrote as evidence in the postwar trials of Nazi perpetrators, as well as his memoirs of the deportation, which provided valuable information for organizations, associations and research committees. The notes written by Scarpa on the individual texts are interesting. Some of these can also be read in *Da una tregua all'altra* by Marco Belpoliti and Andrea Cortellessa (Milan: Chiarelettere, 2010).

HEINZ RIEDT, GERMANS

The correspondence between Levi and his German translator, Heinz Riedt, is still largely unpublished. I was able to read it thanks to Giovanni Tesio, who made a copy available to me. On the relationship with the DDR, see Gabriella Berolatti's research for her degree thesis, *La casa editrice Aufbau* (University of Turin, academic year 2008–2009). Levi's correspondence with Riedt, edited by M. Mengoni, which contains many more letters which reveal the relationship between the two authors is imminent. On this topic, M. Mengoni's lecture, *Primo Levi e i tedeschi* can now be found in *Lezioni Levi* published by Mondadori.

UMBERTO SABA

For a more in-depth look at the correspondence between Levi and Umberto Saba, see the essay by Walter Barberis, '*Primo Levi e "un libro fatale"* ' in *Atlante della letteratura italiana, Vol. 3: Dal Romanticismo a oggi* (edited by S. Luzzatto and G. Pedullà; Turin: Einaudi, 2012). For further discussion of the Shoah, see Enzo Traverso, *Auschwitz e gli intellettuali. La Shoah nella cultura del dopoguerra* (Bologna: il Mulino, 2004).

WHY *IF THIS IS A MAN* WAS REJECTED BY EINAUDI

We recommend reading Luisa Mangoni's, *Pensare i libri. La casa editrice Einaudi dagli anni trenta agli anni sessanta* (Turin: Bollati Boringhieri, 1999) to find out more about the history of the Einaudi publishing house and the events around Levi's first book and subsequent publications. The story of the publisher's rejection of the book is framed in the context of publishing approaches of the time and other books bearing witness to the deportation that were beginning to come out after the war. Transcriptions of the editorial discussions on these topics can be found in a book edited by Tommaso Munari, *I verbali del mercoledì, riunioni editoriali Einaudi 1943–1952* (Turin: Einaudi, 2011).

Is *If This is a Man* a Comedy or a Tragedy?

Giorgio Agamben's 'Comedìa', published for the first time in *Paragone* 346, in December 1976, is the text to read. It is now in Agamben, *Categorie italiane* in a new edition published by Laterza (Rome-Bari, 2010). In this book, there are at least three complementary essays to delve deeper into the question: ' "Corn": dall'anatomia alla poetica'; 'Il sogno della lingua'; 'Il dettato della poesia'. We also recommend Andrea Cortellessa's Afterword, 'Profanare il dispositivo'. The core work on the subject of tragedy is George Steiner's *The Death of Tragedy*, first published by Faber and Faber in 1961 and translated into Italian by Garzanti.

Chance

The theme of chance was explored by Mario Perniola in *Transiti* (1985), later reprinted by Castelvecchi (Rome, 1998): *L'arte dell'occasione* and *L'occasione come opportunità permanente*. Paul Valéry also refers to this concept in the first volume of his *Quaderni* (Milan: Adelphi, 1985): chance is seen as a divinity which is analogous, but different, to Fortune.

The Truce

There are no comprehensive studies focused solely on Levi's second book. However, a good introduction can be found in Giovanni Tesio's article, *Tutta l'Odissea in un quaderno* (published in a special issue of *La Stampa* on *The Truce*, 9 February 1997). Lucia Sgueglia's article,

'A est di cosa? Per una geografia della Tregua', is included in Marco Belpoliti and Andrea Cortellessa, *Da una tregua all'altra* (2010). The article is taken from Sgueglia's doctoral thesis at the University of Rome, La Sapienza: *L'Europa orientale nella narrativa italiana del secondo dopoguerra. Inferni, ritorni, nostalgie, patrie e peripli.* The chapter 'Esili, odissee, esodi: il ritorno dal Lager' is particularly relevant here. Jean-Philippe Bareil has explored some aspects of the theme of travel in Levi in his book *Exil et voyage littéraire dans l'œuvre de Primo Levi* (Paris: Éditons Messène, 1998). Another reference is *La prova* (M. Belpoliti; Turin: Einaudi, 2007), an account of a journey following the places mentioned in *The Truce*, which was documented in a film by Davide Ferrario, *La strada di Levi* (2007). The notes Levi wrote for the school edition of *The Truce* for the series 'Letture per la scuola media' (Turin: Einaudi, 1965) are very revealing. On the subject of the American translation and the title indicated by Levi, see the articles by Sergio Luzzatto, 'Primo Levi su "un oceano dipinto"' and Domenico Scarpa, 'Artigliato al petto dalle rime marinare' (*Il Sole 24 Ore*,19 June 2011).

CLAY/MUD ·

Regarding the theme of clay/mud, a good place to start is Alexander Graham Cairns-Smith's book, *Sette indizi sull'origine della vi*ta (Naples: Liguori, 1986), which Levi reviewed. Further references can be found in Mario Porro's 'Scienza', in the Primo Levi issue of *Riga*. For assonances with Bachelard and an important exploration of scientific themes, see Porro's book, *Primo Levi* (Bologna: il Mulino, 2017). His *Letteratura come filosofia naturale* (Milan: Medusa, 2009) explores Levi's work, but also makes comparisons with Gadda and Calvino.

TRAIN, JOURNEY

There are no detailed studies on the negative or positive presence of trains in Levi's works, but there are a few mentions in various books.

We recommend in particular, Wolfang Schvelbusch, *Storia dei viaggi in ferrovia* (Turin: Einaudi, 1988). On travel in general, see Patrick Pauletto, 'Frontiere' in *Riga* (13) (1997).

SPACE TRAVEL

This is a theme less-often associated with Levi, which intersects with his interest in the moon, an issue that attracted many writers in the second half of the twentieth century. For an overview, see Stefano Catucci, *Learning from the Moon* (Macerata: Quodlibet, 2013), and Carmelo Colangelo, *La verità errante. Viaggi spaziali alla prova del pensiero* (Naples: Liguori, 2009). Freeman Dyson wrote *Disturbing the Universe* (New York: Harper & Row, 1979), a book that Levi read and probably commented on, which is mentioned in one of his poems and which also interested Calvino.

MAPS

Levi had an evident passion for maps and diagrams of all kinds. He drew several of them during his life, including the map of the Monowitz camp in various letters. These can be found in the illustration to the *Enciclopedia Einaudi* edited by Ruggiero Romano, a historian who was also a scholar of Raymond Queneau.

SELF-COMMENTARY

The notes Levi wrote for the school editions of *If This is a Man* and *The Truce*, published by Einaudi in the series 'Letture per la scuola media' were long neglected by critics in their interpretations of the two books. The notes can now be read in *Opere complete*, *Vol.* 1 (2016). They probably originate from Levi's correspondence with Heinz Riedt, his German translator. His notes for *The Periodic Table* are also interesting. A handwritten note is also present in *The Wrench*. The 1983 school edition in the same series was edited by Gian Luigi Beccaria. Cavaglion discussed the subject of in Levi's self-commentary in his essay 'Il termitaio. Primo Levi e "Se questo è un uomo" ' (in *Primo Levi: un'antologia della critica*, 1997).

Music

For the time being, there are no specific studies dedicated to music and noise in Levi's works. There are mentions in various essays, but nothing in depth. There are some radio interviews on the subject in *Opere complete, Vol. 3* (2017). Versions of *If This is a Man* and *The Truce* which were dramatized for radio are available in the RAI archives. *If This is a Man* was also adapted for theatre. The radio scripts of Levi's first two books can now be found in *Opere complete, Vol. 1* (2016).

Theatre

Luca Scarlini's essay, 'Teatro' (in *Riga* 13 [1997]), deals extensively for the first time with the theatrical value of Levi's works and his collaboration with avant-garde directors.

If This is a Dream

On the subject of the dreams reported by deportees, see Viktor E. Frankl, *Uno psicologo nei lager* (Milan: Ares, 1995), and Bruno Bettelheim, *The Informed Heart: Autonomy in a Mass Age* (Glencoe: The Free Press, 1960, translated into Italian by Adelphi as *Il cuore vigile* (Milan, 1988; previously entitled *Il prezzo della vita*). *Sopravvivere* (Milan: Feltrinelli, 1981), collects texts published in journals in the United States, including the first seed of Bettelheim's *The Informed Heart*. Bettelheim's Afterword to Charlotte Beradt's, *The Third Reich of Dreams* (Wellingborough: Aquarian Press, 1985) is also worth reading. Reinhart Koselleck examines the same theme in his Preface to *Terrore e sogno. Osservazioni metodologiche su esperienze del tempo nel Terzo Reich*, now available as *Futuro passato* (Genoa: Marietti, 1986). Jean Cayrol, *Il ritorno di Lazzaro* (Milan: Medusa, 2008) also looks at deportees' dreams. There is an interesting comparison with Kafka's dreams in Gaspare Giudice's *Sogni* (Palermo: Sellerio, 1990). On the subject of dreams in general from the point of view of neurological research, see Peretz Lavie, *Il meraviglioso mondo del sogno* (Turin: Einaudi, 1999) and Piero Salzarulo, *La fine del sogno. Le porte del risveglio* (Turin: Bollati Boringhieri, 1999). For the theme of the veil, we suggest reading a wonderful essay by Francesca Rigotti, 'Il velo e il fiume. Riflessioni sulle metfore dell'oblio' (*Iride* 8, 1995). On the subject of the transmission of dreams, see *Aspetti scientifici della parapsicologia* (Turin: Boringhieri, 1973) edited by Roberto Cavanna.

WHY PRIMO LEVI CAN BE CONSIDERED A POLITICAL WRITER

For an in-depth look at Levi's political reflections, his ideas about the Cold War, Israel, Zionism and the Italian political events of the 1960s and 70s, see Andrea Rondini's book, *Anche il cielo brucia. Primo Levi e il giornalismo* (Macerata: Quodlibet, Macerata, 2012). Many themes are addressed here, in the context of Levi's ongoing collaboration with newspapers and magazines: the Moro case, Chernobyl, the Six-Day War, the invasion of Lebanon, etc. Other references can be found in *Primo Levi* (*Riga* 38, 2017).

NATURAL HISTORIES, SCIENCE FICTION, HYBRIDS

Giuseppe Grassano was among the first critics to tackle Levi's short stories, both in his monographic study published by Nuova Italia and in *La 'musa stupefatta'. Note sui racconti fantascientifici* (1991), now in *Primo Levi: un'antologia della critica* (1997). On Levi's short stories in general, see Enrico Mattioda, *Primo Levi* (2011), which is full of ideas and original analyses. Angela Di Fazio, *Altre simulacri. Automata, vampiri e mostri nella storia dei racconti di Primo Levi* (Pisa: ETS Editions, 2012) is worthy of note, as is Cavaglion's essay on the figure of the centaur, 'Primo Levi era un centauro?' (in *Ebrei senza sapere*; Naples: L'Ancora del Mediterraneo, 2002).

SCIENTIFIC AMERICAN

For Italo Calvino, see *Cronologia cosmicomica* compiled by Claudio Milanini in *Calvino: Tutte le cosmicomiche* (Milan: Mondadori, 2002). Regarding links to Giorgio de Santillana, we recommend, Domenico Scarpa's entry, 'L'esordio della iperstoria' in *Atlante della letteratura, Vol. 3*. On Levi's predilection for *Scientific American*, Enrico Mattioda, 'Scientific American' come fonte d'ispirazione (in *Primo Levi*, 2011) is a useful introduction.

RADIO, TELEVISION

Regarding the radio recordings of Levi's stories and his participation in the adaptations of his first two books for the radio, see Gabriella Poli and Giorgio Calcagno, *Echi di una voce perduta* (1992). See also transcriptions of radio interviews in *Conversazioni e interviste 1963–1987* (1997). On the writer's participation in television broadcasts, see the essay by Frediano Sessi, 'Entre témoignage et fiction: Primo Levi à la télévision italienne' (in *Primo Levi à l'œuvre*, 2008). There is also a radio text inspired by Levi with an introductory note by the author in *Intervista aziendale*.

CINEMA

For further information on this topic, see Andrea Rondini's essay, 'Bello e falso. Il cinema secondo Primo Levi' (*Studi novecenteschi* 1 [2007]). On visual themes in Levi in general, see Enrico Mattioda, 'Schemi visivi' (in *La visione del mondo di Primo Levi*, 2000) and Andrea Cortellessa,

Il film della memoria. Primo Levi 'in the eye of history' (in *Da una tregua all'altra*, 2010), which contains an extensive bibliography on the relationship between images and the Shoah.

FLAWS OF FORM

For an in-depth study, see the chapter in Enrico Mattioda, *Primo Levi* (2011) entitled, *L'ispirazione scientifica: da Vizio di forma al Sistema periodico*. On Levi's stories, see Fabiano Baldasso, *Il cerchio di gesso* in *Primo Levi narratore e testimone* (Bologna: Pendragon, 2007), which explores the relationship between narration and bearing witness. The book is very useful in connecting science fiction to testimony and to fiction in general.

GAMES, INVENTING, CREATION/EVOLUTION

Essential reading for an in-depth examination of these themes is Stefano Bartezzaghi's *Le cosmichimiche di Primo Levi: Gioco, osservazione linguistica, invenzione*, originally published in 1997. This is now available in *Scrittori giocatori* (Turin: Einaudi, 2010), alongside two other essays taken from conference proceedings ('Primo Levi inventore' and 'Primo Levi giocatore'), which contain a comment and a brief bibliography for further study. On the theme of games, see also, again by Bartezzaghi, *Una telefonata con Primo Levi* (Turin: Einaudi, 2012), which examines the relationship between Levi and game expert, Giampaolo Dossena, and among Levi, Calvino and Queneau. See also Gordon, *Primo Levi's Ordinary Virtues* (2001). In *Outrageous Fortune. Luck and the Holocaust* (Turin: Einaudi, CPL Editions, 2017), Gordon explored the theme of chance. We also recommend a curious essay on numbers in Levi by Raniero Speelman, 'I numeri di Primo Levi' (in *Voci dal mondo per Primo Levi*, 2007).

In Voice and in Writing, Conversations and Interviews

In order to understand the oral aspect of Levi's work, his television interviews (which can be seen on YouTube) are the place to start. His radio interviews, some of which have been transcribed in *Conversazioni e interviste 1963–1987* (1997) are also interesting. An almost complete collection of Levi's conversations is now available in *Opere complete, Vol. 3* (2017). Regarding the issue of whether interviews can be considered a literary genre, see Roland Barthes' *Dalla parola alla scrittura, Interviste 1962–1980* (Turin: Einaudi, 1986) and his essay 'Ascolto' (in *L'ovvio e l'ottuso*; Turin: Einaudi, 1985). Alongside Levi's interviews, it is worth reading Pier Paolo Pasolini's interview, *Il sogno del centauro*, edited by J. Duflot (Rome: Editori Riuniti, 1994). For an exploration of oral and narrative traditions, a parallel reading of Levi's interviews with Mario Rigoni Stern's, *Il coraggio di dire di no* (edited by G. Mendicino; Turin: Einaudi, 2013) and Nuto Revelli's, *Il testimone. 1963–2003* (edited by M. Cordero; Turin: Einaudi, 2014), is very revealing. On Levi as a teller of stories in both oral and written form, see Walter Benjamin, 'Il narratore. Considerazioni sull'opera di Nicola Leskov' (in *Angelus Novus*, edited by R. Solmi; Turin: Einaudi, 1962), Daniele Giglioli's essay, 'Narratore' (in *Primo Levi, Riga* 13 [1997]), and especially Roberto Ciccarelli, 'Primo Levi. Del pensiero narrativo' (in *Primo Levi. L'atopia letteraria. Il pensiero narrativo. La scrittura e l'absurdo*; Naples: Liguori, 2000).

The Periodic Table, 'Vanadium' and the Grey Doctor Müller

Further reading regarding the fantastic yet realistic family tree at the beginning of *The Periodic Table*, see Alberto Cavaglion, *Notizie da Argon* (Turin: Instar Libri, 2006). For Levi as a chemist, see Luigi Dei, 'L'arte letteraria di un chimico' (in *Voci dal mondo per Primo Levi*, 2007); Cesare Cases, 'L'ordine delle cose e l'ordine delle parole' (1987), now in *Primo Levi: un'antologia della critica* (edited by E. Ferrero; Turin:

Einaudi, 2006) is essential reading. See, in addition, Giancarlo Borri, *Primo Levi tra scienza e letteratura* (in *Primo Levi: memoria e invenzione*, 1995); Jean-Philippe Bareil, 'Le Système périodique, de l'autobiographie scientifique au métier de vivre' (in *Shoah, mémoire et écriture: Primo Levi et le dialogue des savoirs*, 1997); and JoAnn Cannon, 'Chemistry and Writing in *The Periodic Table*' (in *Reason and Light: Essay on Primo Levi*, 1990). On the links between the story 'Carbon' and Levi as a narrator of micro-stories, see Carlo Ginzburg, 'Microstorie: due o tre cose che so di lei' (1984), in *Il filo e le tracce. Vero, falso, finto* (2006).

SCIENCE, CHEMISTRY, PAINT, SYMMETRY/ASYMMETRY

To find out more about Levi's interest in science, a good starting point is the conversation between Levi and Tullio Regge, *Dialogo* (Milan: Comunità, 1984), commissioned and edited by Ernesto Ferrero and reprinted several times by Einaudi. Additionally, Cesare Cases and Ruggero Pierantoni's, *Il sistema Aperiodico*, in the conference proceedings published under the title *Primo Levi come testimone* (1990). One of the first to deal systematically with science in Levi was Giancarlo Borri in *Le divine impurità. Primo Levi tra scienza e letteratura* (Rimini: Luisé Editore, 1991). Another important contribution is Mario Porro's essay 'Scienza' (in *Primo Levi, Riga* 13 [1997]), and later published as *La cultura ibrida di Primo* Levi in *Letteratura come filosofia naturale* (2009). The essay reconstructs Levi's epistemology, as well as the relationship between science and literature in the light of twentieth-century philosophy. We also recommend reading Cesare Cases, 'Sodio e potassio: scienza e visione del mondo in Primo Levi' (in *Primo Levi come testimone*, 1990). Enrico Mattioda's *L'ordine del mondo* (Naples: Liguori, 1998) is also noteworthy. He goes into greater depth in the chapter 'L'ispirazione scientifica: da Vizio di forma al Sistema periodico' in *Levi* (Rome: Salerno Editrice, 2011). This book contains interesting references to chaos theory and homèostasis. See also Alberto Cavaglion's essay 'Asimmetrie' (in *Primo Levi, Riga* 13 [1997]); and Federico Pellizzi's 'Asimmetria e preclusione' (in *Mémoire oblige. Riflessioni sull'opera di Primo Levi* (edited by A. Neiger; Trento: Università degli Studi di Trento, 2009). On the same subject and on the *Auschwitz Report*, see Martina Mengoni's, ' "Doktor": Primo Levi, Medical Art and Fantastic Science, with a Leopardian Plot' [*Intersections* 34 (1) (April 2014)]. Antonio Di Meo's, *Primo Levi e la scienza come metafora* (Soveria Mannelli: Rubbettino, 2011) examines Levi's relationship with science; see in particular his treatment of 'chirality'', or non-symmetrical symmetry, 'low chemistry' and odours. Finally, see Daniele Orlandi's *Le chimiche di Primo Levi* (Rome: Odradek, 2013).

MOUNTAIN CLIMBING

This great passion of Levi's, which also played a role in his survival in the Lager, is mentioned in various biographies, but there are no specific studies published on the subject. There is a reference to it in an interview by Alberto Papuzzi, a journalist from *La Stampa* who accompanied Levi on various excursions in *Conversazioni e interviste 1963–1987* (1997), also included in the third volume of *Opere complete* (2017).

THE WRENCH, WORK, HAND

For further reading on *The Wrench*, we recommend the Preface and Notes to the school edition (Turin: Einaudi, 1983) by Gian Luigi Beccaria under the guidance of Levi. Levi's interest in work and workers can be explored in Giuseppe Varchetta, *Ascoltando Primo Levi. Organizzazione, narrazione, etica* (Milan: Guerini e Associati, 1991). The author studies the psychology of organizations and is a scholar of labour issues. We also recommend the essay 'Mano/cervello' by Paola Valabrega (in *Primo Levi, Riga* 13 [1997]). See also Marcello Verdelli's essay 'La chiave a stella e la scrittura "in bolla d'aria" ' in *Primo Levi:*

memoria e invenzione (1995). Luigi Cerruti's 'Una vita concreta: Materia, materiali e lavoro umano in Primo Levi' (in *Voci dal mondo per Primo Levi*, 2007) examines what he calls 'the concrete life': labour issues and materials.

CHARLES DARWIN, CLAUDE LÉVI-STRAUSS

Levi talks about Charles Darwin, the father of evolutionism, in various interviews and newspaper articles. Darwin is also included in his personal anthology, *The Search for Roots*. There is no published research on Levi's interest in Darwin. In contrast, Levi's relationship to the anthropologist Lévi-Strauss, whose two books Levi translated, is well documented. Mario Porro, Antonio Di Meo, Franco Baldasso and Enrico Mattioda have all written about the influence of science and animal behaviourism on Levi's work. Federico Pellizzi, 'La lettura del mondo umano: L'antropologia rovesciata di Primo Levi' (in *Ricercare le radici. Primo Levi lettore–Lettori di Primo Levi. Nuovi studi su Primo Levi*, edited by R. Speelman, E. Tinello and S. Gaiga; Utrecht: Igitur Publishing, 2014). Martina Mengoni has analysed the correspondence between Levi and Lévi-Strauss in her essay, 'Epifania di un mestiere. La corrispondenza etnografica tra Primo Levi and Claude Lévi-Strauss' (*Italianistica* 1 [2015]).

WHAT LITERARY LANGUAGE DOES PRIMO LEVI USE?

The most extensive study on Levi's language is Pier Vincenzo Mengaldo's *Lingua e scrittura in Levi* (1990), now included in *Primo Levi: un'antologia della critica* (1997). Jane Nystedt's contributions include: 'Lunghezza della frase e interpunzione: mezzi stilistici in Primo Levi' [*Studi di linguistica teorica e applicata* 21(1–2) (1992)]; *Forestierismi nel lessico di Primo Levi* (Turkey: Italianistica scandinava, atti del terzo congresso degli italianisti scandinavi, Università di Turku, 1992); and *Le opere di Primo Levi viste al computer. Osservazioni stilo linguistiche* (*Acta Universitatis Stockholmienis*, 1993). Anna Laura Lepschy and Giulio Lepschy's essay, 'Primo Levi's Languages' (in *Primo Levi*, 2007) is also recommended. Stefano Bartezzaghi's work deals with language and linguistic games, as well as games in general. See *Le cosmichimiche di Primo Levi. Gioco, osservazione linguistica, invenzione* originally published in 1997 (now available in *Scrittori giocatori*, 2010). Giuliano Mori's, 'Morte e vita sono in potere della lingua. Primo Levi e la ricerca della lingua di Adamo' (in *Ricercare le radici*, 2014).

THE SEARCH FOR ROOTS, PRIMO LEVI'S REVERSED ROOTS

The most all-encompassing study is Giorgio Bertone's essay 'Antologia' (in *Primo Levi*, *Riga* 13 [1997]). We also recommend the chapter 'Le radici e l'Es' in E. Mattioda, *Primo Levi* (2011). Italo Calvino's review of Levi's personal anthology, *Le quattro strade di Primo Levi* (in *Primo Levi*, *Riga* 13 [1997]) is of course essential reading. An interesting reference to Roger Vercel's *Tempesta* (Rome: Nutrimenti, 2013), a book Levi included in the anthology that he read in the Lager infirmary on the day the extermination camp was abandoned and survivors were forced to march. This is contained in the Afterword to the Italian translation by Andrea Cortellessa, *Una radice di Primo Levi*. On Parini and other authors in the personal anthology, see Andrea Rondini, 'Parini, Primo Levi and communication' (*Studi sul Settecento e l'Ottocento* 1 [2006]).

ALESSANDRO MANZONI

An essay exploring the relationship between Levi and Manzoni by Mirna Cicioni, 'Un'amicizia asimmetrica e feconda: Levi e Manzoni' (in *Voci dal mondo per Primo Levi*, 2007), lists the Manzoni quotes throughout Levi's work and comments on Levi's use of parody and irony when he cites Manzoni.

DANTE ALIGHIERI

Critics from Turin, in particular, have explored the relationship between Levi and Dante in a number of essays. Lorenzo Mondo's 'Primo Levi e Dante' (in *Primo Levi*, edited by G. Ioli, 1995) is recommended. Also, Giorgio Calcagno, 'Dante dolcissimo padre' (in *La visione del mondo di Primo Levi*, 2000); and *Demetrio Paolin, La memoria e l'oltraggio. Primo Levi interprete di Dante* (*Levia Gravia* 8 [2007]). The notes to the school edition of *If This is a Man*, edited by Giovanni Tesio (Turin: Einaudi, 1992), indicate the Dante citations in the text. On the subject of Dante's presence in *If This is a Man*, see also Cavaglion's detailed commentary on the edition edited by the Centro Internazionale di Studi Primo Levi in Turin (Turin: Einaudi, 2012), which contains a wealth of references. On the Dantean figure of Ulysses in Levi, see the essay by Piero Boitani, *L'ombra di Ulisse* (Bologna: il Mulino, 1992), the book by François Rastier, *Ulisse ad Auschwitz* (Naples: Liguori, 2009), and Risa Sodi, *A Dante of Our Time: Primo Levi and Auschwitz* (1990).

GIACOMO LEOPARDI

Studies on the relationship between Levi and Leopardi are beginning to emerge. Older studies include Anna Baldini, 'Primo Levi e i poeti del dolore (Da Giobbe a Leopardi)' (*Nuova rivista di letteratura italiana* 1 [2002]); Marco Vianelli, ' "Madre è di parto e di voler matrigna": Primo Levi lettore di Leopardi' (*Critica letteraria* 3 [2004]); Primo Novella, ' "Al di là della siepe": Sondaggi sul leopardismo di Primo Levi' (in *Nemla Italian Studies* 32 [2009–10]).

CHARLES BAUDELAIRE

The quotations from Baudelaire in *If This is a Man* were pointed out by Levi himself in his letters to his German translator, Heinz Riedt, and then taken up by Giovanni Tesio. Cavaglion points out several quotes in his annotated edition of *If This Is a Man* (2012).

FRANÇOIS RABELAIS

Although Rabelais is included in Levi's personal anthology, *The Search for Roots*, and there are many direct and indirect citations in Levi's work, not much research has been published on Levi's interest in Rabelais, except for references in monographs on Levi. William Kluback, *Primo Levi, a Friend of Empedocles and Rabelais* (*Journal of Evolutionary Psychology* 18(3–4 [August 1997]) is worth noting.

ART

Levi does not mention art much in his works and as a consequence it has not been a subject of research. An exception is Angela Di Fazio, 'Primo Levi tra arte e letteratura: per una teoria della gestualità rituale' in *Poetiche* 12(1), 2010, later collected in *Altri simulacri. Automi, vampiri e mostri della storia nei racconti di Primo Levi* (2012).

THE BIBLE

In his detailed comments on *If This is a Man* (2012), Cavaglion points out numerous references to the Old Testament, as well as quotations from the Gospels. The Books of Matthew, Mark, and Luke are present in the book. Other quotes are from the Talmud and Jewish legends and stories. See the entry the relationship between Levi and Judaism in this bibliography.

PAIN, HAPPINESS/UNHAPPINESS, ENVY

See *Primo Levi's Ordinary Virtues* by Robert Gordon (2001), which contains numerous observations on these issues, especially on pain. See also Mario Porro, 'La cultura ibrida di Primo Levi' (in *Letteratura come filosofia naturale*, 2009).

HERMANN LANGBEIN

Levi's relationship with the Auschwitz historian is still waiting to be brought into focus through a parallel reading of their works. For biographical data and correspondence between Levi and Langbein, see the biographies of Carole Angier, *The Double Bond* (2002) and Ian Thomson, *Primo Levi* (2002).

MARIO RIGONI STERN

The correspondence between the two writers has not yet been made public, although Rigoni Stern wrote about it in two chapters of *Aspettando l'alba e altri racconti* (Turin: Einaudi, 2004), *La Medusa non ci ha impietriti*, and *Primo Levi, moderno odissea*. With Nuto Revelli, the three writers represent an important chapter in the study of the relationship between literature and the World War II. See Giuseppe Mendicino's various contributions that culminated in his biography of Mario Rigoni Stern, *Un ritratto* (Rome–Bari: Laterza, 2021).

LILITH AND OTHER STORIES

For a new reading of Levi's stories, see Angela Di Fazio, *Altri simulacra: Automi, vampiri e mostri della storia nei racconti di Primo Levi* (2012).

ON PARODY AND PASTICHE IN LEVI

See Mirna Cicioni in *Un'amicizia asimmetrica e feconda: Levi e Manzoni* (in *Voci dal mondo per Primo Levi*). On parody in Italian literature, see the essay by Guglielmo Gorni and Silvia Longhi, *La parodia* (in *Letteratura italiana, Vol. 5: Le questioni*; Turin: Einaudi, 1986).

All Levi's Animals

Primo Levi, *Ranocchi sulla Luna e altri animali* (edited by E. Ferrero; Turin: Einaudi, 2014) contains all of Levi's stories and essays dedicated to animals. Jane Nystedt was one of the first critics to create a database of Levi's reference to animals in 'Primo Levi e il mondo animale', in *Actes du XIIe. Congrès des Romanistes Scandinaves*, Aalborg, 11-15 août 1993 (edited by G. Boysen, vol. 2; Aalborg: Aalborg University Press, 1994). See also Daniela Amsallem, '*Le symbolisme du chien: Primo Levi et la littérature juive après la Shoah*' (*Chroniques italiennes* 33-34 [1993]), and Sophie Nezri-Dufour, 'Le bestiaire poétique de Primo Levi' (*Italies, Revue d'études italiennes* 10 [2006]).

Animal–Man

On this topic, it is worth reading the essay by Mario Porro, *Un etologo nel Lager* in *Al di qua del bene e del male. La visione del mondo di Primo Levi* (2000). Porro addresses the question of the Lager as a biological and social experiment, in the light of authors such as Zygmunt Bauman, Konrad Lorenz and Arnold Gehlen. To explore this topic further, see Massimo Bucciantini, *Esperimento Auschwitz* (Turin: Einaudi, 2011), where the Lager is interpreted as a 'mental experiment' as Galileo and Einstein might have seen it. The chapter on Levi as animal behaviourist by Franco Baldasso in *Il cerchio di gesso. Primo Levi narratore e testimone* (2007) is also interesting. See also Stefano Levi Della Torre, 'Primo Levi etologo' (in *Primo Levi: Scrittura e testimonianza*, edited by D. Meghnagi; Florence: Libri liberi, 2006). On Levi's interest in Konrad Lorenz, see Andrea Rondini, ' "Ve lo giuro": Primo Levi tra Konrad Lorenz e Marco Polo' (*Rivista di letteratura italiana* 3 [2007]).

If Not Now, When?

In all monographs on Primo Levi there is a chapter on the only novel that is intertwined with the theme of Judaism. Among the most recent studies, see Enrico Mattioda, *Primo Levi* (2011). There are several short essays and newspaper articles on the novel, but no specific overall study.

Judaism

Levi gave many interviews on this theme, now collected in Primo Levi, *Conversazioni e interviste 1963–1987* (1997). Massimo Dini and Stefano Jesurum's book, *Primo Levi: Le opere e i giorni* (Milan: Rizzoli, 1991) is an important contribution. Two books that have explored Levi's Judaism are: Vania De Luca, *Tra Giobbe e i buchi neri: Le radici ebraiche dell'opera di Primo Levi* (Naples: Istituto grafico editoriale italiano, 1991) and Sophie Nezri-Dufour, *Primo Levi: una memoria ebraica del Novecento* (Florence: Giuntina, 2002). Alberto Cavaglion has written several essays on the subject. In particular, see 'Argon e la cultura ebraica piemontese' (in *Primo Levi: Il presente del passato*, 1991); and *La scelta di Gedeone: appunti su Primo Levi e l'ebraismo* (*Journal of the Institute of Romance Studies* 4 [1996]). Other essays by Cavaglion on various Jewish subjects are collected in *Il senso dell'arca* (Naples: L'Ancora del Mediterraneo, 2006). See also the essay by Paola Valabrega, 'Primo Levi e la tradizione ebraico-orientale' (in *Primo Levi: un'antologia della critica*, 1997). For an overview of the topic, see also Claudio Magris, *Lontano da dove. Joseph Roth e la tradizione ebraico-orientale* (Turin: Einaudi, 1971), a book that Levi certainly read and that is also important for understanding the setting of *If Not Now, When?* Daniela Amsallem has explored Jewish myths in 'Ebraismo, scienza e creazione letteraria: Primo Levi e i miti ebraici di Lilít e del Golem' (in *L'ebraismo nella cultura italiana del Novecento*, edited by M. Calà and L. De Angelis; Palermo: Palumbo, 1995). See also Stefano Levi Della Torre, 'L'eredità di Primo Levi and David Meghnagi, 'La vicenda ebraica.

Primo Levi e la scrittura', both of which are included in *Primo Levi: un'antologia della critica* (1997). See also Nancy Harrowitz's article in the Jewish cultural journal, *Ha Keillah*, 'Primo Levi's Jewish identity' (in *Primo Levi*, edited by R. Gordon, 2007).

Israel

As yet, no comprehensive essay has been published that addresses Levi's convictions regarding Israel, his criticism of successive Israeli governments in the 1980s, and his position on Zionism. Levi spoke on the subject in numerous interviews, now included, or reported, in *Conversazioni e interviste 1963-1987* (1997) and in the third volume of *Opere complete* (2017). Andrea Rondini discusses the issue in a chapter entitled, 'Pro e contro Israele. Dalla Guerra dei sei Giorni all'invasione del Libano', in *Anche il cielo brucia. Primo Levi e il giornalismo* (2012). For a general overview of Italian culture's relationship with Israel, see Matteo Di Figlia, *Israel e la sinistra* (Rome: Donzelli Editore, 2012).

Anti-Semitism

Levi's lecture *L'intolleranza razziale* (1979) still awaits a thorough analysis linking animal behavioral and historical aspects. Levi answered a questionnaire contained in a 1961 issue of the magazine *Storia illustrata* of 1961, where many of the themes he would take up later can be found, another potential area of research.

Franz Kafka

Valentina Di Rosa has examined Levi's translations of Kafka from German in 'Tradurre ed essere tradotti. Primo Levi e la memoria riflessa del tedesco' (*Studi germanici*, 42[2], 2004). For his translation of *The Trial*, see: Arianna Marelli, 'Primo Levi e la traduzione del Processo, ovvero il processo della traduzione'; Silvia Ferrari, 'Cono d'ombra, cono di luce. Primo Levi e la traduzione d'autore del Processo'; and Antonio Castore, 'Per un'etica della traduzione: il problema della comprensione e dello stile nel rapporto tra Primo Levi e Franz Kafka', essays collected in: *Ricercare le radici: Primo Levi lettore – Lettori di Primo Levi.* (2014). For further discussion of the theme of "becoming an animal" in Kafka, see: Gilles Deleuze and Félix Guattari, *Kafka. Per una letteratura minore* (Macerata: Quodlibet, 1996). Regarding Kafka's Judaism see also, George Steiner, *No Passion Spent: Essays 1978-1995* (Yale: Yale University Press, 1998)

PRIMO LEVI AND ITALIAN LITERARY CRITICISM (1947–87)

A partial anthology of literary criticism regarding Levi's work can be found in the issue of *Riga* 13 [1997] on Primo Levi. The bibliographies in the various monographs reference the most relevant articles, especially in Edoardo Bianchini's, *Invito alla lettura di Primo Levi* (2000).

AT AN UNCERTAIN HOUR

Massimo Raffaeli's book on Primo Levi, which comments on numerous poems has an athological slant (*Levi;* Milan: Garzanti Scuola, 1998). See also Cesare Greppi, 'Una figura nella poesia di Primo Levi', in *Primo Levi: memoria e invenzione* (1995). One of the most insightful essays on Levi's poetry is by Italo Rosato: 'Poesia' (in *Primo Levi, Riga* 13 [1997]). Massimo Lollini explored Levi's poetry in 'Poesia e autobiografia' (in *Le forme della poesia*, edited by R. Castellana and A. Baldini; Siena: University of Siena, 2006), as did Emanuele Zinato, in 'Primo Levi poeta-scienziato: figure dello straniamento e tentazioni del non-senso' (in *Letteratura come storiografia?* Macerata : Quodlibet, 2015). Regarding the publication of *The Bremen Inn* (*L'osteria di Brema*) (1975) at Scheiwiller, see Lorenzo Marchese's dissertation, *Scrivere ad ora incerta. Sulla poesia di Primo Levi* (Pavia: University of Pavia, 2010/ 2011). On the relationship between poetry and Judaism see, Sophie

Nezri-Dufour, 'Primo Levi, Jewish Poet of Memory' (in *Voci dal mondo per Primo Levi*, 2007).

OTHER PEOPLE'S TRADES, ENCYCLOPEDIA, COMPUTER

Italo Calvino dwells on the encyclopedic aspects of Levi's work in the newspaper article 'Le quattro strade di Primo Levi' (*La Repubblica*, June 11, 1981). For a more in-depth study we recommend Enrico Mattioda's essay, *L'ordine del mondo* (1998).

ITALO CALVINO

Giorgio Bertone's essay, 'Italo Calvino e Primo Levi' (in *Italo Calvino. Il castello della scrittura*; Turin: Einaudi, 1994) is a good place to start exploring the relationship between the two authors. Mario Porro also analyzed the relationship in *Letteratura come filosofia naturale* (2009). For a general overview, see Pierpaolo Antonello, *Il Ménage a quattro. Scienza, filosofia, tecnica nella letteratura italiana del Novecento* (Florence: Le Monnier, 2005).

ALDOUS HUXLEY

The only available material on the relationship between the two authors is Levi's 1965 article on Huxley, available in the Norton edition of *The Complete Works of Primo Levi* (pp. 2019–22).

PAUL CELAN

On Levi's relationship with Celan, see Massimo Lollini, 'Pre-scrittura e scrittura ultima tra Primo Levi e Paul Celan' (in *Intersezioni* 19[3], December 1999).

TURIN

There is an interesting essay on Levi's relationship to his home in Franco Ferrucci, 'La casa di Primo Levi' (in *Primo Levi come testimone*, 1990).

LIGHT/DARK

Domenico Scarpa's essay, 'Chiaro/oscuro' (in *Primo Levi, Riga* 13 [1997]) is essential reading on this topic. See also 'Oscuro/chiaro' dedicated to Manganelli (in *Giorgio Manganelli*, edited by M. Belpoliti and A. Cortellessa, *Riga* 25 [2006]).

STORIES AND ESSAYS, THE LAST CHRISTMAS OF THE WAR

With regard to these two volumes, please refer to the in-depth analyses in the various monographs on Levi, particularly the parts dedicated to the short stories.

EDITORIAL CONSULTANT AND TRANSLATOR

On the relationship between Levi and the Einaudi and Boringhieri publishing houses, see Luisa Mangoni, *Pensare i libri. La casa editrice Einaudi dagli anni trenta agli anni sessanta* (1999). For Paolo Boringhieri, see Giulia Boringhieri's *Per un umanesimo scientifico. Storia di mio padre, di libri e di noi* (Turin: Einaudi, 2010). Tommaso Munari's *Centolettori. I pareri di lettura dei consulenti Einaudi 1941–1991* (Turin: Einaudi, 2015) provides details on Levi's opinion of Gadda. Other editorial opinions are preserved in the Einaudi Archives. On Levi's translations, and translations of Levi's works, see Ann Goldstein and Domenico Scarpa, *In un'altra lingua* (Turin: Einaudi, 2015) where Goldstein discusses editing the translation of Levi's *Complete Works* into English and Scarpa examines the issue of translation and the value of words starting with Levi's lexicon.

THE DROWNED AND THE SAVED

On the history of the book, it is worth reading two reviews that appeared when it first came out: Pier Vincenzo Mengaldo, 'Ricordando con lucidità gli orrori dei Lager' (1986), now in *Primo Levi*, *Riga* 13 [1997]) and Cesare Cases, 'Levi ripensa l'absurd' (*L'indice dei libri del mese*, July 1986). George Steiner, 'Contabilità della tortura' (1988), in *Primo Levi* (*Riga* 13 [1997]), and Fabrizia Ramondino, 'Bel Ami a Auschwitz' (*Linea d'ombra* 70, April 1992) are also worth reading. See also: the chapter in Enrico Mattioda's book, 'Tra le pieghe del male' (in *Primo Levi*; 2011); Mario Porro's essay 'Un etologo nel Lager' (in *La visione del mondo di Primo Levi*, 2000); David Bidussa, 'I limiti della testimonianza e le inquietudini della memoria', also published as a preface to the paperback edition of *I sommersi e i salvati* (Turin: Einaudi, 2005), and M. Mengoni, *I sommersi e i salvati di Primo Levi. Storia di un libro* (Macerata-Roma: Quodlibet, 2021).

'THE GRAY ZONE'

Closely linked to *The Drowned and the Saved*, the theme of the gray zone is the most crucial chapter in the book. Further reading on the topic must include the important essay by Martina Mengoni, 'Variazioni Rumkowski: sulle piste della zona grigia' (www.primolevi.it), and, by the same author, 'Storia di Franz, Hans, Chaim. On Two German Sources and a Jewish Dean' (in *Ricercare le radici. Primo Levi lettore – Lettori di Primo Levi*, 2014). See also Anna Bravo, 'La zona grigia' (in *Raccontare per la storia*; Turin: Einaudi, 2014), and Carlo Ginzburg's essay, 'Calvino, Levi e la zona grigia' (www.primolevi.it). In a more philosophical slant, see 'La zona grigia' by Franco Cassano (in *L'umiltà del male*; Rome-Bari: Laterza, 2011). Simona Forti, *I nuovi demoni. Ripensare il male e il potere* (Milan: Feltrinelli, 2012) is essential reading as it examines Primo Levi, as well as Hannah Arendt and Michel Foucault who are challenged by Levi on the question of power relations.

See in particular the final chapter, 'Poveri diavoli che "adorano" la vita: noi'. The conference proceedings, *La zone grise: entre accommodement et collaboration* (edited by P. Mesnard and Y. Thanassekos; Paris: Kimé, 2010) are very interesting. Alberto Cavaglion wrote about the gray zone in 'Attualità (e inattualità) della zona grigia' (in *Primo Levi. Scrittura e testimonianza*, 2006), previously in *Primo Levi tra i sommersi e i salvati* (*Lo Straniero* 8[48], 2004). On the subject of historical revisionism, see Enzo Colotti, 'Primo Levi e il revisionismo storiografico' (*Primo Levi. Il presente del passato*, 1991). For a general overview, we recommend the ample discussion in Valentina Pisanty, *L'irritante questione delle camere a gas. Logica del negazionismo* (Milan: Bompiani, 1998).

THE NIGHT OF THE GIRONDISTS

Jacques Presser's book, *The Night of the Girondists* has been reprinted several times by Adelphi. Information on this translation can be found in Ian Thomson's biography, *Primo Levi* (2002) and in Gabriella Poli and Giorgio Calcagno, *Echi di una voce perduta* (1992). Additional information about Presser can be found in Bert de Waart, 'Da De nacht der Girondijnen a La notte dei Girondini' (in *Ricercare le radici. Primo Levi lettore - Lettori di Primo Levi*, 2014), where the difference between the original, German and Italian versions is analyzed. Lina Insana's *Arduous Tasks: Primo Levi, Translation and the Transmission of Holocaust Testimony* (Toronto: University of Toronto Press, 2009) is also very interesting, both for the story of the translation and in general. The correspondence between Levi and Hety Schmitt-Maass can be found in the Stadtarchiv in Wiesbaden.

JEAN AMÉRY

Jean Améry's book *Jenseits von Schuld und Sühne: Bewäitigungsversüche eines Überwältigten* (*Beyond Guilt and Atonement: Attempt to Over-come a Defeat*) (Munich: Szczesny Verlag) came out in 1966 and was immediately translated into Italian as *Intellettuali ad Auschwitz* (Turin: Bollati Boringhieri, 1987) after Levi's death, with an introduction by Claudio Magris. Guia Risari was one of the first to write a book on the figure of Améry, *Jean Améry. Il risentimento come morale* (Milan: Franco Angeli, 2002), to which we refer for a general overview of the figure of the Viennese intellectual and essayist. Pier Paolo Portinaro dealt with this subject in an essay, 'Il sopravvissuto e la morte. La testimonianza di Jean Améry' (*Comunità* 189–90, May 1988). Cesare Segre compared Levi and Améry in his essay, 'Un dissenso istruttivo: Primo Levi e Jean Améry' (in *Ritorno alla critica*; Turin: Einaudi, 2001). Enzo Traverso also compares Levi and Améry in the chapter 'Intellettuali a Auschwitz: Jean Améry e Primo Levi', in *Auschwitz e gli intellettuali* (2004), which traces a profile of European intellectuals in the Lager. Franca Molino Signorini's '"Uomini fummo . . .". Riflessioni su Primo Levi e Jean Améry' (*La Rassegna Mensile di Israel* 57[3–4], September–December 1991) is also worthy of note. A revealing essay by Jean Améry on suicide is *Levar la mano su di sé* (Turin: Bollati Boringhieri, 1990), which opens with Innocenzo Cervelli's, 'Suicidio e libertà di morire', which is very useful for placing Améry's ideas in context. Correspondence among Améry, Levi and Hety Schmitt-Maass can be found in the Stadtarchiv of Wiesbaden.

Hannah Arendt

Reference is made to *Eichman in Jerusalem. A Report on the Banality of Evil* (London: Penguin, 1964). For a general framework, see 'Banalità del male' by Simona Forti (in *I concetti del male*, edited by P.P. Portinaro; Turin: Einaudi, 2002), which also deals with the gray zone in the definition given by Levi. Simona Forti returned to the theme in her crucial study of power relations: *I nuovi demoni. Ripensare male e potere* (Milan: Feltrinelli, 2012), where she expands her interpretation in the context of twentieth-century European thought. For those who want to go into further detail regarding the debate around Arendt's book, we recommend the biography by Elisabeth Young-Bruehl, *Hannah Arendt* (Turin: Bollati Boringhieri, 1990). The correspondence between Arendt and Gershom Scholem is collected in *Due lettere sulla banalità del male* (Rome: Nottetempo, 2007), previously published in 1985 in *Fine secolo*. The interview where Levi mentions Hannah Arendt and her theory of the 'banality of evil' is by Giorgio Segrè (in *Ha-Tikwa*, April 1979). For Levi's writings at the time of the Eichmann trial, see *Così fu Auschwitz* (2015). We recommend Elias Canetti's *Potere e sopravvivenza* (Milan: Adelphi, 1974), as well as Hannah *Arendt and Primo Levi. Narrazione e pensiero* (edited by N. Mattucci and A. Rondini; Lecce-Rovato: Pensa Multimedia, 2013), which contains several essays comparing the two authors' points of view regarding the Shoah, Judaism, etc.

BRUNO BETTELHEIM

The essays on the Nazi camps written by the psychoanalyst upon his arrival in the United States during the 1940s, were collected in *Sopravvivere* (1981). His earlier book, written in 1960, was first translated into Italian as *Il prezzo della vita* (1965), and later as *Il cuore vigile* (1988). Levi talks extensively about Bettelheim in his interview with Anna Bravo and Federico Cereja (*Intervista a Primo Levi, ex deportato*, 2011), recorded in January 1984 (now in volume III of *Opere complete;* 2017). Levi also mentions him in his conversation with Risa Sodi (in *Conversazioni e interviste*, 1997), now in the third volume of *Opere complete* (2017).

SIGMUND FREUD

The relationship between Levi and Freud has not yet been investigated systematically. There are various references scattered throughout Levi's work, as well as in the monographs, but there is no overarching reference book on the subject. For puns and slips of the tongue, see the chapter on Levi in Stefano Bartezzaghi, *Scrittori giocatori* (2010).

VARLAM ŠALAMOV

On Levi's relationship to the theme of the extermination camps, read Francesco M. Cataluccio, 'Lager e gulag in Primo Levi' (in *Nazismo, Fascismo, Communismo: totalitarismi a confronto*, edited by M. Flores; Milan: Bruno Mondadori, 1998). An interesting conversation between Piero Sinatti and Gustaw Herling can be found in *Ricordare, raccontare: conversazione su Šalamov* (Naples: L'Ancora del Mediterraneo, 1999). Domenico Scarpa reflected on the two authors in, 'Lager and Gulag: Levi and Herling Writers of *Responsibility*' (in *Lo Straniero*, 1, no. 1, summer 1997). Šalamov's stories were published in their entirety in *I racconti di Kolyma* (Turin: Einaudi, 1999).

WHO WAS CHAIM RUMKOWSKI?

For information on the origins and process of writing the story, see Ian Thomson's biography (2002). Martina Mengoni researches Levi's sources in her essay, 'Variazioni Rumkowski: sulle piste della zona grigia' (www.primolevi.it). Saul Bellow's books, *Mr Sammler's Planet* (New York: Viking, 1970) and *The Bellarosa Connection* (New York: Penguin, 1989) are relevant. James Atlas's *Bellow: A Biography* (New York: Modern Library, 2002) reveals details about his relationship with Hannah Arendt. Philip Roth's review of *Mr Sammler's Planet*, 'Re-reading Saul Bellow', can be found in *The New Yorker* (October 1, 2000). An interesting article by Massimo Mila, 'Il sapiente con la chiave a stella' (*La Stampa*, 14 April 1987) is now collected in *Scritti civili* (edited by A. Cavaglion; Turin: Einaudi, 1995).

SHAME

On the theme of shame in general, see *Senza vergogna* (M. Politi; Milan: Guanda, 2010). Marco W. Battacchi's *Vergogna e senso di colpa* (Milan: Cortina, 2002) provides an important analysis of the chapter *Shame* in

The Drowned and the Saved. Jean-Paul Sartre's *Being and Nothingness* (1943) translated into Italian by Il Saggiatore in 1965 is essential reading, in particular the chapter 'The Look'. Another important book is Tzvetan Todorov's, *Facing the Extreme: Moral Life in the Concentration Camps* (New York: Henry Holt, 1997). Gregory Bateson's double bind concept (1973) was developed in *Verso un'ecologia della mente* (Milan: Adelphi, 1977). R. D. Laing's work, *The Divided Self* (Harmondsworth: Penguin, 1960) is also relevant, as is Jean Améry's *Intellettuale a Auschwitz* (Turin: Bollati Boringhieri, 1987). For further in-depth examination of this topic, see Enrico Mottinelli, *La neve nell'armadio. Auschwitz e la 'vergogna del mondo'* (Florence: Giuntina, 2013).

COLOUR

Neither color nor description of landscape or description in general have never been researched as significant themes in Levi's work. Hints can be found in Massimo Bucciantini, *Esperimento Auschwitz* (2011). On the theme of color in general, we recommend Michel Pastoureau, *I colori del nostro tempo* (Milan: Ponte alle Grazie, 2010) and Philip Ball, *Bright Earth: The Invention of Color* (New York: Vintage, 2008).

MEMORY

In almost every monograph or extensive essay dedicated to Levi, memory plays an important role: memory in relation to bearing witness, historical memory, memory as a psychological problem, and more. We suggest starting with the short paper by Massimo Raffaeli, 'Memoria/ricordi in Primo Levi' (in *Primo Levi, Riga* 13 [1997]). Stefano Bartezzaghi dealt with the theme of voluntary and involuntary memory in his chapter on Levi in *Scrittori giocatori* (2010). One cannot help but link memory to its opposite, oblivion, as Maurice Halbwachs suggests in *La memoria collettiva* (Milan: Unicopli, 1987). On the subject of memory, see Yosef Hahim Yerushalmi's, *Zakor* (Florence: Giuntina,

2011) and the volume he edited, *Usi dell'oblio* (Parma: Pratiche Editrice, 1990), in particular his essay, 'Riflessioni sull'oblio'. On historical memory, see Federico Cereja, 'Primo Levi e la costruzione della memoria storica' (in *Primo Levi testimone e scrittore di storia*, 1999).

HUMOUR

The first person to talk about Levi as a humorist was Massimo Mila in the article 'Il sapiente con la chiave a stella' (in *La Stampa*, April 14, 1987; later published in M. Mila, *Scritti civili*, 1995). See also Mirna Cicioni, 'Un'amicizia asimmetrica e feconda: Levi e Manzoni' (in *Voci dal mondo per Primo Levi*, 2007), where she discusses Levi's irony and self-irony. By the same author, see '"Un riso che direi sabbatico": aspetti dell'umorismo di Primo Levi' (in *Italian Culture*, 2000) and 'Primo Levi's Humour' (in *Primo Levi*, edited by R. Gordon, 2007). Finally, Martina Di Florio Gula, 'Tra i sorrisi di Primo Levi. Alcuni appunti sugli aspetti comici e umoristici de La tregua' (in *neMLA Italian Studies* 32, 2009–10).

CALVINO, LEVI AND BLACK HOLES

On Levi's references to "Scientific American", it is worth reading the chapter 'L'ispirazione scientifica: da Vizio di forma al Sistema periodico' by Enrico Mattioda in the book *Primo Levi* (2011). Regarding Calvino and cosmological themes, see Calvino's works collected in *Italo Calvino. Encyclopedia: arte, scienza e letteratura* (edited by M. Belpoliti; *Riga 9* [1995]). In the same book, you can find the essay by Mario Porro, 'Letteratura come filosofia naturale', later included in *Letteratura come filosofia naturale* (2009). See also Domenico Scarpa, 'La scoperta letteraria dei buchi neri' (in *Ai margini della letteratura. Le scritture contaminate*, edited by A. Ottieri; *Sinestesie. Rivista di studi sulle letterature e le arti europee*, 2006) and the chapter, 'Sfuggire a un mondo di pietra:

tra Lévi-Strauss, Prigogine e Stendhal' by Massimo Bucciantini, in *Italo Calvino e scienza* (Rome: Donzelli Editore, 2007).

SUICIDE

The two biographies of Levi by Carole Angier and Ian Thomson help to reconstruct the last period of the writer's life by offering different interpretations of his suicide in the light of a deep depression. Giovanni Falaschi's essay, 'L'offesa insanabile. L'imprinting del Lager su Primo Levi' (in *Allegoria*, May-August 2001), and 'Tre coppie nella bufera' (in *Ebrei, ebraismo, Lager. Dieci lezioni*, edited by G. Falaschi; Foligno: Editoriale Umbra, 2014) explore the relationship between Levi and Vanda Maestro. Francesco Lucrezi dealt with the theme of Levi's death in *La parola di Hurbinek* (Florence: Giuntina, 2005). David Mendel described the months leading up to his suicide from the point of view of a doctor in 'Un incontro con Primo Levi' (*L'Indice dei libri del mese* 11[5], May 1994). Primo Levi's writing on Vanda Maestro can now be read in *Così fu Auschwitz* (2015).

WORKS CITED

AGAMBEN, Giorgio, 1996. *Categorie italiane. Studi di poetica*. Venice: Marsilio. [*The End of the Poem: Studies in Poetics* (Daniel Heller-Roazen trans.). Stanford: Stanford University Press, 1999].

———. 2005. *Profanazioni*. Roma: Nottetempo. [*Profanations* (Jeff Fort trans.). New York: Zone, 2007].

ALIGHIERI, Dante. 1972. *Divina Commedia. Inferno* (Natalino Sapegno commentary). Florence: La Nuova Italia.

AMÉRY, Jean. 1987. *Intellettuali ad Auschwitz*. Turin: Bollati Boringhieri. [*At the Mind's Limits: Contemplations by a Survivor on Auschwitz and Its Realities* (Sidney Rosenfeld and Stella P. Rosenfeld trans). Bloomington: Indiana University Press, 1980].

AMSALLEM, Daniela. 1993. 'Le symbolisme du chien: Primo Levi et la literature juive après la Shoah'. *Chroniques Italiennes* 33–34: 27–44.

ANGIER, Carole. 2004. *Il doppio legame: Vita di Primo Levi*. Milan: Mondadori. [*The Double Bond: Primo Levi; A Biography*. New York: Farrar, Straus and Giroux, 2002].

ANISSIMOV, Myriam. 1999. *Primo Levi: o la tragedia de un optimista*. Milan: Baldini & Castoldi. [*Primo Levi: Tragedy of an Optimist* (Steve Cox trans.). London: Aurum Press, 1998].

ANTELME, Robert. 1997. *La specie umana*. Turin: Einaudi. [*The Human Species* (Jeffrey Haight and Annie Mahler trans). Marlboro: Marlboro Press, 1992].

ATLAS, James. 2003. *Vita di Saul Bellow*. Milan: Mondadori. [*Bellow: A Biography*. New York: Random House, 2000].

BARBERIS, Walter. 2012. 'Primo Levi e "un libro fatale" ' in Luzzatto, Sergio, Pedullà, Gabriele, Scarpa and Domenico (eds), *Atlante della letteratura italiana: Dal Romanticismo a oggi*, VOL. 3. Turin: Einaudi.

BARENGHI, Mario. 2000. 'La memoria dell'offesa. Ricordare, raccontare, comprendere', in Mattioda, Enrico (ed.), *Al di qua del bene e del male. La visione del mondo di Primo Levi* (Milan: Franco Angeli).

———. 2013. *Perché crediamo a Primo Levi*. Turin: Einaudi.

BARTEZZAGHI, Stefano. 1997. 'Cosmichimiche' in Marco Belpoliti (ed.), *Riga* 13, special issue on Primo Levi.

BARTHES, Roland. 1986. *La grana della voce*. Turin: Einaudi. [*The Grain of the Voice: Interviews, 1962–1980* (Linda Cloverdale trans.). New York: Hill & Wang, 1985].

BATTACCHI, Marco. 2002. *Vergogna e senso di colpa. In psicologia e nella letteratura*. Milan: Cortina.

BELLOW, Saul. 1992. *Il circolo Bellarosa*. Milan: Mondadori. [*The Bellarosa Connection*. London: Penguin, 1989].

———. 2009. *Il pianeta di Mr. Samler*. Milan: Mondadori. [*Mr. Sammler's Planet*. New York: Viking, 1970].

BELPOLITI, Marco. 1996. *L'occhio di Calvino*. Turin: Einaudi.

BETTELHEIM, Bruno. 1965. *Il prezzo della vita*: l'autonomia individuale in una società di massa. Milan: Adelphi. [*The Informed Heart*: Autonomy in a Mass Age. Glencoe, IL: The Free Press, 1960].

———. 1981. *Sopravvivere*, Feltrinelli, Milano. [*Surviving and Other Essays*. New York: Knopf, 1979].

BEROLATTI, Gabriella. 2008–09. *La casa editrice Aufbau*, Università degli Studi di Torino.

BERTONE, Giorgio. 1994. 'Italo Calvino e Primo Levi' in *Italo Calvino. Il castello della scrittura*. Turin: Einaudi.

BIDUSSA, David. 1997. 'Verbi' in Marco Belpoliti (ed.), *Riga* 13, special issue on Primo Levi.

BLOOM, Solomon F. 1948. 'Dictator of the Łódz´ Ghetto. The Strange History of Mordechai Chaim Rumkowski'. *Commentary* (December).

BOITANI, Piero. 1992. *L'ombra di Ulisse*. Bologna: Il Mulino.

BOLOGNA, Corrado (ed.). 1977. *Liber monstrorum*. Milan: Bompiani.

BOROWSKI, Tadeusz. 1988. 'Prego, signori, al gas' in *Paesaggio dopo la battaglia*. Turin: Quadrante edizioni. [*This Way for the Gas, Ladies and Gentlemen*. London: Penguin, 1992].

BUCCIANTINI, Massimo. 2011. *Esperimento Auschwitz/Auschwitz Experiment*. Turin: Einaudi [bilingual edition].

CAIRNS-SMITH, Alexander Graham. 1986. *Sette indizi sull'origine della vita*. Naples: Liguori. [*Seven Clues to the Origin of Life*: A Scientific Detective Story. Cambridge: Cambridge University Press, 1985].

CALVINO, Italo. 1946. 'Le capre ci guardano'. *l'Unità*, 17 November. Reprinted in Mario Barenghi (ed.), *Saggi*, VOL. 2 (Milan: Mondadori, 1995).

———. 1981. 'Le quattro strade di Primo Levi', *la Repubblica*, 11 June. Reprinted in Mario Barenghi (ed.), *Saggi*, VOL. 2.

———. 1983. *Palomar*. Turin: Einaudi. [*Mr. Palomar* (William Weaver trans.). San Diego: Harcourt Brace Jovanovich, 1985].

———. 1984. 'L'orecchio, il cacciatore, il pettelogo'. *La Repubblica*, 12 August.

———. 1985. 'Il romanziere e il suo suggeritore'. *Corriere della Sera*, 19 October.

———. 1991. *I libri degli altri*. Turin: Einaudi.

———. 2000. *Lettere 1940–1985*. Milan: Mondadori. [*Letters 1941–1985* (Michael Wood ed., Martin McLaughlin trans.). Princeton: Princeton University Press, 2013].

CANETTI, Elias. 1972. *Massa e potere*. Milan: Rizzoli. [*Crowds and Power* (Carol Stewart trans.). New York: Viking, 1962].

———. 1974. *Potere e sopravvivenza*. Milan: Adelphi. [*The Conscience of Words* (Joachim Neugroschel trans.). New York: The Seabury Press, 1979].

CASES, Cesare. 1987. 'L'ordine delle cose e l'ordine delle parole'. *L'indice dei libri del mese* 10 (November): 25–31.

CAVAGLION, Alberto. 1991. 'Argon e la cultura ebraica piemontese' in Consiglio Generale del Piemonte-Aned (ed.), *Primo Levi: Il presente del passato*. Milan: Franco Angeli.

———. 1993. *Primo Levi e Se questo è un uomo*. Turin: Loescher.

———. 2012. 'Commento' in Primo Levi, *Se questo è un uomo*. Turin: Einaudi.

CAVANNA, Roberto. 1973. *Aspetti scientifici della parapsicologia*. Turin: Bollati Boringhieri.

CHÉROUX, Clément. 2001. *Memoria dei campi. Fotografie dei campi di concentramento e di sterminio nazisti*. Rome: Contrasto.

DELEUZE, Gilles. 1996. *Critica e clinica*. Milan: Cortina. [*Essays Critical and Clinical* (Michael A. Greco and Daniel W. Smith trans). Minneapolis: University of Minnesota Press, 1997].

—— and Félix Guattari. 1975. *Kafka. Per una letteratura minore*. Milan: Feltrinelli. [*Kafka: Toward a Minor Literature* (Dana Polan trans.). Minneapolis: University of Minnesota Press, 1986].

DE WAART, Bert. 2014. 'Da De nacht der Girondijnen a La notte dei Girondini: motivi, prototesti e strategie della traduzione leviana' in Raniero Speelman, Elisabetta Tonello and Silvia Gaiga (eds), *Ricercare le radici: Primo Levi lettore-lettori di Primo Levi*. Utrecht: Igitur.

DOSSENA, Giampaolo. 1988. *La zia era assatanata*. Milan: Rizzoli.

DOUGLAS, Mary. 1975. *I simboli naturali*. Turin: Einaudi. [*Natural Symbols: Explorations in Cosmology*. London: Barrie & Rockliff, 1970].

DYSON, Freeman. 1981. *Turbare l'universo*. Turin: Bollati Boringhieri. [*Disturbing the Universe*. New York: Harper & Row, 1979].

EINAUDI, Giulio. 1997[1991]. 'Primo Levi e la Casa editrice Einaudi' in Ernesto Ferrero (ed.), *Primo Levi: un'antologia della critica*. Turin: Einaudi.

FALASCHI, Giovanni, ' "L'offesa insanabile": l'imprinting del lager su Primo Levi'. *Allegoria* 13(38) (2001): 5–35.

FORTI, Simona. 2012. *I nuovi demoni*. Milan: Feltrinelli. [*New Demons: Rethinking Power and Evil Today* (Zakiya Hanafi trans.). Stanford: Stanford University Press, 2014].

FRANKL, Viktor. 1995. *Uno psicologo nei lager*. Milan: Ares. [*From Death-Camp to Existentialism: A Psychiatrist's Path to a New Therapy*. Boston: Beacon Press, 1961; later renamed *Man's Search for Meaning: An Introduction to Logotherapy*].

GINZBURG, Carlo. 1986. 'Spie: radici di un paradigma indiziario' in *Miti, emblemi, spie: morfologia e storia*. Turin: Einaudi. ['Clues: Roots of a Scientific Paradigm'. *Theory and Society* 7(3) (May 1979): 273–88].

———. 2020. 'Calvino, Manzoni e la zona grigia'. 26 April. Avalable at https://www.primolevi.it/it/calvino-manzoni-zona-grigia-carlo-ginzburg.

GORDON, Robert. 2003. *Primo Levi: le virtù dell'uomo normale*. Rome: Carocci. [*Primo Levi's Ordinary Virtues: From Testimony to Ethics* (Oxford: Oxford University Press, 2001)].

———. 2006. 'Introduction' in Primo Levi and Leonardo De Benedetti, *Auschwitz Report* (London: Verso, 2006).

GORNI, Guglielmo and Silvia Longhi. 1986. 'La parodia' in Roberto Antonelli and Angelo Cicchetti (eds), *Letteratura italiana: Le questioni*. Turin: Einaudi.

GRASSANO, Giuseppe. 1981. *Primo Levi*. Florence: La Nuova Italia.

GREPPI, Cesare. 1995. 'Una figura nella poesia di Primo Levi' in Giovanna Ioli (ed.), *Primo Levi: memoria e invenzione*. San Salvatore Monferrato: Edizioni della Biennale 'Piemonte e letteratura'.

HALBWACHS, Maurice. 1987. *La memoria collettiva*. Milano: Unicopli. [*On Collective Memory* (Lewis A. Coser ed. and trans.). Chicago: University of Chicago Press, 1992].

HERLING, Gustaw. 1958. *Un mondo a parte*. Bari: Laterza. [*A World Apart* (Andrzej Ciolkosz trans.). London: Joseph Heinemann, 1951].

———. 1999. *Ricordare, raccontare: conversazione su Salamov*. Naples: L'Ancora del Mediterraneo.

HILBERG, Raul. 1995. *La distruzione degli ebrei d'Europa*. Turin: Einaudi. [*The Destruction of the European Jews*. Chicago: Quadrangle Books, 1961].

INSANA, Lina. 2009. *Arduous tasks: Primo Levi, Translation and the Transmission of Holocaust Testimony*. Toronto: University of Toronto Press.

JESURUM, Stefano. 1987. *Essere ebrei in Italia*. Milano: Longanesi.

KÖNIG, Joel. 1973. *Sfuggito alle reti del nazismo*. Milan: Mursia.

KOSELLECK, Reinhard. 1991. 'Prefazione' in Charlotte Beradt, *Il Terzo Reich dei sogni*. Turin: Einaudi. ['Terror and Dream: Methodological Remarks on the Experience of Time During the Third Reich' in *Futures Past: On the Semantics of Historical Time* (Keith Tribe trans.). New York: Columbia University Press, 2004, pp. 205–21].

LA FAUCI, Nunzio and Liana Tronci. 2014. 'Noi in Se questo è un uomo' in Maria Janner, Chiara Maria, Mario Della Costanza and Paul Sutermeister (eds), *Noi – Nous – Nosotros*. Bern: Peter Lang.

LAING, Ronald David. 1969. *L'io diviso*. Turin: Einaudi. [*The Divided Self: An Existential Study in Sanity and Madness*. Harmondsworth: Penguin, 1960].

LAVIE, Peretz. 1999. *Il meraviglioso mondo del sonno*. Turin: Einaudi. [*The Enchanted World of Sleep*. New Haven: Yale University Press, 1996].

LEROI-GOURHAN, André. 1977. *Il gesto e la parola*. Turin: Einaudi. [*Gesture and Speech* (Anna Bostock Berger trans.). Cambridge, MA: The MIT Press, 1993].

LESKOV, Nikolai. 1967. *Il viaggiatore incantato*. Turin: Einaudi. [*The Enchanted Wanderer and Other Tales* (Richard Pevear and Larissa Volokhonsky trans). New York: Vintage, 2014].

LEVI, Fabio. 'L'incontro con Primo Levi'. *Passato e presente* 89(2) (2013): 28–31.

LÉVI-STRAUSS, Claude. 1984. *Lo sguardo da lontano*. Turin: Einaudi. [*The View from Afar* (Joachim Neugroschel and Phoebe Hoss trans). Chicago: University of Chicago Press, 1986].

———. 1985. *La via delle maschere*. Turin: Einaudi. [*The Way of the Masks* (Sylvia Modelski trans.) Seattle: University of Washington Press, 1982].

LORENZ, Konrad. 1985. 'L'analogia come fonte di conoscenza'. *Pegaso*. Reprinted in *Vorrei diventare un'oca*. Padua: Muzzio Editore, 1997. ['Analogy as a Source of Knowledge'. *Science* 185(4147) (19 July 1974): 229–34].

MAETERLINCK, Maurice. 2012. *La vita delle api, la vita delle termiti, la vita delle formiche*. Rome: Newton Compton.

MAGRIS, Claudio. 1971. *Lontano da dove: Joseph Roth e la tradizione ebraico-orientale*. Turin: Einaudi.

MANGANELLI, Giorgio. 1994. *Il rumore sottile della prosa*. Milano: Adelphi.

MANGONI, Luisa. 1999. *Pensare i libri*. Turin: Bollati Boringhieri.

MATTIODA, Enrico. 2011. *Levi*. Rome: Salerno Editore.

MAZZOLENI, Oscar. 1998. *Franco Antonicelli: cultura e politica: 1925–1950*. Turin: Rosenberg & Sellier.

MENDELEEV, Dmitri I. 1992. *Sullo spiritismo*. Turin: Bollati Boringhieri.

MENGALDO, Pier Vincenzo. 1990. 'Lingua e scrittura in Levi' in Primo Levi, *Opere, III: Racconti e saggi*. Turin: Einaudi.

MENGONI, Martina. 2015. 'Epifania di un mestiere: La corrispondenza etnografica tra Primo Levi e Claude Lévi-Strauss'. *Italianistica* 44(1) (2015): 111–31.

MESNARD, Philippe. 2008. *Primo Levi: una vita per immagini*. Venice: Marsilio.

MILANINI, Claudio. 2002. 'Cronologia cosmica' in Italo Calvino, *Tutte le Cosmicomiche*. Milan: Mondadori.

MONDO, Lorenzo, 'Primo Levi e Dante', in Ioli, Giovanna (a cura di), *Primo Levi. Memoria e invenzione*, cit.

NABOKOV, Vladimir. 1982. *Lezioni di letteratura*. Milan: Garzanti. [*Lectures on Literature* (Fredson Bowers ed., John Updike introd.). New York: Harvest, 1980].

NISSIM, Luciana. 2008. *Ricordi della casa dei morti*. Florence: Giuntina.

NYSTEDT, Jane. 1992. 'Lunghezza della frase e interpunzione: mezzi stilistici in Primo Levi'. *Studi italiani di linguistica teorica e applicate* 21(1–3): 85–106.

ORENGO, Nico. 1987. 'Natalia Ginzburg: nessuno censurò Primo Levi'. *La Stampa*, 12 June.

PASOLINI, Pier Paolo. 1972. *Empirismo eretico*. Milano: Garzanti. [*Heretical Empiricism* (Louise K. Barnett trans.) Bloomington: Indiana University Press, 1988].

POLI, Gabriella and Giorgio Calcagno. 1992. *Echi di una voce perduta*. Milano: Mursia.

POLIAKOV, Léon. 1955. *Il nazismo e lo sterminio degli Ebrei*. Turin: Einaudi.

PORRO, Mario. 1997. 'Scienza' in Marco Belpoliti (ed.), *Riga 13*, special issue on Primo Levi.

PRESSER, Jacques. 1976. *La notte dei Girondini*. Milan: Adelphi, 1976. [*The Night of the Girondists* (Foreword by Primo Levi). London: Harper Collins, 1992].

PRIGOGINE, Ilya and Isabelle Stengers. 1981. *La nuova alleanza. Metamorfosi della scienza.* Turin: Einaudi. [*Order Out of Chaos: Man's New Dialogue with Nature.* New York: Flamingo, 1984].

RAFFAELI, Massimo (ed.). 1998. *Primo Levi.* Milano: Garzanti Scuola.

REITLINGER, Gerald. 1962. *La soluzione finale.* Milano: Il Saggiatore. [*The Final Solution.* London: Sphere, 1971].

RIGOTTI, Francesca. 1995. 'Il velo e il fiume. Riflessioni sulla metafora dell'oblio'. *Iride* 8(14): 131–51.

ROSATO, Italo. 1989. 'Primo Levi: sondaggi intertestuali'. *Autografo* 17: 31–43.

———. 1997. 'Poesia' in Marco in Belpoliti (ed.), *Riga* 13, special issue on Primo Levi.

ROTH, Philip. 2004. 'Recensione a *Il pianeta di Mr. Sammler*' in *Chiacchiere di bottega.* Turin: Einaudi. ['Rereading Saul Bellow' in *Shop Talk.* London: Jonathan Cape, 2001].

RUDNICKI, Adolf. 1967. 'Il commerciante di Łódz´ in *I topi.* Milan: Mondadori.

RUFFINI, Elisabetta. 2006. *Un lapsus di Primo Levi.* Bergamo: Assessorato alla cultura.

RUOZZI, Gino. 1992. *Forme brevi.* Pisa: Editrice Goliardica.

SHALAMOV, Varlam. 1999. *I racconti di Kolyma.* Turin: Einaudi. [*Kolyma Tales* (Donald Rayfield trans.). New York: New York Review of Books, 2018].

SARTRE, Jean Paul. 2008. *L'essere e il nulla.* Milan: Il Saggiatore. [*Being and Nothingness: An Essay in Phenomenological Ontology* (Sarah Richmond trans.). London: Routledge, 2020].

SCARLINI, Luca. 1997. 'Teatro' in Marco Belpoliti, (ed.), *Riga* 13, special issue on Primo Levi.

SCARPA, Domenico. 2006. 'Calvino, Levi e la scoperta letteraria dei buchi neri'. *Sinestesie: rivista di studi sulle letterature e le arti europee* 4 (1–2): 297–308.

———. 1997. 'Chiaro/oscuro' in Marco Belpoliti, (ed.), *Riga* 13, special issue on Primo Levi.

SCHOLEM, Gershom. 1995. *Alchimia e Kabbalah*. Turin: Einaudi. [*Alchemy and Kabbalah* (Klaus Ottmann trans.). Putnam, CT: Spring, 2006].

—— and Hannah Arendt. 2007. *Due lettere sulla banalità del male* (Rome: Nottetempo, 2007) [' "Eichmann in Jerusalem": An Exchange of Letters between Gershom Scholem and Hannah Arendt'. *Encounter* 22(1) (January)].

SEGRE, Cesare. 1988. 'Introduzione' in Primo Levi, *Opere*. Turin: Einaudi.

——. 1996. ' "Se questo è un uomo" di Primo Levi' in Alberto Asor Rosa (ed.), *Letteratura Italiana Einaudi. Le Opere*. Turin: Einaudi.

SEMPRÚN, Jorge. 1996. *La scrittura e la vita*. Parma: Guanda. [*Literature or Life* (Linda Cloverdale trans.). London: Penguin, 1998].

SOLZHENITSYN, Alexander. 2006. *Una giornata di Ivan Denisovič*. Turin: Einaudi. [*One Day in the Life of Ivan Denisovich* (Ralph Parker trans.). Harmondsworth: Penguin, 1963].

SONTAG, Susan. 1978. *Sulla fotografia: realtà e immagine nella nostra società*. Turin: Einaudi. [*On Photography*. New York: Farrar, Straus and Giroux, 1977].

SPEELMAN, Raniero. 2005. 'Primo Levi nei Paesi Bassi' in Giovanni Tesio (ed.), *Diffusione e conoscenza di Primo Levi nei paesi europei*. Turin: Centro Studi Piemontesi.

STEINER, George. 1965. *Morte della tragedia*. Milan: Garzanti. [*The Death of Tragedy*. London: Faber and Faber, 1961].

——. 1997. *Nessuna passione spenta*. Milan: Garzanti. [*No Passion Spent: Essays 1978–1995*. New Haven, CT: Yale University Press, 1996].

SULLAM Calimani, Anna-Vera. 2001. *I nomi dello sterminio*. Turin: Einaudi.

TESIO, Giovanni. 1985. 'Premesse su Primo Levi poeta'. *Studi Piemontesi* 14(1) (March): 12–23.

——. 1987. 'Primo Levi tra ordine e caos'. *Studi Piemontesi* 16(2) (November): 281–92.

——. 1991. 'Su alcune giunte e varianti di Se questo è un uomo' (1977) in *Piemonte letterario dell'Otto-Novecento* (*da G. Faldella a P. Levi*). Rome: Bulzoni.

————. 1997a. 'Introduzione e Note' in Primo Levi, *Se questo è un uomo*. Turin: Einaudi Scuola.

————. 1997b. 'Tutta l'Odissea in un quaderno'. *La Stampa*, special supplement, 9 February.

————. 2018. *Primo Levi: Ancora qualcosa da dire. Conversazioni e letture tra biografia e invenzione*. Novara: Interlinea.

THOMSON, Ian. 2003. *Primo Levi*. London: Vintage.

TODOROV, Tzvetan. 1996. *Gli abusi della memoria*. Naples: Ipermedium. [*Memory as a Remedy for Evil* (Gila Walker trans.). London: Seagull Books, 2010]

————. 2011. *Di fronte all'estremo*. Milan: Garzanti. [*Facing the Extreme: Moral Life in the Concentration Camps* (Arthur Denner and Abigail Pollak trans). New York: Henry Holt, 1996].

VALABREGA, Paola. 1982. 'Primo Levi e la tradizione ebraico-orientale'. *Studi Piemontesi* 11(2) (November): 296–310.

VALERY, Paul. 1985. *Quaderni I*. Milan: Adelphi. [*Cahiers/Notebooks, Vol. 1* (Brian Stimpson, Paul Gifford and Robert Pickering eds). New York: Peter Lang, 2010.].

VINCENTI, Fiora. 1973. *Invito alla lettura di Primo Levi*. Milano: Mursia.

VON FRISCH, Karl. 1976. *Il linguaggio delle api*. Turin: Bollati Boringhieri. [*The Dance Language and Orientation of Bees* (Leigh Chadwick trans.). Cambridge, MA: Harvard University Press, 1967].

————. 1978. *Gli insetti padroni della terra?* Milan: Sugarco Edizioni.

WEINRICH, Harald. 1999. *Lete*. Bologna: il Mulino.

YERUSHALMI, Yosef Hayim. 1983. *Zakhor*. Parma: Pratiche. [*Zakhor: Jewish History and Jewish Memory*. Seattle: University of Washington Press, 1982].

————. 1996. *Il Mosé di Freud*. Turin: Einaudi. [*Freud's Moses: Judaism Terminable and Interminable*. New Haven, CT: Yale University Press, 1993].

CREDITS FOR PHOTOGRAPHS

p. xx. Portrait with His Mother: courtesy of proprietor Giulia Colombo Dierna

p. 84. Portrait of a Student (*c.*1937): copyright *La Stampa*, Italiana Editrice S.p.a.

p. 106. Photo of the False Identity Card (*c.*1942): copyright *La Stampa*, Italiana Editrice S.p.a.

p. 212. Portrait of a Chemist (1952): courtesy of proprietor Giovanna Balzaretti

p. 254. Portrait of the Family (1963): photograph published in *Gente*, 1963

p. 312. Portrait of Levi Smoking and Debating (1978): copyright Giuseppe Varchetta

p. 324. Portrait with an Owl Mask (1986): copyright Mario Monge

p. 400. Portrait with a Personal Computer (1986): copyright Mario Monge

p. 476. Portrait of a Retired Chemist (*c.*1986): copyright Bernard Gotfryd

p. 568. Levi's Hall and Stairwell (*c.*1987): copyright *La Stampa*, Italiana Editrice S.p.a.

INDEX OF NAMES

The index includes the names of authors or persons referred to in the body of the text, but not the character present in Primo Levi's books, with the exception of Vanda Maestro, Jean Samuel and Lorenzo Perrone, when they're referred to by their full name.

Bartezzaghi, Stefano, 185, 206–8, 475, 538, 540–1, 577, 592, 597, 610, 612

Barthes, Roland, 85, 593

Bascom, Willard, 547

Bateson, Gregory, 359, 582, 612

Battacchi, Marco Walter, 611

Battaglia, Roberto, 96

Baudelaire, Charles, 299–301, 598

Beccaria, Cesare, 492

Beccaria, Gian Luigi, 264, 589, 595

Beckett, Samuel, 54, 146

Begin, Menachem, 424

Belli, Giuseppe Gioachino, 288, 291, 302, 454, 472

Bellow, Saul, 91, 225, 499, 526, 529, 611

Belpoliti, Marco, 471, 572–3, 585, 587

Benedetti, Arrigo, 97

Benjamin, Walter, 429, 512, 593

Benzi, Rosanna, 138

Berio, Luciano, 195

Berolatti, Gabriella, 81, 585

Bertone, Giorgio, 143, 577, 597, 605

Bettelheim, Bruno, 64, 89, 151–2, 165, 513–6, 589, 610

Bianucci, Piero, 200, 218, 353

Biasin, Gian Paolo, 576–7

Bidussa, David, 278, 577, 583–4, 607

Bissolati, Leonida, 94

Bloom, Solomon F., 485, 526

Bobbio, Norberto, 2, 157, 577, 579

Bocca, Giorgio, 200

Boccaccio, Giovanni, 323

Boitani, Piero, 294–5, 598

Bolis, Luciano, 94

Bollati, Giulio, 130, 191, 280, 282–3, 471

Bologna, Corrado, 328

Borges, Jorge Luis, 176, 206, 370, 443, 538

Boringhieri, Paolo, 48–50, 469, 471, 606

Borowski, Tadeusz, 64

Bosco Coletsos, Sandra, 472

Bosshammer, Friedrich, 71, 74–5

Bragg, William, 248–9, 288

Bravo, Anna, 60, 62, 317, 513, 579, 582, 607, 610

Brecht, Bertolt, 528

Bregstein, Philo, 499

Brod, Max, 426

Brown, Fredric, 184, 286

Bruck, Edith, 61

Bruno, Giovanna, 56, 147

Berger, Egon, 96

Bruzzone, Anna Maria, 61

Bucciantini, Massimo, 534, 601, 612, 614

Buczkowski, Leopold, 530

Cairns-Smith, Alexander Graham, 137, 350–1, 587

Cajumi, Arrigo, 52, 99, 458

Calcagno, Giorgio, 167, 487, 497, 573, 591, 598, 608

Calvino, Italo, xviii, xix, 23, 50, 52, 58, 98–9, 114, 130, 132, 141, 143, 151, 173–6, 178–80, 185, 188–92, 207, 217–8, 220–24, 228, 280, 286–7, 321, 330, 338, 345, 350, 361–2, 364–7, 378, 391, 448, 454, 458–61,

467, 477, 543–5, 547–51, 577, 587–8, 591–2, 597, 605, 607, 613–4

Camilleri, Andrea, 194

Camon, Ferdinando, 60, 80, 555–7, 560, 562, 567

Canetti, Elias, 510, 578, 610

Caravaggio (Michelangelo Merisi), 303

Carducci, Giosuè, 100, 305, 439–40, 442–3

Carena, Carlo, 282

Carné, Marcel, 201

Carrouges, Michel, 337

Cases, Cesare, 185, 459, 471, 479, 593–4, 607

Cavaglion, Alberto, 41, 48, 54, 68, 70, 223, 297, 299–300, 394, 417, 570, 575, 577, 580–1, 583–4, 589, 591, 593–4, 598–9, 602, 608, 611

Cavanna, Roberto, 590

Cecchi, Emilio, 447–8

Celan, Paul, 454, 462, 464, 605

Celati, Gianni, 339–40

Cerati, Roberto, 180

Cereja, Federico, 60, 62, 513, 579, 582, 610, 613

Chagall, Marc, 322, 410

Chateaubriand, François-René, 274

Chéroux, Clément, 8

Chesterton, Gilbert Keith, 358

Chiesa, Adolfo, 214

Cimabue (Cenni di Pepo), 303

Cingolani, Paolo, 194

Clausius, Rudolf, 551

Collodi, Carlo, 77

Conrad, Joseph, 139, 176, 228, 246, 252, 266–7, 319, 363, 454, 504

Contini, Gianfranco, 180

Cortázar, Julio, 323

D'Alembert, Jean-Baptiste Le Rond, 454

D'Annunzio, Gabriele, 275, 296, 523

D'Arrigo, Stefano, 77, 286, 288

Darwin, Charles, 105, 166, 211, 244, 269–72, 288, 299, 343, 350, 363, 379, 410, 454, 461, 596

Davico Bonino, Guido, 280

De Benedetti, Giacomo, 3, 93

De Benedetti, Leonardo, 4, 7–12, 71–2, 171, 556, 564, 580

De Bosio, Gianfranco, 56, 147

De Filippo, Eduardo, 92

Deleuze, Gilles, 100, 426–8, 604

Del Giudice, Daniele, 572, 578

Delmastro, Sandro, 252

del Piombo, Sebastiano, 303

Derer, Condrea, 177

De Sade, Marquis (Donatien Alphonse-François), 528

De Sanctis, Fabrizio, 214

de Santillana, Giorgio, 188, 591

de Waart, Bert, 496, 608

Di Ciaula, Tommaso, 268

Diderot, Denis, 454

Dierna, Emilio, 47

Dini, Massimo, 602

Diwan, Fiona, 418

Döblin, Alfred, 531

Doré, Gustave, 281, 284, 295, 303, 391

Dossena, Giampaolo, 270, 592

Douglas, Mary, 472

Dresner, Lisa, 95

Durkheim, Émile, 375

Dyson, Freeman, 141, 588

Egri, Marta, 56, 147

Eichmann, Otto Adolf, 71–4, 156, 158, 240, 500, 506–9, 512, 524, 528, 610

Einaudi, Giulio, 98, 130, 282, 411, 425, 435, 470, 472, 561

Eisenstein, Sergei, 370

Eliot, Thomas Stearns, 148, 439, 559

Éluard, Paul (Eugéne Grindel), 440

Escher, Maurits Cornelis, 190, 228, 289

Fabiani, Enzo, 216

Fabre, Jean-Henri, 334

Fadini, Edoardo, 147, 176–7, 219–20

Falaschi, Giovanni, 557–63, 566–7, 614

Farmer, Philip José, 370

Faurisson, Robert, 163, 481

Fellini, Federico, 372

Fenoglio, Edmo, 134, 195

Fenoglio, Beppe (Giuseppe), 264, 436

Ferrero, Ernesto, 204, 214, 228, 471, 574, 577, 593–4, 601

Flaubert, Gustave, 285, 287–8

Flores d'Arcais, Paolo, 492

Flory, Paul, 384

Foa, Anna (Yona, Anna), 13–14, 16, 23–4, 37–43, 45–6, 318, 485

Foà, Arturo, 73

Foà, Luciano, 49–50, 52, 471–3, 482, 495–6

Fonzi, Bruno, 577

Fornari, Franco, 525

Forti, Simona, 509–11, 607, 609

Fortini, Franco (Franco Lattes), 442–3, 464, 577

Fossati, Paolo, 471

Frankl, Viktor, 151–2, 589

Freud, Sigmund, 274, 284, 333, 360, 374, 516–7, 539, 610

Fromm, Erich, 486

Fruttero, Carlo, 146, 175

Funke, Otto, 82

Gadda, Carlo Emilio, 77, 177, 194, 402, 470, 587, 606

Galante Garrone, Alessandro, 20, 110

Galvani, Luigi, 330

Gambarotta, Bruno, 199

Garosci, Aldo, 52

Gattermann, Ludwig, 249, 472

Giani, Gian Domenico, 194

Gigli, Lorenzo, 52

Gilman, Henry, 471

Ginzburg, Carlo, 361, 548, 579, 594, 607

Ginzburg, Leone, 20, 92

Ginzburg, Natalia, xviii, 18–20, 92, 97, 99–100, 132, 229, 279, 464

Giolitti, Antonio, 95

Giudice, Gaspare, 590

Gogol, Nikolai Vasilyevich, 132

Goldoni, Carlo, 77

Layzer, David, 548–9
Leopardi, Giacomo, 290, 297–9, 306, 337–8, 364, 455, 517, 598
Lerner, Gad, 161, 424
Leroi-Gourhan, André, 269, 367
Leskov, Nikolai Semyonovich, 261
Lessing, Josef, 73
Levi, Alberto, 193
Levi, Anna Maria, 20, 272, 525–6
Levi, Cesare, 1
Levi, Fabio, 75, 473, 580
Lévi-Strauss, Claude, 272, 362, 375, 472, 474, 550, 596
Leydi, Roberto, 261
Liebig, Justus von, 456–7
Lombroso, Cesare, 244, 271, 329, 351, 461
London, Jack (John Griffith), 176, 252, 339–40, 357, 363
Longhi, Silvia, 600
Lopez, Guido, 420
Lorenz, Konrad, 166, 356, 363, 371, 375, 425, 601
Lo Surdo, Antonino, 384
Lucentini, Franco, 175
Luria, Salvador, 207
Luzzati, Emanuele, 468
Luzzati, Ester, 1

Machiavelli, Niccolò, 361
Machiedo, Mladen, 185, 217–18, 433
Maestro, Vanda, 70, 72, 119, 564–5, 567, 614
Maeterlinck, Maurice, 330, 334
Magris, Claudio, 417–19, 577, 602, 609

Malvano, Maria Vittoria, 18
Manganelli, Giorgio, 194, 452, 606
Mangoni, Luisa, 95, 98, 585, 606
Mann, Thomas, 39, 74
Mantell, Gideon Algernon, 329
Manzini, Raffaella, 418
Manzoni, Alessandro, 28, 99, 104, 121, 169, 181, 229, 253, 260, 265, 277, 285, 290–2, 297, 407, 485, 494, 498, 537, 543, 597
Marché, Pieralberto, 56, 58, 147–8, 313, 580
Marchese, Lorenzo, 552, 604
Marchesi, Concetto, 77
Marchesini, Pieralberto, 56, 58, 147–8, 313, 580
Marino, Gianlorenzo, 248
Marinuzzi Jr., Gino, 56, 147
Maršálek, Hans, 490
Martini, Massimo, 489
Marx, Karl, 271–2, 379
Mastronardi, Lucio, 264
Mastrostefano, Ennio, 200
Mattioda, Enrico, 189, 190–1, 576, 578, 590–2, 594, 596–7, 602, 605, 607, 613
Maupassant, Guy de, 323
Mauriac, François, 66
Mauss, Marcel, 375
Mayr, Otto, 189
Meinert, Joachim, 81–3
Melozzo da Forlì, 382
Melville, Herman, 20, 246, 252, 286, 454
Memling, Hans, 491

Mendel, David, 67, 150, 307–8, 409, 414, 566, 614

Mendeleev, Dmitri Ivanovich, 143, 218, 221, 223, 230, 248–9, 351

Meneghetti, Egidio, 77

Mengaldo, Pier Vincenzo, 67, 70, 146, 275–8, 459, 577, 584, 596, 607

Mengele, Josef, 516

Mengoni, Martina, 525–6, 530, 533, 585, 595–6, 607, 611

Mesnard, Philippe, 107, 574, 581

Meyer, Ferdinand (Dr Müller), 230, 233–43, 501

Mezzanzani, Silvia, 189

Miccinesi, Mario, 575

Milanini, Claudio, 188, 189, 591

Milano, Paolo, 194

Millu, Liana, 61

Minsky, Marvin, 189

Momigliano, Franco, 525

Mondo, Lorenzo, 221, 488, 598

Mondolfo, Luciano, 146

Monge, Mario, 325–6, 401–2, 432, 444, 477

Monod, Jacques, 549

Montaigne, Michel Eyquem de, 165, 306, 361

Montale, Eugenio, 337, 447–8

Morante, Elsa, xviii

Moravia, Alberto, xviii, 148

Moro, Aldo, 162, 314

Morpurgo, Lucia, 255, 434

Morris, Desmond, 139, 364

Mosso, Angelo, 351

Munari, Bruno, 50

Musatti, Cesare, 525

Nabokov, Vladimir, 192–3, 335–6

Nascimbeni, Giulio, 415

Nasser, Gamal Abdel, 423

Nebbia, Franco, 198

Nenni, Pietro, 95

Newton, Isaac, 364, 550

Nietzsche, Friedrich, 340, 381–2

Nirenstein, Alberto, 52

Nissim, Luciana, 8, 17–18, 70, 525, 564–5

Nolte, Ernst, 554

Norzi, Livio, 182, 193

Nyiszli, Miklós, 516

Nystedt, Jane, 343, 354, 368, 596, 601

Offenbach, Jacques, 144

Olivero, Ernesto, 135

Orengo, Nico, 18–19

Orthel, Rolf, 499

Ortona, Ada, 193

Ortona, Silvio, 15–16, 193, 252, 431, 456

Orwell, George (Eric Blair), 388

Ozick, Cynthia, 532–3

Paladini, Carlo, 109

Pansa, Giampaolo, 161, 424

Paoletti, Pier Maria, 297

Papuzzi, Alberto, 200, 252, 595

Parini, Giuseppe, 286, 597

Pasolini, Pier Paolo, xviii, 2, 202, 593

Pastoureau, Michel, 538, 612

Patroni Griffi, Giuseppe, 194

Pavese, Cesare, 18–19, 93–4, 96–100, 193, 264, 279, 443

Pellico, Silvio, 168, 452

Penrose, Roger, 544

Perec, George, 350, 384

Perrone, Lorenzo, 66

Picasso, Pablo, 303

Pierce, John, 189

Pighin, Otello, 77

Pinelli, Giuseppe, 162

Pirandello, Luigi, 77, 426

Pirie, Norman Wingate, 190

Pliny the Elder (Gaius Plinius
    Secundus), 177

Plutarch, 381

Pochettino, Alfredo, 247

Poli, Francesco, 261

Poli, Gabriella, 257, 482, 497, 573, 591,
    608

Poliakov, Léon, 66, 525–6

Polidori, Gianni, 46, 56, 58, 147

Polo, Marco, 454, 601

Ponchiroli, Daniele, 129

Pons, Silvia, 7

Porro, Mario, 244–6, 249, 305, 397,
    460, 577, 587, 594, 596, 600–1, 605,
    607, 613

Pound, Ezra, 464

Pratolini, Vasco, 194

Presser, Jacques, 166, 472, 482–3, 495–
    7, 499–501, 522, 608

Prigogine, Ilya, 549–51

Pushkin, Alexander Sergeyevich, 132

Quartucci, Carlo, 194–5

Quasimodo, Salvatore, 443

Queneau, Raymond, 189, 206, 222,
    345, 370, 391, 454, 460, 588, 592

Rabelais, François, 117, 177, 184, 206,
    272, 284, 301–2, 319, 435, 450, 599

Raboni, Giovanni, 492, 577

Raffaeli, Massimo, 299

Ravenna, Eloisa, 74–5

Regge, Tullio, 200, 244, 251, 594

Reitlinger, Gerald, 525–6

Renoir, Pierre-Auguste, 303

Revelli, Nuto, 310, 593, 600

Rho, Anita, 18

Riedt, Heinz, 22, 59, 76–9, 144, 256,
    301, 585, 588, 598

Rieser, Tina, 193

Rigoni Stern, Mario, 280, 310, 398,
    577, 593, 600

Rigotti, Francesca, 590

Rock, Irvin, 190

Rolfi, Lidia Beccaria, 61, 503, 514, 579

Romano, Ruggiero, 448, 456, 588

Rosato, Italo, 433, 441, 443, 577, 604

Rosenthal, Raymond, 532

Rosny, J. H. (Joseph Henri Honoré
    Boex), 472

Rostand, Jean, 175, 188

Roth, Philip, 229, 268, 325, 473, 531,
    611

Rouault, Georges, 303

Rousseau, Jean-Jacques, 88

Rousset, David, 96

Rudnicki, Adolf, 526, 530

Ruffini, Elisabetta, 8, 49

Rumkowski, Chaim, 167, 237, 318,
    484, 488, 495, 511–12, 522–31, 533,
    607, 611

Russell, Bertrand, 286, 308, 454

Ruzante (Angelo Beolco), 77

Saba, Umberto, 585
Sacerdoti, Franco, 564
Saint-Exupéry, Antoine de, 140
Salvarani, Brunetto, 418
Samuel, Jean, 17, 37–8, 109, 197, 581
Sapegno, Natalino, 341
Sartre, Jean-Paul, 612
Savinio, Alberto (Andrea de Chirico), 194
Scaglione, Massimo, 147–8, 193–4, 196–7
Scarlini, Luca, 146, 202, 577, 589
Scarpa, Domenico, 14, 72–3, 75, 220, 291, 440, 465, 550–4, 573–5, 577–8, 580, 584–5, 587, 591, 606, 611, 613
Scelba, Mario, 183
Scheiwiller, Vanni, 4, 431, 434–5, 439, 552, 604
Schmitt, Carl, 510
Schmitt-Maass, Hety, 76, 79, 222, 233, 260, 484, 608–9
Scholem, Gershom, 351, 512–13, 610
Schwarz-Bart, André, 499
Sciascia, Leonardo, xviii, 180, 280, 356, 467
Segre, Cesare, 68, 278, 442, 471, 560, 581, 609
Segré, Giorgio, 508, 610
Semprún, Jorge, 579
Sereny, Gitta, 500
Serres, Michel, 550
Sessi, Frediano, 197, 574–5, 591
Shakespeare, William, 439, 531, 533
Shalamov, Varlam, 517–21
Silori, Luigi, 136
Singer, Isaac Bashevis, 419

Singer, Israel Joshua, 419
Sinigaglia, Alberto, 440
Socrates, 364
Sodi, Risa, 60, 201, 420, 437, 514, 516, 576, 598, 610
Sodoma (Giovanni Antonio Bazzi), 303
Soldati, Mario, 201
Solmi, Sergio, 175, 177, 345, 460
Solzhenitsyn, Aleksandr Isayevich, 340, 519
Sontag, Susan, 1–2
Spadi, Milva, 202
Spaini, Alberto, 472
Spallanzani, Lazzaro, 330
Speelman, Raniero, 500, 592, 596
Spellanzon, Cesare, 52
Spielberg, Steven, 201
Spitzer, Leo, 553
Stalin, Joseph Vissarionovich, 116, 520
Stangl, Franz, 500
Steiner, George, 102, 429, 579, 586, 604, 607
Steiner, Jean-François, 499
Stengers, Isabelle, 549–50
Sterne, Laurence, 301
Stockhausen, Karlheinz, 195
Sullam Calimani, Anna-Vera, 66, 583
Swift, Jonathan, 184, 186, 286, 289, 328
Székács, Vera, 60

Tchaikovsky, Pyotr Ilyich, 145
Tesio, Giovanni, 31, 53, 110, 113–14, 116–17, 171, 213, 222, 284, 290, 293, 409, 463, 562–4, 566–7, 573–4, 580–1, 585–6, 598–9